FOURTH EDITION

THE HAGUE ABDUCTION CONVENTION

Practical Issues and Procedures for Family Lawyers

JEREMY D. MORLEY

AMERICAN BAR ASSOCIATION
Family Law Section

Cover design by Sara Wadford/ABA Design.

Printed in the United States of America.

29 28 27 26 25   5 4 3 2 1

To Eriko, Rick, Julie, and Hannah, with love.

Contents

Preface

PURPOSE OF THIS BOOK

The purpose of this book is to explain as clearly as possible to family lawyers how the Hague Convention on the Civil Aspects of International Child Abduction works in the United States. The Convention operates in this country in ways that are different than in other Hague countries. This is because of the federal legislation that implements the treaty, the concurrence of federal and state jurisdiction, the lack of a specialized group of judges who handle cases under the Convention, the uniform state legislation on child custody jurisdiction, and a host of other factors.

VOLUMINOUS LITIGATION

The treaty itself is short and to the point. Yet the Convention has spawned voluminous litigation, most especially in the United States. There are several reasons for this:

- The key terms in the Convention are ambiguous and either completely or mostly undefined. One might, at first glance, expect that straightforward terms such as "habitual residence," "rights of custody," and even "grave risk of harm" might be easy to apply in a consistent manner. That has proven not to be the case. The key terms have been subjected to a cascade of judicial interpretation in the United States, which has sometimes been contradictory and often confusing.
- The United States allows Hague cases to be brought before unspecialized judges with no experience in handling them. Somewhat hypocritically, the U.S. State Department asks other countries to limit the number of courts or judges that can handle Hague cases in their countries and to train those judges in how to handle these cases, but there is no such limitation or specialization in the United States. Federal and state courts have concurrent jurisdiction and Hague cases can go to whichever court in a local county handles family law matters. Because there are several thousand such counties in the United States as well as many federal districts, a Hague case can be brought before any one of thousands of courts in the United States.

- Until 2020, the U.S. Supreme Court had never ruled on the key issue in most Hague Convention cases, which is that of determining the "habitual residence" of the child. The various U.S. federal circuits had developed a variety of conflicting rules and burdens of proof about habitual residence, which were confusing and spawned a deluge of appeals, with no guidance from the only court that could "lay down the law." The Supreme Court then adopted a "totality-of-the-circumstances" test for interpreting the term "habitual residence." While logically correct, the test provides little or no guidance as to how to apply it and how to weigh the circumstances.
- The treaty is supposed to have one autonomous meaning throughout the world, but the common law system, which allows interpretation to develop on a case-by-case basis, seems not to work so well when decisions are supposed to yield a consensus in an international environment.
- Even though the treaty is intended to be merely procedural in nature, a parent who has brought a child to another country in search of a "better" forum for a child custody case may be desperate to prevent the child's return since the custody case will normally be heard in the original forum. Likewise, the parents of children who have been snatched by the other parent may be just as desperate to have the "home court advantage" of having their child custody case being heard "at home" instead of "away." The differences between the custody decisions that are rendered in the courts of different countries may theoretically be minimal, yet parents suspect—often with very good reason—that the real-world outcomes will be completely different depending on which country's courts decide the case.
- When children are the subject of international family law disputes, the challenges are often great and the emotions generally run high. Simply put, money can be divided but children cannot. Divorcing parents who stay in the same town can often make sensible arrangements to share the parenting of their children, and, if they cannot, a local court can issue appropriate orders and also enforce them as needed. But when the parents cannot even agree on which country to live in, all bets are off. Consequently, Hague cases are often litigated.
- Neither the Convention nor the International Child Abduction Remedies Act, which brought the Convention into U.S. law, contain any provision for mediation. There are special challenges

to the use of mediation in Hague cases, because the cases are required to be concluded with great speed and a petitioner generally does not want to yield on that and the opportunities for compromise are limited in this area because a child can realistically live in only one country at a time. Nonetheless, mediation of Hague cases has become the norm in several countries, with significant success.

HANDLING HAGUE CASES

Handling Hague abduction cases is challenging and fulfilling. Hague cases are usually tried very quickly. Indeed, they are supposed to be entirely concluded within just six weeks, although that target date is very rarely applied in U.S. cases. They require an intimate knowledge of the Convention and of the voluminous case law that has developed around it. They also require a complete understanding of international child custody law in general and in particular, for U.S. practitioners, of the relationship between the Hague Convention and the Uniform Child Custody Jurisdiction & Enforcement Act.

The Convention is misunderstood by very many family lawyers and, dare I say it, by family judges. A lawyer in a Hague case sometimes needs to provide a quick but respectful education to judges who have not handled any or many such cases before.

I have had the good fortune to have handled Hague cases in many jurisdictions throughout the United States and sometimes in foreign countries also, usually working collaboratively with local lawyers in each jurisdiction. I have also submitted expert evidence to courts throughout the United States and around the world about how the Convention might apply in other countries and as to the compliance with the provisions of the Convention that may be expected by the courts in such countries. Additionally, I have lectured on the Convention before federal and state judges in New York state, at international conferences of family law practitioners, and at venues such as the Foreign Ministry of Japan. And I consult almost daily with lawyers and clients around the world about specific matters concerning the Convention. It is fulfilling and exciting work.

About the Author

Jeremy D. Morley is a hugely experienced New York "lawyer's lawyer" who focuses on international family law. He assists lawyers and clients throughout the United States and around the world with Hague Convention and other international family law cases.

He and his team have prosecuted, defended, and liaised on numerous Hague Convention cases, and Jeremy has counseled, liaised with, advised, and supported lawyers and their clients around the world in many thousands of international family law matters.

Jeremy has taught in law schools in the United States, Canada, and England. He regularly lectures on international child abduction and other international family law topics to the judiciary, bar associations, and others. He is a member of the International Academy of Family Lawyers. He co-chaired the International Family Law Section of the New York State Bar Association and the International Family Law Committee of the International Law Section of the American Bar Association. He is also the author of *International Family Law Practice*, a leading treatise on international family law in the United States that is updated regularly.

Jeremy is frequently asked to appear as an expert witness on international child abduction prevention and recovery issues, as well as many other matters concerning international child custody and international divorce. He is also a frequent guest on television and radio shows on the topic of international child abduction and international divorce law and has been featured in the print media on numerous occasions.

Jeremy maintains a voluminous website on international family law at www.international-divorce.com. He may be reached there.

Introducing the Hague Abduction Convention

1

§ 1.01 INTRODUCTION

The purpose of this book is to provide legal practitioners in the United States and overseas with an introduction to the operation in the United States of the Hague Convention of 25 October 1980 on the Civil Aspects of International Child Abduction (the "Hague Convention" or the "Convention").

The Convention is an international treaty that seeks to protect children from the harmful effects of abduction and retention across international boundaries by providing a procedure to bring about their prompt return. It has been signed by more than 100 countries, including the United States. It provides that a child who has been taken to or retained in a foreign country without the consent of a person with "rights of custody" over the child under the law of the child's "habitual residence" must be returned to the habitual residence unless one of six exceptions applies.

This book is primarily concerned with what are sometimes referred to as "incoming" abductions, meaning abductions from other countries into the United States.

U.S. courts have no jurisdiction under the Convention in the case of "outgoing" abductions from the United States to other countries, with limited exceptions, because those cases must be brought in the courts of the foreign country to which the child has been abducted. The primary exception to this principle is that the judicial or administrative authorities of the country to which a child has been taken may, before ordering the child's return, request that the applicant obtain from the authorities of the state of the habitual residence of the child a decision or other determination that the removal or retention was "wrongful" within the meaning of the Convention (Article 15 of the Convention).

Nonetheless, the Convention does not prevent a left-behind parent whose child has been removed from the United States from bringing suit to establish custody in a state court in the United States if there is jurisdiction in the state court within the meaning of the Uniform Child Custody Jurisdiction and Enforcement Act (UCCJEA) or equivalent legislation. Nor does it preclude the registration and enforcement of a foreign country's custody order under the UCCJEA.

§ 1.02 A REVOLUTIONARY TREATY

The Convention is a revolutionary document. Its drafters determined that it is wrong that parents should be permitted to take their children to another country in search of a friendlier forum for a child custody case, and that it would be far better to order the return abducted children to their habitual residence so that the courts there may determine what is best for them. It embodies the brave decision, made thus far by more than 100 countries, to defer any decision about what is best for wrongfully removed or retained children until they have been returned to the country from which they have been taken.

The Convention provides an extremely simple and relatively unambiguous remedy that is expressly designed to act as a general deterrent to prevent parents from taking their children across international borders without the other parent's consent. That remedy is to send the child "back home" forthwith.

The fundamental idea underlying the Convention is that "we will return children to you so that in the future you will do the same for us." It works only because each country has agreed to trust the other "Hague partner" countries to do the same thing when similar cases come before their courts.

However, when a purported abduction is by a parent who has brought a child "back home" to the primary care provider's country of origin, it may require a judge who is extremely committed to the treaty to follow its precepts, sometimes even in the face of public opinion and a judge's own sense of right and wrong.

The Convention requires judges to be brave enough to implement its terms even in the face of concerns that, for any particular child who is before the court, the result of a return order might not be in that child's best interests. It sometimes compels courts to have kids put on planes, sometimes forcibly, to go back to the place from which they were taken, even in the face of a parent's frantic pleas that she brought the child "home" to avoid injustice overseas.

The treaty embodies the "greater good" theory. The best interests of any particular child might perhaps not be served by returning that child to the country from which he or she was removed, usually by a loving parent. But the interests of children at large are best served by ensuring that parents who abduct their children are not rewarded for doing so.

Although family lawyers and judges are trained to consider nothing but the best interests of the child in any child custody case before them, the Hague Convention requires that "best interests" should not be considered and that the child must instead be sent back to the country from which his or her parent has fled.

On its face, the treaty is purely a jurisdiction-selection document. The Convention does not resolve any of the substantive issues concerning what is best for a child. It simply provides for the prompt return of an abducted child so that the courts in the jurisdiction from which the child was taken may make those decisions.

The Convention resulted from a consensus that international child abduction is a terrible thing. In the *Abbott* case in the U.S. Supreme Court, Justice Kennedy, writing the majority opinion, said, "An abduction can have devastating consequences for a child." He quoted with approval language and studies showing that "[s]ome child psychologists believe that the trauma children suffer from these abductions is one of the worst forms of child abuse"; that studies have shown that separation by abduction can cause psychological problems ranging from depression and acute stress disorder to posttraumatic stress disorder and identity-formation issues; and that a child abducted at an early age can experience loss of community and stability, leading to loneliness, anger, and fear of abandonment; and that abductions may prevent the child from forming a relationship with the left-behind parent, impairing the child's ability to mature.[1]

§ 1.03 A FUNDAMENTAL MISCONCEPTION

It must be acknowledged that the Hague Convention was drafted upon the basis of a fundamental misconception. When it was negotiated, it was anticipated that the abductors would mostly be noncustodial fathers. In fact, most parental international child abductors are the custodial parents of their children, most of whom are the children's mothers, as the

1. Abbott v. Abbott, 560 U.S. 13, 130 S. Ct. 1983, 1996 (U.S. 2010).

U.K. Supreme Court has expressly acknowledged.[2] One might well ask whether such a clear-cut but sometimes harsh and blunt remedy as prompt return would have been adopted had the drafters understood this essential fact.

Although some claim that most mothers who wrongfully remove their children across international borders are fleeing domestic violence, that is not consistent with what I see in running a very busy international family law practice. In my experience, most abducting parents are mothers who have been living in another country in relationship with a national of that country or with a person who is located in that country for business, career, or educational reasons. When the relationship breaks down, she simply wants to "go home" with her child to her country of origin.

Such mothers often feel alone, that they are "fish out of water" in a foreign land without family or strong friends. They may not know the language or the culture. They may well have enjoyed living overseas while the relationship was strong but now that the relationship is over, they feel isolated and often scared. They may well be unfamiliar with the local legal system and they are probably unfamiliar with local social services programs. They may well have been cut off financially, both as to ongoing support and as to their access to bank accounts and credit cards. They may be unable to work because they do not have a work visa, or they lack the necessary language skills or know-how. Theirs may have been an "arranged marriage," where the couple does not necessarily know each other prior to getting married. Once the relationship is over, if not before, their in-laws may well have taken "his side" in the disputes that arise and may raise new complaints and demands and assert additional pressures. These mothers very often feel utterly betrayed and completely out of place. They certainly may have been abused, most often psychologically and sometimes physically. They desperately want to go home to their family, their friends, and the environment that they know and in which they feel safe.

The appropriate solution for such expat parents should be to seek a relocation order from the courts in the country in which they and their children are currently located. This is where the theory may fall down. Winning international relocation cases in most jurisdictions is tough and seems to be getting tougher. There is an inverse relationship between the difficulty of obtaining a local court's permission to relocate with a child and the frequency of parental abduction of their children. In recent years, there seems to be a trend toward making international relocation

2. *Re* E [2011] UKSC 27 [2011] FLR 758.

even harder to obtain, resulting in part from a desire to serve the interests of children in having both parents in their life and the interests of both parents in having their children in their life. I would submit that unfortunately the trend is often counterproductive. It is unfair to the expat parent who is stranded in a foreign country and it is unfair to the child whose primary care provider is upset, angry, and beaten down and whose parents are at each other's throats. The stranded parent often feels that they have no choice but to run away with their children.

However, all cases are unique—and especially in this area of the law—and generalizations are dangerous.

§ 1.04 PARTIES TO THE CONVENTION

The Convention was drafted under the auspices of the Hague Conference on Private International Law (the "Hague Conference"), which is a global intergovernmental organization based in the Hague in the Netherlands. The Convention was approved unanimously by the 23 member states at the Fourteenth Session of the Hague Conference in 1980.

In order to be able to bring a case under the Hague Convention, a petitioner must establish that, on the date of the wrongful taking or the wrongful retention of the child, the Convention was actually in force between the two countries, that is, between the country of the child's habitual residence on the relevant date and the country in which the child is currently located.

Currently, more than 100 states are Contracting Parties to the Convention. However, the Convention is not in force between all of these states because many states have not accepted the accessions of all other Contracting States. The Convention provides that it will not enter into force between an existing Contracting State and a newly acceding state unless and until the existing state expressly accepts the accession of the new state.[3]

Thus, Article 38 of the Convention provides that the accession of a new state will have effect only as regards the relations between the acceding state and those Contracting States that have declared their acceptance of the accession.

When a country accedes to the Convention, the U.S. State Department reviews the new signatory's domestic legal and administrative systems to determine whether the necessary legal and institutional mechanisms are in place for it to implement the Convention and to provide effective

3. Hague Convention, Arts. 38 and 39.

legal relief under it. If it determines that a country has the capability and capacity to be an effective treaty partner, the State Department declares its acceptance of the accession by depositing a written instrument with the Hague Permanent Bureau. Only then does the Convention enter into force between the United States and the acceding country. The State Department posts these details on its website and the Permanent Bureau maintains a current status list on its website.

Currently, the United States has a Hague Convention treaty relationship in force with 89 countries and territories.[4] Thus, although Russia, by way of example, has signed the Convention, the United States had not accepted it as a treaty partner as of the date this book was completed. As a result, the Convention cannot currently be invoked in respect of children abducted between Russia and the United States. The website of the Hague Conference contains a spreadsheet showing the acceptance of accessions to the Convention.[5]

Once a country's accession is accepted, the Convention enters force on the first day of the third calendar month thereafter.[6] A wrongful removal or retention preceding such date will not be covered by the Convention. For this purpose, the term "retention" means a singular and not a continuing act. Accordingly, when a child was retained before the effective date of the U.S. acceptance of Thailand's accession, the Convention could not be utilized to secure the child's return even though the retention continued after such date.[7]

§ 1.05 THE HAGUE CONFERENCE

The Permanent Bureau of the Hague Conference monitors and supports international implementation on a continuing basis. It maintains a website, http://www.hcch.net, which is a useful source of information concerning the operation of the Convention. It also maintains the "INCADAT" database, which contains leading decisions concerning the Convention from courts around the world, searchable summaries of decisions, and compendia of legal analyses.

---

4. As of June 2024. The list is available at https://travel.state.gov/content/travel/en/International-Parental-Child-Abduction/abductions/hague-abduction-country-list.html (last visited Feb. 13, 2025).

5. Currently available at https://assets.hcch.net/docs/33bba6da-cb14-4c0e-bdc0-826c56051633.pdf.

6. Convention, Art. 38.

7. Marks v. Hochhauser, 876 F.3d 416 (2d Cir. 2017).

In addition, official publications of the Hague Conference may be useful sources of information about the operation and interpretation of the Convention. The Conference publishes *Guides to Good Practice*, which may provide authoritative assistance in the interpretation of the provisions of the treaty. Indeed, the concurring judges in the Supreme Court's *Chafin* case found that to be the case,[8] as have courts in other cases.[9]

The most recent such guide is the *Guide to Good Practice Child Abduction Convention: Part VI—Article 13(1)(b),* published in early 2020, prepared by a working group chaired by the Honorable Diana Bryant (Australia), and composed of judges, government officials (e.g., Central Authority personnel), academic/cross-disciplinary experts, and private practitioners from many jurisdictions around the world.

In addition, the Hague Conference periodically publishes the *Judges' Newsletter on International Child Protection*, which generally contains extensive information on the operation of the Convention globally and other materials concerning the Convention.

§ 1.06 THE PÉREZ-VERA REPORT

Professor Elisa Pérez-Vera, the Convention's "Rapporteur," wrote a legislative history of the Convention. It is known as the "Pérez-Vera Report" and is frequently used to assist in interpreting the key terms and intent of the Convention. The Second Circuit has stated, "We have repeatedly observed that the Pérez–Vera Report is 'an authoritative source for interpreting the Convention's provisions.'"[10] The report may be accessed at Appendix 2 to this treatise.

The U.S. Supreme Court has frequently cited the Pérez-Vera Report in its opinions concerning the Convention. In *Golan*, the Court stated, "The explanatory report for the Convention . . . is 'recognized by the [Hague] Conference as the official history and commentary on the Convention and is a source of background on the meaning of the provisions of the Convention.'"[11] Justice Ginsburg, to a significant extent, relied on the Pérez-Vera Report in the U.S. Supreme Court's unanimous ruling concerning habitual residence in *Monasky*.[12] Likewise, in the *Abbott* case,[13]

---

8. Chafin v. Chafin, 133 S. Ct. 1017, 1030 (concurring opinions) (U.S. 2013).

9. *See, e.g.*, Madrigal v. Tellez, 848 F.3d 669 n.3 (5th Cir. 2017); Gil-Leyva v. Leslie, 780 Fed. Appx. 580, 598 (10th Cir. 2019).

10. Guzzo v. Cristofano, 719 F.3d 100, 106 n.4 (2d Cir. 2013).

11. Golan v. Saada, 596 U.S. 666, 142 S. Ct. 1880, 1880 n.8 (2022).

12. Monasky v. Taglieri, 140 S. Ct. 719, 726–27.

13. *Chafin*, 133 S. Ct. at 1029; *Abbott*, 560 U.S. 13, 130 S. Ct. 1983.

the Court stated, "We need not decide whether this Report should be given greater weight than a scholarly commentary," noting that the Report has been cited as the "official history" of the Convention and "a source of background on the meaning of the provisions of the Convention." On the other hand, the Court also stated that the Report itself states that it was not approved by the Conference, and that "it is possible that, despite the Rapporter's [sic] efforts to remain objective, certain passages reflect a viewpoint which is in part subjective."[14]

The Report should always be checked whenever a term in the Convention is in dispute.

§ 1.07 U.S. EXECUTIVE BRANCH INTERPRETATION

Some courts have placed significant weight on the interpretation of the Convention made by or proposed by the Executive Branch of the U.S. government.

Thus, the U.S. State Department's initial legal analysis of the Convention, which is attached as Appendix 4, has been cited by many courts as a source of interpretative assistance.[15] It states in the Introduction that it was expressly prepared "to facilitate understanding of the Convention by the Senate and the use and interpretation of the Convention by parents, judges, lawyers and public and private agency personnel." For example, the State Department's Legal Analysis has been afforded significance when interpreting the word "settled" in Article 12 of the Convention[16] and in interpreting the human rights exception contained in Article 20.[17]

In some cases, the opinions of the Solicitor-General in amicus briefs or the opinions of the State Department in answers to questionnaires submitted by the Hague Conference have been scrutinized and given significance.[18]

In the *Lozano* case, the Supreme Court relied significantly on the fact that the State Department, not only in its original legal analysis but also in its amicus brief in the pending case, had taken a certain position on the appropriate interpretation of a key provision in the Convention. The Court stated that, "[a]s this Court has previously explained (in the context of the

14. *Monasky*, 140 S. Ct. at 726, n.2.

15. *E.g.*, Yaman v. Yaman, 730 F.3d 1 (1st Cir. 2013); Krefter v. Wills, 623 F. Supp. 2d 125 (D. Mass. 2009).

16. Cuenca v. Rojas, 99 F.4th 1344, 1350 (11th Cir. 2024).

17. Galaviz v. Reyes, 95 F.4th 246 (5th Cir. 2024).

18. *E.g.*, *Yaman*, 730 F.3d 1; Blondin v. Dubois, 238 F.3d 153, 159 (2d Cir. 2001).

Convention, in fact), the State Department's interpretation of treaties 'is entitled to great weight.'"[19]

§ 1.08 THE PURPOSE OF THE TREATY

It is often of substantial importance in a Hague case for the petitioner to remind the court of the purpose of the Convention. The Hague process is unusual and it may be surprising to a judge who is not fully familiar with such cases, especially if the judge has a background in handling conventional child custody cases, where the emphasis is always on the best interests of the child. Indeed, the decision in many cases reflects a struggle between the instinct of a judge to do what is in the best interests of the child and the philosophy of the Hague Convention that the best interests determination should be left to the courts of the child's prior habitual residence.

The treaty is founded on four fundamental principles:

- The unauthorized international removal or retention of a child by a parent is normally wrongful when it violates the rights of another parent who has a custodial right concerning the child.
- The wrongful removal or retention of a child is normally prejudicial to the child's welfare and it will normally be in the best interests of the child to return to the state of habitual residence.
- The courts of the child's country of habitual residence are normally best placed to determine the merits of a custody dispute.
- The expeditious return of abducted children to the country of their habitual residence best serves these principles.

Accordingly, the recital provisions of the Convention state that its purpose is "to protect children internationally from the harmful effects of their wrongful removal or retention and to establish procedures to ensure their prompt return to the State of their habitual residence, as well as to secure protection for rights of access."

Article 1 provides that the central purposes of the Convention are to secure the "prompt return" of children who have been wrongfully removed to or retained in any Contracting State; and to ensure that rights of custody and access under the law of one such state are effectively respected in the other states.

The treaty provides a specific mechanism to handle international child abductions in all cases, which all treaty partners have elected to

---

19. Lozano v. Montoya Alvarez, 134 S. Ct. 1224, 1238 (2014).

follow and are required to follow. That method is to return abducted children promptly to their prior habitual residence, unless one of a very limited number of exceptions applies. Articles 11, 12, and 13 impose that duty upon all courts in all Contracting States.

The United States brought the Convention into U.S. law by means of the International Child Abduction Remedies Act (ICARA).[20] Congress expressly declared in ICARA its findings that:

- The international abduction or wrongful retention of children is harmful to their well-being;
- People should not be permitted to obtain custody of children by virtue of their wrongful removal or retention;
- International abductions and retentions of children are increasing; and
- Only concerted cooperation pursuant to an international agreement can effectively combat this problem.

The U.S. Supreme Court has reviewed the Convention in five cases. In the *Abbott*[21] case, the Court stated that the purpose of the Convention is "to prevent harms resulting from abductions" which "can have devastating consequences for a child" and may be "one of the worst forms of child abuse." The Court also referred with approval to findings that international child abduction can cause substantial problems for children.

In *Chafin*, the Supreme Court found that the petitioner was correct to emphasize that both the Hague Convention and ICARA stress the importance of the prompt return of children wrongfully removed or retained, and the Court stated that although it was also sympathetic to the concern that shuttling children back and forth between parents and across international borders may be detrimental to those children, the courts can achieve the ends of the Convention and ICARA—and protect the well-being of the affected children—by expediting proceedings and granting stays where appropriate.[22]

In *Lozano*, the Court explained that in order to secure the prompt return of children wrongfully removed to or retained in any Contracting State, and to ensure that rights of custody and of access under the law of one Contracting State are effectively respected in the other Contracting States, the Convention's "central operating feature" is the return of the child, which in effect lays venue for the ultimate custody determination in

20. 22 U.S.C. § 9001 (Appendix 3 to this book).
21. *Abbott*, 130 S. Ct. 1983, 1987.
22. *Chafin*, 133 S. Ct. at 1026–27.

the child's country of habitual residence rather than the country to which the child is abducted.[23]

In *Golan*[24] and *Monasky*, the Court observed that it is the Convention's "core premise" that the interests of children in matters relating to their custody are best served when custody decisions are made in the child's country of "habitual residence."[25]

Other courts have explained, for example, that the Convention procedures are designed "to restore the status quo prior to any wrongful removal or retention and to deter parents from engaging in international forum shopping in custody cases."[26]

The Convention provides a simple remedy to a complex problem but in many ways simplicity is its strength. Most critically, the Convention is not intended or designed to settle international custody disputes, but rather to ensure that cases are heard in the proper court.[27] Article 19 of the Convention expressly states, "A decision under this Convention concerning the return of the child shall not be taken to be a determination on the merits of any custody issue." Indeed, any consideration of the best interests of the child is generally out of bounds in a Hague case, although once an exception has been established, the courts have a discretion to return a child and at that stage courts will consider what is best for the child, as well as the purposes of the Convention, in applying that discretion.

§ 1.09 CUSTODY JURISDICTION AND THE HAGUE CONVENTION

The Hague Convention is not a jurisdiction-selection treaty. In the United States, it does not supersede the UCCJEA. A case brought pursuant to the Convention does not determine the custody of the child but merely determines where the child should be located while determinations about the child's best interests are being made. A Hague decision does not in and of itself create custody jurisdiction or establish custody jurisdiction and does not trump the jurisdictional provisions of the UCCJEA.

Unfortunately, many courts—including the highest—have made simplistic statements that confuse and misstate the issue. For example, the Seventh Circuit has stated as follows:

23. *Lozano*, 134 S. Ct. at 1228.
24. Golan v. Saada, 142 S. Ct. 1880, 1888 (2022).
25. *Monasky*, 140 S. Ct. at 722.
26. Baxter v. Baxter, 423 F.3d 363 (3d. Cir. 2005) (citation omitted).
27. *In re* B. Del C.S.B., 559 F.3d 999 (9th Cir. 2009).

> As the Supreme Court explained in a decision that takes center stage in this dispute, "[t]he Convention's return requirement is a provisional remedy that fixes the forum for custody proceedings." Monasky v. Taglieri, 589 U.S. 68, 72, 140 S.Ct. 719, 206 L.Ed.2d 9 (2020) (quotation omitted).[28]

But the jurisdictional standards contained in the UCCJEA are not the same as the Convention's provisions concerning the authority of a court to return a child under the Convention.

Proceedings under the UCCJEA do not conflict with, and are not preempted by, proceedings under the Hague Convention because the two laws address different objectives. The Convention focuses on returning children who have been wrongfully removed from their place of habitual residence, whereas the UCCJEA provides the rules that determine which jurisdiction decides custody disputes.[29]

Thus, a New York court correctly ruled that because, at the time a custody case was commenced in New York, the child's "home state" was New York, the New York courts had custody jurisdiction of the child, even though a court in the Dominican Republic had refused to return the child to New York under the Hague Convention. The child's mother had taken the child to the Dominican Republic without the father's consent. She defended a Hague case in that country on the grounds of domestic violence. The Dominican court upheld her claims and refused to return the child to the United States on the ground of the grave risk exception to the Convention. The New York court then ruled that it retained home state jurisdiction and that that jurisdiction was not preempted by the Convention.[30]

Likewise, a Kansas court was required to apply the UCCJEA jurisdictional standards to determine whether it had child custody jurisdiction even though a court in the Netherlands had refused to return children under the Convention.[31]

In a Colorado case, the federal district court judge stated that a Hague Convention proceeding determines which country should address custody issues. In a subsequent state court custody proceeding, the Colorado Court of Appeals politely corrected the federal court's misstatement.[32]

---

28. Baz v. Patterson, 100 F.4th 854 (7th Cir. 2024).
29. *In re* T.L.B., 272 P.3d 1148 (Colo. App. 2012).
30. Katz v. Katz, 117 A.D.3d 1054, 986 N.Y.S.2d 611 (2d Dept. 2014).
31. Interest of S.L., 503 P.3d 244, 265 (Kan. Ct. App. 2021).
32. *In re T.L.B.*, 272 P.3d at 1156.

Hague cases do not decide custody jurisdiction. In *Redmond*, the Seventh Circuit held that the Convention "targets international child abduction; it is not a jurisdiction-allocation or full-faith-and-credit treaty."[33]

The confusion on this issue is enhanced by virtue of the fact that, in many foreign countries, custody jurisdiction is based on the habitual residence of the child, which is the same standard that must be satisfied in any Hague Convention case. However, the UCCJEA (as currently enacted[34]) does not make any mention of "habitual residence" and is founded, instead, on the concept of the "home state," which is a term completely unique to U.S. jurisprudence. Courts in foreign countries may treat the custody jurisdiction and Hague Convention issue of habitual residence as being identical, but U.S. custody jurisdiction rules require that the two issues be kept carefully separate.

Nonetheless, Article 16 of the Convention effectively bars a court in the United States that may conceivably have home state jurisdiction under the UCCJEA from making any child custody determination if a Hague Convention petition to return the child to its habitual residence is brought in a court in the United States and is not denied. This is discussed in § 2.13 Stay of Custody Proceedings.

§ 1.10 BEST INTERESTS AND THE HAGUE CONVENTION

The central tenet of the Hague Convention is that, although any custody determination must be based on an analysis of the child's best interests, that issue should be decided by the courts of the country in the habitual residence from which the child was taken and not by the courts of the country to which a child was wrongfully removed or in which the child was wrongfully retained.

The drafters of the Convention acted on the fundamental premise that the best way to deter international child abduction is to ensure that international child abduction is not rewarded. In particular, forum shopping in such cases should be discouraged. They determined that the best solution

33. Redmond v. Redmond, 724 F.3d 729, 741 (7th Cir. 2013).

34. The 2013 Amendments to the UCCJEA would modify the UCCJEA and would incorporate the term "habitual residence" to comport with the 1996 Hague Convention on Jurisdiction, Applicable Law, Recognition, Enforcement, and Co-operation in respect of Parental Responsibility and Measures for the Protection of Children, to which the United States is not yet a party.

is to return abducted children promptly to their habitual residence, whose courts are the most appropriate to determine the best interests of children.

States adopted the Convention because they agreed with this philosophy and they expected that their treaty partners would adhere to it. When the United States was considering whether to adopt the Hague Convention, the U.S. State Department explained to Congress that,

> The Convention is premised upon the notion that the child should be promptly restored to his or her country of habitual residence so that a court there can examine the merits of the custody dispute and award custody in the child's best interests.

It specifically explained that the grave risk exception "was not intended to be used by defendants as a vehicle to litigate (or relitigate) the child's best interests."[35]

Undoubtedly, the Hague Convention adopted a "greater good" premise, meaning that it is intended to discourage international child abduction in general even if in any specific case it might perhaps be best for that particular child not to be returned. However, the drafters of the Convention recognized that a balance must be struck between the interests of children in general in not being wrongfully taken from their habitual residence and the need to protect individual children in specific, extreme and unusual cases. For this reason, while the Convention contains certain exceptions to the rule requiring a child's prompt return to the habitual residence, the exceptions are carefully delineated, they are to be narrowly interpreted and even if they are established the courts nonetheless retain a discretion to order the child's return.

Courts in the United States have adhered to this philosophy consistently. They have upheld the fundamental principle that the Convention is clear that a court considering a Hague petition should not consider matters relevant to the merits of the underlying custody dispute, such as the best interests of the child, as these considerations are reserved for the courts that have child custody jurisdiction. The Seventh Circuit explained, "The Convention seeks to promote the best interests of the child by entrusting custody proceedings to the country where the child is at home."[36]

Indeed, the Ninth Circuit refused to grant comity to a Greek order in a Hague case because it concluded that the Greek court had "strayed from the objective inquiries prescribed by the Convention" and had focused on

35. Hague International Child Abduction Convention: Text and Legal Analysis, 51 Fed. Reg. 19494 (1984).

36. Baz v. Patterson, 100 F.4th 854, 871 (7th Cir. 2024).

matters largely irrelevant to its ultimate decision, such as the details of the breakdown of the parties' relationship and the father's alleged infidelity and failure to be the sole breadwinner for the family.[37]

On the other hand, Baroness Hale insisted in a leading English case that "[t]hese children should not be made to suffer for the sake of general deterrence of the evil of child abduction worldwide."[38] Justice Thomas cited that quotation in the Supreme Court's opinion in *Lozano v. Montoya Alvarez*, stating that,

> We agree, of course, that the Convention reflects a design to discourage child abduction. But the Convention does not pursue that goal at any cost. The child's interest in choosing to remain, Art. 13, or in avoiding physical or psychological harm, Art. 13(b), may overcome the return remedy.[39]

§ 1.11 THREATS TO THE CENTRAL TENET

The central idea underlying the Convention has been under threat on two fronts.

First, in Europe the European Court of Human Rights (the ECHR) embarked on an interpretation of the Convention that required European countries to apply a best interests test in Hague cases. In 2010, the ECHR ruled in *Neulinger & Shuruk v. Switzerland*[40] that the European Convention on Human Rights requires that courts in states that are parties to the European Convention may not return an abducted child to its habitual residence, even when the child's return is mandated by the Hague Convention, unless it is first established that it is in the best interests of both the child and the child's family to do so. The ECHR decision in *Neulinger* was heavily criticized for having overruled 30 years of international case law, for discounting the fundamental purposes of the Hague Convention of deterring international child abduction, for rewarding international child abduction, and for ensuring that any Hague case that follows its precepts will be lengthy and expensive as well as often unfair to the left-behind parent who must now defend what could be almost a custody case on the taking parent's home turf.[41]

---

37. Asvesta v. Petroutsas, 580 F.3d 1000 (9th Cir. 2009).
38. *In re* M, [2008] 1 A.C. 1288, 1310 (Eng. 2007).
39. *Lozano*, 134 S. Ct. at 1235.
40. Neulinger & Shuruk v. Switzerland, 41615/07 [2010] ECHR 1053.
41. Jeremy D. Morley, *The Hague Abduction Convention and Human Rights: A Critique of the* Neulinger *Case*, 4 Int'l Acad. Matrimonial Law. J. (2011).

The ECHR followed the *Neulinger* case in subsequent cases. In *Šneersone and Kampanella v. Italy*,[42] the ECHR applied *Neulinger* to override an Italian return order since the Italian courts had not conducted an in-depth examination of the entire family situation and of a whole series of factors, in particular of a factual, emotional, psychological, material and medical nature, and made a balanced and reasonable assessment of the respective interests of each person, with constant concern for determining what the best solution would be for the abducted child in the context of an application for his return to his country of origin.

But in *X v. Latvia*,[43] decided in 2013, the Grand Chamber of the ECHR changed course and ruled that a European court's obligation to protect a child's "best interests" would be satisfied in a Hague case, as distinct from a custody case, by complying with a twofold procedural obligation: on the one hand, by examining the allegations of a "serious risk" to the child in the event of return, and demonstrating such examination through a reasoned decision on this point; and on the other, by satisfying themselves that adequate safeguards were provided in the state of habitual residence (in this case, Australia), particularly through tangible protection measures in the event of a known risk. Subsequent cases in Europe show that the Convention is generally being applied appropriately in many, but certainly not all, European countries.

The second front of the attack on the central idea of the Hague Convention comes from advocates of domestic violence victims who contend that the Convention does not provide sufficient protection for women who take their children back to their country of origin when fleeing domestic violence. Although this campaign is directed primarily at an effort to expand the grave risk of harm exception to the Convention, it is sometimes expressed in broader terms as seeking to subordinate all Hague cases to a best interests test. Its influence has been felt in other countries that have enacted legislation that might weaken the application of the Convention in their countries, by expanding the definition of the grave risk of harm exception (e.g., Australia,[44] Switzerland,[45] and Japan[46]).

Of course, the underlying theory of the Convention—that a decision that applies the Convention should make little difference to the ultimate

42. Šneersone & Kampanella v. Italy, (ECHR Application no. 14737/09).

43. X v. Latvia (ECHR Application no. 27853/09).

44. Family Law (Child Abduction Convention) Regulations 1986, as amended in 2022.

45. *See* https://www.international-divorce.com/notes_on_switzerland.

46. *See* http://www.international-divorce.com/japan_hague_convention_practical.

outcome of a case in the long run because the Hague Convention merely determines whether a child should be returned to the country of habitual residence but does not determine the ultimate child custody issues—is, in reality, a pure fiction. Even among the treaty partners to the Convention, there is far less uniformity in the way that courts decide custody cases than the theory claims. All treaty partners claim that their laws are based on the fundamental concept that the best interests of a child must prevail. Translating that concept into reality produces wildly divergent results in practice.

Such inconsistent results are magnified enormously by the fact that there may be enormous delays before a case can be heard; that there may be enormous logistical difficulties for a parent who accompanies a child who is returned to the habitual residence; that local courts may act parochially in favor of the local left-behind parent; that the returning parent may be branded an "international child abductor"; and that restoring the child to the post-abduction, pre-return status quo will uproot the child yet again. Moreover, the returning parent may be in financial ruin, since she may well be unemployed and perhaps unemployable in the original habitual residence, she may well have exhausted her financial resources by defending the Hague case in the U.S. case, she will almost certainly be the subject of an enormous award against her of legal fees and expenses, especially if the petitioner was represented by pro bono counsel whose theoretical hourly rates are high and who have thrown many lawyers into the case, she will often face a contested divorce case in the place to which she is being returned and she must fund and provide the emotional strength to fight what is likely to be a hotly contested custody case in that country.

Notwithstanding these pressures, courts in the United States have generally remained steadfast to the principle that the purpose of the Convention is best fulfilled by interpreting the exceptions narrowly and by avoiding "best interests" analyses in Hague cases except for limited and well-defined circumstances.

§ 1.12 ESSENCE OF THE CONVENTION

Article 12 of the Convention requires judicial authorities in the state in which a child is found to order the return of the child if an application for such relief is made by a person who has a "right of custody" over the child under the laws of the child's "habitual residence" immediately before the removal or retention and if the judicial authorities in the state in which the child is located determine that the child was "wrongfully" removed or retained within the meaning of Article 3 of the Convention, and no exception applies. Article 11 calls for the expeditious conclusion of the proceedings.

The Convention provides for six exceptions to the obligation to return. Although the exceptions are often referred to as "defenses" or "affirmative defenses," they are not complete defenses because the Convention provides that, even if any of several of the exceptions are established, and perhaps all of them, the judicial authorities nonetheless have the authority to order the child's return if they determine that it is appropriate to do so.

Article 3 provides the key definition of a wrongful removal or retention. It states that a child's removal to, or retention in, another state is wrongful if:

> a) it is a breach of rights of custody attributed to a person, an institution or any other body, either jointly or alone, under the law of the State in which the child was habitually resident immediately before the removal or retention; and b) at the time of removal or retention those rights were actually exercised, either jointly or alone, or would have been so exercised but for the removal or retention.

A reading of Article 3 shows that its application hinges on three key terms, these being "child," "rights of custody," and "habitual residence."

§ 1.13 THE KEY TERMS IN THE HAGUE CONVENTION

§ 1.13.1 "Child"

The Convention applies only in respect of children under the age of 16. Article 4 provides that "The Convention shall cease to apply when the child attains the age of 16 years." This means that if a case is commenced while a child is under that age, the case must terminate upon the child reaching the age of 16.

§ 1.13.2 "Rights of Custody"

A petitioner in a Hague case must establish that he or she had a "right of custody" over the child under the law of the child's habitual residence. This does not require that there must have been a custody order in place before the child was taken. It means that the law in question gave certain rights to the petitioner that are sufficient to constitute a custody right. The U.S. Supreme Court has ruled that a parent's right to prevent international travel, known as a *ne exeat* right, is a "right of custody" within the meaning of the Convention.

§ 1.13.3 "Habitual Residence"

The key term "habitual residence" is not defined in the Convention. In many judicial circuits in the United States there was a heavy presumption that a child's habitual residence should be determined by "the last shared intent" of the child's parents, unless it is clearly shown that the child has become acclimatized to another jurisdiction. The courts in other circuits looked primarily at the position of the child reviewed objectively without regard to parental intention. The U.S. Supreme Court in *Monasky* has now overruled all of those cases by determining that the test is that of the "totality of the circumstances."

§ 1.14 OVERVIEW OF THE EXCEPTIONS

Although the purpose of the Convention is to address the harmful effects of international child abduction by ensuring the prompt return of the child to the state of habitual residence, where any custody/access and related issues should be resolved, there may be exceptional circumstances allowing for the non-return of the child. Therefore, the Convention provides that there are six exceptions to the requirement that wrongfully removed or retained children must be returned.

The exceptions must be applied restrictively.[47] The Explanatory Report states that the exceptions "must be applied only so far as they go but no further," thus "in a restrictive fashion if the Convention is not to become a dead letter." It notes that

> a systematic invocation of the [...] exceptions, substituting the forum chosen by the abductor for that of the child's residence, would lead to the collapse of the whole structure of the Convention by depriving it of the spirit of mutual confidence which is its inspiration.[48]

The *Guide to Good Practice* explains that although the exceptions derive from a consideration of the interests of the child, they do not authorize a Hague case to turn into a custody case. The exceptions should not deal with issues of custody or mandate a full "best interests' assessment" for a child within return proceedings. "The competent court or authority seized of return proceedings must apply the provisions of the Convention

47. *Guide to Good Practice Child Abduction Convention: Part VI - Article 13(1)(b)*, para. 25.

48. Perez-Vera Report, para. 34.

and avoid intervening on questions that are for the State of habitual residence to decide."[49]

Although the Convention clearly provides that any one exception is sufficient to authorize a refusal to return a child, there is an ambiguity in ICARA, which was resolved by the Third Circuit. 22 U.S.C 9003(e)(2) provides that in an action for the return of a child, a respondent who opposes the return of the child has the burden of establishing

> **(A)** by clear and convincing evidence that one of the exceptions set forth in article 13b or 20 of the Convention applies; and
>
> **(B)** by a preponderance of the evidence that any other exception set forth in article 12 or 13 of the Convention applies.

A literal meaning of the provision would require a respondent to prove both an exception described in (A) and an exception described in (B). But that interpretation would yield an absurd result. It would contravene the provisions of the Convention itself. Accordingly, in *Monzon*, the court correctly held that a respondent need demonstrate only one affirmative defense to prevail in a case under the Convention, as courts had consistently always allowed.[50]

The six exceptions are as follows:

1. The Consent Exception

If the petitioning parent is proved to have consented to the child being taken to live in the new jurisdiction, this will act as a complete exception in a Hague case.

The key to the consent inquiry is the petitioner's subjective intent. In many cases, a parent allows a child to be taken out of the habitual residence and then there is a dispute as to whether the permission was for a temporary visit or permanent relocation. In such cases, it is critical to focus on what the petitioner actually contemplated and agreed to in allowing the child to travel outside its home country. The burden of proof rests with the respondent to establish that the petitioner harbored a subjective intent to permit the respondent to remove and retain the child for an indefinite or permanent time period.

2. The Acquiescence Exception

Acquiescence by the left-behind parent is also an exception to a Hague petition, but it is far harder to prove than consent. It requires either some

49. *Guide*, *supra* note 39, para. 26.
50. Monzon v. De La Roca, 910 F.3d 92 (3d Cir. 2018).

kind of formality, such as testimony in a judicial proceeding, or a convincing written renunciation of rights, or a consistent attitude of acquiescence over a significant period of time.

3. The Child's Objections Exception

Another exception is that the child objects to being returned and has attained an age and degree of maturity at which it is appropriate to take account of its views. For this exception, there is a two-fold test:

1. Does the child object to being returned to its place of habitual residence? and
2. Has the child obtained an age and degree of maturity at which it is appropriate to take account of its view?

An objection is not the same as a preference. A child's mere preference for one country or another is insufficient. In assessing the maturity level of the minor child, the court must consider the extent to which the child's views have been influenced by an abductor, or if the objection is simply that the child wishes to remain with the abductor.

There is no defined age at which the Convention considers children to be sufficiently mature for their views to be taken into account. It depends entirely on the child.

4. The One Year and Settled Exception

There is also an exception to the obligation to return a child if both of the following are established: That more than one year has elapsed from the date of the alleged wrongful removal or retention to the date that a Hague case is commenced; and that the child is now settled in the new environment.

The date of a wrongful retention may be difficult to establish. Some courts in the United States, but not in other countries, previously ruled that if a child has been concealed so that the left-behind parent does not know where the child is located the one-year period does not start to run until the parent learns of the child's location. Such cases have been overruled.[51] The degree to which a child is now settled in a new environment generally requires an application of a "totality of the circumstances" test.

5. The Human Rights Exception

Another possible exception is that the return of the child "would not be permitted by the fundamental principles of the requested State relating to

51. *Lozano*, 134 S. Ct. 1224.

the protection of human rights and fundamental freedoms."[52] This provision was intended to deal with the rare occasion when the return of a child would utterly shock the conscience of the court or offend all notions of due process. However, it is almost never utilized by the courts.

6. The Grave Risk of Harm Exception

Finally, Article 13(b) of the Hague Convention provides that a court is not bound to order the return of the child if the petitioner establishes that there is a grave risk that his or her return would expose the child to physical or psychological harm or otherwise place the child in an intolerable situation.

The grave risk of harm "defense" is raised in almost every Hague case, but it is successful in only a handful.

The language of the exception is extremely loose. Because a parent who takes a child away from the other parent invariably has a reason to blame that parent, counsel for a respondent is always required to consider the exception and often there is enough evidence to at least make out a viable claim. On the other hand, the exception requires proof of "grave risk" by clear and convincing evidence and the drafting history of the Convention establishes that the drafters intended its terms to be narrowly interpreted.

§ 1.15 UNIFORM INTERPRETATION

The Convention anticipates that its terms will be interpreted uniformly by all treaty partners. This is often expressed by stating that there should be an "autonomous" definition of Hague Abduction Convention terms. ICARA expressly recognizes "the need for uniform international interpretation of the Convention."[53] The U.S. Supreme Court has expressly endorsed this approach. Thus, in *Monasky*, the Supreme Court expressly adopted an interpretation of the term "habitual residence" that accorded with "the views of our treaty partners" and citing cases from the U.K., Canada, European Union, Australia, and New Zealand.[54]

§ 1.16 UNIFORM TRUST

The Convention rests upon the basic premise that the authorities in one treaty partner country will trust the authorities in another treaty partner

52. Convention, Art. 20.
53. 22 U.S.C. § 9001(b)(3)(B).
54. *Monasky*, 140 S. Ct. at 727–28.

country to handle custody cases appropriately and fairly. The concept is that abducted children should be returned forthwith to the country of the child's habitual residence in order that the courts in that original country should decide what is best for the child.

This is similar to the approach that is followed in the United States by means of the Uniform Child Custody Jurisdiction and Enforcement Act, which treats foreign countries as if they were sister states unless a party meets a very heavy burden of proving that the child custody laws of the foreign country violate fundamental provisions of human rights.[55]

However, as more countries become parties to the Convention the disparity among the legal systems of the treaty partners is growing. Some new treaty countries have substantive family law provisions that differ in substance or in practice from the "best interests" approach that is fundamental to U.S. jurisprudence pursuant to which custody is based not on arbitrary norms of age, gender, or religion but on a considered analysis of the circumstances of each child. Others have legal systems that do not provide any effective enforcement of family law orders. Some provide little or no financial support to a custodial mother. Others require a mother with residential custody to keep the child in the location designated by the father.

The tension in this approach is vividly seen in the somewhat typical case of a mother who moved to the father's country of origin at his request; gave birth to their child there (or took their child there); has always been the child's primary care provider; and who now, upon the relationship with the father having ended, faces loneliness, despair, psychological and perhaps physical abuse, and economic distress. Such a mother will invariably want to "go home" with her child and, indeed, will believe that she has the perfect right to do so. If she then exercises what might be a moral right to do so, without the father's consent, and if the father initiates a Hague case against her, she will normally be forced to return to the habitual residence with the child and will be told that she can request international child relocation from the courts of the habitual residence. To add insult to injury, not only will she normally have hired her own counsel to defend her in the Hague case (often spending her last savings) but she will normally be compelled under ICARA to pay the legal expenses and travel and other expenses of the father (who often will have a team of world class pro bono lawyers, who will demand that she pay their fees at their full hourly rates). The idea that the courts in the habitual residence will then order that she—a proven international child

55. *See* Jeremy D. Morley, International Family Law Practice ch. 7 (2020).

abductor—may relocate the child back to her country of origin, is usually quite fanciful.

Indeed, if the law in the habitual residence does not adequately protect the rights of a child to have both parents in its life, that might be deemed to create a grave risk of harm to the child.

Nonetheless, the fundamental purpose of the Convention is deterrence, which is fulfilled by rarely permitting an exception in the typical scenario just described.

§ 1.17 STEP-BY-STEP ANALYSIS IN ANY HAGUE CASE

The structure of the Convention requires a court in any Hague case to follow a step-by-step process in order to apply the Convention logically and correctly.[56] Those steps are as follows:

1. The court should first determine the date of the allegedly wrongful removal or retention of the child.
2. The court should then determine in what country the child was habitually resident immediately prior to that date.
3. The next step is to ascertain whether the Convention was in force at the time of the wrongful removal or retention between the country of habitual residence and the United States.
4. Next, the court must determine the legal rights concerning the child possessed by the petitioning parent (or authority) at that time under the law of the child's habitual residence and whether or not those rights constitute "rights of custody" within the meaning of the Convention.
5. The court must then determine whether the petitioner was exercising those custody rights at the time of removal or retention.
6. It must determine whether the removal or retention breached those custody rights.
7. It must determine whether any exceptions to the Conventions have been established.
8. If an exception is established, the court must determine whether to exercise its discretion to nonetheless return the child.
9. Next, if the child is to be returned to its country of habitual residence it must determine the conditions under which the return shall be made.
10. Finally, if a petition is granted, it must determine the legal fees and expenses, if any, to be paid by the respondent.

56. Tsai-Yi Yang v. Fu-Chiang Tsui, 499 F.3d 259 (3d Cir. 2007).

§ 1.18 ACCESS CLAIMS

The Convention contains certain provisions concerning the protection of a left-behind parent's rights of access to a child. In particular, Article 21 of the Convention provides that an application "to make arrangements for organizing or securing the effective exercise of rights of access" may be presented to the Central Authorities of the Contracting States in the same way as an application for the return of a child. The Central Authority in the United States is the Department of State.

However, the Convention contains no provision for the judicial enforcement of access rights. That is in sharp contrast to Article 12 of the Convention, which addresses wrongful removal and return claims, specifically refers to the initiation of judicial proceedings, and grants judicial authority to provide expedited relief in the case of the wrongful removal or retention of children.

Accordingly, the Fourth Circuit ruled in *Cantor* that neither the Convention nor ICARA provides any authority for federal courts to exercise jurisdiction over access claims, as opposed to claims for the return of children.[57] Other federal courts have stated that access claims are far better left to the state courts.[58]

However, the Second Circuit ruled in *Ozaltin*[59] that it did have jurisdiction over a petitioner's access claims. In that case, the mother removed children from their habitual residence in Turkey. The father petitioned for the return of the children to Turkey, and, pursuant to Article 21, for an order enforcing the visitation rights granted to him by a Turkish family court. The appeal court upheld the district court's return order as well as its ruling that it had jurisdiction under ICARA § 9003(b) to consider the father's access claim and that the mother must comply with the visitation order entered by the Turkish court pending her return of the children to Turkey.

Ozaltin may well be appropriately limited to holding that a federal court has the power to enforce a court order that gives visitation rights to a petitioner but that it does not hold that a federal court has the power to establish a visitation order. In other words, the Second Circuit found that federal courts have jurisdiction to consider and, where appropriate, give effect to orders entered in foreign states regarding a parent's rights

57. Cantor v. Cohen, 442 F.3d 196 (4th Cir. 2006).

58. Janzik v. Schand, No. 99-C-6515, 2000 WL 1745203 (N.D. Ill. 2000); Fernandez v. Yeager, 121 F. Supp. 2d 1118, 1126 (W.D. Mich. 2000); Bromley v. Bromley, 30 F. Supp. 2d 857 (E.D. Pa. 1998).

59. Ozaltin v. Ozaltin, 708 F.3d 355 (2d Cir. 2013).

of access, but this does not allow a federal court to create such rights.[60] The distinction is sensible, and indeed consistent with ICARA § 9001(b)(4), which states, "The Convention and this chapter empowers courts in the United States to determine only rights under the Convention and not the merits of any underlying child custody claims."

In any event, if the left-behind parent has a court order from the child's home state, the UCCJEA provides an excellent and effective remedy for the enforcement of all of the terms of any such order if the foreign jurisdiction was the child's "home state" within the meaning of the UCCJEA.

It should be noted that some countries, such as Australia and New Zealand, have made specific statutory provisions for the enforcement in their domestic courts of Hague access claims.[61]

§ 1.19 RELATIONSHIP OF THE CONVENTION TO THE UCCJEA

The Hague Convention operates independently of the UCCJEA. The UCCJEA (or its predecessor, the Uniform Child Custody Jurisdiction Act) has been incorporated into the law of all U.S. states.

A left-behind parent often has the choice of proceeding under the UCCJEA instead of under the Hague Convention. If a child's "home state" (as that term is defined in UCCJEA section 102(7)) is a foreign country, then, as far as U.S. courts are concerned, courts of that country have primary jurisdiction to make a custody order (section 201), and they generally have "continuing exclusive jurisdiction" concerning custody of the child so long as one parent continues to reside in the country of habitual residence or the "substantial connection" provisions of section 201 are met.[62]

Section 105 of the UCCJEA requires courts in the United States to enforce custody determinations of other countries if jurisdiction was in substantial compliance with the requirements of the act, provided only that the foreign custody law does not violate human rights.

It may well be preferable (and sometimes may be the only option) for a left-behind parent to bring suit under the UCCJEA instead of under the Hague Convention. There are several reasons for this:

60. As was expressly determined in Done v. Pichardo, 2018 WL 1930081 (N.D. Ga. Apr. 24, 2018).

61. *State Central Authority & Quang* [2009] FamCA 1038; *Gumbrell v Jones* [2001] NZFLR 593.

62. UCCJEA § 202.

- The UCCJEA requires a court in the U.S. state in which a child is located to register and enforce a custody order issued by the child's home state, even if the home state is a foreign country. This means that the primary venue for the litigation is the jurisdiction from which the child was taken. It allows the left-behind parent to bring suit on his or her home turf, which is likely to be far more convenient and comfortable than a distant and unfamiliar American court. The left-behind parent can use a local lawyer in the home state to handle the bulk of the work, and the local court will most likely be more sympathetic.
- The foreign country will normally be the child's home state for UCCJEA purposes once the child has lived there for six months. However, that may or may not be sufficient to constitute habitual residence. In any event, if habitual residence is to be an issue in a Hague case it is an expensive issue to prove since it is extremely fact-based and often requires lawyers to collect, evaluate, and present extensive evidence and extensive testimony.
- The UCCJEA does not permit the alleged abductor to assert in the U.S. court any of the exceptions that can be asserted in a Hague case. Registration of a foreign custody order can be contested only on the following grounds: that (1) the issuing court had no jurisdiction to enter the child custody determination; or (2) the foreign child custody determination has been vacated, stayed, or modified by a court having proper jurisdiction to modify same; or (3) notice or an opportunity to be heard was not given to the person contesting jurisdiction provided he or she was entitled to receive notice.[63] There are no other defenses. By contrast, exceptions are invariably claimed in Hague Convention cases and, if one exception is upheld, return may be denied.
- Many countries are not parties to the Hague Convention. A case can be brought under the UCCJEA to register and enforce a foreign custody order issued by any country in the world provided only that the country was the child's "home state," that the action was initiated in compliance with U.S. concepts of due process, and that the defendant cannot establish that the foreign custody law violates human rights.
- The Hague Convention does not effectively provide for the enforcement of access rights. The UCCJEA has no such restriction.

63. *Id.* § 305.

- The Hague Convention applies only in respect of children under the age of 16.
- Hague cases generally raise "interesting" (i.e., expensive) issues. UCCJEA enforcement cases generally (but not always) do not. Therefore, UCCJEA cases are generally substantially cheaper.

On the other hand, it might be better in many cases to bring suit under the Hague Convention, instead of under the UCCJEA, for a variety of reasons:

- The courts in the child's habitual residence might not exercise custody jurisdiction if the child is no longer located there. From a U.S. perspective the courts of that country might have jurisdiction but if those courts do not have jurisdiction under their own jurisdictional rules and if there was no custody order in place prior to the child's removal, there will be no foreign custody order to register and enforce in the United States.
- If the foreign country was not the home state for purposes of the UCCJEA, because the child lived there for less than six months (unless he or she was a baby less than six months old), a custody order issued by a court in that country will generally not be enforceable under the UCCJEA since it will not have been "a child-custody determination made in a foreign country under factual circumstances in substantial conformity with the jurisdictional standards of this [Act]."[64]
- If proper notice or a proper opportunity to be heard was not provided by the foreign court, this should be fatal to an effort to register and enforce the order in the United States. UCCJEA § 305(d)(3) requires that a registered order be vacated if the person contesting registration was entitled to receive proper notice (as required by the UCCJEA) but such notice was not received.
- If the courts in the child's habitual residence act slowly it may be better to bring a Hague case forthwith in the place where the child is currently located.
- If the courts of the habitual residence will not handle the custody case unless and until the child is returned there, it would be possible for the left-behind parent to wait until the U.S. court has custody jurisdiction, usually after six months, and then to sue for custody in the U.S. state where the child is located. In such a situation, however, a Hague case would invariably be a far wiser

64. *Id.* § 105(b).

course, since it would be much quicker, and it would not open the door to a full-blown best interests analysis.

- Financial considerations might favor a Hague case, especially if the foreign country provides legal aid to its nationals for Hague cases but not for UCCJEA cases. Moreover, in an incoming-abduction case to the United States, the left-behind parent might be entitled to reimbursement of legal fees and other related expenses, if the taking parent is found to have abducted the child.

The fact that the UCCJEA and the Hague Convention are entirely separate creatures was well illustrated in a 2012 Colorado decision.[65] There, a respondent mother "won the battle but lost the war," because although she successfully defended the father's petition under the Hague Convention, the father was able to enforce a custody order under the UCCJEA that required the children's return to Canada. The left-behind father filed a Hague petition in a Colorado state court seeking the return to Canada of children born out of wedlock. The mother filed in another Colorado state court under the UCCJEA for an allocation of parental responsibilities. The petition in the Hague case was dismissed because the mother established the exception of grave risk of harm in that returning the children would risk subjecting them to sexual abuse. The proceedings were then consolidated in one proceeding and that court ruled that Canada had jurisdiction under the UCCJEA because it was the "home state." However, the court ordered that the children would remain in Colorado under temporary emergency jurisdiction until a Canadian court took action. The mother appealed. During the pendency of her appeal, the Canadian court entered an order awarding sole custody and guardianship to the father. The Canadian court rejected the allegations of the father's abuse and ordered a brief period of reintegration therapy before the children would be reunited with him.

The mother argued, to no avail, that her victory in the Hague case should act as a bar against contradictory results in a UCCJEA case, under concepts of issue and claim preclusion (or res judicata). But the court held that the issues in a Hague case are entirely different than those in a UCCJEA case. Subject matter jurisdiction to determine parental responsibilities or custody is not decided in a Hague Convention action. Rather, the Hague action concerned only the return of the children, and there was no identity of claims or issues.

---

65. *In re T.L.B.*, 272 P.3d 1148.

Similarly, it is firmly established that a left-behind parent may participate in a custody case in the state court in the place where the child is now located and then, if dissatisfied by the result, may thereafter initiate a Hague case in the federal court. The Ninth Circuit has held that it would undermine the very scheme created by the Hague Convention and ICARA to hold that a Hague Convention claim is barred by a state court custody determination, simply because a petitioner did not raise his Hague Convention claim in the initial custody proceeding.[66]

Indeed, it is also well established that federal courts have the power to vacate state custody determinations and other state court orders that contravene the treaty. The Rooker–Feldman doctrine prohibiting federal court review of state court actions does not bar a federal district court adjudicating a Hague Convention proceeding from vacating a state court's custody order or its order enjoining removal of the child from its jurisdiction.[67]

§ 1.20 HAGUE CONVENTION AND CRIMINAL LAW

The Hague Convention is a purely civil law remedy, even though it uses the criminal terminology of "abduction" and "wrongful" removal or retention.

The United States has enacted federal legislation to prevent children from being removed from or retained out of the United States by one parent without the consent of the other parent or a court order,[68] but such legislation, as well as criminal provisions in state statutes concerning custodial interference, do not normally have any significant bearing on the Hague Convention process.

However, the issue of criminality may arise in connection with a claim that returning the child to the habitual residence will endanger the child since the parent who took the child may face arrest in that country. Child abduction is a criminal offence in many countries, including Argentina, Belgium, Canada, China (Hong Kong SAR), Croatia, Denmark, Finland, France, Germany, Iceland, Israel, Italy, Malta, New Zealand, Panama, Sweden, Switzerland, and the United Kingdom. However, definitions as to what precisely constitutes the offence vary from one country to another. In some jurisdictions (e.g., the U.K.), only wrongful removal

66. Holder v. Holder, 305 F.3d 854 (9th Cir. 2002).
67. Mozes v. Mozes, 239 F.3d 1067 (9th Cir. 2001); *Holder*, 305 F.3d 854.
68. The International Parental Kidnapping Crime Act 1993, 18 U.S.C. §1204.

of a child constitutes a criminal offence, whereas in other jurisdictions wrongful retention can also be a criminal offence. In some countries (e.g., Austria, Poland, and Slovakia) parental child abduction is an offence only if the abducting parent has no parental responsibility or custody rights. Legislation in certain countries creates an offence specifically relating to abduction by parents (e.g., Canada and Finland), whereas in other countries only a more general offence of abduction exists, which in most instances can be applied to parents and third parties alike (e.g., New Zealand, Slovakia, and Switzerland).[69]

In *Madrigal*, the Fifth Circuit ruled that the fact that the respondent mother faced arrest in Mexico if she returned there did not establish that the child faced a grave risk of harm if returned to Mexico. U.S. courts should not second-guess foreign courts, and the possible separation of a child from a parent is not sufficient to trigger the grave risk of harm exception.[70]

The California Court of Appeal held that a trial court had overstepped its bounds by making a return order contingent on the left-behind father providing an assurance from the Italian government that it would not arrest or prosecute the returning mother.[71]

In sharp contrast, the First Circuit upheld a requirement that the petitioner should secure the dismissal of German criminal charges against the respondent prior to returning the child, although the only issue on appeal on this issue concerned whether the requirement provided enough protection to the respondent.[72]

§ 1.21 WHAT THE HAGUE CONVENTION IS NOT

It is important to note what the Hague Convention is not, and what it does not handle, since there is often a false perception among family lawyers who do not handle many international cases, and even among judges, that it is far broader than it really is.

1. The Convention does not provide for the international registration of custody orders. Indeed, other countries, with very few

---

69. This paragraph is based on the *Hague Conference Guide to Good Practice, Part III*, para. 1.3, *available at* www.hcch.net.

70. Madrigal v. Tellez, 848 F.3d 669 (5th Cir. 2017).

71. Maurizio R v. LC, 201 Cal. App. 4th 616, 644 (2011).

72. Kufner v. Kufner, 519 F.3d 33 (1st Cir. 2008).

exceptions, do not have any such registration procedures, unlike the UCCJEA.

2. The Convention does not deal with the international service of process. That is the province of the Hague Convention of 15 November 1965 on the Service Abroad of Judicial and Extrajudicial Documents in Civil or Commercial Matters.
3. The Convention does not deal with international child support.
4. The Convention does not deal with international divorce jurisdiction, although in practice it may have a momentous impact on the jurisdictional issues.
5. The Convention does not deal with international travel of children, except to the extent that courts may be more inclined to allow a child to travel to a country that is a compliant Convention partner and less likely to allow such travel to a country that is not a compliant treaty partner, because if a child is retained in a foreign Hague country the left-behind parent will normally have the right to initiate proceedings in the foreign country to seek the child's return.
6. The Convention does not deal with international relocation of children, except to the very limited extent that it contains (relatively toothless) provisions about rights of access. Some courts place inappropriate reliance on the Hague Convention as a reliable device that will ensure that the terms of a U.S. court order setting forth the rights of a non-relocating parent will be enforced in the foreign country pursuant to the Convention. The Hague Convention is not effective in that regard.
7. The Convention does not provide any substantive rights.
8. The Convention does not allow the court in which a Hague Convention action is filed to consider the merits of any underlying child custody claims, except that, in the exercise of its discretion once a Hague exception has been established, the court may consider such factors as it deems appropriate.
9. Neither the Convention nor ICARA nor any other treaty or legislation authorizes the U.S. Secretary of State to re-abduct an abducted child or to take any other direct action to take back an abducted child.
10. The State Department does not initiate Hague court cases. This is in sharp contrast to the procedures in several other countries, whose Central Authorities are the initiating agency.

11. There is no international court for Hague cases. Cases brought under the Convention are decided by courts in the place where the abducted child is currently located.
12. Submitting an application to the State Department does not constitute the commencement of a judicial proceeding and—critically—it does not stop the clock on the running of the one-year period in Article 12.

Instead, the Hague Convention establishes only a procedure to be used between countries who are treaty partners under the Convention by which the return of children under the age of 16 years may be accomplished if their removal or retention is determined to be "wrongful" under the Convention.

§ 1.22 CASES IN OTHER COUNTRIES UNDER THE HAGUE CONVENTION

The procedures that are employed in the United States to process cases under the Convention are not the same as those followed in other countries. Although all treaty partners are required to follow the provisions that are contained in the Convention, they are free to do so in conformity with their own judicial systems and processes. The Convention requires expeditious action, with Article 2 stating that Contracting States "shall use the most expeditious procedures available," but it does not specify the form that that will take.

Merely by way of example, in Australia jurisdiction to hear abduction cases at first instance is concentrated to the justices of the general or trial division of the Family Court. The Commonwealth Central Authority is appointed within the Commonwealth Attorney General's Department. The Commonwealth Attorney General appoints a Central Authority for each Australian state. This is usually the secretary or head of the state's child welfare department, who then has available the services of trained child protection workers, emergency accommodation, and a working relationship with the police. Abduction applications are normally prosecuted by the state's Central Authority, without cost to the left-behind parent. A parent may choose instead to prosecute their own case to the exclusion of the state Central Authority, but it is most unusual.

In Sweden, the Department for Consular Affairs and Civil Law at the Ministry for Foreign Affairs is the designated Central Authority. The Central Authority handles the administrative duties in Convention cases but does not initiate judicial proceedings. All cases brought under the Convention in Sweden are heard by family judges within the Stockholm City Court. The court is obliged to handle the case with expedience. Cases should be dealt with within six weeks and in the event that the process lasts for a longer period of time the court is obliged to inform the applicant, upon his/her request, about the reasons causing the delay. Appellate courts are also required to give priority to Hague Convention cases regarding wrongful detention or abductions.

Swedish legislation recognizes the child's right to have an opportunity to express his or her views during the procedure, unless that would be improper in respect to the child's age and maturity. The assessment of younger children's statements must be made by people with certain knowledge in this area, usually by the social welfare board's social workers.

§ 1.23 HAGUE CONVENTION AND ASYLUM STATUS

A grant of asylum to a parent who has abducted a child and a grant of asylum to an abducted child do not bar the return of the child to the country of habitual residence pursuant to the Hague Convention. Arguments that an order of return would threaten the sovereignty of the executive branch or violate U.S. public policy or human rights have not succeeded.

The Fifth Circuit considered such matters in *Sanchez*,[73] in which three children sought reversal of the district court's finding under the Convention that they should be returned to their mother in Mexico. While their appeal was pending, the children were granted asylum in the United States pursuant to 8 U.S.C. § 1158, which states that "the Attorney General . . . shall not remove or return the alien to the alien's country of nationality." This grant of asylum is discretionary and requires that the recipient have suffered past persecution or demonstrate a "well-founded fear of persecution on account of race, religion, nationality, membership in a particular social group, or political opinion." On appeal, the children argued that the grant of asylum superseded the district court's order. The Fifth Circuit rejected this argument, refusing to hold that there was no authority to support a claim that the grant of asylum must be revoked before the children could be returned to Mexico. It further held that, despite similarities, the asylum finding that the children had a well-founded fear of persecution did not substitute for or control a finding under Article 13(b) of the Convention about whether return would expose

73. Sanchez v. R.G.L., 761 F.3d 495 (5th Cir. 2014).

them to physical or psychological harm or otherwise place them in an intolerable situation.

Nonetheless, the court recognized that the factors relevant to an asylum grant may also be relevant to whether the Hague Convention exceptions to return should apply. It remanded the case for the district court to consider the newly available evidence associated with the asylum proceedings.

In *Salame*,[74] the Sixth Circuit followed *Sanchez*, even though the children were granted asylum *before* the district court ordered return of the children. The district court made independent findings on whether the children would face an intolerable situation or a grave risk of harm in Venezuela, considering all of the offered, admissible, and relevant evidence, and it found that such evidence did not satisfy the Hague Convention test in Article 13(b). On appeal, the court ruled that the prior consideration of similar concerns in a different forum may be relevant, but a grant of asylum did not strip the district court of its authority to make controlling findings regarding the circumstances that the children might face upon return. The court also noted the difference in evidentiary burdens between asylum proceedings and those under the Convention's framework. To be granted asylum, eligibility must be shown by a preponderance of the evidence, whereas for an Article 13(b) affirmative defense to apply, the respondent must establish the exception by clear and convincing evidence. Additionally, the opportunity for participation by interested parties may be different—here, the left-behind parent did not participate in the asylum proceedings.

Counsel seeking a more extensive reliance on the relevance of the respondent's asylum status or that of the child should review the dissent in the *Salame* case and the judge's reference in that case to a Canadian case holding that a finding of refugee status by the Canadian authorities "gives rise to a rebuttable presumption that the removal of the child from Canada will expose the child to a risk of prosecution, that is, to a risk of harm."[75]

74. Salame v. Tescari, 29 F.4th 763 (6th Cir. 2022).
75. A.M.R.I. v. K.E.R., [2011] ONCA 417.

Procedural and Practical Issues

2

§ 2.01 ROLE OF CENTRAL AUTHORITY

The Convention requires each treaty party to establish a Central Authority to handle certain administrative functions, with responsibility for providing assistance in both "outgoing" cases in which a child is taken away from a country and "incoming" cases in which a child has been brought into the country.[1]

The drafters of the Convention anticipated that Central Authorities would be able to help secure the return of abducted children without the need for the left-behind parent to resort to the courts for relief.

The United States has designated the State Department's Office of Children's Issues in the Bureau of Consular Affairs as its Central Authority for both incoming and outgoing cases. Until October 2008, the National Center for Missing & Exploited Children was the Central Authority for incoming cases.[2]

For outgoing cases, the State Department helps to process applications for a child's return, transmits the applications to the Central Authority in the place where the child is currently located, and provides information about the options and resources available in the foreign country.

In some countries, for incoming cases, the designated Central Authority takes a leading role in overseeing the entire process and in

1. Hague Convention, Arts. 6, 7.
2. FR Doc. E8-25929 filed 10-29-08.

appointing—and even supervising—lawyers to handle Hague cases in the courts. For example, in Australia, the Central Authority initiates Hague cases, is the plaintiff in any such Hague case against an abducting parent, and its lawyers in such cases do not take instructions relating to the conduct of the case directly from the left-behind parent, who is not a party to the legal proceedings.[3] In Germany, the German Central Authority appoints an attorney to represent the left-behind parent in court hearings or the parent can choose to hire a private German attorney.[4]

In sharp contrast, the U.S. Central Authority does not undertake any such work and it is unable to do so. It is not the responsibility of the U.S. State Department to initiate or prosecute Hague Convention cases or to be involved in any significant way in a Hague judicial proceeding. Article 8 of the Convention provides that any person, institution, or other body claiming that a child has been removed or retained in breach of custody rights may apply either to the Central Authority of the child's habitual residence or to the Central Authority of any other Contracting State for assistance in securing the return of the child. However, it is critical to understand that the Office of Children's Issues has no judicial function and it has no authority to secure a child's return pursuant to the Convention.

It is recommended that a petitioning parent should retain private counsel to initiate a Hague case in court in the United States. It is also strongly recommended that the original Hague application should be prepared by retained and experienced counsel, since a poorly drafted document might include inadvertent and inappropriate admissions and might not take advantage of the inclusion of helpful documents, which will be admissible in court if so included. Indeed, it is usually absolutely crucial that knowledgeable international family law counsel is consulted concerning the entire process and, in many cases, concerning the interplay between the Hague Convention and the UCCJEA. Such issues are entirely beyond the responsibility of the staff at the Office of Children's Issues and are beyond the knowledge or experience of most family lawyers who do not generally handle such cases.

The specific services that the U.S. Secretary of State's Office of Children's Issues provides for incoming abduction cases include:

3. http://travel.state.gov/abduction/country/country_507.html.
4. http://travel.state.gov/abduction/country/country_491.html#convention.

- Accepting applications for return or access from foreign Central Authorities;
- Assisting left-behind parents in locating their children within the United States;
- Attempting to achieve voluntary returns or access where possible;
- Assisting left-behind parents with securing attorneys, including attorneys willing to work on a pro bono or reduced-fee basis for qualified parents; and
- Assisting with the safe return of children to their habitual residence abroad.

The submission of an application to the Office of Children's Issues does not constitute the initiation of judicial proceedings, does not stop the clock for purposes of the "one year and settled" exception to the Convention, and does not require the alleged abductor to take or not to take any action. The Office does not appoint attorneys for a left-behind parent and it does not file return petitions with the courts. The responsibility for starting a Hague case in an appropriate court in the United States rests exclusively with the left-behind parent.

The Office of Children's Issues prepares annual reports for Congress on the compliance by other treaty partners of their responsibilities under the Convention.

Before 2015, the obligation to submit such reports was governed by the International Child Abduction Remedies Act, 22 U.S.C. § 911. The reports identified countries that were "Not Compliant with the Convention" or that showed "Patterns of Noncompliance with the Convention." They listed cases that remained open and active for 18 months or more after a Convention application was filed, and listed countries with "enforcement concerns."

Starting in 2015, pursuant to the International Child Abduction Prevention and Return Act (ICAPRA), the Department is required to provide substantially more detailed compliance reports.[5] In particular, for each country with respect to which there were five or more pending abduction cases during the preceding year relating to children whose habitual residence is the United States, the State Department must provide specifics about such factors as cases that have been delayed, situations where children have not been located, and court orders that have not been enforced.

5. 22 U.S.C.A. § 9111.

The views expressed in the annual reports are of great importance in many cases in which judicial applications are made in U.S. courts to enjoin a parent from taking a child overseas or to permit foreign visits by a child or even international relocations of a child with one parent when the other parent objects. However, for obvious reasons, the State Department reports have been prepared "diplomatically" and many international family lawyers find that the State Department's reports have been far too conservative and restrained in their criticisms of the practices of many U.S. treaty partners. In addition, the criteria contained in ICAPRA concerning the State Department's reports are both arbitrary and limited. Consequently, while the State Department also reports on the noncompliance of some non-Hague countries, it fails to make such determinations concerning many other such countries that clearly do not expeditiously return internationally abducted children. This can create a major problem when courts consider whether to allow visits of children to such countries.

§ 2.02 THE INTERNATIONAL CHILD ABDUCTION REMEDIES ACT

In the United States, the Hague Convention is integrated into law by means of the International Child Abduction Remedies Act, known as ICARA.[6] ICARA is important in several respects.

First, it contains Findings and Declarations that may be useful to cite in Hague cases.[7] Those findings are that:

- The international abduction or wrongful retention of children is harmful to their well-being;
- Persons should not be permitted to obtain custody of children by virtue of their wrongful removal or retention; and
- International abductions and retentions of children are increasing, and only concerted cooperation pursuant to an international agreement can effectively combat this problem.

The declarations include the fact that:

- "In enacting this Act the Congress recognizes (A) the international character of the Convention; and (B) the need for uniform international interpretation of the Convention" and that

6. 22 U.S.C. § 9001 *et seq.*
7. *Id.* § 9001.

- "The Convention and this Act empower courts in the United States to determine only rights under the Convention and not the merits of any underlying child custody claims."

Second, the definitions section of ICARA defines "rights of access" as used in the Convention to mean "visitation rights."[8] This is of significance in distinguishing rights of custody and rights of access.

Third, ICARA gives state and federal courts concurrent jurisdiction to handle Hague cases.[9]

Fourth, ICARA provides that a person seeking to initiate judicial proceedings under the Convention may do so by filing a petition in any court having such jurisdiction "in the place where the child is located at the time the petition is filed."[10] Thus, it effectively requires that a case be commenced only in a court in the United States that is geographically in the place where the child is actually located at the time of the filing.

Fifth, ICARA provides that notice of an action brought under the Convention shall be given "in accordance with the applicable law governing notice in interstate child custody proceedings."[11]

Sixth, the law also provides the burdens of proof that govern the conduct of Hague trials.[12] Specifically, the petitioner has the burden to establish by a preponderance of the evidence that the child has been wrongfully removed or retained within the meaning of the Convention. The respondent then has the burden to establish by clear and convincing evidence that one of the exceptions set forth in Article 13b (grave risk of harm) or Article 20 (human rights and fundamental freedoms) of the Convention applies and by a preponderance of the evidence that any other exception set forth in Article 12 or 13 of the Convention applies.

Seventh, the act provides that the term "commencement of proceedings," as used in Article 12 of the Convention, means the filing of a petition in accordance with ICARA with respect to the return of a child located in the United States.[13] This is of substantial importance whenever the exception of "one year and settled" is raised.

Eighth, the act provides that full faith and credit shall be accorded by both state and federal courts to the judgment of any other such court

8. *Id.* § 9002(7).
9. *Id.* § 9003(a).
10. *Id.* § 9003(b).
11. *Id.* § 9003(c).
12. *Id.* § 9003(e).
13. *Id.* § 9003(f)(3).

ordering or denying the return of a child, pursuant to the Convention, in an action brought under ICARA.[14]

Ninth, the act provides for provisional remedies. Specifically, it states that any court in a Hague case may take (or cause to be taken) measures under federal or state law, as appropriate, to protect the well-being of the child involved or to prevent the further removal or concealment before the final disposition of the petition. However, it also states that no such court may order a child removed from a person having physical control of the child "unless the applicable requirements of State law are satisfied."[15]

Tenth, the act contains a significant provision concerning the admissibility of documents.[16] It provides that no authentication shall be required in order for any application, petition, document, or information to be admissible in court in a Hague case if the Hague application is submitted to the U.S. Central Authority or the petition is submitted in a Hague case or the document or information is included with such application or petition or is provided after such submission and relates to the application or petition.

Finally, the act provides that, if a petition is successful, the parent who has taken a child away from its habitual residence must pay the legal fees and travel expenses of the petitioning parent.[17]

§ 2.03 CONCURRENT JURISDICTION

The federal and state courts have concurrent jurisdiction in cases brought in the United States under the Convention. ICARA provides that "[t]he courts of the States and the United States district courts shall have concurrent original jurisdiction of actions arising under the Convention."[18]

In many countries, Hague cases are channeled to a limited number of "Hague judges," who have special training and experience in handling these cases. Indeed, the U.S. State Department has frequently lobbied other countries to provide such training and judicial concentration in Hague cases. However, Hague cases in the United States can be brought before either federal or state judges wherever the child is located, without regard to whether the judge has any special training or experience in such matters. Most judges in the United States who might be called upon

---

14. *Id.* § 9003(g).
15. *Id.* § 9004(b).
16. *Id.* § 9005.
17. *Id.* § 9007(b).
18. *Id.* § 9003(a).

to handle Hague cases have never done so previously. In this author's experience, it happens quite often that judges in Hague cases report that "this is my first Hague case" and therefore sometimes ask the lawyers to provide explanatory information concerning the Hague process.

The completely different backgrounds of family court judges and federal judges means that the choice of either the state system or the federal system might have a major impact on the outcome of the case. Depending on the issues in the case, litigants and counsel may prefer—or may not prefer—a family court judge who has experience in child custody cases or a federal judge who usually does not have any such experience.

In practice, the vast majority of Hague cases in the United States are brought in federal court. This may be for a variety of reasons. One is that petitioners often prefer to bring the case in a court that is not accustomed to applying "best interests" analyses in conventional child custody cases. Another is that swift action might be more likely in a federal court, whose dockets are shorter and whose enforcement procedures are clear and forceful.

If the case is initiated in a state court, the respondent has the absolute right to remove it to the federal court, provided that the specific procedural requirements of the federal removal statute are satisfied.[19] That statute expressly provides that any civil action brought in a state court of which the district courts of the United States have original jurisdiction, may be removed by the defendant to the federal district court for the district and division embracing the place where such action is pending. A respondent desiring to remove a case must file a notice of removal in the federal district court for the district and division within which the state case is pending, within 30 days after the receipt by the respondent, through service or otherwise, of a copy of the initial pleading (or the summons) in the case.[20]

In addition, respondent's counsel must ensure that respondent does not waive the right to remove by engaging in litigation conduct in the state court that is not merely defensive in nature. If such conduct is a "clear and unequivocal" demand for affirmative relief or affirmative action from the state court, as opposed to merely defensive conduct and conduct which is preliminary, it may constitute such a waiver.[21]

---

19. 28 U.S.C. § 1441.
20. *Id.* § 1446.
21. Resolution Trust Co. v. Bayside Developers, 43 F.3d 1230 (9th Cir. 1994).

§ 2.04 THE HAGUE APPLICATION

Each Central Authority has developed an application form that must be carefully completed. Article 8 of the Convention requires that the application should contain:

- Information concerning the identity of the applicant, of the child and of the person alleged to have removed or retained the child;
- Where available, the date of birth of the child;
- The grounds on which the applicant's claim for return of the child is based; and
- All available information relating to the whereabouts of the child and the identity of the person whom the child is presumed to be with.

Article 8 also provides that the application may be accompanied or supplemented by:

- An authenticated copy of any relevant decision or agreement;
- A certificate or an affidavit emanating from a Central Authority, or other competent authority of the state of the child's habitual residence, or from a qualified person, concerning the relevant law of that state; and
- Any other relevant documents.

Although the application is not a court document, it is important that it be prepared with care and thoroughness—and generally by a lawyer who is well experienced in handling Hague cases. This is because:

a. Article 30 of the Convention provides that any such application, together with any documents and any other information appended to it, shall be admissible in the courts of the Contracting States. This means that the statement of the factual basis for the claim should be complete and should contain no inappropriate admissions.
b. The description of the grounds of the application should satisfy the requirements of the Convention. In particular, it is important that the applicant should describe the "rights of custody" that he or she possesses under the law of the habitual residence. If the parents are unmarried and/or there is no order from a court in the habitual residence, it is usual for the application to be accompanied by an affidavit from a lawyer in that country setting forth the legal basis of the applicant's custodial rights in respect of the child.

c. In some jurisdictions outside the United States, a Hague judicial proceeding cannot be commenced unless and until the Hague application has been reviewed and approved by the Central Authority in that country. Indeed, some Central Authorities—Australia being just one example—review the merits of a Hague application to determine whether a prima facie case is presented. Accordingly, particularly in such cases, the application should be drafted so as to be a stand-alone convincing presentation of the applicant's prima facie case.

Article 8 provides that the application may be filed with a Central Authority in a country other than the one in the country from which the child was removed. It is sometimes preferable to file the application in the country in which the child is now located, since that may expedite the case and might be procedurally simpler. Some Central Authorities, including the U.S. Central Authority in outgoing cases, may take a considerable period of time to review applications before forwarding them to the Central Authority in the country in which the child is currently located. Decisions about where to file the application should not be made without securing specialist and experienced advice.

§ 2.05 INITIATING THE CASE

Hague Convention cases in the United States are generally commenced by means of a petition. The petition should, at a minimum:

- Assert that the case concerns a child under the age of 16;
- Assert that the child is located within the jurisdiction of the court;
- Identify the country of habitual residence (within the meaning of the Convention) of the child as of the relevant date;
- Assert that the Hague Convention was in force between the foreign country and the United States on the relevant date;
- Assert that the petitioner had "rights of custody" under the law of the habitual residence as of the relevant date and that such rights were then being actually exercised or would have been actually exercised but for the child's removal or retention;
- Assert that the respondent removed the child to the United States or retained the child in the United States in breach of the petitioner's rights of custody, and identify the date of the removal or retention;
- Assert that such removal or retention was "wrongful" within the meaning of Article 3 of the Convention;

- Demand that the court should order the return of the child forthwith;
- Demand that necessary expenses incurred by or on behalf of the petitioner, including court costs, legal fees, and transportation costs related to the return of the child; and
- Demand any interim relief sought by the petitioner, supporting such demand with details of the reasons for such relief.

For evidentiary reasons, it may well be sensible to include evidentiary materials in the petition. See § 2.16. The petition may request that the court issue a show cause order directing that service be made on the respondent in a specified manner, scheduling an extremely prompt initial hearing or pretrial conference, and immediately ordering injunctive relief. The usual interim relief that is sought on an immediate basis is an injunction prohibiting the removal of the children from the jurisdiction and directing the respondent to bring the children to the court and deliver to the court the respondent's and the child's passports and all other travel documents.

The petitioner might also request such provisions as:

- An order directing that the name of the child be entered into the national police computer system (N.C.I.C.) missing person section; and
- An order requiring the respondent to allow and facilitate calls or visits between the petitioner and the child.

Article 8 of the Convention identifies the persons who may be petitioners in a Hague Convention case. It states that,

> Any person, institution or other body claiming that a child has been removed or retained in breach of custody rights may apply either to the Central Authority of the child's habitual residence or to the Central Authority of any other Contracting State for assistance in securing the return of the child.

This means that the petitioner must be a person, institution, or other body who possesses, and has exercised, custody rights over the child under the law of the child's habitual residence. Although this is typically the left-behind parent, there may be situations in which a person other than a biological parent has actually been exercising custody of the child and is, therefore, eligible to seek the child's return pursuant to the Convention. Thus, the Royal Borough of Kensington & Chelsea (RBKC) was an appropriate petitioner in a case in which it had custody rights over a child when she was taken from England to New York because before the child was removed, the Family Court in London had issued two ne exeat orders prohibiting the removal of the child from the United Kingdom; and under the law of the United Kingdom, the RBKC was delegated the authority to enforce the rights of the High Court relating to the child.[22]

The State Department Legal Analysis provides various further examples.

- One example would be a grandparent who has had physical custody of a child following the death of the parent with whom the child had been residing. If the child is subsequently removed from the custody of the grandparent by the surviving parent, the aggrieved grandparent could invoke the Convention to secure the child's return. In another situation, the child may be in the care of foster parents.
- If custody rights exercised by the foster parents are breached, for instance, by abduction of the child by its biological parent, the foster parents could invoke the Convention to secure the child's return.
- Institutions such as public or private childcare agencies also may have custody rights that would be remediable under the Convention if they were breached. If a natural parent relinquishes parental rights to a child and the child is subsequently placed in the care of an adoption agency, that agency may invoke the Convention to recover the child if the child is abducted by its parent(s).

§ 2.06 WHO MAY BE NAMED AS A RESPONDENT?

Neither the Convention nor ICARA expressly defines who must or may be named as respondents in a Hague case. ICARA provides that notice of an action "shall be given in accordance with the applicable law governing notice in interstate child custody proceedings." This refers to the UCCJEA (or the UCCJA in Massachusetts). Section 205(a) of the UCCJEA provides that

> notice and an opportunity to be heard . . . must be given to all persons entitled to notice under the law of this state as in child custody proceedings between residents of this state, any parent

22. Royal Borough of Kensington & Chelsea v. Bafna-Louis, 2023 WL 6867135 (2d Cir. Oct. 18, 2023).

> whose parental rights have not been previously terminated, and any person having physical custody of the child.

In one case, service on the director of an institution that was charged lawfully with directing the placement of the children with a foster parent was held to be sufficient, even though the foster parent was not served. The director had knowledge of the children's location and, as director of child placement, had authority over the agency to direct their placement. That was enough to oversee the children's return.[23]

There is also authority for including as party respondents those individuals beside the taking parent who have aided the alleged abduction, either by participating in the abduction process or sheltering the abducted child. The Perez-Vera Report expressly "contemplates the possibility of people, other than the father and mother, to become the active subjects in such actions, for example a more or less distant relative or one of the adoptive parents, etc."[24] and states that the Convention upholds the view that the wrongful acts are not to be limited to parents,

> Since the idea of "family" was more or less wide, depending on the different cultural conceptions which surround it, it was felt better to hold a wide view which would, for example, allow removals by a grandfather or adoptive father to be characterized as child abduction, in accordance with the Convention's use of that term.[25]

Indeed, the Convention is especially designed to deter "those close to [a child], such as parents, guardians, or family members," from unilaterally taking or keeping the child out of the country of habitual residence with an intent "to establish artificial jurisdictional links" to a more sympathetic forum for a custody dispute.[26] Thus, when the children's father and grandmother each participated in planning or implementing the abduction and then in concealing the child, they were both appropriate respondents.[27]

In one case,[28] the respondents included the abducting father's unrelated friends who helped him. The court ruled that the friends were "not related to the children and presumably have no stake in the outcome of

23. Sanchez v. R. G. L. *ex rel.* Hernandez, 761 F.3d 495 (5th Cir. 2014).
24. Perez-Vera Report, para. 55.
25. Perez-Vera Report, para. 81.
26. Gitter v. Gitter, 396 F.3d 124, 129–30 (2d Cir. 2005).
27. Lops v. Lops, 140 F.3d 927 (11th Cir. 1998).
28. Neves v. Neves, 637 F. Supp.2d 322 (W.D.N.C. 2009).

the custody case that is currently pending in Germany. Nevertheless, the Court is mindful that the Patels' assistance was integral to Respondent Neves's plans."[29] The friends' assistance included making the travel arrangements, allowing the father and children to live in one of their houses, and ignoring the mother's efforts to locate her children.

A benefit of adding additional respondents is that all of them may be subject to interim injunctions in accordance with 22 U.S.C. § 9004(a) and to liability for the petitioner's legal fees and expenses pursuant to 22 U.S.C. § 9007(b)(3).[30] Thus, a person who conspires with a parent to wrongfully remove or retain a child is as responsible as the abducting parent to pay the petitioner's fees and expenses.[31]

Courts in other countries routinely include respondents who are not parents or even blood relatives. Rule 12.3(1) of the U.K.'s Family Procedure Rules 2010 Practice Directions governing Hague Convention proceedings authorize including as respondents (1) the person alleged to have brought the child into the U.K.; (2) the person with whom the child is alleged to be; (3) any parent or guardian of the child who is within the U.K. and is not otherwise a party; (4) any person in whose favor a decision relating to custody has been made if that person is not otherwise a party; and (5) any other person who appears to the court to have sufficient interest in the welfare of the child. Likewise, the Supreme Court of Israel awarded attorneys' fees against both the abducting mother and the mother's new husband, who had helped her.[32]

§ 2.07 VENUE

ICARA provides that a Hague judicial proceeding shall be brought "in the place where the child is located at the time the petition is filed."[33] Venue is determined solely in accordance with ICARA, not in accordance with the child custody jurisdictional rules of the UCCJEA.[34]

29. *Id.* at 347.

30. Litowchak v. Litowchak, 2015 WL 7428573 (D. Vt. 2015).

31. Hirts v. Hirts, 152 Fed. Appx. 137 (3d Cir. 2005) and see parties' briefs available at 2005 WL 4829185 and 2005 WL 4829186; likewise, we are informed that fees were awarded against both respondents in *Lops*, 140 F.3d 927.

32. G. v. G., 14 August 1995, C.A. 5532/93, *available at* www.incadat.com/en/case/355.

33. 22 U.S.C. § 9003(b).

34. Baz v. Patterson, 100 F.4th 854 (7th Cir. 2024). Similarly, *see* Lops v. Lops, 140 F.3d 927 (11th Cir. 1998).

The Ninth Circuit has recognized that the word "located" has a particular meaning in the context of ICARA, that is distinct from "a traditional residency test." It means "the place where the abducted children are discovered," and is more equivalent to the concept of physical presence. "This kind of common-sense definition makes sense in the context of the ICARA and the Hague Convention, concerned as they are with the Hague Convention's consistent application across borders."[35]

In one case the petitioner brought his case in Nevada, where he reasonably believed the children were located, rather than in California, where the mother claimed they were actually located. Although the Magistrate Judge determined that the children were indeed in Nevada on the date the petition was filed, she recommended against being too exacting about the precise location of the child if the petitioner genuinely believed the children were in that location. The district judge refused to accept that recommendation, holding that "[u]nder ICARA, jurisdiction exists only where the children are physically present at the time of filing."[36]

If a case is commenced in a district or division based upon an erroneous but good faith belief that the child is located there, courts have the power to transfer the case to the district where the child is actually located.[37]

§ 2.08 AGE OF THE CHILD

Article 4 of the Convention states that it "shall cease to apply when the child attains the age of 16 years." The State Department's legal analysis of the Convention explains that "[t]he Convention applies only to children under the age of sixteen (16). Even if a child is under sixteen at the time of the wrongful removal or retention as well as when the Convention is invoked, the Convention ceases to apply when the child reaches sixteen."[38]

Since the power of a court to apply the Convention ceases the moment a child turns 16, a court took action specifically intended to enable the conclusion of a case before the next birthday of a 15-year-old child.[39]

---

35. Holder v. Holder, 305 F.3d 854, 869 (9th Cir. 2002) n.5; citing *Lops*, 140 F.3d 937.

36. Gee v. Hendroffe, 2014 WL 60325 (D. Nev. 2014).

37. Flores Perla v. Perla Velasquez, 2016 WL 3878495 (D. Md. 2016).

38. Appendix Four, p. 6.

39. Gaudin v. Remis, 379 F.3d 631, 638 (9th Cir. 2004).

§ 2.09 SERVICE OF PROCESS

The Convention itself does not contain any specific notice requirements, but ICARA provides that notice should be given "in accordance with the applicable law governing notice in interstate child custody proceedings."[40]

The "law governing notice in interstate child custody proceedings" is set forth in the Uniform Child Custody Jurisdiction & Enforcement Act as enacted in each state (except Massachusetts, which has still adopted only the prior version) and also in the federal Parental Kidnapping Prevention Act of 1980. The UCCJEA, as adopted for example in New York, provides that, "[b]efore a child custody determination is made under this article, notice and an opportunity to be heard in accordance with the standards of section seventy-five-g of this article must be given to all persons entitled to notice under the law of this state."[41] The UCCJEA further provides that notice may be given "in a manner prescribed by the law of this State for service of process or by the law of the state in which the service is made" and "[p]roof of service may be made in the manner prescribed by the law of this State or by the law of the State in which the service is made."[42]

Both statutes have been used in Hague cases to determine the appropriate standard for service.[43]

In some cases, federal courts have authorized substituted service in any manner reasonably effective to give the respondent notice of the suit.[44]

Service that does not comply with the requirements of proper service under the UCCJEA has been held to be insufficient even if the respondent receives actual notice of the petition.[45] Nonetheless, in that case the court concurred in the magistrate judge's discretionary determination to extend the time for service is appropriate, because forcing the husband to recommence the action beyond the one-year time period would bar his claim for immediate return of the children, and since mother had actual notice, she would not be prejudiced. Other cases have upheld service when the respondent had notice without having actually being served. In one case, federal marshals made several attempts to personally serve the respondent at her last two known New York addresses, petitioner mailed the relevant

---

40. 22 U.S.C. § 9003(c).
41. N.Y. Dom. Rel. Law § 76-d(1).
42. UCCJEA § 108; N.Y. Dom. Rel. Law § 75-g.
43. Brooke v. Willis, 907 F. Supp. 57 (S.D.N.Y. 1995).
44. Hernandez v. Erazo, 2022 WL 17490682 (W.D. Tex. Oct. 31, 2022).
45. Ebanks v. Ebanks, 2007 WL 2591196 (S.D.N.Y. Sept. 6, 2007).

papers to those addresses, respondent engaged in evasive tactics, and the petitioner claimed to have informed the respondent of the proceedings.[46]

If the taking parent does not have physical custody of the child, notice shall be given not only to that parent but also to whoever has physical custody of the child. This might be a child protective service agency or a foster care service.

2.10 TEMPORARY RESTRAINING ORDER

A petitioner in a Hague Convention case may seek, and a court will often issue, an ex parte temporary restraining order at the outset of the case. ICARA provides that a court "may take or cause to be taken measures under Federal or State law, as appropriate, to protect the well-being of the child involved or to prevent the child's further removal or concealment before the final disposition of the petition."[47]

Pursuant to Federal Rule of Civil Procedure 65(b)(1), such an order may be issued without notice to the adverse party only upon a showing that "immediate and irreparable injury, loss, or damage will result to the movant before the adverse party can be heard in opposition" and the movant's attorney "certifies in writing any efforts made to give notice and the reasons why it should not be required."

Temporary restraining orders are "designed to preserve the status quo until there is an opportunity to hold a hearing on the application for a preliminary injunction."[48]

Any such order "must state the date and hour it was issued; describe the injury and state why it is irreparable; state why the order was issued without notice; and be promptly filed in the clerk's office and entered in the record."[49] A temporary restraining order may not remain in effect for more than 14 days unless extended by the court for good cause or the adverse party consents.[50] Local rules must be carefully checked before any such application is filed.

A petitioner must establish "(1) the likelihood that the movant ultimately will prevail on the merits of the claim, (2) the irreparable nature of the threatened injury and the reason that notice is impractical, (3) the

---

46. Brooke v. Willis, 907 F. Supp. 57, 60 (S.D.N.Y. 1995).

47. Fed. R. Civ. P. 65(b)(2).

48. United States v. Kaley, 579 F.3d 1246, 1264 (11th Cir. 2009) (quoting 11A C. Wright, A. Miller & M. Kane, Fed. Prac. & Proc.: Civil § 2951, at 253 (2d ed. 1995)).

49. Fed. R. Civ. P. 65(b)(2).

50. *Id.*

harm that might result absent a restraining order, and (4) the nature and extent of any public interest affected.[51]

To succeed on a petition filed under the Hague Convention, Petitioner must establish (1) that the children were habitually resident abroad at the time Respondent removed them to the United States; (2) that the removal was without Petitioner's consent and constituted a wrongful breach of Petitioner's custody rights under the law of the habitual residence; and (3) that Petitioner was actually exercising those custody rights at the time of the removal.

In order to establish the irreparable nature of the threatened injury and the reason that notice is impractical, the petitioner should normally allege and establish that the respondent may attempt to further remove the children and hinder the proceedings, causing irreparable injury to Petitioner. It has been held that the denial of a parent's lawful right to connect with and visit a child constitutes irreparable harm.[52]

In support of the allegation that the public interest will be served by issuing a temporary restraining order, the petitioner should explain the purpose of the Hague Convention and cite the extensive U.S. statutory and case law support of that purpose.

For a useful overview of the elements of an application for an ex parte temporary restraining order, see Gaston.[53]

§ 2.11 EXPEDITIOUS PROCEDURES

Speedy resolution of return applications is essential to the operation of the Convention. The obligation to complete Hague cases expeditiously is supported by the following provisions in the Convention:

- The preamble to the Convention states, "The States signatory to the present Convention . . . Desiring . . . to establish procedures to ensure their prompt return to the State of their habitual residence . . ."
- Article 1 of the Convention states, "The objects of the present Convention are—a. to secure the prompt return of children wrongfully removed to or retained in any Contracting State."
- Article 2 of the Convention requires Contracting States to "use the most expeditious procedures available" to implement the objects of the Convention.

51. *Id.*
52. Morgan v. Morgan, 289 F. Supp. 2d 1067, 1070 (N.D. Iowa 2003).
53. Gaston v. Gutierrez, 2024 WL 4045599 (M.D. Fla. Aug. 1, 2024).

- Article 11 of the Convention states, "The judicial or administrative authorities of Contracting States shall act expeditiously in proceedings for the return of children. If the judicial or administrative authority concerned has not reached a decision within six weeks from the date of commencement of the proceedings, the applicant or the Central Authority of the requested State, on its own initiative or if asked by the Central Authority of the requesting State, shall have the right to request a statement of the reasons for the delay."

The Hague Conference *Guide to Good Practice* under the Convention, Part II—Implementing Measures repeatedly demands that states act expeditiously in such cases.[54] In particular, the *Guide to Good Practice* insists that:

- "Expeditiousness is essential at all stages of the Convention process including appeals."
- "Expeditious procedures should be viewed as procedures which are both fast and efficient."
- "Almost all aspects of implementation (*e.g.* the investment of adequate resources and powers in Central Authorities, the allocation of jurisdiction among courts/administrative authorities, the procedures to be followed both at first instance and on appeal, and the ready availability of appropriate advice, assistance and representation) may have a bearing on the speed with which applications are processed."

The subsequent Hague Conference *Guide to Good Practice* under the Convention, Part VI—Article 13(1)(b) explains that there is a "double aspect" to the duty to return the child *forthwith*: "firstly, the use of the most speedy procedures known to their legal system; secondly, that applications are, so far as possible, to be granted priority treatment."[55]

The International Child Abduction Prevention and Return Act of 2014 requires the U.S. State Department to scrutinize more diligently the performance of other countries in returning abducted children expeditiously and to employ enhanced methods to cause noncomplying countries to improve their performance. Congress also recognizes that "people in glass houses should not throw stones." Accordingly, the law expressly states that it is "the sense of Congress that the United States should set

54. https://assets.hcch.net/docs/de043c72-ee0e-477b-8bae-53726a4b8545.pdf.

55. https://assets.hcch.net/docs/225b44d3-5c6b-4a14-8f5b-57cb370c497f.pdf at para. 21.

a strong example for other Convention countries in the timely location and prompt resolution of cases involving children abducted abroad and brought to the United States."[56]

In *Chafin*, the U.S. Supreme Court instructed that,

> Importantly, whether at the district or appellate court level, courts can and should take steps to decide these cases as expeditiously as possible, for the sake of the children who find themselves in such an unfortunate situation. Many courts already do so.[57]

The concurring opinion of Justice Ginsburg, joined by Justices Scalia and Breyer, stresses that stays pending the conclusion of appeals in Hague cases must be handled with extreme expedition.[58]

In *Monasky*, the Supreme Court explained that clear error review of trial court decisions in Hague cases "speeds up appeals and thus serves the Convention's premium on expedition."[59]

Unfortunately, the U.S. practice does not always meet the requirements of the treaty. Hague cases can take years to complete in the United States. There is no extrajudicial oversight of judicial compliance with the obligation to resolve cases promptly. The courts have not developed any significant body of law that implements the obligation of prompt resolution.

The State Department's annual Compliance Reports are filled with complaints about the delays in the courts of other countries. Such complaints are totally appropriate. But who is evaluating the very sorry and frankly embarrassing performance of U.S. courts, at least at the appeal level?

The *Abbott* case,[60] which went to the U.S. Supreme Court, illustrates the problem. The child, then age 9 or 10, was taken from Chile to the United States in August 2005. A Hague case was commenced in a U.S. District Court in Texas in May 2006. The district court rendered its decision in July 2007, a delay of 14 months. The Fifth Circuit rendered its decision in September 2008, a delay of another 14 months. The Supreme Court granted certiorari in June 2009, a delay of another nine months. It ruled on the case in May 2010, a delay of another 11 months, but it remanded the case to the Fifth Circuit. In August 2010, the Fifth Circuit

---

56. 22 U.S.C. § 9001 *et seq*.
57. Chafin v. Chafin, 133 S. Ct. 1017, 1027 (2012).
58. *Id.* at 1030–31.
59. Monasky v. Taglieri, 140 S. Ct. 719, 730 (2020).
60. Abbott v. Abbott, 130 S. Ct. 1983 (2010).

remanded the case to the original district court. The case then died of its own accord once the child reached the age of 16. The wrongfully removed child was never returned to Chile.

Nonetheless, many courts do cite the need to resolve Hague cases expeditiously. The Ninth Circuit held that a district court's utilization of a magistrate to conduct a hearing in a Hague case was justified, in part, by the need to promote a speedy resolution of such cases.[61] The Seventh Circuit upheld a district court's refusal to allow additional discovery for the same reason, noting, "The Convention and its implementing Act are chock full of the language of urgency and in no uncertain terms contemplate expedited procedures to guarantee that children are returned quickly to the correct jurisdiction."[62]

It may be appropriate when the case is commenced to inform the court of this obligation and even to remind the court of it from time to time as the matter proceeds. Article 11 of the Convention provides that if the judicial or administrative authority concerned has not reached a decision within six weeks from the date of commencement of the proceedings, the applicant or the Central Authority of the requested state, on its own initiative or if asked by the Central Authority of the requesting state, shall have the right to request a statement of the reasons for the delay. The State Department's Office of Children's Issues will normally send a letter to the court advising it of the need for prompt action, as well as other legal requirements such as the stay of final custody orders imposed by Article 16 of the Convention.

The necessity for expeditious resolution of Hague cases has also been held to preclude the denial of a Hague petition on a merely "without prejudice" basis. In one case, the Second Circuit overruled a district court's denial of a Hague petition "without prejudice to renewal" if certain contingencies occurred thereafter. The circuit court ruled that dismissals must be with prejudice since, inter alia, such cases must be concluded expeditiously and finally.[63] The same court relied on the need for expedition by upholding a district court's decision to hold expedited proceedings, to decline to hear testimony from certain witnesses, and to decline to interview children in camera (both parties filed expert affidavits based on interviews with the children).[64] The need for expeditious resolution of a case often arises when stays pending appeal of a return order are

61. Holder v. Holder, 392 F.3d 1009 (9th Cir. 2004).
62. Norinder v. Fuentes, 657 F.3d 526 (7th Cir. 2011).
63. Ermini v. Vittori, 758 F.3d 153 (2d Cir. 2014).
64. Velozny *ex rel.* R.V. v. Velozny, 2021 WL 5567265 (2d Cir. Nov. 29, 2021).

requested by a respondent who is ordered to produce a child for return to the child's habitual residence. In *Chafin*, the Supreme Court ruled that courts in Hague cases should apply the traditional factors in determining whether to grant such stays pending appeal but that the ends of the Convention can be met by expedited proceedings.[65]

Expeditiousness has also been cited as a reason to return a child forthwith, rather than waiting for the beginning of the child's next school year.[66] And it provides a clear basis to provide a court with a substantial degree of discretion to determine the procedures necessary to resolve a Hague proceeding and some latitude to deviate from ordinary rules of procedure that might delay a final resolution.[67]

In sharp contrast are cases in which a circuit court remands a case for additional evidence concerning issues not fully resolved in prior proceedings. In *Walker*, the Seventh Circuit overruled the denial of a return petition after a two-day hearing, but instead of ordering the children's return, and although stating that "we regret the need to prolong this case any further," it remanded the case to the district court because "[s]everal crucial issues were not fully developed in the previous proceedings, and these gaps in the record must be filled before a final decision is rendered."[68] The Seventh Circuit specifically identified potential issues concerning the parties' last shared intentions, the effect of the petitioner's participation on U.S. divorce proceedings, and whether the children had attained an age and degree of maturity at which it is appropriate to take account of their views. In sharp contrast, the U.S. Supreme Court in *Monasky* elected not to remand the case to give the lower courts an opportunity to apply the Supreme Court's newly adopted totality-of-the-circumstances standard, which it would ordinarily do, because a remand "would consume time when swift resolution is the Convention's objective."[69]

Even when a remand is ordered, the need for expedition may be a valid reason for a district court to decide the remanded issue without conducting another hearing.[70]

Nonetheless, the need for expedition does not justify inappropriate haste. Thus, the Ninth Circuit has held that "courts should not allow haste to overwhelm a respondent's right to develop the psychological evidence needed to make out a viable Article 13(b) defense where she has alleged

65. *Chafin*, 568 U.S. at 178.
66. Mendoza v. Silva, 987 F. Supp. 2d 883 (N.D. Iowa 2013).
67. Gil-Leyva v. Leslie, 780 Fed. Appx. 580 (10th Cir. 2019).
68. Walker v. Walker, 701 F.3d 1110, 1123 (7th Cir. 2012).
69. *Monasky*, 140 S. Ct. 731.
70. Radu v. Shon, 62 F.4th 1165 (9th Cir. 2023).

with considerable particularity that the petitioner has engaged in domestic violence. Accordingly, we hold that the district court abused its discretion by denying Lazaro's application for a psychological examination of S.L.C. in the face of her specific allegations that Colchester had engaged in spousal and child abuse."[71]

§ 2.12 THE INITIAL APPEARANCE

At the first appearance before the court, petitioner's attorney will normally explain the petitioner's theory of the case and will ask the court to schedule a final hearing on the matter on as expeditious a basis as possible.

The court at this time will normally set a complete schedule for the entire case, usually by ordering a hearing in the case at a date certain that is well within the six-week schedule called for by the treaty.

The court will also generally hear and resolve any prehearing issues that either party might raise. Such issues may include the following:

- Whether discovery should be permitted and, if so, upon what terms;
- Whether the matter is to be heard by a federal magistrate and, if so, upon what terms;
- Whether interim relief should be ordered, or continued if previously ordered;
- Whether a guardian ad litem should be appointed for the child;
- Whether a psychological evaluation of the child should be authorized;
- Whether telephone or video testimony should be permitted; and
- Whether witness affidavits should be accepted in evidence.

§ 2.13 DISCOVERY

Discovery has generally been permitted in Hague cases but it must be balanced against the requirement that Hague cases should be concluded quickly.[72] There are no special procedural rules prescribing the course of action for a federal court when a petition under the Convention and

71. Colchester v. Lazaro, 16 F.4th 712 (9th Cir. 2021).

72. Robert v. Tesson, 507 F.3d 981 (6th Cir. 2007); Rigby v. Damant, 486 F. Supp. 2d 222 (D. Mass. 2007); Raijmakers-Eghaghe v. Haro, 131 F. Supp. 2d 953 (E.D. Mich. 2001).

ICARA is filed, and the legislative history of ICARA provides little by way of enlightenment.[73]

Although Hague cases brought in a federal court are subject to the Federal Rules of Civil Procedure, they must also proceed expeditiously in conformity with the terms of the Convention. In *Norinder*,[74] the Seventh Circuit was asked to overturn a district court return order on the ground that the respondent's request for additional discovery had been denied. The court reviewed the district court's orders and determined that that court had acted properly, especially in light of the failure of respondent's attorneys to seek the requested additional discovery on a timely basis. The court stated that the adjudication of a petition for return of a child is much like a district court's exercise of equitable power in the context of a preliminary injunction or a temporary restraining order. In both circumstances, discovery often must proceed quickly, the district court must apprise itself of the relevant facts, and a decision must be rendered on an expedited basis. The Tenth Circuit has ruled similarly.[75]

On the other hand, other courts have ruled that discovery is not allowed in a Hague case.[76] Moreover, in some cases courts have ruled that summary judgment without discovery may be an appropriate way of handling Hague cases.[77] Indeed, in one case the court entered summary judgment sua sponte.[78]

Counsel for a party who wants discovery may cite:

- *Colchester v. Lazaro*,[79] holding that a district court's wholesale denial of discovery in general, and of psychological examination in particular, was unreasonable.
- *Norinder v. Fuentes*, which is discussed previously.
- *Rigby v. Damant*,[80] in the district court, which required both parties to submit to discovery even during a pending appeal.
- *Rigby v. Damant*,[81] in which the First Circuit dismissed the appeal of a district court ruling that had extended the time to complete discovery over petitioner's strong objections.

---

73. Zajaczkowski v. Zajaczkowska, 932 F. Supp. 128 (D. Md. 1996).
74. *Norinder*, 657 F.3d 526.
75. West v. Dobrev, 735 F.3d 921 (10th Cir. 2013).
76. McClary v. McClary, 2007 WL 3023563 (M.D. Tenn. 2007).
77. March v. Levine, 249 F.3d 462 (6th Cir. 2001); *McClary*, 2007 WL 3023563.
78. Menachem v. Frydman-Menachem, 240 F. Supp. 2d 437 (D. Md. 2003).
79. Colchester v. Lazaro, 16 F.4th 712 (9th Cir. 2021).
80. Rigby v. Damant, 486 F. Supp. 2d 222 (D. Mass. 2007).
81. Rigby v. Damant, 486 F.3d 692, 693 (1st Cir. 2007).

- *Sasson v. Sasson*,[82] which confirmed that the parties had conducted expedited discovery.
- *Anderson v. Acree*,[83] in which a district court cited to petitioner's deposition for evidence in making its findings.
- *Steffen F. v. Severina*,[84] which stated that the need for discovery had resulted in the Hague proceeding not being tried until eight months after the petition was originally filed.

Counsel may also cite authorities in non-Hague cases that stress the value of discovery, such as the Supreme Court's landmark decision in *Hickman v. Taylor* that stated, "The pre-trial deposition-discovery mechanism established by Rules 26 to 37 is one of the most significant innovations of the Federal Rules of Civil Procedure. . . . Thus civil trials in the federal courts no longer need be carried on in the dark" [85] and the Fifth Circuit's endorsement of "the proposition that discovery . . . together with pretrial procedures make a trial less a game of blind man's bluff and more a fair contest with the basic issues and facts disclosed to the fullest practicable extent." [86]

On the other hand, counsel for a party opposing discovery may cite:

- *West v. Dobrev*,[87] in which the Tenth Circuit ruled that neither the Hague Convention nor ICARA, nor the due process clause of the Fifth Amendment, require that discovery be allowed as a matter of right in cases arising under the Convention.
- *March v. Levine*,[88] in which the district court asserted that there is no requirement under the Hague Convention or under ICARA that discovery be allowed or that an evidentiary hearing be conducted.
- *March v. Levine*,[89] in which the Sixth Circuit ruled that Hague cases are unique and that the treaty requires the use of "the most expeditious procedures available" because its nature is one of an

82. *In re* Application of Sasson v. Sasson, 327 F. Supp. 2d 489 (D.N.J. 2004).

83. Anderson v. Acree, 250 F. Supp. 2d 872 (S.D. Ohio 2002), *subsequent determination*, 250 F. Supp. 2d 876 (S.D. Ohio 2002).

84. Steffen F. v. Severina P., 966 F. Supp. 922 (D. Ariz. 1997).

85. Hickman v. Taylor, 329 U.S. 495 at 500–01, 67 S. Ct. 385 at 388–89 (1947).

86. Dollar v. Long Manufacturing, 561 F.2d 613, 619 (5th Cir. 1977).

87. West v. Dobrev, 735 F.3d 921(10th Cir. 2013).

88. March v. Levine, 136 F. Supp. 2d 831 (M.D. Tenn. 2000), *aff'd*, 249 F.3d 462, 2001 Fed. App. 0126P (6th Cir. 2001).

89. March v. Levine, 249 F.3d 462, 2001 Fed. App. 0126P (6th Cir. 2001).

emergency and it seeks a speedy and immediate solution to the cases involved.

- *Holder v. Holder*,[90] which stated that trial courts are permitted wide leeway to fashion procedures that affect the Convention's aim of expediting Hague petitions and determined that a magistrate's conduct of a prompt evidentiary hearing without discovery was appropriate.
- *Menachem v. Frydman-Menachem*,[91] which held that there is no requirement, under the Convention or under ICARA, that discovery be allowed or that an evidentiary hearing be conducted. The court could properly resolve ICARA cases on the basis of affidavits and other evidence, without resorting to a full trial on the merits or a plenary evidentiary hearing.

A district court in New York stressed the value of deposition testimony in a Hague case, especially that of the petitioner (the court stating that "[h]is testimony is pivotal to understanding whether the six children are habitually resident in Guatemala, and presumably to support his opposition to the defenses under the Convention that the children have indicated they will assert"), but refusing to require him to appear in the United States for a deposition when a video deposition would be sufficient.[92]

§ 2.14 STAY OF CUSTODY PROCEEDINGS

Article 16 of the Convention provides that after receiving notice of the wrongful removal or retention of a child in the sense of Article 3, the judicial or administrative authorities of the Contracting State to which the child has been removed or in which it has been retained shall not decide on the merits of rights of custody until it has been determined that the child is not to be returned, or unless an application under the Convention is not lodged within a reasonable time.

The article applies only to courts in the country to which a child has been taken.[93] It does not prevent a court in the country of the child's habitual residence from initiating or continuing to consider and determine a

90. Holder v. Holder, 2003 WL 24091906 (W.D. Wash. 2003), *aff'd*, 392 F.3d 1009 (9th Cir. 2004).

91. Menachem v. Frydman-Menachem, 240 F. Supp. 2d 437 (D. Md. 2003).

92. Teller v. Helbrans, 2019 WL 3779863 (E.D.N.Y. 2019).

93. Griffin v. Sebuliba, 2009 WL 972862 (E.D. Wis. 2009).

custody proceeding concerning the child.[94] Indeed, it is frequently advisable for a left-behind parent to initiate custody proceedings in the country from which a child has been wrongfully removed or retained.

Although the article expressly bars a state court only from *deciding the merits* of a custody case unless and until a pending Hague case has been dismissed, the State Department's analysis asserts that a state court is barred from "considering the merits" of such a case during the specified time period.[95] Since the purpose of the Convention is to "provide for a reasoned determination of where jurisdiction over a custody dispute is properly placed" it is thus "consistent with this purpose that it is the custody determination, not the Hague Convention Petition, that should be held in abeyance if proceedings are going forward in both state and federal courts."[96]

Indeed, Article 16 precludes any custody case if a Hague case has been commenced "until it has been determined that the child is not to be returned under this Convention." For this reason, once it is ordered that a child shall be returned to the habitual residence no case can be pursued in the United States for custody of the child. This principle has been applied as a basis for the dismissal of custody cases.[97]

Article 16 gives force to the Supreme Court's statement in *Monasky*[98] that, upon a child's return pursuant to a Hague Convention order, "the custody adjudication will proceed in that forum" and the Second Circuit's statement in *Mota*[99] that "the Convention's focus is simply upon whether a child should be returned to her country of habitual residence for custody proceedings."

ICARA empowers federal courts to vacate state custody determinations and other state court orders that contravene the Convention, as applied by the federal court.[100] In *Mozes*, the Ninth Circuit held that "Congress has expressly granted the federal courts jurisdiction to vindicate rights arising under the Convention. . . . Thus, federal courts must have the power to vacate state custody determinations and other state court orders that contravene the treaty." Federal courts have also stated that

94. Ozaltin v. Ozaltin, 708 F.3d 355, 377 (2d Cir. 2013).

95. Text and Legal Analysis, at 10494.

96. Yang v. Tsui, 416 F.3d 199, 203 (3d Cir. 2005).

97. Tyszka v. Tyszka, 200 Mich. App. 231, 503 NW2d 726 (Mich. Ct. Apps. 1993); Tabacci v. Harrison, 200 WL 190576 (N.D. Ill. 2000).

98. *Monasky*, 140 S. Ct. 719 at 723–24.

99. Mota v. Castillo, 692 F.3d 106, 112 (2d Cir. 2012).

100. Mozes v. Mozes, 239 F.3d 1067, n.55 (9th Cir. 2001); Silverman v. Silverman, 338 F.3d 886 (8th Cir. 2003).

state court custody matters "should be held in abeyance" if proceedings are going forward in both state and federal courts.[101]

In one case, a federal district court issued an order staying a state court custody proceeding pending the federal court's determination of the Hague case.[102] But another district court has held that it had no such power.[103]

For these reasons, and in light of the Hague Convention policy that signatory countries should return wrongfully removed children expeditiously and through any appropriate remedy, the Ninth Circuit overturned a district court ruling that a left-behind parent was precluded from pursuing his Hague claim pending the resolution of his state court appeal in his divorce case pending in California.[104] The court below was held to have been entirely wrong in its decision that a Hague Convention claim is barred by a state court *custody* determination, simply because a petitioner did not raise his *Hague Convention* claim in the initial custody proceeding. The circuit court explained that the typical Hague Convention case involves at least the potential for two competing custody orders, one in the children's habitual residence, and one in the country to which the children have been taken. To hold that a left-behind parent is barred, in such a case, from raising a Hague Convention claim in a subsequent federal proceeding just because he or she did not raise it in the state custody proceeding, would render the Convention an incompetent remedy for the very problem that it was ratified to address.

Claims that a federal court may not handle a Hague case when some of the issues are before a state court are often presented under the theory that a federal court must abstain under the Supreme Court's *Younger*[105] doctrine when there is an ongoing state proceeding that implicates important state interests and that affords an adequate opportunity to raise the federal issues. This does not apply merely because a state court handling a custody case might consider some of the issues that would apply in a Convention case unless the left-behind parent actually asserts a claim in the state court under the Convention and that issue is then litigated in the state court.[106]

---

101. *Yang*, 416 F.3d 199.

102. Friedrich v. Thompson, 1999 WL 33954819 (M.D.N.C. 1999).

103. *Rigby*, 486 F. Supp. 2d 222.

104. *Holder*, 305 F.3d 854.

105. Younger v. Harris, 401 U.S. at 37, 91 S. Ct. 746.

106. Barzilay v. Barzilay, 536 F.3d 844, 850 (8th Cir. 2008) ("The pendency of state custody proceedings therefore does not support Younger abstention in the Hague Convention context."); Gaudin v. Remis, 415 F.3d 1028, 1034 (9th Cir. 2005) (Younger abstention "is equally inappropriate in the case of an ICARA petition."); *Yang*, 416 F.3d 201–03.

§ 2.15 GUARDIANS/LAWYERS FOR CHILDREN

Courts in some cases have appointed independent experts or lawyers to represent the interests of the child or to determine the factual circumstances of allegations concerning a child. Courts have sometimes appointed an attorney to act in the dual role of both the guardian ad litem and the child's attorney.[107] Cases in which such appointments have been made are usually those in which the respondent has asserted an exception based either upon a claim of grave risk of harm to the child or based on the objections of a mature child.

In one "exceptional" case, the Fifth Circuit upheld its reversal of a Hague return order and ordered that a guardian ad litem should be appointed to represent the interests of the children. After the children had been taken from Mexico to the United States without their mother's consent, and after the court below had ordered their return under the Convention, they had been granted asylum by the U.S. government based on a fear that they would be persecuted if they were returned to Mexico. The issues raised in the asylum application paralleled a potential "grave risk" defense under the Convention, but those issues had not been fully reviewed by the trial court. The trial court had refused to appoint a guardian ad litem, but no respondent in the case was making an effort to represent the children's interests, because the abducting respondents had disclaimed any responsibility for the children. Accordingly, the Fifth Circuit required the appointment of a guardian ad litem.[108]

In another case, "at the request of the parties" the court appointed a person to act as "guardian ad litem" for the children.[109] The guardian facilitated videoconferences between the children and the petitioner and provided the court with a report concerning issues pertaining to the allegations of grave risk of harm to the children and of the extent to which they were settled in New York as compared to Poland.

And, in another case, a district court appointed a guardian ad litem because it found that there were fundamental and significant differences in the positions of the parties concerning how the children had been treated and how they might be impacted if it ordered their return to Mexico.[110]

107. Kufner v. Kufner, 519 F.3d 33 (1st Cir. 2008); Wasniewski v. Grzelak-Johannsen, 2007 WL 1461794 (N.D. Ohio, 2007).

108. *Sanchez*, 761 F.3d 495.

109. *In re* Filipczak, 2011 WL 6980845 (S.D.N.Y. 2011).

110. Lieberman v. Tabachnik, 2007 WL 4548570 (D. Colo. 2007).

The guardians' duties were to include the following:

(1) To investigate all aspects of the social background of each of the minor children by talking to the Petitioner, Respondent, the minor children, reviewing court records from legal proceedings in Mexico and engaging in any further fact inquiry or investigation that the Guardian Ad Litem deems appropriate;

(2) To investigate Respondent's allegations of abuse, mistreatment of each of the minor children for the purpose of determining if Respondent's allegations are accurate, truthful and verifiable;

(3) To provide facts, evidence and recommendations, as to each child, concerning whether returning said child to Mexico would expose him or her to a grave risk of physical or emotional harm or otherwise subject the child to an intolerable situation; and

(4) To investigate the wishes of the children and their respective maturity levels (to the extent that these issues relate to exceptions within ICARA) and make appropriate recommendations on this point.[111]

The arguments in support of a request for an appointment of a guardian may include a claim that neither parent is best suited to represent the interests of the child; that a child may not wish to disclose certain facts to one parent (whether that be as to the child's wishes to return or not or as to facts concerning a parent's abuse or threats); that a child may express a desire to testify or not to testify to an independent person; and that a trained expert may better elicit relevant facts from a child.

In sharp contrast, a district court in Idaho refused to appoint a guardian ad litem when, although the parties' disagreed as to the outcome of the case, their respective positions evidenced that the child's fundamental interests were well represented by the parents, who were each represented by counsel who presented thoughtful and well-articulated arguments and evidence. The court further cited the fact that it was empowered only to determine the rights under the Hague Convention, not the merits of the underlying custody dispute between the parties.[112]

The arguments against such an appointment might include the assertion that Hague cases should proceed expeditiously;[113] that appointing

111. *Id.* at *2.

112. Pennacchia v. Hayes, 2016 WL 9045965 (D. Idaho 2016).

113. Pinto Quintero v. De Loera Barba, 2019 WL 1386556 (W.D. Tex. 2019).

such a representative invites or strays too close to a forbidden "best interests" analysis; and that it creates unnecessary expense.

§ 2.16 INTERVENTION BY A CHILD

Intervention by a child pursuant to Federal Rule of Civil Procedure 24 might be allowed in special circumstances. When in one case a district court permitted intervention only as to one specific issue, the First Circuit insisted that "we doubted very many" cases would require intervention on behalf of the children involved, but that we "refuse to endorse a blanket rule . . . that intervention is impermissible in Hague Convention cases."[114]

The mere fact that the children in question had obtained certain rights as asylees did not provide a basis for them to intervene in the Hague case. The Fifth Circuit determined that, while their interests were not being represented by the respondents, that would likely be remedied by the appointment of a guardian ad litem.[115]

§ 2.17 EVIDENCE

Counsel must pay close attention to the rules contained in the Convention and in ICARA concerning the admissibility of evidence. They are designed to make Hague cases easier to present and faster to complete, especially for the benefit of a petitioner.

Article 30 of the Convention provides that any application submitted to the court, together with any documents and other information appended to it, shall be admissible in evidence.[116] This is an invitation to include in the petition, or perhaps in any answer to the petition or any answer to any motion submitted by the petitioner, any and all material (even if voluminous) that a party might wish to offer in evidence.

ICARA contains a similar provision. It provides that no authentication is required of any Hague return petition, or any other documents or information included with the petition or provided thereafter that relates to the petition, in order for the documents to be admissible in court.[117] That language has been held to be sufficient to override an otherwise-valid

---

114. Walsh v. Walsh, 221 F.3d 204, 213 (1st Cir. 2000).

115. *Sanchez,* 761 F.3d 508.

116. Hague Convention on the Civil Aspects of International Child Abduction, Art. 30.

117. 42 U.S.C.A. § 11605.

hearsay objection to witness affidavits since the materials were attached to the petition.[118]

The Convention also provides that a court may take judicial notice directly of the law of the country of habitual residence, and of judicial or administrative decisions formally recognized in that country, without the traditional requirements of proof.[119] In one case, the parties had spent considerable energy "wrangling" over the propriety and legitimacy of offering certain translations of the voluminous record of German proceedings. The court admitted translated documents with the proviso that the other side would be provided the opportunity to confirm the accuracy of the translations and, if necessary, to offer evidence to challenge or clarify translated material. The court also stated that where possible, it would rely only on translations that bear official certification (either American or German).[120]

Otherwise, rules of evidence in Hague cases are governed by the applicable court rules. In state courts, the type of evidence admissible in a Hague proceeding is a matter of local law and will vary by state.

There are general rules of relevance and admissibility that are applied by federal courts. The First Circuit has held that the Federal Rules of Evidence apply in Hague cases when a full trial is held. It took issue with the district court's conclusion that, under Federal Rule of Evidence 1101(b), "the summary character of Hague Convention proceedings does not require application of the Federal Rules of Evidence regarding hearsay." The First Circuit insisted that, although summary proceedings certainly may occur in cases under the Convention, "this was not one" because the district court had conducted a full trial and it should have applied federal evidence rules.[121] Thus, courts will likely apply the Federal Rules in conventional federal Hague cases.[122]

Courts have recognized that special accommodation may be necessary or appropriate for foreign petitioners or foreign witnesses to provide their testimony remotely, as an exception to the basic rule that, at trial, the witnesses' testimony must normally be taken in open court.[123] Federal

---

118. *In re* Walsh, 31 F. Supp. 2d 200, 202 n.1 (D. Mass. 1998), *aff'd in part, rev'd in part on other grounds*, 221 F.3d 204 (1st Cir. 2000).

119. Convention, Art. 14.

120. Kufner v. Kufner, 480 F. Supp. 2d 491 (D.R.I. 2007), *aff'd*, 519 F.3d 33 (1st Cir. 2008).

121. Danaipour v. McLarey, 386 F.3d 289 (1st Cir. 2004).

122. Brosselin v. Harless, 2011 WL 6130419 (W.D. Wash. 2011).

123. Fed. R. Civ. P. 43(a).

Rule of Civil Procedure 43(a) requires that remote testimony is waived only, "for good cause in compelling circumstances and with appropriate safeguards, the court may permit testimony in open court by contemporaneous transmission from a different location." The necessary safeguards in such cases include proper identification of the witnesses, the lack of any outside influence on the witness, and accurate transmission of testimony.[124] These issues may be overcome by, for example, requiring that a notary identify the witness and swear that witness in remotely, ensuring that the witness is alone in the room and has been provided with the documentary evidence in advance, and requiring the movant to pay all costs associated with the remote testimony and requiring that it be tested with the court's IT personnel prior to the trial it which it is used.[125]

Courts have permitted parties to testify via live video testimony[126] and have permitted experts or other witnesses to so testify also.[127] Such remote testimony is especially appropriate in a Hague Convention case, given the need for expedition, and particularly if the witness is unable to obtain a visa.[128] Yet not all courts have been so accommodating.[129] Indeed, a petitioner's request to testify by video from a military base in Germany was denied, even though he asserted his active military service, the financial burden of traveling from Germany to California, and the burden of traveling with a medical condition, as was his request for his parents to testify by video from Los Angeles because of high gas prices and COVID concerns, in the face of evidence that the petitioner and his parents were planning to visit Disneyland three weeks after the hearing.[130]

For a discussion of the admissibility of evidence concerning the grave risk exception, see § 8.07.

§ 2.18 CHILD'S TESTIMONY

The testimony of the child who is the subject of a Hague petition may be heard in a Hague case when appropriate.[131] The Convention does not contain any express provision on this issue, except that the existence of the mature child exception obviously invites a focus on a child's opin-

124. *Gil-Leyva*, 780 Fed. Appx. 580.
125. *See, e.g.*, Alcala v. Hernandez, 2015 WL 1893291 (D.S.C. 2015).
126. Haimdas v. Haimdas, 720 F. Supp. 2d 183 (E.D.N.Y. 2010).
127. Clarke v. Clarke, 2008 WL 5191682 (E.D. Pa. 2008).
128. *Haimdas*, 720 F. Supp. 2d 183; Alcala, 2015 WL 1893291.
129. *Gil-Leyva*, 780 Fed. Appx. 580.
130. Krause v. Krause, 2022 WL 1292261 (E.D. Cal. Apr. 29, 2022).
131. Romero v. Bahamonde, 857 Fed. Appx. 576 (11th Cir. 2021).

ions. The opinion of the child is obviously central to that exception and is frequently permitted on that issue.[132]

The testimony of a child has also been permitted as to facts concerning habitual residence in a case in which the district court determined, based on expert evidence, that the child was sufficiently mature to testify and the legal standard defining a child's habitual residence in terms of the child's perspective established that that was central to the question of her habitual residence.[133]

A child's testimony has also been permitted as to the grave risk exception,[134] but very often the courts make it quite clear that the weight they will give to such testimony may be less than that given to the testimony of other witnesses, depending on the age and maturity of the child and the extent to which the child's testimony is independent.[135] In often-quoted language, the Second Circuit has stated that, "if a child's testimony is germane to the question of whether a grave risk of harm exists upon repatriation, a court may take it into account."[136]

But a child was properly not allowed to testify when a child psychiatrist testified that further questioning of the child could be harmful and would not be informative, and when the children's wishes warranted little weight due to their young ages, lack of maturity, and susceptibility to parental influence.[137]

The Permanent Bureau of the Hague Conference has taken a strong stand that children should be heard in Convention cases, reflecting a broad consensus among Contracting States.[138] A special commission set up under the auspices of the Hague Conference specifically recommended that children should be given an opportunity to be heard, unless it would be inappropriate in light of the child's age or degree of maturity.

Since the Convention was drafted, there has been a clear international trend toward recognizing "a child's right to be heard." This has been reflected in international and regional instruments adopted since the 1980 Convention. The Permanent Bureau has collected data on this issue. Of 43 countries that submitted country profiles to the Bureau, ten

---

132. Dubikovskyy v. Goun, 54 F.4th 1042, 1048 (8th Cir. 2022); Falk v. Sinclair, 2009 WL 4110757 (D. Me. 2009).

133. Karkkainen v. Kovalchuk, 445 F.3d 280 (3d Cir. 2006).

134. Romero v. Bahamonde, 857 Fed. Appx. 576, 583 (11th Cir. 2021).

135. Blondin v. Dubois, 238 F.3d 153 (2d Cir. 2001); *Falk*, 2009 WL 4110757.

136. *Blondin*, 238 F.3d 166.

137. *Kufner*, 519 F.3d 33.

138. Report issued November 2011, *available at* http://www.hcch.net/upload/wop/abduct2012pd14e.pdf.

states indicated that the child is always heard in return proceedings, 24 states advised that it depended on the circumstances of the case and the discretion of the judge, and only a few states limited hearing the voice of the child to cases where an Article 13(b) claim is raised.

However, the ways in which children are heard varies internationally. In some courts, the child may be interviewed directly, either by an independent expert or through a child's own representative. Also, the age at which a child may be interviewed directly differs from country to country. Some experts stressed that what was important was that the child's voice be heard, and not necessarily the method by which the child's voice was heard.

In many cases, the child's testimony is elicited by means of interviews with the judge, often in a separate room rather than in the open courtroom. For example, in Blondin, the appeals court stated with approval that "[b]oth the District Court and Dr. Solnit interviewed Marie–Eline, on different occasions. Judge Chin interviewed the children together in his chambers without their mother present; he gave them toys to play with while they talked to him and he did not wear his judicial robe. . . . Dr. Solnit testified that he interviewed the children with a colleague, in a playroom, where they also played with toys."[139]

In one case,[140] a father's claim on appeal that he was denied the opportunity to cross-examine his child was not upheld when he had insisted that the child should not appear in court and should instead be interviewed in chambers; he had submitted numerous questions for the district court to ask the child, which it did; he had listened as the district court posed his questions as well as those submitted by the other party; he was then afforded the opportunity to submit any follow-up questions to the district court to pose to the child in chambers but chose not to; he was also afforded the opportunity to submit evidence to rebut the child's testimony and he did so; and he offered no argument as to what precisely he was denied the opportunity to ask or introduce through a process designed to protect his daughter from being directly questioned by her parents about her relationships with her parents.

Of course, there is all the difference in the world between allowing a child's voice to be heard and the extent to which the child's views are or should be taken into account. That will vary not only with the age and maturity of the child but, most significantly, with the specific issue that is in dispute in the Hague case.

---

139. *Blondin*, 238 F.3d at 167.

140. Romero v. Bahamonde, 857 Fed. Appx. 576, 581 (11th Cir. 2021).

§ 2.19 USE OF FOREIGN CASE LAW

Congress has expressly declared that in enacting ICARA it recognized "the international character of the Convention" and the need for "uniform international interpretation of the Convention."[141] It is entirely appropriate to cite foreign case law in any Hague case and to stress that an appropriate goal of jurisprudence concerning the Convention is to promote uniformity.

The U.S. Supreme Court considered international cases to a significant extent in the *Abbott* case.[142] It stated that in interpreting any treaty, the opinions of "our sister signatories" are "entitled to considerable weight" and that that was particularly so when, as in ICARA, Congress has directed that "uniform international interpretation of the Convention" is part of the Convention's framework.[143] Specifically, it cited cases from the courts of England, Australia, Israel, Austria, South Africa, Germany, Canada, and France, and concluded that there was an "emerging international consensus" that ne exeat rights are rights of custody, even if that view was not generally formulated when the Convention was drafted in 1980.

In *Lozano*,[144] the Supreme Court was very strongly influenced by the weight of international authorities in rejecting the adoption by some U.S. circuits of the American doctrine of equitable tolling in Hague Convention cases. Justice Thomas stated that,

> It is our "responsibility to read the treaty in a manner 'consistent with the *shared* expectations of the contracting parties.'" *Olympic Airways* v. *Husain*, 540 U. S. 644, 650 (2004) (quoting *Air France* v. Saks, 470 U. S. 392, 399 (1985); emphasis added). Even if a background principle is relevant to the interpretation of federal statutes, it has no proper role in the interpretation of treaties unless that principle is shared by the parties to "an agreement among sovereign powers. *Zicherman* v. *Korean Air Lines Co.*, 516 U. S. 217, 226 (1996).
>
> Lozano has not identified a background principle of equitable tolling that is shared by the signatories to the Hague Convention. To the contrary, Lozano concedes that in the context of the Convention, "foreign courts have failed to adopt equitable

141. 42 U.S.C.A. § 116011(b)(3).
142. *Abbott*, 130 S. Ct. 1983.
143. *Id.*
144. Lozano v. Montoya Alvarez, 134 S. Ct. 1224, 1233 (2014).

tolling . . . because they lac[k] the presumption that we [have]."

Since the effectiveness of the Hague Convention requires that countries enforce the treaty uniformly, it is extremely appropriate that courts should encourage counsel to refer to international case law in Hague cases in order to allow the courts to render decisions that take account of the international interpretation of key terms of the treaty. The Ninth Circuit has stated that "the drafters intended that the Convention be interpreted uniformly across jurisdictions in order to avoid forum shopping."[145] For these reasons, counsel should not hesitate to appropriately cite foreign law in support of a position in a Hague case. U.S. courts have frequently relied on foreign authorities in their opinions.

Thus, in one case,[146] the Ninth Circuit was unable to locate an American authority in which the court considered whether immigration status could serve as the sole basis for holding that a child was not "settled" in a new location within the meaning of Article 12. The court cited the rule that in interpreting international treaties, the opinions of other signatories are entitled to considerable weight[147] and it then considered an English case on point.[148] The court ultimately decided to adopt a similar analysis to that which had been adopted in England in concluding that a child who, with her mother, did not have immigration status could nonetheless be "settled" within the meaning of Article 12, despite her unlawful status.[149]

In *Monasky*,[150] the Supreme Court relied extensively on international case law in interpreting the key term of habitual residence. The court purposely selected the test of the totality of circumstances in order to become aligned with "[t]he 'clear trend' among our treaty partners . . . to treat the determination of habitual residence as a fact-driven inquiry into the particular circumstances of the case." The court relied in particular on rulings from the European Union, the United Kingdom, Canada, Australia, and New Zealand.

Of course, consideration of the decisions of foreign courts in Convention cases does not mean that foreign case law must always be followed. In Golan, the Supreme Court considered but did not apply U.K. authority

---

145. Valenzuela v. Michel, 736 F.3d 1173, 1176 (9th Cir. 2013).

146. *In re* B. Del C.S.B., 559 F.3d 999 (9th Cir. 2009).

147. Air France v. Saks, 470 U.S. 392, 105 S. Ct. 1338 (1985).

148. C (A Child) (Child Abduction: Settlement), Re, 2006 WL 1518692, [2007] 1 F.C.R. 649, [2006] 36 Fam. Law 828, [2006] 2 F.L.R. 797, [2006] EWHC 1229 (U.K. Fam Div 2006).

149. *In re* B. Del C.S.B., 559 F.3d 999 (9th Cir. 2009).

150. *Monasky*, 140 S. Ct. 728.

for the proposition that consideration of ameliorative measures is always required upon a finding of a grave risk of harm within the meaning of Article 13 of the Convention.[151]

§ 2.20 ARTICLE 15 DECLARATIONS

Article 15 of the Convention provides that the authorities of a Contracting State may, prior to making a return order, request that the applicant obtain from the authorities of the child's state of habitual residence a decision or other determination that the removal or retention was wrongful within the meaning of Article 3 of the Convention.

This is not a procedure that U.S. courts have pursued. Thus, when a request was made for a stay of a Hague hearing pending a request to the court in the habitual residence for a ruling on the rights of custody under the foreign law, the motion was flatly rejected.[152] There appears to be no reported decision in which a U.S. court has made a request for an Article 15 declaration, although a circuit court has expressly encouraged a district court to do so.[153] A court's failure to request a determination from foreign authorities is not an appealable error, since the process is purely discretionary.[154]

Courts in other countries have stated that requests under Article 15 should rarely be made, because they cause delay and confusion.[155]

American courts have been asked by courts in foreign jurisdictions to make Article 15 declarations. An example is *Sorenson*,[156] in which a father brought a Hague action in Australia alleging that the child's mother had wrongfully retained their child there. To facilitate this claim, the Australian court asked the father to file a petition to the District Court of Minnesota for a determination of the child's habitual residence under the Convention. Upon receiving the petition, the district court held a bench trial, and concluded that Australia was the child's habitual residence. That decision was then upheld on appeal.

In some cases, parties have initiated an Article 15 proceeding in the country of the alleged habitual residence of a child, seeking a quick declaration by a court in that jurisdiction to the effect that the child was

151. Golan v. Saada, 596 U.S. 666, 142 S. Ct. 1880, 1880 n.7 (2022).

152. Basil v. Ibis Aida de Teresa Sosa, 2007 WL 226459 (M.D. Fla. 2007).

153. *In re* Application of Adan, 437 F.3d 381, 394 (3d Cir. 2006).

154. Viragh v. Foldes, 612 N.E.2d 241, 247 n.11 (Mass. 1993).

155. Re D. (A Child) (Abduction: Rights of Custody) [2007] 1 AC 619 (England); Fairfax v. Ireton [2009] NZFLR 433 (NZ CA) (New Zealand).

156. Sorenson v. Sorenson, 559 F.3d 871 (8th Cir. 2009).

wrongfully removed from or retained away from the habitual residence. They have then contended that the U.S. court must extend "full faith and credit" to such determinations pursuant to ICARA, which provides that

> [f]ull faith and credit shall be accorded by the courts of the States and the courts of the United States to the judgment of any other such court ordering or denying the return of a child, pursuant to the Convention, in an action brought under this chapter.[157]

U.S. courts have refused to be bound by such rulings.[158] In *Feder* the petitioner on his own initiative asked the Family Court of Australia for a determination of the child's habitual residence. The respondent received notice of the proceeding but did not enter an appearance. The Australian court ruled in favor of the petitioner on the habitual residence issue. The district court in Minnesota held that it did not appear that the Australian Family Court had jurisdiction to determine the issue of the child's habitual residence, since the Convention left that issue to the judicial or administrative authorities of the country in which the child is living at the time of the petition and Article 15 applies only if the request for a foreign decision is made by the authorities in the state to which the child has been taken.

§ 2.21 COMITY AS TO FOREIGN HAGUE ORDERS

Since some parents travel with their children between different countries, questions may arise as to competing decisions in Hague cases.

ICARA provides, "Full faith and credit shall be accorded by the courts of the States and the courts of the United States to the judgment of any other such court ordering or denying the return of a child, pursuant to the Convention."[159] This does not apply to judgments issued by courts outside the United States.[160]

Although foreign judgments are not entitled to full faith and credit, comity is at the heart of the Hague Convention. Accordingly, American courts will normally accord considerable deference to foreign adjudications as a matter of comity.[161]

157. 22 U.S.C. § 9003(g).

158. Feder v. Evans-Feder, 866 F. Supp. 860 (E.D. Pa. 1994); Muhlenkamp v. Blizzard, 521 F. Supp. 2d 1140 (E.D. Wash. 2007).

159. Act, 22 U.S.C. § 9003(g).

160. Diorinou v. Mezitis, 237 F.3d 133 (2d Cir. 2001).

161. Miller v. Miller, 240 F.3d 392, 400 (4th Cir. 2001); *Diorinou*, 237 F.3d 133.

Nonetheless, it is well established that a U.S. court may properly decline to extend comity to a foreign court's determination if (1) it clearly misinterprets the Hague Convention, or (2) contravenes the Convention's fundamental premises or objectives, or (3) fails to meet a minimum standard of reasonableness.[162]

For such reasons, the Ninth Circuit in *Asvesta* refused to grant comity to a Greek court's decision. There, the mother took the child to Greece but the Greek court refused to return the child on multiple grounds, including the father's alleged consent, his failure to establish that he was exercising his custodial rights to the child, and "a severe danger" that the child's return to the United States would "expose him to mental tribulation, since he will be deprived of his mother's presence, affection, love and care." The father subsequently "re-abducted" the child to Washington state and the mother then initiated a Hague proceeding there. The district court gave comity to the Greek order and ruled that the child must be returned to Greece. The Ninth Circuit overturned the district court holding that "the Greek court's analysis of the merits of Petroutsas' Hague petition misapplies the provisions of the Convention, relies on unreasonable factual findings, and contradicts the principles and objectives of the Hague Convention."[163]

In contrast, in *Smedley*,[164] in which children had been taken back and forth between North Carolina and Germany, the Fourth Circuit upheld the lower court's extension of comity to a German court order in a prior Hague case in that country "because the German court's decision neither clearly misinterpreted the Hague Convention nor failed to meet a minimum standard of reasonableness."

§ 2.22 INTERIM REMEDIES

Interim remedial measures may well be required before the court can hear a Hague Convention case. ICARA authorizes a petitioner to request remedies to protect the well-being of the child or to prevent the child from being abducted or concealed again before final disposition of the case.[165] The request for provisional remedies may be made in the original petition or in a separate pleading filed immediately prior to filing the petition for return.

---

162. Asvesta v. Petroutsas, 580 F.3d 1000, 1014 (9th Cir. 2009).
163. *Id.* at 1010, 1014.
164. Smedley v. Smedley, 772 F.3d 184, 189 (4th Cir. 2014).
165. 22 U.S.C. § 9004.

The kinds of relief that a petitioner may seek pending the outcome of a Hague case include orders to:

- Permit the petitioner to have immediate physical custody of the child;
- Permit the petitioner to have interim access to the child;
- Prohibit the respondent from removing the child from the jurisdiction;
- Direct the respondent to post a bond; and
- Requiring the respondent to surrender passports to the court.

Thus, in *Souratgar*, after hearing the testimony from the petitioner and his investigators, the court granted the father's application for an order directing the U.S. Marshal to take "all necessary and lawful steps" to remove the child from his mother's custody and deliver him into the custody of the petitioner. Petitioner was ordered to surrender his passport and post a $10,000 bond.[166]

In one case, the district court held that the petitioning father was entitled to the issuance of an ex parte temporary restraining order prohibiting the mother from removing the child from the jurisdiction of the court pending a hearing on the merits of the father's petition. The court found that the father had made an adequate showing that the mother and her boyfriend were likely to flee the state with the child if given advance notice of the father's intent to seek a temporary restraining order; that there was a risk of irreparable harm if the temporary restraining order did not issue; that the balance of hardships was in the petitioner's favor; and that it was in the public interest to maintain the status quo pending a hearing on the merits.[167]

In another case in which an ex parte injunction was granted, the court held that if the respondent were to flee the jurisdiction with the children, the very purpose of the Convention and the ICARA would be defeated. "This, by definition, is irreparable harm."[168]

Although a petitioner might request that the child be picked up by the U.S. Marshal or local law enforcement either before or when the respondent is served with the petition, ICARA contains an express "limitation

---

166. Souratgar v. Fair, 2012 WL 6700214, at *1 (S.D.N.Y. 2012), *aff'd sub nom.* Souratgar v. Lee, 720 F.3d 96 (2d Cir. 2013).

167. Morgan v. Morgan, 289 F. Supp. 2d 1067 (N.D. Iowa 2003).

168. Application of McCullough on Behalf of McCullough, 4 F. Supp. 2d 411 (W.D. Pa. 1998). Likewise see Lawrence v. Lewis, 2015 WL 1299285 (S.D. Ohio 2015).

on authority," stating that "no court exercising jurisdiction" in a Hague case may order a child removed from a person with physical control over the child unless "the applicable requirements of State law are satisfied."[169]

If the child's safety in the respondent's care is an issue, the court should consider alternate placement during the pendency of the case. This might be with the petitioner, unless it is unsafe to do so, provided that measures are taken to ensure the petitioner cannot leave with the child before the petition is resolved.[170]

Rule 65(c) of the Federal Rules of Civil Procedure requires that the movant post a security bond in the event that the court grants a temporary restraining order. Indeed, in one case, the court ordered the petitioner to surrender his passport and post a bond.[171] However, the bond requirement can be waived, in the court's discretion, in a Hague case as in other cases.[172]

Moreover, despite the fact that ICARA states that "[a] respondent is entitled to notice of the proceedings in accordance with the applicable law governing notice in interstate child custody proceedings,"[173] nothing in the statute appears to prevent a temporary restraining order without notice that maintains the status quo as to physical custody.[174]

§ 2.23 FUGITIVE DISENTITLEMENT DOCTRINE

Some use has been made of the "fugitive disentitlement" doctrine in Hague cases. Under that equitable doctrine, a fugitive from justice may not seek relief from the judicial system whose authority he or she evades.

The Sixth Circuit applied the doctrine in 1995.[175] There a father had pleaded guilty to a felony theft charge in Texas. He was given ten years' probation, but he then left for France with his wife and children in violation of the terms of probation. His wife subsequently brought the children back to the United States to live, and he responded by initiating a Hague case for the return of the children to France. The Sixth Circuit applied the fugitive disentitlement doctrine to deny the father the right to bring the case.

169. 22 U.S.C. § 9004(b).

170. *Souratgar*, 2012 WL 6700214, at *1, *aff'd sub nom. Souratgar*, 720 F.3d 96.

171. *Id.*

172. *Lawrence*, 2015 WL 1299285.

173. 22 U.S.C. § 9003(c).

174. *Lawrence*, 2015 WL 1299285.

175. *In re* Prevot, 59 F.3d 556 (6th Cir. 1995).

The First Circuit refused to apply the doctrine in *Walsh*[176] on the grounds that (1) the doctrine should not apply unless there is a strong connection between the fugitive status and the petition; and (2) it is not appropriate to apply the doctrine to the detriment of a child. In that case, the father was a fugitive. It was arguable there was some connection between his crime and the allegations of child abduction, but the court found that the connection was not strong enough to support the application of the doctrine. In any event, the court also held that applying the fugitive disentitlement doctrine would impose too severe a sanction in a case involving parental rights.

In another Sixth Circuit case,[177] the doctrine was not applied where the petitioner was in breach of civil orders, even though arrest warrants were outstanding against him arising out of criminal contempt orders. The child's grandparents alleged that he had killed the child's mother, but he had not been indicted for that. On the other hand, the Eleventh Circuit applied the doctrine in *Pesin*[178] to preclude any consideration of a mother's appeal from a Hague return order, on the ground that she had repeatedly defied court orders, had ignored contempt sanctions, and had become a fugitive after the issuance of a bench warrant for her arrest.

The doctrine seems to have been used in Hague cases exclusively in the United States and not in any other countries.

§ 2.24 SUBJECT MATTER JURISDICTION

As categorically explained by the Second Circuit,[179] a court has subject matter jurisdiction if, on the relevant date, the child was habitually resident in a Contracting State and the court hearing the petition is in a Contracting State. Consent (or lack of it) is not a jurisdictional requirement for a petition brought under the Convention. Neither the Convention's jurisdictional provisions nor U.S. domestic jurisdictional law requires that the removal be wrongful or without consent. While consent and wrongful removal bear on the merits of a petition under the Convention, those issues have nothing to do with jurisdiction, whether treaty or domestic. As for domestic law, ICARA explicitly authorizes either federal district courts or

176. *Walsh*, 221 F.3d 204.
177. *March*, 249 F.3d 462.
178. Pesin v. Rodriguez, 244 F.3d 1250 (11th Cir. 2001).
179. Tereshchenko v. Karimi, 102 F.4th 111 (2d Cir. 2024).

state courts to hear a petition brought under the treaty. Such jurisdiction does not extend to children who are located outside the United States.[180]

§ 2.25 PRIMA FACIE CASE

A parent seeking the return of a child under the Convention must prove by a preponderance of the evidence that (1) the child was habitually resident in one State and has been removed to or retained in a different State; (2) the removal or retention was in breach of the petitioner's custody rights under the law of the State of habitual residence; and (3) the petitioner was exercising those rights at the time of the removal or retention. Each of these essential elements is discussed later, in the body of this treatise.

The issue of consent is relevant both in connection with a petitioner's proof of a prima facie case and as to a respondent's assertion of consent as an express exception to the obligation to return a child even after a prima facie case has been established.

The question arose in *Tereshchenko*[181] of whether a father could establish that his rights of custody had been breached even though he had consented to the mother's removal of their children from Ukraine because of the war in that country. The court held that such a breach was established because the mother had taken the children to undisclosed locations, including the United States, and had retained the children in the United States without the father's consent. Those actions violated the father's custody rights under Ukrainian law.

§ 2.26 UNCLEAN HANDS

The doctrine of unclean hands, whereby "the doors of a court of equity" should not be open to one tainted with inequitableness or bad faith relative to the matter in which relief is being requested, has been held not to apply in a Hague Convention case to bar a petitioner's case. In particular, if a child's habitual residence was procured by means of fraud on the other parent, such misconduct will not require the dismissal of a petition if the child has become well-settled in that location; otherwise, the Convention's goal of protecting the well-being of the child, of restoring the status quo before the child's abduction, and of ensuring that rights of

180. 22 U.S.C. § 9003(b); Stone v. U.S. Embassy Tokyo, 2020 WL 4260711 (D.D.C. July 24, 2020).

181. *Id.*

custody arising in one country are effectively respected in other countries would be undermined.[182]

The same has been held to apply to other equitable defenses such as equitable estoppel, since they are not mentioned in the Convention, would weaken the purpose of the Convention, and therefore have been held to be not properly raised as defenses to a petition for return of a child.[183]

However, the unclean hands doctrine may be used in determining whether legal fees and expenses should be awarded in favor of a successful petitioner.[184]

§ 2.27 PLACE OF RETURN

The Convention does not expressly identify the place to which an abducted child is to be returned. Article 12 simply states that "the authority concerned shall order the return of the child." It is usually assumed that a child who is to be "returned" under the Hague Convention should be returned to the habitual residence from which the child was abducted. This is consistent with the dictionary definition of the word "return": "to come or go to a place again; to come back or go back again; to bring, give, send, or take (something) to the place that it came from or the place where it should go."[185]

However, the matter was dealt with at length in the Perez-Vera Report, which makes it clear that the "return" can be to a place other than the original habitual residence, if, for example, the petitioner has relocated. The Report states that the drafters of the Convention did not accept a proposal that the return of the child should always be to the state of its habitual residence before its removal, since "including such a provision in the Convention would have made its application so inflexible as to be useless." The Report further states that when the applicant no longer lives in what was the state of the child's habitual residence prior to its removal, the return of the child to that state might cause practical problems that would be difficult to resolve, and that "the Convention's silence on this matter must therefore be understood as allowing the authorities of the

---

182. Karpenko v. Leendertz, 619 F.3d 259 (3d Cir. 2010). *See also* Tsuruta v. Tsuruta, 76 F.4th 1107 (8th Cir. 2023).

183. *See, e.g., In re* Application of Stead v. Menduno, 77 F. Supp. 3d 1029 (D. Colo. 2014).

184. Souratgar v. Lee Jen Fair, 818 F.3d 72 (2d Cir. 2016).

185. Merriam-Webster Dictionary.

State of refuge to return the child directly to the applicant, regardless of the latter's present place of residence."[186]

The State Department's commentary on the Convention contains similar language:

> The Convention does not technically require that the child be returned to his or her State of habitual residence, although in the classic abduction case this will occur. If the petitioner has moved . . . the child will be returned to the petitioner, not the State of habitual residence.[187]

In *Gaudin*, the Ninth Circuit recited such authorities with apparent approval.[188]

More recently, the Hague Conference *Guide to Good Practice* has declared that,

> The Convention does not specify to whom the child should be returned. In particular, it does not require the return of the child to the care of a left-behind parent. Nor does the Convention specify to what location in the State of habitual residence the child should be returned. This flexibility is deliberate and reinforces the underlying concept that the issue of who will care for the child upon the child's return should be determined by the competent court or authority in the State of habitual residence in accordance with the law governing rights of custody, including any order that may apply as between the parents or other interested persons.[189]

The Second Circuit in *Tereshchenko* stated that "the Convention's text cannot be read to bar categorically the return of a child to a petitioner in a country other than the place of habitual residence."[190] In that case, in which there was a grave risk of returning the children to Ukraine, where a state of war prevailed, the appeals court upheld the district court's ruling that the children should be sent to France, where the left-behind father resided, holding that "[w]e see no reason why the Convention would categorically bar district courts from, as an ameliorative measure, ordering

186. Perez-Vera Report, para. 110.

187. Text and Legal Analysis, 51 Fed. Reg. 10404.

188. Gaudin v. Remis, 282 F.3d 1178 (9th Cir. 2002).

189. Guide to Good Practice Child Abduction Convention: Part VI—Article 13(1)(b), para. 20.

190. Tereshchenko v. Karimi, 102 F.4th 111, 133 (2d Cir. 2024).

a child to temporarily reside in a third country to mitigate a grave risk of harm in the state of habitual residence."[191] However, the circuit court found that the district court had taken a step too far by ordering that the children should reside in France with the father. That provision was too open-ended, since it in effect granted the father permanent custody over the children in France even though the courts in Ukraine had child custody jurisdiction. Instead, the district court was directed to fashion a limited and temporary order that should direct the children to stay with the father in France, commit him to making the children available for the Ukrainian custody proceedings as required by those courts, and direct the parties to abide by the final custody determination of those courts. Such tailoring, the court held, would help ensure that the order serves the goals of the Convention and would align more closely with the Convention's general principle that the best interests of the child are well served when decisions regarding custody rights are made in the country of habitual residence.

On the other hand, the English Court of Appeal held that the return contemplated is a return to the country of the child's habitual residence, and not to the custody of the primary custodial parent.[192] However, such reasoning has been criticized as not taking into account the Perez-Vera Report.

Subsequent cases in Australia,[193] British Columbia, Canada,[194] and Israel[195] have acknowledged that courts have flexibility in ordering the place to which return shall be made, as to both the particular country to which return shall be made and as to the specific place within such country.

What if the petitioner has relocated permanently to the same country as that in which the respondent and child are located? The Ninth Circuit has held that a case may not be brought or maintained under those circumstances. It held that, where "[a] petitioner moves permanently to the same country as the abductor, the petition is moot because no effective relief remains for us to grant."[196] The case was remanded on that issue, and on appeal from a district court ruling that the petitioner had moved permanently from Canada to Hawaii the circuit court then ruled that

---

191. *Id.* at 134.
192. Re A (A Minor) (Abduction) [1988] 1 FLR 365.
193. Murray v. Director, Family Services (1993) FLC 92-416.
194. Matzke v. Matzke, 2009 BCSC 1532.
195. G. v. B., 25 April 2007, Court for Family Matters, Beersheva.
196. *Gaudin*, 282 F.3d 1178.

the applicable test in such a case was that of domicile. Even though she appeared to have moved fully to Hawaii, she was precluded from having a U.S. domicile because of her visa status. Therefore, the Hague case was not moot, and her petition was upheld.[197] The outcome would be different if the left-behind parent went to the abducted-to country only temporarily.

§ 2.28 ARRANGEMENTS FOR RETURN

Article 12 of the Convention provides that children shall be "returned forthwith," at least when they were away from their habitual residence for less than one year prior to the commencement of the case. A return to the country of habitual residence does not mean that the child must be "turned over" to the petitioner. Often the child will be returned to the habitual residence in the care of the abducting parent pending the determination of the substantive custody case in the foreign country.

There has been considerable variation in the court's treatment of return provisions.

- Some courts simply provide that the child shall be returned forthwith to the habitual residence.[198]
- Some courts provide that the petitioner "is hereby **AWARDED** physical custody of D.I.R.A. for the purpose of returning D.I.R.A. to his country of habitual residence, Mexico. Respondent . . . **SHALL SURRENDER** D.I.R.A. to the custody and possession of Petitioner **within SEVEN (7) days** of the date of this Order."[199]
- The Fifth Circuit remanded a case to the district court "for it to decide the details of that prompt return, including the financial considerations."[200]
- The respondent may be ordered:
  - To "immediately provide Petitioner . . . with any and all passports or travel documents belonging to" the child.[201]
  - To pay the cost of "the child's transportation to Petitioner's home in Iceland."[202]

197. *Gaudin*, 379 F.3d 631.
198. *In re* R.V.B., 29 F. Supp. 3d 243, 260 (E.D.N.Y. 2014).
199. Saldivar v. Rodela, 879 F. Supp. 2d 610 (W.D. Tex. 2012).
200. Sealed Appellant v. Sealed Appellee, 394 F.3d 338, 347 (5th Cir. 2004).
201. Judge v. Williams, 2011 WL 3100346 (E.D.N.C. 2011).
202. Nelson v. Petterle, 782 F. Supp. 2d 108, 1095 (E.D. Cal. 2011).

- That failure to comply with the terms of this order "shall constitute contempt of court and may result in imposition of a fine and/or imprisonment."[203]
- That the "United States Marshals Service is directed to assist in the execution of this Order as necessary, and the United States Marshals Service may enlist the assistance of other law enforcement authorities as necessary to aid in any respect of securing the safe return of child to Iceland."[204]

Some courts impose conditions on a return, as discussed further in the next section. Such conditions have included the following:

- "The Return is conditioned on the undertaking that the children receive psychological counseling to deal with the divorce of their parents and their re-integration into their Mexican school and life." [205]
- "Petitioner shall immediately withdraw any criminal complaints against Respondent in Mexico relating to her retention of the children in the United States to facilitate her return to Mexico, and shall file in this Court written confirmation of the dismissal of all criminal proceedings against Respondent in Mexico relating to her retention of the children in the United States as soon as possible, but no later than 30 days."[206]
- "Petitioner shall also undergo anger management counseling or some other form of counseling to deal with his angry outbursts toward the children."[207]

§ 2.29 UNDERTAKINGS

If a court decides that a child must be returned to its country of habitual residence, it might in some circumstances make the return contingent upon certain "undertakings" from the petitioning parent. However, the Supreme Court ruled in *Golan* that neither the Convention nor ICARA requires that an analysis of potential ameliorative measures must be made once a district court makes a finding of grave risk of harm under Article

---

203. *Id.* at 1096.
204. *Id.*
205. Jaet v. Siso, 2009 WL 35270 (S.D. Fla. 2009).
206. *Id.*
207. *Id.*

13(b).[208] Thus, *Golan* authorizes undertakings but holds that the Convention does not require them.

There is significant authority for the proposition that undertakings should not be required unless the respondent has established an Article 13(1)(b) grave risk exception. In *Simcox*, the Sixth Circuit held that, "[a] bsent a grave risk finding, the Convention leaves no room for a court to establish, as the district court did in this case, ameliorative undertakings designed to protect children against the risk of harm upon their return."[209] But a district court decision in favor of undertakings "where the potential for harm is real, even if it does not meet the Article 13(b) definitions," was affirmed by the First Circuit in *Kufner*.[210]

Before the Supreme Court's ruling in *Golan*, some courts insisted that they were obliged to consider the appropriateness of such short-term orders designed to be in effect until the courts in the habitual residence are able to step in and issue their own orders.[211] These may include orders that direct the petitioner to:

- Pay for the respondent and child to travel to the country where the child habitually resides;[212]
- Make appropriate housing arrangements for the respondent and child in the country where the child habitually resides;[213]
- Pay temporary living expenses for the respondent and child in the country of the child's habitual residence;[214]
- Secure the dismissal of criminal charges against the respondent arising from the removal of the children;[215]
- Expeditiously obtain medical procedures for a child;[216]
- Not unreasonably oppose mother's efforts to obtain visitation and counseling for herself to increase visitation to point of joint custody;[217] and

---

208. Golan v. Saada, 142 S. Ct. 1880 (2022).

209. Simcox v. Simcox, 511 F.3d 594, 608 (6th Cir. 2007).

210. *Kufner*, 480 F. Supp. 2d 515 n.34, *aff'd*, 519 F.3d 33 (1st Cir. 2008).

211. *Kufner*, 480 F. Supp. 2d 515 n.34, *aff'd*, 519 F.3d 33; Rial v. Rijo, 2010 WL 1643995 (S.D.N.Y. 2010).

212. Krefter v. Wills, 623 F. Supp. 2d 125 (D. Mass. 2009).

213. *Id.*

214. *Id.*

215. *Kufner*, 480 F. Supp. 2d 491, *aff'd*, 519 F.3d 33 (1st Cir. 2008).

216. *Id.*

217. *Id.*

- Have no contact or limited (e.g., supervised) contact with the child once the child returns to the country of the habitual residence.

Any such measures should be limited in scope and time and should further the Convention's goal of ensuring the prompt return of the child to the habitual residence, so that that jurisdiction can resolve the custody dispute.[218]

The issue of undertakings is discussed more fully in Chapter 8.

§ 2.30 LEGAL FEES AND EXPENSES

Article 26 of the Convention provides that, "upon ordering the return of a child or issuing an order concerning rights of access under the Convention, the judicial or administrative authorities may, where appropriate, direct the person who removed or retained the child, or who prevented the exercise of rights of access, to pay" the applicant's fees and costs. Thus, Article 26 provides that such a direction is discretionary.

ICARA expands Article 26 by providing that any court that orders the return of a child under the Hague Convention "shall order" the respondent to pay "necessary expenses" incurred by or on behalf of the petitioner, including court costs, legal fees, foster home or other care during the course of proceedings in the action, and transportation costs related to the return of the child, "unless the respondent establishes that such order would be clearly inappropriate."[219]

ICARA goes beyond the discretion that is authorized in the Convention and includes a mandatory obligation to impose necessary expenses, unless the respondent establishes that to do so would be clearly inappropriate. This reflects an affirmative intention on the part of Congress to impose fees in favor of the petitioner and against the respondent in return actions filed under this statute.[220]

Consequently, awards are generally made whenever a return order is issued.

However, it is not a two-way fee award process. A respondent who succeeds in securing the dismissal of a Hague petition is not entitled to an award of legal fees against the petitioner.[221]

---

218. *Danaipour*, 286 F.3d 1.

219. 22 U.S.C. § 9007(b).

220. Salazar v. Maimon, 750 F.3d 514, 519–20 (5th Cir. 2014).

221. Mata-Cabello v. Thula, 67 F.4th 5 (1st Cir. 2023); Cuellar v. Joyce, 603 F.3d 1142 (9th Cir. 2010).

The purpose of these provisions is not only to compensate the bearers of the expenses incurred but also to provide an additional deterrent to wrongful international child removal and retention.[222] "Mandatory fee shifting discourages manipulation of the judicial process for purposes of delay and encourages the prompt return of the child."[223]

However, the Second Circuit has insisted that Congress did not provide that the provision's added deterrence was so overriding that courts *must* award fees regardless of the circumstances of a particular case. Rather, "a common sense interpretation of the text" indicates that, *even if* an award of fees would serve a deterrent purpose, that purpose must give way if awarding fees would be "clearly inappropriate."[224]

The statute does not condition the court's obligation to award fees on a trial on the merits or upon a judicial determination of wrongful retention. Thus the Fifth Circuit has ruled that the fact that a mother prevailed through settlement of a Hague case, rather than after a hearing, in securing an order that provided for her child's return did not preclude an award of attorney fees to her as the prevailing party.[225]

The respondent has the burden to establish that a fee/expense order would be clearly inappropriate.[226] Although previously awards were invariably made whenever a return order was issued, in recent years, the courts have exercised a greater degree of discretion. The Second Circuit has ruled that the appropriateness of such costs "depends on the same general standards that apply when attorney's fees are to be awarded to prevailing parties only as a matter of the court's discretion," and that "there is no precise rule or formula for making these determinations, but instead equitable discretion should be exercised in light of the [relevant] considerations."[227]

Some circuits have established a two-factor test: (1) whether respondent had "a good faith belief that her actions in removing or retaining a child were legal or justified" and (2) respondent's ability to pay and whether an award of fees would impair her ability to care for her child.[228]

222. Saldivar v. Rodela, 894 F. Supp. 2d 916, 926 (W.D. Tex. 2012).

223. *Maimon*, 750 F.3d 520; *see also* Onrust v. Larson, 2015 WL 697142 (S.D.N.Y. 2015).

224. *Lee Jen Fair*, 818 F.3d 80.

225. *Id.*

226. Whallon v. Lynn, 356 F.3d 138 (1st Cir. 2004); *Ozaltin*, 708 F.3d 375.

227. *Ozaltin*, 708 F.3d 377.

228. Rath v. Marcoski, 898 F.3d 1306, 1311 (11th Cir. 2018) (citing *Ozaltin*, 708 F.3d 375–76); *see also Fuentes*, 657 F.3d 536–37.

In *Ozaltin*, the court stated that where the respondent had a "reasonable basis for thinking at the time of removing the children to the United States . . . that her actions were consistent with [the law of the country of habitual residence]," that belief, even if mistaken, "is a relevant equitable factor when considering whether a costs award is appropriate."[229] But when the respondent engaged in a "furtive removal" of a child without the petitioner's knowledge and devised a litigation strategy designed to impede any attempt by the petitioner to recover the child, her good faith claim was necessarily rejected.[230]

However, an award of fees and costs is "appropriate" when the case is not a "difficult" one and "falls squarely within the heartland of the Hague Convention."[231]

In considering the relevant equitable factors, acts of domestic violence may also be relevant. In *Souratgar*,[232] the Second Circuit held that the petitioning father's multiple and unilateral acts of intimate partner violence against the mother, who fled the marital home and later fled the country with the parties' child, made any award of the father's expenses "clearly inappropriate." It was most significant that the violence did not stop when the mother fled the marital home, that the removal of the child from the country of habitual residence was related to the violence, and that no countervailing factors favored the father.

There is authority for the proposition that a respondent's dire financial situation may require some reduction in the reimbursement of legal fees.[233] The disparity of resources between the parties has led some district courts to refuse any reimbursement[234] and has led other courts to deny an award of attorneys' fees but to allow an award of out-of-pocket expenses.[235] In one case, the respondent's "straitened financial circumstances" justified a 46 percent reduction in the fee award,[236] whereas in another case a 15 percent reduction was required because "a fee award

229. *Ozaltin*, 708 F.3d 375.

230. *Marcoski*, 898 F.3d 1306.

231. *Cuellar*, 603 F.3d 1143.

232. *Lee Jen Fair*, 818 F.3d 72.

233. Rydder v. Rydder, 49 F.3d 369, 373–74 (8th Cir. 1995).

234. *In re* Polson, 578 F. Supp. 2d 1064, 1072 (S.D. Ill. 2008); Montero-Garcia v. Montero, 2013 WL 6048992 (W.D.N.C. 2013); Vale v. Avila, 2008 WL 5273677, at *2 (C.D. Ill. 2008); Silverman v. Silverman, 2004 WL 2066778, at *4 (D. Minn. 2004).

235. Mendoza v. Silva, 987 F. Supp. 2d 910 (N.D. Iowa 2014).

236. *Rydder*, 49 F.3d 369.

which unduly limited respondent's ability to support his children would be 'clearly inappropriate.'"[237]

The degree of inappropriateness will be increased if, for example, the respondent would be "unable to absorb the necessarily minimal expenses for her family in addition to any fee award, [so that] an award of fees would impair significantly her ability to care for her children."[238] But where an apparently destitute respondent had the ability to earn substantial income as a doctor, the court refused to reduce the fee award,[239] and when a respondent was unemployed and had no assets in the United States but owned a building in Germany that could be rented for $2,000 a month, an award was not "clearly inappropriate."[240] However, the fact that a respondent owes considerable sums to his own lawyer does not render a fee award clearly inappropriate.[241]

The fact that a respondent is wealthy does not operate as a countervailing factor that would justify an award of fees to a petitioner who is found to have engaged in unilateral and intimate partner violence against the respondent.[242]

In considering the issue of appropriateness, a court may consider the conduct of a respondent in evading service for over two months, refusing to abide by the custody decision of a court in the country of habitual residence of the child after having agreed to accept whatever it would decide, and presenting new defenses on the eve of trial.[243]

In a case with multiple respondents, the courts may apportion responsibility among the respondents according to their respective degrees of responsibility for the commission of the wrongful acts.[244]

In many cases, petitioners are represented by pro bono counsel. The question then arises as to whether a petitioner receiving free representation may be awarded legal fees. The argument against any such award is that ICARA requires that the fees be "necessary" fees incurred by or on behalf of the petitioner. On the other hand, withholding fees from pro bono counsel would discourage pro bono representation and undermine

---

237. Berendsen v. Nichols, 938 F. Supp. 737 (D. Kan. 1996).

238. *Silverman*, 2004 WL 2066778, at *4.

239. Norinder v. Fuentes, 2010 WL 4781149 (S.D. Ill. 2010), *aff'd*, 657 F.3d 526 (7th Cir. 2011).

240. Neves v. Neves, 637 F. Supp. 2d 322, 345 (W.D.N.C. 2009).

241. *Cuellar*, 603 F.3d 1143.

242. Jimenez Blancarte v. Ponce Santamaria, 2020 WL 428357 (E.D. Mich. 2020).

243. Tereshchenko v. Karimi, 2024 WL 3342759 (S.D.N.Y. July 9, 2024).

244. Neves v. Neves, 2009 WL 1563893 (W.D.N.C. 2009).

the Convention's policy of effective and speedy return of abducted children. The Ninth Circuit has awarded legal fees for pro bono counsel in such circumstances, stressing that

> [a]n award of fees in this case will encourage other lawyers to advance legal services to impecunious clients in the expectation that they will be compensated if successful. This will help ensure that the Convention not go unenforced merely because a parent whose child is abducted lacks the resources to pay for counsel.[245]

Other courts have also awarded fees for pro bono counsel.[246] But if attorney fees and costs are excessive, the court can consider whether petitioner would have permitted counsel to expend the same amount of resources if she had been required to actually pay for the services.[247]

In determining the amount of reasonable attorney's fees to award under ICARA, federal courts typically apply the lodestar method.[248] Under that method, the court multiplies the number of reasonable hours expended by a reasonable hourly rate. In determining what is "reasonable," a district court's discretion should be guided by the following factors: (1) the time and labor expended; (2) the novelty and difficulty of the questions raised; (3) the skill required to properly perform the legal services rendered; (4) the attorney's opportunity costs in pressing the instant litigation; (5) the customary fee for like work; (6) the attorney's expectations at the outset of the litigation; (7) the time limitations imposed by the client or circumstances; (8) the amount in controversy and the results obtained; (9) the experience, reputation, and ability of the attorney; (10) the undesirability of the case within the legal community in which the suit arose; (11) the nature and length of the professional relationship between attorney and client; and (12) attorneys' fees awards in similar cases.[249]

Case law construing what is a "reasonable fee" in other federal shifting statutes has been held to apply in Hague cases. Thus, in submitting a fee petition, counsel should exercise proper billing judgment and exclude any hours that are "excessive, redundant, or otherwise unnecessary." If a court determines that the number of hours is unreasonably high, it may attempt to identify specific hours that should be eliminated, or it may

245. *Cuellar*, 603 F.3d 1142.

246. *Haimdas*, 720 F. Supp. 2d 183.

247. Cillikova v. Cillik, 2016 WL 541134, at *5, n.2 (D.N.J. 2016).

248. *Neves*, 637 F. Supp. 2d 322; Wasniewski v. Grzelak-Johannsen, 549 F. Supp. 2d 965 (N.D. Ohio 2008); Distler v. Distler, 26 F. Supp. 2d 723 (D.N.J. 1998).

249. *Neves*, 637 F. Supp. 2d 322.

simply reduce the award.[250] In one case, the court reduced the requested fee by 25 percent because of "rampant block billing," meaning the timekeeping method by which each lawyer and legal assistant enters the total daily time spent working on a case, rather than itemizing the time expended on each specific task.[251]

ICARA provides that other "necessary expenses" may also be awarded. This will include such expenses as the airfare and hotel expenses of the petitioner.[252] In one case, it was held to include transportation and lodging for an attorney to attend oral argument and post-argument mediation, as well as the cost of shipping briefs and other filings to the court.[253] Hague cases frequently require the assistance of foreign counsel, and courts will include the reasonable charges of such counsel in a fee award if the petitioner shows that the work in question was necessary and that the fees are reasonable.[254] On the other hand, a petitioner is not entitled to recover expenses that are merely incidental to the preparation of cases and are part of attorney office overhead.[255]

A petitioner may be entitled to recover investigation costs if such costs are "necessary" to secure the return of the child.[256] But investigative fees incurred after the issuance of a warrant have not been allowed.[257]

Counsel for a petitioner must pay attention to local rules concerning attorney's fee applications. In one case, a successful petitioner was not entitled to any award of attorney's fees, because he had failed to comply with a local rule requiring that a motion for attorney fees be filed within 30 days of entry of final judgment.[258]

Although some courts conduct evidentiary hearings on the attorney's fee issue, the Fifth Circuit has ruled that the trial court has broad discretionary powers to determine whether any such hearing is required.[259] In sharp contrast, a petitioner's six-year delay in renewing a motion for fees and expenses did not bar the motion when respondent failed to establish prejudice resulting from the delay.[260]

---

250. Rath v. Marcoski, 2017 WL 9401107 (M.D. Fla. 2017).
251. Harvey v. Means, 2024 WL 4144155 (W.D. Wash. Sept. 11, 2024).
252. *Id.*
253. *Cuellar*, 603 F.3d 114.
254. *Neves*, 637 F. Supp. 2d 322.
255. Freier v. Freier, 985 F. Supp. 710 (E.D. Mich. 1997).
256. *Neves*, 637 F. Supp. 2d at 344.
257. *In re* One Infant Child, 2014 WL 704037 (S.D.N.Y. Feb. 20, 2014).
258. *Pesin*, 244 F.3d 1250.
259. *Maimon*, 750 F.3d 514.
260. Sewald v. Reisinger, 2015 WL 6964290 (M.D. Fla. 2015).

Counsel for a respondent should warn the client of the potentially enormous financial exposure if the petition is successful. Particularly in cases in which the petitioner is represented by pro bono counsel, the fees can be astronomical. Respondents often insist that their lawyers assert every possible defense, raise every possible claim, use every scrap of potential evidence, and make every possible motion. One often wonders if their lawyers have fully warned them that they will not only have to pay hefty legal fees to their own lawyer, but they are also likely to have to pay the mammoth fees and expenses of the other side.

§ 2.31 STAYS PENDING APPEAL

Neither the Hague Convention nor ICARA provide any standard for the granting of a stay pending appeal of an order directing, or refusing to direct, the return of children to foreign countries. Accordingly, the normal criteria governing stays in other proceedings apply in Hague cases.[261]

The basic rule, certainly in federal courts, is that a motion for a stay pending appeal is evaluated according to four criteria: (1) the likelihood that appellant will prevail in the appeal, (2) irreparable harm to the appellant if the stay is not granted, (3) irreparable harm to the appellee if the stay is granted, and (4) whether the public interest would be affected by the stay.[262] These factors are the linchpin for any decision regarding whether to stay a case pending appeal.

In *Chafin*, the U.S. Supreme Court ruled that:

> Ms. Chafin is correct to emphasize that both the Hague Convention and ICARA stress the importance of the prompt return of children wrongfully removed or retained. We are also sympathetic to the concern that shuttling children back and forth between parents and across international borders may be detrimental to those children. But courts can achieve the ends of the Convention and ICARA—and protect the well-being of the affected children—through the familiar judicial tools of expediting proceedings and granting stays where appropriate.[263]

261. Kijowska v. Haines, 463 F.3d 583 (7th Cir. 2006).

262. Hilton v. Braunskill, 481 U.S. 770 (U.S. 1987); Mohammed v. Reno, 309 F.3d 95 (2d Cir. 2002).

263. *Chafin*, 133 S. Ct. 1027.

The court further stated that,

> Courts should apply the four traditional stay factors in considering whether to stay a return order: "(1) whether the stay applicant has made a strong showing that he is likely to succeed on the merits; (2) whether the applicant will be irreparably injured absent a stay; (3) whether issuance of the stay will substantially injure the other parties interested in the proceeding; and (4) where the public interest lies."[264]

A respondent will of course claim irreparable injury by virtue of the child being sent away from a place where it has been residing. Such an argument was accepted in *Kijowska*,[265] in which the court granted a stay because the child had been living in the United States for more than a year and to have sent her to Poland at a time when the appeal was pending could have caused serious harm to the child by reuniting her with her mother for only a short period of time if the district court's order were reversed. In *Simcox*,[266] the court granted a stay citing evidence of physical abuse, the father's threats to subject the mother to criminal prosecution in the overseas country, and a nearly year-long delay between the time of the alleged abduction and the filing of a petition for return.

A petitioner will normally claim that the public interest requires that returns be made promptly and not be delayed by the appeal process. In *Friedrich*, the court noted that, staying the return of a child in an action under the Convention should "hardly be a matter of course" since it is the aim of the Convention to secure the prompt return of abducted children.[267] Some courts have applied this precedent.[268] Other courts have noted that granting a stay pending appeal "qualifies as an 'extraordinary remedy' which should not routinely be granted since to do so would 'undermine' the stated policy concerns in the Hague Convention."[269] By contrast, some courts have provided time prior to an ordered return for the respondent to file in the circuit appellate court for an emergency stay.[270]

264. *Id.* at 1026–27.
265. *Haines*, 463 F.3d 583.
266. *Simcox*, 511 F.3d 594.
267. Friedrich v. Friedrich, 78 F.3d 1060 (6th Cir. 1996).
268. *Haimdas*, 720 F. Supp. 2d 183.
269. Avendano v. Smith, 2011 WL 5223041 (D.N.M. 2011).
270. Garcia v. Varona, 2011 WL 3805778 (N.D. Ga. 2011).

Respondents should normally propose to the court that the appeal proceedings should be accelerated, as was done in *Tereshchenko*, *Kijowska*, *Simcox*, and *Koch*.[271] Some courts have required that a respondent file a substantial bond in order to secure a stay pending appeal.[272]

An excellent example of a district court and an appellate court fashioning a procedure to accommodate both the time constraints of the Convention and the right of an appellant to have his day in an appellate court prior to the drastic step of sending the child overseas is provided by the Second Circuit case of *Diorinou v. Mezitis*.[273] There the following events occurred, as described in Second Circuit opinion:

- The district court ordered the father forthwith to return the children to their residence in Greece.
- The district court "helpfully" stayed its order for a few days to permit the father to seek a stay pending appeal from the Second Circuit.
- A Second Circuit judge extended that stay for a few more days.
- The Second Circuit then expedited the appeal, scheduled oral argument (after prompt briefing) for three days later, and extended the stay until disposition of the appeal.
- The Second Circuit also directed that, pending appeal, the father should transfer care and temporary custody of the children to their mother in New York, and it required her to surrender her passport and those of the children to the district court.
- The Second Circuit also invited the views of the U.S. Department of State on the pending appeal, which it received, "with extraordinary promptness."
- The Second Circuit rendered its opinion early the next month.

The English courts have adopted a procedure for the prompt handling of appeals in Hague cases that might serve as a model for courts in the United States. Appeals in England must be lodged within 14 days of the first instance decision. Resolution of appeals is expedited through a fast-tracking appellate procedure. Convention appeals can be scheduled for

---

271. Tereshchenko v. Karimi, 102 F.4th 111, 124 (2d Cir. 2024); *Haines*, 463 F.3d 583; *Simcox*, 511 F.3d 594, 2007 Fed. App. 0502P; Koch v. Koch, 450 F.3d 703 (7th Cir. 2006).

272. Bekier v. Bekier, 248 F.3d 1051 (11th Cir. 2001).

273. *Diorinou*, 237 F.3d 133.

final determination within a week of the appeal being lodged, particularly when an immediate return order has been issued. The target of six weeks is for resolution of the case in its entirety, including all appeals.[274] Unfortunately, the issue has not been significantly addressed in the United States, and a resolution of the matter is urgently required.

The seriousness of this issue is borne out by just about any case in which, on appeal, a return order was eventually overturned. A striking illustration of the need for liberal stays pending appeal in Hague cases (with expedited consideration of the appeal) is provided by the Third Circuit's two appeals in the *Adan* case, details of which are in Chapter 8. There a district court refused to accept a mother's claim of sexual misconduct leading to a grave risk of harm. The Third Circuit remanded the case,[275] but the district court again issued a return order. The district judge refused to grant a stay pending appeal. The mother petitioned for reconsideration, and another judge in the district court refused to grant a stay. In fact, that judge concluded that the mother's chance of success on the merits of any appeal was small.[276] Finally, the Third Circuit granted a stay and was sufficiently outraged at the district court's conduct, and at its errors in barring relevant evidence, that from the bench it ordered the immediate reversal of the district court's orders, and the matter was remanded to that court with instructions that the Hague petition must be immediately dismissed.[277] Had no stay of the lower court order been issued, the appeal would in fact have likely been entirely moot.

The refusal of many circuit courts to grant stays of return orders pending appeals—often in the name of the policy of expeditious conclusion of Hague cases—does not serve the Hague process well. It means that there are plenty of appeals against the dismissals of Hague petitions, because there is no need for a stay pending the appeal, and far less appeals of return orders. A significant element of the appropriate solution would be to place Hague appeals of return orders on a fast track, as the treaty requires, rather than to deprive respondents of their right to appeal.

---

274. Jeremy D. Morley, *U.S. Hypocrisy Concerning International Child Abduction*, http://www.international-divorce.com/us-hypocrisy-concerning-international-child-abductions.

275. *In re* Application of Adan, 437 F.3d 381 (3d Cir. 2006).

276. Adan v. Avans, 2007 WL 2212711 (D.N.J. 2007).

277. *In re* Application of Adan, 544 F.3d 542 (3d Cir. 2008).

§ 2.32 STANDARD OF REVIEW ON APPEAL

In *Monasky*, the Supreme Court reviewed the appropriate standard of review in Hague Convention cases, at least as far as habitual residence issues are concerned.[278]

The Court explained that neither the Convention nor ICARA prescribes modes of appellate review, other than the directive to act "expeditiously." It further stated that:

- Absent a treaty or statutory prescription, the appropriate level of deference to a trial court's habitual-residence determination depends on whether that determination resolves a question of law, a question of fact, or a mixed question of law and fact.
- Generally, questions of law are reviewed *de novo* and questions of fact, for clear error, while the appropriate standard of appellate review for a mixed question depends on whether answering it entails primarily legal or factual work.
- A child's habitual residence presents a "mixed question" of law and fact—albeit barely so. The inquiry begins with a legal question: What is the appropriate standard for habitual residence?
- Once the trial court correctly identifies the governing totality-of-the-circumstances standard, however, what remains for the court to do in applying that standard is to answer a factual question: Was the child at home in the particular country at issue? The habitual-residence determination thus presents a task for fact-finding courts, not appellate courts, and should be judged on appeal by a clear-error review standard deferential to the factfinding court.
- As a deferential standard of review, clear-error review speeds up appeals and thus serves the Convention's premium on expedition.

The same reasoning has been applied concerning other exceptions in the Convention. The First Circuit explained that, like the habitual residence determination at issue in *Monasky*, the "grave risk" and "now settled" defenses require the trial court to identify a broad standard and then answer the factual questions of whether return would expose the abducted child to grave risk of harm or whether the abducted child is "now settled." On appeal, once it is shown that the trial court applied the correct legal standard, appellate review is limited to clear error review.[279] Likewise, see, for example, *Tereshchenko*[280] and *Vieira*.[281]

278. *Monasky*, 140 S. Ct. 730.
279. Da Silva v. De Aredes, 953 F.3d 67 (1st Cir. 2020).
280. Tereshchenko v. Karimi, 102 F.4th 11 (2d Cir. 2024).
281. Vieira v. De Souza, 22 F.4th 304 (1st Cir. 2022).

Habitual Residence 3

§ 3.01 INTRODUCTION

Determining the child's "habitual residence" is a threshold issue in any Hague Convention case.[1] It is often outcome-determinative, because, if the court concludes that the country from which the child was removed was not the country of the child's habitual residence, the Convention will not apply and the petition must be dismissed.[2] Habitual residence is the central concept on which "the entire system" is based.[3]

Courts in the United States have scrutinized the phrase extensively and in the past there was substantial diversity in the way that it was interpreted in different circuits and by many state courts. The term is also extremely fact sensitive. Lawyers must often conduct an intense fact investigation and, given the strict timeline of most Hague cases, they must usually do so with great urgency.

The fundamental reasons for the difficulty in interpreting the phrase are that it is not defined in either the Convention or in ICARA; that it consists of two inherently ambiguous terms; and, most significantly, that international relationships are often messy and confusing. Thus:

- Spouses and partners travel to other countries with all manner and kind of intentions, purposes, hopes, dreams, and aspirations;

1. Feder v. Evans-Feder, 63 F.3d 217 (3d Cir. 1995).
2. Mozes v. Mozes, 239 F.3d 1067 (9th Cir. 2001).
3. Guzzo v. Cristofano, 719 F.3d 100 (2d Cir. 2013).

- Initial moves to a new country may be intended to be permanent, or for a defined period of time, or purely tentative and uncertain;
- Some parents agree to "shuttle" arrangements, whereby children or families are to go back and forth after designated periods of time or upon certain events;
- Intentions may differ between the parents of a child and may or may not be openly—or even accurately—described at the time;
- One partner may tell the other partner one thing while telling family or friends a quite different story;
- Ideas about residency may change over time as family members adjust or do not adjust to new circumstances, as children are born or develop, as marriages improve or deteriorate, as careers develop or fail, as economic conditions fluctuate over time, as parents "back home" get old or sick, as in-laws provide support or interfere, and so on;
- Children may or may not adjust to their new environment in ways that are difficult to predict; and
- When parents separate, they may do so in ways that are both confused and confusing, they may make promises that they do or do not intend to keep, and they may make threats upon which they may or may not intend to act.

Before the 2020 Supreme Court decision in *Monasky*, the uncertainty about habitual residence in the United States, and the extremely subjective nature of the interpretation adopted by the majority of the circuits, stood in sharp contrast to the more "objective" interpretation adopted by most other countries. This created many adverse consequences, including the following:

- There was an explosion of litigation concerning the interpretation of habitual residence in Hague cases in the United States.
- There was a surge in appeals to circuit courts on the issue of habitual residence.
- Hague cases have been far more expensive to litigate than would be the case if the term had been afforded a clear and standard interpretation.
- Hague Convention cases have taken far longer than would be the case if the term were clear. The U.S. majority interpretation of habitual residence, established primarily by the Ninth Circuit in the *Mozes* case, and the Second Circuit in the *Gitter* case, spawned a morass of case law that overlaid the plain meaning of "habitual residence" with a tangled web of rules,

presumptions, conditions, maxims, and guidelines that makes any trial of a Hague habitual residence case uncertain, expensive, and confusing.

- By delaying the resolution of Hague Convention cases, the United States was in derogation of its obligation to resolve such cases expeditiously.
- The United States may well have been in breach of its treaty obligation under the Hague Convention to promote a consistent interpretation of the Convention and to afford "considerable weight" to the opinions of our sister signatories in interpreting any treaty.[4]
- The U.S. courts may well have been acting contrary to the instructions of Congress, which directed in the International Child Abduction Remedies Act (ICARA) that there should be a "uniform international interpretation of the Convention."[5]

These problems have been reduced by the Supreme Court's decision in *Monasky*, which not only provided a standard—though very loose—interpretation of the term but also provided that there should be great deference to the decisions of the trial courts in applying that standard.

§ 3.02 "HABITUAL RESIDENCE" AND "HOME STATE"

The term "habitual residence," as used in the Convention, has nothing to do with the test for a "home state" under the Uniform Child Custody Jurisdiction & Enforcement Act (UCCJEA). Indeed, a child may have a "home state" in the country in which he has been living for the past six months and a "habitual residence" in the place where he lived previously.[6]

The home state concept is far simpler and easier to apply. It is carefully defined in the UCCJEA, is fundamentally based on a specific period of time (six months), is purposefully based on the term "living" rather than the looser word "residency," and is based upon a consideration of the situation of only the child in a particular jurisdiction and not upon the location of the child's parents.[7]

---

4. Abbott v. Abbott, 130 S. Ct. 1983, 1993 (2010).
5. ICARA, 42 U.S.C. § 11601(b)(3)(B).
6. *E.g.*, Baz v. Patterson, 100 F.4th 854, 865 (7th Cir. 2024).
7. However, recent cases on the issue of whether the time a child has spent away from a place is a "temporary absence" from the place where the child has primarily been living have opened the door to some such issues in UCCJEA cases. *See, e.g.*, Sajjad v. Cheema, 428 N.J. Super. 160 (App. Div. 2012).

Although there are sometimes difficulties in determining the home state when the child spends time in more than one jurisdiction, or when a child is removed from a jurisdiction without the consent of a parent, those challenges are minimal when compared to the enormous difficulties that arise in interpreting the term "habitual residence."

The fact that habitual residence is used in the United States for Hague Convention purposes but not for child custody jurisdiction purposes creates confusion and difficulty. It is often said that the Hague Convention does not determine child custody but merely determines which court is entitled to decide custody; but that statement is actually incorrect. A child could be returned to a habitual residence that is not the child's home state. For example, if the return is from the United States to most foreign countries, the U.S. determination of habitual residence might well suffice to enable the foreign court to assume custody jurisdiction under its own laws, but a court in the United States might nonetheless continue to have "home state" jurisdiction under the UCCJEA.[8]

§ 3.03 "HABITUAL RESIDENCE" AND "DOMICILE"

Nor is habitual residence the same as domicile. Domicile is a term of great vintage in the common law, but it is quite different from habitual residence. A child acquires a domicile of origin upon birth. Every independent person may acquire a domicile of choice in a country by residing there with the intention of permanent or indefinite residence. During minority, a child's "domicile of dependency" changes to match that of the adult on whom the child is dependent. In many common law jurisdictions, the precise rules about domicile are enshrined in legislation. A child may be domiciled in a place where he has never lived, as where his parents have relocated from their own domicile only temporarily to the country in which the child was born, but his habitual residence may well be in the country of his birth.

Domicile in civil law jurisdictions is quite different. For example, the place of domicile under Dutch law is the place where a person is officially registered at a specific address according to the municipal personal data records, but the official address does not need to be the address where the registered person actually lives or resides.

The Hague Conference on Private International Law deliberately chose "habitual residence" for its factual character, making it the

8. *See, e.g., In re* T.L.B., 272 P.3d 1148, 1156 (Colo. App. 2012).; Redmond v. Redmond, 724 F.3d 729, 741 (7th Cir. 2013).

foundation for the Convention's return remedy in lieu of formal legal concepts like domicile and nationality.[9] Interpretations of domicile provide no useful assistance to the understanding of habitual residence as that term is used in the Hague Convention.

§ 3.04 DRAFTING HISTORY

The drafters of the Convention purposely left the term "habitual residence" undefined. The Perez-Vera Report merely states that the overwhelming and fundamental purpose of the Convention is to return a child taken out of its habitual environment (without the consent of the custodial/left-behind parent) to the child's home and that the habitual residence of the child is "a question of pure fact, differing in that respect from domicile."[10] The drafters left it to the courts of the various nations to interpret the term but they supplied no definition in the Convention and no useful guide in the *travaux preparatoires.*

An important goal for the drafters of the Convention was that it would be interpreted and applied uniformly. That is, there should be an "autonomous" meaning of the term, with consistently standard interpretation worldwide. Such hopes have proven specious. With no international court to render any interpretation, the courts in contracting states have gone their own ways. There has been a deluge of litigation on the issue and a mind-boggling array of differing and often-conflicting interpretations both within the United States and globally.

The failure of courts to develop an international consensus as to the meaning of the term was confirmed at the Fifth Meeting of the Hague Conference's Special Commission to Review the Operation of the Hague Convention. The Permanent Bureau reported merely that, after intense expert discussion:

- It could make no recommendation regarding the issue of habitual residence;
- There was a divergence in the case law as to the weight to be attached to the shared intention of custodians about their future residence and that of the child; and
- Many experts agreed that the use of a strict definition for habitual residence would go against the spirit of the Convention, noting

9. Monasky v. Taglieri, 589 U.S. 68, 78, 84, 140 S. Ct. 719 (2020).
10. Perez-Vera Report, paras. 11 & 66.

> that habitual residence was above all a question of fact to be decided on a case-by-case basis.[11]

Putting a brave face on a serious matter, the experts declared that it had been wise of the drafters of the Convention not to define the concept and that it was the role of judges to exercise their discretion on this matter.

§ 3.05 DATE OF A WRONGFUL REMOVAL

The first step in determining a child's habitual residence is to fix the date on which the alleged wrongful removal or retention took place. The text of the Convention directs courts to only one point in time in determining habitual residence: the time "immediately before the removal or retention."[12] In a wrongful taking case there is little or no question about the date of the event since it occurs on the date that the child is removed from the country in which the child was living.

§ 3.06 DATE OF A WRONGFUL RETENTION

Determining the date of a wrongful retention may be far more difficult than in a case of wrongful removal. It can often be unclear exactly when a wrongful retention has occurred, because, for example, the parents might have agreed to a temporary trip away from the place where the child has been living but the subsequent date when that is converted into a retention is often unclear. Complications can often arise because retaining parents may conceal their true intentions or lie about them. In many cases, temporary vacations overseas become permanent relocations, either because the taking parent tricks the other parent or because during a vacation the taking parent has a change of mind.

In such cases, courts must decide whether the wrongful act occurred on:

- The date that the child should have been returned, such as the date that a planned vacation was scheduled to end or the date on the airline return tickets; or
- The date that the retaining parent subjectively decided to not return the child; or
- The date that the retaining parent communicated the intention to not return the child; or

11. *Available at* http://www.hcch.net/upload/concl28sc5_e.pdf.
12. Hague Convention, Art. 3.

- The date that the left-behind parent understood, or should have understood, that the other parent was not intending to return the child; or
- The earliest or the latest of any such event.

The Perez-Vera Report provides some assistance. It states that

> [t]he fixing of the decisive date in cases of wrongful retention should be understood as that on which the child ought to have been returned to its custodians or on which the holder of the right of custody refused to agree to an extension of the child's stay in a place other than that of its habitual residence.[13]

It is also significant, and may prove helpful in many cases, that it has been held that the retention of a child for purposes of the Convention "is a singular and not a continuing act."[14] Therefore, once a wrongful retention has occurred, the parents' discussions about subsequent return dates will not create a new act of wrongful retention and will not toll the relevant date of wrongful retention or create a new date of wrongful retention.[15]

§ 3.06.1 Clear Return Date

If the evidence establishes that the parties agreed on a specific return date, the analysis is likely to be easier than if the return date was open-ended. Such a circumstance corresponds to the first part of the Perez-Vera Report's definition: the retention in such cases is "wrongful" if the child is not returned by the date "on which the child ought to have been returned to its custodians." Thus, when the petitioner has consented to the child's travel abroad only until a specific date, courts have concluded that the retention becomes "wrongful" after that date.[16]

But if a parent consents to an extension of the child's stay abroad, the retention becomes wrongful at the conclusion of the extension.[17]

Even after an initial instance of wrongful retention, a parent may extend authorization for the child to remain outside the country of habitual residence. This extension will postpone the date of wrongful

13. Perez-Vera Report, para. 108.

14. Marks ex rel. SM v. Hochhauser, 876 F.3d 416 (2d Cir. 2017).

15. Swett v. Bowen, 2024 WL 2034713 (S.D.N.Y. May 7, 2024).

16. *E.g.*, Demaj v. Sakaj, 2013 WL 1131418, at *3, *7 (D. Conn. 2013); Velasquez v. Green, 2012 WL 2885662 (E.D. Tex. 2012), *report and recommendation adopted*, 2012 WL 6569792.

17. *In re* Cabrera, 323 F. Supp. 2d 1303, 1312–13 (S.D. Fla. 2004).

retention for determining whether the well-settled defense is available.[18] But a parent was held not to have consensually extended the authorized time for the child to remain away from the habitual residence in Chile by merely acceding to circumstances that she subjectively felt she could not change after the child's wrongful retention. Specifically, the left-behind parent could not meaningfully consent to the father's continued retention because she lacked any practical ability to control the father's decisions, had already filed a police report in Chile, and did not have any firm belief that the father would return the child at the end of the extension.[19]

§ 3.06.2 Anticipatory Breach

More controversial is the issue of whether a parent's announced refusal to return the child, if made prior to the date of the child's required return, is itself a wrongful retention that constitutes the date of the wrongful retention. There is substantial authority in support of the proposition that it is the date of a pre-return date refusal that is the date of the wrongful retention.

In *Baz*,[20] the father brought his child from Germany to Illinois for agreed parenting time pursuant to a German consent order, but before the agreed return date he filed a case in Illinois for a temporary exclusive custody order in violation of the German order. The Seventh Circuit upheld the district court's ruling that the date of wrongful retention was the date when the father filed his Illinois case, since that was when the mother learned the true nature of the situation.

In *Abou-Haidar*,[21] the D.C. Circuit Court stated, "There is some intuitive logic to the notion that, when the parents agreed that the child would remain in a certain place until a specified date, no retention occurs before that date as long as the child remains there." It then found that the "fundamental flaw with this theory" is that, by filing a case for custody in D.C. court and stating that she intended to remain in Washington with the child, the mother thereby rejected and sought to depart from the previous mutual arrangement.

Similarly, the Second Circuit in *Marks*[22] upheld the lower court's determination that, when a mother took a child from Thailand for an agreed three-week trip to New York, the retention occurred when, after

18. Urquieta v. Bowe, — F.4th —, 2024 WL 4630284 (2d Cir. Oct. 31, 2024).
19. *Id.*
20. Baz v. Patterson, 100 F.4th 854, 865 (7th Cir. 2024).
21. Abou-Haidar v. Sanin Vazquez, 945 F.3d 1208, 1218 (D.C. Cir. 2019).
22. Marks *ex rel.* SM v. Hochhauser, 876 F.3d 416 (2d Cir. 2017).

only two weeks in New York, the mother told the father that she would not return the child. Even though after two weeks she was still allowed to remain in New York with the child for another week without violating her promise to return on the ticketed departure date, the retention was wrongful from the date that she stated that she would not do so. Likewise, see *Stein*,[23] holding that, "[i]n cases where the petitioning parent originally consented to the child's stay outside its habitual residence, wrongful retention occurs on the date that the petitioning parent is informed that the co-parent will not be returning the child to its country of habitual residence."

In *Lomanto*,[24] a father initially consented to the children traveling from Spain to the United States to visit the mother's family and provided a letter authorizing the travel with no return date. The original plan was for the mother to return to Spain with the children at the end of August. Although the exact date changed a few times, the final agreed-upon plan was for the children to return on August 28, 2021. But on August 24, 2021, the mother told one of the children that they would not return to Spain and would stay in New York City, where she had already enrolled the children in school. One child and then the mother told this to the father the same day. The father reported to the police in Spain the next day that his children had been "kidnapped." The district court held, and the Second Circuit affirmed, that the date of the wrongful retention was August 24, not August 28.

On the other hand, there is some older authority for the proposition that even a clearly articulated decision in advance of an agreed return date not to return the child does not constitute the date of a wrongful retention. In *Toren*,[25] the parents had agreed that their children would spend a fixed amount of time in the United States before returning home to Israel. The mother filed for divorce and custody of the children in Massachusetts before the scheduled return date. Did the one-year period commence on the date that the mother filed the demand for custody, or served the demand, or on the scheduled return date? The court held that the wrongful act did not occur until the scheduled return date, even in the face of clear evidence that the mother had made and communicated her decision not to return before that date. It ruled that,

---

23. Stein *ex rel.* J.S. v. Kohn, 2024 WL 4848986, at *1 (2d Cir. Nov. 21, 2024).

24. Lomanto v. Agbelusi, 2023 WL 4118124 (S.D.N.Y. June 22, 2023), *aff'd*, 2024 WL 3342415 (2d Cir. July 9, 2024).

25. Toren v. Toren, 191 F.3d 23 (1st Cir. 1999).

> [t]o the extent that the father's argument is based on the mother's future intent, the father is seeking a judicial remedy for an anticipatory violation of the Hague Convention. But the Hague Convention only provides a cause of action to petitioners who can establish actual retention. Therefore, we do not see how a petitioner like the father, alleging only an anticipatory retention, can invoke the protections of the Hague Convention.

Following *Toren*, a district court in the same circuit likewise held that the date of wrongful retention was the date the child was scheduled to return home, not when the father had earlier told the mother that he would not do so.[26] The court stated that the wisdom of this approach was illustrated by the specific facts of the case because, although the respondent had told the petitioner that he intended not to return the child on the appointed date, the petitioner credibly testified that she continued to expect that the respondent would indeed return the child on that date and, indeed, she had gone to the airport to meet the scheduled flight. Similarly, a district court in Florida[27] held that the date of wrongful retention begins when the agreed date for return passes, not when the earlier notice of an intent is given.

In apparently sharp contrast, the D.C. Court of Appeals ruled that an unlawful retention can occur before the return date agreed upon by the parties if the actions of one parent demonstrate a departure from the agreement.[28] The parents had agreed that the child would be with the mother in the United States for a period of up to three years and would then return home to France, but, after less than a year, the mother filed a custody petition and told the father that she intended to remain in the United States with the child. The Court of Appeals held that the mother had committed a wrongful retention of the child at the time that she made unilateral actions to assert custody, which amounted to a declaration that she then rejected and sought to depart from the previous mutual arrangement concerning the return of the child. The court distinguished *Toren* on the basis that there was no clear communication in that case that the retaining parent would not actually return the child home.

A district court in Georgia considered a case in which the parents had agreed that the mother would travel to the United States with their child for a six-week visit but, shortly after arriving in the United States, she told the father that she intended to remain in the United States with the

26. Falk v. Sinclair, 2010 WL 723744 (D. Me. 2010).
27. Chechel v. Brignol, 2010 WL 2510391 (M.D. Fla. 2010).
28. Abou-Haidar v. Sanin Vazquez, 945 F.3d 1208 (D.C. Cir. 2019).

child. The court ruled that, although the communication of an "anticipatory refusal" to return was probably sufficient to have allowed the father to file a Hague case, the father had the right to wait to file suit until after the retention became wrongful, which was on the date that the mother had previously agreed to return the child.[29]

Courts in other countries have been divided on this issue. An English court accepted the concept that an announced refusal to return would constitute a wrongful retention, even though it preceded the scheduled return date.[30] A Scottish court rejected that approach.[31]

§ 3.06.3 Open Return Date

If the overseas visit has no fixed return date, courts have generally held that the wrongful act occurs when the left-behind parent withdraws his or her consent to the child being retained away from the habitual residence.

In *Karkkainen*,[32] the petitioner allowed her child to travel to the United States and did not set an explicit return date. Addressing the question of when the retention became wrongful, the Third Circuit explained that there was "unrebutted evidence in the record showing that, by mid-July 2003, [petitioner] had withdrawn her consent to have [the child] remain in the United States beyond August 10, 2003 and that the Respondents were fully aware of this." The Court thus concluded that the retention became wrongful on August 10, because the petitioner had "unequivocally communicated" to the respondents that she did not consent to the child remaining in the United States beyond that date.

As a New York district court explained,[33] although the Third Circuit did not cite the Perez-Vera Report for this point, its conclusion mirrors the second half of the Report's description of when a retention becomes wrongful. Because the petitioner in *Karkkainen* did not set a return date when she permitted the child to leave, it was difficult to determine when the child "ought to have been returned." The Third Circuit concluded, however, that the retention became wrongful when the petitioner communicated to respondents that she "had withdrawn her consent to have [the child] remain in the United States" beyond a certain date—or, in other words, when "the holder of the right of custody refused to agree to

29. Philippopoulos v. Philippopoulou, 461 F. Supp. 2d 1321 (N.D. Ga. 2006).
30. Re S. (Minors) (Child Abduction: Wrongful Retention), [1994] Fam 70.
31. Watson v. Jamieson, 1998 SLT 180.
32. Karkkainen v. Kovalchuk, 445 F.3d 280, 286, 290 (3d Cir. 2006).
33. Taveras v. Morales, 22 F. Supp. 3d 219 (S.D.N.Y. 2014).

an extension of the child's stay in a place other than that of its habitual residence."[34]

In *Slagenweit*,[35] the parents had agreed that their child would reside temporarily with the father in the United States and eventually return to her mother in Germany, but they set no specific date for the child's return. The court fixed the date of wrongful retention as the date when the father "clearly" communicated to the mother his intention to keep the child on a permanent basis in the United States, rather than the date that the child came to live with the father. The court determined that this occurred when the noncustodial parent first asked that the child be returned to her in Germany and the custodial parent refused.

In *Blackledge*,[36] the Third Circuit "built on" its decision in *Karkainnen*, holding that the retention date is the date beyond which the noncustodial parent no longer consents to the child's continued habitation with the custodial parent and instead seeks to reassert custody rights, as clearly and unequivocally communicated through words, actions, or some combination thereof. It explained that that determination is, by necessity, fact intensive and will vary with the circumstances of each case. In some cases, the notice date and actual expiration date will coincide, but in other cases the notice will indicate a future date as the date consent will be withdrawn, in which case that latter date, depending on the facts of the case, will constitute the expiration date and, hence, the retention date.

Applying that formulation, the court in *Blackledge* held that the retention date was not the date that the father stated that he wanted his son returned to him in Germany but was the date when he filed his Hague Convention petition, since only then did he seek to reassert his custody rights and unequivocally withdrew his consent for son to reside in the United States.

In *Abou-Haidar*,[37] the parties agreed to stay with their child in the United States for at least 18 months before returning to France. After 11 months the mother filed a case for custody in Washington, D.C. The father submitted a Hague application to the French Central Authority, which rejected it on the basis that the retention of the child was not unlawful since the child's presence in the United States was the result of both parents' agreement. The D.C. district court and circuit courts disagreed.

34. Perez-Vera Report, para. 108.

35. Slagenweit v. Slagenweit, 841 F. Supp. 264 (N.D. Iowa 1993), *vacated as moot*, 43 F.3d 1476 (8th Cir. 1994).

36. Blackledge v. Blackledge, 866 F.3d 169 (3d Cir. 2017).

37. Abou-Haidar v. Vazquez, 945 F.3d 1208 (D.C. Cir. 2019).

The D.C. Circuit did not view the question of wrongful retention as a jurisdictional matter. The date of wrongful retention is the date consent is revoked, or when the petitioner learns the true nature of the situation, or when the respondent no longer consents to the child's continued habitation with the custodial parent and instead seeks to reassert custody rights, as clearly and unequivocally communicated through words, actions, or some combination thereof. In the pending case, that was the date that the mother informed the child's father that she was seeking primary physical custody in the state court.

However, in *Zuker*,[38] the court concluded that a retention does not become wrongful until the petitioner asks that the child be returned and the respondent refuses. In that case, a mother took her child from Argentina for an agreed temporary vacation in Massachusetts. They stayed initially with her family. The court ruled that the wrongful retention occurred on the date that, with the knowledge of the father, the mother moved with the child into her own apartment in Massachusetts, since "it was by *that* act" that the mother communicated to the father that she was not going back to Argentina. Before that date the mother had decided that she would stay in America with the child, but she never communicated that fact to the father. In fact, the parents had at least tacitly agreed that mother and child would remain in United States for some period of time. The court held that it would be unfair to the father to hold that the wrongful act occurred before he even knew about it.

The *Zuker* case has been extensively criticized and expressly called into doubt as inconsistent with the Perez-Vera Report and the reasoning in the *Karkkainen* case.[39]

§ 3.07 OVERVIEW OF HABITUAL RESIDENCE

Once the court has determined the date of the allegedly wrongful act, it must then determine where the child was habitually resident at that moment in time.

Before the seminal decision of the U.S. Supreme Court in *Monasky v. Taglieri*, there were fundamental differences within the circuits as to the criteria that must be focused on to make the required determination. Fundamentally, the dispute concerned whether the court should focus on parental intentions or on the child's viewpoint, but highly technical

38. Zuker v. Andrews, 2 F. Supp. 2d 134 (D. Mass. 1998).

39. *E.g.*, Castillo v. Castillo, 597 F. Supp. 2d 432 (D. Del. 2009); *Morales*, 22 F. Supp. 3d 219, n.15.

subsidiary elements also developed. All those issues were upended by the Supreme Court's establishment of a new standard, that of totality of the circumstances. However, the approaches were not fixed and conclusive, except in those circuits in which they were clearly and expressly set forth.

The first approach focused primarily on parental intention, with a subsidiary look at acclimatization. Six courts of appeals—the First, Second, Fourth, Seventh (to some extent), Ninth, and Eleventh Circuits—adopted this approach, although there were variations between the circuits.[40] The parents' "last shared intent" regarding their child's habitual residence was presumed to be controlling, although the presumption could be rebutted in exceptional cases if the child had sufficiently acclimatized to its new surroundings as to render a return order unfair or seriously damaging.

Courts taking this approach held that a child had acquired a new habitual residence only if it was established that the parents had a shared and settled purpose to do so, unless there was strong proof of the child's acclimatization. The inquiry focused on the state of mind of each of the parents, and whether their intent was shared. This might be revealed by considering, for example, whether or not they intended their move with the child to a new place to be permanent or merely temporary, how long they intended to stay in the new country and whether they had any plans to return to a previous residence. It was possible, using this approach, to find that a child remained habitually resident in a prior country of residence despite having resided for some years in a new country, even attending school and assimilating into the new community.[41]

The second approach was the "child-centered approach." It was followed in the Sixth Circuit. Here the courts looked exclusively at the child's objective circumstances and past experiences. Relevant inquiries included whether or not the child was attending school, the child's participation in other cultural activities such as sports teams and religious organizations, and the child's overall level of acclimatization and integration into the community. The inquiry did not consider parental intent, which

40. Key cases include the following: Nicolson v. Pappalardo, 605 F.3d 100 (1st Cir. 2010); Gitter v. Gitter, 396 F.3d 124 (2d Cir. 2005); Hofmann v. Sender, 716 F.3d 282 (2d Cir. 2013); *Cristofano*, 719 F.3d 100; Maxwell v. Maxwell, 588 F.3d 245 (4th Cir. 2009); Larbie v. Larbie, 690 F.3d 295 (5th Cir. 2012); Redmond v. Redmond, 724 F.3d 729 (7th Cir. 2013); Koch v. Koch, 450 F.3d 703 (7th Cir. 2006); *Mozes*, 239 F.3d 1067; Ruiz v. Tenorio, 392 F.3d 1247 (11th Cir. 2004).

41. *See, e.g.*, Ruiz v. Tenorio, 392 F.3d 1247 (11th Cir. 2004); Murphy v. Sloan, 764 F.3d 1144 (9th Cir. 2014).

was deemed to be entirely irrelevant in determining the child's habitual residence.[42]

The third approach—which was followed by the Third and Eighth Circuits—required a mixed inquiry into both the child's circumstances and the shared intentions of the child's parents. How much weight should be given to each factor was unclear. Sometimes evidence of shared parental intent to abandon an old habitual residence and acquire a new one was held to trump any evidence of acclimatization from the child's perspective.[43] In other cases, sufficient evidence of acclimatization sufficed to defeat evidence of shared intent.[44] In jurisdictions following this approach, the inquiry might shift from case to case so that arguments based on both parental intentions and the child's circumstances needed to be presented.

The Seventh Circuit, in both *Kijowska*[45] and *Redmond*,[46] straddled the various approaches. It stated in *Redmond* that "conventional wisdom thus recognizes a split between the circuits" that follows a standard focusing on the parents' perspectives and "those that use a more child-centric approach." The court insisted that, "in substance, all circuits—ours included—consider both parental intent and the child's acclimatization, differing only in their emphasis." It also stated, in seeming anticipation of *Monasky*, that "[t]he habitual-residence inquiry remains essentially fact-bound, practical, and unencumbered with rigid rules, formulas, or presumptions."[47]

It then applied the test asked in another case: "Simply put, would returning the children to [the other country] be tantamount to sending them home?"[48]

The disagreement among the circuits on the interpretation of habitual residence was in derogation of the congressional call for a "uniform international interpretation of the Convention."[49] If the various parts of the United States could not agree on one interpretation, how could the United States expect other countries to do so?

42. *See, e.g.*, *Ruiz*, 392 F.3d 1247; Friedrich v. Friedrich, 983 F.2d 1396 (6th Cir. 1993); Simcox v. Simcox, 511 F.3d 594 (6th Cir. 2007).

43. *See, e.g.*, *Gitter*, 396 F.3d 124.

44. *See, e.g.*, *Koch*, 450 F.3d 703.

45. Kijowska v. Haines, 463 F.3d 583 (7th Cir. 2006).

46. *Redmond*, 724 F.3d 729.

47. *Id.* at 746.

48. *Id.* at 747.

49. 22 U.S.C. § 9001(b)(3)(B).

Worse still, such inconsistencies encouraged forum shopping within the United States. Given the dramatic differences in the way that this key term was interpreted, it made perfect sense for a parent who was considering taking a child from a country that might or might not be deemed to be the habitual residence of the child to take legal advice before choosing exactly where in the United States to live. The difference between how the law was interpreted, for example, on either side of the Hudson River might have been completely decisive, with New York looking primarily at the last shared parental intention and New Jersey looking far more at the actual "conditions on the ground."

§ 3.08 THE *MONASKY* CASE: OVERVIEW

In its seminal ruling in *Monasky v. Taglieri*,[50] the U.S. Supreme Court changed "overnight" the U.S. jurisprudence on the interpretation of the term "habitual residence" in a Hague Convention case. It held that a child's habitual residence depends on the totality of the circumstances specific to the case, not on categorical requirements such as an actual agreement between the parents. Of at least equal importance, the Supreme Court ruled that, providing that the trial court has correctly identified the governing standard, its application of that standard answers the merely factual question of whether the child was at home in the particular country at issue. Such deference to trial courts' decisions has drastically reduced the role of appeals courts in overseeing the application of the Hague Convention.

The *Monasky* case concerned a child who was born in Italy to an American mother and Italian father who had married in the United States and had then moved to Milan, Italy, for their careers. Within a year of arriving in Italy, their relationship deteriorated, but the mother became pregnant. The father moved to Lugo, another city in Italy, while the mother stayed in Milan. She considered returning to the United States but remained in Italy and she and the father made preparations to take care of the child in Italy. They acquired a larger apartment in Milan, inquired about childcare, and made purchases for the needs of their child in Italy. Once the baby was born, the mother informed the father that she wanted a divorce and planned to return to the United States, but she then agreed to join the father in Lugo with the baby. When the baby was six weeks old, the parents argued, and the mother moved with the baby to a safe house

50. Monasky v. Taglieri, 140 S. Ct. 719, 206 L. Ed. 2d 9 (2020).

and reported abuse to the police. Two weeks later, she left Italy with the child and moved to Ohio to live with her parents.

The U.S. District Court for the Northern District of Ohio granted the father's Hague petition to return the child to Italy. Although the Sixth Circuit precedents generally applied a test of acclimatization, the child in this case was too young to have become acclimatized, so the court applied a test of the parents' shared intention. Since the last shared intention (or agreement) had been to live in Italy, it was Italy that was the child's habitual residence. That decision was upheld by the Sixth Circuit before a divided three-judge panel and then a divided en banc panel.

The Supreme Court granted certiorari to resolve the differences between the circuits on how to determine a child's habitual residence. It did so by ruling that a child's habitual residence depends on the totality of the circumstances specific to the case. Although the courts below had applied the wrong test, the Supreme Court did not remand the case to allow the courts below to apply the correct test because nothing in the record suggested that the district court would appraise the facts differently on remand. Accordingly, the ruling stood that the child was habitually resident in Italy on the date her mother took her to the United States, because she had been born in Italy, where her parents had lived for the previous two years, and then lived in Italy for the first two months of her life before her mother took her to live in the United States.

§ 3.09 THE *MONASKY* CASE: FUNDAMENTAL STATEMENTS

The most significant statements made by the Supreme Court in *Monasky* include the following:

a. We begin with the text of the treaty and the context in which the written words are used.[51]
b. The Hague Convention does not define the term "habitual residence."[52]
c. A child "resides" where she lives. See Black's Law Dictionary 1176 (5th ed. 1979).[53]
d. Her residence in a particular country can be deemed "habitual," however, only when her residence there is more than transitory.[54]

51. *Id.* at 726.
52. *Id.*
53. *Id.*
54. *Id.*

e. "Habitual" implies "customary, usual, of the nature of a habit."[55]
f. The Hague Convention's text alone does not definitively tell us what makes a child's residence sufficiently enduring to be deemed "habitual."[56]
g. It surely does not say that habitual residence depends on an actual agreement between a child's parents.[57]
h. But the term "habitual" does suggest a fact-sensitive inquiry, not a categorical one.[58]
i. The Perez-Vera report refers to a child's habitual residence in fact-focused terms: "the family and social environment in which [the child's] life has developed."[59]
j. What makes a child's residence "habitual" is "some degree of integration by the child in a social and family environment."[60]
k. The place where a child is at home, at the time of removal or retention, ranks as the child's habitual residence.[61]
l. Because locating a child's home is a fact-driven inquiry, courts must be sensitive to the unique circumstances of the case and informed by common sense.[62]
m. For older children capable of acclimating to their surroundings, courts have long recognized, facts indicating acclimatization will be highly relevant.[63]
n. Because children, especially those too young or otherwise unable to acclimate, depend on their parents as caregivers, the intentions and circumstances of caregiving parents are relevant considerations.[64]
o. No single fact, however, is dispositive across all cases.[65]
p. Common sense suggests that some cases will be straightforward: Where a child has lived in one place with her family indefinitely, that place is likely to be her habitual residence.[66]

55. *Id.*
56. *Id.*
57. *Id.*
58. *Id.*
59. *Id.*
60. *Id.*
61. *Id.*
62. *Id.* at 727.
63. *Id.*
64. *Id.*
65. *Id.*
66. *Id.*

q. But suppose, for instance, that an infant lived in a country only because a caregiving parent had been coerced into remaining there. Those circumstances should figure in the calculus.[67]

r. "Facts that courts have considered include: a change in geography combined with the passage of an appreciable period of time, the age of the child, the immigration status of the child and the parent, academic activities, social engagements, participation in sports programs and excursions, meaningful connections with the people and places in the child's new country, language proficiency, and the location of personal belongings."[68]

s. "The aim: to ensure that custody is adjudicated in what is presumptively the most appropriate forum—the country where the child is at home."[69]

t. "Our conclusion that a child's habitual residence depends on the particular circumstances of each case is bolstered by the views of our treaty partners. ICARA expressly recognizes 'the need for uniform international interpretation of the Convention.'"[70]

u. "The bottom line: There are no categorical requirements for establishing a child's habitual residence—least of all an actual-agreement requirement for infants."[71]

v. "An infant's mere 'physical presence' . . . is not a dispositive indicator of an infant's habitual residence. But a wide range of facts other than an actual agreement, including facts indicating that the parents have made their home in a particular place, can enable a trier of fact to determine whether an infant's residence in that place has the quality of being 'habitual.'"[72]

In addition, the Supreme Court ruled that the habitual-residence determination presents a task for factfinding courts, not appellate courts, and should be judged on appeal by a clear-error review standard deferential to the factfinding court. This means that the opportunity for appealing issues of habitual residence is substantially constrained.

67. *Id.*
68. *Id.* at n.3.
69. *Id.* at 727.
70. *Id.* at 728.
71. *Id.*
72. *Id.* at 729.

§ 3.10 CIRCUIT COURT CASES AFTER *MONASKY*

As of the date of final editing of this book, there had not yet been a case in which a federal circuit court overruled a district court's determination of habitual residence. The significant circuit court rulings are as follows.

In *Nisbet*,[73] the mother, a U.S. citizen, had lived in Scotland (except for two brief periods in Jersey, a British Crown Dependency) for seven years, in the home of the father, a British citizen. Their children were British citizens. In June 2022, the mother removed the children from Scotland to Oregon without the father's prior knowledge or consent. At that time, the older child, born in Jersey, was age 4½ and had lived in Scotland with his mother since late 2018, except for part of 2019 in Jersey. The younger child, then age 2½, was born in Scotland and had never lived anywhere else. The children had never stepped foot in the United States. They attended school in Scotland and received their medical care there. The Ninth Circuit upheld, despite a powerful dissent, the district court's ruling that the children were not habitually resident in Scotland and had no habitual residence at that time. The courts stressed the facts that the children had few friends in Scotland and no meaningful relationship with their father (who lived in England) and that their mother's U.K. visa was about to expire. The courts were clearly substantially influenced by the fact, recited in the opening sentence of the circuit court's opinion, that the father had killed his own mother in Jersey, had pleaded guilty to manslaughter based on diminished responsibility, and was in indefinite psychiatric confinement in England.

In *Goldstein*,[74] the 11th Circuit considered the impact on the determination of habitual residence of the parents' intention to return to Israel after the passage of some time or a change in circumstances in Israel, as compared to the passage of a few months of having lived in Florida. The parties, with their young children, led a transitory international lifestyle. They left Israel after the Hamas attack on October 7, 2023. There was evidence that they agreed to stay in Florida until the end of the war or for six months to one year. The mother filed for the return of the children four months after the children were in Florida.

The 11th Circuit upheld the district court's decision that the children were habitually resident in Florida because there was evidence that they were in school in Florida, had doctors and therapists there, and participated in a thriving social community. The circuit court stressed that

73. Nisbet v. Bridger, 124 F.4th 577 (2d Cir. 2024).
74. Goldstein v. Simon, 2024 WL 4284921 (11th Cir. Sept. 25, 2024).

the shared intent of the parties is not dispositive as to habitual residence but that the parties' intent to remain in Florida for a period of six to 12 months, or until the end of the war, was a factor that supported the habitual residence in Florida. The district court's opinion noted that a relatively short stay can be sufficient to establish a new habitual residence, regardless of the parents' hope to someday return to their prior residence. The district court noted further that the parties' dispute as to whether the evidence was sufficient to establish that the children had previously been habitually resident in Israel was not significant because the relevant issue is where a child is at home "at the time of removal or retention."[75]

Horacius,[76] in which the 11th Circuit upheld the district court's finding that the child was habitually resident in Canada, not the United States, illustrates the extent to which an appeals court defers to the lower courts' decisions on this issue as a result of *Monasky*. The parties lived in Canada and when their child was nine months old, they took the child to Florida. The father, a U.S. and Canadian citizen originally from Haiti, obtained a Florida driver's license, a Florida notary commission, and a Florida concealed weapons permit, and he registered to vote in Florida. After nearly a year in Florida, the father returned to live in Canada without the child and then demanded that the child should return to Canada. The mother refused to comply. The father did not file his Hague Convention petition for another 21 months. The district court found that the mother's evidence that the parents intended to live permanently in Florida was not credible. It relied on the retention of their personal effects in storage in Canada and the father's assertion that he never intended to live in Florida permanently. The circuit court stated that "it is a close call" but it did not have a "definite and firm conviction that a mistake has been committed" and, since the district court had correctly identified the applicable totality-of-the-circumstances standard, it upheld the district court's ruling in the absence of clear error.[77]

Baz[78] illustrates the limited significance of a parental agreement as to their future intentions for their family. The parties resided with their child in Illinois. They entered into a stipulated judgment in settlement of a custody case in Illinois authorizing the mother to take the child to live primarily in Germany but stipulating that the child would also spend considerable time with the father in Illinois; that the habitual residence

75. *Id.* at *2 (citing Monasky, 140 S. Ct. at 77).
76. Horacius v. Richard, 2024 WL 3580772 (11th Cir. July 30, 2024).
77. *Id.* at *2.
78. Baz v. Patterson, 100 F.4th 854 (7th Cir. 2024).

of the child would remain in Illinois; that neither parent had consented or acquiesced to the permanent removal of the child from the United States; and that so long as at least one parent resides in Illinois, the Illinois Circuit Court would retain exclusive and continuing jurisdiction. Despite that judgment the district court ruled, after the father refused to return the child to Germany, that the child had become habitually resident in Germany. On appeal, the Seventh Circuit upheld that determination, holding that a parental agreement about a child's future habitual residence should not be given decisive effect and that the totality-of-the-circumstances test had been correctly identified and applied by the district court.

Tsuruta[79] concerned the impact of spousal control and coercion in selecting a place to reside. The respondent asserted that Japan was not the child's habitual residence because she had been coerced into living there, in that her husband had required her to sign a marriage license in Japan that she did not understand, had controlled their finances and all important decisions, and had isolated their child from her by only speaking Japanese. The district court held that although the respondent had mixed feelings about being in Japan and was, at times, reluctant to be there, this did not amount to coercion and did not significantly undermine the other evidence suggesting that Japan was the child's home—including the fact that the child had spent most of her time in Japan for several years before the relevant date, had attended school and daycare, and had participated in activities there. The Eighth Circuit affirmed the district court's decision but, while noting that the respondent had cited two cases for the proposition that one parent being coerced into living in a country is relevant to the habitual residence determination because it affects the intent of the parents, did not address the issue of the relevance of coercion to a habitual residence determination because the district court had found that there was no coercion.[80]

In *Rodrigues*,[81] the circuit court held that the district court did not clearly err by weighing the competing evidence and finding that the

79. Tsuruta v. Tsuruta, 76 F.4th 1107 (8th Cir. 2023).

80. Application of Ponath, 829 F. Supp. 363, 368 (D. Utah 1993) ("Petitioner's coercion of respondent by means of verbal, emotional and physical abuse removed any element of choice and settled purpose which earlier may have been present in the family's decision to visit Germany."); Tsarbopoulos v. Tsarbopoulos, 176 F. Supp. 2d 1045, 1049 (E.D. Wash. 2001) ("The verbal and physical abuse of one spouse by the other is one of several factors in the Court's determination of the existence of 'shared intent' to make a place the family's 'habitual residence.'").

81. Rodrigues Dos Santos Argueta v. Argueta-Ugalde, 2023 WL 4635901 (6th Cir. July 20, 2023).

child's connections to Brazil were stronger than the connections she had formed during her four months in the United States. The district court had properly noted that, although the child had established some friendships in the United States, most of her family and relationships remained in Brazil and she had continued to be connected to those relationships through video calls. Moreover, the district court did not clearly err when it found that the family intended to maintain Brazil as a home base for the children. The circuit court further found that the district court's decision to compare the connections that the child had formed in Brazil to her connections in the United States in determining habitual residence is supported by case law that recognizes as a relevant consideration the fact that a child has had alternating residences or has moved frequently.

In *Harm*,[82] the mother took the parties' child from Ireland, where the father was from, to New Orleans, where she was originally from, and retained the child there. The mother was a well-known musician who spent considerable time traveling internationally. The Fifth Circuit court upheld the district court decision that the child was not habitually resident in Ireland even though the child, a toddler, had primarily lived there for the prior ten months, the parents had applied for residency in Ireland, the child attended a toddler group there, and the parents stated their intention for Ireland to be their "home base."

In *Grano*, the Second Circuit upheld a district court determination that the parents' last shared intention was that the child should remain in Spain and then discounted that determination in light of *Monasky* and focused on the objective facts that the child spent less than three months of his life in New York before moving to Spain for nearly a year, and while in Spain, his family built a home, discussed long-term education for him, took him to see doctors, and more generally went about living a life there that was settled, not transient.[83]

In *Farr*, the Ninth Circuit upheld a decision, made pursuant to the pre-*Monasky* law applicable in that circuit that the parties had not intended to abandon the infant children's habitual residence in the United States when they moved to Mexico for an intended period of three to five years, and there was evidence that they considered "home" to be in the United States, even though they lived in Mexico for three years before the abduction. The Ninth Circuit held that the totality of the circumstances

82. Harm v. Lake-Harm, 16 F.4th 450 (5th Cir. 2021).

83. Grano v. Martin, 443 F. Supp. 3d 510 (S.D.N.Y. 2020), *aff'd*, 2020 WL 4045801 (2d Cir. 2020).

supported the district court's finding that the children's habitual residence was the United States, not Mexico.[84]

§ 3.11 INTERNATIONAL AUTHORITIES

The terms employed in an international treaty, and specifically in the Hague Convention, are intended to be interpreted autonomously, as the U.S. Supreme Court expressly ruled in *Abbott*[85] when interpreting the term "rights of custody." This means that the courts should not rely on local law usages of a legal term but instead should strive for international consistency in how the term is interpreted. Indeed, Congress expressly directed in ICARA that "uniform international interpretation of the Convention" is part of the Convention's framework.[86]

Thus, the meaning of the term "habitual residence" should not be drawn from domestic law or from other conventions, but rather from the object and purpose of the Convention and should be aligned with international interpretations.

A review of the international case law indicates that there is a developing international consensus concerning the interpretation of habitual residence that the U.S. Supreme Court has now determined should be the law that applies in the United States.

§ 3.11.1 The European Union

The 27 sovereign countries of the European Union (EU) apply a common set of rules governing jurisdiction and the recognition and enforcement of judgments in matters of parental responsibility, including custody, access, and child abduction. Habitual residence is the primary connecting factor used in these harmonized rules and has twice been interpreted by the Court of Justice of the European Union (CJEU). This guidance is binding in all EU Member States.

In one case,[87] the CJEU ruled that the term

> must be interpreted as meaning that it corresponds to the place which reflects some degree of integration by the child in a social and family environment. To that end, in particular the duration,

84. Farr v. Kendrick, 2020 WL 4877531 (9th Cir. 2020). Fact analysis based in part on review of district court docket.

85. Abbott v. Abbott, 130 S. Ct. 1983, 176 L. Ed. 2d 789 (2010).

86. 22 U.S.C. § 9001(b)(3)(B).

87. Proceedings brought by A (Case C-523/07) [2010] Fam. 42. *Also available at* http://eur-lex.europa.eu/LexUriServ/LexUriServ.do?uri=CELEX:62007CJ0523:EN:HTML.

> regularity, conditions and reasons for the stay on the territory of a member state and the family's move to that state, the child's nationality, the place and conditions of attendance at school, linguistic knowledge and the family and social relationships of the child in that state must be taken into consideration. It is for the national court to establish the habitual residence of the child, taking account of all the circumstances specific to each individual case.

Advocate General Kokott referred to this approach as designating the child's "actual centre of interests."[88]

The CJEU reaffirmed this factually oriented approach, in which parental intention is only one of the factors that may be relevant, in *Mercredi v. Chaffe*.[89] The court clarified that the age of a child is relevant to the way in which habitual residence is to be ascertained. It specified that as "a general rule, the environment of a young child is essentially a family environment, determined by the reference person(s) with whom the child lives, by whom the child is in fact looked after and taken care of."

§ 3.11.2 The United Kingdom

The interpretation in U.K. courts of "habitual residence," as that term is used in the Hague Abduction Convention and in Article 8 of the European Union's Council Regulation (EC) 2201/2003, shifted away from a substantial reliance on parental intention in a series of cases, including the decisions of the U.K. Supreme Court in *A v. A (Children: Habitual Residence)* [2013] UKSC 60, *Re LC (Children)* [2014] UKSC 1, and *Re B (A Child)* [2016] UKSC 4.

In *Re LC (Children) (International Abduction: Child's Objections to Return)*, Lord Wilson noted that the CJEU interpretation of the habitual residence of children actually reflected the intentions of the drafters of the 1980 Hague Convention. Referring to the Pérez–Vera Report, he stated that it was

> satisfactory that, 30 years after the Convention was adopted, in a case (*Proceedings brought by A*, cited above) unrelated to the [1980 Hague] Convention, the CJEU should have formulated a test for habitual residence, which now falls to be applied as fully

88. *Id.* ¶ 28.

89. Mercredi v. Chaffe (Case C-497/10 PPU) [2012] Fam 22. *Also available at* https://eur-lex.europa.eu/legal-content/EN/TXT/?uri=CELEX:62010CJ0497.

to Convention proceedings as to other proceedings, in terms so intriguingly close to what its signatories had in mind.

In *AR v. RN*[90] the mother of two children who were born and raised in France brought them to Scotland pursuant to an agreement with the children's father, who remained in France. After just four months in Scotland, the mother brought a custody case in Scotland seeking an interdict against the father removing them from Scotland. The father promptly brought a Hague case. The lower court in Scotland found that the children were still habitually resident in France because the move to Scotland had not been intended by both parents to be permanent. That ruling was overturned on appeal and the U.K. Supreme Court upheld that decision.

The U.K. Supreme Court stated that, for the purposes of habitual residence, it is the stability of the residence that is important, not whether it is of a permanent character; that there is no requirement that the child should have been resident in the new country for a particular period of time or that one or both parents intended to reside there permanently or indefinitely; that the focus must be upon the situation of the child; that the intentions of the parents are merely one of the relevant factors; that there is no rule that one parent cannot unilaterally change the habitual residence of a child; and that it is necessary to assess the degree of the integration of the child (or, in the case of an infant or young child, the degree of integration of those on whom the child is dependent) into a social and family environment in the new country.

In *AR*, the absence of a joint parental intention to live permanently in Scotland was not decisive, nor was an intention to live in a country for a limited period inconsistent with becoming habitually resident there. The important question was whether the residence had the necessary quality of stability, not whether it was necessarily intended to be permanent.

Following the children's move with their mother to Scotland, their life there had the necessary quality of stability. For the time being, their home was Scotland. Their social life and much of their family life was there. The longer time went on, the more deeply integrated they had become into their environment in Scotland. Accordingly, their habitual residence had shifted to Scotland.

The current law on habitual residence was usefully summarized by an English High Court judge[91] as follows:

90. AR v. RN [2015] UKSC 35.
91. EE and ME (Children) (Habitual Residence) [2016] EWHC 3363 (Fam).

(1) Habitual residence is a question of fact and not a legal concept.
(2) The essentially factual and individual nature of the inquiry should not be glossed with legal concepts which would produce a different result from that which the factual enquiry would produce.
(3) The test adopted by the European Court, which must be applied in cases in the U.K., is that habitual residence is "the place which reflects some degree of integration by the child in a social and family environment."
(4) To that end, in particular the duration, regularity, conditions and reasons for the stay on the territory of a member state and the family's move to that state, the child's nationality, the place and conditions of attendance at school, linguistic knowledge and the family and social relationships of the child in that state must be taken into consideration.
(5) It must be shown that the child's presence in the country in question is not in any way temporary or intermittent but rather of a lasting character.
(6) The social and family environment of an infant or young child is shared with those (whether parents or others) on whom he is dependent. Hence it is necessary to assess the integration of that person or persons in the social and family environment of the country concerned.
(7) This is a child-centered approach. It is the child's habitual residence which is in question. It is the child's integration which is under consideration. Each child is an individual with his own experiences and his own perceptions. These are not necessarily determined by the decisions of his parents. The environment of an infant or very young child is (one hopes) a family environment and so determined by reference to the person with whom he lives. But once the child leaves the family environment and goes to school, his social world widens and there are more factors to be taken into account. Furthermore, where parents are separated, there may well be two possible homes in which the children can live, and the children will be well aware of this. This may well affect the degree of their integration in a new environment.
(8) The modern concept of a child's habitual residence operates in such a way as to make it highly unlikely, albeit conceivable,

that a child will be in limbo. The concept operates in the expectation that, when a child gains a new habitual residence, he loses his old one. Simple analogies are best: consider a see-saw. As, probably quite quickly, he puts down those first roots which represent the requisite degree of integration in the environment of the new state, up will probably come the child's roots in that of the old state to the point at which he achieves the requisite de-integration (or, better, disengagement) from it.

(9) In identifying the point at which habitual residence was lost and gained, the court might find that:
  (a) The deeper the child's integration in the old state, probably the less fast his achievement of the requisite degree of integration in the new state; and
  (b) The greater the amount of adult pre-planning of the move, including pre-arrangements for the child's day-to-day life in the new state, probably the faster his achievement of that requisite degree; and
  (c) were all the central members of the child's life in the old state to have moved with him, probably the faster his achievement of it and, conversely, were any of them to have remained behind and thus to represent for him a continuing link with the old state, probably the less fast his achievement of it.

§ 3.11.3 Australia

The Australian position is set forth in the landmark ruling of the High Court of Australia in *LK v. Director-General, Department of Community Services* [2009] HCA 9.[92] The case concerned four Israeli-born children, who moved to Australia with their Australian-born mother, with the father's consent, on condition that they would return to Israel if the father decided he wanted to live with the family. The mother and children settled into a family home in Australia, the children went to school there, the mother obtained government benefits, and the older children took up sports and music lessons. Just two months later the father asked the mother to return the children to Israel but the mother refused. The High Court ruled that the children were no longer habitually resident in Israel. The decisive factor was that when they left Israel both parents agreed that

92. LK v. Director-General, Department of Community Services [2009] HCA 9.

unless there was a reconciliation, they would stay in Australia. The possibility that the children might again take up habitual residence in Israel (if their parents were reconciled) did not prevent the loss of their habitual residence there meanwhile.

In reaching this conclusion, the High Court affirmed that in determining habitual residence, intention was not to be given controlling weight. And like the courts of England and Ireland, it refused to embrace the principle of abandonment, holding that "[a]bsence of a final decision positively rejecting the possibility of returning to Israel in the foreseeable future is not necessarily inconsistent with ceasing to reside there habitually."[93]

§ 3.11.4 New Zealand

The New Zealand courts have given detailed consideration to United States case law on habitual residence. The New Zealand Court of Appeal has described its approach as taking a middle course between *Mozes* and the child-centered approach. All relevant facts are weighed, with the settled purpose of the parents as one significant factor, but not as important as it was seen to be by the *Mozes* Court. In addition, unlike in *Mozes*, the concentration is on parental purpose as to the quality and length of residence in the new state, rather than as to abandonment of the previous habitual residence.[94]

§ 3.11.5 Canada

The leading case in Canada is *Balev*,[95] in which the Supreme Court of Canada adopted a fluid and flexible "hybrid" approach to determine habitual residence. It held that a trial judge should determine the focal point of the child's life immediately prior to the removal or retention and consider all relevant links and circumstances within the child's life. This includes "the child's links to and circumstances in country A; the circumstances of the child's move from country A to country B; and the child's links to and circumstances in country B." No single factor should dominate the analysis. The judge should be free to consider the entirety of the circumstances when assessing habitual residence and "while courts allude to factors or considerations that tend to recur, there is no legal test for habitual residence and the list of potentially relevant factors is not closed."

93. *Id.* at ¶ 33.
94. S.K. v. K.P. [2005] 3 NZLR 590.
95. Office of the Children's Lawyer v. Balev, 2018 SCC 16, [2018] 1 S.C.R. 398.

In providing further guidance, the majority set out a number of possible factors to consider, such as the duration, regularity, conditions, and reasons for a child's stay in a jurisdiction, and the child's nationality. The relevant considerations may also vary according to the age of the child concerned, with younger children being more closely tied to the family environment and to their primary caregiver. The majority acknowledged that under the hybrid approach, the circumstances of the parents, including their intentions, may be important factors, particularly in the case of infants or young children; however, the intention of the parents are not meant to be determinative, and they cautioned against overreliance on parental intention. The child is the focus of the analysis and parental intention is only relevant as a tool to assess the child's connections to a given country.

In *Beairsto v. Cook*,[96] Beveridge J.A. concluded a child's habitual residence had changed to Nova Scotia and discussed *Balev* in this context. The mother was a Canadian citizen who gave birth to the parties' child in Washington state. The relationship was intermittent prior to the birth and after. The mother resided with the father for only 42 days following the birth of the child and then returned to Nova Scotia, following an incident of domestic violence. The father had consented to the stay in Canada with the child on a temporary basis; however, the plans for the couple, ongoing, were described as vague. There was some evidence that the relationship between the mother and the father was abusive. The father revoked his consent after five months, and then, six months later, he started a Hague Convention application. The Nova Scotia Court of Appeal concluded that by the time the father revoked his consent, in June 2017, the child's habitual residence was in Nova Scotia.

§ 3.11.6 Hong Kong

The Hong Kong Court of Appeal follows the U.K. and European authorities. In a case in which the children were taken to Hong Kong from New Jersey for what was intended to be a temporary period of up to two years, and in which the mother then stated that she would not return them at the end of that period, the Hong Kong court expressly held that "the absence of a joint parental intention to live permanently in Hong Kong is by no means decisive."[97]

96. Beairsto v. Cook, 2018 NSCA 90, [2018] N.S.J. No. 489 (QL).
97. LCYP v. JEK, [2015] HKCA 407; CACV 98/2015 (27 August 2015).

§ 3.11.7 Israel

Although the courts in Israel had previously issued contradictory opinions on habitual residence, they appear to have been resolved by the decision of the Supreme Court of Israel in 2013.[98] The court stated that habitual residence was an issue of pure fact, which should be determined on the basis of the facts in each case from the perspective of the child. Parental intention was a relevant fact but should not be given independent weight.

§ 3.11.8 Conclusion as to International Authorities

There appears to be an international consensus outside the United States that in the determination of the habitual residence of a child, parental intention should not be given controlling weight, and that an existing habitual residence does not have to be abandoned before a new one is acquired. There is also consensus that once a child has resided and gone to school for an appreciable period of time in a new country on an indefinite basis, the child is habitually resident in the new country.

§ 3.12 POSSIBILITY OF NO HABITUAL RESIDENCE OR MULTIPLE HABITUAL RESIDENCES

There is authority, pre-*Monasky*, for the proposition that a child might have no habitual residence. It was thought that this might apply to an infant who is born in a country that is not the shared habitual residence of the parents.[99] Thus, the Third Circuit held that where parental conflict is contemporaneous with the birth of the child, no habitual residence may ever come into existence,[100] and the Fifth Circuit considered that it also might apply when the parents have been in lengthy disagreement about where to live and the family has made multiple cross-border moves.[101]

However, *Monasky* disapproved of any such approach, which would mean that the Hague Convention could not be invoked, particularly when the purported lack of a habitual residence resulted from parental disagreement. The Supreme Court upheld the view that that approach would create a presumption of no habitual residence for infants, leaving the population

98. L.S. v. G.S, RFam 7784/12.
99. *In re* A.L.C., 607 Fed. Appx. 658 (9th Cir. 2015).
100. Delvoye v. Lee, 329 F.3d 330 (3d Cir. 2003).
101. Berezowsky v. Ojeda, 765 F.3d 456 (5th Cir. 2014).

most vulnerable to abduction of the least protected.[102] That was adopted by the Second Circuit in *Grano*[103] but was not in *Nisbet*.

In *Nisbet*,[104] the Ninth Circuit upheld the district court's determination that the children had no habitual residence. It held that, "[w]hile a finding of no habitual residence is rare and should be disfavored, it is not a clear error to render such a finding if the totality of the circumstances of a particular case so warrants. . . . We agree that a finding of no habitual residence should not be made lightly, but we do not see a clear error in finding no habitual residence in the unusual circumstances of this case."[105] That ruling yielded a fierce dissent.

The facts in *Nisbet* were unusual, not so much in those concerning the children (the younger child, age 2½, had always lived in Scotland, and the older child, age 4½, had lived there for well over two years; they went to school in Scotland and had their medical treatment there; and the mother, a U.S. citizen, had lived in Scotland for seven years except for some time in Jersey, a Crown Dependency) but because the father had killed his own mother, had pleaded guilty to manslaughter based on diminished responsibility, and was sentenced to indefinite psychiatric confinement in England.

The U.K. Supreme Court has held that except in special and most unusual circumstances a child should not be left "in limbo" with no habitual residence.[106] Specifically, the court ruled:

> I conclude that the modern concept of a child's habitual residence operates in such a way as to make it highly unlikely, albeit conceivable, that a child will be in the limbo in which the courts below have placed B. The concept operates in the expectation that, when a child gains a new habitual residence, he loses his old one. Simple analogies are best: consider a see-saw. As, probably quite quickly, he puts down those first roots which represent the requisite degree of integration in the environment of the new state, up will probably come the child's roots in that of the old

102. Monasky v. Taglieri, 140 S. Ct. 719, 728 (2020).

103. Grano v. Martin, 443 F. Supp. 3d 510, 535 (S.D.N.Y. 2020), *aff'd*, 821 F. App'x 26 (2d Cir. 2020).

104. Nisbet v. Bridger, 124 F.4th 577 (2d Cir. 2024).

105. *Id.* at 587–88.

106. Re B (A Child) [2016] UKSC 4 at 45, [2016] AC 606. Subsequently in AC v. NC [2021] EWHC 946 (Fam), a U.K. court stated that for a child to have no habitual residence "is vanishingly unlikely. . . . Limbo must be near-impossible." Likewise *see* Re J & H, [2024] EWHC 1395 at ¶ 27 (Fam).

state to the point at which he achieves the requisite de-integration (or, better, disengagement) from it.

As to whether a child can have more than one habitual residence for purposes of the Convention, the authorities overwhelmingly support the proposition that a child may have only one habitual residence at any point of time.[107] Rather than referencing "*a* state" of habitual residence or "the *states*" of habitual residence, the Convention repeatedly refers to "*the state*" of habitual residence. The Perez-Vera Report similarly makes clear that a child may have only one habitual residence country at a time. Courts have rejected a contrary suggestion in the *Mozes* case.

In a "shuttle custody" situation, the Ninth Circuit adopted the theory of alternating habitual residences, rather than considering the possibility of concurrent habitual residence.[108]

§ 3.13 PRE-*MONASKY*: THE FIRST U.S. APPROACH: PARENTAL INTENT PREEMINENT

Before the *Monasky* case, the Second Circuit and five other circuits applied a heavy presumption that a child's habitual residence should be determined by the shared intent of those entitled to fix the child's residence (usually the parents) at the latest time that their intent was shared.[109]

This presumption could be overcome only if "the evidence unequivocally points to the conclusion that the child has acclimatized to the new location and thus has acquired a new habitual residence, notwithstanding any conflict with the parents' latest shared intent."[110] The Second Circuit ruled that this presumption was difficult to rebut: only in "relatively rare circumstances" will "the child's acclimatization to [a particular] location . . . be so complete that serious harm to the child can be expected to result from compelling his return to the family's intended residence."[111]

The most significant cases on the parental intent approach—subsequently overruled by *Monasky*—were *Mozes* and *Gitter*. In *Mozes*,[112] the parents and their children had lived all of their lives in Israel. The parents then agreed that the mother and children would spend 15 months in

107. *See* Didon v. Castillo, 838 F.3d 313 (3d Cir. 2016), and cases cited therein.

108. Valenzuela v. Michel, 736 F.3d 1173, 1178–79 (9th Cir. 2013).

109. *Gitter*, 396 F.3d 124; *Nicolson*, 605 F.3d 100; *Maxwell*, 588 F.3d 245; *Koch*, 450 F.3d 703; *Mozes*, 239 F.3d 1067; *Ruiz*, 392 F.3d 1247.

110. *Gitter*, 396 F.3d 124.

111. *Id.*; *see also Mozes*, 239 F.3d at 1079; *Ruiz*, 392 F.3d at 1254.

112. *Mozes*, 239 F.3d 1067.

California before returning to live in Israel, while the father would stay at home in Israel through that same period. The Ninth Circuit ruled that the family had never abandoned its habitual residence in Israel, which precluded the habitual residence from shifting to California.

The court held that a determination that a child has acquired a new habitual residence must be based on the intention of the person or persons entitled to fix the child's residence (i.e., the parents or guardians).

In *Gitter*,[113] the Second Circuit built on the opinions presented in the *Mozes* case and refined it into a two-pronged test to determine if a new forum has superseded an old one. If a petitioner satisfied either prong, he had established habitual residence.

The first prong was that a court should determine the parents' (or other custodians') most recent "shared intent" regarding where the child should live by considering the parents' representations and actions.

The second prong was that a new habitual residence was established if the child had "acclimatized" to its new surroundings; that is, if "the objective facts point unequivocally to a person's ordinary or habitual residence being in a particular place."

In *Poliero v. Centenaro*,[114] the court held that parents who lived with their four children in Italy and then moved with all of the children to New York—and spent two full years living in New York with the children attending two academic years of school in New York—did not have a shared intent to abandon Italy as the habitual residence of the children. The key factors militating against the acquisition of a new habitual residence in New York were that the parents came to New York in an effort to repair their marriage, initially for a test period of one year and then they extended it for another year; that the parents kept a house in Italy; that they retained personal belongings in Italy; that they leased apartments in New York to coincide with the children's school year; and that they maintained continuous contacts with Italy.

In *Daunis*,[115] (another United States/Italy case) the Second Circuit held that three years of residency in Italy was not sufficient to establish habitual residence when the children had in fact spent up to half of that time back in the United States, the parents had agreed to spend only a limited but unspecified amount of time overseas and the parties had signed (but apparently had not filed) a separation agreement that purported to

---

113. *Gitter*, 396 F.3d 124.
114. Poliero v. Centenaro, 373 Fed. Appx. 102 (2d Cir. 2010).
115. Daunis v. Daunis, 222 Fed. Appx. 32 (2d Cir. 2007).

give primary custody of the children to the wife and stated that the children would reside with her (presumably in New York).

In *Guzzo*,[116] (yet another U.S./Italy case), the Second Circuit held that even if the parties' child was previously habitually resident in Italy, the child's habitual residence changed to the United States after the parties reached a settlement agreement that demonstrated that the parents' shared intent was that the child, who was then less than three years old and had been living with the mother in New York for several months, should reside in New York.

In *Mota*[117] and *Hofmann*,[118] the Second Circuit applied the parental intent test but ruled that an express, implied, or inferred condition on a shared relocation agreement barred a change of habitual residence when the condition was not satisfied.

Great confusion arose (again, pre-*Monasky*) about the concept of abandonment in determining habitual residence. The key *Mozes/Gitter* cases stated that evidence of the abandonment of the prior habitual residence was a key element of an intention to establish a new habitual residence. This emphasis on the need to prove the abandonment of the prior habitual residence before a new habitual residence could be established was one of the key elements of distinction between the majority U.S. approach and the consensus in most other countries.

Thus in *Ruiz v. Tenorio*[119] the Eleventh Circuit accepted the finding of the trial court that the left-behind father had not met his burden of proving that he and his wife—who moved from California to Mexico with their children "in order to save their marriage" and who kept the children in Mexico for almost three years—had actually formed a shared intention to abandon their habitual residence within the United States.

The *Ruiz* case was criticized as producing absurd results, but it was followed in other circuits.[120]

In *Murphy*,[121] the child went from California to Ireland with her Irish mother with the consent of the father in California. The child spent three years in school in Ireland while spending many holidays in the United States. The father retained the child in California and asserted that the time in Ireland was a mere trial. The Ninth Circuit held that the facts did not evince a shared, settled intent to abandon the United States as the

116. *Cristofano*, 719 F.3d 110.
117. Mota v. Castillo, 692 F.3d 108, 116 (2d Cir. 2012).
118. *Hofmann*, 716 F.3d 282.
119. *Ruiz*, 392 F.3d 1247.
120. Sanchez-Londono v. Gonzalez, 752 F.3d 533, 540 (1st Cir. 2014).
121. *Murphy*, 764 F.3d 1144.

child's residence. Moreover, although facts demonstrating that a child has become acclimatized to a new habitual residence might in some cases be sufficient to allow abandonment to be inferred, the objective facts "must point unequivocally" to the child's habitual residence being in the new country. The court cautioned that courts should be slow to infer from contacts with the new country that an earlier habitual residence had been abandoned, because the inquiry is fraught with difficulty and because readily inferring abandonment would circumvent the purposes of the Convention.

Thankfully, *Monasky* has overruled all of this jurisprudence.

§ 3.14 PRE-*MONASKY*: THE SECOND U.S. APPROACH: THE OBJECTIVE CIRCUMSTANCES TEST

In the landmark *Friedrich* case,[122] the Sixth Circuit held that parental intent is irrelevant to a child's habitual residence and that the determination of a child's habitual residence should be based only on the objective circumstances of the child, such as the child's physical presence in a country, the duration of residency, and evidence of acclimatization.

This line of authority will likely be useful in applying the new totality-of-circumstances test in the future, except for the issue of parental intent.

In *Friedrich*, a German father sought the return of his one-and-a-half-year-old child, whom his wife (a member of the U.S. Army stationed in Germany) had taken to the United States. The mother argued that the United States was the child's habitual residence because she had always intended to return to the United States with the boy when she was discharged from the military.

The Sixth Circuit rejected that argument. It held that the determination of habitual residence "must focus on the child, not the parents, and examine past experience, not future intentions."[123]

It also held that habitual residence should not be determined through the technical rules governing legal residence or common law domicile; that a person can have only one habitual residence; and that a child's habitual residence is not determined by the nationality of his primary care giver.

Under these principles, the court found the case to be simple. The boy had been born in Germany and had resided there exclusively at the time

122. *Friedrich*, 983 F.2d 1396.
123. *Id.*

of his removal. As a result, Germany was the child's country of habitual residence.

The Sixth Circuit revisited the issue in 2007 in *Robert v. Tesson*.[124] That case concerned twin boys born to American parents. The family moved between the United States and France, spending substantial periods of time in both countries. The children then lived with the mother in Colorado for ten months, at the end of which time the mother terminated her apartment lease in Denver, shipped several boxes of possessions to France, gave a French address as her forwarding address, and took the children back to France. The parents then enrolled the children in school in France. Three weeks later she took the children back to the United States, where she retained them, leading to the father's initiation of Hague proceedings.

The court reviewed the entire issue of the interpretation of the term habitual residence. It strongly criticized the parental intention approach, especially as applied by the Eleventh Circuit in *Ruiz v. Tenorio*.[125] There, a child was found to have retained a habitual residence in the United States notwithstanding his having been resident in Mexico for 32 months. The Sixth Circuit held that that result had "turned the Convention on its head" since the child had been taken out of the family and social environment in which his life had developed and had been returned to the nation of the abductor simply because she had held personal reservations about the original move to Mexico.

The Sixth Circuit insisted that the *Mozes* rule was inconsistent with the Convention's goal of deterring parents from crossing borders in search of a more sympathetic court, because by considering the subjective intentions of the parents it empowered a future abductor to lay the foundation for an abduction by expressing reservations over an upcoming move.

The court ruled that a child-centered approach to habitual residence was in accordance with the recommendation in the Perez-Vera Report that children should be regarded as individuals and not merely as their parents' property.

For these reasons, the *Robert* court concluded that the *Friedrich* reasoning better served the purposes of the Hague Convention than the interpretation espoused in *Mozes*. It modified the *Friedrich* finding only to the extent of accepting some of the Third Circuit's reasoning in the *Feder* case and held that a child's habitual residence is the nation where, at the time of the removal, "the child has been present long enough to allow

124. *Robert*, 507 F.3d 981.
125. *Ruiz*, 392 F.3d 1253.

acclimatization, and where this presence has a degree of settled purpose from the child's perspective."[126]

In determining the degree of acclimatization that was required in such a case, the Sixth Circuit found that the Third Circuit case of *Karkkainen v. Kovalchuk*[127] provided helpful guidance. There the court had:

- Considered parental conduct to be relevant, not to determine parental intent, but only to the extent that it "colored" the child's attitude to her stay in a new country;
- Held that academic activities are among the most central in a child's life and therefore highly suggestive of acclimatization;
- Found that social engagements, participation in sports programs and excursions, and meaningful connections with the people and places in the U.S. all pointed to the child being acclimatized;
- Held that the fact that the child had brought more personal belongings with her than usual, in anticipation that she would remain in the new location, was evidence of a settled purpose to reside here; and
- Determined that the child's own stated desire to reside in the U.S., combined with her parents' communication to her that she was free to act on this desire, was a significant factor in determining that she had a settled purpose to reside in the United States.

Applying this test to the facts of the case at bar, the Sixth Circuit in *Robert* held that most of the evidence suggested that the boys would have perceived their stay in France to be merely a temporary journey before they were to return to a permanent residence in the United States.

During the ten months preceding their return to France, the children had attended an American kindergarten, vacationed with their mother's family in Yellowstone National Park, visited their maternal grandmother in Baton Rouge, formed meaningful relationships with their American relatives, and participated in excursions throughout the United States. This "America-centered experience" contrasted dramatically with the fact that during the same period, the children had had scant contact with their father, which contact could have helped them maintain a sense of French identity; that they had been "largely ignored" by their French relatives; and they had celebrated holidays and birthdays almost exclusively with the American side of their family. In effect, the boys' ties with France were cut while they lived in Denver.

126. *Robert,* 507 F.3d at 998.
127. *Karkkainen,* 445 F.3d 280.

Upon their return to France the boys were enrolled in school and they spoke perfect French, but these factors did not outweigh the facts that:

- Their French father did little to welcome them to France or communicate that they should expect a long stay. Indeed, they received a "cool reception" from him at the airport upon their arrival in France. He did not hug or even acknowledge the boys, and he even expressed surprise that they had actually come to France in the first place.
- They brought only two seasons worth of clothing to France, which suggested a return to the United States when the weather became warmer.
- The actual length of the boys' stay in France was only three weeks, hardly enough time for them to become "acclimatized" to a new residence, and far less than the ten months they had recently spent in the United States.
- The house in which they stayed was a "hazard-riddled construction site" with no interior walls, "primitive" bathroom facilities, an "open staircase" and floorboards that were only partially laid.
- They had few experiences that would have acclimatized them to their new surroundings, or which would indicate a settled purpose to remain in France.

Accordingly, the court in *Robert* found that the children's habitual residence was in the United States.

Some of these authorities might still have relevance in the post-*Monasky* era.

§ 3.15 PRE-*MONASKY*: THE THIRD U.S. APPROACH: THE BLENDED TEST

Even before *Monasky*, the Third and Eighth Circuits adopted an interpretation of habitual residence that blended an objective consideration of the child's factual experiences with a consideration of parental intent as an additional but subsidiary factor. This approach appears to be essentially the same as the Supreme Court's totality-of-circumstances test, and therefore the case law that applied the blended approach might well prove to be extremely helpful in future cases throughout the United States.

The Third Circuit held that a child's habitual residence was the place where the child had been physically present for an amount of time sufficient for acclimatization and had a degree of settled purpose from the child's perspective. It stated that the inquiry should focus on the child, but it must consider the parents' present, shared intentions regarding their child's presence in a particular location.[128] How much weight should be given to each factor was unclear. Sometimes evidence of shared parental intent to abandon an old habitual residence and acquire a new one would trump any evidence of acclimatization from the child's perspective. In other cases, sufficient evidence of acclimatization should defeat any evidence of shared intent. The inquiry might shift from case to case so that arguments based on both parental intentions and the child's circumstances should be presented.

The key Third Circuit cases are *Feder*,[129] *Delvoye*,[130] *Whiting*,[131] *Adan*,[132] *Karkkainen*,[133] *Yang*,[134] and *Karpenko*.[135]

The Eighth Circuit similarly looked to the child's objective circumstances to determine his habitual residence while also allowing consideration of parental intent as one factor. In that circuit, the factors relevant to the determination of habitual residence were included "the settled purpose of the move to the new country from the child's perspective, parental intent regarding the move, the change in geography, the passage of time, and the acclimatization of the child to the new country."[136]

The key decision in the Eighth Circuit was *Silverman*,[137] which was followed in and applied by the Circuit Court there in *Sorensen*[138] and *Barzilay*.[139]

Silverman was an en banc decision. The parents had lived in the United States as husband and wife for ten years and their two children were born in the United States. They moved to Israel as a family in July 1999, but the mother was torn about the move and went to Israel in an effort to reconcile the couple's failing marriage. Two months later she announced that she wanted to return to the United States. Meanwhile, the

128. Tsai-Yi Yang v. Fu-Chiang Tsui, 499 F.3d 259 (3d Cir. 2007).
129. *Evans-Feder*, 63 F.3d 217.
130. *Delvoye*, 329 F.3d 330.
131. Whiting v. Krassner, 391 F.3d 540 (3d Cir. 2004).
132. *In re* Application of Adan, 437 F.3d 381, 392 (3d Cir. 2006).
133. *Karkkainen*, 445 F.3d 291.
134. *Tsai-Yi Yang*, 499 F.3d 259.
135. Karpenko v. Leendertz, 619 F.3d 259 (3d Cir. 2010).
136. Barzilay v. Barzilay, 536 F.3d 844, 851–52 (8th Cir. 2010).
137. Silverman v. Silverman, 338 F.3d 886 (8th Cir. 2003).
138. Sorenson v. Sorenson, 559 F.3d 871 (8th Cir. 2009).
139. Barzilay v. Barzilay, 600 F.3d 912 (8th Cir. 2010).

parents swore in bankruptcy court and represented on a tax return that they still lived in Minnesota. The mother took the children back to the United States after only 11 months in Israel.

The court stated the basic principles that should govern the case, as follows:

- A person may have only one habitual residence.
- The court must focus on the child, not the parents.
- The court must examine past experience, not future intentions.
- Habitual residence may only be altered by a change in geography and the passage of time.
- Habitual residence must encompass some form of "settled purpose."
- The settled purpose need not be to stay in a new location forever, but the family must have a "sufficient degree of continuity to be properly described as settled."
- The determination of "settled purpose" must be determined from the children's perspective, including the family's change of geography along with their personal possessions and pets, the passage of time, the family abandoning its prior residence and selling the house, the application for and securing of benefits only available to immigrants, the children's enrollment in school, and, to some degree, both parents' intentions at the time of the move.

The Eighth Circuit majority applied those above-stated principles as follows:

- It reviewed the district court opinion that had found that the Silvermans' habitual residence never changed from Minnesota to Israel. That decision had been made despite the district court having found that:
    - The parents sold their home in Minnesota prior to their move to Israel;
    - The mother wanted to move to Israel to raise her children;
    - The move was set up by the parents to be permanent;
    - The family shipped their household goods to Israel prior to their move;
    - The family rented an apartment in Israel; and
    - The children were enrolled in school in Israel and participated in activities there.

- The critical facts for the district court had been that:
  - The mother was prevented from leaving Israel by virtue of the father having obtained a restraining order from October to November of 1999; and
  - The father would not have allowed the mother to leave Israel with the children from October 1999 until June 2000.
- Applying these facts to the Hague Convention, the district court had concluded that despite the intent that was present at the time of the move to Israel and the outward appearance of a permanent move, the mother's unilateral desire to return to the United States (coupled with the alleged abuse from October 1999) eliminated the settled intent necessary to establish habitual residence.
- The circuit court ruled that the district court had erred. The court should have looked at the habitual residence of the children at the time the mother removed them from Israel in June 2010, keeping in mind that they could only have had one habitual residence.
- The court below should have determined the degree of settled purpose from the children's perspective, including:
  - The family's change in geography along with their personal possessions and pets;
  - The passage of time;
  - The family abandoning its prior residence and selling the house;
  - The application for and securing of benefits only available to Israeli immigrants;
  - The children's enrollment in school; and
  - To some degree, both parents' intentions at the time of the move to Israel.
- Fairly assessing these facts, there was only one acceptable legal conclusion regarding the children's habitual residence: they were habitual residents of Israel.

In *Cohen*,[140] the Eighth Circuit held that a child's habitual residence was in the United States when he had moved with his mother from Israel to Missouri with the father's consent for three to five years (he claimed) or indefinitely (as the mother claimed). The father demanded the child's return after two years. By then, the child had lived in the United States for a significant portion of his life, primarily spoke English, and had little

140. Cohen v. Cohen, 858 F.3d 1150 (8th Cir. 2017).

connection to Israel. From his perspective, his family had moved to the United States indefinitely and established a home there; his mother had obtained employment, had purchased a vehicle, and had rented an apartment for the family in United States; and the child attended school and speech therapy classes, had a pediatrician, socialized with friends, and had extended family in the United States.

Again, some of these authorities might still have relevance in the post-*Monasky* era.

§ 3.16 POLICY CONSIDERATIONS

Faced with the fact that such a fundamental term has been given such contradictory interpretations and applications by courts in the United States, it may well be necessary for counsel and the courts in future cases to consider and apply the underlying policy considerations.

§ 3.17 "FACTS ON THE GROUND" CONCERNING HABITUAL RESIDENCE

Whether the focus before *Monasky* was on "acclimatization" or on "settled purpose from the child's perspective," the "facts on the ground" regarding the child's habitual residence are the most significant factors in any contested habitual residence case.

Although there is no limit to the potential facts that might be identified, the following are the types of facts that were considered in pre-*Monasky* cases, all of which are likely to be potentially relevant under the current totality-of-the-circumstances test:

- *Academic activities*. School is among the most central elements in a child's life. Continuous school attendance is highly suggestive of acclimatization. Accordingly, to establish acclimatization, counsel should look first and foremost to a child's academic circumstances.[141] However, in *Murphy*,[142] three years in school in Ireland, as well as other strong ties to Ireland, were insufficient to establish acclimatization to Ireland because she also maintained broad and deep "family, cultural, and developmental ties to the United States"; spent Halloween, Thanksgiving, Easter, and summers in the United States while living in Ireland; "maintain[ed] a relationship with Sloan's extended family";

141. *Evans-Feder*, 63 F.3d 217.
142. *Murphy*, 764 F.3d 1144.

"maintain[ed] a community in Mill Valley"; and "receive[d] her dental and medical care in California" while living overseas.

- *Social and family life.* The location of a child's friends and the depth of the friendships are highly significant factors, as are his relationships with family members.[143] See, for example,
    - *Silvestri,*[144] finding that the "children have made friends in school as well as friends they see after school" after they moved to the United States;
    - *Jenkins,*[145] affirming that a child was acclimatized to life in the United States after only five months since he was attending preschool, was "doing well in that environment, having attained both Hebrew and English language skills commensurate with his age and learning opportunities," and enjoyed "a weekly routine that involved visits to the Air Force museum in Dayton, frequent summertime visits to fountains in a nearby water park, weekly trips to the synagogue with his grandmother, and attendance at numerous birthday parties for young friends from both preschool and synagogue";
    - *Redmond,*[146] finding acclimatization after child spent three years in Illinois, where he had frequent contact with his extended American family, attended school, and played on a children's baseball team; and
    - *Karkkainen,*[147] finding acclimatization after less than three months in the United States because the child had enrolled in school, attended extracurricular classes, and had developed relationships with her American family.
- *Extracurricular activities.* Participation in sports programs and excursions and meaningful connections with the people and places in the child's new country all point to the child being acclimatized.[148] Relevant cases include:
    - *Barzilay,*[149] in which children were found to have had acclimatized to the United States primarily because they attended schools here.

143. *Sorenson*, 559 F.3d 871.
144. Silvestri v. Oliva, 403 F. Supp. 2d 378, 386 (D.N.J. 2005).
145. Jenkins v. Jenkins, 569 F.3d 549 (6th Cir. 2009).
146. *Redmond*, 724 F.3d 729, 743, 747.
147. *Karkkainen*, 445 F.3d 293–94.
148. *Evans-Feder*, 63 F.3d 224.
149. *Barzilay*, 600 F.3d 912.

- *Feder*,[150] citing a four-year-old's attendance in preschool and enrollment in kindergarten for the following year during family's stay of less than six months in Australia as evidence that Australia had become the child's habitual residence. *Roche*,[151] in which schooling and academic activities in the United States supported the conclusion that young children had acclimatized to the United States after 26 months since "[a]cademic activities are among the most central in a child's life and are therefore highly suggestive of acclimatization."
- *Silvestri*,[152] concluding that the withdrawal of children from school in Argentina and their enrollment in a U.S. school was evidence of the United States becoming their habitual residence.

- *Length of time.* The length of timc that a child has spent in the location is obviously of critical importance.[153] Even the circuits that favor reliance on parental intent to determine the child's habitual residence agree that if, at the relevant moment, a person has been living in one country "for a sufficiently long period" "questions as to the purpose of the residence become irrelevant."[154] In *Shalit*,[155] the Ninth Circuit upheld a ruling that a child who spent three years in a new country was habitually resident there, stating that "[i]t is undisputed that by the summer of 1998, [the child] had lived in Israel with his father for approximately three years and held a round-trip ticket to return after approximately two weeks. Three years is certainly enough time for [the child] to be considered 'settled' in Israel, regardless of [the mother]'s claimed intention to have him return permanently to Alaska at some point in the future."

§ 3.18 PARENTAL UNCERTAINTY

Several courts ruled before *Monasky* that a settled purpose was not voided by the fact that one parent has great uncertainty about a new location.

---

150. *Evans-Feder*, 63 F.3d 217.
151. Roche v. Hartz, 783 F. Supp. 2d 995 (N.D. Ohio 2011).
152. *Oliva*, 403 F. Supp. 2d 378.
153. *Sorenson*, 559 F.3d 871.
154. *Mozes*, 239 F.3d 1067; *Gitter*, 396 F.3d 124.
155. Shalit v. Coppe, 182 F.3d 1124 (9th Cir. 1999).

- In *Silverman*, the mother had great qualms about moving to Israel. She had wanted to return to the United States within two months of her arrival. However, this was held to be insufficient to overcome the fact that the family unit had elected to move to Israel.[156]
- In *Feder*, the Third Circuit emphasized the need to look at both parents' intentions and the lifestyle of their son, but it discounted the relevance of the mother's plan to return to the United States if the marriage failed while in Australia.[157]
- Even in *Mozes*, which has been overruled by *Monasky*, the Ninth Circuit ruled that when courts find that a family has jointly taken all the steps associated with abandoning habitual residence in one country to take it up in another, they are generally unwilling to let one parent's alleged reservations about the move stand in the way of finding a shared and settled purpose.[158]
- In *Koch*, when the parents moved from the United States to Germany, they talked frequently of returning to live in the U.S. once they had saved sufficient funds, but this hope had to be viewed in light of the fact that the family actually established themselves in Germany. Although they shared a subjective wish to someday return to the United States, habitual residence is not determined by wishful thinking alone.[159]

Such cases might still have relevancy, especially if the child is an infant.

§ 3.19 CONDITIONAL MOVES

Courts in circuits that adopted the now-overruled parental intention rule often refused to find that a change in habitual residence had occurred when one parent intended to move to the new country of residence on a trial or conditional basis. Indeed, many couples undergoing marital problems make attempts at reconciliation. In international relationships, this can take the form of an agreement for one spouse to move to the other spouse's country conditionally, to see if their problems can be resolved. If the reconciliation is not successful, the spouse who moved may attempt to return to his or her home country with their children. However, if they

---

156. *Silverman*, 338 F.3d 886.
157. *Evans-Feder*, 63 F.3d 217.
158. *Mozes*, 239 F.3d 1067.
159. *Koch*, 450 F.3d 703.

have spent an extended period of time in the country of relocation, notwithstanding parental intentions, the child or children may have acclimatized and could be found to have acquired a settled purpose.

Indeed, the *Gitter* case was itself a conditional relocation case. There the Second Circuit upheld the district court's finding that the parents agreed to move to Israel on a conditional basis—namely, that Mrs. Gitter would be satisfied with the new arrangements. The court remanded the case to the district court to determine whether this was an exceptional case in which there was evidence of acclimatization by the child sufficient to trump the lack of a shared parental intention.

In some cases, even an extended conditional relocation was found to have not resulted in a change of habitual residence. For example, in *Ruiz v. Tenorio*,[160] the Eleventh Circuit found that despite the fact that the children had been in Mexico for three years, their habitual residence had not changed, based in significant part on the mother's assertion that the family's move from the United States was conditioned on the fact that if the marriage did not work out, she was free to return.

Likewise, in *Papakosmas*,[161] the Ninth Circuit upheld a finding that a move from California to Greece had been conditional and for that reason held that the habitual residence of the child in the United States had never been abandoned. Similarly, in *Maxwell*,[162] the Fourth Circuit ruled that a mother's relocation to Australia with her four children was conditional on reconciling with her Australian husband. The district court's finding that her testimony on that issue was more credible; was supported by evidence that she had left many possessions behind in North Carolina; had reserved round trip tickets for herself and the children; had traveled with Australian tourist visas that limited their stay in Australia to three months; and had maintained her local financial accounts (North Carolina Medicare insurance, and the lease and insurance on her vehicle). Since the children had been in Australia for only a few weeks before the mother had brought them back to North Carolina, there was no strong case of acclimatization and the court denied the Hague petition.

One of the leading cases in a "blended approach" circuit, the *Feder* case,[163] is itself a conditional relocation case. It clearly illustrates the differences between the interpretation of habitual residence between the Second and Third Circuits. The family lived in the United States. The

160. *Ruiz*, 392 F.3d 1247.
161. Papakosmas v. Papakosmas, 483 F.3d 617 (9th Cir. 2007).
162. *Maxwell*, 588 F.3d 245.
163. *Evans-Feder*, 63 F.3d 217.

father took a new job in Australia. The mother agreed to go there on a conditional basis in order to try and resolve their marital problems. She returned to the United States with the child after just six months, having determined that the marriage could not be saved. The Third Circuit accepted that the mother had always intended to leave Australia if her marriage did not improve. Nonetheless, the court found that the couple had a settled purpose to live as a family in the place where the father had found work.

§ 3.20 IMPLIED OR INFERRED CONDITIONS

Some courts in parental intention circuits upheld claims that a condition on a relocation might be implied or inferred, sufficient to prevent a child's habitual residence from being changed.

In *Mota,*[164] the Second Circuit upheld the decision of a district court to infer such a condition from the circumstances even though the parent who thereby benefited had testified that there had been no such agreement. In that case, the parents of a child who habitually resided in Mexico with her mother agreed that the mother and child would join the father in New York in order to reunite their family and live there indefinitely. The mother gave the child to third parties to take her to New York, where she was reunited with her father. However, U.S. border guards prevented the mother from entering the country illegally. She tried a second time but was deported.

The Second Circuit upheld the finding that the mother's consent to her daughter's relocation was impliedly conditioned upon her own ability to join the family in New York and that the failure of this condition annulled her consent. There was no direct evidence of any agreement between the parents concerning the condition and the mother testified that there was no such agreement. Nonetheless, the court upheld the district court's finding that such a condition could—and should—be "reasonably inferred" from the circumstances, because the mother was a devoted mother who "more likely than not . . . intended for [the child] to live in the United States *only if* she herself could join the household and continue to raise her child."

Thus, *Mota* reaffirmed the rule that if the parents' agreement to their child's relocation is subject to a condition precedent, there is no shared intent to relocate unless the condition is fulfilled. *Mota* also established

164. *Castillo*, 692 F.3d 108.

that the existence of a condition to an agreed relocation can be established by inference from the circumstances of the case.

In *Hofmann*,[165] the Second Circuit ruled that Canada was the country of the children's habitual residence even though the mother and children had come to New York with the father's consent and had lived there for one and a half years. The court held that the parties did not have a shared intent at the time the father consented to the move to New York, because the father intended for the children to reside habitually in New York only if he was also resident in New York in the same home as his children and his wife, but the wife had served him with divorce papers instead.

In the future, such issues may still have some significance in the application of the totality-of-the-circumstances test, but they are unlikely to be decisive.

§ 3.21 SABBATICALS AND TIME-LIMITED OVERSEAS POSTINGS

Before *Monasky*, the outcome of cases that arose when families moved overseas for a sabbatical or a time-limited position in a foreign country hinged on how much weight a court gave to the shared intentions of the parents versus the circumstances of the child.

Courts in a parental intent circuit generally deemed a sabbatical or similar relatively short-term foreign posting to be insufficient to cause a change in habitual residence.

- A district court in Colorado (in the Tenth Circuit) ruled that when the family had moved from Colorado to Switzerland for the father's sabbatical of less than one year, and the father had brought the child back to Colorado several months later, the child's habitual residence in Colorado had never been abandoned.[166]
- In *Mozes*,[167] the mother relocated from Israel to Los Angeles with her four children, leaving the father behind in Israel, on the understanding that the move was intended to be temporary and that at the end of 15 months in the United States she and the children would return to Israel. Many of the factors that were indicative of acclimatization were present from the children's perspective. They had settled into their new home in Beverly Hills; they were

165. *Hofmann*, 716 F.3d 282.
166. *In re Morris*, 55 F. Supp. 2d 1156 (D. Colo. 1999)
167. *Mozes*, 239 F.3d 1067.

enrolled and participating full time in schools and social, cultural, and religious activities; they had successfully completed a year of school in the United States; they had quickly learned English; they had made new friends; and they were accustomed to and thriving in their new life in Beverly Hills. But because there was no indication that the parents had intended the move to be permanent, there was no "settled intention" on the part of the parents for the children to have acquired a new habitual residence, and hence, the children had not acquired one.

In sharp contrast, courts in circuits that focused on the child's circumstances discounted parental intention when a child was found to be settled in the new environment. Thus:

- In *Sorensen*,[168] the Eighth Circuit focused on the child's circumstances rather than on parental intent. Here, a child moved with her parents to Australia after her father took a job there on a three-year contract. Her parents' marriage deteriorated and her father moved back to the United States. Her mother chose to remain in Australia. The court held that the fact that the move had initially been indefinite, coupled with evidence of the child's acclimatization (she spoke English with an Australian accent), indicated that, for purposes of the Convention, her habitual residence was Australia. The parental intent was considered only for the purpose of establishing that Australia was the child's residence from *her* perspective, not her parents' perspective.
- In *Cohen*,[169] the Eighth Circuit upheld a trial court decision that focused on the child's circumstances rather than the father's claim that the child's move from Israel to the United States was intended to be limited in duration. From the child's perspective, his habitual place of residence was the United States, because he primarily spoke English, attended school, socialized with friends, and participated in local activities.

Post-*Monasky*, courts have generally held that it is inappropriate to prioritize the purpose of a move overseas over the actual circumstances of the children at the time as of which habitual residence is being determined.

In *Goldstein*,[170] the 11th Circuit upheld the district court's decision that the children were habitually resident in Florida notwithstanding

168. *Sorenson*, 559 F.3d 871.
169. *Cohen*, 858 F.3d 1150.
170. Goldstein v. Simon, 2024 WL 4284921 (11th Cir. Sept. 25, 2024).

evidence of the parents' intention to stay in Florida only for six months to a year or until the hostilities in Israel after October 7, 2023, had ceased or substantially reduced. The court focused on the facts that the children were in school in Florida, had doctors and therapists there, and participated in a thriving social community.

In *Baz*,[171] the fact that a stipulated judgment in Illinois authorized the mother to take the child to live primarily in Germany, but ordered that the child's habitual residence would remain in Illinois, was not sufficient to overcome the district court's totality-of-the-circumstances determination in favor of the child's habitual residence having been shifted to Germany.

However, in *Roberts*,[172] the district court expressed uncertainty as to the extent to which it should consider parental intention in a case concerning a five-year-old child of a U.S. military family in England who moved from Hawaii to England for the father's tour of duty there, which was projected to last for up to three years. The court decided that it need not decide that issue, primarily because the child had lived in England for only ten months, which was too short for a child to acclimate. However, the court was clearly influenced by the fact that the family clearly planned to return to the United States in the future.

§ 3.22 MULTIPLE MOVES

The increasing trend of multiple or "nomadic" residences creates particular challenges in determining the habitual residence of children.

In a case in the Sixth Circuit,[173] the child, whose parents were Brazilian and Mexican, moved from the family's home in Brazil, together with her mother's other two children, first to China for six months, then to Brazil for eight months, then back to China for another nine months, then to Brazil for five months, to Mexico for eight months, and finally to Michigan for four months before the date of her alleged wrongful retention there. The Sixth Circuit upheld the trial court's decision that the child's habitual residence was Brazil, not the United States, because she had spent half of her life in Brazil, was in constant communication with her Brazilian extended family throughout her travels to different countries, and returned to Brazil twice to reside indicating that Brazil was her home base, and because the time in Mexico was intended to be transitory. Moreover, during the four months of her stay in the United States, although the

---

171. Baz v. Patterson, 100 F.4th 854 (7th Cir. 2024).
172. Roberts v. Roberts, 2024 WL 5191971 (E.D. Va. Dec. 20, 2024).
173. Argueta v. Argueta-Ugalde, 2023 WL 4635901 (6th Cir. July 20, 2023).

child had developed some meaningful connections with her classmates, there was no evidence that those connections were more meaningful than those she had developed in either Mexico or China; she had video calls with her family in Brazil on a weekly basis and the last shared intention of the parents was that she would go back to Brazil.

§ 3.23 COERCION

The *Monasky* court stated that coercive conduct by a petitioning parent might be relevant to a habitual residence evaluation. Justice Ginsburg stated that "where a child has lived in one place with her family indefinitely, that place is likely to be her habitual residence. But suppose, for instance, that an infant lived in a country only because a caregiving parent had been coerced into remaining there. Those circumstances should figure in the calculus."[174]

Such a claim succeeded in a case in which a father levied many demands on the caregiving mother in exchange for his signature and money—including daily hours-long phone calls—and he threatened her, in ways that could also harm the children, when she did not meet his demands.[175]

There is no other reported post-*Monasky* case in which allegations of coercion have helped to establish a finding of habitual residence. Indeed, such arguments have failed in those cases in which such allegations have been made because, even if well-founded, they cannot override other evidence concerning the child's home. For example, in *Tsuruta*,[176] the Eighth Circuit rejected the mother's substantial claims of coercion—which included claims that she had had to sign a Japanese marriage license that she did not understand and that she had a complete lack of financial and decision-making control in a country in which she did not understand the language—because there was no physical abuse, violence, or threats of violence, and the limited evidence of control by the husband did not significantly undermine the other evidence suggesting that Japan was the child's home.

Similarly, in *Grano*,[177] the Second Circuit held that, although the father had previously coercively controlled the mother, her decision to move with the child from New York to Spain to live with the father was

174. Monasky v. Taglieri, 589 U.S. 68, 78 (2020).
175. Nisbet v. Bridger, 124 F.4th 577 (2d Cir. 2024).
176. Tsuruta v. Tsuruta, 76 F.4th 1107, 1110–11 (8th Cir. 2023).
177. Grano v. Martin, 443 F. Supp. 3d 510, 540–41 (S.D.N.Y. 2020), *aff'd*, 821 Fed. Appx. 26 (2d Cir. 2020).

made at a time when she was no longer living with him and therefore, she was no longer so much subject to his control that her decision-making was "obliterated."

§ 3.24 HABITUAL RESIDENCE OF INFANTS

In *Monasky*,[178] the Supreme Court stated that the habitual residence of an infant raises different issues than arise in respect of older children. Older children are capable of acclimating to their surroundings, whereas children who are too young to acclimate are entirely dependent on their parents as caregivers. The court held that an infant's mere physical presence is not a dispositive indicator of an infant's habitual residence, but that where a child has lived in one place with her family indefinitely, that place is likely to be her habitual residence. It further held that there "are no categorical requirements for establishing a child's habitual residence—least of all an actual-agreement requirement for infants," and that a wide range of facts other than an actual agreement, including facts indicating that the parents have made their home in a particular place, can enable a trier of fact to determine whether an infant's residence in that place has the quality of being "habitual."

In any future Hague Convention concerning the habitual residence of children, the *Monasky* ruling will be of decisive importance, and older authorities, particularly from circuits that focused on parental intention must be discounted.

Nonetheless, the following is a summary of the prior case law, since courts and counsel will likely review such authorities and may find useful guidance from them.

When a child is born in the place where the parents have their habitual residence, the child should normally be regarded as a habitual resident of that country.[179] However, the mere place of birth is not automatically the child's habitual residence.[180] If the parents never shared an intent for the child to reside in the United States and were themselves living in different countries and in conflict as to where to reside the child is not habitually resident in the United States and will have no habitual residence. In such circumstances, the Hague Convention cannot be invoked.[181]

---

178. Monasky v. Taglieri, 140 S. Ct. 719, 728 (2020).

179. Nunez-Escudero v. Tice-Menley, 58 F.3d 374, 379 (8th Cir. 1995); *Friedrich*, 983 F.2d 1401-02.

180. Holder v. Holder, 392 F.3d 1009, 1020 (9th Cir. 2004).

181. *In re* A.L.C., 607 Fed. Appx. 658 (9th Cir. 2015).

The Fifth Circuit has held that parental intentions should be dispositive in determining habitual residence where the child is so young that he or she cannot possibly decide the issue of residency.[182] In that regard, the court held that the necessary intention for the purpose of establishing that a habitual residence has shifted after a consensual move is that the parents had a mutual intent to abandon the original habitual residence.

When the issue arises in other circuits, the courts must necessarily recognize that a newborn or extremely young infant lacks the relative cognizance to attach anything remotely approaching a "settled purpose" to the objective, factual circumstances surrounding the child's presence in a given location. Very young children and infants have no academic engagements or social connections that can be analyzed, and any personal belongings are likely to be limited, as is an ability to express a desire or understanding that a move is to be temporary or permanent. It is generally accepted that an infant cannot really acquire a habitual residence apart from its parents, so the parents' intentions are usually the most relevant area of inquiry in the determination of an infant's habitual residence.

The issue has been before the Third Circuit on several occasions. In *Delvoye v. Lee*,[183] a mother who lived in New York traveled to Belgium, the father's native country, to give birth to their child. She returned to New York with the child when she was two months old. The father asserted that, because the child had lived all of her (then short) life in Belgium at the time she was removed by her mother, Belgium should be deemed her habitual residence. The Third Circuit disagreed. It held, "Where a child is born while his mother is temporarily present in a country other than that of her habitual residence it does seem that the child will normally have no habitual residence until living in a country on a footing of some stability."[184]

In *Whiting v. Krassner*,[185] the Third Circuit stated that an inquiry that focuses more on the circumstances of the child was appropriate for children of at least four years of age or older, whereas the *Delvoye* approach, focusing more on shared parental intent, is appropriate for children up to 18 months of age. The precise cutoff between a focus on acclimatization and a focus on shared parental intentions was left unclear. In that case, the parents agreed that their one-year-old child would relocate with her mother from New York to Canada for a period of at least two years, but

182. *Berezowsky*, 765 F.3d 456.
183. *Delvoye*, 329 F.3d 330.
184. *Id.*
185. *Krassner*, 391 F.3d 540.

the father brought her back to the United States after just a few weeks in Canada. The court declared that the child's habitual residence was in Canada based upon the parental intention that she should be there for at least two years.

The Third Circuit did not consistently apply these competing approaches. In *In re Application of Adan*,it found that a child who was at least four years old was habitually resident in Argentina based, at least in part, on an analysis that focused not on the child but rather on the shared intent of the parents, stating that "[w]hen a child is too young to have an intent regarding her habitual residence, the touchstone inquiry is 'shared parental intent.'"[186]

In *McKie v. Jude*,[187] a district court in Kentucky clearly had great difficulty in applying the Sixth Circuit test in *Friedrich* to the facts of the case before it. The child was born in Canada with a congenital health problem. The parents brought him to the mother's family home in Kentucky for a visit. He was ten weeks old. The Canadian father consented to the child staying in Kentucky for three months for medical treatment and then consented to additional extensions as required for medical treatment purposes. The mother retained the child in Kentucky. Applying the test of last shared parental intention, the court concluded that the intention was to retain the child in Kentucky indefinitely for as long as medical treatment was needed. However, the court also considered the situation assuming that the Sixth Circuit were to apply "the seemingly hard-line *Friedrich* analysis even in the case of a newborn child" and were to look solely to physical presence and acclimatization prior to wrongful retention. Here the Court's "alternative, albeit less convincing" conclusion was that the child's physical presence and acclimatization for 11 months in the United States prior to his retention becoming wrongful warranted a finding that the child was habitually resident in the United States immediately before his wrongful retention.

Even in a "parental intention" circuit, the focus on parental intention as the only or primary element of inquiry in determining an infant's habitual residence was not followed by the Seventh Circuit in *Kijowska v. Haines*.[188] There, the court determined the habitual residence of an infant who had spent six months in Poland with her mother by considering the infant's acclimatization in Poland, in addition to the shared intent of the

186. *In re* Application of Adan, 437 F.3d 381, 392 (3d Cir. 2006).
187. McKie v. Jude, 2011 WL 53058 (E.D. Ky. 2011).
188. *Haines*, 463 F.3d 583.

parents, or lack thereof, to establish that the child's habitual residence was Poland and not the United States.

§ 3.25 RE-ABDUCTION

Can a habitual residence be established by means of abducting a child? Yes, at least if the left-behind parent did not pursue available remedies under the Hague Convention.

In *Moreno*,[189] a mother abducted a child from Michigan to Ecuador. Seven years later, the father refused to return the child to Ecuador after an agreed visit to Michigan. The father had not attempted to secure the child's return from Ecuador under the Convention. The Sixth Circuit ruled that the child's habitual residence was Ecuador despite the initial abduction, stating that if Convention procedures are not fully pursued when a child is first abducted, it makes little sense to categorically permit later self-help abduction in the other direction, after the child has been acclimatized in the second country. Permitting re-abduction results in a total disregard for the limits that the Convention puts on the remedy for the first abduction, such as time limits, and exceptions for the child's welfare or mature preference. And permitting abduction for a second time carries the same threat to the child's well-being of being torn from an accustomed residence. The court insisted that the Convention scheme achieves its purposes only if Convention processes are applied, with applicable exceptions, each time a child is abducted from a country in which the child has been acclimatized.

In *Ovalle*,[190] a mother removed the child from Florida to Guatemala where they then lived stably for some months. The father did not seek the child's return under the Convention but instead he re-abducted her by means of a trick. The child's habitual residence was in Guatemala, at least for purposes of the mother's subsequent Hague petition seeking to remedy the re-abduction, given the father's reliance on self-help, and, in part, his "failure to 'pursue his legal remedy' under the Hague Convention."

§ 3.26 USEFUL EVIDENCE

Winning the issue of habitual residence depends in large part on gathering the best evidence. Any presentation should be buttressed by as much supporting evidence as possible.

---

189. Moreno v. Zank, 895 F.3d 917 (6th Cir. 2018).

190. Ovalle v. Perez, 681 F. App'x 777, 779 (11th Cir. 2017). Likewise, *see* Asumadu v. Baffoe, WL 3957696 (D. Ariz. 2010), *aff'd*, 765 Fed. Appx. 200 (2019).

Relevant evidence may include

- **Schools.** What evidence exists that the child has attended school in the new country, has adjusted or not to school, has performed better or worse in school?
- **Friends.** Has the child made new friends, misses old friends, participated in activities with new friends, is involved or not in new activities or similar activities as before?
- **Family.** How much contact has the child had with family in the new country as compared to before, and how much contact with the family in the prior place of residency?
- **Place of residence.** Is the child in a stable environment in the new country; are they settled into a stable residence or are they transient or merely "camped out"?
- **Organizations.** Has the child joined sports, cultural, or religious organizations, participated in group activities?
- **Language.** Has the child coped with a new language?
- **Emotions.** Is the child happy or not, complaining or not, missing the old home or not?

Relevant considerations bearing on the parties' intent include

> parental employment in the new country of residence; the purchase of a home in the new country and the sale of a home in the former country; marital stability; the retention of close ties to the former country; the storage and shipment of family possessions; the citizenship status of the parents and children; and the stability of the home environment in the new country of residence.[191]

In considering this issue, counsel should evaluate the following types of evidence concerning the parents' move overseas:

- **Airline tickets.** Did they have one-way or round-trip tickets? If round trip, was that because it was cheaper? Or was the plan to return to the United States in the future solely for a visit?
- **Residence.** Compare the circumstances of the parents' old and new residences. Did they buy a new house in the new country? Did they rent on a long-term basis? If they had a short-term lease did that give them the right to stay longer? Did they contact real estate agents in the new country? What representations did they make? Did they take only a short-term lease? Stay with family?

---

191. *Maxwell*, 588 F.3d 245.

"Camp out" with friends? Did they retain their old house? Did they terminate the lease? Did they retain rights to return to the old house? Did they plan to return to another location in the United States?

- **Immigration.** Did the parents apply for immigration in the new country? With what type of visa did they enter the new country? Have they applied for other visas? What representations did they make when applying for visas? Did they retain an immigration lawyer? Obtain all immigration-related documents.
- **Tax returns.** Did they file taxes in the new residency? In the old residency? What addresses did they use on their tax forms?
- **Employment.** Did they end employment in the former residence? Did they obtain new employment in the new country? Long-term or short-term? Examine the circumstances under which they left a prior position and acquired a new position. Review employment contracts, job applications, resignation letters, and e-mails concerning new and potential employment.
- **Business.** Did a parent set up a business in the new country or terminate or retain a business in the former country? What were the reasons for any such steps?
- **Education.** Did the parents enroll the children in school in the new country, make inquiries as to schools or submit applications to schools? Obtain all completed application or registration forms. What did they tell the old school? Examine any plans for a family member to go to school or college or take courses in the new country or to continue with education in the prior location.
- **Possessions.** What happened to the parties' furnishings, automobiles, memorabilia, etc.? Did they buy or lease a car in the new location? Did they sell their belongings before leaving? Were they put in storage and, if so, where? Obtain shipping documents.
- **Announcements.** Did the parents announce their move and, if so, to whom? Any farewell parties?
- **Finances.** Were they looking to make a fresh start after financial reversals in the former location? Did they set up new bank accounts? Did they retain old accounts? Did they use the old accounts?
- **Driver's licenses.** Did they apply for new licenses? Did they renew their licenses in their place of former residence?
- **Health.** Did they apply for new health insurance? Did they join the new country's health support programs? Did they retain health insurance in the "old country"?

- **Memberships.** Did they join clubs in the new location? Religious organizations? Social organizations? Sports clubs? Did they retain memberships in such organizations in the place of their former residence?

Specific documents to look for include e-mails, text messages, letters, cards and notes between the parents and with relevant third parties such as friends, employers, leasing agents, shipping companies and lawyers; applications forms for visas, schools, colleges, jobs, business matters, residences, financing, etc.; statements made on social networking sites; and receipts for such items as shipping, storage, and car leases.

Rights of Custody 4

§ 4.01 CONVENTION PROVISIONS AS TO "RIGHTS OF CUSTODY"

In order to establish that a child has been wrongfully taken or retained within the meaning of the Hague Convention, a petitioner must establish that the child was removed from the habitual residence "in breach of rights of custody attributed to a person, an institution or any other body, either jointly or alone, under the law of the State in which the child was habitually resident immediately before the removal or retention."[1]

The petitioner must also establish that "at the time of the removal or retention those rights were actually exercised, either jointly or alone, or would have been so exercised but for the removal or retention."[2] The requirement that the custodial rights were "actually exercised" is also set forth in Article 13 of the Convention, which provides that,

> [T]he judicial or administrative authority of the requested State is not bound to order the return of the child if the person . . . oppos[ing] its return establishes that . . . the person . . . having the care of the person of the child was not actually exercising the custody rights at the time of removal or retention.

1. Hague Convention, Art. 3(a).
2. Hague Convention, Art. 3(b).

The requirements concerning actual exercise of custody rights that are stated in both Articles 3 and 13 should be interpreted identically. Efforts to secure a different standard of review in Article 13 as compared to Article 3 have failed. The issue was well-reviewed in a case in Delaware.[3]

The existence of rights of custody and the exercise of such rights must be established by a preponderance of the evidence.[4]

Article 3 makes it clear that the jurisdiction whose law determines the nature of the rights possessed by the complaining party is that of the habitual residence of the child "immediately before" the allegedly wrongful taking or retention.

The Convention does not provide a complete definition of the term "rights of custody," but it does provide some assistance. The following provisions are significant in this respect:

1. The Convention provides that the rights of custody "may arise in particular by operation of law or by reason of a judicial or administrative decision, or by reason of an agreement having legal effect under the law of that State."[5]
2. The Convention provides that rights of custody "shall include rights relating to the care of the person of the child and, in particular, the right to determine the child's place of residence."[6]
3. The Convention distinguishes "rights of custody" from mere "rights of access" and states that the latter "shall include the right to take a child for a limited period of time to a place other than the child's habitual residence."[7]

The background report of the Convention provides some further guidance. It states that the law of the child's habitual residence is invoked in "the widest possible sense and that the sources from which custody rights derive are all those upon which a claim can be based within the context of the legal system concerned."[8] The report also establishes that the intention of the Convention is to protect all the ways in which custody of children can be exercised, and that the Convention favors a flexible interpretation

---

3. Lopez v. Bamaca, 2020 WL 1915260 (D. Del. 2020).
4. 22 U.S.C. § 9003(e).
5. Hague Convention, Art. 3.
6. Hague Convention, Art. 5.
7. *Id.*
8. Whallon v. Lynn, 230 F.3d 450 (1st Cir. 2000).

of the terms used, so as to allow the greatest possible number of cases to be brought into consideration.[9]

§ 4.02 STEP-BY-STEP ANALYSIS

If there is also a dispute as to whether the left-behind parent had a "right of custody," the court handling a Hague case must act as follows:

- First the court should determine the relevant date. This is the date of the alleged wrongful taking or wrongful retention. See § 3.05 and § 3.06 for a discussion of this issue.
- Next, the court should determine the habitual residence of the child on that date.
- Then the court must consult the law of the habitual residence to determine the "content" of the rights that the petitioner had in respect of the child on the relevant date under that country's law.
- Finally, the court should follow the Convention's text and structure to decide whether the right at issue is a "right of custody."

The issue is not whether the right is a custodial right under the domestic law of the forum but whether the autonomous international meaning of the term is satisfied. In this regard the U.S. Supreme Court has stated that,

> This uniform, text-based approach ensures international consistency in interpreting the Convention. It forecloses courts from relying on definitions of custody confined by local law usage, definitions that may undermine recognition of custodial arrangements in other countries or in different legal traditions, including the civil-law tradition.[10]

Nor is the issue whether the courts in the habitual residence have given rights that they have labeled as "custody" to the petitioner, but whether the complete "bundle of rights" possessed by the petitioner under the law of the habitual residence as of the relevant date satisfies the autonomous meaning of the term "rights of custody." Although the law of the country where a child habitually resides determines the content or scope of parental rights, whether those rights constitute "rights of custody" under Article 5(a) of the Convention is a matter to be determined by the court hearing the case in the place where the child is currently located

9. Furnes v. Reeves, 362 F.3d 702 (11th Cir. 2004).
10. Abbott v. Abbott, 560 U.S. 1, 130 S. Ct. 1983 (2010).

by applying the autonomous meaning of "rights of custody" under the Convention.

Put another way, while the *definition* of "rights of custody" under the Convention is an issue of treaty interpretation and does not depend on the domestic custody law of the country of habitual residence, the *substance* of those custody rights is provided by the domestic law of the country in which the child was habitually resident immediately before the wrongful removal or retention.[11]

The Convention's intent is to protect *all* the ways in which custody of children can be exercised, and the Convention favors a flexible interpretation of the terms used, which allows the greatest possible number of cases to be brought into consideration. Indeed, the violation of a *single* custody right suffices to make removal wrongful.[12]

This factor is well illustrated by those cases in which the U.S. courts have considered the rights of a parent under the law of a Central or South American country. In some such cases, the foreign court may have issued an order giving sole custody to the respondent but nonetheless the foreign law may provide that the other parent has so-called *patria potestas* rights. Such rights give the "noncustodial" parent, by default, certain elements of "parental authority/responsibility" concerning the child. U.S. courts have generally held that such default rights are sufficient to create a Hague Convention "right of custody."[13]

Thus, in *Palencia*, although the parents were unmarried and the Guatemalan Civil Code provided that an unmarried mother has sole custody of the child, there were other provisions of the Code that gave some rights to unmarried fathers. The court held that the father had Hague Convention rights of custody based on expert evidence that the task of the noncustodial parent did not consist of mere supervision, but rather that he or she maintained a parental role and had a right to take on an active position that involved collaborating with the custodial parent in terms of raising, protecting, and assisting the minor.[14]

In *Whallon v. Lynn*, the First Circuit held that a left-behind parent without physical custody of his child possessed rights of custody under Article 3 of the Hague Convention, because under Mexican law he automatically had *patria potestas* rights. These rights gave him a meaningful,

11. *Id.*; Ozaltin v. Ozaltin, 708 F.3d 355 (2d Cir. 2013).

12. Palencia v. Perez, 921 F.3d 1333 (11th Cir. 2019).

13. *Lynn*, 230 F.3d 450; Lalo v. Malca, 318 F. Supp. 2d 1152 (S.D. Fla. 2004); Giampaolo v. Erneta, 390 F. Supp. 2d 1269 (N.D. Ga. 2004).

14. *Palencia*, 921 F.3d 1333.

decision-making role in the life and care of the child and were not mere visitation rights.[15] The court explained that *patria protestas* is defined broadly in Mexican law as authority over a child to provide comprehensive physical, mental, moral, and social protection of the minor child, including responsibility for the child's guardianship and education. Consequently, it encompasses more than mere visitation rights.

Claims that the parties' divorce or custody decree has superseded and eliminated the father's *patria potestas* rights are successful only if the decree issued by the governing court in the child's habitual residence clearly extinguished those rights. A good summary of the applicable case law is set forth in a Colorado case.[16]

Similarly, in *Furnes v. Reeves*,[17] the Eleventh Circuit found that a left-behind father who did not have physical custody of his child pursuant to a so-ordered Norwegian custody agreement had a right of custody. This was because under Norwegian law, when a child lives permanently with only one parent, even though the parent with residency has unilateral decision-making authority "concerning important aspects of the child's care," the noncustodial parent retains the joint right "to make decisions for the child in personal matters."

§ 4.03 PROOF OF FOREIGN LAW

Because the analysis of what rights the left-behind parent had must be made under the law of the habitual residence, it is often necessary to retain an expert in the law of the foreign country to establish just what rights the petitioning parent had at the time that the child was removed from the jurisdiction. The failure to provide such evidence can be fatal to a petitioner's case.[18] But the Ninth Circuit has insisted that courts "nonetheless have an 'independent obligation to adequately ascertain relevant foreign law, even if the parties' submissions are lacking.'"[19]

Article 14 of the Convention permits courts to

> take notice directly of the law of, and of judicial or administrative decisions, formally recognized or not in the State of the habitual residence of the child, without recourse to the specific

15. *Lynn*, 230 F.3d 458–60.
16. Marriage of Morales and Meixueiro, 546 P.3d 639 (Colo. Ct. App. 2024).
17. *Furnes*, 362 F.3d 702.
18. Livingstone v. Livingstone, 2023 WL 8524922 (10th Cir. Dec. 8, 2023).
19. Radu v. Shon, 62 F.4th 1165, 1173 (9th Cir. 2023).

procedures for the proof of that law or for the recognition of foreign decisions which would otherwise be applicable.

The Perez-Vera Report states that "proof of the substantive law of the State of the child's habitual residence may be established by either certificates or affidavits, that is to say documents which include solemn statements for which those who make them assume responsibility."[20] Thus, an attorney's declaration as to the application of another country's law is generally acceptable in Hague Convention cases.[21]

Although the standards for proof of foreign law are relaxed under the Convention, the court may take into account the source of the information. In *Shalit*, the Ninth Circuit stated that a court should review more skeptically an assertion as to the contents of the foreign law if, for example, it was provided by a party's own attorney.[22]

Attorneys may need to pay careful attention to any conflict of laws issues under the law of the foreign country. Civil law countries may not apply their domestic family law to child custody cases concerning foreigners. The "law" that is referred to in Article 3 of the Convention encompasses the conflict of law rules of the state of habitual residence. For this reason, the respondent's motion for summary judgment in *Shalit* was granted. The petitioner's lawyer described the law of Israel as to child custody but ignored the conflict of law issue in concluding that the petitioner had rights of custody under Israeli law. The Ninth Circuit ruled that the inquiry into whether the petitioner had custody rights necessarily entailed a determination of whether Israel would apply its own law or U.S. law in the circumstances of the case.

Article 15 of the Convention authorizes a court to direct the petitioner to obtain, from authorities in the state where the child habitually resides, a decision or other determination that the removal was wrongful within the meaning of Article 3.

The Convention also provides a further mechanism to simplify the identification of a petitioner's rights of custody under a foreign law. Article 7(e) of the Hague Convention provides that the Central Authorities should "provide information about the law of their State in connection with the application of the Convention." Some courts have relied upon the views of the Central Authority in the country of habitual residence. In one case, a New Jersey district court had guidance from the Argentine

20. Perez-Vera Explanatory Report, para. 101, at 456–57.
21. *Lynn*, 230 F.3d 455.
22. Shalit v. Coppe, 182 F.3d 1124 (9th Cir. 1999).

Central Authority and the Argentine Embassy in the United States.[23] Likewise, a district court in Georgia relied upon information submitted by the Argentine Central Authority about Argentine law[24] and a court in New Hampshire relied on the advisory opinion of the German Central Authority as to German law.[25]

A case in Israel illustrates that the process can vary in accordance with the local judicial and administrative procedures. The parents were not married and lived with their children in the Netherlands. Under the law of the Netherlands, an unmarried father only acquires rights of custody in relation to his child if he registers those rights. The father applied for access and custody to a court in Rotterdam, which ordered access once every other weekend and directed the Netherlands Bureau of Child Welfare to draft a report in relation to custody and access, but on the day that the mother left for Israel he had mere access rights over the child and he only obtained an injunction against the mother leaving the day after he left with the parties' younger child. The father applied to the Family Court in Israel for a return order. That court applied Israeli law, which presumed the identity of laws and held that the father had rights of custody that had been breached and ordered the return of the children. On appeal, the Israeli District Court requested an Article 15 opinion from the Netherlands Court as to whether the father had custody rights. That court held that it did not have jurisdiction to give such an opinion, which should be given by the Central Authority for the Netherlands. The Central Authority then issued an opinion that the Netherlands court order about access had not changed the fact that the mother had the sole right to determine the child's place of residence. On that basis, the Israel appeal court dismissed the Hague petition and the Israeli Supreme Court refused leave to appeal.[26]

§ 4.04 AGREEMENTS CONCERNING CUSTODY

What if the child's parents have signed an agreement concerning their custodial rights? Article 3 states that rights of custody may arise "by reason of an agreement having legal effect under the law of [the state of habitual residence]." Thus, it is clear that the effect of the agreement must be tested under the foreign law.

23. Adan v. Avans, 2007 WL 1850910 (D.N.J. 2007).

24. *Erneta*, 390 F. Supp. 2d 1269.

25. Currier v. Currier, 845 F. Supp. 916 (D.N.H. 1994).

26. HSB v. AAK RFamA 9441/12, *available at* https://www.incadat.com/en/case/1300.

Basically, if under the law of the child's habitual residence such an agreement is without force or effect, because it was never filed in court or approved or "so ordered" by a judge, it will not have any effect in establishing a right of custody for purposes of the Convention.[27] On the other hand, if under the law of the habitual residence an agreement concerning custody between the parents can be legally sufficient to cause a transfer of custody then the terms of that agreement must be scrutinized to determine if it is indeed a legally sufficient agreement under the foreign law.

In *Ogawa*,[28] the parents entered into a written agreement that was binding under Japanese law concerning the custody of their children who lived in Japan. The agreement gave "parental authority over" the children solely to the mother, with some access rights to the father, but it also stated that the father would continue "to maintain the right of custody" of the children. However, the father failed to provide any evidence to the court as to the nature or content of any specific residual rights that the father maintained. The mother's expert established that, under Japanese law, the mother's exclusive parental authority was fully valid, even though it was not issued by a court order, and it gave her unrestricted parental authority, including the right to remove the children. Accordingly, the father had no right of custody and his Hague application was dismissed.

In *Yang*,[29] where the child was consensually taken by the father from her habitual residence in British Columbia, Canada, to Pennsylvania, the father established that under British Columbia's Family Relations Act a legally binding custody agreement did not need to be filed with a court or even be memorialized in writing and could be established by an oral agreement or unsigned documents, such as e-mails. However, the evidence that he adduced purporting to establish the existence of such an agreement was found to be insufficient for the purposes of the British Columbia law.

§ 4.05 COMPETING CUSTODY ORDERS

What if custody orders have been issued in different jurisdictions that provide differing custodial rights? In *Miller*,[30] there were custody issues from courts in New York and Ontario, Canada. When the father removed the child from Canada, he asserted, as a defense in the mother's Hague

27. *Currier*, 845 F. Supp. 916; *Coppe*, 182 F.3d 1124.
28. Ogawa v. Kang, 946 F.3d 1176 (10th Cir. 2020).
29. Yang v. Tsui, 499 F.3d 259 (3d Cir. 2007).
30. Miller v. Miller, 240 F.3d 392 (4th Cir. 2001).

Convention case in North Carolina, that he had sole custody under a New York order. The Fourth Circuit held that the first step is to determine the child's habitual residence. It upheld the lower court's ruling that on the date of removal the child was habitually resident in Canada. The next step was to determine the rights of the parents under Canadian law. Since there was a pending custody order of a court in Ontario, the terms of that order were binding on the U.S. Hague Convention court notwithstanding the existence of an order from the New York court, which was perhaps fully binding under the laws of New York and throughout the United States. Since the father's conduct was wrongful under the laws of the habitual residence, the mother's prima facie case was established.

§ 4.06 NE EXEAT CLAUSE

There was previously great controversy as to whether a parent's right to prevent international travel, known as a ne exeat right, is a "right of custody." The U.S. Supreme Court in *Abbott v. Abbott* settled the issue by holding that such a right is, indeed, a "right of custody" under the Hague Convention. The Supreme Court overruled the Fifth Circuit and a line of cases that had originated with a Second Circuit decision in 2000[31] and had been followed in some but not all circuits.

The case concerned a British father and an American mother who had moved with their son from Hawaii to Chile, where they had separated. A Chilean court had assigned daily care and control of the child to the mother, with mere visitation rights to the father. The mother then covertly took the child to Texas. The father brought suit in Texas under the Convention seeking the child's return to Chile.

The mother argued that the Hague case must be dismissed because the father had no rights of custody. In response, the father established that a Chilean statute gave him a ne exeat right, meaning that he had a right to veto the custodial parent from removing the child from the jurisdiction. The issue was whether that statutory right constituted a "right of custody" within the meaning of the treaty.

"No," said the trial court, the Fifth Circuit and three dissenting Supreme Court judges, all of whom followed the Second Circuit's majority opinion in *Croll v. Croll* and declared that the ne exeat right was more akin to a right of access than to a right of custody.

"Yes," said the Supreme Court majority,[32] stating that:

31. Croll v. Croll, 229 F.3d 133 (2d Cir. 2000).
32. Abbott v. Abbott, 560 U.S. 1, 130 S. Ct. 1983 (2010).

- Otherwise the Convention would be rendered meaningless in many cases where it is most needed since ne exeat rights can only be honored with a return remedy because these rights depend on the child's location being away from its habitual residence;
- The Convention's purpose of deterring child abductions by parents who are looking for a friendlier custody forum would otherwise be compromised; and
- International case law, including decisions favoring such an interpretation from the courts in the United Kingdom, Australia, South Africa, New Zealand, and Israel, should be respected; and
- Article 5(a) of the Convention defines "rights of custody" to include the right to determine the child's place of residence.

Thus, an incarcerated father in Brazil whose custodial rights were removed still maintained his ne exeat right when he refused to consent to a "vacation trip" to Orlando, which forced the mother to obtain travel authorization from a Brazilian court to overrule the father's objection. That right alone was sufficient to establish that he maintained a right of custody under Article 3.[33]

An interesting and unresolved question is whether a parent with mere access rights possesses a right of custody if the child's removal violates a criminal law in the habitual residence that results from the interference with such access rights.[34] There would be a strong argument in favor of finding that the left-behind parent does, indeed, possess a right of custody in such a situation, because the removal would not be criminal if the left-behind parent consented. Accordingly, the parent with "mere" access would in fact have a broader right to veto the removal of the child, such that the decision in *Abbott* that a ne exeat right is a right of custody for Hague Convention purposes should govern the matter.

§ 4.07 RIGHTS OF CUSTODY ATTRIBUTED TO AN INSTITUTION

Article 3 expressly provides that custody rights may be attributed to an "institution or another body." The purpose of this is to allow institutions and other bodies who have children in their care to assert the exercise of rights of custody.[35]

---

33. Da Silva v. Vieria, 2020 WL 5652710, at *4 (M.D. Fla. 2020).

34. For example, removal of a child from the United States with intent to obstruct the lawful exercise of parental rights, which "includes visiting rights," constitutes international parental kidnapping. 18 U.S.C.A. 1204.

35. Perez-Vera Report, para. 80.

Thus, the Royal Borough of Kensington & Chelsea (RBKC) was an appropriate petitioner in a case in which it had custody rights over a child when she was taken from England to New York because before the child was removed, the Family Court in London had issued two ne exeat orders prohibiting the removal of the child from the United Kingdom; and under the law of the United Kingdom, the RBKC was delegated the authority to enforce the rights of the High Court relating to the child.[36] Similarly, an English social service agency with court-ordered responsibility to supervise a neglected child because of parental neglect,[37] and an Italian public service agency whose consent was required before a parent could remove the child from Italy,[38] both had rights of custody within the meaning of the Convention.

What if a parent has applied to a court in the habitual residence for custodial rights and the child is removed while the case is pending? In one case, the Fourth Circuit left that issue open. The English House of Lords had decided that a court would have such a right of custody if the pending application to the court raised matters of custody within the meaning of the Convention.[39] The Fourth Circuit was faced with a case in which a noncustodial mother had asked a court in Scotland to bar the father of her child from taking the child out of the country.[40] The father had represented to that court that he would not do so, but he removed the child before any order was issued. The district court ruled that the Scottish court had a right of custody because of the pending proceedings and relied on the House of Lords case as a precedent. The Fourth Circuit ruled that it was not necessary to decide whether a court could have a right of custody because the mother was asking for nothing more than a ne exeat right, which was not a right of custody. That decision has, of course, been abrogated by the *Abbott* case.

§ 4.08 EXERCISE OF RIGHTS OF CUSTODY

Every petitioner must also establish that he or she was actually exercising his custody rights at the time of removal or retention. The Convention does not define the term "actual exercise."

---

36. Royal Borough of Kensington & Chelsea v. Bafna-Louis, 2023 WL 6867135 (2d Cir. Oct. 18, 2023).

37. East Sussex Children Services v. Morris, 919 F. Supp. 2d 721 (N.D. W. Va. 2013).

38. Cascio v. Pace, 992 F. Supp. 2d 856 (N.D. Ill. 2014).

39. *In re* H (A Minor), [2000] 2 A.C. 291.

40. Fawcett v. McRoberts, 326 F.3d 491 (4th Cir. 2003).

Courts have expressed great reluctance to find that a petitioner has not exercised custody rights. They have recognized that wrongful removal claims often arise amidst "confusing dynamics of quarrels and informal separations [which] make it difficult to assess adequately the acts and motivations of a parent" and that "[r]eading too much into a parent's behavior during these difficult times could be inaccurate and unfair."[41]

The Sixth Circuit has ruled that only "acts that constitute clear and unequivocal abandonment of the child" can cause a person with valid custody rights to be deemed as having failed to "exercise" those rights under the Hague Convention.[42] It stated that once a court determines that the parent exercised custody rights in any manner, it should completely avoid the question of whether or not the parent exercised the custody rights well or badly, since such matters go to the merits of the custody dispute and are, therefore, beyond the subject matter jurisdiction of the federal courts.

Most courts have followed this approach.[43] The Fourth Circuit ruled that it would "liberally" find "exercise" whenever a parent with de jure custody rights keeps, or seeks to keep, any sort of regular contact with his or her child.[44]

The courts explain that "sound policy reasons" support this liberal standard, because (1) U.S. courts are not well equipped to determine whether the courts of a child's habitual residence would conclude that a parent with de jure custody rights has nevertheless forfeited those rights "because he or she was not acting sufficiently like a custodial parent"; (2) any determination that a parent has failed to behave in a sufficiently parent-like fashion comes dangerously close to an adjudication on the merits of the parents' custody dispute, which is something the Convention expressly reserves for the courts of the child's habitual residence; and (3) the "confusing dynamics" of domestic strife "make it difficult to assess adequately the acts and motivations of a parent."[45]

Courts hold that the abandonment test is "easy" for a petitioner to meet, as "very little is required of the applicant in support of the allegation that custody rights have actually been or would have been exercised." A petitioner "need only provide some preliminary evidence that he or she actually exercised custody of the child, for instance, took physical care of

41. Bader v. Kramer, 484 F.3d 666 (4th Cir. 2007).

42. Friedrich v. Friedrich, 78 F.3d 1060 8 (6th Cir. 1996).

43. *See, e.g., Bader*, 484 F.3d 666; Baxter v. Baxter, 423 F.3d 363 (3d Cir. 2005); Sealed Appellant v. Sealed Appellee, 394 F.3d 338 (5th Cir. 2004); Walker v. Walker, 701 F.3d 1110 (7th Cir. 2012).

44. *Bader*, 484 F.3d 671.

45. *Walker*, 701 F.3d 1121.

the child."[46] For example, a petitioner can show the exercise of custody rights by demonstrating that he or she kept, or sought to keep, some sort of regular contact with the child.[47]

What if the petitioner had not paid child support in violation of a support order? A Massachusetts court took this argument seriously but found that the petitioner had been paying "some level" of child support and had also had some communication with and made some visits to see the child, which vitiated the claim that he had clearly and unequivocally abandoned his custody rights.[48]

The fact that the father allegedly emptied out his joint account with the mother and cut her off financially was insufficient to establish that he had clearly and unequivocally abandoned the child to the extent that he was not actually exercising custody rights in respect of the child. In any event, he saw the child often and kept the child overnight on several occasions with the mother's consent, and although he did not see the child for an extended period of time, that was because the mother took the child to an undisclosed location, and the father had frequently sent texts and e-mails asking her to let him see the child.[49]

Failure to pay child support after the date of the wrongful taking or retention is entirely insufficient because non-exercise is evaluated as of the date of the alleged wrongful act.[50]

---

46. *In re* Adan, 437 F.3d 381, 391 (3d Cir. 2006) (citing Hague Convention Analysis, 51 Fed. Reg. at 10,507).

47. *See, e.g.*, *Tsai-Yi Yang*, 499 F.3d at 277 (finding no abandonment where petitioner attempted to speak with child "whenever" possible).

48. Krefter v. Wills, 2009 WL 1582912 (D. Mass. 2009).

49. *In re* ICJ, 13 F.4th 753 (9th Cir. 2021).

50. Walker v. Walker, 701 F.3d 1110, 1121 (7th Cir. 2012).

Consent and Acquiescence

5

§ 5.01 CONVENTION PROVISIONS AS TO CONSENT AND ACQUISCENCE

The Convention provides that a court need not order the return of a child if the left-behind parent either consented to the child's removal or retention or acquiesced in the child's removal or retention. Article 13(a) states that:

> [t]he judicial or administrative authority of the requested State is not bound to order the return of the child, if the person, institution or other body which opposes its return establishes that—(a) the person, institution or other body having the care of the person of the child . . . had consented to or subsequently acquiesced in the removal or retention.

The exceptions of consent and acquiescence are separate and distinct. Either consent or acquiescence alone can extinguish the right of return under the Convention.[1]

A respondent opposing the return of a child on the grounds of consent or acquiescence must prove that either exception applies by a preponderance of the evidence.[2] Once a petitioner has established a wrongful

1. Gonzalez-Caballero v. Mena, 251 F.3d 789, 794 (9th Cir. 2001).
2. 22 U.S.C. § 9003(e)(2)(B).

removal or retention, the burden then shifts to the respondent to establish the consent or acquiescence exception.[3]

While the consent exception concerns the petitioner's conduct before the child's removal or retention, the acquiescence exception considers whether the petitioner agreed to the removal or retention after it occurred. Courts have held that the consent and acquiescence inquiries are mutually exclusive. They consider the petitioner's conduct prior to the removal of the child when evaluating consent, although evidence after the removal may also have a bearing on the issue, and will then address the separate issue of whether the petitioner subsequently agreed to or accepted the removal or retention of the child.[4]

Even if either exception is established, courts retain the discretion to return or not return a child if doing so would further the aims of the Convention.

§ 5.02 CONSENT

§ 5.02.1 Meaning of the Term

The Convention does not define consent and the legislative history of ICARA does not provide any guidance. The issue is whether the respondent has proved by a preponderance of the evidence that the petitioner had the subjective intent to permit the respondent to "remove and retain the child for an indefinite or permanent time period."[5] The consent exception applies when a petitioning parent agrees to a removal or retention before it takes place. The consent may be made expressly or implied from the petitioner's conduct.[6]

There are no formal requirements to prove consent. Courts consider the specific facts and circumstances of each case in determining whether the left-behind parent had agreed to the removal or retention of the child.

In examining consent, it is important to consider what the petitioner actually contemplated and agreed to by allowing the child to travel outside its home country. The nature and scope of the petitioner's consent, and any conditions or limitations, should be taken into account. The mere fact that a petitioner allows a child to travel with the other parent, and knows their location and how to contact them, does not constitute consent to removal or retention under the Convention.[7]

---

3. Padilla v. Troxell, 850 F.3d 168, n.7 (4th Cir. 2017).
4. Friedrich v. Friedrich, 78 F.3d 1060 (6th Cir. 1996).
5. Choi v. Kim (In re Kim), 404 F. Supp. 2d 495 (S.D.N.Y 2005).
6. Walker v. Walker, 701 F.3d 1110, 1122 (7th Cir. 2012).
7. Baxter v. Baxter, 423 F.3d 363 (3d Cir. 2005).

The key to the consent inquiry is the petitioner's subjective intent as evinced by the petitioner's statements or conduct.[8]

§ 5.02.2 Relevant Evidence

The consent to the removal of the child need not be in writing. Consent may be evinced by the petitioner's statements or conduct, which can be rather informal.[9] On the other hand, courts have cautioned that every word and action during the separation of the parties should not be scrutinized to the extent that one passing statement in an e-mail or otherwise (possibly out of context) should necessarily suffice.[10]

To establish consent, a court focuses on the parties' conduct prior to the removal or retention.[11] But the conduct of either parent after the child's removal can be useful in determining whether consent was present at the time of removal.[12]

The types of evidence that are relevant to the issue of consent may include:

- Testimony of the parties and any witnesses, either as to express permission to travel with a key focus being on whether any time limit was imposed, or as to such factors as suggesting that the child will have a better life in the new country[13] or that the petitioner had told the respondent that she could no longer care for the child because she was pregnant and her boyfriend had left her;[14]
- E-mail exchanges between the parties concerning any such issues;[15]
- Evidence regarding the taking parent's behavior when removing the children;[16] and
- Any other circumstantial evidence.

Circumstantial evidence tending to indicate that the petitioner did, indeed, consent to the child's removal or retention may include the following:

---

8. Larbie v. Larbie, 690 F.3d 295 (5th Cir. 2012).
9. *Baxter*, 423 F.3d 363; *Gonzalez-Caballero*, 251 F.3d 789.
10. Simcox v. Simcox, 511 F.3d 594 (6th Cir. 2007).
11. *Padilla*, 850 F.3d n.7.
12. *Gonzalez-Caballero*, 251 F.3d 789.
13. *Id.*
14. *Friedrich*, 78 F.3d 1060.
15. *Padilla*, 850 F.3d 168; *Choi*, 404 F. Supp. 2d 495.
16. *Simcox*, 511 F.3d 594.

- The respondent had made substantial preparations for the proposed move, such as selling furniture and household items, packing moving boxes, and the left behind parent verbally agreed to the relocation before his last-minute purported retraction.[17]
- The petitioner met with an immigration consultant to discuss political asylum in the United States for his wife and children, sent clothes for the winter, and knew that the wife was registering the children in school.[18]
- The petitioner sent his wife and children to the United States on a one-way ticket, deposited monthly support funds, participated in arranging schooling and housing, and transported respondent's car and her and the children's personal property to the U.S.[19]
- The mother who was herself a lawyer and who authorized her child to go to New York with the father had herself become enamored with the apparently lucrative lifestyle of a New York lawyer and had engaged in a "scorched earth policy" of looking for a job in New York.[20]
- The left-behind parent supplied the father with the child's birth certificate, passport, and other documents and accompanied the father to government offices to secure required exit paperwork for the child. The left-behind father participated in extensive preparations for the mother's and child's trip, packed belongings, transferred title to the couple's car, invited a male friend to move into the house after his family's departure, stated on Facebook that the departure was "my loss of my family" and that "my baby girl" had been "ripped away," and changed his status on Facebook from "married" to "single" (but note that while all of this evidence was deemed to be relevant in this matter, the court ultimately ruled that the accumulation of evidence was insufficient).[21]
- After the date of the purportedly wrongful retention, the parents had acted consistently with the fact that they expected that the child would remain in New York and would not be returned to Canada, including the facts that the respondent applied for law school in New York, that she sought to obtain a visa allowing the

17. *In re* D.A., 2015 WL 2344079 (E.D.N.Y. 2015).
18. Delgado v. Osuna, 2015 WL 5095231 (E.D. Tex. 2015).
19. Culculoglu v. Culculoglu, 2013 WL 4045905 (D. Nev. 2013).
20. *In re* Kim, 404 F. Supp. 2d 495 (S.D.N.Y. 2005).
21. *Gonzalez-Caballero*, 251 F.3d 789.

petitioner to relocate to the United States, and that the petitioner, upon learning of that, stated, "Wow, she's [the child] going to be a New Yorker now."[22]

Circumstantial evidence tending to indicate the lack of consent may include such facts as:

- Before the child was removed, and promptly after learning that the mother was about to do so, the father flew to the city where the mother and child were living to confront the mother, obtained legal advice, secured a statement from the mother that she was open to continuing to work on their marriage, attempted to persuade the mother to return, and reserved a ticket for her to do so.[23]
- The parents contemplated the possibility of relocating to the United States together as a family at some point, depending on the father's job prospects and other factors, but agreed that no firm plan was in place as of the date the child was removed.[24]
- Prior to the child's removal, the left-behind father consulted an attorney for the purpose of initiating custody proceedings in Spain and told the mother that he planned to file a custody proceeding.[25]
- Before she took the children out of Argentina the mother asserted, in a police complaint against the father, that she wanted to have the father respond to her claims of abuse so that she could take her children out of the country with his authorization, since all her family was in the United States and he had left her alone with the minor children.[26]
- The father had maintained the children's health insurance in Colombia and had enrolled the children for school in Colombia.[27]
- The left-behind parent vigorously and promptly objected to the retention and initiated legal proceedings or took other action.[28]

22. *In re* Kim, 404 F. Supp. 2d 495 (S.D.N.Y. 2005).
23. Nicolson v. Pappalardo, 605 F.3d 100 (1st Cir. 2010).
24. *Baxter*, 423 F.3d 363.
25. Moreno v. Martin, 2008 WL 4716958 (S.D. Fla. 2008).
26. Mendez Lynch v. Mendez Lynch, 220 F. Supp. 2d 1347 (M.D. Fla. 2002).
27. Garcia v. Angarita, 440 F. Supp. 2d 1364 (S.D. Fla. 2006).
28. Garcia v. Varona, 806 F. Supp. 2d 1299 (N.D. Ga. 2011); *Baxter*, 423 F.3d 363.

Consent may be established by inference. For example, in *Gonzalez-Caballero*, the fact that "there was no evidence that [petitioner] objected to [the child] becoming an American citizen" was the first item of substantial evidence cited by the district court and the Ninth Circuit in their analysis of the evidence that established petitioner's consent.[29] In the same case, the fact that petitioner supplied substantial documentation to the respondent was a strong indication that the child's flight to the United States was not intended to be merely temporary. Likewise, in Delgado, consent was based primarily on inference from circumstance. The court in that case concluded, "the Court finds that the informal conduct/acts of Petitioner lead to the conclusion that Petitioner consented."[30]

If there is evidence that the taking parent removed the child in a "deliberately secretive" manner, that determination will be deemed to be "extremely strong evidence" that the other parent would not have consented to the removal.[31] Thus, even though a father had sent an e-mail to the mother that could be interpreted as indicating his consent, the fact that the mother left with the children at midnight after the father had fallen asleep and hid the father's passport and identification papers to prevent his pursuit, constituted far stronger evidence.[32]

§ 5.02.3 Temporary or Permanent Consent

A frequent issue is whether a left-behind parent consented to merely an overseas visit or to a permanent removal. The issue is what the petitioner actually contemplated and agreed to in allowing the child to travel outside the home country. It is incumbent on the respondent alleging consent to establish that an agreement permitting a child's visit to a foreign country was in fact permission to a permanent relocation.

In one case, the court resolved conflicting testimony by determining that the parents had agreed that the child would stay in New York if the father were accepted to law school there. The court held that there was no apparent time limit to the consent and that the petitioner had the subjective intent to permit the child to remain with her husband once he earned acceptance to law school in New York.[33]

Mere reliance on travel authorization documents will generally not establish consent to a permanent removal. Such documents usually only permit a parent to remove a child from the child's habitual residence,

29. *Gonzalez-Caballero*, 251 F.3d 789.
30. *Delgado*, 2015 WL 5095231, at *11.
31. *Friedrich*, 78 F.3d 1060.
32. Simcox v. Simcox, 511 F.3d 594 (6th Cir. 2007).
33. *Simcox*, 511 F.3d 594.

are typically open-ended, and commonly do not include a return date. However, the specific language in a travel document will be of critical importance. A document entitled "Permission to Travel" indicates that the consent was for a temporary visit, not a permanent relocation. If such a document were to refer to "relocation" rather than "travel" it is far more likely that consent would thereby be established.[34]

Courts may allow the introduction of extrinsic testimony as to the nature and meaning of the travel document. In one case, the notary before whom a travel document was executed testified as to what was said by the child's parents at the time of the event. In his testimony he stated that the father had stated, before signing the travel authorization, that

> he did not wish to lose his daughter, he wanted her with him and that the permission was being given . . . on a temporary basis was held to strongly suggest that the parties never agreed that the document was intended to authorize a permanent relocation.[35]

Thus, a consent defense will fail where a petitioner granted permission for a child to travel for a finite time and did not give permission for the child to move indefinitely to another country.[36]

§ 5.02.4 Conditional Consent

If the petitioner's agreement to a removal was subject to a condition precedent that was not satisfied, the consent exception cannot be established. Thus:

- Although a father consented to his children moving with his wife from Canada to New York, his consent was implicitly conditioned on his intended move to join them there and reside with them as an intact family unit. The condition was not fulfilled because his wife served him with divorce papers when he went to join them.[37]
- When a mother consented to the child's removal to the United States from Mexico on the implied condition that she would be able to join her child and the child's father at a later date, and she was then unable to cross the border into the U.S., the consent was subject to an unsatisfied condition precedent.[38]

34. *Martin*, 2008 WL 4716958.

35. *Id.*

36. Panteleris v. Panteleris, 601 F. App'x 345, 352 (6th Cir. 2015).

37. Hofmann v. Sender, 716 F.3d 282 (2d Cir. 2013); likewise see Nissim v. Kirsh, 394 F. Supp. 3d 386 (S.D.N.Y. 2019).

38. Mota v. Castillo, 692 F.3d 108, 112–13 (2d Cir. 2012).

- When a father allowed his wife to take their son to the United States and it was agreed that he would join would join them there a few months later and he was open to the idea of looking for work there, all based on them being an intact family, the consent was both limited and conditional.[39]
- If an allegation were true that parents agreed that the father and child would relocate first to the United States and that the father would then petition for the mother to immigrate to the U.S., then the consent was conditional and, because the condition was not met, it was invalidated.[40]

§ 5.02.5 Limited Consent

The extent of a consent must be examined. A parent's agreement that the other parent could and should remove the children from their habitual residence in Ukraine, for safety in light of the war in that country, did not constitute consent to the children then being secreted in an undisclosed foreign country.[41]

§ 5.02.6 Retraction of Consent

What if a parent consents to the permanent removal of a child but later has a change of heart and revokes the consent?

If the consent is revoked before the child is removed, the consent exception may well not be fulfilled.

In one case, a mother entered into a private written agreement in Germany giving custody of her children to their father and implicitly allowing him to remove them from Germany. However, she explicitly rescinded that agreement before he removed the children. The court held that a hastily-drafted and soon-rued written agreement was insufficient indication of consent because the consent was revoked prior to the removal or retention of the child.[42]

That ruling is supported by English authority.[43]

On the other hand, the First Circuit has ruled that consent prior to the removal of the child is sufficient for the purpose of establishing a change of habitual residence, even if one parent revokes the consent prior to the child's relocation. Thus, where the last shared intention of the parents was

39. *Baxter*, 423 F.3d 363.
40. Cocom v. Timofeev, 2019 WL 76773 (D. S.C. 2019).
41. Tereshchenko v. Karimi, 102 F.4th 111 (3d Cir. 2024).
42. Currier v. Currier, 845 F. Supp. 916 (D.N.H. 1994).
43. Re. P-J (Children) (Abduction: Habitual Residence: Consent), [2009] EWCA Civ 588.

that the child should be relocated to the United States from Argentina, the fact that the father changed his mind and sought to prevent the child from leaving after the mother had relocated in anticipation of the planned relocation of the child, did not vitiate the fact that the last shared intention of the parents was that the child would move to the States.[44]

However, if the parent has a change of heart after the child is removed, and does not revoke the consent until then, it will be too late. In one case, the court found that the petitioner's "post hoc" regret that she had agreed to allow her daughter to remain in New York while she attended school in Canada reflected "an attempt at revocation or modification of the previously-provided consent" to leave her daughter in New York. The petitioner's change of heart was insufficient to "revive her right to return under the Convention."[45]

In another case, the mother of a young child living in Panama allowed the father to take the child to live in the United States, but promptly after the child left, she claimed that the visit was to be for no more than two weeks and she contacted the police and other authorities in Panama and received special permission to travel to the United States. The Ninth Circuit held that her purported revocation of her prior consent came only after the child had already been taken to the U.S. and that it was too late.[46]

Likewise, there is authority that, if a child is already in the new location for a visit and the other parent then agrees that the child may stay and live in that country, the consent is effective as soon as it is given and may not be retracted even if the retraction occurs promptly thereafter.[47]

§ 5.03 ACQUIESCENCE

Article 13(a) provides an exception to a Hague petition if the petitioner "subsequently acquiesced in the removal or retention" of the child. The exception addresses the issue of whether, after the alleged wrongful taking or retention, the petitioner agreed to or accepted the removal or retention of the child.

As with consent, neither the Convention nor ICARA defines acquiescence. The drafting history provides no significant assistance.

Courts in the United States have consistently taken the position that the exception of acquiescence requires a higher degree of formality than the consent exception and that it requires, as set forth in *Friedrich*:

---

44. Mendez v. May, 778 F.3d 337 (1st Cir. 2015).
45. *In re Kim*, 404 F. Supp. 2d 495.
46. *Gonzalez-Caballero*, 251 F.3d 789.
47. Cascio v. Pace, 992 F. Supp. 2d 856 (N.D. Ill. 2014).

- An act or statement with the requisite formality, such as testimony in a judicial proceeding;
- A convincing written renunciation of rights; or
- A consistent attitude of acquiescence over a significant period of time.[48]

When attempting to characterize ambiguous conduct as a basis for inferred acquiescence, courts employ a subjective inquiry into the intent of the parent who is claimed to have acquiesced.[49]

Because of the high burden required by the *Friedrich* test, the acquiescence defense is extremely difficult to prove and has rarely succeeded.

Thus:

- An isolated statement by the petitioner is insufficient. In one case, testimony that the petitioner stated that he was not seeking custody of the child because he did not have the means to take care of him, made to the respondent's commanding officer, was insufficient evidence of subsequent acquiescence.[50]
- A petitioner's visits to a child after the child's removal will not constitute acquiescence. Specifically, a mother's arranged visits to see her child and indirect methods of communicating to the child were held to be insufficient to constitute acquiescence.[51]
- A failure of the left-behind parent to raise the issue of a child's wrongful removal in conversations with the taking parent does not suggest acquiescence.[52]
- A parent's failure to object to the retention of a child before initiating Hague litigation does not constitute acquiescence.[53]
- Interactions between the parents in public settings will not constitute acquiescence. In one such case on this issue, the court explained that acquiescence is not determined by the outside world's perception.[54]
- Delay in commencing the Hague case or taking other action does not constitute acquiescence.[55]

---

48. *Friedrich*, 78 F.3d 1060.
49. Darin v. Olivero-Huffman, 746 F.3d 1 (1st Cir. 2014).
50. *Id.*
51. Boquet v. Ouzid, 225 F. Supp. 2d 1337 (S.D. Fla. 2002).
52. *Martin*, 2008 WL 4716958.
53. *Angarita*, 440 F. Supp. 2d 1364.
54. Pesin v. Osorio Rodriguez, 77 F. Supp. 2d 1277 (S.D. Fla. 1999).
55. *Darin*, 746 F.3d 1; *Angarita*, 440 F. Supp. 2d 1364; Whallon v. Lynn, 230 F. 3d 450 (1st Cir. 2000).

Efforts by the left-behind parent to reconcile the relationship with the taking parent are generally entirely insufficient to constitute acquiescence. Thus, when a father sent tuition payments and monthly stipends to his wife, who had taken their children from Venezuela to the United States, and shipped the children's clothing and belongings to her, this was not sufficient to constitute a consistent attitude of acquiescence over a significant period of time.[56] Specifically, the Court in *Pesin* stated, "Courts examining the tension between reconciliation and acquiescence have been careful not to confuse the former for the latter."[57]

Another Florida court stated that the Hague Convention encourages the parties to engage in informal discussions prior to initiation of formal proceedings, and that claims that such negotiations established acquiescence inappropriately confuses acquiescence with negotiation and attempted reconciliation.[58]

In one case, the left-behind father wrote a series of letters to the mother in which he had stated that she could temporarily keep the children in Massachusetts. The court determined that the letters merely indicated that he wanted to reunite the family and that the agreement about the temporary residence of the children was merely for the period of attempted reconciliation. Throughout the reconciliation period, the father kept in continual contact with his children by writing letters and calling on the phone. Once the father realized that repairing the marriage was futile, he filed a petition under the Convention for the return of his children. There was no acquiescence.[59]

Although it has often been stated that the defense requires an inquiry solely into the subjective intent of the left-behind parent, the First Circuit has insisted that a parent's words or actions might constitute acquiescence regardless of intent if they show clearly that the wronged parent was not insisting on the child's summary return.[60] However, even when analyzing a written agreement between the parties, or an affidavit signed by a left-behind parent, the courts will likely consider any ambiguity in favor of that parent. Thus, when parents traveled to the United States with their son for a visit and the mother refused to return, the father signed an ambiguous affidavit authoring the mother to provide for the care and supervision of the child. A decision that this constituted acquiescence

56. *Osorio Rodriguez*, 77 F. Supp. 2d 1277.
57. *Id.* at 1259.
58. *Mendez Lynch*, 220 F. Supp. 2d 1347.
59. Wanninger v. Wanninger, 850 F. Supp. 78 (D. Mass. 1994).
60. *Nicolson*, 605 F.3d 100.

was overturned. The Fourth Circuit stated, "We emphasize, the defense of acquiescence calls for definiteness and clarity, i.e., a 'clear and unequivocal expression of an agreement' or 'a convincing written renunciation of rights.'" Moreover, the father's circumstances were such that he could not remain in the United States and he signed the document under virtual duress.[61]

§ 5.04 CONSENT, ACQUIESCENCE AND PARALLEL LITIGATION

Hague cases are often initiated at the same time that child custody cases between the parties are pending, or shortly thereafter. Indeed, a cause of action under the Convention might be interposed in a state court custody case, although that will normally require that the custody claims be stayed. The participation of the parties in such litigation, and the positions taken by the parties there, can have a substantial impact on the Hague case and can be deemed in some cases to amount to acquiescence (or perhaps consent).

In *Larbie*,[62] the Fifth Circuit ruled that a parent's consent for a particular tribunal to make a final custody determination—which may be established by entry of a temporary custody order—may suffice to establish an affirmative defense under the Convention. In that case, after the date that a child was allegedly wrongfully retained in Texas by his father away from his prior residence in England, the mother initiated a divorce and custody suit in Texas, filed a counter-petition seeking affirmative relief, exercised custody pursuant to a temporary order issued by the Texas court, recognized and obeyed orders entered by that court on multiple occasions, paid sanctions imposed by the courts for discovery abuses, participated in the divorce trial and appealed it, as well as moved to modify its terms, and at no time even while temporarily in England did she initiate custody proceedings there. Although the district court had determined that the mother had attended the final divorce proceedings "under compulsion of the Texas court's order," thereby belying the voluntariness of her participation, the Fifth Circuit held that the totality of the mother's conduct left no doubt that she had given clear and unequivocal consent for the Texas court to make a final custody determination.

---

61. *Darin*, 746 F.3d 1.
62. *Larbie*, 690 F.3d 295.

In *Nicolson*,[63] an Australian left-behind father brought suit under the Hague Convention in federal court in Maine but also brought suit in state court in Maine for a temporary order of protection. His attorney then agreed on his behalf to an order in the state court case giving him "temporary parental rights and responsibilities (custody)" of the child "to be amended by court of competent jurisdiction." The First Circuit held that if the father had thereby consented to custody jurisdiction in Maine that would have constituted acquiescence within the meaning of the Convention even through his subjective intent was not to do so. However, because it was ambiguous whether the reference to a "court of competent jurisdiction" meant a Maine or an Australian court, there was no "clear and unequivocal expression of an agreement" to have final custody determined in Maine court, nor "a convincing written renunciation of rights" to that effect.[64]

This means that counsel must be most wary of a permitting or causing a client to initiate or participate in custody litigation in which a different position is to be taken than that which might need to be taken in a Hague abduction case.

§ 5.05 DISCRETION

Once the respondent establishes that petitioner consented to the relocation of the child to the United States, the strict language of Article 13 that the court is "not bound" to order the child's return may afford the court a limited discretion to return the children notwithstanding consent.

There is no reported U.S. case that the author could find in which a court has ever returned a child despite the "consent" defense having been established. However, a district court has ruled that if the "affirmative defense" of consent, or any other alleged defenses were established, it would nonetheless exercise its discretion and would order the child's return. In support of its "equitable decision" in that regard, it cited (1) steps taken by the mother to sever the child's relationship with the father, including not disclosing where the child was living, not allowing the child to have any regular contact with the father, taunting the father about her possession of the child, and not allowing the father to meaningfully participate in the child's life; (2) the fact that if the child remained in the U.S., it would be virtually impossible for him to see his father ever again, at least until he reached the age of 18, since the

63. *Nicolson*, 605 F.3d 100.
64. *Id.* at 108.

father was prohibited from entering the U.S.; and (3) an order denying the father's request to return the child would have the effect of sanctioning the mother's unilateral action to abduct the child in violation of Mexican and international law.[65]

In contrast, in *In re Kim*,[66] the court, having found that consent had been established, ruled that it would be inappropriate to exercise its discretion to return the child because that "would not be appropriate to further the goals of the Hague Convention" and "there is nothing from the record that would suggest that Respondent behaved as he did because he believed New York would be a more hospitable forum to have a custody battle."

For a further discussion on the discretion to return a child notwithstanding a finding that an exception to the Convention has been established, see § 6.18, § 7.09, and § 8.33.

65. Vite-Cruz v. Sanchez, 360 F. Supp. 3d 34 (D. S.C. 2018).
66. *In re Kim*, 404 F. Supp. 2d 495.

One Year and Settled

6

§ 6.01 INTRODUCTION

Article 12 of the Hague Convention contains the so-called one-year-and-settled exception. It is designed to avoid the unfairness that would result if a left-behind parent were permitted to secure a return order even after delaying the case for an inordinate period of time if the child has become settled in the new home. The second sentence of the article provides that:

> The judicial or administrative authority, even where the proceedings have been commenced after the expiration of the period of one year referred to in the preceding paragraph, shall also order the return of the child, unless it is demonstrated that the child is now settled in its new environment.

The two elements of the exception are that (1) at least one year must have elapsed between the wrongful removal of the child and the filing of a petition for that child's return under the Convention; and (2) the child must be "settled" in its current environment. ICARA requires the petitioner to prove each of these elements but only by a preponderance of the evidence, rather than by the clear and convincing evidence standard that applies to the grave risk of harm exception.[1]

In most cases, the first branch of the exception is relatively objective because the question of whether a period of one year has passed from the date of wrongful removal or retention of the child to the date that a Hague

1. 22 U.S.C. § 9003(e)(2)(B).

petition is filed in a court of law can be measured objectively. Nonetheless, there can be serious difficulties in determining the correct starting date of the one-year period in those cases in which an agreed overseas visit becomes a wrongful retention. Thus, it is often unclear exactly when discussions about potentially keeping a child for longer than the agreed period become an actual determination to breach such an agreement. It also may not be appropriate to insist that the one-year period begins with a decision to keep the child for longer than was agreed unless that decision is communicated to the other parent. Furthermore, it may be unfair to deem even a communicated decision to breach a promise to return as the commencement date, instead of the actual date that the child is supposed to be returned, because it can be well argued that an anticipated breach of such a promise does not become wrongful until the scheduled return date is reached.

The first branch of the exception is also difficult to apply when the child's whereabouts are unknown. ICARA provides that a Hague case must be commenced "in the place where the child is located at the time the petition is filed." This means that a left-behind parent who knows that the child is somewhere in the United States but does not know the specific location may be unable to commence a Hague case. The courts have struggled with this issue and American courts have dealt with it differently than the courts in most other countries.

The second branch of the exception, as to whether the child has become well-settled in a new location, is extremely fact sensitive and requires a court to consider detailed evidence concerning the child's precise circumstances, connections, education, friends, activities, and stability.

It is also critical to understand that, even if a respondent successfully proves each of the elements of the exception, a petitioner may nonetheless assert that the court has the power to exercise a discretion to order the child's return. In the case of other exceptions, a clear discretion exists but the language of the "one-year-and-settled" exception is less clear.[2]

§ 6.02 PURPOSE OF THE EXCEPTION

The "one-year-and-settled" exception is intended to prevent serious and long-lasting harm to a child that might result if the child is returned to the former habitual residence after the passage of a substantial period of time.

2. *See* § 6.17.

Although the Convention is designed to avoid any consideration of the best interests of the child, the drafters added the exception in order to allow some consideration of some "best interests" factors, albeit in extremely limited form, once the necessary prerequisites are established.

The Explanatory Report to the Convention states that fixing a one-year time limit, although arbitrary, was "the least bad answer" to the concerns of when children could be considered well-settled in their new environment.[3]

It is important to note that the exception was drafted with the understanding that courts would comply with their duty to try Hague cases expeditiously. That is why the starting date of the judicial proceeding was treated as the relevant date. However, in the real world, although Hague cases are generally concluded quickly at the trial level in courts in the United States, appeals can delay the resolution of cases for months and often for years. Such delays significantly undercut the intent of the exception that abducted children should be sent back to their habitual residence quickly, before they have become settled in their new environment.

§ 6.03 WHEN THE ONE-YEAR PERIOD COMMENCES

The first element of the exception is that at least a year has elapsed from the date of the wrongful removal or retention of the child to the date of the commencement of the proceedings to secure the child's return.

The one-year period commences on the date of the wrongful taking or retention. In the case of a wrongful taking, the date is simply the date upon which the child is taken out of the habitual residence. However, far more difficulty arises in cases of wrongful retention, because it is often difficult to pin down the point at which a consensual temporary trip to a foreign country is converted into one parent's unilateral retention. The issues are often complicated because retaining parents often hide their true intentions or lie about them. In many cases, temporary vacations overseas become permanent relocations, either because the taking parent tricked the other parent or because during a vacation the taking parent had a change of mind.

A detailed discussion of this issue may be found at § 3.06. Some courts have held that the date of the wrongful retention is not necessarily the same for purposes of determining whether a left-behind parent may commence a Hague proceeding as it is for determining whether the

3. Perez-Vera Report, para. 107.

one-year period has started to run. The issue arises when a taking parent declares that he or she will not return the child on the agreed return date. The weight of the authorities favors the principle that the wrongful act does not occur until the date of the scheduled return even if a petitioner might perhaps be able to bring suit even before that date based upon the anticipatory breach of the agreement.

Thus, in *Philippopoulos*[4] the court held that the one-year period did not start to run until the scheduled return date had passed, notwithstanding the mother's prior announcement that she was not returning the child. However, the court also stated, by analogy to the contract law doctrine of anticipatory breach, that "Petitioner probably could have filed suit immediately upon learning of Respondent's intention to wrongfully retain the child, Petitioner also had the right to wait to file suit until after the retention became wrongful."[5]

A district court in Florida has asserted that where there is an agreement to return a child on a date certain, "courts have uniformly held that the wrongful retention begins when the agreed date passes, not when the earlier notice of intent is given."[6] This is supported by the First Circuit ruling in *Toren*.[7]

Finally in this regard, it is clear that a respondent cannot interpose the one-year-and-settled exception if the one-year anniversary occurs after the commencement of judicial proceedings but while those proceedings are still in progress.[8]

§ 6.04 WHEN PROCEEDINGS COMMENCE

Article 12(a) of the Convention states that the one-year period runs from the date of wrongful retention to "the date of the commencement of the proceedings before the judicial or administrative authority of the Contracting State."

ICARA provides that commencement of proceedings consists of "filing a petition for the relief sought in any court which has jurisdiction of

4. Philippopoulos v. Philippopoulou, 461 F. Supp. 2d 1321 (N.D. Ga. 2006).
5. *Id.* at 1325.
6. Chechel v. Brignol, 2010 WL 2510391 (M.D. Fla. 2010).
7. Toren v. Toren, 191 F.3d 23 (1st Cir. 1999); followed in Falk v. Sinclair, 692 F. Supp. 147 (D. Me. 2010).
8. Slagenweit v. Slagenweit, 841 F. Supp. 264 (N.D. Iowa 1993), *vacated as moot*, 43 F.3d 1476 (8th Cir. 1994).

such action"[9] and that the term "commencement of proceedings" as used in Article 12 of the Convention means, with respect to the return of a child located in the United States, "the filing of a petition in accordance with subsection (b) of this section."[10] The court that has the requisite jurisdiction is an appropriate state court or federal court "in the place where the child is located at the time the petition is filed."[11]

Accordingly, it is entirely insufficient to merely file a Hague application with a Central Authority or to undertake self-help measures. That applies even if the left-behind parent believed in good faith that filing the application was sufficient.[12]

The one-year clock continues to run until an actual petition for the return of the child under the Convention is filed in a court that has jurisdiction of the case. Thus, when a left-behind father filed a request for the return of his children with the French Central Authority, who in turn contacted the U.S. State Department, all before the end of the one-year period, the "proceedings" were not "commenced" until he subsequently filed a petition in court.[13]

§ 6.05 NO TOLLING OF THE ONE-YEAR PERIOD

Some U.S. courts previously held that if one year had elapsed and it was clear that the child had settled into the new environment, the one-year period could be equitably tolled if the abducting parent had concealed the location of the child.[14] The purpose of equitable tolling was to prevent a parent who abducts and conceals a child from being rewarded for such misconduct.

The Supreme Court overruled all such cases in *Lozano v. Alvarez*,[15] and definitively held that tolling should not be allowed in Hague Convention cases. The court found that equitable tolling is a particularly American concept and that it had not been applied in other jurisdictions in Hague cases, citing cases from England, Canada, New Zealand, and Hong Kong.

9. 22 U.S.C. § 9003(b).
10. *Id.* § 9003(f)(3).
11. *Id.* § 9003(b).
12. Monzon v. De La Roca, 910 F.3d 92 (3d Cir. 2018).
13. *In re* Wojcik, 959 F. Supp. 413 (1997).
14. Duarte v. Bardales, 526 F.3d 563 (9th Cir. 2008); Furnes v. Reeves, 362 F.3d 702 (11th Cir. 2004).
15. Lozano v. Montoya Alvarez, 134 S. Ct. 1224 (2014).

The court also stressed that it is not

> true that an abducting parent who conceals a child's whereabouts will necessarily profit by running out the clock on the 1-year period [because] American courts have found as a factual matter that steps taken to promote concealment can also prevent the stable attachments that make a child "settled."

§ 6.06 THE "SETTLED" REQUIREMENT

Even if more than a year has passed since the date of wrongful removal, the respondent must still demonstrate, by a preponderance of the evidence, "that the child is now settled in its new environment."[16]

The term "settled" is not defined in the Convention or in ICARA. The Perez-Vera Report acknowledges the difficulty of determining what makes a child well settled. It states that "it would seem logical to regard such a task as falling upon the abductor or upon the person who opposes the return of the child, whilst at the same time preserving the contingent discretionary power of internal authorities."[17] Congress followed this advice in drafting ICARA. The burden of proving that a child is well settled in the new environment falls upon the respondent by a preponderance of the evidence.[18] The State Department has noted that proving that a child is settled in the new environment should require "nothing less than substantial evidence of the child's significant connections to the new country."[19]

Since Article 12 provides that the child must be returned "unless it is demonstrated that the child is now settled in its new environment," the court should determine whether the child is settled at the time the defenses are considered, not whether the child was settled at the commencement of the proceedings.[20]

The child must have more than a better material existence in the new home; rather, "there must be *substantial* evidence of *significant* connections to the new environment."[21] To defeat a petition, it must be established that specific actions by the removing parent and the child demonstrate that they have substantial connections to their new home.

16. Hague Convention, Art. 12.
17. Perez-Vera Report, para. 109.
18. 42 U.S.C. § 9003(e)(2)(B).
19. 51 Fed. Reg. at 10,509.
20. Lopez Moreno v. Zank, 2020 WL 4583755 (W.D. Mich. 2020).
21. Cabrera v. Lozano, 323 F. Supp. 2d 1303 (S.D. Fla. 2004).

The context should also take into account the concern expressed in the *Friedrich* case that "[a] removing parent must not be allowed to abduct a child and then—when brought to court—complain that the child has grown used to the surroundings to which they were abducted."[22]

The question of whether specific actions demonstrate a sufficiently substantial connection requires a fact-intensive, ad hoc inquiry. Courts have the discretion to consider "any relevant factor concerning a child's living arrangements in determining whether a child is settled in her new environment."[23] One court noted that settled is not "a legal term of art."[24] A typical set of factors that courts consider include "the child's age, the stability of the child's new residence, whether the child attends school, daycare or church regularly, the stability of the removing parent's employment, and whether the child has friends and relatives in the new area."[25] Although these factors are for the most part standard in all cases, there are other issues considered by the courts, such as whether the removing parent is legally in the United States.[26]

To the extent that Article 12 permits a court to deny repatriation on this basis, it effectively allows the court to reach the underlying custody dispute, even though that is a matter that is generally outside the scope of the Convention.[27]

Although there is "nothing magical" about one year, its basic purpose is designed to serve the best interests of the child.[28] Thus, although the Convention's aim is to return the child without considering the custody merits, the drafters of the Convention realized that at some point, a child may become so settled in his or her new country that repatriation might no longer be in the child's best interests. The defense "protect[s] a child's interest in remaining in a place she is settled."[29] However, given the Convention's underlying goals, "nothing less than substantial evidence of the child's significant connections to the new country is intended to suffice to

22. Friedrich v. Friedrich, 78 F.3d 1060 (6th Cir. 1996).

23. Lops v. Lops, 140 F.3d 927 (11th Cir. 1998).

24. Robinson v. Robinson, 983 F. Supp. 1339 (D. Colo. 1997).

25. *Cabrera*, 323 F. Supp. 2d 1303.

26. *In re* Koc, 181 F. Supp. 2d 136 (E.D.N.Y. 2001); Lopez v. Alcala, 547 F. Supp. 2d 1255 (M.D. Fla. 2008).

27. *Blondin IV*, 238 F.3d at 164; *In re* Lozano, F. Supp. 2d, 2011 WL 3667444 (S.D.N.Y. 2011).

28. *In re* Robinson, 983 F. Supp. 1339 (D. Colo. 1997).

29. *Alvarez*, 697 F.3d 54, *aff'd sub nom.* Lozano v. Montoya Alvarez, 572 U.S. 1, 134 S. Ct. 1224, 188 L. Ed. 2d 200 (2014); *de Aredes*, 953 F.3d 67.

meet the respondent's burden of proof."[30] In addition, the court must also consider evidence concerning the child's contacts with and other ties to her state of habitual residence.

§ 6.07 GENERAL PRINCIPLES

The case law establishes some general principles, as follows:

1. To find that a child is now settled in its new environment, the proponent of the exception must produce "substantial evidence of the child's significant connections" to the new environment.[31]
2. "Settled" should be viewed to mean that the child has significant emotional and physical connections demonstrating security, stability, and permanence in its new environment.[32]
3. The State Department[33] has interpreted "settled" to relate not just to the child's situation in her new residence but to her situation in her country of habitual residence. This requires weighing evidence of the child's significant connections to the new country and to the country of habitual residence.[34]
4. A child is "settled" when a preponderance of the evidence shows that the child has significant connections to the new home that indicate that the child has developed a stable, permanent, and nontransitory life in the new country to such a degree that return would be to the child's detriment.[35]
5. Where the child may have a more comfortable material existence is not relevant. Courts have repeatedly stated that being well adjusted means more than a mere comfortable material existence.[36] There must be substantial connections amounting to more than a mere enjoyable material lifestyle. As one court stated, "even if the home of [a petitioner] were a grim place to raise a child in comparison to the pretty, peaceful streets of

---

30. State Dep't Legal Analysis § III(I)(1)(c), 51 Fed. Reg. at 10,509.

31. *Andrews*, 2 F. Supp. 2d 134, *aff'd*, 181 F.3d 81 (1st Cir. 1998); *In re* Robinson, 983 F. Supp. 1339 (D. Colo. 1997); *In re* Koc, 181 F. Supp. 2d 136 (E.D.N.Y. 2001).

32. *Alvarez*, 697 F.3d 56–57, *aff'd sub nom.* Lozano v. Montoya Alvarez, 572 U.S. 1, 134 S. Ct. 1224, 188 L. Ed. 2d 200 (2014).

33. State Department Legal Analysis, Appendix 4 at 10,509.

34. Fernandez v. Bailey, 909 F.3d 353 (11th Cir. 2018).

35. *Bailey*, 909 F.3d 353.

36. *Lops*, 140 F.3d 927, *cert. denied*, 525 U.S. 1158 (1999); Koc v. Koc, 181 F. Supp. 2d 136 (E.D.N.Y. 2001).

Ironton, Ohio, that fact would be irrelevant to a federal court's obligation under the Convention."[37]

6. Although "settled" is not a legal term of art, and is not defined in the Convention or ICARA, the reference to "significant connections" reflects the objective of the Convention to have children promptly returned and to have custody matters decided in the state with the strongest interest in the child's care, protection, training, and personal relationships.[38]
7. In determining whether a child has "significant connections to the new country," the court should consider the "totality of the circumstances."[39] A court may consider "any factor relevant to a child's connection to his living arrangement."[40] These factors include (1) child's age; (2) stability and duration of child's residence in new environment; (3) whether child attends school or daycare consistently; (4) whether child has friends and relatives in new area; (5) child's participation in community or extracurricular school activities, such as team sports, youth groups, or school clubs; and (6) respondent's employment and financial stability.[41]
8. The analysis is different from a "best interests" analysis. In one case, the court stated that it did not deny that the child appeared content in her current situation or that the respondent is a good mother. On the contrary, the evidence showed that the child was developing well and was happily situated in her apartment with her mother and grandmother. Those facts, however, were more relevant to a determination of the child's "best interests," "which is a line of inquiry that is inappropriate for the court to undertake under the Convention."[42]
9. Although all of these factors, when applicable, may be considered in the "settled" analysis, ordinarily the most important

37. *Friedrich*, 78 F.3d 1060.

38. *In re* Robinson, 983 F. Supp. 1339 (D. Colo. 1997); *In re* Koc, 181 F. Supp. 2d 136 (E.D.N.Y. 2001).

39. Da Silva v. De Aredes, 953 F.3d 67 (1st Cir. 2020).

40. *Alvarez*, 697 F.3d 57, *aff'd sub nom.* Lozano v. Montoya Alvarez, 572 U.S. 1, 134 S. Ct. 1224, 188 L. Ed. 2d 200 (2014).

41. *In re* B. Del C.S.B. 559 F.3d 999 (9th Cir. 2009); Habrzyk v. Habrzyk, 775 F. Supp. 2d 1054 (N.D. Ill. 2011).

42. *Habrzyk*, 775 F. Supp. 2d 1054.

is the length and stability of the child's residence in the new environment.[43]

10. Although all returns will necessarily involve some level of disruption to the child or children involved, disruption should not be considered per se detrimental. Rather, the "settled" inquiry requires courts to carefully consider the totality of the circumstances.[44]
11. The court may rely in part or even entirely on evidence that post-dates the petition's filing, since the text of the Convention explicitly contemplates a court considering the child's circumstances after the petition has been filed without reference to the child's prior situation.[45]
12. Concealing the child's location does not necessarily prevent the child from being settled in a new environment, despite the Supreme Court's acknowledgment in *Lozano*[46] that "steps taken to promote concealment can also prevent the stable attachments that make a child 'settled.'" The cases cited by the Supreme Court specifically connected the misconduct to the child's being settled. In one case, concealed children were not settled when their mother "took active and consistent steps to prevent contact between the children and their father,"[47] and in another case a child was not settled when the mother "purposely kept [the child] out of all community activities, sports, and even church to avoid detection by the father."[48]

§ 6.08 BURDEN OF PROOF

As with respect to the exception as a whole, the burden is firmly on the respondent to establish that the child is sufficiently settled.[49]

Nonetheless, in one case, the court seemed to steer particularly close to shifting the burden to the petitioner to disprove the claim. In *Wojcik*, the court pointed out that the "father has no evidence that the children have maintained any ties to France," and that the mother testified that the

43. *In re* B. Del C.S.B. 559 F.3d 999 (9th Cir. 2009).
44. *Bailey*, 909 F.3d 353.
45. Da Costa v. de Lima, 94 F.4th 174 (1st Cir. 2024).
46. *Lozano*, 517 U.S. at 17.
47. Mendez Lynch v. Mendez Lynch, 220 F. Supp. 2d 1347, 1363 (M.D. Fla. 2002).
48. Wigley v. Hares, 82 So. 3d 932, 942 (Fla. Dist. Ct. App. 2011).
49. 22 U.S.C. § 9003(e)(2)(B).

father's own family "was indifferent to the children at best."[50] This was despite a finding that the father had "met his burden of proving . . . that his daughters were wrongfully retained." Although these comments were made after the court had pointed out that the children were attending school, had regular contact with family and friends in the United States, attended church, and participated in community activities, the focus on the petitioner appeared to almost shift the burden of proof to him. After showing that the respondent had made a prima facie case for the children being well settled, the court examined whether the respondent had demonstrated that the children were *not* well settled, or at the least would be better settled were they to return to their habitual residence of France. The court also pointed out that the father had presented no testimony to rebut the mother's statements detailing how the children were well settled in their new community.

§ 6.09 AGE

The age of the child is one factor that must be considered in determining whether a child is sufficiently settled. It is well established that very young children may not have meaningful connections to their environment, even if a year has passed, because such children can more easily adapt to their new environment than older children.[51]

A child's age may even be a threshold issue before the court will determine that a child is well settled. Some courts require that the child be of a minimum age before considering any other aspect of the well-settled issue. Thus, a three-year-old child who was wrongfully removed from her home in Spain and then lived at a fixed location in the United States, where she attended daycare and spent substantial time with family members, was held to not be sufficiently settled so as to preclude being returned to Spain, largely on account of her young age.[52] The district court found that it was questionable whether such a young child "has the developmental capacity to engage meaningfully in such activities and be considered settled due to them."[53]

Likewise, in *Blanc v. Morgan*, a child aged four, who lived with her mother and grandmother in a stable home, was found not to be sufficiently "settled" even though her mother had stable employment and the child regularly attended daycare, was enrolled in summer camp, and had

50. Wojcik v. Wojcik, 959 F. Supp. 2d 413 (E.D. Mich. 1997).
51. David S. v. Zamira S., 574 N.Y.S.2d 429 (1991).
52. Moreno v. Martin, 2008 WL 4716958 (S.D. Fla. Oct. 23, 2008).
53. *Id.* at *21.

developed bonds with her grandmother and aunt. The district court found that there was insufficient evidence that the child was so extensively involved in activities or had developed connections within the community such that she would suffer an undue disruption if she were returned.[54]

In one case, the court stated that "courts generally conclude that repatriation of an infant is less burdensome on the child that repatriating an older child, who is more likely to have memories of the United States and more ties to the country."[55]

On the other hand, some courts have found that preschool children are old enough to have become sufficiently settled for purpose of the exception. In *Muhlenkamp*, a child who was three and a half years old, with an American passport and American birth certificate, was found to be sufficiently settled in the United States based on the testimony of the child's daycare provider and a report that the child was performing at an academic level two to three times above age group, and the fact that child had a "strong core" of friends.[56] In *Zuker v. Andrews*, a child who was four years and two months old was "settled" based on the child's attendance at daycare for 21 months; a record of thriving academically and socially; and the testimony of the executive director of a daycare center that the child had established relationships with teachers, children, and other staff.[57] In *Robinson*, the court determined that a five-year-old child could form such meaningful connections and be well settled in the new environment.[58]

§ 6.10 STABILITY OF RESIDENCE

The stability of the child's residence is an extremely significant factor. A child who has resided in the same location for a significant period of time since the removal is far more likely to be found to be settled than a child who has been constantly moved from place to place. Frequent relocations within the new jurisdiction, which render it difficult to foster ongoing friendships and connections with a community, certainly increase the possibility that the child is not well settled.

In a Florida case,[59] the instability of residence was a dispositive reason for finding that the child had not settled into a new community. The

54. Blanc v. Morgan, 721 F. Supp. 2d 749 (W.D. Tenn. 2010).
55. Taveras v. Morales, 22 F. Supp. 3d 219, 236 (S.D.N.Y. 2014).
56. Muhlenkamp v. Blizzard, 521 F. Supp. 2d 1140 (E.D. Wash. 2007).
57. Zuker v. Andrews, 2 F. Supp. 2d 134 (D. Mass. 1998).
58. *Robinson*, 983 F. Supp. 1339.
59. *Martin*, 2008 WL 4716958.

child, abducted from Spain to Florida, then lived in "at least five different residences" in 18 months. Even though the different residences were in the same geographic area, the court concluded, "*a fortiori*, that a three-year-old child who has moved five times in just one and a half years is not well settled."

In an Illinois case,[60] the fact that the child had moved three times during the 17 months between her removal from Poland and the filing of the Hague petition, during which she had spent several weeks in Canada in a hotel, had then lived in the home of her aunt and uncle, and had then moved to the apartment in which she currently resided with her mother and grandmother, was "further evidence" that the child was not "settled."

In a New York case[61] the court found that a child was not sufficiently settled despite her excellent English and academic performance because she had moved to three new homes and been in three different schools in less than three years, which had prevented her from making close friends or being involved in afterschool activities.

Likewise, even though a nine-year-old child had lived in the United States for two and a half years, had consistently attended and performed well in school, played soccer and had friends, she was found to be not settled, in substantial part because she had changed residences five times and changed schools once.[62] And a nine-year-old child was found not "settled" despite evidence that he was doing well in school because, among other facts, he had resided in three different locations and had attended three different schools in the two years since he had been wrongfully retained.[63]

But when a child had resided in a few homes since his arrival in the United States, the fact that he had resided peacefully for the past ten months in one house with his mother and family members supported a finding of a stable residence.[64]

In at least one case, the stability of residence was the determining factor in a court finding that children had settled into their community.[65] The petitioner argued that, because the extended family of the children lived in Argentina, they were not settled in New Jersey. The court rejected this argument and found the children well settled in their new home because

60. *Habrzyk*, 775 F. Supp. 2d 1054.
61. *In re* Koc, 181 F. Supp. 2d 136, 154 (E.D.N.Y. 2001).
62. *In re* Ahumada Cabrera, 323 F. Supp. 2d 1303 (S.D. Fla. 2004).
63. Lutman v. Lutman, 2010 WL 3398985 (M.D. Pa. 2010).
64. Bejarno v. Jimenez, 2020 WL 4188212.
65. Silvestri v. Oliva, 403 F. Supp. 2d 378, 388 (D.N.J. 2005).

they had remained in the same town since their arrival in the United States, and the children had attended the same school throughout.

In its decision in *Lozano*,[66] the Supreme Court stressed the fact that concealing a child is a factor of great significance in this regard. The Court (Justice Thomas) stated that:

> American courts have found as a factual matter that steps taken to promote concealment can also prevent the stable attachments that make a child "settled." See, *e.g.*, *Mendez Lynch v. Mendez Lynch,* 220 F.Supp.2d 1347, 1363-1364 (M.D.Fla.2002) (children not settled when they "lived in seven different locations" in 18 months); *Wigley v. Hares,* 82 So.3d 932, 942 (Fla.App.2011) ("The mother purposely kept him out of all community activities, sports, and even church to avoid detection by the father"); *In re Coffield,* 96 Ohio App.3d 52, 58, 644 N.E.2d 662, 666 (1994) (child not settled when the abducting parent "was attempting to hide [child's] identity" by withholding child from school and other organized activities). Other signatories to the Hague Convention have likewise recognized that concealment may be taken into account in the factual determination whether the child is settled. See, *e.g.*, *Cannon,* [2005] 1 W.L.R., ¶¶ 52-61. See also*Kubera,* 3 B.C.L.R. (5th), ¶ 47, 317 D.L.R. (4th), ¶ 47; *A.C. v. P.C.*, [2005] HKEC 839, ¶ 39, 2005 WL 836263, ¶ 39.

§ 6.11 PRESENCE OF RELATIVES

Whether or not there are other relatives in the child's life may be a significant factor in determining whether the child is well settled in their new environment. A stable family life often includes the presence of relatives.

For example, in *Moreno*, the fact that the removed child "has few relatives in her new environment" was relevant to the question of well-settled status.[67] However, the presence of the child's mother, an aunt and uncle, and a half-sister of the mother in Florida was outweighed by the presence of the father, a grandfather, aunt, uncle, and grandmother in Spain.

In *Robinson*, the court found that the involvement of the respondent's family in the child's life was significant, such activity having included helping the children with school and providing rides to extracurricular

66. *Lozano*, 134 S. Ct. 1236.
67. *Martin*, 2008 WL 4716958.

activities such as "Cub Scouts, Kampus Club, hockey and soccer."[68] Although such evidence of familial involvement was secondary to evidence of adjusting well to the new community, there was no doubt that the involvement and assistance of a stable family facilitated their adjustment.

In a state court case in Texas, the benefit of having relatives nearby was more than offset by the criminal record of the removing parent. After abducting her children from their habitual residence, the police had arrested the respondent for kidnapping and pressed charges. Because of this criminal history, the respondent "added to the instability and unrest suffered by her children when they were uprooted, placed in foster care, and went on to maintain a different residence with their maternal grandparents."[69] Even though there were relatives available, the mother's criminal record had made it all but impossible for the children to adjust to their new community, because they had lived in several different residences and had little stability.

§ 6.12 EMPLOYMENT OF THE PARENT

The employment history and economic stability of the removing parent is a factor that may be important to determining whether the child is well settled. A stable income can often yield a stable residence and an environment in which a child can more easily adjust, adapt, and settle. However, stable parental employment is more usually cited as one factor among many rather than as the dispositive factor.[70]

In some cases, even regular employment may not suffice. In *Lops*,[71] the court noted that the employment of the respondent was limited to "a few hours each week and that it was the respondent's mother who worked and cared for the children." Further, the respondent was potentially subject to prosecution in state and federal courts for several outstanding misdemeanors and felonies related to his abduction of the children. Those factors were decisive in the court's determination that the children were not well settled, even though more than two years had passed since their removal from their former home.

In *Matovski*,[72] the court concluded that the mother's inconsistent employment history was not a major factor because the children and

68. *Robinson*, 983 F. Supp. 1339.
69. In the Interest of A.V.P.G., 251 S.W.3d 117, 126 (Tex. App. 2008).
70. *Oliva*, 403 F. Supp. 2d 378; *Robinson*, 983 F. Supp. 1339.
71. *Lops*, 140 F.3d 927.
72. Matovski v. Matovski, 2007 WL 2600862 (S.D.N.Y. 2007).

mother were financially supported by the children's grandparents, with whom the children and mother lived, rendering their overall financial stability "reasonably assured."

The trial court in *In re Lozano*[73] followed *Matovski* in a case in which the respondent mother was unemployed and she and the child were entirely dependent on respondent's sister and the sister's partner for financial support. The court held that such factors did not negate the fact that the child was well settled because there was nothing to suggest that the financial and other support was in jeopardy, or was unlikely to continue for the foreseeable future.

By contrast, in *Koc*,[74] the court viewed the financial dependence of the mother and child on the mother's parents as a significantly negative factor but there they also received support from public services and they had lived with the child's grandparents for only the first three months of the 27 months that they had been living in New York prior to the filing of the petition.

§ 6.13 CONCEALMENT

Those courts that applied equitable tolling to the one-year period in Article 12 cited the fact that parents who abduct their children should not be encouraged to conceal their children in order to benefit from the running of the one-year period. Although the Supreme Court rejected this argument in *Lozano*, Justice Thomas asserted in the majority opinion that American courts have found as a factual matter that steps taken to promote concealment can also prevent the stable attachments that make a child "settled" and that other signatories to the Convention have likewise recognized that concealment may be taken into account in the factual determination whether the child is settled.[75] In support of that assertion he cited a case in which children were found not to be settled when they had lived in seven different locations in 18 months,[76] a case in which the child was not settled when the mother had purposely kept him out of all community activities, sports, and even church to avoid detection by the father,[77] and a case where a child was not settled when the abducting

73. *In re* Lozano, 2011 WL 3667444 (S.D.N.Y. 2011).
74. *In re* Koc, 181 F. Supp. 2d 136, 154 (E.D.N.Y. 2001).
75. *Lozano*, 134 S. Ct. 1236.
76. Mendez Lynch v. Mendez Lynch, 220 F. Supp. 2d 1347, 1363–64 (M.D. Fla. 2002).
77. Wigley v. Hares, 82 So.3d 932, 942 (Fla. App. 2011).

parent was attempting to hide the child's identity by withholding him from school and other organized activities.[78]

§ 6.14 IMMIGRATION STATUS

Consideration in a Hague case of the immigration status of a removing parent is somewhat controversial. Several district courts have held that the lack of legal immigration status in the United States will weigh significantly against a finding that the child is "settled."[79] Indeed, some courts have deemed the taking parent's illegal immigration status to be a dispositive issue against a finding that the child is "settled" regardless of how well settled in fact the child might otherwise be. In a case in which the child had been living in the United States for over two years, the first issue was the uncertain immigration status of the mother and her child.[80] The immigration status made it impossible for the father to obtain a visa to visit the child, and made it extremely difficult for the mother to find a stable job or residence. Accordingly, it was found that the child was not sufficiently settled.

In another case, the fact that the removing parent was not in the country legally, and was "subject to deportation at anytime," was a major factor in the district court ordering the return of a child to the habitual residence.[81] The court even seemed to reach the merits of the removing parent's asylum claim, finding it "not [to] appear meritorious."

In sharp contrast, the Ninth Circuit in the significant case of *In re B. del C.S.B* has more flatly rejected the idea that immigration status should render an otherwise settled child not settled. It ruled that immigration status should be a significant factor only if there is an immediate and concrete threat of deportation.

At first instance in that case, the lower court in California was concerned that, because the removing parent and her child were in the United States illegally, deportation was a possibility at any time. It held that this was not merely one additional factor among many that should be weighed equally with other factors in determining whether the child was well settled, but that it represented "a constant danger to [the child's] well-being, threatening to undermine each and every connection to her community

---

78. *In re* Coffield, 96 Ohio App. 3d 52, 58, 644 N.E.2d 662, 666 (1994).
79. *In re* Ahumada Cabrera, 323 F. Supp. 2d 1303 (S.D. Fla. 2004).
80. *In re* Koc, 181 F. Supp. 2d 136 (E.D.N.Y. 2001).
81. *Alcala*, 547 F. Supp. 2d 1255.

that she has developed."[82] For this reason it ruled that the one-year-and-settled exception had not been established, even though the child had developed significant connections to the United States.

On appeal, the Ninth Circuit insisted that the child's current immigration status "cannot undermine all of the other considerations which uniformly support a finding that she is 'settled' in the United States." It ruled that, "if a child has been living in a new country for a long enough period of time, an ordinary person could conclude that the child is 'now settled' in that country, regardless of his immigration status."[83]

The key elements of the Ninth Circuit's reasoning were as follows:

- Neither the text of the Convention nor the history of its adoption suggests that lawful immigration status is a prerequisite, or even a factor of great significance, for a finding that a child is "settled" in a new environment. The text of Article 12 does not define the term "settled," nor does it state how the fact that a child is now settled in its new environment is to be proved. Article 12's use of a relatively broad, undefined term is consistent with the Convention drafters' desire to avoid linking the determination of which country should exercise jurisdiction over a custody dispute to idiosyncratic legal definitions.
- Where the Convention fails to define a word or phrase, courts interpret the term according to its "ordinary and natural meaning" rather than a rigid technical or legal definition.
- As with habitual residence, if a child has been living in a new country for a long enough period of time, an ordinary person could conclude that the child is "now settled" in that country, regardless of his immigration status. Moreover, it would be an "odd result indeed" if a child may be habitually resident, but not settled, in a country in which he does not have legal status. By acknowledging that an undocumented child may be habitually resident within the meaning of Article 3, the courts have already accepted the principle that a child may remain in a place in which he lacks legal status for the duration of custody proceedings because of his close ties to that country.

82. *In re* B. Del C.S.B., 525 F. Supp. 2d 1182, 1195 (C.D. Cal. 2007).
83. *In re* B. Del C.S.B., 559 F.3d 999 (9th Cir. 2009).

- The English courts have ruled that the illegal immigration status of a mother and child does not bar a finding that the child is "settled."[84]
- On a practical level, it makes little sense to permit immigration status to serve as a determinative factor in the Article 12 "settled" analysis. Although there are undoubtedly real risks posed by illegal status, the reality is that millions of undocumented immigrants are presently living in the United States, many of whom will remain here permanently without ever having any contact with immigration authorities. The Department of Homeland Security estimates that the unauthorized immigrant population in the United States numbered 11.6 million in January 2008. The majority of these undocumented immigrants are long-term residents and they are unlikely to face removal, especially if they are law-abiding.
- In light of the discretionary federal power to grant relief from deportation, one cannot realistically determine that any particular undocumented child will in fact be deported until after deportation proceedings have been completed. Indeed, undocumented immigrants, and undocumented children in particular, benefit from significant protections under state and federal law.
- In the future the child might face difficulties as a result of her undocumented immigration status but the Convention is concerned with the *present*, and not with determining the best interests of the child in the long term. The determination of future well-being is left to the court conducting custody proceedings.

In *Cuenca*,[85] the 11th Circuit followed *In re B. del C.S.B.* and held that the fact that a child lacks permanent legal immigration status does not categorically preclude a finding that the child is "settled" in the United States. In that case, the court rejected the suggestion that district courts should attempt to prejudge the merits of an immigration petition because, in general, district courts have no role in immigration proceedings and are not in the best position to predict how an immigration judge or the Board of Immigration Appeals may rule.[86]

84. *Re* C (A Child) (Child Abduction: Settlement), [2006] EWHC (Fam) 1229, 2006 2 F.L.R. 797, 2006 WL 1518692.

85. Cuenca v. Rojas, 99 F.4th 1344 (11th Cir. 2024).

86. *Id.*

It is now well established that courts look to the totality of the circumstances in determining whether a child is now settled, and that immigration status is relevant but usually not dispositive.[87] For example, in *Lozano*, the Second Circuit insisted that an abducted child's immigration status should be only one of many relevant factors in determining whether the child is now settled, and its weight "will necessarily vary."[88]

However, in *Wigley*, the Ninth Circuit relied on a mother's illegal immigration status as a significant factor in holding that the child had not become settled, despite the fact that the court acknowledged that she might have been able to achieve legal status because she married a few days prior to the hearing.[89] And the fact that the respondent and the child were not merely illegally present in the United States but were actively involved in removal proceedings and were both within current DHS civil enforcement priorities as new immigration violators was a significant factor that militated against a finding of being settled.[90]

Even if immigration status is less of a significant factor in weighing *against* whether a child is settled, it remains unlikely that the immigration status of the parent will ever weigh *in favor* of a respondent's case. In *Moreno*, the respondent argued that because she was a legal permanent resident in the United States, her child was necessarily well settled. The court said that although "immigration status is a factor in deciding whether a child is well settled in her new environment . . . alone it suggests little about significant connections that [the child] may have established."[91] Puzzlingly, the opinion further stated that there was "no guarantee that [the child] will actually obtain U.S. citizenship if she remains." As a lawful permanent resident, the child could be just as settled in the United States as an American citizen.

§ 6.15 SOCIAL LIVES OF THE CHILDREN

Perhaps the single most important factor in establishing the well-settled exception is showing the stable and happy social life of the removed child. Courts are significantly more likely to find a child well settled if the child attends school, has a network of friends, and attends various

87. Alcala v. Hernandez, 826 F.3d 161 (4th Cir. 2016).

88. *Alvarez*, 697 F.3d 56, *aff'd sub nom.* Lozano v. Montoya Alvarez, 572 U.S. 1, 134 S. Ct. 1224, 188 L. Ed. 2d 200 (2014).

89. Wigley v. Hares, 2011 WL 3111898 (Fla. App. 2011).

90. Hernandez v. Garcia Pena, 820 F.3d 782 (5th Cir. 2016).

91. Moreno v. Martin, No. 08-22432-CIV, 2008 WL 4716958 (S.D. Fla. Oct. 23, 2008).

community activities. The extent and quality of the child's social relationships may be fully evaluated by the court.

Certainly, if a child does not attend school, it will be difficult to establish that the child is well settled.[92] School is the primary activity of children, and the place where they are likely to make the most friends, take part in the most extracurricular activities, and best settle into their new communities.

In an Ohio case, the court found it significant that the child's social life was limited to close friends and relatives of the removing parent, rather than friends of the child himself, even though more than three years had passed since the wrongful removal.[93] Further, the court held that because the child was apparently not enrolled in school or in any other activities, the respondent "was attempting to hide [the child's] identity," which had resulted in the child being effectively hidden from the left-behind parent and the entire outside world.

When a child was enrolled in school but was often tardy or absent, this weighed against her being settled.[94] And, in *Bocquet*,[95] the court found that the burden of proving that the child was settled had not been met, in large part because there was no evidence that the child had been in school, been involved in a play group, attended any religious institution, played in any organized sport teams, or established any other significant connections.

By contrast, a finding that the child was popular, did well in school, and regularly attended community events was sufficient to find that the child was well settled.[96] In another case, the fact that the children had attended the same schools for their entire time in the United States and had developed a number of friendships at school appeared to be enough for the court to find that the children were well settled in their new home.[97]

However, a similar amount of social activities was insufficient in a case involving a boy in Puerto Rico who attended "school in Puerto Rico and has good grades, has friends, goes to the movies and plays sports."[98] The court found the child not well settled because his mother and sister remained in Argentina, and had always lived in Argentina before his abduction into Puerto Rico. The fact that the boy had done well in Puerto

92. *Hares*, 2011 WL 3111898.
93. *In re* Coffield, 644 N.E.2d 662 (Ohio App. 1994).
94. *De Aredes*, 953 F.3d 67.
95. Bocquet v. Ouzid, 225 F.Supp.2d 1337 (S.D. Fla. 2002).
96. *Blizzard*, 521 F. Supp. 2d 1140.
97. *See* Arboleda v. Arenas, 311 F. Supp. 2d 336 (E.D.N.Y. 2004).
98. Gonzalez-Locicero v. Nazor Lurashi, 321 F. Supp. 2d 295 (D. P.R. 2004).

Rico did not make him better settled in his new environment; rather, the court emphasized the hazy work and residence history of the respondent.

A child's language may also be relevant in this regard. In one case, the child spoke Polish as her first language, and knew only a few words in English. The court stated that although this fact did not necessarily weigh against a finding that she was settled in Illinois, that the child spoke Polish did indicate that her return to Poland would be less likely to cause her harm or "undue disruption."[99]

§ 6.16 EDUCATION

Attendance at school is a most significant factor, as just discussed, since it is generally the focus of a child's social life. Both attendance and performance at school are also important factors in and of themselves. Courts generally should consider as a now settled factor "whether the child attends school or day care consistently."[100] However, the fact that a child who was engaged in school for more than two years was repeatedly tardy and absent throughout both years was a factor that weighed against a finding that she was settled.[101]

§ 6.17 EXPERT TESTIMONY

Some courts have allowed and relied on expert testimony as to the well-settled exception. Indeed, a district court in Washington state on its own initiative appointed a child psychologist as an expert to assist the court in making its decision. The court primarily wanted the expert to obtain greater input from the child himself concerning his life in Mexico and in the United States, as well as a professional opinion as to how well the child had adjusted to life in the United States and his relationship with his parents. The court had determined initially that the child's older sister would not be returned to Mexico because she objected to being returned and she was of sufficient age and maturity. The younger child was too young and immature for the objection exception to apply. Nonetheless, his opinions and perspective were relevant in consideration of the "settled" defense.[102]

---

99. *Habrzyk*, 775 F. Supp. 2d 1054.

100. *Alvarez*, 697 F.3d 57, *aff'd sub nom.* Lozano v. Montoya Alvarez, 572 U.S. 1, 134 S. Ct. 1224, 188 L. Ed. 2d 200 (2014).

101. *De Aredes*, 953 F.3d 67.

102. Etienne v. Zuniga, 2010 WL 4918791 (W.D. Wash. 2010).

In one case, the Ninth Circuit, upholding the district court's finding that the child was now settled in Arizona, relied substantially on the fact that a child psychology expert had testified that the child had a "normal" emotional status for a five-year-old child, and was "well acclimated" to her home and community, and, in particular, that the child had friends with whom "she's very involved," and that she liked her school and teacher.[103]

§ 6.18 EXISTENCE OF A DISCRETION

There was previously some uncertainty as to whether a court may return a child even though the elements of a one-year-and-settled-defense are established.[104]

The existence of such a discretion is not stated in the language of Article 12. Indeed, Article 12 provides that, if a wrongful removal or retention has been proven, then if "a period of less than one year has elapsed from the date of the wrongful removal or retention, the authority concerned *shall order* the return of the child forthwith" but if "the proceedings have been commenced after the expiration of the period of one year referred to in the preceding paragraph, *shall also order* the return of the child, unless it is demonstrated that the child is now settled in its new environment."

On its face, that language affords no discretion if the elements of the defense have been established. Indeed, the language is quite different from the language in Article 13, which expressly provides that the judicial authorities are "not bound" to order the return of a child if one of the conditions described in that article are established.

Nonetheless, most courts that have considered the issue have ruled or opined in favor of the existence of a discretion. The First Circuit reviewed the issue at length and expressly held that the Convention does not prevent the district court from ordering return of "now settled" children.[105] The Eleventh Circuit has come to the same conclusion.[106] Such courts have cited Article 18 of the Convention, which provides, "The provisions of this Chapter do not limit the power of a judicial or administrative authority to order the return of the child at any time." Likewise, in his

103. Margain v. Ruiz-Bours, 592 Fed. Appx. 619, 620–21 (9th Cir. 2015).

104. Antunez-Fernandes v. Connors-Fernandes, 259 F. Supp. 2d 800 (N.D. Iowa 2003); Rivera Rivas v. Segovia, 2010 WL 394778 (W.D. Ark. 2010).

105. Yaman v. Yaman, 730 F.3d 1 (1st Cir. 2013).

106. *Bailey*, 909 F.3d 353.

concurring opinion in the Supreme Court ruling in *Lozano*, Justice Alito insisted that nothing in Article 12 or elsewhere in the Convention prevents a court from ordering a child's return whenever equitable considerations impel it to do so.[107]

Similarly, the Ninth Circuit went out of its way, having agreed with the district court that the child was settled in its new environment, to note that no equitable factors counseled against the application of the Article 12 exception, as the record supported the district court's conclusion that the petitioner had not been diligent in locating the child.[108]

Likewise, the Second Circuit stated in the first *Blondin* case that, "if more than one year has passed, a demonstration that the child is now settled in its new environment may be a *sufficient* ground for refusing to order repatriation," and in the second *Blondin* case that, even if the exception is established, "the district court is not necessarily bound to allow the child to remain with the abducting parent."[109]

It is clear that such a discretion has been recognized in some foreign decisions, but those cases have been based in part on the domestic legislation pursuant to which the Convention was brought into domestic law. Thus, in New Zealand domestic legislation, implementing the Convention expressly provides for an exercise of judicial discretion where settlement is established.[110]

English case law formerly favored the existence of such a discretion but that was based in large part on giving an expansive interpretation to Article 18 of the Convention (as recently cited by the Eleventh Circuit). However, the House of Lords subsequently declared that Article 18 is of no relevance to this issue because it merely contemplates powers conferred by the ordinary domestic law rather than by the Convention itself.[111] Nonetheless, Baroness Hale declared in that case that she had reached the conclusion, "not without considerable hesitation," that Article 12 does indeed allow for a discretion to return a settled child pursuant to the Convention procedures. She felt that the words "shall . . . unless" in Article 12(2) left the matter open and that to hold otherwise would be inconsistent with all the other exceptions to the rule of return. Furthermore, she stated that a discretion recognizes the flexibility in the concept

107. *Lozano*, 134 S. Ct. 1237–38.

108. *Margain*, 592 Fed. Appx. 621.

109. Blondin v. Dubois, 238 F.3d 153 (2d Cir. 2001); Blondin v. Dubois, 189 F.3d 240 (2d Cir. 1999); *applied in* Lomanto v. Agbelusi, 2024 WL 3342415 (2d Cir. July 9, 2024).

110. Sec. 106, N.Z. Care of Children Act, 2004.

111. Re. M & Anor (Children), [2007] UKHL 55.

of settlement, which may arise in a wide variety of circumstances and to very different degrees; that allowing a discretion acknowledges that a late application may be the result of active concealment as to the child's location; and that it would leave the court with all options open.

§ 6.19 EXERCISE OF DISCRETION

In *Fernandez,*[112] the Eleventh Circuit took the unusual step of overturning the district court's decision not to return children who had become settled in the United States during the period of more than one year prior to the left-behind father's filing of his Hague petition. It did so because of the unusual facts of the case. The children's American mother had wrongfully removed the boys to the United States for the second time in five years in violation of court-ordered exit restrictions. The Panamanian courts were deeply involved in multiple issues related to the children's custody. And the father was not able to enter the United States to see his children or to litigate custody issues in person. The circuit court held that the district court abused its discretion by not sufficiently weighing the audacity and significance of a second wrongful removal.

In contrast, in *Cuenca,*[113] the 11th Circuit held that the district court did not abuse its discretion in declining to order the child's return to Venezuela pursuant to the settled exception, notwithstanding the mother's wrongful conduct in removing the child from his home in violation of his father's custody rights and her initial dishonesty in informing the father that she planned to return with the child even as she applied for asylum. It was relevant that the mother had informed the father almost immediately that she had taken the child to Florida, that the father did not file his petition until more than one year after learning of the abduction, and that the child had developed stable and enduring ties in Florida. The court also stated that "returning a settled child is the exception rather than the rule."

In *Lomanto,*[114] the Second Circuit upheld the refusal of a district court to order the return of children who were wrongfully retained away from their habitual residence in Spain where the respondent established the defense of one-year-and-settled in respect of both children and the objections of a mature child in respect of one of the two children. The circuit court held that, while a district court may exercise its discretion to order the return of children in order to further the aims of the Convention even

112. *Bailey*, 909 F.3d 353.
113. Cuenca v. Rojas, 99 F.4th 1344, 1352–53 (11th Cir. 2024).
114. Lomanto v. Agbelusi, 2024 WL 3342415 (2d Cir. July 9, 2024).

in cases where affirmative defenses are established, here, the district court declined to do so, explaining that, in addition to deterrence of wrongful removal or retention, the Convention has "an interest in the welfare of the children and their interests in remaining settled."[115]

A district court in Iowa exercised such a discretion in *Antunez-Fernandes*. There, the court found that "even under the most generous reading," the petitioner filed more than a year after removal. The court noted that, "by all accounts, the children are performing very well scholastically and have healthy relationships with fellow students . . . active in curricular and extra-curricular programs."[116] Despite finding that over a year had passed between the taking and the filing, and that the children had settled into their community, the court ordered that the children be returned to their habitual residence in France. This was because the mother's activities "are exactly what the Hague Convention seeks to remedy. By bringing the children into the United States and into a community where her extended family is already well established, she knowingly and successfully created language, cultural, distance and financial barriers" with their father.[117]

The court took special note of the various ex parte procedures that the mother had taken once arriving in the United States in an attempt to prevent the father from having any contact with her or the children. Because of those proceedings, and because of the mother's refusal to maintain the children's French language, despite her own fluency, the court was more inclined to exercise its discretion and grant a petition to return the children to their habitual residence. Ultimately, the court granted the petition even though the respondent proved both elements of the exception.

A New York district court upheld an Article 12 discretion in deciding that, even if the exception had been established, it would be inequitable to apply it on the facts of the particular case. The court was greatly influenced by the fact that case had been filed just 25 days after the end of the one-year period and that the left-behind parent had spent considerable time searching for the child. Although it did not apply equitable tolling, it used the residual discretion as the appropriate way of achieving what it considered an equitable result.[118]

115. *Id.* at *3.
116. *Antunez-Fernandes*, 259 F. Supp. 2d 814.
117. *Id.* at 815.
118. *In re* Filipczak, 2011 WL 6980845 (S.D.N.Y. 2011).

In another New York case, the court simply stated that the discretion existed but it saw no reason to exercise it because there was no evidence that the relocation was motivated by a desire to remove the children to a jurisdiction more favorable to her custody claim.[119]

§ 6.20 APPELLATE REVIEW STANDARD

The 11th Circuit in *Cuenca*[120] considered in depth the appropriate standard of appellate review in a Hague Convention case of whether a child is "settled." It held that, like the analogous concept of a child's "habitual residence," the determination of whether a child is settled begins with the selection of the appropriate legal framework: a case-specific totality-of-the-circumstances analysis. It adopted the language in *Monasky* that, once the trial court correctly identifies the governing totality-of-the-circumstances standard, "what remains for the court to do in applying that standard"[121] is classic fact-finding work, for which the court must marshal and weigh evidence, make credibility judgments, and consider multifarious, fleeting, special, narrow facts specific to the child's circumstances. The assessment of whether a child is settled thus presents a task for fact-finding courts, not appellate courts, and should be judged on appeal by a clear-error review standard deferential to the fact-finding court. A factual finding is clearly erroneous when a review of the entire record leaves the appellate court with the definite and firm conviction that a mistake has been committed. But even if the district court finds that a wrongfully removed child is "now settled in its new environment," that court has the discretion to order the child returned to the country where he or she habitually resided at the time of the removal. The appeals court should then review the district court's ultimate decision whether to return a child for abuse of discretion.

119. Gwiadowski v. Gwiadowski, 2015 WL 14436 (E.D.N.Y. 2015).
120. Cuenca v. Rojas, 99 F.4th 1344, 1350 (11th Cir. 2024).
121. *Id.* at 1350, citing *Monasky*, 589 U.S. at 84.

The Child's Objections 7

§ 7.01 INTRODUCTION

Article 13 of the Convention authorizes a court to refuse to order the return of a child if it finds that "the child objects to being returned and has attained an age and degree of maturity at which it is appropriate to take account of its views." The Article requires the court to take into account information relating to the social background of the child provided by the Central Authority or other competent authority of the child's habitual residence.

The "mature child's objection" exception was the result of a debate among the drafters of the Convention as to the inclusion of a clause that would give some weight to the wishes or objections of children involved in Hague proceedings. The Convention applies only to children under the age of 16, because it was thought that children over that age, who might be better categorized as young adults at that point, almost certainly have asserted a degree of independence and are capable of making decisions for themselves regarding their futures. Some drafting nations had specific statutory provisions that allowed for a child's wishes to be heard in some hearings, while others did not have the laws and procedures in place to explicitly recognize or allow for a child to be heard. The clause in the Convention, as it stands in Article 13, represents a compromise.

The Perez-Vera Report explains that the drafters could not agree to a set age when a child's objections would be taken under consideration.

The Rapporteur's observations follow [1]—in verbatim form, since some courts treat her report as a source of significant authority:

> The Convention also provides that the child's views concerning the essential question of its return or retention may be conclusive, provided it has, according to the competent authorities, attained an age and degree of maturity sufficient for its views to be taken into account. In this way, the Convention gives children the possibility of interpreting their own interests. Of course, this provision could prove dangerous if it were applied by means of the direct questioning of young people who may admittedly have a clear grasp of the situation but who may also suffer serious psychological harm if they think they are being forced to choose between two parents. However, such a provision is absolutely necessary given the fact that the Convention applies, *ratione personae*, to all children under the age of sixteen; the fact must be acknowledged that it would be very difficult to accept that a child of, for example, fifteen years of age, should be returned against its will. Moreover, as regards this particular point, all efforts to agree on a minimum age at which the views of the child could be taken into account failed, since all the ages suggested seemed artificial, even arbitrary. It seemed best to leave the application of this clause to the discretion of the competent authorities.

Thus, the drafters agreed to disagree. They left ample discretion to the factfinder in each individual case for a child's objections to play a large part in the case if the child is of a sufficient age as well as maturity to have his or her opinions considered.

Consequently, a court may refuse repatriation *solely* on the basis of a considered objection to returning by a sufficiently mature child.[2] The result is that when a respondent parent claims that a child objects to being returned, a fierce judicial battle may ensue as to the effect to be given to the child's words, which must often be analyzed and dissected with great care in the context of the child's age, maturity, social context, parental influence, demeanor, self-confidence, genuineness, psychological profile, and a host of other factors. Which of those factors will be determinative in any particular case before any particular judge is difficult to predict.

---

1. Perez-Vera Report, para. 30.
2. De Silva v. Pitts, 418 F.3d 1279 (10th Cir. 2007).

Some commentators and judges have been critical of the maturity exception. A broad interpretation of the clause may conflict with the purpose of the Convention itself. When the objections of a child are given sufficient weight by the factfinder and the ruling is made based on these objections, the fact that an abduction has occurred is essentially ignored, thus overriding the rights and legal status of the left-behind parent. Such a result may be equitable when balancing the many considerations of an individual case, but it might contradict and undermine the purpose of the Convention, which is to prevent child abductions and effectuate a speedy return of children to their home countries.

On the other hand, an unduly narrow interpretation of the child's objections clause might summarily and unfairly dismiss a child's strong and maturely-formed opinions about his future and create an arbitrary result that will inure to the child's detriment.

§ 7.02 BURDEN OF PROOF

The burden rests firmly on the respondent to establish the elements of the child's maturity exception by a preponderance of the evidence.[3]

The effect of the burden of proof is to require a court at first instance to make detailed rulings on the various elements of the exception and, if finding that the exception has been established, to explain the rationale for such a finding. In *England v. England*,[4] the district court ruled that the child, aged 13, was sufficiently mature and had expressed a clear objection to being returned. On appeal, the Fifth Circuit found that the burden of proof was "salient" and had not been satisfied because the party opposing the return of the child had failed to establish the child's maturity by a preponderance of the evidence, especially in light of evidence in the record that showed that the child had endured turbulent times with "four mothers in twelve years" (due to some time in foster care and orphanages), was diagnosed with ADD and learning disabilities, and was "scared and confused by the circumstances producing this litigation."[5] An oft-cited dissent in that case scolds the majority for failing to accept the 13-year-old's objection to a return without any stringent legal or logical reasoning why they did so and for overruling the district judge who was the only judge who had observed the child.

3. 22 U.S.C. § 9003(e)(2)(B).
4. England v. England, 234 F.3d 268 (5th Cir. 2000).
5. *Id.* at 273.

The Fifth Circuit has also held that whether the child has reached an appropriate age and degree of maturity is a factual determination and thus subject to clear error review.[6]

An extensive review of the case law shows that there is no clear framework to analyze the exception in the United States. There is no well-established all-encompassing precedent to instruct and help judges confronted with the exception, except to apply common sense to a difficult task on a case-by-case basis. Predictably, this has led to some confusion and scattered results as to how the exception is to be applied in each case.

The Tenth Circuit has noted, "Given the fact-intensive and idiosyncratic nature of the inquiry, decisions applying the age and maturity exception are understandably disparate."[7] There the court compared:

- An Ohio case which considered the views of an eight-year-old child who was composed, calmly and readily answered questions, pointed to New Zealand on a globe, and indicated her understanding of the difference between truth and falsehood and of her obligation to tell the truth;[8] and
- A Michigan case in which the court ordered limited discovery, including psychological reports and in-camera interview to gather enough information to pursue issue of eight-year-old child's wishes;[9] with
- A New Jersey case which held, without discussion, that the exception "simply does not apply to a nine-year-old child";[10] and
- A previously described Fifth Circuit case, reversing a district court that had taken a 13-year-old child's wishes into account where the child had learning disabilities, had had four mothers in 12 years, had attention deficit disorder, took Ritalin, and was scared and confused.[11]

The child's wishes can be the sole reason that a court refuses to order the return of the child to his or her habitual residence.[12] However, some courts have asserted that a court must apply a stricter standard in

6. Vasconcelos v. Batista, 512 Fed. Appx. 403 (5th Cir. 2013).
7. De Silva v. Pitts, 481 F.3d 1279 (10th Cir. 2007).
8. Anderson v. Acree, 250 F. Supp. 2d 876 (S.D. Ohio 2002).
9. Raijmakers-Eghaghe v. Haro, 131 F. Supp. 2d 953 (E.D. Mich. 2001).
10. Tahan v. Duquette, 259 N.J. Super. 328, 613 A.2d 486 (1992).
11. *England*, 234 F.3d 272–73.
12. Blondin v. Dubois, 189 F.3d 240, 247 (2d Cir. 1999).

considering a child's wishes when those wishes are the sole reason underlying a repatriation decision and not part of some broader analysis.[13]

The confusion and disparate results in the United States do not appear to be shared with other countries that are signatories to the Hague Convention. Granted, the child's objections defense is interpreted and adjudicated differently in many countries that are Convention members. A brief look at how the legal system in the United Kingdom effectively analyzes this defense can provide a good example at how the United States system might evolve as far as providing a framework for analysis for this 13(b) defense.

The English courts have established a logical framework for the analysis of a child's objections. In one case,[14] the court noted that only in exceptional cases should a return not be immediately ordered, and that if there is the slightest taint of undue influence from a parent to a child's objections, the objections should be given little or no weight. A court welfare officer will be appointed to the matter, whose role is to interview the child and make sure that the child's objections are heard. There is no similar automatic appointment mechanism in the United States. The Court of Appeal has outlined three proper inquiries that a court in the United Kingdom should make when presented with the objections of a child:

> The first question to be considered is whether or not the objections to return are made out. The second is whether the age and maturity of the child are such that it is appropriate for the court to take account of those objections (unless that is so, the defense cannot be established). Assuming a positive finding in that respect, the court moves to the third question, whether or not it should exercise its discretion in favour of retention or return.[15]

That case also describes the further analysis under the first two questions, mainly to seek out exactly why the child objects and also if the child is, indeed, mature enough to have those objections noted by the court.

The results in each case are still shaped by the specific and distinct facts of each matter. Lord Justice Ward provides a well-accepted list of considerations to take into account when trying to determine how

13. *De Silva*, 481 F.3d 1279; Yang v. Tsui, 499 F.3d 259 (3d Cir. 2007); Dubikovskyy v. Goun, 54 F.4th 1042 (8th Cir. 2022).

14. S v. S (Child Abduction) (Child's Views) [1992] 2 FLR 492.

15. Re M. (A Child) (Abduction: Child's Objections to Return) [2007] EWCA Civ 260, [2007] 2 FLR 72.

appropriate it is to give the proper weight to a child's objections.[16] He stated that the following matters should be examined:

(a) What is the child's own perspective of what is in her interests, short, medium and long term? Self-perception is important because it is *her* views which have to be judged appropriate.

(b) To what extent, if at all, are the reasons for objections rooted in reality or might reasonably appear to the child to be so grounded?

(c) To what extent have those views been shaped or even colored by undue influence and pressure, directly or indirectly exerted by the abducting parent?

(d) To what extent will the objections be mollified on return and, where it is the case, on removal from any pernicious influence from the abducting parent?

§ 7.03 SIMILAR CASES, DIFFERENT RESULTS

It is instructive to compare the facts of two very similar U.S. cases that yielded different decisions on the maturity exception issue. These cases illustrate the individualistic nature of decision making in this area and the way in which the selection of different factors to highlight may yield quite different results.

In *Yang*,[17] the parties were unmarried when the mother gave birth to their daughter in 1996 in Pittsburgh. She and the child lived in Taiwan until a relocation to Canada in 2000. The father was married to another woman and largely remained in Pittsburgh, having sporadic communication with the child, occasionally sending money and gifts. The mother became severely ill in 2002 and required surgery followed by a lengthy recovery period. She asked the father to care for the child for at least a few months while she recovered, adding "if anything happens to me, at least you can still raise (the child)." The father agreed, and took her from Canada to Pittsburgh. He later refused to return the child. The Hague case was commenced after the child had been living with her father for only eight months. She was ten years old.

The district court conducted an in-camera hearing and considered reports from a child psychologist and expert witnesses to weigh the

16. Re T. (Abduction: Child's Objections to Return) [2000] 2 FCR 159.
17. Yang v. Tsui, 499 F.3d 259 (3d Cir. 2007).

objections of the child. The child expressed a desire to stay in Pittsburgh. She admitted that she knew that her mother was ill. She stated that she based her decision on wanting to stay at her current school, her preference for living in a house over a small apartment, and because she had friends and brothers close by (she lived with her half-brothers while staying with her father in Pittsburgh). The psychologist's report and testimony were quite favorable to the father and the child, as he stated that the child did not demonstrate any signs of coercion and that he found her to be quite intelligent, going as far as to describe her as a "borderline genius."

In *Castillo*,[18] the child lived in Colombia and came to the United States to visit her father for the summer. He then refused to return her. She was 11 years old when the Hague case was initiated. The court ordered that the child should meet with an attorney to prepare a report as to whether she had attained an age and degree of maturity at which it was appropriate to take into account her views, among other things. The court-appointed attorney's report noted that the child displayed "impressive" maturity for a person her age; she had expressed a strong desire to stay in the United States; she had demonstrated a clear understanding of both the purpose of the meeting and the need for her to answer questions truthfully; she did not demonstrate any signs of being unduly influenced in regard to her responses to the questions; she was quite well adjusted; and she was performing at a high level at her school.

Although one might well have expected that the two cases would have yielded similar outcomes—because the factual scenarios were quite similar (the expert reports reached parallel conclusions, each child demonstrated a clear objection to returning to her country of habitual residence, and each seemed to have reached an age and degree of maturity where their views would be given proper deference). However, that proved not to be the case. The child in *Yang* was returned to Canada, while the child in *Castillo* remained in the United States.

In *Yang*, the district court found that despite the child's intelligence and demeanor, the respondent had failed to meet his burden of proof on the child's objection exception by a preponderance of the evidence due to two reasons. First, the district court found that there was some evidence that the child's testimony had been influenced by the father. Second, the court determined that the lengthy wrongful detention of the child had apparently contributed greatly to her testimony and her positive feelings for Pittsburgh and her surroundings. Hence, the Third Circuit affirmed the

18. Castillo v. Castillo, 597 F. Supp. 2d 432 (D. Del. 2009).

district court's determination that the child must be returned to Canada despite her clear objection.

Conversely, in *Castillo*, the court concluded that there were two fundamental reasons why the child's objection exception should be upheld. First, the child's "particularized objections" evidenced that her desire to remain in the United States was born of "rational comparison" between her life here and her life in Colombia. Second, the child had been in the United States for a lengthy period (19 months) at the time of trial and the initial petition had been filed almost exactly one year after the wrongful retention.

Accordingly, in comparing the two cases all that is clear is that each case will be decided on its own unique facts and that in reality, judges have enormous discretion to select and highlight those facts that will support whatever subjective conclusion they have reached.

§ 7.04 AGE AND MATURITY

The elements of age and maturity are quite obviously intertwined and they are often considered together. Nonetheless they are both elements that need to be considered.

§ 7.04.1 Age of the Child

It is often said that there is no definite line of demarcation as to a child's age below which a court will likely decline to take into account the child's objections. In *Blondin*,[19] the court specifically declined to hold as a matter of law that an eight-year-old girl was too young for her views to be taken into account, and ruled that the district court did not err in finding that a child of that age was mature enough to have her views taken into account. On the other hand, a New Jersey court held that the maturity exception "simply does not apply to a nine year old."[20]

A district court in Ohio accepted the views of an eight-year-old child, as the child was "composed," "calmly and readily answered questions," "pointed to New Zealand on a globe, and indicated her understanding of the difference between truth and falsehood and of her obligation to tell the truth."[21] The court found no evidence of any undue influence, and although the child's objections to a return were not totally conclusive, they did influence the court's ultimate decision not to order a return.

---

19. Blondin v. Dubois, 238 F.3d 153 (2d Cir. 2001).
20. *Duquette*, 259 N.J. Super. 613 A.2d 486.
21. *Acree*, 250 F. Supp. 2d 876.

A district court in Florida held that a nine-year-old boy had attained age/maturity at which it was appropriate to take into account his objections to returning to Argentina.[22] However, the court exercised its discretion to return child nonetheless, because "his memories of Argentina are those of a six year old, he has been in the virtually exclusive custody of his mother in the United States since his removal from Argentina, and his mother has articulated a desire not to return to Argentina since almost the beginning of her arrival" in the United States. A state court in California found that an eight-year-old boy was sufficiently mature for purposes of the exception, based on the fact that he was forthright and unequivocal in his responses to questions and demonstrated a sufficient degree of maturity to raise an objection.[23]

But a nine-year-old boy and ten-year-old boy were not of sufficient age and maturity because although they were "polite, smart boys," they did not seem "to be especially sophisticated or to have reached a maturity beyond their years."[24] And a seven-year-old girl was determined to be "not of sufficient age and maturity to warrant the application of the exception."[25]

Nor is there a specific age that will definitively cause a court to take into account a child's objections. This is consistent with the statement in the Perez-Vera Report that the drafters intended that courts should determine the merits of a child's objections on a case-by-case basis due to the complexities involved in determining whether a child's objections should be duly considered.

However, in one federal case in Puerto Rico, the Magistrate Judge overruled the objections of an otherwise mature 13-year-old, and ordered a return over these objections without an extended discussion explaining the reasoning other than stating that:

> The fact that the child prefers to remain in Puerto Rico, because he has good grades, has friends and enjoys sport activities and outings, is not enough for this Court to disregard the narrowness of the age and maturity exception to the Convention's rule of mandatory return.[26]

---

22. Mendez Lynch v. Mendez Lynch, 220 F. Supp. 2d 1347 (M.D. Fla. 2002).
23. Escobar v. Flores, 183 Cal. App. 4th 737, 107 Cal. Rptr. 3d 596 (Cal. App. 3 Dist. 2010).
24. Hirst v. Tiberghien, 947 F. Supp. 2d 578, 598 (D.S.C. 2013).
25. Rivas v. Segovia, 2010 WL 5394778, at *6 (W.D. Ark. 2010).
26. Gonzalez Locicero v. Nazor Lurashi, 321 F. Supp. 2d 295 (D. Puerto Rico 2004).

§ 7.04.2 Maturity

Maturity is also determined on a case-by-case basis. It is generally tied in with and connected to the age of the child and the clarity, strength, and nature of the child's objections.

Cases that have determined this issue indicate the type of factors that courts consider to be significant:

- In *Simcox*,[27] the Sixth Circuit affirmed a district court finding that a child was not sufficiently mature because he was "preoccupied, disinterested and detached; in short, a typical eight year old boy who strongly desired to be anywhere but in a Judge's chambers answering questions."
- In *Dalsgaard*,[28] the court supported its finding of insufficient maturity by stating that, although the child was "a vibrant, cheerful, and delightful guest in chambers," she had little to say about her parents' dispute and expressed a preference to remain in the United States only in head nods and one-word sentences. The court found that "Her reticent and laconic responses (she had plenty to say about other matters) leave the depth and sophistication of her conviction, and the maturity behind her conviction, highly doubtful."
- In *Khalip*,[29] the court stated that it found that the children's stated reasons and responses revealed that they were not mature enough to understand the full scope of the situation in order to prevent being returned.
- By contrast, in *Carnelli*,[30] the court concluded that the child, who was 14, was sufficiently mature because he had expressed his wishes to stay with his father in a cogent and well-reasoned manner; he had explained that he enjoyed meaningful and close relationships with many family members also living in or near his father's home; he had testified that he was happy with his schooling, where he enjoyed friendships; he had achieved good grades; he had contrasted his prior itinerant and somewhat lonely previous lifestyle in Argentina; and he had testified that while he spoke a little Spanish, he was not fluent in the language.

27. Simcox v. Simcox, 511 F.3d 594 (6th Cir. 2007).
28. Dalsgaard v. Montoya, 2011 WL 5037223 (M.D. Fla. 2011).
29. Khalip v. Khalip, 2011 WL 2490983 (E.D. Mich. 2011).
30. Carnelli v. Paz, 2011 WL 1983360 (D.N.J. 2011).

- In *In re D.A.*,[31] the court solicited counsel to provide proposed questions and then interviewed the child in the jury room, with all counsel present but discretely out of the child's sight. The court concluded that the child was "an unusually poised and mature adolescent, who is comfortable with adults, and engaged readily and openly with the Court"; that he was "perceptive, bright, forthright, rational, friendly, credible, and serious about his education; and that his "answers and demeanor evinced clarity about his wishes and the reasons for them, and complete awareness of the consequences of the court proceeding."
- Finally, in *Etienne*,[32] the court concluded, after interviewing the child in chambers with counsel present, that she had displayed a thorough understanding of the purpose of the interview; was articulate and specific in her answers; asked for clarification when she did not understand a question; added specificity to her answers when asked to do so; discussed at length her life in Mexico and her life in the United States with respect to her friends, school, church, and family; and was clear in her preference for remaining in the United States and in her objection to being returned to Mexico.

§ 7.05 EXPERT EVIDENCE

Some courts have permitted and relied on expert testimony as to the issue of a child's maturity. Indeed, in some cases, the judges themselves have required such testimony. Other courts have either precluded such testimony or have given little or no weight to it.

In *Haimdas*,[33] the court permitted a forensic psychologist who was licensed as a psychologist in the District of Columbia, Maryland, Pennsylvania, and Virginia to evaluate the children and offer an expert opinion on their maturity levels. However, the judge barred the expert testimony of a marriage and family therapist who was licensed to practice as such in the states of Florida, Georgia, and North Carolina, because he had never been licensed to practice psychology anywhere.

Then, having allowed the forensic psychologist to testify, the judge ultimately stated that he gave "no weight" to such evidence because the "expert" opinions regarding the potentially distorting effects of the

31. *In re* D.A., 2015 WL 2344079 (E.D.N.Y. 2015).
32. Etienne v. Zuniga, 2010 WL 2262341 (W.D. Wash. 2010).
33. Haimdas v. Haimdas, 2010 WL 652823 (E.D.N.Y. 2010).

parents' protracted custody battle, parental alienation, and the ping-pong lifestyle that the children had experienced, as well as their notable verbal abilities and overall intelligence, "essentially confirmed the obvious." Moreover, the expert's opinions as to the children's answers to test and interview questions "veered into credibility-assessment territory" and the credibility and weight of testimony were questions to be decided exclusively by the court.

On the other hand, in *Andreopoulos*,[34] the court relied in part on the testimony of a therapist, who was qualified as an expert in providing psychotherapy and treating and evaluating children, that met with the child individually for several hours over three different sessions and concluded that the child demonstrated an age-appropriate maturity level. It should be noted, however, that the judge relied also on the fact that the child testified twice during the proceedings, and that the judge also spoke with him once in chambers.

In *Garcia*,[35] the court's conclusion that the children were insufficiently mature was based in significant part on the expert testimony of a court-appointed psychologist.

Finally, in *Ostevoll*,[36] the court relied on expert testimony that the children in question were sufficiently mature.

§ 7.06 GUARDIAN AD LITEM

In several cases in which there has been an issue concerning the age, maturity, and opinions of the child, courts have appointed guardians ad litem to assist in the process. The appointee may be a lawyer, but in some cases has been a psychologist.

In a federal case in Texas,[37] the Fifth Circuit approved of the district court's procedure in interviewing the child during which time she was represented by an attorney ad litem.

In Colorado, a district court treated the respondent's pro se "request for assistance" as a motion to appoint a guardian ad litem.[38] The court granted the motion and directed the guardian to investigate all aspects of the social background of each of the children, to investigate their wishes and their respective maturity levels (to the extent that those issues related to exceptions within ICARA) and to make appropriate recommendations

---

34. Andreopoulos v. Nickolaos Koutroulos, 2009 WL 1850928 (D. Colo. 2009).
35. Garcia v. Angarita, 440 F. Supp. 2d 1364 (S.D. Fla. 2006).
36. Ostevoll v. Ostevoll, 2000 WL 1611123 (S.D. Ohio 2000).
37. *Batista*, 512 Fed. Appx. 403.
38. Lieberman v. Tabachnik, 2007 WL 4548570 (D. Colo. 2007).

on these points. The court then took significant account of the guardian ad litem's report, which concluded that he had concern as to whether the children's wishes were grounded in independence and not subject to influence by either parent.

In a federal case in Rhode Island, the court appointed a "guardian ad litem and attorney" to prepare a report on the relevant issues, which included a determination of the wishes of the children and their age and maturity.[39]

Likewise, a guardian ad litem was appointed in a district court case in Massachusetts to assess the children's degree of maturity and to determine their wishes.[40]

§ 7.07 CLARITY AND STRENGTH OF OPINION

Case law establishes that it is entirely insufficient for a child to express a mere preference for one country or another.[41] The Fifth Circuit has stated that,

> There is a substantive difference between preferring to live in one of two countries—when living in either country would be acceptable—and affirmatively objecting to returning to one country—when living in that country would be unacceptable. Only an objection is sufficient to trump the Convention's strong presumption in favor of return.[42]

The child must clearly express an objection to being returned to the former habitual residence.

There is a fundamental distinction between the need in a Hague case for a child's objections to be expressed with strength and clarity, as compared to the relevance of a child's wishes, as expressed in a custody case.[43]

- In *Dubikovskyy*,[44] the court overturned a district court decision that had held that the child objected to being returned to Switzerland. The Eighth Circuit read the transcript of the trial judge's interviews with the child and concluded that the child, whose native language was not English, had stated that she

39. Kufner v. Kufner, 480 F. Supp. 2d 41 (D.R.I. 2007), *aff'd,* 519 F.3d 33 (1st Cir. 2008); Carlson v. Carlson, 651 F. Supp. 3d 516 (D.R.I. 2023).

40. McManus v. McManus, 354 F. Supp. 2d 62 (D. Mass. 2005).

41. *Tsui*, 499 F.3d 279.

42. Rodriguez v. Yanez, 817 F.3d 466, 477 (5th Cir. 2016).

43. Morrison v. Dietz, 2008 WL 4280030 (W.D. La. 2008).

44. Dubikovskyy v. Goun, 54 F.4th 1042 (8th Cir. 2022).

"objected" to being returned but in fact appeared merely to be expressing preferences. The court stated, "If given two choices, country A and country B, an objection to living in A will almost always (although not invariably) indicate a preference for living in B. But a preference to live in B does not necessarily indicate an objection to living in A. In this case, M.D.'s testimony fails to show by a preponderance of the evidence that she 'objected' to returning to Switzerland. Rather, when asked why she would be 'unhappy,' or 'dissatisfied' if she had to go back to Switzerland, M.D. consistently responded with reasons why she preferred to stay in Missouri."[45]

- In *Haimdas*,[46] the court found that an older child had a strong commitment to staying with his younger brother. The two children had long been "the only constant presence in one another's lives" and they operated "as a team." Although the older child expressed a preference to remain in the United States, the court determined that that preference would "evaporate" if his brother were returned to England. Accordingly, the court found that his objection to return to England was not sufficiently strong.
- In *Falk*,[47] the child stated that she wanted to stay in Maine and expressed strong negative feelings about her German school. Nonetheless, her expression of a mere preference to remain in the respondent's country was not enough to disregard the narrowness of the age and maturity exception to the Convention's rule of mandatory return.
- In *Trudrung*,[48] the child indicated more of a preference to remain in the United States rather than an objection to being returned to Germany. During an in camera examination, the child testified several times that he would "prefer" to stay here but expressed no strong objection to returning to Germany. Accordingly, the exception was found to not have been established.
- In *Alcala*,[49] the child expressed an unequivocal desire to remain in the United States. But his reasons were deemed to be mere preferences for one parent or one lifestyle over another. The court stated that the reasons for wanting to remain in the United

45. *Id.* at 1049.
46. Haimdas v. Haimdas, 720 F. Supp. 2d 183 (E.D.N.Y. 2010).
47. Falk v. Sinclair, 692 F. Supp. 2d 147 (D. Me. 2010).
48. Trudrung v. Trudrung, 686 F. Supp. 2d 570 (M.D.N.C. 2010).
49. Alcala v. Hernandez, 2015 WL 4429425 (D.S.C. 2015), *aff'd*, 826 F.3d 161 (4th Cir. 2016).

States must be "born of rational comparison" between the child's life in the new country as compared to the habitual residence. Here however the child had merely identified such factors as that his father in Mexico had not played with him or helped him; that he had no toys in Mexico; that he had to sleep in a bed with his grandmother; and that he had a room, friends, and by contrast he had his own toys in the United States.

Moreover, there is some authority in support of the proposition that the views of a child who has been away from the habitual residence for a substantial period of time should be discounted because the child will obviously not usually want to be uprooted again.

- In *Yang*,[50] the Third Circuit affirmed a decision to override a child's wish to remain in the United States because her lengthy stay had apparently contributed greatly to her positive feelings for Pittsburgh and her surroundings.
- In *Gatica*,[51] the court upheld a Magistrate Judge's decision to give little weight to a child's views because the child had already been in her mother's exclusive custody for over 18 months and "would thus naturally prefer to remain in the United States instead of moving once again and changing her social environment."
- In *Khalip*,[52] the court likewise stated in support of its decision denying the exception that, "as one would expect from children of this age, each articulated a natural desire to stay with their mother in an environment that they have become accustomed to and in which they are now comfortable."

However, the court in *Castillo* used the fact that the child had been away from the habitual residence for a long time to reach the converse result, since it would be natural for a child to want to stay in the place where she had become well established and such wishes should be upheld.[53]

§ 7.08 UNDUE INFLUENCE

If a child's views are the apparent result of coaching or undue influence by a parent, a court will generally discount the child's objection entirely.

---

50. *Tsui*, 499 F.3d 279.
51. Gatica v. Martinez, 2011 WL 2110291 (S.D. Fla. 2011).
52. *Khalip*, 2011 WL 2490983.
53. *Castillo*, 597 F. Supp. 2d 432.

In a Hague proceeding, in which emotions usually run high, the abducting parent will often both limit the child's communication with the left-behind parent and attempt to coach the child to express ideas to the court that are too sophisticated to come from a child's tender mind. Conversely, a left-behind parent might be able to speak to the child by telephone or the Internet and might try to influence the child in these communications.

In order to ascertain whether a child is expressing mature and independent opinions, or coached and pressured opinions, judges may conduct preliminary in-camera interviews with the child. This is generally appropriate since judges have a great deal of discretion when scrutinizing a 13(b) defense under a Hague case. In many cases, judges have asserted that it is best to isolate the child alone in a comfortable environment in order to best hear the child's objections and opinions. Alternatively, the judge will invite counsel into the interview with the child.

Often the court will appoint a guardian ad litem, independent counsel, or a court-appointed psychiatrist to provide a report on the child's maturity level and on whether there has been any undue influence from either parent. It is rare to place a child on the stand, and far more frequent for the judge to rely in his or her own interview of the child and a report from an appointed psychologist or guardian ad litem in making the appropriate determinations as to the child's testimony and objections.

The court will also consider reports offered by experts hired by petitioner or respondent.

This testimony of the child might well be insufficient to establish the necessary level of maturity and the independence of the child's views. A respondent should sometimes be urged to hire an expert to testify on these issues. Although the burden of proof is merely at the level of the preponderance of the evidence, it remains a steep hurdle to clear to effectively persuade a judge that a child's objections should be determinative of the ultimate issue. Thus, in *Haimdas*,[54] where the judge interviewed the children in camera, and the only expert report was offered by the petitioner, the court "easily found" that the respondent did not prove by a preponderance that the children were sufficiently mature for the court to take their views into account.

However, expert reports on this specific issue tread a fine line between opining on a child's level of maturity and assessing the credibility of a witness. Witnesses may not opine as to the credibility of the testimony of other witnesses at the trial. The decisions as to whose testimony to

54. *Haimdas*, 720 F. Supp. 2d 183.

credit and which permissible inferences to draw are within the province of the trier of fact.[55] Courts may well prefer not to rely upon the assertions of "hired gun" experts. In *Haimdas*, the court gave no weight to the testimony of the petitioner's expert (a psychologist) and stated that his report "essentially confirmed the obvious" and "veered into credibility-assessment territory."[56]

Other outcomes are possible. A judge might find evidence of parental influence without classifying it as "undue." Or a court might rule that the child's views should be heard on the record not only because the child has reached both an age and a degree of maturity, but also because of the tremendous amount of time consecutively spent with one parent (the abductor), the child's views hence have been molded by the wrongful abduction. Thus, the court is likely to find in this situation that the child's opinions have been tainted and are therefore unduly influenced and not worthy of ultimate consideration.

In one case, the court found that evidence from the child's adult sibling concerning the child was helpful. The judge credited such testimony that, since moving to the United States, her brother was "finally happy and he's where he wants to be with people that love him and people he wants to be around"; whereas he had been "miserable" in Greece.[57]

The case law establishes only that there is a wide range of potential results.

- The *Robinson* case in Colorado illustrates the fact that it is improper for a parent to unduly influence the child and doing so will generally bar any application of the child's objection exception.[58] Children aged six and ten were wrongfully taken by their mother to Colorado from their habitual residence in England. The six-year-old was deemed to be too young to have her views heard by the court, but the ten-year-old was interviewed in-camera by the judge and a letter that he wrote to the judge was admitted into evidence. The opinion noted that the Department of State's Legal Analysis of the Convention emphasized that any use of the child's objection was discretionary because of "the potential for brain washing" of the child by the alleged abductor.

55. U.S. v. Scop, 846 F.2d 135 (2d Cir. 1988); Chacko v. DynAir Svcs., Inc., 272 Fed. Appx. 111 (2d Cir. 2008).

56. *Haimdas*, 720 F. Supp. 2d 183.

57. *In re* D.A., 2015 WL 2344079 (E.D.N.Y. 2015).

58. *In re* Robinson, 983 F. Supp. 1339, 1343–44 (D. Colo. 1997).

The judge acknowledged that it is not easy to clearly identify when an influence becomes undue and specifically noted that "there will always be some influence . . . and it is unrealistic, indeed inhuman to expect a caring parent not to influence the child's preference."[59] Nonetheless, the court ruled that the parental pressure on the child was undue, based largely on the fact that the child reported that his counselor had given him a "few ideas" for his letter to the judge, along the lines of "I like it here and I'm settled in, yeah." The judge noted the importance of the specific term "settled" in Hague cases and concluded that the ten-year-old had been unduly influenced by his mother and his counselor.

- In *Lieberman*,[60] the court appointed a guardian ad litem to investigate the wishes of the children (who were 14, 12, and 10 years old) and their respective maturity levels to the extent that these issues related to exceptions within ICARA and make appropriate recommendations. The guardian reported that the children had been exposed to a "great deal of information and statements about their father that has caused them to turn against him" and recommended that the children be returned to Mexico. The judge allowed the two older children to testify in court after an in-camera meeting with all three children. As a result of their testimony, the judge concluded that, although the children had demonstrated composure in dealing with a difficult situation and appeared to be articulate, he could not be sure that the opinions they expressed were those of the children themselves. Accordingly, he refused to hold that the exception had been established. The key factor was that each child gave an identical response—that "I know because I lived it"—when asked whether the respondent had a role in forming their opinions. The court felt that the children could not have all given the same exact response to the same exact question unless they had been coached, to some degree.
- The *Kofler*[61] case demonstrates that even if a degree of influence on the children has been found, it does not necessarily rise to the level sufficient to preclude a judge from accepting their opinions. The children were 11, 13, and 15 at the time of trial. The judge met with them in chambers, but in the presence of counsel for both sides. The two older children expressed some stress at the

59. *Id.* at 1343.
60. *In re* Lieberman, 625 F. Supp. 2d 1109, 1114 (D. Colo. 2008).
61. Kofler v. Kofler, 2007 WL 2081712 (W.D. Ark. July 18, 2007).

breakup of their parent's marriage, and both stated a desire to stay with their mother in the United States. The youngest child was silent as to any opinion on the pending litigation during this initial meeting. The court subsequently received letters written by all three children, apparently at the behest of their mother. The letters contained telling passages, such as: "I do not want to go back to Germany. I do not want you to send me back," "We tried many years in Germany, giving him chance after chance. Why would I want to live there anymore? It's great here and I want to stay here in America. I have dreams here that I didn't have in Germany" and "Just to make it clear . . . I want to stay here with my mom."

The petitioner vehemently argued that the letters had been penned with coaching from respondent. The judge then ordered and conducted a meeting with each child in chambers, again in the presence of counsel. The meetings revealed that the children were sincere as to the content of their letters and that it had been their own decision to write to the court, albeit, with their mother's knowledge and some coaxing as to what to put in the letters if they wished to stay in the United States. The judge found all of the children to be of sufficient age and maturity to have their objections and wishes considered, and found that although the children had been "coached" by the mother to some degree, the collective objections to being returned were not a distinct product of undue influence. Accordingly, the court refused to order the children's return.

- The *Giampaolo* case[62] establishes that a court may refuse to give any weight to a mature child's testimony simply because the child has spent so much time with the taking parent and away from the left-behind parent that it would be inappropriate to do so. The mother wrongfully removed the child from Argentina to the United States and then lived with the child for the next two years in various locations in the U.S., without disclosing her location to the left-behind father and with only sporadic communication with him. The court met the child, then aged ten, in chambers with counsel for both sides present and determined that she was "articulate, intelligent, and mature." The child convinced the court that she wanted to stay in the United States. She explicitly mentioned that she would have better opportunities in the United

62. Giampaolo v. Ernetta, 390 F. Supp. 2d. 1269, 1275 (N.D. Ga. 2004).

States, that she enjoyed her school and her friends, that she very much liked her mother's new husband, and that she thought that her father only wanted her return to make her mother "mad and sad." Nonetheless, the court ruled that the child's objection was due to her being accustomed to her new life, and that, viewing the testimony "in its entirety," the child had simply internalized mother's preference for her to remain here and was influenced by the mother over the past two years in coming to this point. Consequently, the child was ordered to be returned to Argentina.

The result may seem harsh because the objecting child was both old enough and mature enough to have her views heard. The judge's decision was not expressly based on any specific testimony elicited from the child and was not based on an expert's opinion. It simply was the fact that the mere passage of time and the amount of time spent with the abducting parent had presumably influenced the child's objection to the point where her views could not be determinative in the case. A fundamental policy of the Convention is not to reward concealment and abduction. Here the abducting mother went to great lengths to conceal her location and substantial efforts to prevent the left-behind father from communicating with his daughter.

- In *Gonzalez*,[63] the court interviewed a 13-year-old child alone in chambers and determined that he was "well spoken and assertive in his answers when he was asked whether he wanted to return to Argentina and he answered he wanted to stay with respondent in Puerto Rico" and found that "at the age of 13, the child has attained an age and degree of maturity at which it is appropriate to take account of his views." Nonetheless, the court refused to rule that the child's objections were dispositive, for two reasons. First, the child conceded that his father had prompted him to write a letter to his mother saying that he did not want to return to Argentina. Second, the court felt that the child's views were too heavily influenced by his father due to the 16 months of exclusive custody that his father had before the case went to trial. However, unlike in *Giampaolo*, the respondent had made no efforts to conceal the child.
- In *In re D.A.*,[64] the court interviewed the child in the jury room and found that, although he was clearly close to and influenced

63. *Gonzalez Locicero*, 321 F. Supp. 2d 295.
64. *In re* D.A., 2015 WL 2344079 (E.D.N.Y. 2015).

to an extent by his mother, he harbored disappointment and some resentment toward his father. Nonetheless the court decided that his relationship with and feelings toward his parents had not clouded his judgment about his own situation or his wishes about his place of residence. Indeed, his reasons for wanting to remain in the United States were rational and sincere, and he seemed genuinely happy about living in the United States. The court noted that "all children are influenced to some degree by their parents" but that even though he confirmed that he felt that he "had to be strong" for his mother, that simply meant comforting her as much as he could so that she would feel better and not be sad. The court found that there was no hint that he felt that he had to lie about, or overstate, his desire to remain in the United States in order to "be strong" for his mother.

- Finally, in *Leites*,[65] the court adhered to a 13-year-old child's objections and refused to order her return after determining that she was mature enough to have her objections heard because she felt that she had been negatively affected by her parents' bickering in Argentina, and that her home in the United States would potentially provide her with a better opportunity to succeed in the future. Notably, the court determined that the child had developed that opinion before she had come to the United States, and hence, that it was not the product of undue influence.

§ 7.09 DISCRETION

Even if the mature child's objection is established, the Convention nonetheless still affords the court discretion to order the child's return. The Convention does not provide any limitation on what appears to be an unfettered discretion. Article 13 merely states that courts "may also refuse to order the return of the child" if "the child objects to being returned and has attained an age and degree of maturity at which it is appropriate to take account of its views."

The case law on the exercise of the discretion focuses on the issue of whether a return would further the purposes of the Convention. Thus the Tenth Circuit has stated that even if the respondent meets his or her burden of proving the affirmative defense, the court retains the discretion to order the return of the child "if it would further the aim of the Convention

65. Leites v. Mendiburu, 2008 WL 114954, at 6 (M.D. Fla. Jan. 9, 2008).

which is to provide for the return of a wrongfully removed child."[66] In this regard, courts have frequently taken the position that the "preference for repatriation" and the "narrow compass of the exceptions" are necessary for the Convention to serve its purpose to preserve the pre-abduction status quo and deter parents from crossing international boundaries in search of a more sympathetic court.[67]

In *Mendez Lynch*,[68] the older child, but not his younger brother, had attained an age and degree of maturity to make it appropriate to take his views into account. The court also found that the older child objected to being returned to Argentina. However, the court stated that the child's memories of Argentina were three years old and had likely resulted from the fact that he had lived with his mother throughout that time and that she had stated that she did not wish to return there. Consequently, the court found that return of the child to Argentina would further the aims of the Hague Convention, and it therefore exercised its discretion to so order despite the child's clear view.

In *Yang*,[69] the Third Circuit upheld the lower court's finding that the child was insufficiently mature but also agreed that, in any event, this was not an appropriate case in which to apply the exception, because the attachment that the child had to Pittsburgh and her family there had been created by virtue of the father's wrongful retention after a planned three-week visit. It was not during that three-week period that the child had grown attached to her family and life in Pittsburgh. Rather, it was the passage of time during the subsequent years of wrongful retention and litigation of the case that created her desire to remain in Pittsburgh. If the exception were applied in such circumstances, it would encourage parents to wrongfully retain a child for as long as possible. A lengthy wrongful retention could enable the child to become comfortable in his or her new surroundings, which would likely create a desire to remain in the new home. The application of the exception would reward the father for violating the mother's custody rights and defeat the purposes of the Convention.

Similarly, in *Garcia*,[70] an Illinois district court declined to apply the exception since the child's objections were based almost entirely on his

66. *De Silva*, 481 F.3d 1279.

67. Friedrich v. Friedrich, 983 F.2d 1396 (6th Cir. 1993); *In re* Kim, 404 F. Supp. 2d 495 (S.D.N.Y. 2005).

68. *Mendez Lynch*, 220 F. Supp. 2d 1347.

69. Tsai-Yi Yang v. Fu-Chiang Tsui, 499 F.3d 259 (3d Cir. 2007).

70. Garcia v. Pinelo, 2015 WL 4910654 (N.D. Ill. 2015).

concern about his or his mother's ability to travel to and from Mexico. It stated that,

> The crucial point on this issue is this: if [respondent] wrongfully retained [the child] in the United States, then the travel restriction that is the basis for [the child's] objection was created by that wrongful retention and [respondent's] own conduct in violating the immigration law of the United States.

To allow the child's wrongful retention and the respondent's immigration status to create the circumstances that led to the child's objections would "reward [respondent] for violating [petitioner's] custody rights, and defeat the purposes of the Convention."[71]

In sharp contrast, the English House of Lords took a diametrically opposite approach in a case in 2007.[72] Although the lower courts had determined that the children were sufficiently mature and clearly objected to being returned, they had nevertheless applied the discretion to return the children because the policy of the Convention was that international child abduction should not be rewarded absent except in exceptional cases. The House of Lords overruled those decisions. It held that they had been wrong to focus so much on the "comparative moral blameworthiness" of the parents and the policies of the Convention. The Convention allowed a court not to return children if the various elements of the exceptions were satisfied and a further gloss that would further limit the application of the exceptions should not normally apply. It held that there should have been more of a "child-centric" analysis in considering the discretion and less of a focus on the policies of the Convention. Specifically,

> once the discretion comes into play, the court may have to consider the nature and strength of the child's objections, the extent to which they are "authentically (his) own" or the product of influence of the abducting parent, the extent to which they coincide or are at odds with other considerations which are relevant to . . . welfare, as well as general Convention considerations. . . . The older the child, the greater the weight that (his) objections are likely to carry. But that is far from saying that the child's objections should only prevail in the most exceptional circumstances.

71. *Id.* at 784.
72. *In re* M. (Children) (Abduction: Rights of Custody) [2007] UKHL 55.

In *Laguna*,[73] the court ruled that because there was nothing in the request that would suggest that the respondent had come to the United States in search of a jurisdictional home court advantage, it would not be appropriate for the court to exercise the discretion to return the child once it upheld the objection of a mature child exception.

73. *Laguna*, 2008 WL 1986253 (E.D.N.Y. 2008).

Grave Risk of Harm

8

§ 8.01 INTRODUCTION

Article 13(b) of the Convention provides a discretionary exception to the obligation to order the return of a wrongfully removed or retained child if the respondent can establish that the child would face a grave risk of physical or psychological harm or an otherwise intolerable situation upon being returned. The provision reads in full as follows:

> Notwithstanding the provisions of the preceding Article, the judicial or administrative authority of the requested State is not bound to order the return of the child if the person, institution, or other body which opposes its return establishes that . . .
>
> (b) there is a grave risk that his or her return would expose the child to physical or psychological harm or otherwise would place the child in an intolerable situation. . . .
>
> In considering the circumstances referred to in this Article, the judicial and administrative authorities shall take into account the information relating to the social background of the child provided by the Central Authority or other competent authority of the child's habitual residence.

Thus, in some circumstances, it may be possible to show that returning a child to the habitual residence would constitute a "grave risk" of harm that overrides any harm that the child may have experienced from the abduction alone. This would then authorize a court to decline to return the child.

The Perez-Vera Report explains that the grave risk exception is based on the recognition that the interest of the child in not being removed from the habitual residence without sufficient guarantees of its stability in the new environment should give way to the primary interest of any person in not being exposed to physical or psychological danger or being placed in an intolerable situation.[1]

The "grave risk" exception is one of the most heavily litigated provisions in the Convention. There are several reasons for this:

- First, there is there a lack of clarity as to what exactly constitutes a grave risk of harm or intolerable situation beyond the general consensus that the "grave risk" threshold is high. The language in Article 13(b) is loose and the literal meanings of the key terms are extremely broad.
- Second, courts in the U.S.—and indeed among all contracting nations—have not applied the provision uniformly.
- Third, all grave risk cases are extremely fact sensitive.
- Fourth, application of the exception is discretionary. Even if a respondent proves by clear and convincing evidence that return would subject a child to a grave risk of harm or an otherwise intolerable situation, the court is still permitted to grant a petitioner's application for return. Neither the Convention nor ICARA provides any specific guidelines as to the issues to be considered in applying the discretion.
- Fifth, there is considerable uncertainty as to the appropriateness of undertakings as a means of ensuring that any risks a child will face upon return are adequately mitigated by conditions placed on the return order.

§ 8.02 THE PEREZ-VERA REPORT

The Perez-Vera Report contains a substantial discussion of the history and purpose of the "grave risk" exception. It explains that

> the interest of the child in not being removed from its habitual residence . . . gives way before the primary interest of any person in not being exposed to physical or psychological danger or being placed in an intolerable situation.[2]

1. Perez-Vera Report, para. 29.
2. *Id.*, para. 34.

The Report further states that to view the defenses more broadly would frustrate the core purpose of the Hague Convention, which is to preserve the status quo and deter parents from seeking custody of their child through, in effect, forum shopping.[3]

Indeed, the Report insists[4] that:

- It would seem necessary to underline the fact that the three types of exception to the rule concerning the return of the child must be applied only so far as they go and no further. This implies above all that they are to be interpreted in a restrictive fashion if the Convention is not to become a dead letter.
- In fact, the Convention as a whole rests upon the unanimous rejection of this phenomenon of illegal child removals and upon the conviction that the best way to combat them at an international level is to refuse to grant them legal recognition.
- The practical application of this principle requires that the signatory States be convinced that they belong, despite their differences, to the same legal community within which the authorities of each State acknowledge that the authorities of one of them—those of the child's habitual residence—are in principle best placed to decide upon questions of custody and access.
- As a result, a systematic invocation of the said exceptions, substituting the forum chosen by the abductor for that of the child's residence, would lead to the collapse of the whole structure of the Convention by depriving it of the spirit of mutual confidence which is its inspiration.

§ 8.03 STATE DEPARTMENT ANALYSIS

The Text and Legal Analysis of the Convention written by the U.S. Department of State in 1985 to assist the Senate in considering whether to ratify the Convention, provides further analysis.[5]

It asserts that wrongfully removed children are "deprived of the stable relationships which the Convention is designed promptly to restore" and that the "overriding objective" of the Convention is "to spare children

3. *Id.*
4. *Id.*
5. Text and Legal Analysis, at 10494.

the detrimental emotional effects associated with transnational parental kidnapping."[6]

It states that,

> This provision was not intended to be used by defendants as a vehicle to litigate (or relitigate) the child's best interests. Only evidence directly establishing the existence of a grave risk that would expose the child to physical or emotional harm or otherwise place the child in an intolerable situation is material to the court's determination. The person opposing the child's return must show that the risk to the child is grave, not merely serious.[7]

It states further that Article 13(b) is to be "narrowly construed"[8] because in drafting Articles 13 and 20, the representatives of countries participating in negotiations on the Convention were aware that any exceptions had to be drawn "very narrowly lest their application undermine the express purposes of the Convention—to effect the prompt return of abducted children."[9]

This Text and Legal Analysis is frequently cited in support of a narrow interpretation of the grave risk exception.[10]

§ 8.04 GUIDE TO GOOD PRACTICE

In addition, official publications may be useful sources of information and guidance about the operation and interpretation of the Convention. The Conference publishes *Guides to Good Practice*, which may provide authoritative assistance in the interpretation of the provisions of the treaty. Indeed, the concurring judges in the Supreme Court's *Chafin* case found that to be the case,[11] as have courts in other cases.[12]

The *Guide* is the *Guide to Good Practice Child Abduction Convention: Part VI—Article 13(1)(b)*. It was prepared by judges, government officials (e.g., Central Authority personnel), academic/cross-disciplinary experts, and private practitioners from many jurisdictions around the world and published in early 2020 by the Hague Conference. It is another

6. *Id.*
7. *Id.*
8. *Id.*
9. *Id.*
10. *E.g.*, Baxter v. Baxter, 423 F.3d 363, 373 (3d Cir. 2005).
11. Chafin v. Chafin, 133 S. Ct. 1017, 1030 (concurring opinions) (U.S. 2013).
12. *See, e.g.*, Madrigal v. Tellez, 848 F.3d 669, n.3 (5th Cir. 2017); Gil-Leyva v. Leslie, 780 Fed. Appx. 580, 598 (10th Cir. 2019).

source of highly authoritative guidance concerning the grave risk of harm exception. Practitioners should consult the *Guide* in cases of uncertainty as to the applicability of the exception and cite it as appropriate.[13]

§ 8.05 THE BURDEN OF PROOF

ICARA provides that a respondent asserting the grave risk of harm exception has the burden of establishing by "clear and convincing evidence" that Article 13(b) applies.[14] The burden of proof for this exception is higher than for all but one of the other exceptions available under the Convention, which need be established by a mere "preponderance of the evidence."[15]

However, while a respondent must establish the Article 13(b) exception by clear and convincing evidence, "subsidiary facts" that support a finding of grave risk "need only be established by a preponderance of the evidence."

Thus, in *Danaipour v. McLarey*,[16] a district court stated that there "may be twenty facts, each proved by a preponderance of the evidence, that in the aggregate create clear and convincing evidence." There, the court found that such evidence constituted clear and convincing evidence that the petitioning father had sexually abused one of the two children that his wife had taken to the United States. Finding that a return would subject the children to grave psychological harm, the court ruled that the 13(b) exception applied. In affirming that judgment, the First Circuit held that the district court had properly considered "as a subsidiary finding in support of its grave risk conclusion" that the father was not apparently willing to follow a psychologist's recommendation that he apologize to his daughter as a contribution to her healing process.[17] Other courts have applied a similar evidentiary standard.[18]

As a result of the high burden of proof, it is generally incumbent on a respondent who alleges that there has been a history of physical or sexual abuse to provide corroboration of the events when the petitioner denies them. Thus, in *Mauvais*, the First Circuit found that there was competing "he said, she said" testimony from both parties, with little independent evidence corroborating the respondent's testimony, and no

13. *E.g.*, Gil-Leyva v. Leslie, 780 F. App'x 580, 598 (10th Cir. 2019).
14. 22 U.S.C. § 9003(e)(2)(A).
15. *Id.* § 9003(e)(2)(B).
16. Danaipour v. McLarey, 386 F.3d 289 (1st Cir. 2004).
17. *Id.* at 301.
18. *See, e.g.*, Elyashiv v. Elyashiv, 353 F. Supp. 2d 394 (E.D.N.Y. 2005).

clear acceptance by the district court of the respondent's narrative over the petitioner's. Accordingly, it upheld the district court's finding that the respondent had failed to meet her burden of proof.[19]

On the other hand, the high burden of proof on a respondent does not require that proof of past sexual abuse rise to "a reasonable degree of medical certainty."[20]

§ 8.06 THE DISTINCTION BETWEEN HAGUE CASES AND CUSTODY CASES: AVOIDING A "BEST INTERESTS" ANALYSIS

Both the Convention and ICARA draw a sharp line between custody proceedings and Hague proceedings. The purpose of the Convention is to return abducted children to their habitual residence so that the courts there can decide what is in the children's best interests. The Convention is somewhat akin to a jurisdiction-selection treaty and Hague proceedings are not the forum in which to litigate or relitigate the substantive aspects of a custody case.[21] ICARA expressly provides, "The Convention and this chapter empower courts in the United States to determine only rights under the Convention and not the merits of any underlying child custody claims."[22] Thus:

- In *Abbott*,[23] the Supreme Court stated that the Convention "is based on the principle that the best interests of the child are well served when decisions regarding custody rights are made in the country of habitual residence" and that ordering a return remedy "does not alter the existing allocation of custody rights,"[24] but does allow the courts of the home country to decide what is in the child's best interests. The court stated that it is the Convention's premise that courts in Contracting States will make this determination in a responsible manner.
- In *Whallon*,[25] the First Circuit stressed that, while returning the child to Mexico might lead to a separation of siblings, that kind of issue should not be heard in a Hague case. To conclude

19. Mauvais v. Herisse, 772 F.3d 6, 19 (1st Cir. 2014).
20. Yaman v. Yaman, 730 F.3d 1 (1st Cir. 2013).
21. *Text and Legal Analysis*, at 10494.
22. 22 U.S.C. § 9001(b)(4).
23. Abbott v. Abbott, 130 S. Ct. 1983 (U.S. 2010).
24. Hague Convention, Art. 19.
25. Whallon v. Lynn, 230 F.3d 450 (1st Cir. 2000).

otherwise, it asserted, would risk substituting a best interest of the child analysis for the analysis the Convention requires.

- In *Asvesta*,[26] the Ninth Circuit refused to apply the decision of a Greek court in a Hague case because that court had violated the fundamental rule that "a court considering a Hague petition should not consider matters relevant to the merits of the underlying custody dispute such as the best interests of the child, as these considerations are reserved for the courts of the child's habitual residence."
- In *Blondin*, the Second Circuit explained that courts considering a Hague petition cannot make inquiries as to who is the better parent or where the child would be happiest.[27]

Indeed, Article 16 of the Convention expressly forbids courts in the requested state from making decisions on the merits concerning custody rights unless they have determined that the child is not to be returned. Likewise, Article 19 states that a decision regarding return, standing alone, is not considered a determination on the merits of an underlying custody dispute.

For these reasons, a court in a Hague case must issue a once-only decision as to whether or not the child should be returned to its habitual residence. It may not deny a petition "without prejudice to renewal" in the future if certain factors concerning the child should change.[28] Once a determination properly applying the Convention to the facts at hand has been made, all other issues leave the realm of the treaty's domain. "The Convention is not, and cannot be, a treaty to enforce future foreign custody orders, nor to predict future harms or their dissipation."[29] Thus, the Convention

> is not concerned with establishing the person to whom custody of the child will belong at some point in the future, nor with the situations in which it may prove necessary to modify a decision . . . on the basis of facts which have subsequently changed.[30]

---

26. Asvesta v. Petroutsas, 580 F.3d 1000 (9th Cir. 2009).

27. Cuellar v. Joyce, 596 F.3d 505 (9th Cir. 2010); Nunez-Escudero v. Tice-Menley, 58 F.3d 374 (8th Cir. 1995); Blondin v. Dubois, 189 F.3d 240 (2d Cir. 1999); *In re* Koc, 181 F. Supp. 2d 136 (E.D.N.Y. 2001).

28. Ermini v. Vittori, 758 F.3d 153, 167–68 (2d Cir. 2014).

29. Perez-Vera Report, para. 36.

30. *Id.*, para. 71.

However, there is a fine line between "best interests" and "grave risk," and that line becomes even murkier when accommodating the fact that even if grave risk is established the court maintains a discretion to order the child's return. Indeed, the Perez-Vera Report expressly acknowledged that each of the terms used in Article 13(b) "is the result of a fragile compromise" reached during the original negotiation sessions.[31]

§ 8.07 EVIDENCE

In order to establish the grave risk exception, a respondent must typically show that the child was harmed in its state of habitual residence or faces a likelihood of harm if returned. The evidence that is offered at the hearing must focus on those issues and not on other matters that would be relevant to a custody determination. The State Department has stated that "[o]nly evidence directly establishing the existence of a grave risk that would expose the child to physical or emotional harm or otherwise place the child in an intolerable situation is material to the court's determination."[32]

Some state courts have been restrictive in ruling on the admissibility of evidence. For example:

- In *Tahan v. Duquette*,[33] the Superior Court of New Jersey upheld a trial court's decision to deny a petitioner the opportunity to present evidence of the child's "dreams and desires, his nightmares and fears," as well as psychological profiles, evaluations of parental fitness, and evidence concerning the lifestyle and quality of the child's relationships with family in the state of habitual residence. The court rejected the petitioner's claim that this evidence was necessary to establish the alleged psychological harm.
- In *In re Coffield*,[34] the Court of Appeals of Ohio emphasized that "testimony concerning the nature of the child's life in this country [i]s irrelevant to the determination under Article 13(b)." Hence, it upheld a trial court's decision to deny a respondent's motion for psychological testing of himself, the petitioning mother, and the child, which the respondent claimed was necessary to prove that he was "the better parent." The court's denial was based on the fact that psychological testing would not "produce evidence as to the basic environment in Australia [the habitual residence]

31. *Id.*, para. 116.
32. *Text and Legal Analysis*, at 10494.
33. Tahan v. Duquette, 259 N.J. Super. 328 (N.J. Super. A.D. 1992).
34. *In re* Coffield, 96 Ohio App. 3d 52 (Ohio Ct. App., Portage County 1994).

and the type of individuals . . . with whom [the child] would have to live." The Superior Court also upheld the trial court's refusal to allow a respondent father to submit evidence concerning the mother's lifestyle and the way she raised the child before the abduction because such information is relevant to a plenary custody proceeding, not a Hague case.

On the other hand, Article 13 provides that the court "shall take into account the information relating to the social background of the child." Accordingly, it has been held that the court may consider the environment in which the child will reside upon returning to the home country.[35] In *Nunez-Escudero*, the Eight Circuit remanded a case in which the trial court had barred such testimony, insisting that it was "too narrow and mechanical" to exclude any focus on the people involved. The circuit court upheld the view that, in order to determine whether a realistic basis exists for apprehensions concerning the child's physical safety or mental well-being, a court may evaluate the surroundings to which the child is to be sent and the basic personal qualities of those located there. However, its instruction to the lower court was hardly specific, because it merely instructed the court to consider evidence as to whether the return of the child to Mexico would subject him to a grave risk of harm or otherwise place him in an intolerable situation but not to consider evidence relevant to custody or the best interests of the child."

In *Silva*,[36] the Eleventh Circuit held that it was error for a district court to conclude that a single witness's testimony—in this case, the testimony of the mother concerning the father's abusive conduct—is necessarily insufficient to satisfy the clear-and-convincing-evidence standard to establish the grave risk defense. It was also error for the district court to conclude that the father's testimony about the mother's allegations lacked credibility and "made no sense" but to then fail to consider that as substantive evidence that corroborated the mother's testimony regarding the alleged abuse.

A parent's conduct after the time of an alleged abuse may be significant. Thus, a parent's voluntary agreement to allow the allegedly abusive parent to have shared custody of the child tended to disprove her claim that the other parent was abusive and dangerous.[37]

---

35. *Nunez-Escudero*, 58 F.3d 374.
36. Silva v. Dos Santos, 68 F.4th 1247, 1259 (11th Cir. 2023).
37. De Freitas Pinto v. Barone, 2017 WL 2779700 (S.D. Cal. 2017).

§ 8.08 EXPERT TESTIMONY

The presentation of compelling expert testimony may be important for both parties when the respondent raises the grave risk exception. Such testimony may be critical for a respondent wishing to prove a grave risk of harm, particularly in domestic violence cases when most of the evidence and witnesses are located in the child's state of habitual residence and physical injuries are no longer observable. Due to the private and often secret nature of domestic abuse, a psychologist's expert examination and opinion may be one of the few ways to prove psychological harm.

Although it may be dilatory and expensive to travel to meet with experts, a petitioner should also make every effort to present countervailing expert testimony. Failure to do so might be fatal to a Hague petition, especially if the respondent has introduced such evidence. The court's opinion in *Blondin*[38] illustrates this point. In that case, the respondent mother presented testimony by a child psychiatry and psychology expert who interviewed her and her children. The expert testified that the children were recovering from trauma arising from the petitioning father's previous physical and emotional abuse, and that they would likely suffer a harmful recurrence of traumatic stress disorder if returned to France. The petitioner's failure to put forth any contravening evidence seemed to seal his fate, with the court stating that:

> Blondin did not present any evidence as to the psychological impact that a return to France would have on the children. We are thus presented with a rare situation in which, for unexplained reasons, no evidence was presented by one party that would contradict the conclusions of an expert procured by the opposing party. Dr. Solnit's conclusions thus stand uncontroverted. They are the only evidence that we and the District Court have available as to whether repatriation to France would cause the children to suffer a recurrence of traumatic stress disorder.[39]

The court had no basis to doubt the lower court's determination that the children would suffer a grave risk of harm. Consequently, the respondent prevailed.

Although there have been cases in which a grave risk of harm was established solely on the basis of testimony by the respondent and other

38. Blondin v. Dubois, 238 F.3d 153 (2d Cir. 2001).
39. *Id.* at 160.

family members, it is more usual for a successful case to be established with the assistance and the testimony of qualified experts.

For example, each party presented the reports of psychologists in *Simcox*,[40] the respondent presented the testimony of a licensed psychologist in *Rodriguez*,[41] and the respondent presented three reports from a child psychiatrist in *Elyashiv*.[42]

It is important that the alleged expert has complete information concerning the matter. When experts claimed that the father's abuse to the mother created a significant risk to the child, while failing to consider the abuse of the mother's new husband against the child, their testimony was rejected.[43] And when a pediatrician testified that the children would be subject to grave risk if returned to Canada, but he had not reviewed the children's Canadian medical records, had never interviewed the father, and relied solely on the mother's allegations, his testimony was deemed "unconvincing."[44]

The court itself may appoint an expert. When a respondent mother alleged that the father had forcefully shaken their baby's head at least six to ten times per month and head-butted her at least two to three times per month, the court ordered an independent examination of the child by a pediatric neurologist.[45] In the context of disputed claims that the child had been subjected to great trauma, and that the child was autistic, the court directed the parties to submit the names of three independent mental health professionals with expertise in childhood autism and then appointed one of them to evaluate the child.[46] And when a mother asserted that the children's father had subjected them to sexual abuse, the court appointed an independent expert in pediatrics, child abuse, child sexual abuse, and child pornography.[47] In some cases, the parties have made a joint request that the court should appoint an independent psychologist to evaluate the children concerning the issues raised in a grave risk claim.[48]

Expert testimony has also been allowed as to the conditions in the location to which the child is potentially to be returned. Such testimony

40. Simcox v. Simcox, 511 F. 3d 594 (6th Cir. 2007).
41. Rodriguez v. Rodriguez, 33 F. Supp. 2d 456 (D. Md. 1999).
42. *Elyashiv*, 353 F. Supp. 2d 394.
43. Rowe v. Vargason, 2011 WL 4529341 (D. Minn. 2011).
44. *Herisse*, 772 F.3d 6.
45. Vasquez v. Colores, 2010 WL 3717298 (D. Minn. 2010).
46. Saada v. Golan, 712 F. Supp. 3d 361 (E.D.N.Y. 2024).
47. Kufner v. Kufner, 480 F. Supp. 2d 491 (D.R.I. 2007), *aff'd on other grounds*, 519 F.3d 33 (1st Cir. 2008).
48. Ortiz v. Martinez, 789 F.3d 722 (7th Cir. 2015).

was decisive in a case in which, although a return to Odessa, Ukraine, was deemed to be too dangerous, conditions in a city in western Ukraine were considered to be sufficiently safe.[49]

§ 8.09 NARROW INTERPRETATION

Any petitioner faced with the respondent's assertion of the grave risk of harm exception will ask the court to interpret the scope of the exception in as narrow a way as possible. The arguments in favor of a narrow interpretation will include the following.

- The legislative history of the Convention and both the language in and the history of ICARA provide strong support for such an interpretation, as explained in detail in previous sections of this chapter.
- ICARA expressly states that "The Congress makes the following findings: Children who are wrongfully removed or retained within the meaning of the Convention are to be promptly returned unless one of the narrow exceptions set forth in the Convention applies."[50]
- In enacting ICARA, Congress explicitly recognized "the need for uniform interpretation of the Convention."[51] A petitioner must therefore impress upon a court the importance of adhering to the established international standard for interpreting the Article 13(b) defense narrowly.
- Thus, the Second Circuit has explained that the "careful and thorough fulfillment of our treaty obligations" does not only protect children abducted to the United States but also serves "to protect American children abducted to other nations whose courts, under the legal regime created by this treaty, are expected to offer reciprocal protection."[52]
- Since Congress has signaled to courts that uniformity is desirable, it is appropriate for counsel to refer to foreign precedent, which generally supports a narrow interpretation of the grave risk exception.

---

49. Yuriiovych v. Hryhorivna, ___ F. Supp. 3d ___, 2024 WL 5241037 (D. Mont. Dec. 23, 2024).

50. 22 U.S.C. § 9001(a)(4).

51. *Id.* § 9001(b)(3)(B).

52. *Blondin*, 189 F.3d 240.

- The U.S. Department of State annually reviews Contracting States' compliance with the Convention and identifies states that fail to consistently apply its provisions. The most commonly cited such deficiency is that some foreign courts have considered and applied a best-interests analysis rather than promptly returning the child to his or her country of habitual residence for resolution there.
- The Special Commission to Review the Operation of the Hague Convention reaffirmed the narrow construction of Article 13(b) in 2006.
- In evaluating any alleged trauma asserted by the respondent, the courts must consider the fact that the act of the respondent in removing or retaining a child away from the habitual residence is itself a harmful act. The fundamental purpose of the Convention is to deter parents from wrongfully removing or retaining a child away from the child's habitual residence, which is generally considered abusive and appalling. The Hague Convention Explanatory Report asserts that international child abduction is reprehensible because:

> the true victim of the "childnapping" is the child himself, who suffers from the sudden upsetting of his stability, the traumatic loss of contact with the parent who has been in charge of his upbringing, the uncertainty and frustration which come with the necessity to adapt to a strange language, unfamiliar cultural conditions and unknown teachers and relatives.[53]

The circuit courts have generally applied a narrow interpretation of the grave risk exception, in decisions that have expressly cited many of the abovementioned authorities. For example, see:

> **First Circuit:** *Viera.*[54] "[E]xceptions to the Hague Convention should be construed narrowly by courts . . . . This serves the Hague Convention's strong presumption in favor of the child's return. . . . The grave risk defense may not be used 'as a vehicle to litigate (or relitigate) the child's best interests.'"

---

53. Explanatory Report at 432 (citing *Questionnaire and Report on international child abduction by one parent*, prepared by Adair Dyer, Prel. Doc. No. 1, Aug. 1977).
54. Vieira v. De Souza, 22 F.4th 304, 309 (1st Cir. 2022), citing Danaipour, 286 F.3d at 14.

Second Circuit: *Souratgar.*[55] "The potential harm to the child must be severe, and the "[t]he level of risk and danger required to trigger this exception has consistently been held to be very high. . . . The grave risk involves not only the magnitude of the potential harm but also the probability that the harm will materialize."

This "'grave risk' exception is to be interpreted narrowly, lest it swallow the rule." *Simcox v. Simcox,* 511 F.3d 594, 604 (6th Cir. 2007); *Blondin II,* 189 F.3d at 246 (warning that permissive invocation of the affirmative defenses "would lead to the collapse of the whole structure of the Convention by depriving it of the spirit of mutual confidence which is its inspiration" (quotation marks and citation omitted))."

Third Circuit: *Adan.*[56] "The Convention's Article 13(b) exception is 'narrowly drawn.'" *See Feder*, 63 F.3d at 226. "Were a court to give an overly broad construction to its authority to grant exceptions under the Convention, it would frustrate a paramount purpose of that international agreement—namely, to 'preserve the status quo and to deter parents from crossing international boundaries in search of a more sympathetic court.'"

Fifth Circuit: *Soto.*[57] "[F]indings of grave risk are rare." *Delgado v. Osuna*, 2015 WL 5095231, at *13 (E.D. Tex. 28 Aug. 2015), *aff'd*, 837 F.3d 571 (5th Cir. 2016). "The person opposing the child's return must show that the risk to the child is grave, not merely serious." Hague International Child Abduction Convention; Text and Legal Analysis, 51 FR 10494–01, 1986 WL 133056 (Mar. 1986). The principles underlying the Hague Convention require the "grave risk must be narrowly construed; otherwise, a broad interpretation would cause the exception to swallow the rule and transform the Convention into an arena for custody disputes." *Tavarez v. Jarrett*, 252 F. Supp. 3d 629, 640 (S.D. Tex. 2017) (citing *England v. England*, 234 F.3d 268, 271 (5th Cir. 2000)). In that regard, courts in Hague Convention cases "must strive always to avoid a common tendency to prefer their own society and culture"; the Hague Convention "deter[s] child abductions by parents who attempt to find a friendlier forum for deciding custodial disputes." *Abbott*, 560 U.S. at 20, 130 S. Ct. 1983.

55. 720 F.3d 96, 103 (2d Cir. 2013).
56. Application of Adan, 437 F.3d 381. 395 (3d Cir. 2006).
57. Soto v. Contreras, 880 F.3d 706, 710–11 (5th Cir. 2018).

Sixth Circuit: *Simcox*.[58] "The "grave risk" exception is to be interpreted narrowly, lest it swallow the rule. *See Friedrich II*, 78 F.3d at 1067. That rule—that "[c]hildren who are wrongfully removed or retained within the meaning of the Convention are to be promptly returned," 42 U.S.C. § 11601(a)(4)—was designed to protect the interests of the state of habitual residence in determining any custody dispute, and to deter parents from unilaterally removing children in search of a more sympathetic forum."

Seventh Circuit: *Norinder*.[59] "We said in *Van De Sande v. Van De Sande* that "[c]oncern with comity among nations argues for a narrow interpretation of the 'grave risk of harm' defense; but the safety of children is paramount." 431 F.3d 567, 572 (7th Cir. 2005). Because the court in this sort of case is responsible for determining which country's courts should adjudicate the domestic dispute and not resolving the dispute itself, we have stressed that the risk of harm must truly be grave. *Id.* at 570. The respondent must present clear and convincing evidence of this grave harm because any more lenient standard would create a situation where the exception would swallow the rule. *Simcox v. Simcox*, 511 F.3d 594, 605 (6th Cir. 2007)."

Ninth Circuit: *Asvesta*.[60] "Further, the Greek Hague court's determination that the child faced a grave risk of harm if returned to the United States relied on an impermissibly broad interpretation of Article 13(b). United States courts have consistently recognized that, like the other exceptions to return of a child under the Convention, Article 13(b)'s exception for grave risk should be "narrowly drawn." *In re Adan*, 437 F.3d 381, 395 (3d Cir. 2006) (citing *Feder*, 63 F.3d at 226); *see also Blondin*, 189 F.3d at 246; *Blondin v. Dubois*, 238 F.3d 153, 162 (2d Cir. 2001) (observing that "grave risk of harm" arises in "situations in which the child faces a real risk of being hurt, physically or psychologically, as a result of repatriation")."

Eleventh Circuit: *Gomez*. "Those defenses—including the 'grave risk' exception at issue in this case—are to be construed narrowly. 22 U.S.C. § 9001(a)(4); *Baran*, 526 F.3d at 1345. As the Convention's official commentary has noted, narrow interpretations

58. *Simcox*, 511 F.3d 604.
59. Norinder v. Fuentes, 657 F.3d 526, 535 (7th Cir. 2011).
60. *Asvesta*, 580 F.3d 1020.

of the exceptions are necessary to prevent them from swallowing the rule and rendering the Convention "a dead letter." Elisa Perez-Vera, Explanatory Report: Hague Conference on Private International Law, in 3 Acts and Documents of the Fourteenth Session 426 (1980) ("Perez-Vera Commentary"), ¶ 34. alternative, "a systematic invocation of the said exceptions, substituting the forum chosen by the abductor for that of the child's residence, would lead to the collapse of the whole structure of the Convention by depriving it of the spirit of mutual confidence which is its inspiration." *Id.*"

§ 8.10 BROADER INTERPRETATION

A respondent asserting the grave risk of harm exception will ask the court to interpret the scope of the exception in as broad as way as possible.

Support for a broader interpretation may be found in the following:

- Article 1 of the Convention proclaims that: "[T]he interests of children are of paramount importance in matters relating to their custody."
- The Perez-Vera Report stated that the Convention was "inspired by the desire to protect children and should be based upon an interpretation of their true interests."[61]
- The Perez-Vera Report stated that the Convention's purposes, however, must "give . . . way before the primary interest of any person in not being exposed to physical or psychological danger or being placed in an intolerable situation."[62]
- The court in *Simcox* asserted that, "although the 'grave risk' threshold is necessarily a high one, there is a danger of making the threshold so insurmountable that district courts will be unable to exercise any discretion in all but the most egregious cases of abuse."[63]
- The court in *Van De Sande*[64] adopted the argument of Professor Weiner that "while the remedy of return works well if the abductor is a non-custodial parent, it is inappropriate when the abductor is a primary caretaker who is seeking to protect herself and the children from the other parent's violence" and that in

61. Perez-Vera Report, para. 24.
62. *Id.* para. 28.
63. *Simcox*, 511 F.3d 594.
64. Van De Sande v. Van De Sande, 431 F.3d 567 (7th Cir. 2005).

such a case the remedy of return "puts the victim's most precious possession, her child, in close proximity to her batterer either without her protection (assuming she does not return with the child), or with her protection, thereby exposing her to further violence."

- Judge Posner in *Van De Sande* cited with approval the view that "[a] typical pattern involves a female U.S. national who has married a male foreign national and moved with her spouse to a foreign country. In most Hague cases invoking grave risk on the basis of domestic violence, the abuse begins before the transnational move. Ultimately, the victim flees with her children back to the United States in order to escape the abuse. The batterer, left behind in the country of habitual residence, then files a petition under the Hague Convention requesting return of the children to adjudicate the custody issues."[65]
- The legislative history of the Convention reveals that the drafters of the Convention and ICARA likely had a particular stereotype in mind when they created these instruments. They anticipated that most abductors would be the foreign noncustodial fathers of children who were being taken from their primary care providers. In such circumstances, a prompt return to the habitual residence makes perfect sense. In fact, most abductors are mothers who are the primary care providers and who want to return to their countries of origin after their relationship breaks down. In many such situations, the mothers have been subjected to domestic violence.
- The enactment of the federal International Parental Kidnapping Crime Act—which recognizes flight from domestic violence as an affirmative defense to the crime of removing or retaining a child outside of the U.S. in violation of custody rights—constitutes an acknowledgment of the role that domestic violence may play in provoking international child abduction.[66] Individual states have provided for similar defenses in state parental kidnapping statutes.

---

65. *Id.* at 568.

66. The act provides that "[i]t shall be an affirmative defense under this section that . . . (2) the defendant was fleeing an incidence or pattern of domestic violence," and that this section does not detract from the Hague Convention. 18 U.S.C. 1204(c)(2)(d) (1994).

- One might argue that the exception should not be defined so narrowly as to defeat the Convention's ultimate purpose. In the domestic violence context, a literal, textual reading of the Convention and its supporting documents might produce an injustice that defeats the overriding purpose of protecting children.

§ 8.11 GRAVE RISK IN GENERAL; WHAT CONSTITUTES A "GRAVE RISK?"

Neither the Convention nor the Explanatory Report nor any U.S. statute defines the term "grave risk of harm" resulting in great uncertainty as to its meaning. However, there is at least significant agreement as to many of the factors that are clearly insufficient to establish to establish a grave risk of harm. These include:

- The best interests of child;
- Adjustment problems (see § 8.12);
- Separation from the primary care provider (see § 8.13);
- Relative happiness or living conditions;
- Financial hardship;
- Poor parenting.

The risks associated with returning a child to a zone of war, famine, or disease[67] or to a sexually abusive situation[68] have been said to exemplify the specific types of risks contemplated by Article 13(b). However, there is no bright line definition of grave risk beyond these extreme examples.

The U.S. Department of State has said that a respondent "must show that the risk to the child is grave, not merely serious."[69] The same report also noted that "[a]n example of an 'intolerable situation' is one in which a custodial parent sexually abuses the child because such circumstances would constitute 'a grave risk of psychological harm.'"

In *Walsh*, the First Circuit explained that the risk of harm "must be a great deal more than minimal":[70]

> Not any harm will do nor may the level of risk of harm be low. The risk must be "grave," and when determining whether a grave risk of harm exists, courts must be attentive to the purposes of the Convention.

---

67. Friedrich v. Friedrich, 78 F.3d 1060 (6th Cir. 1996).
68. Text and Legal Analysis, at 10494.
69. Text and Legal Analysis, at 10510.
70. Walsh v. Walsh, 221 F.3d 204 (1st Cir. 2000).

The Second Circuit has characterized the "grave risk" exception as follows:

> At one end of the spectrum are those situations where repatriation might cause inconvenience or hardship, eliminate certain educational or economic opportunities, or not comport with the child's preferences; at the other end of the spectrum are those situations in which the child faces a real risk of being hurt, physically or psychologically, as a result of repatriation. The former do not constitute a grave risk of harm under Article 13(b); the latter do.[71]

The Tenth Circuit has held, that "'grave risk' means the potential harm to the child must be severe, and the level of risk and danger . . . very high."[72]

In *Simcox*,[73] the Sixth Circuit divided claims of abuse into three categories:

- Cases in which the abuse is relatively minor, such that it is unlikely that the risk of harm caused by return of the child will rise to the level of a "grave risk" or "intolerable situation." In these cases, the exception will not have been established.
- Cases at the other end of the spectrum in which the risk of harm to the child is clearly grave, such as where there is credible evidence of sexual abuse, other similarly grave physical or psychological abuse, death threats, or serious neglect. The crucial facts in *Simcox*—that the father beat the children physically and abused their mother in their presence, and that a psychologist found that the children suffered from post-traumatic stress disorder—were such that they were in this middle category, and accordingly it remanded the case to the district court to determine what conditions could mitigate the grave risk of harm.
- Cases that fall somewhere in the middle, where the abuse is substantially more than minor, but is less obviously intolerable.

In the difficult middle group, the issue of whether the child's return would subject it to a "grave risk" of harm or otherwise place it in an "intolerable situation" is a fact-intensive inquiry that depends on careful consideration of several factors, including the nature and frequency of the

71. *Blondin*, 238 F.3d 162.
72. West v. Dobrev, 735 F.3d 921, 932 (10th Cir. 2013).
73. *Simcox*, 511 F.3d 594.

abuse, the likelihood of its recurrence, and whether there are any enforceable undertakings that would sufficiently ameliorate the risk of harm to the child caused by its return.

The interpretation given by the U.K. Supreme Court might also prove helpful.[74] That court identified the following principles:

- The risk to the child must have reached such a level of seriousness as to be characterized as "grave." It is not enough, as it is in other contexts, that the risk be merely "real."
- Although "grave" characterizes the risk rather than the harm, there is in ordinary language a link between the two. Thus, a relatively low risk of death or really serious injury might properly be qualified as "grave," whilea higher level of risk might be required for other less serious forms of harm.
- The words "physical or psychological harm" gain color from the alternative "or *otherwise*" placed "in an intolerable situation." "Intolerable" is a strong word, but when applied to a child must mean a situation which a particular child in her particular circumstances should not be expected to tolerate. Those words were carefully considered and can be applied just as sensibly to physical or psychological harm as to any other situation.
- Every child has to put up with a certain amount of rough and tumble, discomfort, and distress. It is part of growing up. But there are some things that are not reasonable to expect a child to tolerate. Among these, of course, are physical or psychological abuse or neglect of the child. Among these also, we now understand, can be exposure to the harmful effects of seeing and hearing the physical or psychological abuse of her own parent.
- Article 13(b) is looking to the future: the situation as it would be if the child were to be returned forthwith to her home country. This is not necessarily the same as being returned to the person, institution, or other body who has requested her return, although of course it may be so if that person has the right to demand.
- More importantly, the situation that the child will face on return depends crucially on the protective measures that can be put in place to secure that the child will not be called upon to face an intolerable situation when she gets home.

74. Re E [2011] UKSC 27 [2011] FLR 758.

§ 8.12 ADJUSTMENT PROBLEMS INSUFFICIENT

Despite the somewhat vague pronouncements described in the preceding section and the lack of guidance as to what precisely a grave risk is, authorities generally agree that there are certain risks or circumstances that, standing alone, will typically not sustain the Article 13(b) defense.

For example, courts have made it clear that a respondent—whose unilateral decision to move has necessitated the child's adjustment to a new setting—cannot expect the law to come to her aid on the basis that the child has subsequently adapted to its new residence. A defense will likely fail if it relies on evidence that the child would have difficulty in re-adjusting to its country of habitual residence if returned.

Friedrich[75] illustrates the point. The respondent alleged that her son would suffer grave psychological harm if he were returned to Germany. An expert psychologist testified on her behalf that the child would suffer feelings of loss if forced to leave his mother in the United States, as well as feelings of anger and abandonment. The Sixth Circuit dismissed such concerns as "nothing more than adjustment problems." It insisted that for the purposes of the Convention, "[t]he disruption of the usual sense of attachment that arises during most long stays in a single place with a single parent should not be a 'grave' risk of harm." It refused to "reward" the respondent for removing the child from his habitual residence, insisting that a removing parent must not be allowed to abduct a child and then—when brought to court—complain that the child has grown used to the surroundings to which they were abducted. It explained that, under the logic of the Convention, it is the *abduction* that causes the pangs of subsequent return and that the disruption of the usual sense of attachment that arises during most long stays in a single place with a single parent should not be a "grave" risk of harm for the purposes of the Convention.

The First Circuit in *Walsh*[76] expressly rejected the argument that grave risk of harm could be established by the mere fact that returning the children to the habitual residence would unsettle them, since they had become settled in the United States, since such settlement was an "inevitable consequence" of the removal.

A petitioner faced with the argument that adjustment-related problems constitute a grave risk may also point out that the Convention essentially reserves this issue to Article 12, which implicitly contemplates adjustment problems. That article relieves a court of its obligation to

75. *Friedrich*, 78 F.3d 1060.
76. *Walsh*, 221 F.3d 204.

promptly return a child if the petitioner has waited more than one year after the child's wrongful removal to commence Hague proceedings and the child has become "well settled" in its new location.

Although the Article 12 "well-settled" defense operates independently of Article 13(b), at least one circuit court has said that it is acceptable for a district court to consider the fact that a child is deeply settled in its new environment as one factor in its grave risk assessment. In *Blondin*,[77] a father timely filed his petition within a year of the abduction, precluding the respondent from raising a defense under Article 12. The district court nevertheless took into consideration the fact that the children had become well-settled in the United States, and decided that it would be wrong to remove the children from the home in which they had begun to feel safe and recover from the trauma of their father's abuse, as being returned to France would cause a recurrence of their stress disorder.

The district court's consideration of the fact that the children were well-settled survived review by the Second Circuit. This is because its grave risk finding was not based on a determination that the children would experience the simple adjustment issues described in *Friedrich*. Rather, the children's settled nature was connected to their recovery from trauma and the likely reversal of that progress they would experience if returned. The Second Circuit explained that, in spite of the arbitrary one-year time limit in Article 12, there was no reason to think that evidence that a child is well-settled is completely outside the realm of an Article 13(b) analysis:

> Under Article 13(b), the fact that a child is settled may form part of a broader analysis of whether repatriation will create a grave risk of harm. . . . [I]n the course of an Article 13(b) analysis, a district court may be presented with evidence that a child is now settled in a new environment, and such evidence may be relevant to the issue of grave risk . . . a district court may consider it as part of an analysis under Article 13(b) as long as that factor is not the sole basis for a finding that there is clear and convincing evidence that a grave risk of harm exists.

§ 8.13 SEPARATION FROM PRIMARY CARE PROVIDER

A respondent will typically assert that she cannot return to the habitual residence and that the child will suffer irreparably if returned there without her. In some cases, a respondent presents expert psychological

77. *Blondin*, 238 F.3d 153 ["*Blondin IV*"].

testimony that the child's psychological health and sense of security is dependent on his ability to remain in his mother's (or father's) care. In general, such assertions fall on deaf ears.

In *Souratgar*, the Second Circuit held that the possible loss of access by a parent to the child does not constitute a grave risk of harm per se for Article 13(b) purposes.[78] It explained that, because the Convention defers the determination of custody to courts in the country where the child habitually resides, it is quite conceivable that in some cases one or the other parent might lose legal custody after repatriation and be deprived of access to the child. Courts hold that such issues should be handled by the courts in the habitual residence as part of custody proceedings.[79]

Thus, when a district court factored the possible separation of the child from his mother in assessing whether the return of the child to Mexico constituted a grave risk that his return would expose him to physical or psychological harm or otherwise place him in an intolerable situation, the Eighth Circuit overruled the court below and asserted that it had acted incorrectly in so doing and remanded the case for a determination of whether there truly was a grave risk of harm based exclusively on other factors.[80]

In *Asvesta*, the Ninth Circuit overruled a district court that had granted comity to a Greek Hague decision that had ruled that separating the child from his mother would inherently create a grave risk of harm to the child.[81] The circuit court concluded that, by determining (or assuming) that the child's separation from his mother at a young age would be more traumatic than his separation from his father, the Greek court had stepped out of its role as a Hague Convention tribunal by inquiring into the best interests of the child.

In a California state court case the respondent mother sought to fashion a grave risk claim based on the fact that she would not or could not return with the child to the habitual residence in Italy.[82] She alleged that she feared criminal prosecution there; that the courts in Italy might not treat her fairly; that she would be ostracized; and that she had financial worries about any potential return. The court rejected such claims, for two fundamental grounds:

78. Souratgar v. Fair, 720 F.3d 96 (2d Cir. 2016).

79. Charalambous v. Charalambous, 627 F.3d 462 (1st Cir. 2010).

80. *Nunez-Escudero*, 58 F.3d 374.

81. *Asvesta*, 580 F.3d 1000.

82. Maurizio R. v. L.C., 201 Cal. App. 4th 616, 135 Cal. Rptr. 3d 93 (Cal. App. 2 Dist. 2011).

> First, consideration of a child's bond with the abducting parent or his sense of security in new surroundings are not valid bases for departing from the Convention's fundamental rule of return. The effect of return on a parent-child bond is a "determination pertinent only to the merits of the underlying custody dispute," which must be resolved by the courts of the child's habitual residence.
>
> Second, a parent should not be rewarded for wrongfully abducting a child.

The same case raised the issue of respondent's claim that she could not return to Italy, the child's habitual residence, because she feared criminal prosecution for the crime of child abduction. Again, the claim was rejected. The court held that the Convention was a purely civil remedy and that it does not preclude prosecution of a parent who is a kidnapper. In this regard, it cited *U.S. v. Ventre*,[83] which was a criminal appeal under the International Parental Kidnapping Crime Act. There the court had made it clear that the civil and criminal issues were entirely distinct.

Further substantial authority for the proposition that separation from the primary care provider does not create a grave risk of harm for purposes of Article 13(b) is supplied by the following cases, among many others:

- A district court in Ohio, in *Robert v. Tesson*,[84] was faced with the expert report of a board-certified child psychiatrist who opined that:
    - A protracted separation of the children from their mother, who was their primary caregiver, would subject the children to a grave risk of psychological harm.
    - The mother was the focal point of the children's lives.
    - There was a reasonable medical certainty that the forced protracted separation from their mother represented a grave risk of psychological harm.
    - The loss of a fundamental primary caregiver, especially the maternal caregiver, represents the most stressful life experience that any child may face, with the exception of fears of

83. U.S. v. Ventre, 338 F.3d 1047 (9th Cir. 2003) (*cert. denied,* 540 U.S. 1085, 124 S. Ct. 951, 157 L. Ed. 2d 763).

84. Robert v. Tesson, 2005 WL 1652620 (S.D. Ohio 2005), *report and recommendation adopted*, 2006 WL 1401651 (S.D. Ohio 2006), *aff'd on other grounds*, 507 F.3d 981 (6th Cir. 2007).

annihilation, physical, or sexual abuse without the support of the caregiver to help buffer the insult.

The court ruled that such evidence was insufficient to establish that the risk to the children was "grave," rather than merely "serious." Furthermore, the children had been in the sole custody of the father in France for a four-month period in 2002 and that they sustained no psychological harm whatsoever as a result of their separation from their mother who was working in the United States during this time period. Therefore, the court did not believe that a separation between the children and their mother for the time that it took the French court to determine the custody issues would amount to "forced maternal abandonment" and therefore would not constitute a grave risk of psychological harm.

- A district court in Florida was clearly troubled about returning children to their habitual residence in Mexico in face of abuse that did not rise to the level of being grave and potential separation from their mother who was their primary care provider that could result in severe psychological harm to the children. However, the court ruled that it had failed to find any legal authority to allow this factual finding to impact its legal conclusion regarding the respondent's burdens under the Convention as there was no legal bar to her return to Mexico with the children.[85]
- In a district court case in New York the respondent mother argued that returning the child to Poland would cause her daughter "grave harm" because she would be denied "the benefit of motherly love." The court flatly rejected this theory, holding that "respondent ignores the fact that this is a consequence of choices made by respondent and not one that this Court may consider in determining the questions presented here."[86]
- An English case has reiterated the basic English rule that an abducting parent is not entitled to rely upon harm to the child arising out of her refusal to return with the child, as permitting her so to do would "drive a coach and four through the Convention. In such a situation any risk of harm to the child arises not from the order for return but from the refusal of the abductor to accompany him."[87]

85. Jaet v. Siso, 2009 WL 35270 (S.D. Fla. 2009).
86. *In re* Koc, 181 F. Supp. 2d 136 (E.D.N.Y. 2001).
87. C v. S [2014] EWHC 3799 (Fam).

In contrast are some cases in which the potential separation from the primary care provider was a significant factor in a determination of grave risk of harm. It is noteworthy that in all of the cases cited next the courts found clear and convincing evidence that one or more older siblings were at grave risk of harm if returned to the habitual residence while the court needed to make a decision about the younger children.

- A district court in Washington state relied upon the difficulty or impossibility of the mother returning to Greece as a significant factor (adding to evidence of physical and psychological harm to the children) in support of a finding that grave risk of harm had been sufficiently established.[88] The mother had no resources that would enable her to live in Greece, no place to go to, no facility with the Greek language, and was probably unemployable there. The youngest of the three siblings, as to whom there was less evidence of abuse, had bonded with his siblings and his mother had always been his primary care provider.
- A district court in New York found that two older children had been abused by their father and that returning them to Israel "would surely expose them to a grave risk of both physical and psychological harm" but that the youngest child had not "yet" been physically abused. The court found that this child was "not insulated" from future abuse given her father's inability to control his temper, and his threat to use a sword on her, and that the danger to the child was enhanced sufficiently by the fact that her mother and siblings would likely remain in the United States, which, as a psychologist testified, was "completely terrifying" to her.[89]
- A district court in Pennsylvania found that the older child suffered post-traumatic stress syndrome but not the younger child. As in the previously cited New York case, the court concluded that the younger child was "not insulated" from the likelihood of the petitioner's future abuse and supported its finding by also finding that if returned to Cyprus his mother and sibling would likely stay in the United States, which was likely to cause him harm.[90]

---

88. Tsarbopoulos v. Tsarbopoulos, 176 F. Supp. 2d 1045 (E.D. Wash. 2001).
89. *Elyashiv*, 353 F. Supp. 2d 394.
90. Miltiadous v. Tetervak, 686 F. Supp. 2d 544 (E.D.P.A. 2010).

§ 8.14 SEPARATION FROM SIBLINGS

There is no provision in the Convention that addresses the particular circumstances of sibling separation. If one child has been abused sufficient to create a grave risk of harm but the other child has not suffered such abuse is it necessary to separate siblings?

In some cases, the courts have answered this troubling question by finding that the unscathed sibling is "not insulated" from future abuse given the left-behind parent's past history in respect of the other child or children.[91]

In other cases, the courts have ordered that the abused child need not be returned but that the child who was not abused must be returned to the habitual residence and have placed the blame for any future separation of the siblings on the refusal of the taking parent to return both children. Thus, in *Whallon*,[92] the First Circuit stated, "Whether there is a separation is [the mother's] choice. She may return to Mexico with both her daughters." To rule otherwise, it held, "would risk substituting a best interest of the child analysis for the analysis the Convention requires," which would undercut the Convention's presumption of return where rights of custody have been violated by wrongfully removing a child in situations where that child had a sibling who was not wrongfully removed.

In sharp contrast, the Second Circuit held in *Ermini*[93] that, because there was a grave risk that the psychological health of one sibling would be endangered by his return to Italy, and since the two siblings were close, neither child should be returned. The court simply stated that,

> Moreover, in light of the children's close relationship to each other, and, significantly, the conclusion we reached with respect to abuse, we determine as well that it was not error for the district court to decline to separate the children. *See Ermini,* 2013 WL 1703590, at *17 ('Courts in this Circuit have frequently declined to separate siblings, finding that the sibling relationship should be protected even if only one of the children can properly raise an affirmative defense under the Hague Convention.').

Alternatively, a court might take into account the sibling factor in exercising its discretion whether to return a child even when the grave risk exception has been established.

91. *Elyashiv*, 353 F. Supp. 2d 394; *Tsarbopoulos*, 176 F. Supp. 2d 1045.
92. *Lynn*, 230 F.3d 450.
93. *Ermini*, 758 F.3d 167.

§ 8.15 RELATIVE HAPPINESS OR LIVING CONDITIONS INSUFFICIENT

Since the Convention aims to reserve substantive custody decisions to the state of habitual residence, it is not appropriate for a court to weigh the relative comforts or opportunities available to a child living in the United States versus living abroad in evaluating a Hague petition.[94] The rationale is that this would resemble a best interests determination, which would exceed the court's narrow mandate to review only the merits of the abduction claim. The Supreme Court has explained, "It is the Convention's premise that courts in contracting states will make this determination in a responsible manner."[95]

Pointing to the relevant notion of international comity, the *Friedrich* court explained that:

> [I]f Germany really is a poor place for young Thomas to grow up, as Mrs. Friedrich [the respondent] contends, we can expect the German courts to recognize that and award her custody in America. When we trust the court system in the abducted-from country, the vast majority of claims of harm—those that do not rise to the level of gravity required by the Convention—evaporate."[96]

Moreover, because the record did not suggest that the child would never be able to readjust to his former home, or that "any permanent harm or unhappiness" would result from his return, the grave risk threshold was not met.[97] Even if the father's home were a grim place to raise a child as compared to the pretty, peaceful streets of Ironton, Ohio, that fact would be irrelevant to a federal court's obligation under the Convention. The court was not to debate the relevant virtues of Batman vs. Max und Moritz and Wheaties vs. Milchreis. The exception was not license for a court in the abducted-to country to speculate on where the child would be happiest; that decision was a custody matter and reserved to the court in the country of habitual residence.

The U.S. State Department's legal analysis makes it clear that Article 13(b) is also not intended to encompass situations in which a child would

94. *Friedrich*, 78 F.3d 1060.

95. Abbott v. Abbott, 560 U.S. 1, 19 (2010).

96. *Friedrich*, 78 F.3d 1060. The court also noted that the home of the child's father in Germany was adequate to suit the child's needs and that there was "nothing in the record to indicate that life in Germany would result in any permanent harm or unhappiness" that would rise to the level of a grave risk. *Id.* at 1068.

97. *Id.*

be sent to a home "where money is in short supply, or where educational or other opportunities are more limited."[98]

Acknowledging this point in *Blondin*, the Second Circuit summarized the range of risks a child could face in being returned to his country of habitual residence:

> At one end of the spectrum are those situations where repatriation might cause inconvenience or hardship, eliminate certain educational or economic opportunities, or not comport with the child's preferences; at the other end of the spectrum are those situations in which the child faces a real risk of being hurt, physically or psychologically, as a result of repatriation. The former do not constitute a grave risk of harm under Article 13(b); the latter do.[99]

The Ninth Circuit in *Cuellar* lambasted a district court for "buying" an American father's argument that his child's far better circumstances in the United States as compared to Panama created a grave risk of harm.[100] He claimed that the mother was neglectful and very poor, that the child had grown used to living in America, and that the child's medical needs could not be addressed in Panama. The district court credited the father's testimony about the home where the mother lived with the child: that the home "has no indoor running water"; that "residents in this area use a nearby creek and outhouse for waste disposal"; and that the home "has no climate control, no refrigeration, and very little furniture." The circuit court made it abundantly clear that such evidence came "nowhere close" to establishing a grave risk of harm if the child were returned to Panama to live with her mother.

The court reasoned that billions of people live in similar circumstances and that if that amounted to a grave risk of harm, parents in more developed countries would have unchecked power to abduct children from countries with a lower standard of living. The court also cautioned (having pointed out that the case concerned a U.S. college professor and an exotic dancer whom he had married in Panama) that the time to take considerations about living circumstances into account is "before undertaking the volitional acts that lead to conception."[101] Once the child is

98. Text and Legal Analysis, at 10494.
99. *Blondin*, 238 F.3d 162.
100. *Cuellar*, 596 F.3d 505.
101. *Id.* at 510.

born, it said, the remote parent must accept the country where the child is habitually resident and its legal system as given.

However, in some cases, the courts have considered the extent to which a child has become settled in the new environment after the wrongful taking or retention as compared to a traumatic environment in the habitual residence in support of a finding of grave risk.

The *Blondin*[102] case supports such an approach, since the court held that the fact that a child is settled may form part of a broader analysis of whether repatriation would create a grave risk of harm. Although the ordinary disruptions necessarily accompanying a move would not by themselves constitute such a risk, it held that a district court could consider it as part of an analysis under Article 13(b) as long as that factor is not the sole basis for finding that a grave risk of harm exists. The court found that the district court in this case properly considered the evidence that the children were settled in their new environment as one factor in its grave-risk analysis. The key finding in this regard was that,

> I am convinced that wrenching the children away from the safe, extended-family environment in which they have begun to recover from the trauma caused by their father's abuse would thwart their recovery by causing a recurrence of the traumatic stress disorder they suffered in France, the site of their father's sustained, violent abuse.

In a district court case in New York,[103] the court accepted and cited substantial evidence concerning the children's settled environment in New York in addition to firmly establishing that the petitioner had engaged in substantial domestic violence against the entire family in Mexico. The court found that the children had become well-settled in New York and that,

> This factor, while not dispositive, militates against repatriation. Wrenching the boys from their current stable environment, when they are only now beginning to recover from the trauma inflicted by [the father] in Mexico, could only increase the likelihood and severity of harm of their repatriation.

A district court's case in Arkansas[104] is perhaps the high-water mark of this position. There, the court found that ordering the children to be

102. *Blondin*, 238 F.3d 153.
103. Reyes Olguin v. Cruz Santana, 2005 WL 67094 (E.D.N.Y. 2005).
104. Kofler v. Kofler, 2007 WL 2081712 (W.D. Ark. 2007).

returned to their habitual residence in Germany would be tantamount to requiring them to live with petitioner under conditions that would subject them to a grave risk of psychological harm or otherwise place them in an intolerable situation. That finding was based on findings that:

- The children had a poor relationship with their father;
- The father's live-in girlfriend did not want the children there;
- The father did not provide adequate financial support for the children in Germany, resulting in the children being forced to live in very poor conditions, sometimes without sufficient food; and
- Due to these conditions, the youngest child needed psychological treatment.

The court allowed evidence to be submitted contrasting the conditions in which the mother and children lived in Arkansas with their circumstances in Germany, and casting doubt on the genuineness of the father's desire to have the children live with him. The case was not appealed.

In several cases, respondents have argued that their child faced prejudice if returned to the habitual residence. Such claims have never succeeded, at least in any published case. In two cases concerning alleged racism in Germany, the courts took the allegations seriously, allowed testimony as to some specific acts that the children had experienced and concluded in each case that the evidence fell far short of proof of a grave risk.[105] In one such case, the court concluded that it was unclear that the racism that apparently exists in Germany is more pervasive or problematic than the racism that unfortunately continues to plague the United States.

§ 8.16 FINANCIAL HARDSHIP INSUFFICIENT

Respondents frequently assert that if the child is returned to the habitual residence, they will need to return also, but that they face financial ruin or destitution if they do so. In many cases, a key reason why parents may leave the child's habitual residence is because they are unable to make a living there, either because they do not have a work visa or that they are too ill to work or for other similar reasons. Such claims inevitably do not succeed.

Thus, when a respondent sought to assert that the allegedly inferior economic and educational opportunities in Poland rose to the level of

105. Neves v. Neves, 637 F. Supp. 2d 322 (W.D.N.C. 2009); Sita-Mambwene v. Keeton, 2009 WL 2836430 (E.D. Mo. 2009).

psychological harm or intolerable situation envisioned by Article 13(b), the claim was given short shrift.[106]

In one case, the respondent contended that if she returned to Germany with the child to face a protracted custody proceeding, she would have no way to support herself and the child, and they would end up homeless or living in an equally intolerable situation in Germany.[107] The court noted that a mere shortage of money is not, on its own, sufficient to establish an "intolerable situation." The court noted that the bar for proving the "grave risk" exception is set exceptionally high and the mother had not satisfied this exceedingly high standard.

Similarly, the district court in a case in Mississippi described the acute financial plight of the respondent mother in considerable detail, acknowledging that she and her children had been nearly destitute before she removed the children from Canada, but conceded that such circumstances did not begin to compare with the circumstances of "grave harm" contemplated by the Convention, such as war, famine, or spousal or child physical abuse.[108]

Nonetheless, courts will sometimes condition the return on the petitioner's compliance with specified undertakings requiring them to pay interim sums to the respondent. Indeed, that was the order of the courts in each of the two just-mentioned cases.

Moreover, when grave risk is established, the court may take account of the respondent's financial circumstances in considering whether she will be able to protect her child if the child is returned.[109]

§ 8.17 POOR PARENTING INSUFFICIENT

Clearly, evidence that the petitioner has been a poor or deficient parent is insufficient to establish a grave risk of harm. It is a factor that should be considered by a court handling the custody issue, but it is not determinative in a Hague case.

The father in *Cuellar*[110] alleged that the mother in Panama allowed the child to play in a wheeled walker on a concrete construction platform that had no guardrails; that she fell seven feet off the ground to a concrete platform, landing on her head and was unconscious from the fall; and

---

106. *In re* Koc, 181 F. Supp. 2d 136 (E.D.N.Y. 2001).
107. Krefter v. Wills, 623 F. Supp. 2d 125 (D. Mass. 2009).
108. Wilchynski v. Wilchynski, 2010 WL 1068070 (S.D. Miss. 2010).
109. *Ortiz*, 789 F.3d 722.
110. *Cuellar*, 596 F.3d 505.

that the child was sometimes cared for by a sick relative, had frequent ear infections, and had unexplained burns behind her earlobes. The Ninth Circuit held that the district court had improperly drawn a conclusion about the mother's fitness as a parent and had thereby overstepped its mandate and impermissibly addressed the ultimate question of custody. The court noted that well-cared-for children occasionally have accidents, and that leaving a child with a sick relative may or may not be neglectful, depending on the circumstances.

A father complained in a North Carolina case[111] that the wife and her family in Germany were overly zealous in their pursuit of physical fitness and too strict in disciplining the children. Such claims were deemed entirely insufficient.

On the other hand, the "refusal" of the petitioning mother to parent the child was a highly significant factor in establishing grave risk in a case in Kansas.[112] The evidence indicated that the mother was away from home, ignored the child, and was unstable and that the child was repeatedly absent from school, and had difficulties in school arising from the mother's refusal to parent him. The Tenth Circuit remanded the case so as to allow the mother to put in exculpatory evidence.

A useful comparison was made by a New York district court[113] that contrasted cases in which a grave risk of harm was found based on "serious neglect" by the custodial parent, citing cases in which the custodial parent entirely disregarded a child's needs or actively facilitated a child's harm,[114] as compared to cases in which parental conduct was poor but was a matter reserved for the custody courts.[115]

111. *Neves*, 637 F. Supp. 2d 322.

112. Didur v. Viger, 392 F. Supp. 2d 1268 (D. Kan. 2005), *judgment rev'd on other grounds*, 197 Fed. Appx. 749 (10th Cir. 2006).

113. Swett v. Bowe, 2024 WL 203471 (S.D.N.Y. May 7, 2024).

114. Ischiu v. Garcia, 274 F. Supp. 3d 339, 353–54 (D. Md. 2017) (grave risk found where father "condoned" sexual abuse and child suffered from post-traumatic stress disorder and clinical depression as a result).

115. E.g., Galaviz v. Reyes, 95 F.4th 246, 257–59 (5th Cir. 2024) (grave risk not found despite "unsuitable childcare," children's "poor hygiene," a "lack of educational opportunities," and mother's decision to "obtain[ ] a 'boob job' instead of continuing therapy for her son"; such considerations are "relevant to custody" but not to the grave risk defense); Guerrero v. Oliveros, 119 F. Supp. 3d 894, 913–14 (N.D. Ill. 2015) (grave risk not found although child "was frequently left unsupervised in the street, had lice, and was often dirty," as such "custody issues are expressly reserved" for home country's courts).

§ 8.18 MUST PRIOR HARM BE ESTABLISHED?

The Convention does not explicitly require that a child has experienced harm prior to removal in order for the Article 13(b) exception to apply.

Some courts have refused to return a child to a habitual residence when the petitioner's past conduct created powerful red flags that established a strong likelihood that the child would be exposed to serious risk.

In *Baran v. Beaty*,[116] the Eleventh Circuit held that the district court "was not required to find the child had previously been physically or psychologically harmed; it was required to find returning him to Australia would expose him [to such harm]." It was sufficient that the respondent mother established that the father had a history of alcohol abuse, had threatened to harm the child, had physically abused the mother while she was pregnant and after the child was born, and had endangered the child while drunk.

A district court in New York used similar reasoning in *Elyashiv*.[117] It held that a "likelihood of future abuse" was sufficient to constitute a grave risk of harm. The mother had endured serious domestic violence at the hands of her husband in Israel. The father had also verbally and physically abused the couple's two older children, both of whom a child psychiatrist had diagnosed with post-traumatic stress disorder, but there was no evidence that he had ever abused his youngest child. The court had no problem in concluding that the two older children faced a grave risk of harm if returned to Israel. As for the youngest child, the court stated that even though she had yet to be physically abused by her father, and was not suffering from post-traumatic stress disorder, returning her to Israel would also expose her to a grave risk of physical and psychological harm. In respect to physical harm, "she is not insulated from the likelihood of future abuse," given the father's inability to control his temper, his pattern of domestic abuse, and his threats to physically hurt her. Based on expert testimony that the child was terrified of being separated from her mother and siblings, the court also found that sending her back to Israel without them would expose her to a risk of psychological harm.

In *Simcox*,[118] the Sixth Circuit echoed that position. There was evidence that the petitioning father had frequently verbally and physically abused the respondent mother and their older children. The alleged abuse included belt-whipping, hitting, pulling of the children's hair and ears, repeated beatings, and yelling profanity. However, only the older children

---

116. Baran v. Beaty, 526 F.3d 1340 (11th Cir. 2008).
117. *Elyashiv*, 353 F. Supp. 2d 394.
118. *Simcox*, 511 F.3d 608.

were found to be suffering from post-traumatic stress disorder, and the youngest "appear[ed] to have largely escaped the physical and psychological injuries suffered by her older siblings." Nevertheless, the court upheld the grave risk of harm exception, noting that "nothing in the Convention requires that a child must first be traumatized by abuse before the Article 13b exception applies."

§ 8.19 MUST THE RISK OF HARM BE IMMINENT?

Courts have differed on whether the risk of harm must be imminent upon return. In *Walsh*,[119] for example, the First Circuit held that a district court had erroneously required a showing of an "immediate, serious threat" upon return. The court stated that the risk need only be grave, not immediate.[120]

In contrast, the Ninth Circuit has said that a court should only be concerned with harm that could occur in the immediate future. In *Gaudin*,[121] it reasoned that the Convention and ICARA are only intended to provide "a provisional, short-term remedy in order to permit long-term custody proceedings to take place in the home jurisdiction." It explained that psychological harm is often cumulative, especially in the absence of physical abuse or extreme maltreatment, and that even a living situation capable of causing grave psychological harm over the full course of a child's development is not *necessarily* likely to do so during the period necessary to obtain a custody determination.

The *Friedrich* court also asserted that—other than in cases of serious abuse, neglect, or emotional dependence—a grave risk of harm can only exist when return would subject children to *imminent* danger before the resolution of a custody dispute.[122]

Accordingly, many courts have cited the fact that returning the child to the habitual residence would not put the child in imminent danger as a basis for declaring that grave risk was not established.[123]

However, in a later ruling in a case involving domestic abuse allegations, the Sixth Circuit modified this criterion, making no mention of whether the harm must be imminent.[124]

---

119. *Walsh*, 221 F.3d 204.
120. *Id.*
121. Gaudin v. Remis, 415 F.3d 1028 (9th Cir. 2005).
122. *Friedrich*, 78 F.3d 1060.
123. Stevens v. Stevens, 499 F. Supp. 2d 891 (E.D. Mich. 2007).
124. *Simcox*, 511 F.3d 594.

Similarly, with respect to harm associated with sexual abuse, the First Circuit has indicated that just because a young child will not immediately experience the harmful psychological effects of the abuse upon return does not disprove the possibility that there is a risk of harm in returning the child to the place where the abuse recurred.[125] The court repeated the observation in *Walsh* that the Hague Convention "does not require that the risk be 'immediate'; only that it be grave."

§ 8.20 EXTENT OF HARM

The text of Article 13(b) requires only that the harm be "physical or psychological," but the context makes it clear that the harm must be a great deal more than minimal.[126]

There is strong authority in support of the fundamental proposition that the potential harm to the child must be severe, and that the level of risk and danger required to trigger the exception must be very high.[127]

Cases are judged on their own unique facts and the outcomes are difficult to predict. Written decisions usually do not reveal the full extent of the difficulties that courts have in reaching the right result for the obvious reason that judges are the ones who write their rulings after they have already reached a decision and they highlight those factors that support the conclusions they have already reached.

A district court in Minnesota was faced with a large amount of disturbing evidence about the misconduct of the respondent mother, the petitioning father, and the mother's new husband. Ultimately, the court concluded that it was insufficient to constitute proof of grave risk.[128] The mother claimed, among other things, that the child's father had raped her on three occasions, including when she was pregnant with the child; that he had choked her and threatened to kill her with a knife; that he had forced her into prostitution and had collected the money; and that he had had inappropriate contact with minor girls. She also asserted that he had shaken the child on three occasions. Although the court assumed that such evidence was truthful, it found that it was extremely significant that the mother had admitted that she was not scared of the father, had considered trying to work out an agreement with him to allow them to share custody of the child, and had talked about sending the child to him in Australia full-time. In addition, the court allowed evidence as to the

125. *Danaipour*, 286 F.3d 17.
126. *Walsh*, 221 F.3d 218–19.
127. Souratgar v. Lee, 729 F.2d 96, 103 (2d Cir. 2013).
128. *Rowe*, 2011 WL 4529341.

fact that the mother's current husband, with whom the mother and the child were then living, had been significantly abusive to the child, as well as to the mother, and that the mother was scared of him. Ultimately, the court ruled that the grave risk exception had not been established.

Yet it must be recognized that the Convention "is designed to protect the interests of children and their parents"[129] and that the children's interests may point against return in some circumstances. The Convention explicitly recognizes that the child's interest in avoiding physical or psychological harm, in addition to other interests, "may overcome the return remedy."[130] Courts must remain conscious of this purpose, "bearing in mind that the Convention sets as a primary goal the safety of the child."[131]

§ 8.21 ISOLATED OR SPORADIC ABUSE

A respondent must generally show that the alleged abuse is not merely "isolated or sporadic."[132] Sporadic or isolated incidents of physically disciplining the child, or some limited incidents aimed at persons other than the child, even if witnessed by the child, are generally not grave risks of harm.[133]

In *Foster*,[134] a Pennsylvania district court found that the petitioning father had spanked his son two to four times, called him names, and resorted to other types of physical discipline. However, despite the father's "regrettable" parenting techniques and "overbearing, egotistical, hot-tempered" personality, the court found that the respondent's allegations of abuse were insufficient to establish a grave risk of harm to their son. The court stated that an abusive situation is less likely to be considered "grave" where the allegations of abuse concern isolated or sporadic incidents.

Similarly, in *McManus*,[135] a district court refused to recognize a father's Article 13(b) defense in a case where the petitioning mother was found to have physically or violently disciplined her children on two occasions. The court recognized that the children had suffered physical and psychological distress as a result of their parents' marital and parenting problems, but found that this "serious" harm did not rise to the

---

129. Lozano v. Montoya Alvarez, 572 U.S. 1, 19 (2014) (Alito, J., concurring).
130. *Id.* at 16 (majority opinion).
131. Golan v. Saada, 596 U.S. 666, 668 (2022).
132. Foster v. Foster, 654 F. Supp. 2d 348 (W.D. Pa. 2009).
133. *Lee*, 729 F.2d 103.
134. *Foster*, 654 F. Supp. 2d 348.
135. McManus v. McManus, 354 F. Supp. 2d 62 (2005).

level of gravity required by Article 13(b). In denying the defense, the court distinguished the evidence of "real but sporadic or isolated incidents of physical abuse" in *McManus* from the "sustained pattern of physical abuse and/or a propensity for violent abuse" at stake in other cases in which the defense succeeded.

In a case in Kansas,[136] the court declined to find a grave risk because the respondent mother did not show regularly inflicted abuse but rather described two distinct incidents of physical violence toward herself while the only evidence of violence toward the children was her testimony that he struck them with a belt during meals, apparently because he did not want them speaking during meals.

By contrast, in *Simcox*,[137] the fact that the petitioning father's abuse of his children and wife was not merely "isolated or sporadic" played an important role in the court's determination that the children faced a grave risk of harm. The court distinguished the recurrent beatings, hair pulling, and belt-whippings in the case before it together with psychological abuse (the father's profane outbursts and abuse of the children's mother in their presence), from the two incidents of a mother striking her children in *McManus*.

§ 8.22 GRAVE PHYSICAL RISKS: TERRORISM AND ZONES OF WAR

The grave physical risks asserted under the Convention are often traced to a petitioner's violent nature within the specific home from which the child was removed. However, in some cases, respondents have argued that dangers originating outside the walls of the child's home give rise to grave physical risks that should preclude return.

Respondents frequently rely on *Friedrich v. Friedrich* to support claims that general dangers in the country from which the child was abducted will pose a grave risk of harm to the child if it returns. These claims have been largely unsuccessful. According to Sixth Circuit dicta in *Friedrich*, returning children to "a zone of war, famine, or disease" presumptively imposes a grave risk of imminent, physical harm.[138] However, the case law suggests that a respondent must prove more than a generalized risk of danger in parts of a child's country of habitual residence in order to benefit from the "zone of war" defense.

---

136. Dalmasso v. Dalmasso, 269 Kan. 752 (Kan. 2000).
137. *Simcox*, 511 F.3d 594.
138. *Friedrich*, 78 F.3d 1060.

Such a danger was found on appeal in *Tereshchenko*.[139] The Second Circuit held that the district court's determination that returning children of Ukrainian parents to a city in Ukraine would not expose them to a grave risk of harm was clearly erroneous, since Ukraine was in the midst of an invasion by Russia and was subject to repeated missile attacks, one child was a U.S. citizen, and the State Department had advised that U.S. citizens should not travel to Ukraine due to active armed conflict. But in another case a district court subsequently ruled that, despite the high risk in the city in Ukraine from which the child was abducted, the child should be returned to a city in western Ukraine where the expert evidence established that the risk was lower.[140]

The terrorist bombings in Israel have been a considerable source of litigation with respect to Article 13(b) of the Convention and the "zone of war" classification. However, in two cases, courts have rejected respondents' claims that the situation in Israel constitutes a zone of war as contemplated by the Sixth Circuit and the Convention.

In *Freier*,[141] a mother claimed that she had taken her daughter from the family home in Israel to the United States because of ongoing tension in Israel—including recent skirmishes that occurred 15 to 90 minutes from their home and random car bombings in the country—had created a zone of war. In rejecting her claim, the court pointed to the fact that businesses and schools were open in the area, and the fighting was apparently limited to areas outside the city in which she lived. The court was also swayed by the fact that the mother had spent 14 years raising children in Israel. Her purported anxiety about the turmoil thus seemed questionable. Ultimately, the court ruled that there was not clear and convincing evidence to support a finding that Israel constituted a zone of war under the Convention or the Sixth Circuit standard.

In *Silverman*,[142] the Eighth Circuit affirmed a determination that a mother had wrongfully removed her children from Israel to the United States and rejected the mother's grave risk defense. Her defense failed because she cited only "general regional violence" that threatened every Israeli. This evidence was not sufficient to classify the child's habitual residence as a "zone of war."

---

139. Tereshchenko v. Karimi, 102 F.4th 111 (2d Cir. 2024).

140. Yuriiovych v. Hryhorivna, ___ F. Supp. 3d ___, 2024 WL 5241037 (D. Mont. Dec. 23, 2024).

141. Freier v. Freier, 969 F. Supp. 436 (E.D. Mich. 1996).

142. Silverman v. Silverman, 338 F.3d 886 (8th Cir. 2003).

Several cases have considered the situation in Venezuela. In *Salame*,[143] a parent presented testimony regarding frequent protests, an incident of criminal violence against the family in their home approximately ten years ago, and shortages of gas, water, food, electricity, and medication. But the district court also received evidence that the protests were avoidable, that a nearby grocery store was stocked with food and water, that the mother's home was equipped with a generator, that the family had access to medical care and medication, and that the children would return to their school and soccer teams. The Sixth Circuit held that, although Venezuela was suffering from years-long, well-documented political and socioeconomic crisis, characterized by economic instability, power outages, food and medicine shortages, and violent protests, it was required to consider the particular circumstances to which the children were returning, which, while less stable than those they likely enjoyed in Tennessee, were insufficient to establish an intolerable situation or a grave risk of harm.

Similar claims have been rejected concerning Colombia, Argentina, Guatemala, El Salvador, and Mexico. In one case,[144] a father relied on a State Department travel warning about Colombia directed to American citizens, which cautioned that U.S. citizens in Colombia had been the victims of numerous threats, kidnappings, hijackings, and murders and may be targeted at higher rates in response to U.S. drug policy. The court concluded that, at best the record reflected a general current risk of harm to U.S. citizens in Colombia, but no specific risk of harm either to the child or, more generally, to children who are Colombian as well as American citizens.

In *Mendez Lynch*,[145] a respondent presented the testimony of a political scientist and international affairs professor with expertise in Argentina, the children's state of habitual residence. Although the professor did not characterize Argentina as a zone of war, he described it as a "volatile" place that "could turn violent at any moment." The court found that the testimony of people who lived in the children's home city, to the effect that banks and schools were open and that street demonstrations were not taking place in close proximity to the area to which the children would return, was persuasive.

143. Salame v. Tescari, 29 F.4th 763 (6th Cir. 2022).

144. Hazbun Escaf v. Rodriquez, 200 F. Supp. 2d 603 (E.D. Va. 2002).

145. Mendez Lynch v. Mendez Lynch, 220 F. Supp. 2d 1347, 1350 (M.D. Fla. 2002).

In a case concerning Mexico,[146] the father argued that returning the child to Mexico would expose the child to a grave risk of physical harm due to the spiraling violence and surge in murders in Monterrey and because of specific violent acts that had been committed in the school that the child attended in Monterrey and in the neighborhood where the petitioner resided. The court simply concluded that such evidence was insufficient to find that Monterrey was a "zone of war." Likewise, allegations as to gang activity and threats failed to establish that circumstances in El Salvador constituted a zone of war or that the child was in such specific danger living in El Salvador as to constitute a grave risk of harm.[147]

Foreign courts have used similar logic in evaluating whether a case involves general risks that would not necessarily trigger Article 13(b) versus specific risks to the particular child and his specific place of habitual residence.[148]

Nonetheless, the European Court of Human Rights[149] upheld a Romanian determination that children who had been abducted from Israel should not be returned there because there was a grave risk of harm to the children in light of the purportedly dangerous conditions with terrorism in the communal settlement in Israel where they had been living, based on reports by Amnesty International and the U.S. State Department (which had not mentioned the specific town or area).

§ 8.23 ABUSE OF A PARENT

A difficult situation arises when there is evidence of domestic violence against a parent, but less severe abuse or none at all directed at the child. Typically, if the exception prevails, it is because the respondent has been able to show a strong link between the abuse addressed to the parent and harm to the child.

The Guide to Good Practice stresses the fact that the wording of Article 13(1)(b) makes clear that the issue is whether there is a grave risk that the return would "expose the *child* to physical or psychological harm or otherwise place the *child* in an intolerable situation."[150] But it also

---

146. Vazquez v. Estrada, Slip Copy, 2011 WL 196164 (N.D. Tex. 2011).

147. Salguero v. Argueta, 256 F. Supp. 3d 630 (E.D.N.C. 2017).

148. *See, e.g.*, in Re S (A Child) (Abduction: Grave Risk of Harm) [2002] 1 WLR 3355; *In re* M and another (Children) (Abduction: Rights of Custody) [2007] 3 WLR 975.

149. Raban v. Romania, [2010] ECHR 1625 (26 Oct. 2010).

150. Guide to Good Practice Child Abduction Convention: Part VI—Article 13(1)(b), para. 32.

notes that "harm to a parent, whether physical or psychological, could, in some exceptional circumstances, create a grave risk that the return would expose the child to physical or psychological harm or otherwise place the child in an intolerable situation."[151]

The Article 13(1)(b) exception does not require, for example, that the child be the direct or primary victim of physical harm if there is sufficient evidence that, because of a risk of harm directed to a taking parent, there is a grave risk to the child.[152] But the Article 13(b) inquiry is not whether repatriation would place the respondent parent's safety at grave risk, but whether so doing would subject the child to a grave risk of physical or psychological harm.[153]

Traditionally, the Article 13(b) exception failed under the preceding fact pattern because of the tendency to narrowly interpret its exceptions. For example:

- In a 1995 case, *Nunez-Escudero v. Tice-Menley*,[154] the respondent mother asserted that her husband had physically, sexually, and verbally abused her, causing her to fear for the baby's safety. The Eighth Circuit held that this evidence fell short of the clear and convincing standard because it was general and concerned the problems between the respondent, her husband, and father-in-law. The court insisted that the respondent must prove that the child would face "immediate and substantial risk of an intolerable situation" if returned to the habitual residence.
- In *Tabacchi v. Harrison*,[155] the respondent claimed that her husband had slapped her on at least three occasions, hit her on the head at least twice, threw her down, briefly choked her, hit her in the face with his arm, and smashed household items. However, the court concluded that the evidence showed only a risk to the respondent, not to their daughter, who witnessed only two instances of violence and was never harmed by her father.
- In *Whallon v. Lynn*,[156] the First Circuit held that a husband's verbal abuse of his wife and the parties' oldest child and a single incident of physical shoving of his wife, while regrettable, did

151. *Id.*

152. Guide to Good Practice Child Abduction Convention: Part VI—Article 13(1)(b), para. 33.

153. Souratgar v. Lee, 720 F.3d 96, 102, 104 (2d Cir. 2013).

154. *Nunez-Escudero*, 58 F.3d 374.

155. Tabacchi v. Harrison, 2000 U.S. Dist. LEXIS 1518 (N.D. Ill. Feb. 8, 2000).

156. *Lynn*, 230 F.3d 450.

not rise to the level of harm required to establish a grave risk to the youngest child.

In contrast, some courts adopted a broader approach, most especially the First Circuit in the *Walsh*[157] case in 2000. There the district court had held that the grave risk exception had not been proven despite evidence of the petitioning father's violent conduct against the children's mother (among others), because none of the violence had been directed to the children although they had witnessed much of it. The First Circuit reversed that decision. It cited six primary reasons for doing so:

1. The father had demonstrated an uncontrollably violent temper. His assaults were "bloody and severe." His temper and assaults were "not in the least lessened" by the presence of his two youngest children, who had witnessed his assaults.[158]
2. The father had demonstrated that his violence "knows not the bonds between parent and child or husband and wife, which should restrain such behavior."[159]
3. The father had gotten into fights with persons much younger than he.
4. Credible social science literature establishes that serial spousal abusers are also likely to be child abusers.
5. Both state and federal law have recognized that children are at increased risk of physical and psychological injury themselves when they are in contact with a spousal abuser.
6. The father had a pattern of violence and chronic disobedience of court orders.

Thus, *Walsh* recognized that exposure to domestic violence may be one factor that contributes to a threshold showing of a grave risk of harm. The court placed great weight on the psychological and physical harm to the children resulting from witnessing spousal abuse. It explicitly acknowledged that witnessing spousal abuse could itself create a grave risk of harm.

In *Simcox*,[160] evidence of physical and psychological abuse of the youngest child's mother and siblings was sufficient to warrant a finding of grave risk as to that child. The court held that although that child, "presumably due to her young age, appears to have largely escaped the

157. *Walsh*, 221 F.3d 204.
158. *Id.* at 220.
159. *Id.*
160. *Simcox*, 511 F.3d 594.

physical and psychological injuries suffered by her older siblings, nothing in the Convention requires that a child must first be traumatized by abuse before the Article 13b exception applies."

In *Van de Sande*[161] the Seventh Circuit reversed an order of return where the father had "beat[en] his wife severely and repeatedly in [the children's] presence," and had also threatened to kill them.

In *Davies*, overwhelming evidence of the father's extreme violence and uncontrollable anger, as well as his psychological abuse of the mother over many years, much of which was witnessed by the child, created an unusually grave risk of imminent danger.[162]

The district court in *Tsarbopoulos*[163] also recognized that spousal abuse was a factor to be considered in the determination of whether or not the Article 13(b) exception applies because of the potential that the abuser will also abuse the child.

In a district court case in Pennsylvania,[164] the court held that the father's physical and emotional abuse of the mother had been such that returning the children to Cyprus would expose them to a grave risk of physical or psychological harm. The court accepted the mother's testimony that the father had beaten her repeatedly and, at one point, had broken her nose; that he drank heavily and become enraged at her and the children; and that he kept a gun in the house and had threatened to kill her.

In *Gomez*, the Eleventh Circuit held that a pattern of threats and violence directed against a child's parent but not specifically at a child, posed a grave risk of harm to the child.[165] During a contentious custody battle in Venezuela over their daughter, the child's mother and her husband had made several threats against the father. One death threat occurred in a Venezuelan courtroom. Those threats assumed a new dimension when actual violence began against the father's family. The father's girlfriend was shot while driving, minutes after dropping the father and his daughter off. The father's mother's car was damaged and vandalized. In addition, on at least two occasions, drugs were planted in the car. Fearing for his and his family's safety, the father fled Venezuela for the United States, bringing the child with him in violation of a Venezuelan court's restraining order. Indeed, he forged the mother's signature on an authorization to leave Venezuela.

161. *Van De Sande*, 431 F.3d 567.
162. Davies v. Davies, 717 Fed. Appx. 43 (2d Cir. 2017).
163. *Tsarbopoulos*, 176 F. Supp. 2d 1045.
164. *Miltiadous*, 686 F. Supp. 2d 544.
165. Gomez v. Fuenmayor, 2016 WL 454037 (11th Cir. 2016).

The court held that, where violence is directed at a parent that may threaten the well-being of a child, the grave risk exception may apply. It then upheld the finding of the trial court that the scope and severity of the threats to the father were clearly sufficient to establish a grave risk to his daughter. It held that a child's proximity to actual or threatened violence may pose a grave risk to the child; and that sufficiently serious threats to a parent can pose a grave risk of harm to a child. The court stated that "[r]uling to the contrary would artificially and unrealistically ignore the powerful effect that a pattern of serious violence directed at a parent may have on his children" and that "[s]imilarly, it requires no stretch of the imagination to conclude that serious, violent domestic abuse repeatedly directed at a parent can easily be turned against a child."[166]

The Tenth Circuit's approach in *Gil-Leyva*[167] is instructive. After reviewing evidence that the petitioner father had physically abused the respondent mother, the court reasoned that though this testimony was deeply concerning, and undeniably would figure in any foreign custody proceedings, spousal abuse is relevant for Article 13(b) purposes only if it seriously endangers the child. The court differentiated between evidence of a clear and long history of spousal abuse, which could suffice to show a propensity for child abuse and evidence of isolated incidents of abuse, which generally demonstrate a risk of harm only to the spouse. The court held that, at a minimum, the spouse must draw a connection showing that the risk such abuse poses to her constitutes a grave risk to the children. Here, any argument that such contact would trigger grave psychological harm upon the children's return to Canada rested on mere speculation.

§ 8.24 POST-TRAUMATIC STRESS DISORDER

In many cases, the exception of grave risk of harm has been established when there has been a well-established diagnosis of post-traumatic stress disorder.

The leading case is *Blondin*,[168] where the Second Circuit found that any undertakings would be inadequate to protect the children from a grave risk of harm if they were returned to France because any return to France would trigger a return of their post-traumatic stress disorder, because they associated France with their father's abuse and the trauma they suffered as a result.

166. *Id.* at 1014.
167. *Gil-Leyva*, 780 F. App'x 580.
168. *Blondin*, 238 F.3d 153

Other cases have also based findings of grave risk on psychiatric evidence of post-traumatic stress disorder (PTSD). If the evidence establishes, as in *Blondin*, that any return to the habitual residence is likely to trigger the disorder then such evidence may preclude a return order.[169] However, if the evidence establishes that the disorder will not be triggered if the taking parent returns to the habitual residence with the child, then such evidence may not preclude a return order.[170]

A full examination of the impact of PTSD is contained in the district court decision in the *Golan* case, subsequent to the Supreme Court's remand and subsequent to the tragic death of the child's mother.[171]

§ 8.25 SEXUAL ABUSE

Claims of sexual abuse are generally taken extremely seriously in Hague cases. When any such claim is raised, the court's inquiry must extend to types of abuse other than rape, "particularly when such abuse occurs at the hand of a parent." A court must not assert an "overly restrictive approach" to the type of conduct that constitutes sexual abuse and to the relationship between sexual abuse of a child and grave risk. The proper focus is on the effect on the child and the extent to which a child would be exposed to a risk if returned to the habitual residence.[172]

Nor should a court "overly compartmentalize" its analysis of discrete items of evidence that individually might have an innocent explanation, but which collectively are far less easily explained.[173]

It is not appropriate for a court to decline to resolve a claim of sexual abuse even on the ground that it would be more practical to defer the issue to a court in the country of habitual residence where the sexual abuse is alleged to have occurred.[174] On the other hand, if a court determines that the grave risk standard has not been met, it might nonetheless request the appropriate authorities in the habitual residence to review the issues surrounding the abuse allegations once the child has been returned.[175]

---

169. *Elyashiv*, 353 F. Supp. 2d 394; *Cruz Santana*, 2005 WL 67094.

170. Maurizio R. v. L.C., 201 Cal. App. 4th 616, 135 Cal. Rptr. 3d 93 (Cal. App. 2 Dist. 2011).

171. Saada v. Golan, 712 F. Supp. 3d 361 (E.D.N.Y. 2024).

172. *Danaipour*, 286 F.3d 1.

173. *In re* Application of Adan, 437 F.3d 381 (3d Cir. 2006).

174. *Danaipour*, 286 F.3d 1.

175. Seaman v. Peterson, 766 F.3d 1252 (11th Cir. 2014).

Courts vary in the extent to which corroborating evidence is required when sexual abuse claims are raised.[176]

A court faced with conflicting assertions concerning allegations of sexual abuse will often appoint an independent and well-qualified expert to conduct a thorough investigation of the allegations.[177] Even when a respondent's allegations of such abuse were deemed to be without any real foundation, a district court in Rhode Island found it necessary to appoint a pediatric expert to evaluate the claims.[178]

In one case, the petitioner was a convicted sex offender. However, there was no evidence or assertion that he had sexually abused the child. Although the respondents were concerned that he might do so in the future, they presented no specific evidence that suggested that he might do so. Although they cited a study published by the U.S. Department of Justice on the sexual recidivism rate of male sex offenders, the court held that it did not assist the court in determining the risk that the petitioner poses to the child. Respondents presented no specific evidence that suggested that petitioner might sexually assault the child in the future. Without this evidence, the court could not find that the risk of harm to the child was grave.[179]

Prior determinations in investigations that were conducted in the habitual residence should be considered, but the results are not binding. If they establish that a thorough investigation was made then that fact is of substantial significance.[180] When a court in Mexico had considered—and rejected for lack of evidence—charges based on the same conduct that a respondent subsequently asserted in a Hague case, the Mexican decision was of significance in supporting a finding that the grave risk exception based on sexual abuse claims had not been established.[181]

§ 8.26 NEED FOR MEDICAL TREATMENT OR THERAPY

In extremely special circumstances, it is possible that grave risk of harm could be established by proving that the child would be unable to secure

176. *In re* Application of Adan, 437 F.3d 381 (3d Cir. 2006); Charalambous v. Charalambous, 2010 WL 4115495 (D. Me. 2010), *judgment aff'd on other grounds*, 627 F.3d 462 (1st Cir. 2010).

177. *Danaipour*, 386 F.3d 289; Edoho v. Edoho, 2010 WL 3257480 (S.D. Tex. 2010).

178. *Kufner*, 480 F. Supp. 2d 491, *aff'd*, 519 F.3d 33 (1st Cir. 2008).

179. Guerrero v. Oliveros, 2015 WL 4755437 (N.D. Ill. 2015).

180. *Kufner*, 480 F. Supp. 2d 491, *aff'd*, 519 F.3d 33 (1st Cir. 2008).

181. Stirzaker v. Beltran, 2010 WL 1418388 (D. Idaho 2010).

needed medical treatment or psychological therapy if returned to the habitual residence.

Such an argument succeeded in a case in which the respondent father established the child's return to his mother's custody in Canada would expose him to grave risk of physical or psychological harm or otherwise place him in an intolerable situation. The mother had herself originally brought the child to the United States for the specific purpose of securing therapy for a developmental disorder, which was unavailable in Canada. If he were returned to Canada, the child would be unable to continue therapy with his established therapist.[182]

However, the burden is on the respondent to establish that the required treatment is unavailable in the habitual residence. Thus when a child was brought to the United States to live with her father and receive medical treatment for grand mal epilepsy and the father refused to return her to Germany, his claim of grave risk of harm failed once the court determined that the medical treatment that the child would receive in Germany was equivalent to the care that she was receiving in the United States, even though the father established that the child had made significantly greater progress while in the United States than she had made while living in Germany. Although there would be some temporary confusion and a sense of loss and the child's developmental progress might be set back somewhat, the adjustment period would be temporary and without any long-lasting effect.[183]

In sharp contrast, a Second Circuit case,[184] a Canadian case,[185] and an Australian case[186] all found that the risk of harm in removing an autistic child from his or her current therapy was sufficiently grave as to preclude ordering the child's return to the habitual residence. But note that, in the Second Circuit case, there was strong medical testimony that if the child were removed from his educational program and not provided promptly with an analogous program, he would face a severe loss of the skills that he had successfully developed since beginning his program, including his ability to develop cognitive, linguistic, social, and emotional skills; that any hope for the child to lead an independent and productive life depended on his participation in a program such as the one that he

---

182. *Didur*, 392 F. Supp. 2d 1268, *judgment rev'd on other grounds*, 197 Fed. Appx. 749 (10th Cir. 2006).

183. Slagenweit v. Slagenweit, 841 F. Supp. 264 (N.D. Iowa 1993), *aff'd*, 43 F.3d 1476 (8th Cir. 1994).

184. *Ermini*, 758 F.3d 167.

185. J.M.H. v. A.S., [2010] 367 N.B.R.2d 200 (N.B. Fam. Ct.) (Can.).

186. DP Commonwealth Cent. Auth., [2001] HCA 39 (High Ct. Austl.).

attended on a daily basis; that no such program was available in Italy; and that if the child were to be removed from this program, he would cease to be able to learn to write or to talk and would most likely never learn to read.[187]

Similarly, evidence that a mother had neglected the children's medical care was entirely insufficient when the father claimed that the children had "rotten molars" when in her care and were behind on their vaccinations, that one child had hearing loss requiring hearing aids, and that the other child had an astigmatism requiring eyeglasses, especially when partly rebutted by evidence of some dental treatment.[188]

Any claim that the other country has an inferior health care system should normally be supported by far more than the mere say-so of the respondent parent. There should be clear and convincing evidence both of the child's serious medical needs and of the home country's inability to provide the necessary care.[189] And mere allegations that an area in Guatemala was a place of leprosy and pneumonia from which some people suffered were insufficient without supporting evidence.[190]

§ 8.27 INTOLERABLE SITUATION

Article 13(b) permits a court to decline to return a child if "there is a grave risk that his or her return would expose the child to physical or psychological harm *or otherwise would place the child in an intolerable situation*" (emphasis added). There is some debate as to whether the two clauses in the provision are meant to be read as discrete factors, either of which needs to be satisfied, or whether the "or otherwise intolerable situation" language is merely intended to qualify the first "grave risk" clause.

In some cases, the harm in returning a child may not qualify as a grave risk of physical or psychological harm. A return that results in separating siblings or placing children in foster care when the primary caretaker is fit to care for them, for example, may not pose a grave risk of harm, but may still be considered so offensive as to constitute an "intolerable situation."

Professor Weiner criticizes U.S. courts for generally ignoring the "intolerable situation" phrase, choosing to analyze cases based on the "grave risk" of harm standard. Alternatively, some courts conflate the two phrases, assuming that the "'intolerable situation' language . . . is

---

187. Likewise, *see* Mene v. Sokola, 2024 WL 4227788 (S.D.N.Y. Sept. 17, 2024).

188. Galaviz v. Reyes, 95 F.4th 246, 257–59 (5th Cir. 2024).

189. *Cuellar*, 596 F.3d 505; *Kufner*, 480 F. Supp. 2d 491, *aff'd on other grounds*, 519 F.3d 33 (1st Cir. 2008).

190. Guerra v. Rodas, 2020 WL 2858534 (W.D. Okla. 2020).

coextensive with the 'grave risk of harm' language."[191] She argues that both of these approaches are incorrect because the "intolerable situation" phrase actually constitutes a separate and distinct element within Article 13(b). In support of her assertions, she points to a statement made by an individual involved in drafting the Convention, who said that the phrase "intolerable situation" was meant to be a flexible concept that could address many of the hard cases, including the situation of an abductor fleeing for reasons of domestic violence.

However, the State Department's analysis of Article 13(b) ascribed a far more limited role to the language, stating that:

> An example of an "intolerable situation" is one in which a custodial parent sexually abuses the child. If the other parent removes or retains the child to safeguard it against further victimization, and the abusive parent then petitions for the child's return under the Convention, the court may deny the petition. Such action would protect the child from being returned to an "intolerable situation" and subjected to a grave risk of psychological harm.[192]

The only other guidance that the State Department provides on the meaning of an "intolerable situation" is that it is "not intended to encompass return to a home where money is in short supply, or where educational or other opportunities are more limited than in the requested State."[193]

The extension of the Convention to countries that do not have a developed family law system and to countries with an entirely different view of family roles and parental rights and responsibilities than in the original Hague countries raises particular issues. What if the legal system in the habitual residence provides no significant rights to a parent or decides custody cases on grounds that would not protect the child's right to have both parents in its life? What if the abducting parent was unable to obtain any access to his or her child because the legal system in the country of the child's habitual residence has no provision for enforcement of access rights or bars parents of a certain religion or who do not follow a particular code of conduct from having or enforcing parental rights?

That question arose in a Hong Kong case in which the respondent claimed that if his children were returned to their habitual residence in

---

191. M. Weiner, *Intolerable Situations and Counsel for Children: Following Switzerland's Example in Hague Abduction Cases*, 58 AM. U. L. REV. 335.

192. Text and Legal Analysis, at 10504.

193. Text and Legal Analysis, at 10510.

Japan he would be unable to have any further significant contact with them, because Japanese law does not recognize joint custodial and access rights and is otherwise discriminatory. The court in Hong Kong took the issue seriously but rejected the claim on the basis that the respondent had not offered any effective proof of his claims.

> It is trite law that foreign law is matter of fact, and so the Father must produce factual evidence, usually in the form of an expert report by a lawyer in the relevant jurisdiction, to prove a particular law in that foreign jurisdiction. In the present case, no such evidence has been supplied to the court to substantiate these serious allegations.[194]

§ 8.28 WHETHER RESPONDENT MUST PROVE LACK OF PROTECTION IN HABITUAL RESIDENCE

There is a sharp divergence of opinion and authority as to whether or not a claim of grave risk must be supported by proof that the necessary protection is not available in the habitual residence.

Neither the Convention nor ICARA contains any express requirement that a respondent must prove that a child's state of habitual residence will not adequately protect the child against an alleged risk in order for the respondent to prevail. However, many courts have accepted the narrow *Friedrich* formulation as a governing principle of law. More recently, courts have deviated from that point of view.

§ 8.28.1 Such Proof Is Required

In 1996, the Sixth Circuit issued its landmark opinion in *Friedrich*[195] in which it sought to define the parameters of the Article 13(b) exception. The court asserted that a grave risk of harm for Convention purposes can only exist in two situations. The first is when returning the child would place it in imminent danger before the resolution of a custody dispute—for example, returning the child to a "zone of war, famine or disease." The second is when authorities in the country of habitual residence are unwilling or unable to adequately protect the child from "serious abuse or neglect, or extraordinary emotional dependence."

In *Blondin v. DuBois*,[196] the Second Circuit agreed with the Friedrich statement that grave risk of harm exists "in cases of serious abuse or

194. LPQ v. LYW [2014] HKCU 2976.
195. *Friedrich*, 78 F.3d 1060.
196. *Blondin*, 238 F.3d 153.

neglect, or extraordinary emotional dependence, when the court in the country of habitual residence, *for whatever reason*, may be incapable or unwilling to give the child adequate protection" (emphasis added).

In *Saada*,[197] the court held that even if serious abuse has been established sufficient to trigger the grave risk exception, a court may not deny repatriation on the ground that a grave risk of harm exists under Article 13(b) unless and until it has examined the full range of options that might make possible the safe return of a child to the home country.

Although the Second Circuit mandates such consideration before the grave risk exception may be applied, there is uncertainty as to which party has the burden of proof or if either party does,[198] even though in *Blondin IV*, the court stated, "In cases of serious abuse, before a court may deny repatriation on the ground that a grave risk of harm exists under Article 13(b), it must examine the full range of options that might make possible the safe return of a child to the home country."[199]

The Third Circuit in *Adan*[200] relied on *Blondin* and *Friedrich* as authority that established that a grave risk exception required the respondent to produce clear and convincing evidence not merely of the allegations of abuse that are offered in support of the exception but also to prove that the courts in the country of the child's habitual residence, "for whatever reason, may be incapable or unwilling to give the child adequate protection."

Thus:

- A district court in Kentucky ruled that there was no grave risk of harm because, inter alia, there was no indication that the Irish courts or the Irish authorities were incapable or unwilling to adequately protect the child.[201]
- In *March v. Levine*,[202] the Sixth Circuit explained that a default judgment in a wrongful death action against a petitioning father was not clear and convincing proof that returning the children would put them in imminent harm "such as to a war zone, or to an area of rampant disease or famine," nor were Mexican authorities incapable of protecting them.

---

197. Saada v. Golan, 930 F.3d 533 (2d Cir. 2019).
198. Saada v. Golan, 2020 WL 212886 (2d Cir. 2020).
199. *Blondin*, 238 F.3d 153 at n.11.
200. *In re* Application of Adan, 437 F.3d 381 (3d Cir. 2006).
201. Flynn v. Borders, 472 F. Supp. 2d 906 (E.D. Ky. 2007).
202. March v. Levine, 249 F.3d 462, 471–72 (6th Cir. 2001).

§ 8.28.2 Such Proof Is Not Required

In *Van de Sande*,[203] the Seventh Circuit rejected the proposition that the Convention requires that a court return a child in risk of harm unless the respondent proves that the law and system in the habitual residence will provide inadequate protection.

Its reasoning was that:

- The Convention itself does not contain any such requirement and this could not have been a mere slip in draftsmanship because it redefines the issue that the Convention actually handled. The drafters of the Convention expressly defined the issue as whether or not there was a grave risk of harm, not as whether foreign country has good laws or even as whether it both has and zealously enforces such laws.
- There is a substantial difference between the law on the books and the law as it is actually applied, and nowhere is the difference as great as in domestic relations. Because of the privacy of the family and parental control of children, most abuse of children by a parent goes undetected. To give a father custody of children who are at great risk of harm from him, on the ground that they will be protected by the police of the father's country, would be to act on an unrealistic premise. The rendering court must satisfy itself that the children will in fact, and not just in legal theory, be protected if returned to their abuser's custody.
- If handing over a child to an abusive parent creates a grave risk of harm to the child, in the sense that the parent may with some non-negligible probability injure the child, the child should not be handed over to such a person, however severely the law of the parent's country might punish such behavior. In such a case, any order divesting the abducting parent of custody would have to be conditioned on the child's being kept out of the custody of the abusing parent until the merits of the custody dispute between the parents could be resolved by the court in the abusive parent's country. Whether such a condition would be effective is uncertain.
- Although concern with the comity among nations argues for a narrow interpretation of the "grave risk of harm" defense, the safety of children is paramount.

203. *Van De Sande*, 431 F.3d 567.

In *Baran v. Beaty*,[204] the Eleventh Circuit agreed with the Seventh Circuit based on concerns of practicality. Its viewpoint was that to require a respondent to adduce evidence regarding the condition of the legal and social service systems in a country she has fled creates difficult problems of proof; that the text of the Convention and the commentaries on it place a higher premium on children's safety than on their return; that neither the Convention's official commentary nor the textual analysis of the United States State Department say anything about a reviewing court's duty to assess the home country's ability to protect a child from harm; and that "[c]onsequently, we decline to impose on a responding parent a duty to prove that her child's country of habitual residence is unable or unwilling to ameliorate the grave risk of harm which would otherwise accompany the child's return."

In *Danaipour*,[205] the First Circuit held that because the district court had found that the father had sexually abused his youngest daughter and had reached the conclusion that psychological harm to both children would be a necessary consequence of their return to Sweden, regardless of any possible conditions or undertakings imposed, the court was not required to inquire further into remedies and protections available through Swedish courts in applying the grave-risk exception.

In *Nunez-Escudero*,[206] the Eighth Circuit flatly rejected the father's argument that the "intolerable situation" exception applies only if the government agencies and courts of Mexico are unable to protect the child if he is returned to that country.

§ 8.28.3 Sufficiency of Such Proof

In several cases, the courts have found that a respondent has been able to meet the burden of proving that the authorities in the country of the child's habitual residence are, indeed, unable, unwilling, or unlikely to provide the necessary protection. This might be because the respondent had tried unsuccessfully but diligently to obtain the assistance of the local authorities or because even a strong and willing legal system could not, in fact, provide the necessary protection.

In *Blondin* this was because, although the French authorities were both willing and able to make numerous arrangements and accommodations to facilitate repatriation, they could not provide the necessary protection in the special circumstances of the case because doing so would

204. *Baran*, 526 F.3d 1340.
205. *Danaipour*, 386 F.3d 289.
206. *Nunez-Escudero*, 58 F.3d 374.

require them to fulfill the impossible task of ensuring that a return to France would not trigger a recurrence of traumatic stress disorder in the children. As the site of their trauma, their mere presence in that country would create a significant risk.

Similarly, in *Didur*,[207] there was evidence that the Children's Aid Society in the local area of Canada to which the child would be returned would certainly act diligently to protect the child but it was also established that the petitioning mother was unstable, and had previously fled Canada with the child when those authorities had intervened. Accordingly, the court found that Canada would not be able, in fact, to provide the necessary protection.

In contrast, there are many cases in which the evidence established that there was sufficient protection available in the habitual residence.

In *Saada III*,[208] the petitioner was physically, psychologically, emotionally, and verbally abusive to the respondent, largely in the child's presence. After the circuit order remanded the case to determine whether ameliorative measures would protect the child if he were returned to Italy, the district judge undertook an extensive examination of the measures available to ensure the child's safe return, which included communications with the Italian authorities. Thereafter, the court handling the parties' custody dispute in Italy issued a comprehensive order imposing various measures to facilitate the child's Italian repatriation, including a protective order against the petitioner and an order directing Italian social services to oversee his parenting classes and behavioral and psychoeducational therapy. The order also noted the U.S. court's finding that the petitioner was physically and psychologically violent toward the respondent, sometimes in the presence of the child. Separately, an Italian criminal court dismissed charges that the petitioner initiated against the respondent in connection with the child's removal from Italy, and the petitioner signed a statement agreeing not to pursue future criminal or civil actions against the respondent and submitted it to the Italian court. The court determined that the order of protection was sufficient to ameliorate the grave risk of harm resulting from the child's violent relationship. In addition, the court required the father to pay a substantial sum to cover the mother's living expenses for a year in Italy pending the final outcome of the Italian proceeding.

---

207. *Didur*, 392 F. Supp. 2d 1268, *rev'd on other grounds*, 197 Fed. Appx. 749 (10th Cir. 2006).

208. Saada v. Golan, 2020 WL 2128867 (S.D.N.Y. 2020).

In *Valles Rubio*,[209] the district court found that the respondent met her burden of proving grave risk, since there was clear and convincing evidence that the respondent father had physically and emotionally abused the child, including four beatings with a belt, one beating with a stick, frequent verbal abuse, using the child as a cover to transport firearms in the father's car, and handing the child a loaded firearm while making threatening comments. Nonetheless, the court found that ameliorative measures, such as litigation in Ecuadorian courts, were sufficient to protect the child. The parties were engaged in litigation in Ecuador and submitted a joint status update to the court that provided for weekly visits between the child and his mother's family, daily conversations by video or telephone between the mother and child, and restrictions on any access to firearms. Because the mother had failed to establish on appeal that these measures were inadequate to protect the child, or why she could not avail herself of the Ecuadorian courts or the equitable power of the district court to enforce ameliorative measures for the protection of the child, the Second Circuit affirmed the district court's ruling.

In *Adan*,[210] although a district court concluded that the mother did not produce sufficient evidence that Argentinean courts were without the skill, the expertise, or the concern to deal with the matter, the Third Circuit remanded the case because the lower court had not adequately evaluated the testimony of the mother on this issue. The mother had testified about her numerous experiences with Argentine law enforcement when police officers refused to offer her any assistance, and the fact that the father had violated a temporary restraining order issued by an Argentine court after the police refused to enforce it. Indeed, the father had not contested those allegations. The mother also testified as to the father's alleged bribery of judges and police officers.

On remand,[211] the lower court ruled that it did not find that the Argentine legal system was "incapable of resolving a custody dispute and ensuring the well-being and safety of the child of two Argentine citizens based on generalized allegations of corruption in the Argentine judicial system." To the contrary, it declared itself "confident that the Argentinean courts will more than adequately resolve the interests of the parties and their child." However, upon a further appeal, the Third Circuit dismissed

209. Valles Rubio v. Veintimilla Castro, 2020 WL 2311897 (2d Cir. 2020).
210. *In re* Application of Adan, 437 F.3d 381 (3d Cir. 2006).
211. *In re* Application of Adan v. Avans, 2007 WL 1850910 (D.N.J. 2007).

the petitioner's entire case, from the bench, without providing written reasons.[212]

In *Miltiadous*,[213] the court accepted that there was evidence that the local authorities were unable or unwilling to protect the respondent based on her testimony that she had no legal status in Cyprus; that she had been afraid to call the Cypriot authorities because she feared that the local police, who were well acquainted with the father, would not help; and that she had called the police on one occasion but the father had threatened to "throw her out" of the country and she had been forced to recall her complaint.

A Michigan appellate court[214] held that a lower court had been wrong to find that it would be dangerous to return a child to Mexico because of psychological harm resulting from the petitioner's obsessive and controlling behavior on the child. There was no evidence that the child would be forced to live with her mother if she were returned to Mexico.

But in *Ortiz*, the Seventh Circuit upheld the lower court's request to return a child to Mexico when the left-behind parent had sexually abused her and the mother had no job, no funds, and would almost certainly not have the means to reside independently from the father while custody was being determined.[215]

These cases often become a "battle of the experts," in which the court has to weigh the evidence on one side that the measures that are available in the country of habitual residence are strong and will be effective against the evidence of another expert to the effect that such measures will not provide sufficient protection.[216]

§8.29 ANTICIPATED CIRCUMSTANCES UPON RETURN

The situation that might face the child and perhaps the child's parents upon a return to the country of habitual residence may well be relevant to a grave risk analysis.

This is well illustrated by the ultimate findings in the *Golan* case, although the facts of that case were highly unusual. In the initial proceedings, the district court had held the authorities in Italy would be well able to provide any necessary protection for the child and the mother and had

212. *In re* Application of Adan, 544 F.3d 542 (3d Cir. 2008).
213. *Miltiadous*, 686 F. Supp. 2d 544.
214. Bonilla-Ruiz v. Bonilla, 2004 WL 2883247 (Mich. Ct. App. 2004).
215. *Ortiz*, 789 F.3d 722
216. *See, e.g.*, Mene v. Sokola, 2024 WL 4227788 (S.D.N.Y. Sept. 17, 2024).

ordered that certain measures should be implemented before the child's return. In the later proceeding before the same court, which occurred after the death of the mother, the district court had to consider what would happen in Italy if the child were returned to Milan. The court considered the status of the pending custody case in Milan, received expert evidence from Italian lawyers concerning the likely outcome of those proceedings, and consulted with judges in both countries who were members of the International Network of Judges pursuant to the Hague Conference Protocol on Direct Judicial Communications. The district court ultimately concluded that there was a possibility, the extent of which was uncertain, that the child might be placed in an institution upon his return to Italy. Since he had PTSD, had lost his mother, did not speak Italian, and had no memory of life in Italy, this factor was an additional reason to find that the risk of harm to him if he were returned to Italy would be significant.[217]

8.30 UNDERTAKINGS/AMELIORATIVE MEASURES: AUTHORITY TO REQUIRE

Article 13(b) is permissive. A court may still return a child to the habitual residence even when a respondent has proven that a grave risk or intolerable situation exists. In some cases, courts attach certain conditions, or undertakings, to a return order in an effort to mitigate the risks that might result from the return.

The concept of undertakings is a purely judicial construction. The Convention is silent on the use of undertakings, and they do not have a basis in the implementing legislation of any nation.[218]

The term "ameliorative measures" is also frequently employed. The Supreme Court has found[219] that "Courts of Appeals use the terms 'undertakings' and 'ameliorative measures' interchangeably. See, e.g., Blondin I, 189 F.3d 240, 248 (C.A.2 1999) (referring to 'ameliorative measures'); Simcox v. Simcox, 511 F.3d 594, 604–606 (C.A.6 2007) (referring to 'undertakings'). Although Saada asserts that the latter is broader than the former, he does not argue that the difference is determinative in this case. Accordingly, we use 'ameliorative measures,' the term employed by the Second Circuit in this case."

217. Saada v. Golan, 712 F. Supp. 3d 361 (E.D.N.Y. 2024).
218. *Danaipour*, 286 F.3d 1.
219. Golan v. Saada, 596 U.S. 666, 142 S. Ct. 1880, 1880 n.4 (2022).

In a letter to the British government, cited by the court in *Danaipour*,[220] the United States Department of State expressed the view that undertakings should be used sparingly and should be narrowly tailored to advance the Convention's goal of a prompt return.

On the other hand, courts that are ordering a child's return may well prefer to do so with "strings attached" in the form of undertakings. However, unless they find that a grave risk has been established, or that another exception has been proven, they will normally have no authority to do so. The Sixth Circuit in *Simcox* noted that absent a grave risk finding, the Convention leaves no room for a court to establish ameliorative undertakings designed to protect children against the risk of harm upon their return. For this reason the court pointed out, although the "grave risk" threshold is necessarily a high one, there is a danger of making the threshold so insurmountable that district courts will be unable to exercise any discretion in all but the most egregious cases of abuse.

§ 8.31 APPROPRIATENESS OF UNDERTAKINGS/ AMELIORATIVE MEASURES

The Sixth Circuit[221] has stressed that a determination as to whether undertakings are appropriate in a given case is "inherently fact-bound"; that the petitioner bears the burden of proving that undertakings are valid and feasible; and that, in evaluating whether undertakings can ameliorate a grave risk, "a court should primarily focus on the time period between repatriation and the determination of custody by the courts in the child's homeland."

In returning a child, a district court cannot employ undertakings as a tool to determine whether or not a grave risk exists. In *Danaipour*,[222] the First Circuit insisted that there must be a finding of grave risk or intolerable situation *before* a court can order undertakings. It stated that:

> The trial judge should have taken the steps available to him to determine if sexual abuse occurred; only once he had made such a finding could he ask the right questions about whether the children could be returned to the locale of the abuse. . . . Similarly, if the evaluation exonerated [the father], or even if it was inconclusive, that would also be relevant information to deciding the level of risk, if any, that the girls would face if returned.

220. *Danaipour*, 286 F.3d 1.
221. *Simcox*, 511 F.3d 594. (citing *Danaipour*, 286 F.3d at 21, 26).
222. *Danaipour*, 286 F.3d 1.

The decision of the Sixth Circuit in *Simcox* provides a helpful primer on the law of undertakings, at least as it applies in that circuit, and a useful roadmap for parties, their attorneys and the courts.

The court reviewed the authorities on the appropriateness of undertakings and concluded that it believed that any Hague Convention case dealing with abusive situations should be placed into one of three broad categories:

- In the first category are cases in which the abuse is relatively minor and it is unlikely that the risk of harm caused by return of the child will rise to the level of a "*grave risk*" or otherwise place the child in an "*intolerable situation*" under Article 13(b).

  In these cases, the court stated that undertakings designed to protect the child are largely irrelevant, since the Article 13(b) threshold has not been met and the court has no discretion to refuse to order return, with or without undertakings.
- In the second category are cases at the other end of the spectrum in which the risk of harm is clearly grave, such as where there is credible evidence of sexual abuse, other similarly grave physical or psychological abuse, death threats, and/or serious neglect.[223] The court stated that in these cases, undertakings will likely be insufficient to ameliorate the risk of harm, given the difficulty of enforcement and the likelihood that a serially abusive petitioner will not be deterred by a foreign court's orders. Consequently, the child in such a case should not be returned unless "the rendering court [can] satisfy itself that the children will in fact, and not just in legal theory, be protected if returned to their abuser's custody."[224]
- The third category comprises those cases that fall somewhere in the middle, where the abuse is substantially more than minor but is less obviously intolerable. Whether, in these cases, the return of the child would subject it to a "grave risk" of harm or otherwise place it in an "intolerable situation" is a fact-intensive inquiry that depends on careful consideration of several factors, including the nature and frequency of the abuse, the likelihood of its recurrence, and whether there are any enforceable undertakings that would sufficiently ameliorate the risk of harm to the child caused by its return.

223. *See, e.g., Van De Sande*, 431 F.3d at 571; Walsh, 221 F.3d at 220 (both rejecting undertakings in the face of such evidence).

224. *Van De Sande*, 431 F.3d 567.

The court stated that even for cases in the third category, undertakings should be adopted only where the court satisfies itself that the parties are likely to obey them. Thus, undertakings would be particularly inappropriate, for example, in cases where the petitioner has a history of ignoring court orders.[225] Where a grave risk of harm has been established, ordering return with feckless undertakings would be worse than not ordering it at all.

In applying that framework to the facts of the case before it, the *Simcox* court ruled that it was a Category 2 case. Its analysis was as follows:

- The nature of abuse was both physical (repeated beatings, hair pulling, ear pulling, and belt-whipping) and psychological (the father's profane outbursts and abuse of the children's mother in their presence). Importantly, these were not isolated or sporadic incidents. A psychologist found that all but the youngest were suffering from some level of post-traumatic stress disorder, which a return to Mexico could exacerbate. The youngest child had largely escaped such psychological injuries but the Convention does not require that a child must first be traumatized by abuse before the Article 13(b) exception applies.
- Such abuse was somewhat less serious than the abuse in the *Van De Sande*, *Walsh*, *Elyashiv*, and *Rodriguez* cases, in which other courts have refused to order return.
- But the abuse was decidedly *more* serious than that in those cases cited by the petitioner, in which courts had declined to find a "grave risk" of harm. Those cases were:
    - *McManus*[226] (holding that "two incidents" of a mother striking two of her four children and a generally chaotic home environment was insufficient to establish a grave risk of harm because it did not show "a sustained pattern of physical abuse");
    - *Whallon*[227] (stating that a husband's "verbal abuse and an incident of physical shoving" directed at his wife, while regrettable, were insufficient to establish a "grave risk" of harm to the child, especially where there was no allegation that the father had ever abused the child, either physically or psychologically); and

225. *See Walsh*, 221 F.3d 204 (citing the petitioner's "history of violating [court] orders" in concluding that undertakings would be insufficient to protect the children).
226. *McManus*, 354 F. Supp.2d 62.
227. *Lynn*, 230 F.3d 450.

- *In re D.D.*[228] (finding "no credible evidence that petitioner has ever physically harmed either of the two children" even though he had been verbally abusive).

The *Simcox* court then reviewed the specific undertakings imposed by the district court and determined that they required modification. There were two reasons why the lower court's undertakings were unsatisfactory:

- First, the district court had ordered the mother herself, not just the children, to return to Mexico. Thus, she could arguably defeat the order of return by simply refusing to accompany her children to Mexico. Then, since the condition that the children "remain in [her] custody" would be unfulfilled, the children would not be returned. Further litigation would inevitably ensue. Therefore, there needed to be provision for a contingency to ensure the children's safety and care should the mother choose to remain in the United States.
- Second, the fact that the father had exhibited "an arrogance, a need to be in control and a tendency to act out violently," raised doubts as to the enforceability of the undertakings and as to the father's willingness to abide by them, as did his threats to have his wife arrested upon her return to Mexico.

Accordingly, the case was remanded to the district court to determine what undertakings, if any, would be sufficient to ensure the safety of the children upon their return to Mexico pending the outcome of custody proceedings. It directed that any order on remand should be explicit as to the appropriate and efficacious undertakings that will apply should the mother decline to accompany her children. It suggested that one possibility may be for the father to remain in the United States and surrender his passport for a period of time, as the father had suggested at trial, although the district court should take into account the possible harm to his litigation interest when considering this approach.

The Sixth Circuit also stated that if the district court were to determine that no such arrangement was feasible, or that the only way in which the children could be protected from harm was for them to remain in the custody of their mother, then it might be necessary to deny the petition. It reiterated that the burden for establishing the appropriateness and efficacy of any proposed undertakings rests with the petitioner.

228. *In re* D.D., 440 F. Supp. 2d 1283, 1299 (M.D. Fla. 2006).

By contrast, even though it could not condition a return order on the mother returning with the child, a California appeal court ordered the return of a child to Italy, despite the fact that the mother had established that her son would suffer grave risk if she did not go with him.[229] The court ruled the trial court to appoint a guardian or "child welfare escort" to escort the child back to Italy, for further custody proceedings there, if the mother chose not to accompany her son.

Certainly, it is incumbent on a party who contends that any risk to a child or a parent can be adequately ameliorated by protective undertakings to provide the court with evidence that the undertakings will, in fact, work. Thus, in *Acosta*, the Eighth Circuit rejected undertakings on the ground, inter alia, that the petitioner did not make a specific proposal for appropriate undertakings before the district court and, on appeal, claimed that the court could have ordered the parties to utilize certain services available in Peru, which, according to his Peruvian attorney, included a child's ability to inform his school of any abuse, protection orders, battered women's shelters, and a domestic abuse hotline. The court stated, "[t]hat Peru has services designed to address domestic violence does not, by itself, establish that the children would receive sufficient protection if returned."[230]

§ 8.32 OPPOSING UNDERTAKINGS/AMELIORATIVE MEASURES

Respondents opposing the use of undertakings may have several arguments available to them.

First, there is an argument that placing conditions upon a return clashes with notions of international comity. A presumption that a U.S. court can impose enforceable orders on foreign states invites concerns about U.S. courts exceeding the scope of their authority. In *Danaipour*,[231] the First Circuit held that a district court had "offended notions of international comity" by issuing orders with the expectation that Swedish courts would simply copy and enforce them. The so-called legally and factually erroneous undertakings mandated by the U.S. district court were that Swedish authorities should conduct a forensic evaluation to investigate possible sexual abuse, and that Swedish judicial authorities should

229. Maurizio R. v. L.C., 201 Cal. App. 4th 616, 135 Cal. Rptr. 3d 93 (Cal. App. 2 Dist. 2011).

230. Acosta v. Acosta, 725 F.3d 868, 877 (8th Cir. 2013).

231. *Danaipour*, 286 F.3d 1.

adjudicate the implications of that evaluation. In contrast, in another case, the First Circuit affirmed the district court's conditional order of return, even though it contained several somewhat burdensome conditions, because they required the petitioner but not a foreign court to take the specified actions.[232]

Second, one may question the effectiveness of undertakings, particularly in cases involving severe abuse,[233] or where a petitioner has a history of disobeying court orders.[234] It is well established that where substantial allegations of grave risk to a child are made and a credible threat exists, a court should be "particularly wary" about using potentially unenforceable undertakings to try to protect the child. Thus, undertakings that will protect the child from grave risk for only a very limited time have been held to be insufficient to defeat an Article 13(b) claim.[235] U.S. courts have no real power to enforce their orders across national borders. The Eighth Circuit in *Baran*[236] cited a British study as showing that undertakings orders were violated in two-thirds of child abduction cases and honored in only one-fourth.

Thus, in *Davies*,[237] the court rejected proposed ameliorative measures because it found that petitioner would not abide by a stay-away agreement, respondent would be unable to hide or avoid petitioner on a small island such as St. Martin, the legal system in St. Martin was inadequate to protect respondent and the child from petitioner's abuse, and the child would be severely traumatized if he were returned to St. Martin regardless of whether he resided with petitioner full-time, part-time, or not at all.

Thus, some courts have rejected undertakings outright in abuse cases, most notably, the Seventh Circuit in *Van De Sande*, which asserted that any court imposing undertakings should satisfy itself that the children will "in fact, and not just in legal theory, be protected if returned to their abuser's custody."[238]

---

232. Kufner v. Kufner, 519 F.3d 33 (1st Cir. 2008).

233. *See, e.g.*, U.S. Department of State, Legal Memorandum attached to Brown Letter (If there is "unequivocal evidence" of a grave risk, "it would seem less appropriate for the court to enter extensive undertakings than to deny the return request.").

234. *Simcox*, 511 F.3d 594.

235. *Danaipour*, 286 F.3d 1.

236. *Baran*, 526 F.3d 1340.

237. Davies v. Davies, 717 F. App'x 43, 49 (2d Cir. 2017).

238. *Van De Sande*, 431 F.3d 567.

In *Baran*,[239] the Eighth Circuit upheld the district court's refusal to use undertakings to ameliorate a return order. It cited with approval the lower court's blunt language that,

> For this Court blithely to ship Sam back to Australia subject to elaborately crafted, well-meaning conditions that may or may not be enforced or enforceable by an Australian court would be to abdicate its overarching responsibility to protect this child from harm, while simultaneously entangling this Court in custody matters that exceed its authority and jurisdiction. This the Court will not do.

§ 8.33 TYPES OF UNDERTAKINGS/AMELIORATIVE MEASURES

The types of undertakings that have been employed range from:

- Temporary conditions on the return mechanism, such as allowing one specified parent to return the child at or by a specified time and perhaps even on a specified flight; requiring one parent to pay the travel expenses; and requiring one parent to deliver the child's passport to the other parent; to
- Interim conditions covering the immediate period after a return such as payment for lodging or an apartment; a restraining order against abuse; to
- Longer term conditions, usually to continue until a court in the habitual residence issues its first order, such conditions perhaps including physical custody, interim visitation, and school registration and attendance.

A far better solution might be to require the petitioner to obtain a "mirror" or "safe harbor" order from a court in the habitual residence before the return is accomplished. Indeed, the U.S. State Department has proposed such orders as an alternative to undertakings. They are orders issued by the courts in the habitual residence of the child that contain terms that are requested by the court handling the Hague case. Such orders are becoming increasingly common in cases concerning visitation or relocation of a child to a foreign country, where a parent is concerned

239. *Baran*, 526 F.3d 1340.

that the child might not be returned.[240] The English Court of Appeal has endorsed their use in such cases.[241] However, U.S. courts have not applied this idea. The First Circuit insisted that conditioning a return upon the making of an order by the court in the requested state "would smack of coercion of the foreign court," and "offended notions of international comity."[242]

§ 8.34 JUDICIAL DISCRETION

The court has a discretion to order the child's return to the habitual residence notwithstanding a determination that there would be a grave risk to the child to do so. For obvious reasons, the discretion to order a return in such circumstances has rarely been exercised, if at all.[243]

In one case, the court found, by clear and convincing evidence, that repatriating the child to Hungary, and to proximity to her father, would severely damage her psychological and emotional state. It then considered its discretion to return a child to its home country, regardless of any other determination, if return would further the aims of the Convention. It held that it saw no reason to do so, especially because there was no sign that a respondent's removal of the child, although unlawful, was not "motivated by a desire to go to a jurisdiction more favorable to [her] custody claims."

For further discussion concerning the discretion, see § 5.05, § 6.19, and § 7.09.

§ 8.35 STANDARD OF APPELLATE REVIEW

There is some uncertainty as to the standard of review on appeal in a grave risk case.

Prior to the Supreme Court's ruling in *Monasky*,[244] holding that a district court's determination of habitual residence is subject to deferential appellate review for clear error, most circuit courts had applied de novo

240. *See* Jeremy D. Morley, *Mirror Orders to Help Prevent International Child Abduction*, New York Family Law Monthly (Oct. 2011), available at www.internationalfamilylawfirm.com/2011/10/mirror-orders-to-help-prevent_06.html.

241. *See*, for example, the following English cases: C v. C (Minor: P Rights of Custody Abroad) [1989] 2 All E.R. 465, 471; Re G (a Minor) (Abduction) [1989] 2 FLR 475; Re W (Abduction: Domestic Violence) [2004] EWHC (Fam) 1247.

242. *Danaipour*, 286 F.3d 23 & 25.

243. *In re* D.T.J., 956 F. Supp. 2d 523 (S.D.N.Y. 2013).

244. Monasky v. Taglieri, 589 U.S. 68, 140 S. Ct. 719, 206 L. Ed. 2d 9 (2020).

review to a district court's conclusion whether particular facts establish an exception under Article 13(b).[245]

After *Monasky*, the First Circuit applied the clear error standard,[246] the Eleventh Circuit applied the de novo standard,[247] and the Fifth Circuit stated that "it is not clear-cut" which standard should apply.[248]

---

245. *See, e.g.*, Ermini v. Vittori, 758 F.3d 153, 160 (2d Cir. 2014) (holding "[t]he district court's factual findings are reviewed for clear error, while its application of the Convention to its factual findings is reviewed de novo"); Salame v. Tescari, 29 F.4th 763, 767 (6th Cir. 2022) ("Whether a child would be exposed to a 'grave risk' of harm or returned to an 'intolerable situation' are mixed questions of law and fact that we also review de novo."); Ortiz v. Martinez, 789 F.3d 722, 728 (7th Cir. 2015) ("We review the district court's factual findings for clear error and its conclusion that those facts establish a grave risk of harm de novo."); Acosta v. Acosta, 725 F.3d 868, 874 (8th Cir. 2013) ("A determination of a grave risk of harm under the Hague Convention is a mixed question of law and fact that we review de novo."); Cuellar v. Joyce, 596 F.3d 505, 509 (9th Cir. 2010) ("We review the district court's factual findings for clear error, but determine de novo whether those facts establish a grave risk of harm.").

246. Da Silva v. De Aredes, 953 F.3d 67, 72 (1st Cir. 2020).

247. Silva v. Dos Santos, 68 F.4th 1247, 1253 (11th Cir. 2023).

248. Galaviz v. Reyes, 95 F.4th 246, 251–52 (5th Cir. 2024).

Human Rights Exception

9

§ 9.01 IN GENERAL

Article 20 of the Convention states that "[t]he return of the child . . . may be refused if this would not be permitted by the fundamental principles of the requested State relating to the protection of human rights and fundamental freedoms."

A respondent has the burden of proving an Article 20 exception by clear and convincing evidence.[1]

The State Department Report on the Convention states that the exception is meant to be "restrictively interpreted and applied . . . on the rare occasion that return of a child would utterly shock the conscience of the court or offend all notions of due process."[2] That extreme limitation on the applicability of the article has been endorsed by case law.[3]

This exception was intended to be narrowly applied and is not to be used "as a vehicle for litigating custody on the merits or for passing judgment on the political system of the country from which the child was removed."[4]

1. 22 U.S.C. § 9003(e)(2)(A).

2. Text and Legal Analysis, Pub. Notice 957, 51 Fed. Reg. 10494, 10510 (1986).

3. Souratgar v. Lee, 720 F.3d 96 (2d Cir. 2013); Habrzyk v. Habrzyk, 759 F. Supp. 2d 1014 (N.D. Ill. 2011); Hazbun Escaf v. Rodriquez, 200 F. Supp. 2d 603 (E.D. Va. 2002).

4. Text and Legal Analysis, Pub. Notice 957, 51 Fed. Reg. 10494, 10510 (1986); Galaviz v. Reyes, 95 F.4th 246 (5th Cir. 2024).

Article 20 is directed to concerns about harms arising from the child's return to a particular country. It envisions a limited situation where human rights concerns, most likely defined within the parameters of other international agreements, would prohibit a return.[5]

Article 20 is silent as to whether it applies only to the human rights and fundamental freedoms of the child, or to the parties in the case as well. The district court in *Souratgar* concluded that Article 20 is broad enough to encompass the rights of the parties but only insofar as they relate to the exercise of custody rights of the child.[6]

§ 9.02 APPLICABILITY IN SPECIFIC CASES

There is no reported case in the United States that was not overturned on appeal in which a court did not return a child to the habitual residence based on Article 20.

The Fifth Circuit overturned a district court decision that a child should not be returned to Mexico because of a lack of educational opportunities there for a child with special needs.[7] The district court had focused primarily on the father's actions or inactions regarding the children's education, not on laws or policies of the United States that would prohibit return of the children. Neither the parties nor the district court had pointed to laws of the United States that would prohibit the return of a child to another country if the child's educational opportunities in that country are severely limited, either by a parent's shortcomings or because of that country's educational system. By focusing on the father's actions or inactions, the district court had essentially made an impermissible custody decision. The mother did not present clear and convincing evidence demonstrating that, as a matter of law, the return of the children would utterly shock the conscience or offend all notions of due process.

The court in another case rejected an argument that corruption in Mexico would make a fair custody determination impossible and that the child's rights as a United States citizen would not be protected.[8] The court held that not only were the allegations of corruption in the Mexican judicial system insufficiently established but also that the Hague Convention was expressly intended to prevent a parent removing a child from the child's habitual residence in search of a better forum, even if the purpose of such efforts was to secure a purportedly impartial forum.

5. Aldinger v. Segler, 263 F. Supp. 2d 284 (D.P.R. 2003).
6. Souratgar v. Fair, 2012 WL 6700214 (S.D.N.Y. 2012), *aff'd*, *Lee*, 720 F.3d 96.
7. *Galaviz*, 95 F.4th 246.
8. Stirzaker v. Beltran, 2010 WL 1418388 (D. Idaho 2010).

Several other cases seeking to use Article 20 to prevent returns to Mexico have failed.[9]

On the other hand, in a Canadian case an appeal court remanded a case for a further hearing when the child had been accepted into Canada as a refugee by reason of abuse from her mother in Mexico. Under Canadian law the child's refugee status gave rise to a rebuttable presumption that her return to Mexico would expose her to a risk of persecution. The court required that the hearing should determine the applicability of Article 20 as well as Article 13(b) in such a context.[10]

In another case a respondent argued that Article 20 applied because domestic abuse was a serious problem in Poland, so that returning the child to that country would offend the principles espoused in Illinois laws enacted to protect women and children from abuse. The court ruled summary judgment that the claim must fail for three reasons:[11]

1. Respondent failed to establish that the purported prevalence of domestic abuse in Poland met the "shocks the conscience" standard required to fall under the Article 20 exception.
2. Any claim that the child faced the threat of being a victim of domestic violence if she were returned to Poland was more properly addressed by the "grave risk" exception.
3. Article 20 requires that the fundamental principles of the state should not permit the return of the child; merely offending principles espoused in Illinois laws was insufficient.

It is possible that, as an increasing number of countries accede to the Convention from a wider range of legal systems, there will be more of an effort to use Article 20. For example, Sharia law countries are beginning to accede to the Convention. However, Sharia law bases custody decisions in large part on such factors as the age and gender of the child and upon the parents' adherence to Islam. There is substantial authority in support of the proposition that Sharia law, at least as it is applied in certain countries, violates fundamental principles of human rights, and does not apply the bedrock principle of the best interests of the child that is the basis of Western child custody legislation.[12]

---

9. Castro v. Martinez, 2012 WL 359901 (W.D. Tex. 2012); *In re* Hague Child Abduction Application, 2008 WL 913325 (D. Kan. 2008).

10. A.M.R.I. v. K.E.R., 2011 ONCA 417.

11. *Habrzyk*, 759 F. Supp. 2d 1014.

12. Charara v. Yatim, 78 Mass. App. Ct. 325, 937 N.E.2d 490 (Mass. App. Ct. 2010); El Chaar v. Chehab, 78 Mass. App. Ct. 501, 941 N.E.2d 75 (Mass. App. Ct. 2010).

That issue was before the court in *Souratgar*. The abducting parent argued that if the children were returned to Singapore, the Syariah Courts would have custody jurisdiction and would apply principles that are incompatible with the "relating to the protection of human rights and fundamental freedoms" of this country. The Second Circuit court stated, "While this general assertion might find sympathy among some in this country as a political statement, we decline to make this categorical ruling as a legal matter." In any event, it was not established that the issue of custody is likely to be litigated before Singapore's Syariah Court. Moreover, the court stated that it was mindful of the need for comity, since the treaty is intended "not only to protect children abducted to the United States, but also to protect American children abducted to other nations—whose courts, under the legal regime created by this treaty, are expected to offer reciprocal protection."[13] It insisted that, in the exercise of comity, U.S. courts should trust the courts of the home country to issue whatever orders may be necessary to safeguard children who come before it.

In addition, there may be a need in future cases to consider the case law emanating from the European Court of Human Rights to the effect that Article 8 of the European Convention on Human Rights requires that courts in states that are parties to the European Convention may not return an abducted child to its habitual residence, even when the child's return is mandated by the Hague Convention, unless it is first established that it is in the best interests of both the child and the child's family to do so. This issue is discussed at § 1.11. The U.K. Supreme Court has rejected the contention that the effect of *Neulinger*[14] case in the European Court of Human Rights requires a full "best interests" investigation in any Hague case.[15] The U.K. court noted that the violation of Article 8 in the *Neulinger* case arose from the enormous delay in ordering the child's return. It further noted that simply because the best interests of the child were not expressly made a primary consideration in Convention proceedings did not mean that they were not "at the forefront of the whole exercise"; that the Convention sought to promote both the best interests of children and of the individual child in cases of abduction; and that the best interests of the individual child were well served through the rebuttable assumption that it was best to provide for a prompt return to the state of habitual residence, which would promote the best resolution of any dispute about the child's future.

13. *Lee*, 720 F.3d 108–09.
14. Neulinger & Shuruk v. Switzerland, 41615/07 [2010] ECHR 1053.
15. Re E [2011] UKSC 27 [2011] FLR 758.

The U.K. court did state that it was possible to imagine other, highly unusual, cases in which a return under the Hague Convention might be in violation of the European Convention, such as if a child would be sent to a country where he would face a real risk of torture or inhuman or degrading treatment or punishment or the flagrant denial of a fair trial.

Rights of Access

10

§ 10.01 INTRODUCTION

The Hague Convention contains numerous provisions concerning access rights. However, those provisions have had little utility thus far, certainly in the United States, and it has often been said that the Convention's access provisions have no teeth. This may change in the future, given the Second Circuit's decision in *Ozaltin*,[1] which held that ICARA has created a federal right of action to secure the effective exercise of rights of access protected under the Convention.

§ 10.02 CONVENTION PROVISIONS CONCERNING ACCESS

The Convention's access provisions are as follows:

- The preamble states that the signatory parties desire "to protect children internationally from the harmful effects of their wrongful removal or retention and to establish procedures to ensure their prompt return to the State of their habitual residence, as well as to secure protection for rights of access."

1. Ozaltin v. Ozaltin, 708 F.3d 355 (2d Cir. 2013).

- Article 1 provides that the fundamental objects of the Convention include that of ensuring that access rights, as well as rights of custody, under the law of one Contracting State "are effectively respected in the other Contracting States."
- Article 4 provides that the Convention "shall apply to any child who was habitually resident in a Contracting State immediately before any breach of . . . access rights."
- Article 5 provides that "'rights of access' shall include the right to take a child for a limited period of time to a place other than the child's habitual residence."
- Article 7 obliges Central Authorities to take substantial proactive steps to further the objects of the Convention, such as taking all appropriate measure to locate children, to protect children, to resolve issues, and to provide legal assistance. Such steps also include "f) to initiate or facilitate the institution of judicial or administrative proceedings with a view to obtaining the return of the child and, in a proper case, to make arrangements for organizing or securing the effective exercise of rights of access."
- Chapter IV of the Convention is entitled "Rights of Access." It contains only one article, Article 21. That article provides that,
    - An application to make arrangements for organizing or securing the effective exercise of rights of access may be presented to the Central Authorities of the Contracting States in the same way as an application for the return of a child.
    - The Central Authorities are bound by the obligations of co-operation which are set forth in Article 7 to promote the peaceful enjoyment of access rights and the fulfillment of any conditions to which the exercise of those rights may be subject. The Central Authorities shall take steps to remove, as far as possible, all obstacles to the exercise of such rights.
    - The Central Authorities, either directly or through intermediaries, may initiate or assist in the institution of proceedings with a view to organizing or protecting these rights and securing respect for the conditions to which the exercise of these rights may be subject.
- Article 26 provides that, upon issuing an order concerning rights of access under this Convention, the judicial or administrative authorities may, where appropriate, direct the person who prevented the exercise of rights of access, to pay necessary expenses incurred by or on behalf of the applicant, including the costs of legal representation.

- Article 29 provides that the Convention shall not preclude any person who claims that there has been a breach of access rights from applying directly to the judicial or administrative authorities of a Contracting State, whether or not under the provisions of this Convention.

§ 10.03 ICARA PROVISIONS CONCERNING ACCESS

The provisions about access contained in ICARA are as follows:

- Section 9002(1) defines the term "applicant" to include any person who, pursuant to the Convention, files an application for arrangements for organizing or securing the effective exercise of rights of access pursuant to the Convention.
- Section 9002(7) provides that the term "rights of access" means visitation rights.
- Section 9003(b) provides that any person seeking to initiate judicial proceedings under the Convention for arrangements for organizing or securing the effective exercise of rights of access to a child may do so by commencing a civil action by filing a petition for the relief sought in any court that has jurisdiction of such action and that is authorized to exercise its jurisdiction in the place where the child is located at the time the petition is filed.
- Section 9003(e) provides that a petitioner in an action brought under subsection (b) shall, in the case of an action for arrangements for organizing or securing the effective exercise of rights of access, establish by a preponderance of the evidence that the petitioner has such rights.

§ 10.04 ICAPRA PROVISIONS CONCERNING ACCESS

The 2014 International Child Abduction Prevention and Return Act contains reports and other provisions that are designed to improve compliance with the Hague Convention and to extend the State Department's reporting role to include non-Hague countries. The act contains numerous provisions concerning rights of access that are intended to require oversight of the extent to which other countries comply with the access terms of the Convention as well as with the return obligations.

Unfortunately the act does not grapple with the very real issues, discussed in the next chapter, concerning the inability of the courts in one country to control the exercise by courts in another country of their jurisdiction to modify the terms of provisions in custody orders concerning access whenever a child has become habitually resident in a new country and the courts in that country believe that a modification is required.

§ 10.05 FEDERAL RIGHT OF ACTION CONCERNING ACCESS

The federal courts in the United States previously held that they had no jurisdiction to enforce rights of access.[2] A similar interpretation applied in England.[3]

Thus, the Fourth Circuit in *Cantor*[4] pointed out that Article 21 "does not provide for presentation to a judicial authority," in "sharp contrast to Article 12 "which specifically refers to the initiation of judicial proceedings and grants judicial authority to provide the requisite relief in the event of a child's wrongful removal or retention." The court also relied on the State Department's legal analysis of the Convention, which stated that access rights

> are also protected by the Convention, but to a lesser extent than custody rights. While the Convention preamble and Article 1(b) articulate the Convention objective of ensuring that rights of access under the law of one state are respected in other Contracting States, the remedies for breach of access rights are those enumerated in Article 21. . .[5]

The Fourth Circuit noted that the petitioner could file a claim for visitation in state court under the state's visitation law, or petition the State Department under the Convention.[6]

However, the Second Circuit ruled in *Ozaltin*[7] that ICARA has created a federal right of action to secure the effective exercise of rights of access protected under the Convention, holding that the facilitative role that Central Authorities assume under the Convention did not displace or inhibit the ability of a party to vindicate his or her rights directly in federal or state court. The court relied primarily on the terms of ICARA,

---

2. Cantor v. Cohen, 442 F.3d 196 (4th Cir. 2006).
3. G (A Minor) (Enforcement of Access Abroad), Re, 1992 WL 895736, [1993] 3 All E.R. 657, [1993] 2 F.C.R. 485, [1993] Fam. 216, [1993] Fam. Law 340, [1993] 1 F.L.R. 669, 1-26-1993 Times 895736, [1993] 2 W.L.R. 824 (CA (Civ Div) (1992).
4. *Cantor*, 442 F.3d 200.
5. State Department Legal Analysis, 51 Fed. Reg. 10,494, 10,513.
6. *Cantor*, 442 F.3d 206.
7. *Ozaltin*, 708 F.3d 355.

which has implemented the Convention in U.S. law. Specifically, ICARA provides that,

> Any person seeking to initiate judicial proceedings under the Convention for the return of a child *or for arrangements for organizing or securing the effective exercise of rights of access to a child* may do so by commencing a civil action by filing a petition for the relief sought in any court which has jurisdiction of such action and which is authorized to exercise its jurisdiction in the place where the child is located at the time the petition is filed.[8]

Earlier, but in a case concerning the Alien Tort Claims Act, the Sixth Circuit had arrived at the same conclusion, stating that "unlike [t]he Hague Convention, the ICARA . . . does provide for judicial remedies for non-custodial parents, namely for rights of access claims (e.g., visitation)."[9]

§ 10.06 INTERNATIONAL APPROACHES TO ACCESS PROVISIONS

Article 21 of the Convention has generally been given little effect in other countries. An English judge determined that "[t]here are no teeth to be found in art 21 and its provisions have no part to play in the decision to be made by the judge."[10] However, some countries such as Australia[11] and New Zealand,[12] have made express or implied provision for the enforcement of rights of access in their domestic legislation.

§ 10.07 APPLICABILITY OF ACCESS PROVISIONS

Thus far the federal courts have faced access issues in Hague Convention cases primarily only as to interim access in return cases, that is, as to whether a left-behind parent who has petitioned for the return of a child is entitled to interim access pending the determination of the case. In *Ozaltin*, the trial court ordered interim access in the United States on alternating weekends prior to the children's return to Turkey, in compliance with a prior order of a Turkish court. The issue on appeal essentially concerned

8. 22 U.S.C. 9003(b) (emphasis added).

9. Taveras v. Taveraz, 477 F.3d 767 (6th Cir. 2007).

10. Re G (a minor) (Enforcement of Access Abroad) [1993] 3 All ER 657.

11. Art. 25, Australian Family Law (Child Abduction Convention) Regulations 1986.

12. *See* Gumbrell v. Jones [2001] NZFLR 593.

whether the petitioner should receive a fee award for that portion of the case, as well as for the expense of securing the basic return order.[13]

In a Washington state case, the court allowed interim visitation—including overnight visitation, over the objection of respondent, the child's mother, but with "numerous safeguards"—since although there was no custody order from Germany, the place of the child's habitual residence, the evidence established that by default under German law the petitioner shared equal custodial rights with the respondent.[14]

The Tenth Circuit held that, pursuant to the Younger abstention principle,[15] a district court should have abstained from exercising jurisdiction over a father's claim of access under the Hague Convention when the father was simultaneously seeking such access in a pending state court case under the Uniform Child Custody Jurisdiction and Enforcement Act.[16]

U.S. federal courts have not fully explored the difficult issues that may arise if a petitioner in a foreign country seeks access rights in lieu of a return order or as an alternative to a return order in respect of a child now located in the United States but who was previously habitually resident in that foreign country. If a noncustodial overseas parent has a visitation order from a foreign court, will a U.S. federal court enforce the terms of that order in the face of a claim from the custodial parent that (1) the foreign court did not have jurisdiction under the Uniform Child Custody Jurisdiction & Enforcement Act as enacted in the state where the child is located, or (2) a local state court proceeding is pending seeking to modify the foreign order, or (3) the foreign order will expose the child to grave risk of harm, or (4) the local state court has actually issued a contradictory custody order? Will a federal access order trump a state court order that rules that the state court has modification jurisdiction? These fundamental issues concerning access rights have not yet been resolved.

---

13. *Ozaltin*, 708 F.3d 355.
14. Rehder v. Rehder, 2014 WL 5324295 (W.D. Wash. 2014).
15. Younger v. Harris, 401 U.S. 37 (1971).
16. Dawson v. Dylla, 2021 WL 5232251 (10th Cir. Nov. 10, 2021).

The Hague Convention and International Relocation and Travel

11

§ 11.01 INTRODUCTION

The Hague Convention has a role to play in cases concerning international child visitation and travel. That role will on occasion be of great significance. It also has some significance in international relocation ("move away") cases, but that role is frequently afforded entirely inappropriate significance.[1]

§ 11.02 INTERNATIONAL CHILD RELOCATION

In international child relocation cases, an important issue is whether or not the foreign country to which the child may be relocated will effectively enforce the orders of the U.S. court concerning access for the non-custodial, non-relocating parent.

Parents sometimes cite, as a relevant factor on this issue, the fact that the country in question is—or is not—a party to the Hague Convention. However, the key issue is far narrower than that. The Convention is triggered as an abduction case only if there has been a wrongful removal or retention within the meaning of Article 3. If a court in the United States permits a parent to relocate with a child to another country, that parent's retention of the child in the foreign country is obviously not a wrongful act.

1. The issues in this chapter are discussed in far greater length in the author's treatise, *International Family Law Practice* (2024), available through Westlaw.

The issue in international child relocation cases should be whether or not the Convention, as it is actually applied in the foreign country, will enforce a left-behind parent's right of access. But in most cases the mere fact that a foreign country is a Hague Convention treaty partner provides no assurance whatsoever that access orders issued by a court in the United States will be recognized and enforced after the relocation has taken place.

Courts in the United States must appreciate that, once a child has been lawfully relocated overseas, their extraterritorial jurisdiction will generally be quite limited. Indeed, no other country has adopted the Uniform Child Custody Jurisdiction & Enforcement Act or any law similar to it. The American concept of exclusive jurisdiction continuing in the (American) court that issues an initial custody order, even if the child lives overseas, as long as one parent continues to live in the original state, is completely alien to almost all foreign courts.

In most countries, once a child has been relocated to such a country and is habitually or ordinarily resident there, the local courts will consider that they have exclusive jurisdiction to issue a child custody order or to modify a prior foreign custody order without regard to any claim to the contrary by the courts of the prior habitual residence. A change of habitual residence in favor of the new country is likely to occur promptly after a child is lawfully relocated there, particularly when the child is in school there.

In this context, it must be said that the influential California case of *Condon*[2] makes little sense. In that case, the court conditioned international child relocation on the applicant first obtaining an order from the court in the country to which the relocating parent proposed to move that mirrored the terms of the forum court's order, that acknowledged that the forum court has continuing exclusive jurisdiction concerning all matters as to the child's custody and visitation, and that required the appropriate authorities in the foreign country to enforce such orders. If that condition were actually applied in California, it would preclude any international relocation from that state because, once a relocated child is habitually resident in the foreign country, the courts in that country will invariably have the right and the duty under the laws and the public policy of that country to assume modification jurisdiction without regard to the demands and presumptions of an American court.

Of course, such an order of a court in the United States would nonetheless be binding under the laws of the issuing state, and most likely of

2. *In re* Marriage of Condon, 62 Cal. App. 4th 533, 73 Cal. Rptr. 2d 33 (2d Dist. 1998).

sister states in this country, even if the foreign court has issued a contradictory order. The U.S. orders would bind the relocating parent who has taken the child overseas and might put that parent in jeopardy. In this regard, it would be critical to consider the impact in the U.S. courts of the provisions of the Uniform Child Custody Jurisdiction and Enforcement Act on the extent to which they would have continuing exclusive jurisdiction or continuing jurisdiction. But the orders of a U.S. court would be inconsequential in the foreign country and most likely in other foreign countries also.

Thus, reliance on Article 21 of the Hague Convention to ensure compliance with the visitation provisions of an order permitting international relocation may well be misplaced. Once a foreign court has assumed custody jurisdiction under its own jurisdictional rules, it will make such decisions as it deems fit about custody and access, and Article 21 will not restrain that process in the slightest.

It should be noted that the U.S. approach may be modified to accord with the worldwide standard and with the anticipated accession by the United States to the 1996 Hague Convention on Jurisdiction, Applicable Law, Recognition, Enforcement and Cooperation in Respect of Parental Responsibility and Measures for the Protection of Children (the "1996 Convention"). The basic principle of the UCCJEA—that the court that issues an initial custody order retains the exclusive right to modify the order so long as that state remains the residence of a parent, the child, or a person acting as a parent—is not mirrored in the 1996 Convention. Instead, the Convention provides that modification jurisdiction changes with changes to the child's habitual residence. These terms codify the practice of many countries around the world. The 1996 Convention provides that a country's courts have custody jurisdiction whenever the child is habitually resident there (Article 5), subject to certain limitations for refugee or internationally displaced children with no habitual country of residence (Article 6), and cases of wrongful removal or retention of a child (Article 7). Another country's authorities cannot intervene to protect a child without the express agreement of, or at the express request of, the courts of country where the child is habitually resident (Articles 8 and 9).

In 2013, the Uniform Law Commissioners promulgated a revised UCCJEA, to accommodate the 1996 Convention. The new UCCJEA contains a new Article 4 that is intended to govern cases between states of the United States and foreign countries. In such cases, jurisdiction to issue—and to modify—a custody order (to be referred to as a "measure of protection") will be based on the child's habitual residence, which may shift over time.

Courts have sometimes relied on the fact that a country has not signed the Hague Convention as one reason among others to reject an application for international relocation. Thus, a Delaware court denied a parent's application to relocate a child to Liberia in part because that country was not a signatory to the Convention. The court was also concerned about Liberia's uncertain medical emergency assistance, police presence, and the fact that only financially capable citizens are able to afford running water and electricity.[3]

On the other hand, the New Jersey Supreme Court allowed a parent to relocate to Japan even though at that time Japan had not signed the Convention.[4] There the court relied on the finding of the court below that it expected that the mother would permit visitation by the father even after she relocated with the child to Japan. Although it found that a foreign nation's Hague Convention status was a pertinent factor, it concluded that it was by no means a dispositive factor. It also suggested that trial courts should pursue alternative solutions by encouraging parties to obtain appropriate orders in the foreign nations or enter into contractual agreements that are definitively enforceable in foreign nations.

It should also be noted that there is clearly a relationship between the extent to which the courts in a country are liberal in permitting international relocation and the number of international child abduction cases. When expat parents learn that they are unlikely to be able to win a relocation order through the judicial process, they are far more likely to resort to self-help. This tendency is reinforced by the failure of lawmakers, courts, and scholars to establish rules about international child relocation that provide any real degree of predictability as to when such relocations will be permitted (except for the (somewhat) draconian principle applied in many jurisdictions that international child relocations should not be permitted except in extreme cases).[5]

§ 11.03 INTERNATIONAL CHILD TRAVEL

Cases concerning a child's international travel arise when a parent seeks to enjoin the other parent from taking the child to visit a foreign country, usually because of a fear that the child will not be returned, or when a parent asks for leave to take the child overseas, often for a family visit, notwithstanding the objections of the other parent.

3. J.B. v. A.C., 2009 WL 6303022 (Del. Fam. Ct. 2009).
4. MacKinnon v. MacKinnon, 191 N.J. 240, 252, 922 A.2d 1252 (2007).
5. For an extensive discussion of international child relocation, see Jeremy D. Morley, International Family Law Practice, ch. 8 (Thomson Reuters 2024).

There are two basic issues in these cases. *The first issue* is the extent to which the parent who wants to take the child overseas is a likely child abductor. A body of knowledge has developed, much of it under the auspices of the U.S. Justice Department, as to the factors that tend to indicate that a specific parent presents a significant risk of abducting a specific child. The evidence has formed the basis of the Uniform Child Abduction Prevention Act (UCAPA), adopted in 2006.[6] The purpose of UCAPA, as stated in its preamble, is to identify circumstances indicating a risk of abduction and to provide measures to prevent the abduction of children.

The risk factors are identified in Section 7 of UCAPA. They include evidence that the parent has previously abducted or attempted to abduct the child; has threatened to abduct the child; has recently engaged in activities that may indicate a planned abduction, including abandoning employment, selling a primary residence, terminating a lease, closing bank or other financial management accounts, liquidating assets, hiding or destroying financial documents, or conducting any unusual financial activities; applying for a passport or visa or obtaining travel documents for the respondent, a family member, or the child; or seeking to obtain the child's birth certificate or school or medical records.

Other factors are whether the person has engaged in domestic violence, stalking, or child abuse or neglect; has refused to follow a child-custody determination; lacks strong familial, financial, emotional, or cultural ties to the state or the United States; has strong familial, financial, emotional, or cultural ties to another state or country; is undergoing a change in immigration or citizenship status that would adversely affect the respondent's ability to remain in the United States legally; has had an application for U.S. citizenship denied; has forged or presented misleading or false evidence on government forms or supporting documents to obtain or attempt to obtain a passport, a visa, travel documents, a Social Security card, a driver's license, or other government-issued identification card or has made a misrepresentation to the U.S. government; has used multiple names to attempt to mislead or defraud; or has engaged in "any other conduct the court considers relevant to the risk of abduction."

The second issue in such a case is the extent to which the courts in the country to which the child is to be taken will recognize American custody orders and are likely to expeditiously secure the child's return to the United States. In this regard, the relevant elements to consider are whether the parent is likely to take the child to a country that is not a party

6. *Available at* http://www.nccusl.org/Act.aspx?title=Child%20Abduction%20 Prevention.

to the Hague Convention; whether the country provides for the extradition of abducting parents; whether the authorities in the country have procedures for the return of abducted children and a history of having done so; whether, if the country is a party to the Convention, it is actually in force between the United States and that country; and whether the country is noncompliant according to the most recent compliance report issued by the United States Department of State or lacks legal mechanisms for immediately and effectively enforcing a return order under the Convention.

So far, UCAPA has been enacted in 18 states, but its principles are relevant to any case concerning the propriety of a child's proposed international travel.

The cases establish that the mere fact that a country has or has not signed the Hague Convention is not dispositive, but that it is a highly relevant factor.

- A Delaware court refused to allow a three-week visit of a child to Nigeria. A significant factor was Nigeria's failure to sign the Hague Convention, which meant that "it could be very difficult and time consuming for a U.S. resident to retrieve a child that is taken to Nigeria and kept there."[7]
- A New Jersey court allowed a father to take his daughter for a family visit to Lebanon even though Lebanon had not signed the Hague Convention.[8] The court expressly declined to adopt a "bright-line rule" prohibiting out-of-country visitation by a parent whose country has not adopted the Hague Convention or executed an extradition treaty with the United States. It stated that such a rule would "unnecessarily penalize a law-abiding parent" and that it "could conflict with a child's best interest by depriving the child of an opportunity to share his or her family heritage with a parent." Indeed, the court further insisted that any such rule "would mistakenly change the focus" from the parent to "whether his or her native country's laws, policies, religion or values conflict with our own" which "would border on xenophobia, a long word with a long and sinister past."
- A Wisconsin appeal court upheld a lower court's decision to allow a parent to take children for a family visit to Iran notwithstanding

7. V.U. v. F.U.U., 2008 WL 2898335 (Del. Fam. Ct. 2008).

8. Abouzahr v. Matera-Abouzahr, 361 N.J. Super. 135, 824 A.2d 268 (N.J. Super. A.D. 2003).

evidence that Iran was not a signatory to the Hague Convention, that it did not have diplomatic relations with the United States, and that its courts would not recognize a U.S. custody order.[9] The court below had not ignored this evidence, but had forthrightly addressed it in weighing the benefit of the children going to Iran with their father against the likelihood that they would not be returned, along with the harm to them if they were not returned. The court refused to rule that, as a matter of law, a parent may not take a child to a country that is not a signatory to the Hague Convention if the other parent objects, even if a court finds the parent wishing to take the child intends to return the child and otherwise comply with court orders.

- By contrast, a South Carolina appeal court affirmed a decision that prohibited a father from traveling to Iran with his children.[10] The mother presented evidence of specific threats by the father to relocate the children to Iran and testimony as to the "inherent dangers" in travel with children of Iranian descent to that country and the possibility that the father could easily fly from another country into Iran if he was allowed to travel with the children outside the United States. Furthermore, even if the father had every intention to return the children after their visit to Iran, if he were to become incapacitated while he and the children were there, the mother could do very little to retrieve the children, based on the lack of legal recourse in a country that was not a signatory to the Hague Convention.
- A court in Washington state barred a father from taking a child for a family visit to India based in part on the fact that India was a non-signatory to the Hague Convention and upon findings about the legal impediments to effectuating return of children abducted to India by a parent, such as that abduction by a parent is not a crime in India, there is "no guarantee of enforcing a U.S. parenting order in India," such proceedings can take from six months to a year, and that the "custody order of a foreign state is only one of the factors which will be taken into consideration by a court of law in India."[11]

---

9. Long v. Ardestani, 241 Wis. 2d 498, 624 N.W.2d 405 (Wis. App. 2001).
10. Pirayesh v. Pirayesh, 596 S.E.2d 505 (S.C. Ct. App. 2004).
11. Katare v. Katare, 159 Wash. App. 1017, 2011 WL 61847 (Wash. App. Div. 1, 2011).

- A Louisiana court vacated an order enjoining a parent from taking a child to Nicaragua because the order was based solely on the fact that Nicaragua was not a party to the Hague Convention. The court below was directed to consider all of the risk factors identified in UCAPA.[12]

It may be tempting for a court to go no further than to ascertain whether or not the country of a proposed visit has signed the Convention. In fact, the inquiry should often go much further than that. Questions that may be highly material are:

- Is the Convention actually in force between the United States and the other country?
- Does the foreign country comply with the terms of the Convention? A starting point is to review the annual reports of compliance published by the State Department. If a country is listed as "noncompliant" that is obviously significant. Unfortunately, the State Department is very cautious in applying that label and seems to be even more so as of late as compared to prior years. Furthermore, the State Department's determinations are not based on any overall analysis of the actual likelihood that the courts and other authorities in the foreign country will actually cause the child to be expeditiously returned. Its hands are tied by the provisions of the International Child Abduction Prevention and Return Act of 2014, which provides arbitrary standards that do not reflect the facts on the ground concerning the likelihood that a specific country will actually return an abducted child. Counsel should certainly check for past compliance reports as well as the current report.

  In this author's view, the mere fact that the State Department has not listed a country as not compliant or not fully compliant is not and should not be the end of the inquiry. For example, the Swiss "Federal Act on International Child Abduction and the Hague Conventions on the Protection of Children and Adults"[13] requires Swiss courts to interpret Article 13(b) of the Convention in a manner that is fundamentally at odds with the terms of the treaty. It provides that a best interests test governs the applicability of the exception and it provides that the exception will apply if the taking parent is not in a position to return to the child's

12. Mohsen v. Mohsen, 2008 WL 5352015 (La. App. 1 Cir. 2008).
13. *Available at* http://www.admin.ch/ch/e/rs/2/211.222.32.en.pdf.

habitual residence or if "this cannot reasonably be required from this parent." Such factors must be presented to the court through expert testimony.

- Are there other reasons to believe that the other country may not promptly return the child? Thus, one should consider whether a defense to a potential Hague case could be successfully asserted in the foreign country. For example, Article 13 of the Convention provides that an abducted child need not be returned if the child objects to being returned and has attained an age and degree of maturity at which it is appropriate to take account of its views. This means that if the child is, say, 12 years old, there is a potentially significant risk that the child may successfully oppose a return home. The risk would be accentuated if, for example, the taking parent creates conditions in the new country that cause the child to be infatuated by the new environment or fearful of going back to the former environment. Likewise, if the taking parent has previously made assertions that the other parent has committed domestic violence against the child or the taking parent, then it must be assumed that such allegations, perhaps in an exaggerated form, will provide the basis for a claimed defense to any case under the Convention that is brought in the foreign country, alleging that there will be a grave risk of harm to the child within the meaning of Article 13 of the Convention if the child is returned.

On occasion, the fact that a country is not compliant with its obligations under the Hague Convention, coupled with evidence indicating that the non-custodial parent has threatened to take the child permanently to that country, has led a court to require that all visitation with the child by that parent within the U.S. should be supervised. In *In re Sigmar*,[14] a Texas appeal court displayed little reluctance in telling some blunt truths about Mexico's consistent breach of its obligations under the Hague Convention. Such determinations provided the basis to uphold a decision to require supervision of all visitation in Texas between a father and his son since there was a serious risk that the father might abduct the child to Mexico. The court based its negative findings as to the Mexican legal system and as to safety in that country by relying exclusively on the State Department's published materials, including the State Department evaluations of Mexico's compliance with the Hague Convention, and its

14. *In re* Sigmar, 270 S.W.3d 289 (Tex. App.-Waco 2008).

published warnings concerning travel in certain parts of the country and concerning trafficking in women and children for the purpose of sexual exploitation.

Expert evidence from experienced international family law counsel or other experts—concerning the laws and procedures in the foreign country in international child custody cases, the difficulties of litigating such issues in the foreign courts, the risk factors of potential international child abduction, and the applicability of the well-established body of knowledge concerning the risk factors of potential international child abduction to the alleged facts asserted by the parent who seeks to prevent international child abduction—is generally absolutely essential in such cases. Courts cannot determine whether a foreign legal system is likely to cause an abducted child to be returned without expert testimony.

The author has submitted evidence on such issues in numerous cases concerning the child custody laws and practices of foreign countries of India, Japan, China, France, England, Colombia, Brazil, and many other countries to counsel and courts in many states and countries.[15]

§ 11.04 PROVISIONS OF ORDER AUTHORIZING VISITATION

It may be useful to provide certain language in an order authorizing a child's international travel that will make it easier for a court in the foreign country to make a quick ruling in a Hague case in favor of the left-behind parent.[16] The order might include:

- A provision that the nontraveling parent has specified custody rights over the child;
- A provision that the United States is the habitual residence of the child for purposes of the Convention;
- A representation by the taking parent that he will return the child no later than a specified date and an order that that must be done; and
- Findings, based on the affirmative representation of the taking parent, that (a) such parent knows of no reason why the child should not be returned to his home in the United States, (b) there

15. *See, e.g.*, Lehn v. Al-Thanayyan, 246 Ariz. 277, 438 P.3d 646 (AZ Ct. Apps. 2019); Mahadevan v. Shankar, 2010 ONSC 5608 (CanLII).

16. For an extensive discussion of the prevention of international child abduction, see Jeremy D. Morley, International Family Law Practice, ch. 11 (Thomson Reuters 2024).

is no risk, physical, psychological or otherwise, in returning the child to the United States, (c) the non-traveling parent is a good parent, (d) the child has expressed his wish to return home to the United States after the visit, (e) the child is not sufficiently mature to object to returning to the United States.

- A requirement that the taking parent must sign an updated affidavit containing the abovementioned representations before each and every visit.

However, it is most important for both the U.S. court and the non-traveling parent to understand that such an order will not bind the foreign court and that the extent to which it has some influence in the foreign court will depend on a host of factors that are entirely beyond the control of both the U.S. court and the potentially left-behind parent.

In one American case the parties signed a "Stipulation in Custody" that the habitual residence of the child was in Finland as part of their effort to obtain a visa for the child to visit the United States. The terms of the Stipulation required that it be filed with the Court of Common Pleas of Allegheny County, Pennsylvania. Though the Stipulation was signed by a common pleas judge, the parties never actually filed it with the court. Three years later, the child was retained in the United States after a summer visit. The Third Circuit disregarded the Stipulation on the issue of the child's habitual residence.[17]

Moreover, if the child is of an age and at a level of maturity that might suffice to lead a court to apply the age and maturity exception to the Convention, there will be little that a court in this country can do to preclude a parent who takes a child on a foreign visit from asserting the exception in a Hague case in the foreign country. Similarly, the foreign court in any Convention case will have the duty for itself to determine whether the respondent has established that, if the child is returned, there will be a grave risk that the child will be exposed to physical or psychological harm or will be placed in an intolerable situation.

---

17. Karkkainen v. Kovalchuk, 445 F.3d 280 (3d Cir. 2006).

APPENDIX 1

Hague Convention on the Civil Aspects of International Child Abduction

(Concluded 25 October 1980)

The States signatory to the present Convention,

Firmly convinced that the interests of children are of paramount importance in matters relating to their custody,

Desiring to protect children internationally from the harmful effects of their wrongful removal or retention and to establish procedures to ensure their prompt return to the State of their habitual residence, as well as to secure protection for rights of access,

Have resolved to conclude a Convention to this effect, and have agreed upon the following provisions—

CHAPTER I—SCOPE OF THE CONVENTION

Article 1

The objects of the present Convention are—

a) to secure the prompt return of children wrongfully removed to or retained in any Contracting State; and

b) to ensure that rights of custody and of access under the law of one Contracting State are effectively respected in the other Contracting States.

Article 2

Contracting States shall take all appropriate measures to secure within their territories the implementation of the objects of the Convention. For this purpose they shall use the most expeditious procedures available.

Article 3

The removal or the retention of a child is to be considered wrongful where—

a) it is in breach of rights of custody attributed to a person, an institution or any other body, either jointly or alone, under the law of the State in which the child was habitually resident immediately before the removal or retention; and

b) at the time of removal or retention those rights were actually exercised, either jointly or alone, or would have been so exercised but for the removal or retention.

The rights of custody mentioned in sub-paragraph *a)* above, may arise in particular by operation of law or by reason of a judicial or administrative decision, or by reason of an agreement having legal effect under the law of that State.

Article 4

The Convention shall apply to any child who was habitually resident in a Contracting State immediately before any breach of custody or access rights. The Convention shall cease to apply when the child attains the age of 16 years.

Article 5

For the purposes of this Convention—

a) "rights of custody" shall include rights relating to the care of the person of the child and, in particular, the right to determine the child's place of residence;

b) "rights of access" shall include the right to take a child for a limited period of time to a place other than the child's habitual residence.

CHAPTER II—CENTRAL AUTHORITIES

Article 6

A Contracting State shall designate a Central Authority to discharge the duties which are imposed by the Convention upon such authorities.

Federal States, States with more than one system of law or States having autonomous territorial organisations shall be free to appoint more than one

Central Authority and to specify the territorial extent of their powers. Where a State has appointed more than one Central Authority, it shall designate the Central Authority to which applications may be addressed for transmission to the appropriate Central Authority within that State.

Article 7

Central Authorities shall co-operate with each other and promote co-operation amongst the competent authorities in their respective States to secure the prompt return of children and to achieve the other objects of this Convention.

In particular, either directly or through any intermediary, they shall take all appropriate measures—

a) to discover the whereabouts of a child who has been wrongfully removed or retained;

b) to prevent further harm to the child or prejudice to interested parties by taking or causing to be taken provisional measures;

c) to secure the voluntary return of the child or to bring about an amicable resolution of the issues;

d) to exchange, where desirable, information relating to the social background of the child;

e) to provide information of a general character as to the law of their State in connection with the application of the Convention;

f) to initiate or facilitate the institution of judicial or administrative proceedings with a view to obtaining the return of the child and, in a proper case, to make arrangements for organising or securing the effective exercise of rights of access;

g) where the circumstances so require, to provide or facilitate the provision of legal aid and advice, including the participation of legal counsel and advisers;

h) to provide such administrative arrangements as may be necessary and appropriate to secure the safe return of the child;

i) to keep each other informed with respect to the operation of this Convention and, as far as possible, to eliminate any obstacles to its application.

CHAPTER III—RETURN OF CHILDREN

Article 8

Any person, institution or other body claiming that a child has been removed or retained in breach of custody rights may apply either to the Central Authority of the child's habitual residence or to the Central Authority of any other Contracting State for assistance in securing the return of the child.

The application shall contain—

a) information concerning the identity of the applicant, of the child and of the person alleged to have removed or retained the child;

b) where available, the date of birth of the child;

c) the grounds on which the applicant's claim for return of the child is based;

d) all available information relating to the whereabouts of the child and the identity of the person with whom the child is presumed to be.

The application may be accompanied or supplemented by—

e) an authenticated copy of any relevant decision or agreement;
f) a certificate or an affidavit emanating from a Central Authority, or other competent authority of the State of the child's habitual residence, or from a qualified person, concerning the relevant law of that State;
g) any other relevant document.

Article 9

If the Central Authority which receives an application referred to in Article 8 has reason to believe that the child is in another Contracting State, it shall directly and without delay transmit the application to the Central Authority of that Contracting State and inform the requesting Central Authority, or the applicant, as the case may be.

Article 10

The Central Authority of the State where the child is shall take or cause to be taken all appropriate measures in order to obtain the voluntary return of the child.

Article 11

The judicial or administrative authorities of Contracting States shall act expeditiously in proceedings for the return of children.

If the judicial or administrative authority concerned has not reached a decision within six weeks from the date of commencement of the proceedings, the applicant or the Central Authority of the requested State, on its own initiative or if asked by the Central Authority of the requesting State, shall have the right to request a statement of the reasons for the delay. If a reply is received by the Central Authority of the requested State, that Authority shall transmit the reply to the Central Authority of the requesting State, or to the applicant, as the case may be.

Article 12

Where a child has been wrongfully removed or retained in terms of Article 3 and, at the date of the commencement of the proceedings before the judicial or administrative authority of the Contracting State where the child is, a period of less than one year has elapsed from the date of the wrongful removal or retention, the authority concerned shall order the return of the child forthwith.

The judicial or administrative authority, even where the proceedings have been commenced after the expiration of the period of one year referred to in the preceding paragraph, shall also order the return of the child, unless it is demonstrated that the child is now settled in its new environment.

Where the judicial or administrative authority in the requested State has reason to believe that the child has been taken to another State, it may stay the proceedings or dismiss the application for the return of the child.

Article 13

Notwithstanding the provisions of the preceding Article, the judicial or administrative authority of the requested State is not bound to order the return of the child if the person, institution or other body which opposes its return establishes that—

a) the person, institution or other body having the care of the person of the child was not actually exercising the custody rights at the time of removal or retention, or had consented to or subsequently acquiesced in the removal or retention; or *b)* there is a grave risk that his or her return would expose the child to physical or psychological harm or otherwise place the child in an intolerable situation.

The judicial or administrative authority may also refuse to order the return of the child if it finds that the child objects to being returned and has attained an age and degree of maturity at which it is appropriate to take account of its views.

In considering the circumstances referred to in this Article, the judicial and administrative authorities shall take into account the information relating to the social background of the child provided by the Central Authority or other competent authority of the child's habitual residence.

Article 14

In ascertaining whether there has been a wrongful removal or retention within the meaning of Article 3, the judicial or administrative authorities of the requested State may take notice directly of the law of, and of judicial or administrative decisions, formally recognised or not in the State of the habitual residence of the child, without recourse to the specific procedures for the proof of that law or for the recognition of foreign decisions which would otherwise be applicable.

Article 15

The judicial or administrative authorities of a Contracting State may, prior to the making of an order for the return of the child, request that the applicant obtain from the authorities of the State of the habitual residence of the child a decision or other determination that the removal or retention was wrongful within the meaning of Article 3 of the Convention, where such a decision or determination may be obtained in that State. The Central Authorities of the Contracting States shall so far as practicable assist applicants to obtain such a decision or determination.

Article 16

After receiving notice of a wrongful removal or retention of a child in the sense of Article 3, the judicial or administrative authorities of the Contracting State to which the child has been removed or in which it has been retained shall not decide on the merits of rights of custody until it has been determined that the child is not to be returned under this Convention or unless an application under this Convention is not lodged within a reasonable time following receipt of the notice.

Article 17

The sole fact that a decision relating to custody has been given in or is entitled to recognition in the requested State shall not be a ground for refusing to return a child under this Convention, but the judicial or administrative authorities of the requested State may take account of the reasons for that decision in applying this Convention.

Article 18

The provisions of this Chapter do not limit the power of a judicial or administrative authority to order the return of the child at any time.

Article 19

A decision under this Convention concerning the return of the child shall not be taken to be a determination on the merits of any custody issue.

Article 20

The return of the child under the provisions of Article 12 may be refused if this would not be permitted by the fundamental principles of the requested State relating to the protection of human rights and fundamental freedoms.

CHAPTER IV—RIGHTS OF ACCESS

Article 21

An application to make arrangements for organising or securing the effective exercise of rights of access may be presented to the Central Authorities of the Contracting States in the same way as an application for the return of a child.

The Central Authorities are bound by the obligations of co-operation which are set forth in Article 7 to promote the peaceful enjoyment of access rights and the fulfilment of any conditions to which the exercise of those rights may be subject. The Central Authorities shall take steps to remove, as far as possible, all obstacles to the exercise of such rights.

The Central Authorities, either directly or through intermediaries, may initiate or assist in the institution of proceedings with a view to organising or protecting these rights and securing respect for the conditions to which the exercise of these rights may be subject.

CHAPTER V—GENERAL PROVISIONS

Article 22

No security, bond or deposit, however described, shall be required to guarantee the payment of costs and expenses in the judicial or administrative proceedings falling within the scope of this Convention.

Article 23

No legalisation or similar formality may be required in the context of this Convention.

Article 24

Any application, communication or other document sent to the Central Authority of the requested State shall be in the original language, and shall be accompanied by a translation into the official language or one of the official languages of the requested State or, where that is not feasible, a translation into French or English.

However, a Contracting State may, by making a reservation in accordance with Article 42, object to the use of either French or English, but not both, in any application, communication or other document sent to its Central Authority.

Article 25

Nationals of the Contracting States and persons who are habitually resident within those States shall be entitled in matters concerned with the application of this Convention to legal aid and advice in any other Contracting State on the same conditions as if they themselves were nationals of and habitually resident in that State.

Article 26

Each Central Authority shall bear its own costs in applying this Convention.

Central Authorities and other public services of Contracting States shall not impose any charges in relation to applications submitted under this Convention. In particular, they may not require any payment from the applicant towards the costs and expenses of the proceedings or, where applicable, those arising from the participation of legal counsel or advisers. However, they may require the payment of the expenses incurred or to be incurred in implementing the return of the child.

However, a Contracting State may, by making a reservation in accordance with Article 42, declare that it shall not be bound to assume any costs referred to in the preceding paragraph resulting from the participation of legal counsel or advisers or from court proceedings, except insofar as those costs may be covered by its system of legal aid and advice.

Upon ordering the return of a child or issuing an order concerning rights of access under this Convention, the judicial or administrative authorities may, where appropriate, direct the person who removed or retained the child, or who prevented the exercise of rights of access, to pay necessary expenses incurred by or on behalf of the applicant, including travel expenses, any costs incurred or payments made for locating the child, the costs of legal representation of the applicant, and those of returning the child.

Article 27

When it is manifest that the requirements of this Convention are not fulfilled or that the application is otherwise not well founded, a Central Authority is not bound to accept the application. In that case, the Central Authority shall forthwith inform the applicant or the Central Authority through which the application was submitted, as the case may be, of its reasons.

Article 28

A Central Authority may require that the application be accompanied by a written authorisation empowering it to act on behalf of the applicant, or to designate a representative so to act.

Article 29

This Convention shall not preclude any person, institution or body who claims that there has been a breach of custody or access rights within the meaning of Article 3 or 21 from applying directly to the judicial or administrative authorities of a Contracting State, whether or not under the provisions of this Convention.

Article 30

Any application submitted to the Central Authorities or directly to the judicial or administrative authorities of a Contracting State in accordance with the terms of this Convention, together with documents and any other information appended thereto or provided by a Central Authority, shall be admissible in the courts or administrative authorities of the Contracting States.

Article 31

In relation to a State which in matters of custody of children has two or more systems of law applicable in different territorial units—

a) any reference to habitual residence in that State shall be construed as referring to habitual residence in a territorial unit of that State;

b) any reference to the law of the State of habitual residence shall be construed as referring to the law of the territorial unit in that State where the child habitually resides.

Article 32

In relation to a State which in matters of custody of children has two or more systems of law applicable to different categories of persons, any reference to the law of that State shall be construed as referring to the legal system specified by the law of that State.

Article 33

A State within which different territorial units have their own rules of law in respect of custody of children shall not be bound to apply this Convention where a State with a unified system of law would not be bound to do so.

Article 34

This Convention shall take priority in matters within its scope over the *Convention of 5 October 1961 concerning the powers of authorities and the law applicable in respect of the protection of minors*, as between Parties to both Conventions. Otherwise the present Convention shall not restrict the application of an international instrument in force between the State of origin and the State addressed or other law of the State addressed for the purposes of obtaining the return of a child who has been wrongfully removed or retained or of organising access rights.

Article 35

This Convention shall apply as between Contracting States only to wrongful removals or retentions occurring after its entry into force in those States.

Where a declaration has been made under Article 39 or 40, the reference in the preceding paragraph to a Contracting State shall be taken to refer to the territorial unit or units in relation to which this Convention applies.

Article 36

Nothing in this Convention shall prevent two or more Contracting States, in order to limit the restrictions to which the return of the child may be subject, from agreeing among themselves to derogate from any provisions of this Convention which may imply such a restriction.

CHAPTER VI—FINAL CLAUSES

Article 37

The Convention shall be open for signature by the States which were Members of the Hague Conference on Private International Law at the time of its Fourteenth Session.

It shall be ratified, accepted or approved and the instruments of ratification, acceptance or approval shall be deposited with the Ministry of Foreign Affairs of the Kingdom of the Netherlands.

Article 38

Any other State may accede to the Convention.

The instrument of accession shall be deposited with the Ministry of Foreign Affairs of the Kingdom of the Netherlands.

The Convention shall enter into force for a State acceding to it on the first day of the third calendar month after the deposit of its instrument of accession.

The accession will have effect only as regards the relations between the acceding State and such Contracting States as will have declared their acceptance of the accession. Such a declaration will also have to be made by any Member State ratifying, accepting or approving the Convention after an accession. Such declaration shall be deposited at the Ministry of Foreign

Affairs of the Kingdom of the Netherlands; this Ministry shall forward, through diplomatic channels, a certified copy to each of the Contracting States.

The Convention will enter into force as between the acceding State and the State that has declared its acceptance of the accession on the first day of the third calendar month after the deposit of the declaration of acceptance.

Article 39

Any State may, at the time of signature, ratification, acceptance, approval or accession, declare that the Convention shall extend to all the territories for the international relations of which it is responsible, or to one or more of them. Such a declaration shall take effect at the time the Convention enters into force for that State.

Such declaration, as well as any subsequent extension, shall be notified to the Ministry of Foreign Affairs of the Kingdom of the Netherlands.

Article 40

If a Contracting State has two or more territorial units in which different systems of law are applicable in relation to matters dealt with in this Convention, it may at the time of signature, ratification, acceptance, approval or accession declare that this Convention shall extend to all its territorial units or only to one or more of them and may modify this declaration by submitting another declaration at any time.

Any such declaration shall be notified to the Ministry of Foreign Affairs of the Kingdom of the Netherlands and shall state expressly the territorial units to which the Convention applies.

Article 41

Where a Contracting State has a system of government under which executive, judicial and legislative powers are distributed between central and other authorities within that State, its signature or ratification, acceptance or approval of, or accession to this Convention, or its making of any declaration in terms of Article 40 shall carry no implication as to the internal distribution of powers within that State.

Article 42

Any State may, not later than the time of ratification, acceptance, approval or accession, or at the time of making a declaration in terms of Article 39 or 40, make one or both of the reservations provided for in Article 24 and Article 26, third paragraph. No other reservation shall be permitted.

Any State may at any time withdraw a reservation it has made. The withdrawal shall be notified to the Ministry of Foreign Affairs of the Kingdom of the Netherlands.

The reservation shall cease to have effect on the first day of the third calendar month after the notification referred to in the preceding paragraph.

Article 43

The Convention shall enter into force on the first day of the third calendar month after the deposit of the third instrument of ratification, acceptance, approval or accession referred to in Articles 37 and 38.

Thereafter the Convention shall enter into force—

(1) for each State ratifying, accepting, approving or acceding to it subsequently, on the first day of the third calendar month after the deposit of its instrument of ratification, acceptance, approval or accession;

(2) for any territory or territorial unit to which the Convention has been extended in conformity with Article 39 or 40, on the first day of the third calendar month after the notification referred to in that Article.

Article 44

The Convention shall remain in force for five years from the date of its entry into force in accordance with the first paragraph of Article 43 even for States which subsequently have ratified, accepted, approved it or acceded to it.

If there has been no denunciation, it shall be renewed tacitly every five years.

Any denunciation shall be notified to the Ministry of Foreign Affairs of the Kingdom of the Netherlands at least six months before the expiry of the five year period. It may be limited to certain of the territories or territorial units to which the Convention applies.

The denunciation shall have effect only as regards the State which has notified it. The Convention shall remain in force for the other Contracting States.

Article 45

The Ministry of Foreign Affairs of the Kingdom of the Netherlands shall notify the States Members of the Conference, and the States which have acceded in accordance with Article 38, of the following—

(1) the signatures and ratifications, acceptances and approvals referred to in Article 37;
(2) the accessions referred to in Article 38;
(3) the date on which the Convention enters into force in accordance with Article 43;
(4) the extensions referred to in Article 39;
(5) the declarations referred to in Articles 38 and 40;
(6) the reservations referred to in Article 24 and Article 26, third paragraph, and the withdrawals referred to in Article 42;
(7) the denunciations referred to in Article 44.

In witness whereof the undersigned, being duly authorised thereto, have signed this Convention.

Done at The Hague, on the 25th day of October, 1980, in the English and French languages, both texts being equally authentic, in a single copy which shall be deposited in the archives of the Government of the Kingdom of the Netherlands, and of which a certified copy shall be sent, through diplomatic channels, to each of the States Members of the Hague Conference on Private International Law at the date of its Fourteenth Session.

APPENDIX 2

Explanatory Report Drawn Up by Ms. E. Pérez-Vera

Table des matières	page	Contents of the Report	page
Introduction (Nos 1-8)	426	**Introduction** (Nos 1-8)	426
I *Conclusions des travaux de la Conférence de La Haye de droit international privé* (Nos 1-4)	426	I *Results of the work of the Hague Conference on private international law* (Nos 1-4)	426
II *Objet et plan du présent Rapport* (Nos 5-8)	427	II *Aim and structure of this Report* (Nos 5-8)	427
Première partie – Caractères généraux de la Convention (Nos 9-53)	428	**First Part – General characteristics of the Convention** (Nos 9-53)	428
I OBJET DE LA CONVENTION (Nos 10-34)	428	I OBJECT OF THE CONVENTION (Nos 10-34)	428
A *Délimitation du sujet* (Nos 11-15)	428	A *Definition of the Convention's subject-matter* (Nos 11-15)	428
B *Les objectifs de la Convention* (Nos 16-19)	429	B *The objectives of the Convention* (Nos 16-19)	429
C *Importance accordée à l'intérêt de l'enfant* (Nos 20-26)	430	C *Importance attached to the interest of the child* (Nos 20-26)	430
D *Exceptions à l'obligation d'assurer le retour immédiat des enfants* (Nos 27-34)	432	D *Exceptions to the duty to secure the prompt return of children* (Nos 27-34)	432
II NATURE DE LA CONVENTION (Nos 35-41)	435	II NATURE OF THE CONVENTION (Nos 35-41)	435
A *Une convention de coopération entre autorités* (Nos 35-37)	435	A *A convention of co-operation among authorities* (Nos 35-37)	435
B *Caractère autonome de la Convention* (Nos 38-39)	436	B *The autonomous nature of the Convention* (Nos 38-39)	436
C *Rapports avec d'autres conventions* (No 40)	436	C *Relations with other conventions* (No 40)	436
D *Ouverture de la Convention aux Etats non-membres de la Conférence de La Haye* (No 41)	437	D *Opening of the Convention to States not Members of the Hague Conference* (No 41)	437
III INSTRUMENTS D'APPLICATION DE LA CONVENTION (Nos 42-51)	437	III INSTRUMENTS FOR APPLYING THE CONVENTION (Nos 42-51)	437
A *Les Autorités centrales* (Nos 42-47)	437	A *The Central Authorities* (Nos 42-47)	437
B *La formule modèle* (Nos 48-51)	439	B *The model form* (Nos 48-51)	439
IV STRUCTURE ET TERMINOLOGIE (Nos 52-53)	440	IV STRUCTURE AND TERMINOLOGY (Nos 52-53)	440
A *La structure de la Convention* (No 52)	440	A *The structure of the Convention* (No 52)	440
B *Terminologie utilisée par la Convention* (No 53)	441	B *Terminology used in the Convention* (No 53)	441
Deuxième partie – Commentaire des articles de la Convention (Nos 54-151)	441	**Second Part – Commentary on the specific articles of the Convention** (Nos 54-151)	441
CHAPITRE PREMIER – CHAMP D'APPLICATION DE LA CONVENTION (Nos 54-86)	441	CHAPTER ONE – SCOPE OF THE CONVENTION (Nos 54-86)	441
Article premier – Les objectifs de la Convention (Nos 55-61)	442	*Article 1 – The aims of the Convention* (Nos 55-61)	442
a *Observations générales* (Nos 55-56)	442	*a* *General observations* (Nos 55-56)	442
b *Lettre* a (Nos 57-59)	442	*b* *Sub-paragraph* a (Nos 57-59)	442
c *Lettre* b (Nos 60-61)	443	*c* *Sub-paragraph* b (Nos 60-61)	443

Rapport explicatif de Mlle Elisa Pérez-Vera

Introduction

I *Conclusions des travaux de la Conférence de La Haye de droit international privé*

1 La Convention sur les aspects civils de l'enlèvement international d'enfants a été adoptée en séance plénière le 24 octobre 1980 par la Quatorzième session de la Conférence de La Haye de droit international privé, à l'unanimité des Etats présents.[1] Le 25 octobre 1980, les délégués signèrent l'Acte final de la Quatorzième session contenant le texte de la Convention et une Recommandation qui contient la formule modèle à utiliser pour les demandes de retour des enfants déplacés ou retenus illicitement.

A cette occasion, la Conférence de La Haye s'est écartée de sa pratique, les projets de Conventions adoptés au cours de la Quatorzième session ayant été ouverts à la signature des Etats immédiatement après la séance de clôture. Quatre Etats ont signé la Convention à cette occasion (le Canada, la France, la Grèce et la Suisse), de sorte qu'elle porte la date du 25 octobre 1980.

2 En ce qui concerne le point de départ des travaux qui ont abouti à l'adoption de la Convention, ainsi que les conventions existantes en la matière ou ayant un rapport direct avec elle, nous renvoyons à l'introduction du Rapport de la Commission spéciale.[2]

3 La Quatorzième session de la Conférence, qui a siégé du 6 au 25 octobre 1980, a confié l'élaboration de la Convention à sa Première commission, dont le Président était le professeur A. E. Anton (Royaume-Uni) et le Vice-président le doyen Leal (Canada); l'un et l'autre avaient déjà été respectivement Président et Vice-président de la Commission spéciale. D'autre part, le professeur Elisa Pérez-Vera a été confirmé dans ses fonctions de Rapporteur. M. Adair Dyer, Premier secrétaire au Bureau Permanent, qui avait élaboré d'importants documents pour les travaux de la Conférence, a été chargé de la direction scientifique du secrétariat.

4 Au cours de treize séances, la Première commission a procédé à une première lecture de l'avant-projet élaboré par la Commission spéciale. Simultanément, elle a nommé un Comité de rédaction qui, au fur et à mesure de la pro-

[1] Allemagne, Australie, Autriche, Belgique, Canada, Danemark, Espagne, Etats-Unis, Finlande, France, Grèce, Irlande, Japon, Luxembourg, Norvège, Pays-Bas, Portugal, Royaume-Uni, Suède, Suisse, Tchécoslovaquie, Venezuela et Yougoslavie. Les Représentants de la République Arabe d'Egypte, d'Israël et de l'Italie, quoique ayant pris une part active aux travaux de la Première commission, n'ont pas participé au vote. Le Maroc, le Saint-Siège et l'Union des Républiques Socialistes Soviétiques ont envoyé des observateurs. Au cours des travaux, la Première commission a également disposé du concours précieux des observateurs du Conseil de l'Europe, du Commonwealth Secretariat et du Service Social International.

[2] Rapport de la Commission spéciale, Nos 3 et 7 à 15.

Explanatory Report by Elisa Pérez-Vera

TRANSLATION OF THE PERMANENT BUREAU

Introduction

I *Results of the work of the Hague Conference on private international law*

1 The Convention on the Civil Aspects of International Child Abduction was adopted on 24 October 1980 by the Fourteenth Session of the Hague Conference on private international law in Plenary Session, and by unanimous vote of the States which were present.[1] On 25 October 1980, the delegates signed the Final Act of the Fourteenth Session which contained the text of the Convention and a Recommendation containing the model form which is to be used in applications for the return of children who have been wrongfully abducted or retained.
On this occasion, the Hague Conference departed from its usual practice, draft Conventions adopted during the Fourteenth Session being made available for signature by States immediately after the Closing Session. Four States signed the Convention then (Canada, France, Greece and Switzerland), which thus bears the date 25 October 1980.

2 As regards the starting point of the proceedings which resulted in the adoption of the Convention, as well as the matter of existing conventions on the subject or those directly related to it, we shall refer to the introduction to the Report of the Special Commission.[2]

3 The Fourteenth Session of the Conference, which took place between 6 and 25 October 1980, entrusted the task of preparing the Convention to its First Commission, the Chairman of which was Professor A. E. Anton (United Kingdom) and the Vice-Chairman Dean Leal (Canada), who had already been Chairman and Vice-Chairman respectively of the Special Commission. Professor Elisa Pérez-Vera was confirmed in her position as Reporter. Mr Adair Dyer, First Secretary of the Permanent Bureau, who had prepared important documents for the Conference proceedings, was in charge of the scientific work of the secretariat.

4 In the course of thirteen sittings, the First Commission gave a first reading to the Preliminary Draft drawn up by the Special Commission. At the same time, it named the members of a Drafting Committee which drafted the text

[1] Australia, Austria, Belgium, Canada, Czechoslovakia, Denmark, Finland, France, Germany, Greece, Ireland, Japan, Luxemburg, Netherlands, Norway, Portugal, Spain, Sweden, Switzerland, United Kingdom, United States, Venezuela and Yugoslavia.
Representatives of the Arab Republic of Egypt, Israel and Italy did not participate in the vote, despite having played an active part in the proceedings of the First Commission. Morocco, the Holy See and the Union of the Soviet Socialist Republics sent observers. In the course of the proceedings, the First Commission also had at its disposal the invaluable assistance of observers from the Council of Europe, the Commonwealth Secretariat and International Social Service.
[2] Report of the Special Commission, Nos 3 and 7 to 15.

gression des travaux, a mis les textes au point.[3] Sept autres séances ont été consacrées à la discussion du texte préparé par le Comité de rédaction,[4] ainsi qu'à celle des clauses visant l'application de la Convention au regard des Etats à systèmes juridiques non unifiés («*Application Clauses*») et de la formule modèle[5] rédigées par des Comités *ad hoc*.[6] Les clauses finales, suggérées par le Bureau Permanent, ont été incorporées dans l'avant-projet établi par le Comité de rédaction.

II *Objet et plan du présent Rapport*

5 Le Rapport explicatif d'un texte destiné à devenir du droit positif, c'est-à-dire d'un texte qui devra être invoqué et appliqué, doit remplir au moins deux objectifs essentiels. D'une part, le Rapport doit mettre en relief aussi fidèlement que possible les principes qui sont à la base de la Convention et, quand cela s'avère nécessaire, l'évolution des idées qui ont conduit à consacrer de tels principes parmi les options existantes. Il ne s'agit certes pas de faire état d'une manière exhaustive des positions adoptées tout au long du processus d'élaboration de la Convention, mais le point de vue retenu par celle-ci sera parfois plus facile à comprendre s'il est confronté à d'autres idées avancées.

Or, étant donné que l'avant-projet de Convention préparé par la Commission spéciale a obtenu un large appui[7] et que, par conséquent, le texte définitif maintient l'essentiel de la structure et des principes fondamentaux de l'avant-projet, le présent Rapport final reprendra, surtout dans sa première partie, certains passages du Rapport de la Commission spéciale préparé en avril 1980 à l'intention de la Quatorzième session.[8]

6 Ce Rapport final doit remplir aussi un autre objectif: fournir à ceux qui auront à appliquer la Convention un commentaire détaillé de ses dispositions. Ce commentaire étant en principe destiné à éclairer la teneur littérale des dispositions conventionnelles, nous nous préoccuperons beaucoup moins d'en retracer la genèse que d'en préciser le contenu.

7 Des considérations précédentes nous pouvons conclure que les deux objectifs envisagés sont nettement différenciés et que les méthodes mêmes d'analyse utilisées pour atteindre l'un et l'autre ne peuvent pas être identiques. Toutefois, la référence dans les deux cas à un texte unique, celui de la Convention, impliquera certaines redites, qui nous semblent inévitables. En dépit de ce risque et étant donné le double objectif souligné, nous avons divisé le Rapport en deux parties: la première est consacrée à l'étude des principes généraux qui inspirent la Convention; la seconde est destinée à l'examen du texte article par article.

8 Finalement, comme le soulignait en 1977 le professeur von Overbeck,[9] il semble opportun de rappeler que ce Rapport a été établi, à l'issue de la Quatorzième session, à partir des procès-verbaux et des notes du Rapporteur. Il n'a

[3] Le Comité de rédaction, sous la présidence de M. Leal en tant que Vice-président de la Première commission, comprenait MM. Savolainen (Finlande), Chatin (France), Jones (Royaume-Uni) et le Rapporteur. M. Dyer et plusieurs des secrétaires rédacteurs lui ont fourni un concours extrêmement précieux.
[4] Doc. trav. Nos 45, 66, 75, 78, 79 et 83.
[5] Doc. trav. No 59, complété par la proposition du Secrétariat contenue dans le Doc. trav. No. 71. Le Sous-comité «*Application Clauses*» a décidé de ne pas changer la teneur des articles élaborés à ce sujet par la Commission spéciale (P.-v. No 12).

[6] Le Sous-comité «Formule-modèle», sous la présidence du professeur Müller-Freienfels (République fédérale d'Allemagne), comprenait MM. Deschenaux (Suisse), Hergen (Etats-Unis), Barbosa (Portugal), Minami (Japon) et Mlle Pripp (Suède). Le Sous-comité «*Application Clauses*», présidé par M. van Boeschoten (Pays-Bas), était formé par MM. Hétu (Canada), Hjorth (Danemark), Creswell (Australie), Salem (Egypte) et Mlle Selby (Etats-Unis).
[7] Voir notamment les *Observations des Gouvernements*, Doc. prél. No. 7.
[8] Doc. prél. No. 6.
[9] Rapport explicatif de la Convention sur la loi applicable aux régimes matrimoniaux, *Actes et documents de la Treizième session*, tome II, p. 329.

concurrently with the progress of the main proceedings.[3] Seven other sittings were devoted to a discussion of the text prepared by the Drafting Committee,[4] as well as of clauses relating to the application of the Convention to States with non-unified legal systems ('Application Clauses') and of the model form[5] drafted by *ad hoc* Committees.[6] The final clauses had been suggested by the Permanent Bureau and were incorporated into the preliminary draft Convention drawn up by the Drafting Committee.

II *Aim and structure of this Report*

5 The Explanatory Report on a text which is destined to become positive law, that is to say a text which will require to be cited and applied, must fulfil at least two essential aims. On the one hand, it must throw into relief, as accurately as possible, the principles which form the basis of the Convention and, wherever necessary, the development of those ideas which led to such principles being chosen from amongst existing options. It is certainly not necessary to take exhaustive account of the various attitudes adopted throughout the period during which the Convention was being drawn up, but the point of view reflected in the Convention will sometimes be more easily grasped by being set opposite other ideas which were put forward.
Now, given the fact that the preliminary draft Convention prepared by the Special Commission enjoyed widespread support[7] and that the final text essentially preserves the structure and fundamental principles of the Preliminary Draft, this final Report and in particular its first part, repeats certain passages in the Report of the Special Commission prepared in April 1980, for the Fourteenth Session.[8]

6 This final Report must also fulfil another purpose, *viz.* to supply those who have to apply the Convention with a detailed commentary on its provisions. Since this commentary is designed in principle to throw light upon the literal terms of these provisions, it will be concerned much less with tracing their origins than with stating their content accurately.

7 We can conclude from the foregoing considerations that these two objectives must be clearly distinguished and that even the methods of analysis used cannot be the same for each of them. Nevertheless, the need to refer in both cases to the one text, that of the Convention, implies that a certain amount of repetition will be necessary and indeed inevitable. Despite this risk and in view of the emphasis which is placed on a double objective, the Report has been divided into two parts, the first being devoted to a study of the general principles underlying the Convention, the second containing an examination of the text, article by article.

8 Finally, as Professor von Overbeck emphasized in 1977,[9] it would be as well to remember that this Report was prepared at the end of the Fourteenth Session, from the *procès-verbaux* and the Reporter's notes. Thus it has not

[3] The Drafting Committee, under the chairmanship of Mr Leal as Vice-Chairman of the First Commission, included Messrs Savolainen (Finland), Chatin (France), Jones (United Kingdom) and the Reporter. Mr Dyer and several recording secretaries provided the Committee with extremely valuable assistance.
[4] Working Documents Nos 45, 66, 75, 78, 79 and 83.
[5] Working Document No 59, supplemented by the proposal of the Secretariat in Working Document No. 71. The Subcommittee on 'Application Clauses' decided against changing the terms of the articles on this topic which had been prepared by the Special Commission (*Procès-verbal* No 12).
[6] The 'Model Forms' Subcommittee, under the chairmanship of Professor Müller-Freienfels (Federal Republic of Germany) comprised Messrs Deschenaux (Switzerland), Hergen (United States), Barbosa (Portugal), Minami (Japan) and Miss Pripp (Sweden). The Subcommittee on 'Application Clauses', chaired by Mr van Boeschoten (Netherlands), was made up of Messrs Hétu (Canada), Hjorth (Denmark), Creswell (Australia), Salem (Egypt) and Miss Selby (United States).
[7] See in particular the *Observations of Governments*, Prel. Doc. No 7.
[8] Prel. Doc. No 6.
[9] Explanatory Report on the Convention on the Law Applicable to Matrimonial Property Regimes, *Acts and Documents of the Thirteenth Session*, Book II, p. 329.

donc pas été approuvé par la Conférence et il est possible que, malgré les efforts faits par le Rapporteur pour rester objectif, certains passages répondent à une appréciation partiellement subjective.

Première partie – Caractères généraux de la Convention

9 La Convention reflète, dans son ensemble, un compromis entre deux conceptions, partiellement différentes, du but à atteindre. On perçoit, en effet, dans les travaux préparatoires, la tension existant entre le désir de protéger les situations de fait altérées par le déplacement ou le non-retour illicites d'un enfant et le souci de garantir surtout le respect des rapports juridiques pouvant se trouver à la base de telles situations. A cet égard, l'équilibre consacré par la Convention est assez fragile. D'une part, il est clair que la Convention ne vise pas le fond du droit de garde (article 19); mais d'autre part il est également évident que le fait de qualifier d'illicite le déplacement ou le non-retour d'un enfant est conditionné par l'existence d'un droit de garde qui donne un contenu juridique à la situation modifiée par les actions que l'on se propose d'éviter.

I OBJET DE LA CONVENTION

10 Le titre de ce chapitre fait allusion tant au problème auquel répond la Convention, qu'aux objectifs qu'elle a adoptés pour lutter contre le développement des enlèvements. Après avoir abordé ces deux points, nous traiterons d'autres questions connexes qui nuancent sensiblement la portée des objectifs visés; il s'agit en particulier de l'importance accordée à l'intérêt de l'enfant et des exceptions possibles au retour immédiat des enfants déplacés ou retenus illicitement.

A *Délimitation du sujet*

11 En ce qui concerne la délimitation du sujet,[10] nous nous limiterons à rappeler très brièvement que les situations envisagées découlent de l'utilisation de voies de fait pour créer des liens artificiels de compétence judiciaire internationale, en vue d'obtenir la garde d'un enfant. La diversité des circonstances qui peuvent concourir dans un cas d'espèce fait échouer toute tentative d'établir une définition plus précise d'un point de vue juridique. Cependant, deux éléments se font jour de façon inéluctable dans toutes les situations examinées et confirment la caractérisation approximative que l'on vient d'ébaucher.

12 En premier lieu, dans toutes les hypothèses nous nous trouvons confrontés au déplacement d'un enfant hors de son milieu habituel, où il se trouvait confié à une personne physique ou morale qui exerçait sur lui un droit légitime de garde. Bien entendu, il faut assimiler à une telle situation le refus de réintégrer l'enfant dans son milieu, après un séjour à l'étranger consenti par la personne qui exerçait la garde. Dans les deux cas, la conséquence est en effet la même: l'enfant a été soustrait à l'environnement familial et social dans lequel sa vie se déroulait. D'ailleurs, dans ce contexte, peu importe la nature du titre juridique qui était à la base de

[10] Voir notamment *Questionnaire et Rapport sur l'enlèvement international d'un enfant par un de ses parents*, établi par M. Adair Dyer, Doc. prél. No 1, août 1977, *supra*, p. 18-25 (cité par la suite, «Rapport Dyer»), et Rapport sur l'avant-projet de Convention adopté par la Commission spéciale, Doc. prél. No 6, mai 1980, *supra*, p. 172-173.

been approved by the Conference, and it is possible that, despite the Rapporter's efforts to remain objective, certain passages reflect a viewpoint which is in part subjective.

First Part – General characteristics of the Convention

9 The Convention reflects on the whole a compromise between two concepts, different in part, concerning the end to be achieved. In fact one can see in the preliminary proceedings a potential conflict between the desire to protect factual situations altered by the wrongful removal or retention of a child, and that of guaranteeing, in particular, respect for the legal relationships which may underlie such situations. The Convention has struck a rather delicate balance in this regard. On the one hand, it is clear that the Convention is not essentially concerned with the merits of custody rights (article 19), but on the other hand it is equally clear that the characterization of the removal or retention of a child as wrongful is made conditional upon the existence of a right of custody which gives legal content to a situation which was modified by those very actions which it is intended to prevent.

I OBJECT OF THE CONVENTION

10 The title of this chapter alludes as much to the problem addressed by the Convention as to the objectives by which it seeks to counter the increase in abductions. After tackling both of these points, we shall deal with other connected questions which appreciably affect the scope of the Convention's objectives, and in particular the importance which has been placed on the interest of the child and on the possible exceptions to the rule requiring the prompt return of children who have been wrongfully removed or retained.

A *Definition of the Convention's subject-matter*

11 With regard to the definition of the Convention's subject-matter,[10] we need only remind ourselves very briefly that the situations envisaged are those which derive from the use of force to establish artificial jurisdictional links on an international level, with a view to obtaining custody of a child. The variety of different circumstances which can combine in a particular case makes it impossible to arrive at a more precise definition in legal terms. However, two elements are invariably present in all cases which have been examined and confirm the approximate nature of the foregoing characterization.

Firstly, we are confronted in each case with the removal from its habitual environment of a child whose custody had been entrusted to and lawfully exercised by a natural or legal person. Naturally, a refusal to restore a child to its own environment after a stay abroad to which the person exercising the right of custody had consented must be put in the same category. In both cases, the outcome is in fact the same: the child is taken out of the family and social environment in which its life has developed. What is more, in this context the type of legal title which underlies the exercise of custody rights over the child matters little, since

[10] See in particular the *Questionnaire and Report on international child abduction by one parent*, prepared by Mr Adair Dyer, Prel. Doc. No 1, August 1977, *supra*, pp. 18-25 (hereafter referred to as the 'Dyer Report'), and the Report on the preliminary draft Convention, adopted by the Special Commission, Prel. Doc. No 6, May 1980, *supra*, pp. 172-173.

l'exercice du droit de garde sur la personne de l'enfant: de ce point de vue, l'existence ou l'absence d'une décision relative à la garde ne change en rien les données sociologiques du problème.

13 En second lieu, la personne qui déplace l'enfant (ou qui est responsable du déplacement, quand l'action matérielle est exécutée par un tiers) a l'espoir d'obtenir des autorités du pays où l'enfant a été emmené le droit de garde sur celui-ci. Il s'agit donc de quelqu'un qui appartient au cercle familial de l'enfant, au sens large du terme; en fait, dans la plupart des cas, la personne en question est le père ou la mère.

14 Il est fréquent que la personne qui retient l'enfant essaie d'obtenir qu'une décision judiciaire ou administrative de l'Etat de refuge légalise la situation de fait qu'elle vient de créer; mais si elle n'est pas sûre du sens de la décision, il est aussi possible qu'elle opte pour l'inactivité, laissant ainsi l'initiative à la personne dépossédée. Or, même si cette dernière agit rapidement, c'est-à-dire même si elle évite la consolidation dans le temps de la situation provoquée par le déplacement de l'enfant, l'enleveur se trouvera dans une position avantageuse, car c'est lui qui aura choisi le for qui va juger de l'affaire, un for que, par principe, il considère comme le plus favorable à ses prétentions.

15 En conclusion, nous pouvons affirmer que le problème dont s'occupe la Convention – avec tout ce qu'implique de dramatique le fait qu'il concerne directement la protection de l'enfance dans les relations internationales – prend toute son acuité juridique par la possibilité qu'ont les particuliers d'établir des liens plus ou moins artificiels de compétence judiciaire. En effet, par ce biais, le particulier peut altérer la loi applicable et obtenir une décision judiciaire qui lui soit favorable. Certes, une telle décision, surtout quand elle coexiste avec d'autres décisions de contenu contradictoire rendues par d'autres fors, aura une validité géographiquement restreinte, mais en tout état de cause elle apportera un titre juridique suffisant pour «légaliser» une situation de fait qu'aucun des systèmes juridiques en présence ne souhaitait.

B *Les objectifs de la Convention*

16 Les objectifs de la Convention, qui apparaissent dans l'article premier, pourraient être résumés comme suit: étant donné qu'un facteur caractéristique des situations considérées réside dans le fait que l'enleveur prétend que son action soit légalisée par les autorités compétentes de l'Etat de refuge, un moyen efficace de le dissuader est que ses actions se voient privées de toute conséquence pratique et juridique. Pour y parvenir, la Convention consacre en tout premier lieu, parmi ses objectifs, le rétablissement du *statu quo*, moyennant le «retour immédiat des enfants déplacés ou retenus illicitement dans tout Etat contractant». Les difficultés insurmontables rencontrées pour fixer conventionnellement des critères de compétence directe en la matière[11] ont en effet conduit au choix de cette voie qui, bien que détournée, va, dans la plupart des cas, permettre que la décision finale sur la garde soit prise par les autorités de la résidence habituelle de l'enfant, avant son déplacement.

17 D'ailleurs, bien que l'objectif exprimé au point *b*, «faire respecter effectivement dans les autres Etats contractants les

[11] Une telle option a été rejetée au cours de la première réunion de la Commission spéciale. *Cf. Conclusions des discussions de la Commission spéciale de mars 1979 sur le kidnapping légal*, établies par le Bureau Permanent, Doc. prél. No 5, juin 1979, *supra*, p. 163-164.

whether or not a decision on custody exists in no way alters the sociological realities of the problem.

Secondly, the person who removes the child (or who is responsible for its removal, where the act of removal is undertaken by a third party) hopes to obtain a right of custody from the authorities of the country to which the child has been taken. The problem therefore concerns a person who, broadly speaking, belongs to the family circle of the child; indeed, in the majority of cases, the person concerned is the father or mother.

14 It frequently happens that the person retaining the child tries to obtain a judicial or administrative decision in the State of refuge, which would legalize the factual situation which he has just brought about. However, if he is uncertain about the way in which the decision will go, he is just as likely to opt for inaction, leaving it up to the dispossessed party to take the initiative. Now, even if the latter acts quickly, that is to say manages to avoid the consolidation through lapse of time of the situation brought about by the removal of the child, the abductor will hold the advantage, since it is he who has chosen the forum in which the case is to be decided, a forum which, in principle, he regards as more favourable to his own claims.

15 To conclude, it can firmly be stated that the problem with which the Convention deals – together with all the drama implicit in the fact that it is concerned with the protection of children in international relations – derives all of its legal importance from the possibility of individuals establishing legal and jurisdictional links which are more or less artificial. In fact, resorting to this expedient, an individual can change the applicable law and obtain a judicial decision favourable to him. Admittedly, such a decision, especially one coexisting with others to the opposite effect issued by the other forum, will enjoy only a limited geographical validity, but in any event it bears a legal title sufficient to 'legalize' a factual situation which none of the legal systems involved wished to see brought about.

B *The objectives of the Convention*

16 The Convention's objects, which appear in article 1, can be summarized as follows: since one factor characteristic of the situations under consideration consists in the fact that the abductor claims that his action has been rendered lawful by the competent authorities of the State of refuge, one effective way of deterring him would be to deprive his actions of any practical or juridical consequences. The Convention, in order to bring this about, places at the head of its objectives the restoration of the *status quo*, by means of 'the prompt return of children wrongfully removed to or retained in any Contracting State'. The insurmountable difficulties encountered in establishing, within the framework of the Convention, directly applicable jurisdictional rules[11] indeed resulted in this route being followed which, although an indirect one, will tend in most cases to allow a final decision on custody to be taken by the authorities of the child's habitual residence prior to its removal.

17 Besides, although the object stated in sub-paragraph *b*, 'to ensure that rights of custody and of access under the law

[11] Such an option was rejected in the course of the first meeting of the Special Commission. *Cf. Conclusions drawn from the discussions of the Special Commission of March 1979 on legal kidnapping*, prepared by the Permanent Bureau, Prel. Doc. No 5, June 1979, *supra*, pp. 163-164.

droits de garde et de visite existant dans un Etat contractant», présente un caractère autonome, sa connexion téléologique avec l'objectif «retour de l'enfant» n'en est pas moins évidente. En réalité, on pourrait estimer qu'il ne s'agit que d'un seul objectif considéré à deux moments différents: tandis que le retour immédiat de l'enfant répond au désir de rétablir une situation que l'enleveur a modifiée unilatéralement par une voie de fait, le respect effectif des droits de garde et de visite se place sur un plan préventif, dans la mesure où ce respect doit faire disparaître l'une des causes les plus fréquentes de déplacements d'enfants.
Or, puisque la Convention ne précise pas les moyens que chaque Etat doit employer pour faire respecter le droit de garde existant dans un autre Etat contractant, il faut conclure qu'exception faite de la protection indirecte, qui implique l'obligation de retourner l'enfant à celui qui en avait la garde, le respect du droit de garde échappe presque entièrement au domaine conventionnel. Par contre, le droit de visite fait l'objet d'une régulation incomplète certes, mais indicative de l'intérêt accordé aux contacts réguliers entre parents et enfants, même quand la garde a été confiée à un seul des parents ou à un tiers.

18 Si on admet le bien-fondé des considérations précédentes, il faut en conclure que toute tentative de hiérarchisation des objectifs de la Convention ne peut avoir qu'une signification symbolique. En effet, il semble presque impossible d'établir une hiérarchisation entre deux objectifs qui prennent leurs racines dans une même préoccupation. Car, en définitive, il revient à peu près au même de faciliter le retour d'un enfant déplacé ou de prendre les mesures nécessaires pour éviter un tel déplacement.
Or, comme nous le verrons par la suite, l'aspect que la Convention a essayé de régler en profondeur est celui du retour des enfants déplacés ou retenus illicitement. La raison nous semble évidente: c'est après la retenue illicite d'un enfant que se produisent les situations les plus douloureuses, celles qui, tout en exigeant des solutions particulièrement urgentes, ne peuvent pas être résolues de façon unilatérale par chaque système juridique concerné. Prises dans leur ensemble, toutes ces circonstances justifient à notre avis le développement que la réglementation du retour de l'enfant reçoit dans la Convention et en même temps accordent, sur le plan des principes, une certaine priorité à l'objectif visé. Ainsi donc, bien qu'en théorie les deux objectifs mentionnés doivent être placés sur un même plan, dans la pratique c'est le désir de garantir le rétablissement de la situation altérée par l'action de l'enleveur qui a prévalu dans la Convention.

19 Dans un dernier effort de clarification des objectifs de la Convention, il convient de souligner qu'ainsi qu'il résulte en particulier des dispositions de son article premier, elle ne cherche pas à régler le problème de l'attribution du droit de garde. Sur ce point, le principe non explicite sur lequel repose la Convention est que la discussion sur le fond de l'affaire, c'est-à-dire sur le droit de garde contesté, si elle se produit, devra être engagée devant les autorités compétentes de l'Etat où l'enfant avait sa résidence habituelle avant son déplacement; et cela aussi bien si le déplacement a eu lieu avant qu'une décision sur la garde ait été rendue – situation dans laquelle le droit de garde violé s'exerçait *ex lege* – que si un tel déplacement s'est produit en violation d'une décision préexistante.

C *Importance accordée à l'intérêt de l'enfant*

20 Avant tout, il est nécessaire de justifier les raisons qui nous amènent à insérer l'examen de ce point dans le contexte des considérations sur l'objet de la Convention. Elles apparaissent clairement si l'on considère, d'une part que

of one Contracting State are effectively respected in the other Contracting States' appears to stand by itself, its teleological connection with the 'return of the child' object is no less evident. In reality, it can be regarded as one single object considered at two different times; whilst the prompt return of the child answers to the desire to re-establish a situation unilaterally and forcibly altered by the abductor, effective respect for rights of custody and of access belongs on the preventive level, in so far as it must lead to the disappearance of one of the most frequent causes of child abductions.
Now, since the Convention does not specify the means to be employed by each State in bringing about respect for rights of custody which exist in another Contracting State, one must conclude that, with the exception of the indirect means of protecting custody rights which is implied by the obligation to return the child to the holder of the right of custody, respect for custody rights falls almost entirely outwith the scope of the Convention. On the other hand, rights of access form the subject of a rule which, although undoubtedly incomplete, nevertheless is indicative of the interest shown in ensuring regular contact between parents and children, even when custody has been entrusted to one of the parents or to a third party.

18 If the preceding considerations are well-founded, it must be concluded that any attempt to establish a hierarchy of objects of the Convention could have only a symbolic significance. In fact, it would seem almost impossible to create a hierarchy as between two objects which spring from the same concern. For at the end of the day, promoting the return of the child or taking the measures necessary to avoid such removal amount to almost the same thing.

Now, as will be seen below, the one matter which the Convention has tried to regulate in any depth is that of the return of children wrongfully removed or retained. The reason for this seems clear: the most distressing situations arise only after the unlawful retention of a child and they are situations which, while requiring particularly urgent solutions, cannot be resolved unilaterally by any one of the legal systems concerned. Taken as a whole, all these circumstances justify, in our opinion, the Convention's development of rules for regulating the return of the child, whilst at the same time they give in principle a certain priority to that object. Thus, although theoretically the two above-mentioned objects have to be placed on the same level, in practice the desire to guarantee the re-establishment of the *status quo* disturbed by the actions of the abductor has prevailed in the Convention.

19 In a final attempt to clarify the objects of the Convention, it would be advisable to underline the fact that, as is shown particularly in the provisions of article 1, the Convention does not seek to regulate the problem of the award of custody rights. On this matter, the Convention rests implicitly upon the principle that any debate on the merits of the question, *i.e.* of custody rights, should take place before the competent authorities in the State where the child had its habitual residence prior to its removal; this applies as much to a removal which occurred prior to any decision on custody being taken – in which case the violated custody rights were exercised *ex lege* – as to a removal in breach of a pre-existing custody decision.

C *Importance attached to the interest of the child*

20 Above all, one has to justify the reasons for including an examination of this matter within the context of a consideration of the Convention's objects. These reasons will appear clearly if one considers, on the one hand, that

l'intérêt de l'enfant est souvent invoqué à ce sujet, et d'autre part que l'on pourrait argumenter que l'objectif conventionnel touchant au retour de l'enfant devrait toujours être subordonné à la prise en considération de son intérêt.

21 A cet égard, il a été à juste titre mis en relief que «la norme juridique reposant sur «l'intérêt supérieur de l'enfant» est, à première vue, d'une telle imprécision qu'elle ressemble davantage à un paradigme social qu'à une norme juridique concrète. Comment étoffer cette notion pour décider quel est l'intérêt *final* de l'enfant sans faire des suppositions qui ne prennent leur source que dans le contexte moral d'une culture déterminée? En introduisant le mot «final» dans l'équation, on fait aussitôt naître de sérieux problèmes, puisque l'énoncé général de la norme ne permet pas de savoir clairement si «l'intérêt» de l'enfant qu'il faut protéger est celui qui suit immédiatement la décision, ou celui de son adolescence, de son existence de jeune adulte, de son âge mûr ou de sa vieillesse».[12]

22 D'autre part, on ne doit pas oublier que c'est en invoquant «l'intérêt supérieur de l'enfant» que souvent, dans le passé, les juridictions internes ont accordé finalement la garde en litige à la personne qui l'avait déplacé ou retenu illicitement. Il a pu se trouver que cette décision soit la plus juste; nous ne pouvons cependant pas ignorer le fait que le recours, par des autorités internes, à une telle notion implique le risque de traduire des manifestations du particularisme culturel, social, etc., d'une communauté nationale donnée et donc, au fond, de porter des jugements de valeur subjectifs sur l'autre communauté nationale d'où l'enfant vient d'être arraché.

23 Pour les motifs invoqués, parmi d'autres, la partie dispositive de la Convention ne contient aucune allusion explicite à l'intérêt de l'enfant en tant que critère correcteur de l'objectif conventionnel qui vise à assurer le retour immédiat des enfants déplacés ou retenus illicitement. Cependant, il ne faudrait pas déduire de ce silence que la Convention ignore le paradigme social qui proclame la nécessité de prendre en considération l'intérêt des enfants pour régler tous les problèmes les concernant. Bien au contraire, dès le préambule, les Etats signataires déclarent être «profondément convaincus que l'intérêt de l'enfant est d'une importance primordiale pour toute question relative à sa garde»; c'est précisément dans cette conviction qu'ils ont élaboré la Convention, «désirant protéger l'enfant, sur le plan international, contre les effets nuisibles d'un déplacement ou d'un non-retour illicites».

24 Ces deux paragraphes du préambule reflètent assez clairement quelle a été la philosophie de la Convention à cet égard, philosophie que l'on pourrait définir comme suit: la lutte contre la multiplication des enlèvements internationaux d'enfants doit toujours être inspirée par le désir de protéger les enfants, en se faisant l'interprète de leur véritable intérêt. Or, parmi les manifestations les plus objectives de ce qui constitue l'intérêt de l'enfant figure le droit de ne pas être déplacé ou retenu au nom de droits plus ou moins discutables sur sa personne. En ce sens, il est souhaitable de rappeler la Recommandation 874 (1979) de l'Assemblée parlementaire du Conseil de l'Europe dont le premier principe général dit que «les enfants ne doivent plus être considérés comme la propriété de leurs parents, mais être reconnus comme des individus avec leurs droits et leurs besoins propres».[13]

[12] Rapport Dyer, *supra*, p. 22-23.
[13] Assemblée parlementaire du Conseil de l'Europe. 31ème Session ordinaire, *Recommandation relative à une Charte européenne des droits de l'enfant*. Texte adopté le 4 octobre 1979.

interests of the child are often invoked in this regard, and on the other hand, that it might be argued that the Convention's object in securing the return of the child ought always to be subordinated to a consideration of the child's interests.

21 In this regard, one fact has rightly been highlighted, *viz.* that 'the legal standard 'the best interests of the child' is at first view of such vagueness that it seems to resemble more closely a sociological paradigm than a concrete juridical standard. How can one put flesh on its bare bones without delving into the assumptions concerning the *ultimate* interests of a child which are derived from the moral framework of a particular culture? The word 'ultimate' gives rise to immediate problems when it is inserted into the equation since the general statement of the standard does not make it clear whether the 'interests' of the child to be served are those of the immediate aftermath of the decision, of the adolescence of the child, of young adulthood, maturity, senescence or old age'.[12]

22 On the other hand, it must not be forgotten that it is by invoking 'the best interests of the child' that internal jurisdictions have in the past often finally awarded the custody in question to the person who wrongfully removed or retained the child. It can happen that such a decision is the most just, but we cannot ignor the fact that recourse by internal authorities to such a notion involves the risk of their expressing particular cultural, social etc. attitudes which themselves derive from a given national community and thus basically imposing their own subjective value judgments upon the national community from which the child has recently been snatched.

23 For these reasons, among others, the dispositive part of the Convention contains no explicit reference to the interests of the child to the extent of their qualifying the Convention's stated object, which is to secure the prompt return of children who have been wrongfully removed or retained. However, its silence on this point ought not to lead one to the conclusion that the Convention ignores the social paradigm which declares the necessity of considering the interests of children in regulating all the problems which concern them. On the contrary, right from the start the signatory States declare themselves to be 'firmly convinced that the interests of children are of paramount importance in matters relating to their custody'; it is precisely because of this conviction that they drew up the Convention, 'desiring to protect children internationally from the harmful effects of their wrongful removal or retention'.

24 These two paragraphs in the preamble reflect quite clearly the philosophy of the Convention in this regard. It can be defined as follows: the struggle against the great increase in international child abductions must always be inspired by the desire to protect children and should be based upon an interpretation of their true interests. Now, the right not to be removed or retained in the name of more or less arguable rights concerning its person is one of the most objective examples of what constitutes the interests of the child. In this regard it would be as well to refer to Recommendation 874(1979) of the Parliamentary Assembly of the Council of Europe, the first general principle of which states that 'children must no longer be regarded as parents' property, but must be recognised as individuals with their own rights and needs'.[13]

[12] Dyer Report, *supra*, pp. 22-23.
[13] Parliamentary Assembly of the Council of Europe. 31st Ordinary Session *Recommendation on a European Charter on the Rights of the Child*. Text adopted on 4 October 1979.

En effet, comme l'a souligné M. Dyer, dans la littérature consacrée à l'étude de ce problème, «l'opinion qu'on y trouve le plus souvent exprimée est que la véritable victime d'un «enlèvement d'enfant» est l'enfant lui-même. C'est lui qui pâtit de perdre brusquement son équilibre, c'est lui qui subit le traumatisme d'être séparé du parent qu'il avait toujours vu à ses côtés, c'est lui qui ressent les incertitudes et les frustrations qui découlent de la nécessité de s'adapter à une langue étrangère, à des conditions culturelles qui ne lui sont pas familières, à de nouveaux professeurs et à une famille inconnue».[14]

25 Il est donc légitime de soutenir que les deux objectifs de la Convention – l'un préventif, l'autre visant la réintégration immédiate de l'enfant dans son milieu de vie habituel – répondent dans leur ensemble à une conception déterminée de «l'intérêt supérieur de l'enfant». Cependant, même dans l'optique choisie, il fallait admettre que le déplacement d'un enfant peut parfois être justifié par des raisons objectives touchant soit à sa personne, soit à l'environnement qui lui était le plus proche. De sorte que la Convention reconnaît certaines exceptions à l'obligation générale assumée par les Etats d'assurer le retour immédiat des enfants déplacés ou retenus illicitement. Pour la plupart, ces exceptions ne sont que des manifestations concrètes du principe trop imprécis qui proclame que l'intérêt de l'enfant est le critère vecteur en la matière.

26 D'ailleurs, la réglementation du droit de visite répond aussi au souci de fournir aux enfants des rapports familiaux aussi complets que possible, afin de favoriser un développement équilibré de leur personnalité. Pourtant, ici encore les avis ne sont pas unanimes, ce qui met une fois de plus en relief le caractère ambigu du principe de l'intérêt de l'enfant. En effet, à l'encontre du critère admis par la Convention, certaines tendances soutiennent qu'il est préférable pour l'enfant de ne pas avoir de contacts avec ses deux parents quand le couple est séparé *de jure* ou *de facto*. A cet égard, la Conférence a été consciente du fait qu'une telle solution peut parfois s'avérer la plus souhaitable. Tout en sauvegardant la marge d'appréciation des circonstances concrètes inhérente à la fonction judiciaire, la Conférence a néanmoins préféré l'autre option et la Convention fait prévaloir sans équivoque l'idée que le droit de visite est la contrepartie naturelle du droit de garde; contrepartie qui, par conséquent, doit en principe être reconnue à celui des parents qui n'a pas la garde de l'enfant.

D *Exceptions à l'obligation d'assurer le retour immédiat des enfants*

27 Etant donné que le retour de l'enfant est en quelque sorte l'idée de base de la Convention, les exceptions à l'obligation générale de l'assurer constituent un aspect important pour en comprendre avec exactitude la portée. Il ne s'agit évidemment pas d'examiner ici en détail les dispositions qui établissent ces exceptions, mais d'en esquisser le rôle, en insistant particulièrement sur les raisons qui ont déterminé leur inclusion dans la Convention. De ce point de vue, nous pouvons distinguer des exceptions basées sur trois justifications différentes.

28 D'une part, l'article 13*a* reconnaît que les autorités judiciaires ou administratives de l'Etat requis ne sont pas

[14] Rapport Dyer, *supra*, p. 21.

In fact, as Mr Dyer has emphasized, in the literature devoted to a study of this problem, 'the presumption generally stated is that the true victim of the 'childnapping' is the child himself, who suffers from the sudden upsetting of his stability, the traumatic loss of contact with the parent who has been in charge of his upbringing, the uncertainty and frustration which come with the necessity to adapt to a strange language, unfamiliar cultural conditions and unknown teachers and relatives'.[14]

25 It is thus legitimate to assert that the two objects of the Convention – the one preventive, the other designed to secure the immediate reintegration of the child into its habitual environment – both correspond to a specific idea of what constitutes the 'best interests of the child'. However, even when viewing from this perspective, it has to be admitted that the removal of the child can sometimes be justified by objective reasons which have to do either with its person, or with the environment with which it is most closely connected. Therefore the Convention recognizes the need for certain exceptions to the general obligations assumed by States to secure the prompt return of children who have been unlawfully removed or retained. For the most part, these exceptions are only concrete illustrations of the overly vague principle whereby the interests of the child are stated to be the guiding criterion in this area.

26 What is more, the rule concerning access rights also reflects the concern to provide children with family relationships which are as comprehensive as possible, so as to encourage the development of a stable personality. However, opinions differ on this, a fact which once again throws into relief the ambiguous nature of this principle of the interests of the child. In fact, there exists a school of thought opposed to the test which has been accepted by the Convention, which maintains that it is better for the child not to have contact with both parents where the couple are separated in law or in fact. As to this, the Conference was aware of the fact that such a solution could sometimes prove to be the most appropriate. Whilst safeguarding the element of judicial discretion in individual cases, the Conference nevertheless chose the other alternative, and the Convention upholds unequivocally the idea that access rights are the natural counterpart of custody rights, a counterpart which must in principle be acknowledged as belonging to the parent who does not have custody of the child.

D *Exceptions to the duty to secure the prompt return of children*

27 Since the return of the child is to some extent the basic principle of the Convention, the exceptions to the general duty to secure it form an important element in understanding the exact extent of this duty. It is not of course necessary to examine in detail the provisions which constitute these exceptions, but merely to sketch their role in outline, while at the same time stressing in particular the reasons for their inclusion in the Convention. From this vantage point can be seen those exceptions which derive their justification from three different principles.

28 On the one hand, article 13*a* accepts that the judicial or administrative authorities of the requested State are not

[14] Dyer Report, *supra*, p. 21.

tenues d'ordonner le retour de l'enfant lorsque le demandeur n'exerçait pas de façon effective, avant le déplacement prétendûment illicite, la garde qu'il invoque maintenant, ou lorsqu'il a donné son accord postérieur à l'action qu'il attaque désormais. Il s'agit par conséquent des situations dans lesquelles, ou bien les conditions préalables au déplacement ne comportaient pas l'un des éléments essentiels des relations que la Convention entend protéger (celui de l'exercice effectif de la garde), ou bien le comportement postérieur du parent dépossédé montre une acceptation de la nouvelle situation ainsi créée, ce qui la rend plus difficilement contestable.

29 D'autre part, les alinéas 1*b* et 2 du même article 13 retiennent des exceptions s'inspirant clairement de la prise en considération de l'intérêt de l'enfant. Or, comme nous l'avons signalé auparavant, la Convention a donné un contenu précis à cette notion. Ainsi, l'intérêt de l'enfant de ne pas être déplacé de sa résidence habituelle, sans garanties suffisantes de stabilité de la nouvelle situation, cède le pas devant l'intérêt primaire de toute personne de ne pas être exposée à un danger physique ou psychique, ou placée dans une situation intolérable.

30 De surcroît, la Convention admet aussi que l'avis de l'enfant sur le point essentiel de son retour ou de son non-retour puisse être décisif, si d'après les autorités compétentes il a atteint un âge et une maturité suffisante. Par ce biais, la Convention donne aux enfants la possibilité de se faire l'interprète de leur propre intérêt. Evidemment, cette disposition peut devenir dangereuse si son application se traduit par des interrogatoires directs de jeunes qui peuvent, certes, avoir une conscience claire de la situation, mais qui peuvent aussi subir des dommages psychiques sérieux s'ils pensent qu'on les a obligés à choisir entre leurs deux parents. Pourtant, une disposition de ce genre était indispensable étant donné que le domaine d'application de la Convention *ratione personae* s'étend aux enfants jusqu'à leur seizième anniversaire; il faut avouer que serait difficilement acceptable le retour d'un enfant, par exemple de quinze ans, contre sa volonté. D'ailleurs, sur ce point précis, les efforts faits pour se mettre d'accord sur un âge minimum à partie duquel l'opinion de l'enfant pourrait être prise en considération ont échoué, tous les chiffres ayant un caractère artificiel, voire arbitraire; il est apparu préférable de laisser l'application de cette clause à la sagesse des autorités compétentes.

31 En troisième lieu, il n'existe pas d'obligation de faire revenir l'enfant quand, aux termes de l'article 20, ceci «ne serait pas permis par les principes fondamentaux de l'Etat requis sur la sauvegarde des droits de l'homme et des libertés fondamentales». Nous nous trouvons ici devant une disposition peu habituelle dans les conventions concernant le droit international privé et dont la portée exacte est difficile à établir. En renvoyant au commentaire de l'article 20 pour tenter d'y parvenir, il nous paraît surtout intéressant ici d'en considérer l'origine. Or cette règle est le produit d'un compromis entre délégations favorables et délégations contraires à l'inclusion dans la Convention d'une clause d'ordre public.
Une telle possibilité a été largement débatue au sein de la Première commission, sous des formules différentes. Finalement, après quatre scrutins négatifs et par une seule voix de différence, la Commission a admis la possibilité de rejeter la demande en retour de l'enfant, avec mention d'une réserve faisant état de l'exception d'ordre public sous une formule restreinte en relation avec le droit de la famille et de l'enfance de l'Etat requis. La réserve prévue était formulée littéralement comme suit: «*Contracting States may reserve the right not to return the child when such return would be manifestly incompatible with the fundamental principles of the*

bound to order the return of the child if the person requesting its return was not actually exercising, prior to the allegedly unlawful removal, the rights of custody which he now seeks to invoke, or if he had subsequently consented to the act which he now seeks to attack. Consequently, the situations envisaged are those in which either the conditions prevailing prior to the removal of the child do not contain one of the elements essential to those relationships which the Convention seeks to protect (that of the actual exercise of custody rights), or else the subsequent behaviour of the dispossessed parent shows his acceptance of the new situation thus brought about, which makes it more difficult for him to challenge.

29 On the other hand, paragraphs 1*b* and 2 of the said article 13 contain exceptions which clearly derive from a consideration of the interests of the child. Now, as we pointed out above, the Convention invests this notion with definite content. Thus, the interest of the child in not being removed from its habitual residence without sufficient guarantees of its stability in the new environment, gives way before the primary interest of any person in not being exposed to physical or psychological danger or being placed in an intolerable situation.

30 In addition, the Convention also provides that the child's views concerning the essential question of its return or retention may be conclusive, provided it has, according to the competent authorities, attained an age and degree of maturity sufficient for its views to be taken into account. In this way, the Convention gives children the possibility of interpreting their own interests. Of course, this provision could prove dangerous if it were applied by means of the direct questioning of young people who may admittedly have a clear grasp of the situation but who may also suffer serious psychological harm if they think they are being forced to choose between two parents. However, such a provision is absolutely necessary given the fact that the Convention applies, *ratione personae*, to all children under the age of sixteen; the fact must be acknowledged that it would be very difficult to accept that a child of, for example, fifteen years of age, should be returned against its will. Moreover, as regards this particular point, all efforts to agree on a minimum age at which the views of the child could be taken into account failed, since all the ages suggested seemed artificial, even arbitrary. It seemed best to leave the application of this clause to the discretion of the competent authorities.

31 Thirdly, there is no obligation to return a child when, in terms of article 20, its return 'would not be permitted by the fundamental principles of the requested State relating to the protection of human rights and fundamental freedoms'. Here, we are concerned with a provision which is rather unusual in conventions involving private international law, and the exact scope of which is difficult to define. Although we shall refer to the commentary on article 20 for the purpose of defining such scope, it is particularly interesting to consider its origins here. This rule was the result of a compromise between those delegations which favoured, and those which were opposed to, the inclusion in the Convention of a 'public policy' clause.
The inclusion of such a clause was debated at length by the First Commission, under different formulations. Finally, after four votes against inclusion, the Commission accepted, by a majority of only one, that an application for the return of a child could be refused, by reference to a reservation which took into account the public policy exception by way of a restrictive formula concerning the laws governing the family and children in the requested State. The reservation provided for was formulated exactly as follows: 'Contracting States may reserve the right not to return the child when such return would be manifestly incompatible with the

law relating to the family and children in the State addressed».[15] En adoptant ce texte, on ouvrait une brèche grave dans le *consensus* qui avait présidé fondamentalement jusqu'alors aux travaux de la Conférence; c'est pourquoi, conscientes de ce qu'il fallait trouver une solution largement acceptable, toutes les délégations se sont engagées dans cette voie qui constituait le chemin le plus sûr pour garantir la réussite de la Convention.

32 Le point débattu était particulièrement important, car il reflétait en partie deux conceptions partiellement différentes de l'objectif de la Convention en matière de retour de l'enfant. En effet, jusqu'ici le texte élaboré par la Première commission (en accord avec l'avant-projet préparé par la Commission spéciale) avait limité les exceptions possibles au retour de l'enfant à la considération des situations de fait et de la conduite des parties ou à une appréciation spécifique de l'intérêt de l'enfant. Par contre, la réserve qu'on venait d'accepter impliquait qu'on admettait la possibilité de refuser le retour d'un enfant sur la base d'arguments purement juridiques, tirés du droit interne de l'Etat requis. Droit interne qui aurait pu jouer dans le contexte de la disposition transcrite, soit pour «évaluer» le titre invoqué par le parent dépossédé, soit pour apprécier le bien-fondé juridique de l'action de l'enleveur. Or, de telles conséquences altéraient considérablement un édifice conventionnel construit sur l'idée qu'il fallait éviter le détournement, par voies de fait, de la compétence normale des autorités de la résidence habituelle de l'enfant.

33 Dans cette situation, l'adoption par une majorité[16] rassurante de la formule qui figure à l'article 20 de la Convention représente un louable effort de compromis entre les différentes positions, le rôle accordé à la loi interne de l'Etat de refuge ayant considérablement diminué. D'une part, la référence aux principes fondamentaux concernant la sauvegarde des droits de l'homme et des libertés fondamentales porte sur un secteur du droit où il existe de nombreux compromis internationaux. D'autre part, la règle de l'article 20 va également plus loin que les formules traditionnelles de la clause d'ordre public en ce qui concerne le degré d'incompatibilité existant entre le droit invoqué et l'action envisagée; en effet, pour pouvoir refuser le retour de l'enfant en invoquant le motif qui figure dans cette disposition, l'autorité en question doit constater non seulement l'existence d'une contradiction, mais aussi le fait que les principes protecteurs des droits de l'homme interdisent le retour demandé.

34 Pour clore les considérations sur les problèmes traités à cet alinéa, il semble nécessaire de souligner que les exceptions de trois types au retour de l'enfant doivent être appliquées en tant que telles. Cela implique avant tout qu'elles doivent être interprétées restrictivement si l'on veut éviter que la Convention devienne lettre morte. En effet, la Convention repose dans sa totalité sur le rejet unanime du phénomène des déplacements illicites d'enfants et sur la conviction que la meilleure méthode pour les combattre, au niveau international, est de ne pas leur reconnaître des conséquences juridiques. La mise en pratique de cette méthode exige que les Etats signataires de la Convention soient convaincus de ce qu'ils appartiennent, malgré leurs différences, à une même communauté juridique au sein de laquelle les autorités de chaque Etat reconnaissent que les autorités de l'un d'entre eux – celles de la résidence

[15] Voir P.-v. No 9 et Doc. trav. connexes.
[16] Le texte a été adopté par 14 suffrages positifs, 6 négatifs et 4 abstentions, voir P.-v. No 13.

fundamental principles of the law relating to the family and children in the State addressed'.[15] The adoption of this text caused a serious breach in the consensus which basically had prevailed up to this point in the Conference proceedings. That is why all the delegations, aware of the fact that a solution commanding wide acceptance had to be found, embarked upon this road which provided the surest guarantee of the success of the Convention.

32 The matter under debate was particularly important since to some extent it reflected two partly different concepts concerning the Convention's objects as regards the return of the child. Actually, up to now the text drawn up by the First Commission (like the Preliminary Draft drawn up by the Special Commission) had limited the possible exceptions to the rule concerning the return of the child to a consideration of factual situations and of the conduct of the parties or to a specific evaluation of the interests of the child. On the other hand, the reservation just accepted implicitly permitted the possibility of the return of a child being refused on the basis of purely legal arguments drawn from the internal law of the requested State, an internal law which could come into play in the context of the quoted provision either to 'evaluate' the right claimed by the dispossessed parent or to assess whether the action of the abductor was well-founded in law. Now, such consequences would alter considerably the structure of the Convention which is based on the idea that the forcible denial of jurisdiction ordinarily possessed by the authorities of the child's habitual residence should be avoided.

33 In this situation, the adoption by a comforting majority[16] of the formula which appears in article 20 of the Convention represents a laudable attempt to compromise between opposing points of view, the role given to the internal law of the State of refuge having been considerably diminished. On the one hand, the reference to the fundamental principles concerning the protection of human rights and fundamental freedoms relates to an area of law in which there are numerous international agreements. On the other hand, the rule in article 20 goes further than the traditional formulation of 'public policy' clauses as regards the extent of incompatibility between the right claimed and the action envisaged. In fact, the authority concerned, in order to be able to refuse to order the return of the child by invoking the grounds which appear in this provision, must show not only that such a contradiction exists, but also that the protective principles of human rights prohibit the return requested.

34 To conclude our consideration of the problems with which this paragraph deals, it would seem necessary to underline the fact that the three types of exception to the rule concerning the return of the child must be applied only so far as they go and no further. This implies above all that they are to be interpreted in a restrictive fashion if the Convention is not to become a dead letter. In fact, the Convention as a whole rests upon the unanimous rejection of this phenomenon of illegal child removals and upon the conviction that the best way to combat them at an international level is to refuse to grant them legal recognition. The practical application of this principle requires that the signatory States be convinced that they belong, despite their differences, to the same legal community within which the authorities of each State acknowledge that the authorities of one of them – those of the child's habitual residence – are in

[15] See *P.-v.* No 9 and associated Working Documents.
[16] The text was adopted with 14 votes in favour, 6 against and 4 abstentions, see *P.-v.* No 13.

habituelle de l'enfant – sont en principe les mieux placées pour statuer en toute justice sur les droits de garde et de visite. De sorte qu'une invocation systématique des exceptions mentionnées, substituant ainsi au for de la résidence de l'enfant le for choisi par l'enleveur, fera s'écrouler tout l'édifice conventionnel, en le vidant de l'esprit de confiance mutuelle qui l'a inspiré.

II NATURE DE LA CONVENTION

A *Une convention de coopération entre autorités*

35 En délimitant les buts poursuivis par les Etats contractants, les objectifs d'une convention en déterminent en dernier ressort la nature. Ainsi, la Convention sur les aspects civils de l'enlèvement international d'enfants est avant tout une convention qui cherche à éviter les déplacements internationaux d'enfants en instituant une coopération étroite entre les autorités judiciaires et administratives des Etats contractants. Une telle collaboration porte sur les deux objectifs que nous venons d'examiner, d'une part l'obtention du retour immédiat de l'enfant dans le milieu d'où il a été éloigné, d'autre part le respect effectif des droits de garde et de visite existant dans un des Etats contractants.

36 Cette caractérisation de la Convention peut aussi être effectuée à travers une approche négative. Ainsi, nous pouvons constater avant tout qu'il ne s'agit pas d'une convention sur la loi applicable à la garde des enfants. En effet, les références faites au droit de l'Etat de la résidence habituelle de l'enfant ont une portée restreinte, puisque le droit en question n'est pris en considération que pour établir le caractère illicite du déplacement (par exemple, à l'article 3). En second lieu, la Convention n'est pas non plus un traité sur la reconnaissance et l'exécution des décisions en matière de garde. On a sciemment évité cette option, qui a pourtant suscité de longs débats au sein de la première réunion de la Commission spéciale. Etant donné les conséquences sur le fond de la reconnaissance d'une décision étrangère, cette institution est normalement entourée de garanties et d'exceptions qui peuvent prolonger la procédure. Or, en cas de déplacement d'un enfant, le facteur temps prend une importance décisive. En effet, les troubles psychologiques que l'enfant peut subir du fait d'un tel déplacement pourraient se reproduire si la décision sur son retour n'était adoptée qu'après un certain délai.

37 Une fois acquis que nous nous trouvons devant une convention axée sur l'idée de coopération entre autorités, il faut préciser qu'elle n'essaie de régler que les situations entrant dans son domaine d'application et touchant deux ou plusieurs Etats parties. En effet, l'idée d'une convention «universaliste» (c'est-à-dire dont le domaine s'applique à toute espèce internationale) est difficile à soutenir en dehors des conventions en matière de loi applicable. En ce sens, nous devons rappeler que les systèmes prévus, qu'il s'agisse du retour des enfants ou d'assurer l'exercice effectif du droit de visite, s'appuient largement sur une coopération entre les Autorités centrales reposant sur des droits et des devoirs réciproques. De même, quand des particuliers s'adressent directement aux autorités judiciaires ou administratives d'un Etat contractant en invoquant la Convention, l'application des bénéfices conventionnels répond aussi à une idée de réciprocité qui exclut en principe son extension aux ressortissants des Etats tiers.

Par ailleurs, bien que la Convention n'atteigne la plénitude de ses objectifs qu'entre les Etats contractants, les autorités de chacun de ces Etats ont parfaitement le droit de s'inspirer

principle best placed to decide upon questions of custody and access. As a result, a systematic invocation of the said exceptions, substituting the forum chosen by the abductor for that of the child's residence, would lead to the collapse of the whole structure of the Convention by depriving it of the spirit of mutual confidence which is its inspiration.

II NATURE OF THE CONVENTION

A *A convention of co-operation among authorities*

35 By defining the ends pursued by the Contracting States, a convention's objects in the final analysis determine its nature. Thus, the Convention on the Civil Aspects of International Child Abduction is above all a convention which seeks to prevent the international removal of children by creating a system of close co-operation among the judicial and administrative authorities of the Contracting States. Such collaboration has a bearing on the two objects just examined, *viz.* on the one hand, obtaining the prompt return of the child to the environment from which it was removed, and on the other hand the effective respect for rights of custody and access which exist in one of the Contracting States.

36 This description of the Convention can also be drawn in a negative way. Thus, it can be said at the outset that the Convention is not concerned with the law applicable to the custody of children. In fact, the references to the law of the State of the child's habitual residence are of limited significance, since the law in question is taken into consideration only so as to establish the wrongful nature of the removal (see, for example, article 3). Secondly, the Convention is certainly not a treaty on the recognition and enforcement of decisions on custody. This option, which gave rise to lengthy debates during the first meeting of the Special Commission, was deliberately rejected. Due to the substantive consequences which flow from the recognition of a foreign judgment, such a treaty is ordinarily hedged around by guarantees and exceptions which can prolong the proceedings. Now, where the removal of a child is concerned, the time factor is of decisive importance. In fact, the psychological problems which a child may suffer as a result of its removal could reappear if a decision on its return were to be taken only after some delay.

37 Once it is accepted that we are dealing with a convention which is centred upon the idea of co-operation amongst authorities, it must also be made clear that it is designed to regulate only those situations that come within its scope and which involve two or more Contracting States. Indeed, the idea of a 'universalist' convention (*i.e.* a convention which applies in every international case) is difficult to sustain outwith the realm of conventions on applicable law. In this regard, we must remember that the systems which have been designed either to return children or to secure the actual exercise of access rights, depend largely on co-operation among the Central Authorities, a co-operation which itself rests upon the notion of reciprocal rights and duties. In the same way, when individuals, by invoking the provisions of the Convention, apply directly to the judicial or administrative authorities of a Contracting State, the applicability of the Convention's benefits will itself depend on the concept of reciprocity which in principle excludes its being extended to nationals of third countries.

What is more, although the Convention attains its objectives in full only as among the Contracting States, the authorities in each of those States have the absolute right to be guided

des dispositions conventionnelles pour traiter d'autres situations similaires.

B *Caractère autonome de la Convention*

38 Axée comme elle l'est sur la notion de coopération entre autorités, en vue d'atteindre des objectifs précis, la Convention est autonome par rapport aux conventions existantes en matière de protection des mineurs ou relatives au droit de garde. Ainsi, l'une des premières décisions prises par la Commission spéciale a été d'orienter ses travaux dans le sens d'une convention indépendante, plutôt que d'élaborer un protocole à la *Convention de La Haye du 5 octobre 1961 concernant la compétence des autorités et la loi applicable en matière de protection des mineurs.* Dans cette même optique, elle ne pouvait pas non plus s'en tenir aux modèles proposés par les conventions sur la reconnaissance et l'exécution des décisions en matière de garde, y compris celui de la Convention du Conseil de l'Europe.[17]

39 Cette autonomie ne signifie pas que les dispositions prétendent régler tous les problèmes posés par les enlèvements internationaux d'enfants. Bien au contraire, dans la mesure où les objectifs de la Convention, quoique ambitieux, ont une portée très concrète, le problème de fond du droit de garde se situe hors du domaine d'application de la Convention. Elle est donc appelée à coexister inévitablement avec les règles sur la loi applicable et sur la reconnaissance et l'exécution des décisions étrangères de chaque Etat contractant, indépendamment du fait que leur source soit interne ou conventionnelle.
D'autre part, même dans son domaine propre, la Convention ne prétend pas être appliquée de façon exclusive: elle désire, avant tout, la réalisation des objectifs conventionnels et reconnaît donc explicitement la possibilité d'invoquer, simultanément à la Convention, toute autre règle juridique qui permette d'obtenir le retour d'un enfant déplacé ou retenu illicitement, ou l'organisation d'un droit de visite (article 34).

C *Rapports avec d'autres conventions*

40 La Convention se présente comme un instrument devant apporter une solution d'urgence, en vue d'éviter la consolidation juridique des situations, initialement illicites, provoquées par le déplacement ou le non-retour d'un enfant. Dans la mesure où elle n'essaie pas de trancher sur le fond des droits des parties, sa compatibilité avec d'autres conventions s'impose. Néanmoins, une telle compatibilité ne pouvait être obtenue qu'en assurant l'application prioritaire des dispositions susceptibles de fournir une solution d'urgence et, dans une certaine mesure, provisoire. C'est en effet après le retour de l'enfant à sa résidence habituelle que devront être soulevées, devant les tribunaux compétents, les questions relatives au droit de garde. A ce sujet, l'article 34 déclare que «dans les matières auxquelles elle s'applique, la Convention prévaut sur la *Convention du 5 octobre 1961 concernant la compétence des autorités et la loi applicable en matière de protection des mineurs*, entre les Etats parties aux deux Conventions». D'ailleurs, étant donné qu'on a essayé d'éviter que l'on puisse ajourner l'application des dispositions conventionnelles en invoquant des dispositions qui touchent le fond du droit de garde, le principe incorporé à l'article 34 devrait s'étendre à toute

[17] Il s'agit de la *Convention européenne sur la reconnaissance et l'exécution des décisions en matière de garde des enfants et sur le rétablissement de la garde des enfants*, adoptée par le Comité des Ministres du Conseil de l'Europe le 30 novembre 1979 et ouverte à la signature des Etats membres, au Luxembourg, le 20 mai 1980.

by the provisions of the Convention when dealing with other, similar situations.

B *The autonomous nature of the Convention*

38 The Convention, centred as it is upon the notion of co-operation among authorities with a view to attaining its stated objects, is autonomous as regards existing conventions concerning the protection of minors or custody rights. Thus, one of the first decisions taken by the Special Commission was to direct its proceedings towards the drawing up of an independent Convention, rather than the preparation of a protocol to the *Hague Convention of 5 October 1961 concerning the powers of authorities and the law applicable to the protection of minors.* Seen from this perspective, the Convention could not possibly be confined within the framework provided by the conventions on the recognition and enforcement of custody decisions, including that of the Council of Europe Convention.[17]

39 This autonomous character does not mean that the provisions purport to regulate all the problems arising out of international child abductions. On the contrary, to the extent that the Convention's aims, although ambitious, are given concrete expression, the basic problem of custody rights is not to be found within the scope of the Convention. The Convention must necessarily coexist with the rules of each Contracting State on applicable law and on the recognition and enforcement of foreign decrees, quite apart from the fact that such rules are derived from internal law or from treaty provisions.
On the other hand, even within its own sphere of application, the Convention does not purport to be applied in an exclusive way. It seeks, above all, to carry into effect the aims of the Convention and so explicitly recognizes the possibility of a party invoking, along with the provisions of the Convention, any other legal rule which may allow him to obtain the return of a child wrongfully removed or retained, or to organize access rights (article 34).

C *Relations with other conventions*

40 The Convention is designed as a means for bringing about speedy solutions so as to prevent the consolidation in law of initially unlawful factual situations, brought about by the removal or retention of a child. In as much as it does not seek to decide upon the merits of the rights of parties, its compatibility with other conventions must be considered. Nonetheless, such compatibility can be achieved only by ensuring that priority is given to those provisions which are likely to bring about a speedy and, to some extent, temporary solution. In fact it is only after the return of the child to its habitual residence that questions of custody rights will arise before the competent tribunals. On this point, article 34 states that 'This Convention shall take priority in matters within its scope over the *Convention of 5 October 1961 concerning the powers of authorities and the law applicable in respect of the protection of minors*, as between Parties to both Conventions.' Moreover, since one is trying to avoid delays in the application of the Convention's provisions caused by claims concerning the merits of custody rights, the principle in article 34 ought to be extended to any provision which has a bearing upon custody rights, whatever the reason. On the other hand, as has just been emphasized in the preceding

[17] The *European Convention on Recognition and Enforcement of Decisions Concerning Custody of Children and on Restoration of Custody of Children*, adopted by the Committee of Ministers of the Council of Europe on 30 November 1979 and opened for signing by the Member States at Luxemburg on 20 May 1980.

disposition portant sur le droit de garde, quelle qu'en soit la source. Par contre, comme nous venons de le souligner au paragraphe précédent, les parties peuvent faire appel à toute règle qui facilite la réalisation des objectifs conventionnels.

D *Ouverture de la Convention aux Etats non-membres de la Conférence de La Haye*

41 Sur ce point aussi, la Convention s'est manifestée en tant que Convention de coopération, en déterminant son caractère semi-ouvert. En principe, tout Etat pourra adhérer à la Convention, mais son adhésion «n'aura d'effet que dans les rapports entre l'Etat adhérant et les Etats contractants qui auront déclaré accepter cette adhésion» (article 38). En agissant de la sorte, les Etats contractants ont cherché à maintenir l'équilibre nécessaire entre le désir d'universalisme et la conviction qu'un système de coopération n'est efficace que lorsqu'il existe entre les Parties un degré de confiance mutuelle suffisant.

Plus encore, le choix du système de l'acceptation explicite de l'adhésion par chaque Etat membre, afin que celle-ci devienne effective à leur égard,[18] de préférence au système, plus ouvert, qui entend que l'adhésion produit ses effets sauf dans les rapports avec l'Etat membre qui s'y oppose dans un délai fixé,[19] montre l'importance accordée par les Etats à la sélection de ses cocontractants dans la matière qui fait l'objet de la Convention.

III INSTRUMENTS D'APPLICATION DE LA CONVENTION

A *Les Autorités centrales*

42 Une convention de coopération comme celle qui nous occupe peut en principe s'orienter dans deux directions différentes: imposer la coopération directe entre les autorités internes compétentes dans le domaine d'application de la Convention, ou baser son action sur la création d'Autorités centrales dans chaque Etat contractant, en vue de coordonner et de canaliser la coopération souhaitée. L'avant-projet mis au point par la Commission spéciale consacrait assez nettement le choix fait en faveur de la deuxième option et la Convention elle-même continue à être bâtie, dans une large mesure, sur l'intervention et les compétences des Autorités centrales.

43 Néanmoins, l'admission sans équivoque de la possibilité reconnue aux particuliers de s'adresser directement aux autorités judiciaires ou administratives compétentes dans l'application de la Convention (article 29), accroît l'importance du devoir qui est fait à celles-ci de coopérer, à tel point qu'on pourra qualifier de «système mixte» le système suivi par la Convention du fait qu'en marge des obligations des Autorités centrales, il en introduit d'autres qui sont propres aux autorités judiciaires ou administratives.

44 D'ailleurs, ce serait une erreur de prétendre construire une convention pour lutter contre les enlèvements internationaux d'enfants sans tenir compte du rôle important joué par les autorités judiciaires ou administratives internes dans toutes les questions concernant la protection des mineurs.

[18] A l'instar de l'article 39 de la *Convention sur l'obtention des preuves à l'étranger en matière civile ou commerciale, du 18 mars 1970*, voir P.-v. No 13.
[19] Système consacré, parmi d'autres, dans la *Convention tendant à faciliter l'accès international à la justice*, adopté également au cours de la Quatorzième session de la Conférence.

paragraph, the parties may have recourse to any rule which promotes the realization of the Convention's aims.

D *Opening of the Convention to States not Members of the Hague Conference*

41 On this point also, by virtue of the decision that it be of a 'semi-open' type, the Convention is shown to be one of co-operation. In principle, any State can accede to the Convention, but its accession 'will have effect only as regards the relations between the acceding State and such Contracting States as will have declared their acceptance of the accession' (article 38). The Contracting States, by this means, sought to maintain the requisite balance between a desire for universality and the belief that a system based on co-operation could work only if there existed amongst the Contracting Parties a sufficient degree of mutual confidence.

What is more, the choice of a system based on the express acceptance of accession by each Member State, by which such acceptance becomes effective as amongst themselves,[18] in preference to a more open system by which accession has effect except as regards Member States which raise objections thereto within a certain period of time,[19] demonstrates the importance which the States attached to the selection of their co-signatories in those questions which form the subject-matter of the Convention.

III INSTRUMENTS FOR APPLYING THE CONVENTION

A *The Central Authorities*

42 A convention based on co-operation such as the one which concerns us here can in theory point in two different directions; it can impose direct co-operation among competent internal authorities, in the sphere of the Convention's application, or it can act through the creation of Central Authorities in each Contracting State, so as to co-ordinate and 'channel' the desired co-operation. The Preliminary Draft drawn up by the Special Commission expressed quite clearly the choice made in favour of the second option, and the Convention itself was also built in large measure upon the intervention and powers of Central Authorities.

43 Nevertheless, the unequivocal acceptance of the possibility for individuals to apply directly to the judicial or administrative authorities which have power to apply the provisions of the Convention (article 29), increases the importance of the duty of co-operation laid upon them, so much so that the system adopted by the Convention could be characterized as a 'mixed system', due to the fact that, aside from the duties imposed upon the Central Authorities, it creates other obligations which are peculiar to judicial or administrative authorities.

44 What is more, it would be a mistake to claim to have constructed a convention to counter international child abduction without taking account of the important role played by the internal judicial or administrative authorities in all matters concerning the protection of minors. In this context,

[18] As in article 39 of the *Convention of 18 March 1970 on the Taking of Evidence Abroad in Civil or Commercial Matters*, see *P.-v.* No 13.
[19] The system adopted, among others, by the *Convention on International Access to Justice*, also adopted during the Fourteenth Session of the Conference.

Dans ce contexte, la référence aux autorités administratives doit être comprise comme le simple reflet du fait que, dans certains Etats membres de la Conférence, cette tâche est confiée à des autorités d'une telle nature, tandis que dans la plupart des systèmes juridiques la compétence en la matière appartient aux autorités judiciaires. Somme toute, c'est aux autorités chargées à l'intérieur de chaque Etat de statuer sur la garde et la protection des enfants que la Convention confie le soin de trancher les problèmes posés, qu'il s'agisse du retour d'un enfant déplacé ou retenu illicitement, ou de l'organisation de l'exercice du droit de visite. Ainsi, la Convention fait sienne l'exigence de sécurité juridique qui inspire dans ce domaine tous les droits internes. En effet, quoique les décisions sur le retour des enfants ne préjugent pas du fond du droit de garde (voir article 19), elles vont largement influencer la vie des enfants; l'adoption de telles décisions, la prise d'une semblable responsabilité doivent obligatoirement revenir aux autorités qui sont normalement compétentes selon le droit interne.

45 Cependant, dans ses grandes lignes et dans une large majorité des cas, l'application de la Convention dépendra du fonctionnement des instruments qu'elle-même instituera à cette fin, c'est-à-dire des Autorités centrales. En ce qui concerne leur réglementation par la Convention, la première remarque à faire est que la Conférence a eu conscience des différences profondes existant dans l'organisation interne des Etats membres; c'est la raison pour laquelle la Convention ne précise point quelles doivent être la structure et la capacité d'action des Autorités centrales, deux aspects qui seront nécessairement régis par la loi interne de chaque Etat contractant. L'acceptation de cette prémisse se traduit dans la Convention par la reconnaissance du fait que les tâches assignées en particulier aux Autorités centrales pourront être accomplies soit directement par elles-mêmes, soit avec le concours d'un intermédiaire (article 7). Il est évident, par exemple, que la localisation d'un enfant peut requérir l'intervention de la police; de même, l'adoption de mesures provisoires ou l'introduction de procédures judiciaires sur des rapports privés peuvent tomber hors des compétences susceptibles d'être dévolues aux autorités administratives par certaines lois internes. Néanmoins, dans tous les cas, l'Autorité centrale reste le destinataire des obligations que la Convention lui impose, en tant que «monteur» de la coopération voulue pour lutter contre les déplacements illicites d'enfants. D'autre part, c'est encore pour tenir compte des particularités des différents systèmes juridiques que la Convention admet que l'Autorité centrale pourra exiger que la demande qui lui est adressée soit accompagnée d'une autorisation «par écrit lui donnant le pouvoir d'agir pour le compte du demandeur, ou de désigner un représentant habilité à agir en son nom» (article 28).

46 Par ailleurs, la Convention, suivant une tradition bien établie de la Conférence de La Haye,[20] dispose que tant les Etats fédéraux que les Etats plurilégislatifs ou ayant des organisations territoriales autonomes sont libres de désigner plus d'une Autorité centrale. Pourtant, les problèmes constatés dans l'application pratique des conventions qui prévoient l'existence de plusieurs Autorités centrales sur le territoire d'un seul Etat, ainsi que, tout particulièrement, les caractéristiques spéciales de la matière qui fait l'objet de la présente Convention, ont amené la Conférence, suivant le critère déjà établi par la Commission spéciale, à faire un pas

[20] Par exemple, *cf.* l'article 18, troisième alinéa de la *Convention relative à la signification et la notification à l'étranger des actes judiciaires et extrajudiciaires en matière civile ou commerciale, du 15 novembre 1965. Id.* les articles 24 et 25 de la *Convention sur l'obtention des preuves à l'étranger en matière civile ou commerciale, du 18 mars 1970.*

references to administrative authorities must be understood as a simple reflection of the fact that, in certain Member States, the task in question is entrusted to such authorities, while in the majority of legal systems jurisdiction belongs to the judicial authorities. *In fine*, it is for the appropriate authorities within each State to decide questions of custody and protection of minors; it is to them that the Convention has entrusted the responsibility of solving the problems which arise, whether they involve the return of a child wrongfully removed or retained or organizing the exercise of access rights. Thus, the Convention adopts the demand for legal certainty which inspires all internal laws in this regard. In fact, although decisions concerning the return of children in no way prejudge the merits of any custody issue (see article 19), they will in large measure influence children's lives; such decisions and such responsibilities necessarily belong ultimately to the authorities which ordinarily have jurisdiction according to internal law.

45 However, the application of the Convention, both in its broad outline and in the great majority of cases, will depend on the working of the instruments which were brought into being for this purpose, *i.e.* the Central Authorities. So far as their regulation by the Convention is concerned, the first point to be made is that the Conference was aware of the profound differences which existed as regards the internal organization of the Contracting States. That is why the Convention does not define the structure and capacity to act of the Central Authorities, both of which are necessarily governed by the internal law of each Contracting State. Acceptance of this premise is shown in the Convention by its recognition of the fact that the tasks specifically assigned to Central Authorities can be performed either by themselves, or with the assistance of intermediaries (article 7). For example, it is clear that discovering a child's whereabouts may require the intervention of the police; similarly, the adoption of provisional measures or the institution of legal proceedings concerning private relationships may fall outwith the scope of those powers which can be devolved upon administrative authorities in terms of some internal laws. Nonetheless, the Central Authority in every case remains the repository of those duties which the Convention imposes upon it, to the extent of its being the 'engine' for the desired co-operation which is designed to counter the wrongful removal of children. On the other hand, it is so as to take account of the peculiarities of different legal systems that the Convention allows a Central Authority to require that applications addressed to it be accompanied by a 'written authorization empowering it to act on behalf of the applicant, or to designate a representative so to act' (article 28).

46 In other respects, the Convention follows a long-established tradition of the Hague Conference,[20] by providing that States with more than one system of law or which have autonomous territorial organizations, as well as Federal States, are free to appoint more than one Central Authority. However, the problems encountered in the practical application of those Conventions which provide for several Central Authorities within the territory of a single State, as well as, in particular, the special characteristics of the subject-matter of this Convention, led the Conference to adopt the text previously established by the Special Commission and

[20] Compare, for example, article 18(3) of the *Convention of 15 November 1965 on the Service Abroad of Judicial and Extrajudicial Documents in Civil or Commercial Matters.* Also, articles 24 and 25 of the *Convention of 18 March 1970 on the Taking of Evidence Abroad in Civil or Commercial Matters.*

en avant vers une sorte de «hiérarchisation» des Autorités centrales dans ces Etats. En effet, en nous limitant au deuxième aspect mentionné, si la personne qui a déplacé ou retenu un enfant se sert de l'extrême facilité des communications à l'intérieur d'un Etat, le demandeur ou l'Autorité centrale de l'Etat requérant pourraient être contraints de répéter plusieurs fois leur demande en vue d'obtenir le retour de l'enfant; de surcroît, il existe la possibilité que, même en ayant des raisons sérieuses de croire que l'enfant se trouve dans un Etat contractant, on ignore quelle est l'unité territoriale de sa résidence.

47 Pour fournir une solution à ces situations et à d'autres similaires, la Convention prévoit que les Etats qui établissent plus d'une Autorité centrale, désigneront simultanément «l'Autorité centrale à laquelle les demandes peuvent être adressées en vue de leur transmission à l'Autorité centrale compétente au sein de cet Etat» (article 6). La question est importante, du fait que la Convention limite, dans le temps, l'obligation imposée aux autorités judiciaires ou administratives de l'Etat requis, en ce qui concerne le retour immédiat de l'enfant;[21] une erreur dans le choix de l'Autorité centrale requise peut donc avoir des conséquences décisives pour les prétentions des parties. Or, pour éviter qu'un facteur non prévu par la Convention en modifie l'application normale, il faudra que cette sorte de «super Autorité centrale», envisagée à l'article 6, adopte une attitude active. En effet, puisqu'elle devra servir de pont entre l'Autorité centrale de son propre Etat qui est compétente dans chaque cas d'espèce d'une part, et les Autorités centrales des autres Etats contractants d'autre part, elle se verra contrainte de choisir entre procéder à la localisation de l'enfant pour pouvoir transmettre l'affaire à l'Autorité centrale adéquate, ou transmettre une copie de la demande à toutes les Autorités centrales de l'Etat, ce qui provoquera inévitablement une multiplication des services bureaucratiques. Mais il est hors de doute qu'une telle Autorité centrale jouera un rôle fondamental dans l'application de la Convention quant aux rapports qui affectent les Etats susmentionnés.

B *La formule modèle*

48 Suivant en cela la décision prise par la Commission spéciale lors de sa seconde réunion, la Quatorzième session de la Conférence a adopté, en même temps que la Convention, une Recommandation qui incorpore une formule modèle pour les demandes en vue du retour des enfants déplacés ou retenus illicitement. A son sujet, il convient de faire deux remarques. La première concerne la valeur juridique de la Recommandation en question: pour l'établir, il semble souhaitable de recourir au droit général des organisations internationales. Or, dans cette optique, une recommandation est en substance une invitation non contraignante adressée par une organisation internationale à un, plusieurs ou tous les Etats membres. Par conséquent, les Etats ne sont pas tenus *stricto sensu* d'utiliser la formule modèle contenue dans cette Recommandation; on a même soigneusement évité de la présenter comme une annexe à la Convention.

Les motifs en sont évidents. Avant tout, étant donné l'absence d'expérience internationale préalable dans le domaine couvert par la Convention, on peut penser qu'après quelques années l'application pratique des dispositions

[21] *Cf. infra*, commentaire de l'article 12 de la Convention.

take a step towards creating a sort of 'hierarchy' of Central Authorities in those States. In fact, by confining our discussion to the latter point, we can see that if the person responsible for the removal or retention of a child avails himself of the excellent means of communication within a particular State, the applicant or Central Authority of the requesting State could be forced to re-apply several times in order to obtain the return of the child. Moreover, it is still possible that, even if there are valid reasons for believing that the child is in a Contracting State, the territorial unit of the child's residence will be ignored.

47 The Convention supplies a solution to these and other situations by providing that States which establish more than one Central Authority should at the same time designate 'the Central Authority to which applications may be addressed for transmission to the appropriate Central Authority within that State' (article 6). The matter is important, because the Convention imposes a time-limit upon the duty of judicial or administrative authorities in the requested State for the prompt return of the child;[21] a mistaken choice as to the requested Central Authority could therefore have decisive consequences for the claims of the parties. Now, so as to prevent a factor which was not provided for in the Convention modifying the Convention's normal application, this type of 'super-Central Authority' envisaged in article 6 will have to adopt a positive approach. As a matter of fact, if it is to act as a bridge between on the one hand the Central Authority of its own State which has jurisdiction in each particular case, and on the other hand the Central Authorities of the other Contracting States, it will find itself obliged to choose between proceeding to locate a child in order to transmit the matter to the appropriate Central Authority, and transmitting a copy of the application to all the Central Authorities of the State concerned, which would inevitably cause a great increase in administrative duties. However it is undoubtedly the case that such a Central Authority will play a fundamental role in the application of the Convention in regard to relations affecting the aforementioned States.

B *The model form*

48 Following the decision taken by the Special Commission at its second meeting, the Fourteenth Session of the Conference adopted simultaneously with its adoption of the Convention, a Recommendation containing a model form for applications for the return of children wrongfully removed or retained. Two comments are appropriate here. The first concerns the legal force of this Recommendation. In drawing it up, it seemed advisable to have recourse to the general law governing international organizations. Now, viewed from this perspective, a recommendation is in substance a non-obligatory invitation addressed by one international organization to one, several or all Member States. Consequently, States are not strictly required to make use of the model form contained in the Recommendation; indeed, the Commission took care to avoid presenting the form as an annex to the Convention.

The reasons for this are clear. Most importantly, given the lack of prior international experience in this field, it can well be imagined that, after a number of years, the practical application of the Convention's provisions will result in

[21] *Cf. infra*, the commentary on article 12 of the Convention.

conventionnelles amène à conseiller l'introduction de certaines modifications dans la formule adoptée. Or, il semble préférable de ne pas soumettre une éventuelle révision du texte aux formalités qu'exigerait le droit international public en matière de révision des traités internationaux. On peut d'ailleurs soutenir qu'en marge d'une future action concertée de la Conférence sur ce point, l'adaptation de la formule recommandée aux Etats pourra aussi être l'oeuvre des contacts bilatéraux entrepris par les Autorités centrales, en exécution de l'obligation générale visée à l'article 7, alinéa 2, lettre *i*.

D'autre part, une conséquence directe de la décision de ne pas rendre obligatoire l'emploi de la formule modèle est que la Convention contient une énumération des données que doit nécessairement inclure toute demande adressée à une Autorité centrale (article 8).

49 La deuxième remarque porte sur le domaine d'application et sur la teneur de la formule recommandée. En effet, bien que la Convention règle aussi des aspects importants concernant le droit de visite, la formule proposée se limite à offrir une requête modèle en vue du retour de l'enfant. Ceci montre la polarisation de l'intérêt de la Conférence sur la solution des problèmes posés après le déplacement de l'enfant, tout en mettant en relief l'originalité de la voie choisie pour y parvenir. C'est justement parce que cette voie est nouvelle qu'on a cru souhaitable d'insérer une indication concernant son mode d'utilisation.

50 Quant à la teneur de la formule, elle développe très justement les éléments exigés par la Convention; pourtant, nous voudrions attirer l'attention sur deux points mineurs. D'abord, sur la mention «date et lieu du mariage» des parents de l'enfant concerné: dans la mesure où elle n'est pas suivie, entre parenthèses, de l'expression «s'il y a lieu», il semble qu'on donne un traitement exceptionnel et discriminatoire à la situation des enfants naturels. D'ailleurs, l'absence de cette même expression à côté de la référence à la date et au lieu de naissance de l'enfant s'accorde mal avec la précision dont fait preuve sur ce point l'article 8 de la Convention, quand il ajoute en se référant à la date de naissance, «s'il est possible de se la procurer».

51 D'autre part, on constate un manque de concordance entre le texte français et le texte anglais, du point de vue des «renseignements concernant la personne dont il est allégué qu'elle a enlevé ou retenu l'enfant». A cet égard, il semble préférable de suivre le texte anglais, plus complet, surtout en ce qui concerne la mention de la nationalité du prétendu enleveur, un élément qui sera parfois décisif dans la localisation de l'enfant.

IV STRUCTURE ET TERMINOLOGIE

A *La structure de la Convention*

52 Les articles 1, 2, 3 et 5 définissent le domaine d'application matériel de la Convention, en précisant ses objectifs et les conditions requises pour pouvoir considérer que le déplacement ou le non-retour d'un enfant sont illicites. L'article 4 s'attache au domaine d'application personnel de la Convention, tandis que l'article 35 détermine son application dans le temps. Les articles 6 et 7 sont consacrés à la création des Autorités centrales et à leurs obligations. Les articles 8, 27 et 28 se réfèrent à la saisine des Autorités centrales et aux documents qui peuvent accompagner ou compléter une demande qui leur aurait été présentée. Les articles 9 à 12 et 14 à 19 traitent des différentes voies instaurées pour obtenir le retour d'un enfant, ainsi que de la portée juridique d'une décision à cet effet. Les articles 13 et 20 s'occupent des exceptions à l'obligation générale de renvoyer l'enfant. L'article 21 établit les devoirs spécifiques

certain modifications to the present form being thought advisable. Now, it seems better not to subject future revisions of the text to the formalities required by public international law for the revision of international treaties. Besides, it could be said, in connection with any future concerted action by the Conference in this regard, that adaptation of the form which was recommended to States should also be a matter for bilateral negotiations between Central Authorities, in implementation of their general obligation contained in article 7(2)(*i*).

On the other hand, a direct consequence of the decision not to make the use of the model form obligatory is the catalogue of details which every application to a Central Authority must contain (article 8).

49 The second comment bears upon the sphere of application and the terms of the recommended form. Although the Convention also governs important matters concerning access rights, the model form proposed is merely a model application for the return of the child. This demonstrates the concentration of interest within the Conference on the resolution of problems arising out of the removal of a child, whilst at the same time throwing into relief the novelty of the means chosen to resolve them. It is precisely because the means are new that it was thought advisable to include some indication of the way in which they should be used.

50 The actual terms of the form narrate precisely those points required by the Convention itself. We should however like to draw attention to two minor points. Firstly, the phrase 'date and place of marriage' of the parents of the child in question: in as much as it is not followed, in parentheses, by the words 'if any', it would seem to treat natural children in an exceptional and discriminatory fashion. Moreover, the absence of the same phrase alongside the reference to the date and place of birth of the child compares badly with the precision shown by article 8 of the Convention which adds, referring to the date of birth, the words 'where available'.

51 Secondly, there is an inconsistency between the French and English texts regarding the 'information concerning the person alleged to have removed or retained the child'. It would be advisable to follow the English text here, since it is more comprehensive, especially as regards its reference to the nationality of the alleged abductor, a fact which will sometimes prove decisive in efforts to locate the child.

IV STRUCTURE AND TERMINOLOGY

A *The structure of the Convention*

52 Articles 1, 2, 3 and 5 define the Convention's scope with regard to its subject-matter, by specifying its aims and the criteria by which the removal or retention of a child can be regarded as wrongful. Article 4 concerns the persons to whom the Convention applies, while article 35 determines its temporal application. Articles 6 and 7 are devoted to the creation of the Central Authorities and their duties. Articles 8, 27 and 28 are concerned with applications to Central Authorities and the documents which may accompany or supplement an application to them. Articles 9 to 12, and 14 to 19, deal with the various means established for bringing about the return of a child, as well as the legal significance of a decree to that effect. Articles 13 and 20 concern the exceptions to the general rule for the return of the child. Article 21 lays down the specific duties which the States have taken upon themselves with regard to access rights.

assumés par les Etats à l'égard du droit de visite. Les articles 22 à 26 et 30 (ainsi que les articles 27 et 28 susmentionnés) s'occupent de certains aspects techniques concernant la procédure et les frais qui peuvent découler des demandes introduites par l'application de la Convention. Les articles 29 et 36 reflètent le point de vue non exclusif qui a présidé à l'élaboration de la Convention en précisant, d'une part l'action directe possible des particuliers devant les autorités judiciaires ou administratives des Etats contractants, hors du cadre des dispositions conventionnelles, et d'autre part la faculté reconnue aux Etats contractants de déroger conventionnellement aux restrictions auxquelles le retour de l'enfant peut être soumis d'après la présente Convention. Les articles 31 à 34 ont trait aux Etats plurilégislatifs et aux rapports avec d'autres conventions. Finalement, les articles 37 à 45 contiennent les clauses finales.

B *Terminologie utilisée par la Convention*

53 Selon une tradition bien établie de la Conférence de La Haye, la Convention a évité de définir les termes utilisés, sauf ceux contenus à l'article 5 sur les notions de droit de garde et de droit de visite, indispensables pour établir le domaine d'application matériel de la Convention. Ceci sera examiné dans son contexte. Nous voulons simplement considérer ici un aspect qui concerne la terminologie et qui mérite, à notre avis, un bref commentaire. Il s'agit du manque de concordance entre le titre de la Convention et la terminologie utilisée dans son texte. En effet, tandis que le premier emploie l'expression «enlèvement international d'enfants», les dispositions conventionnelles ont recours à des périphrases ou, en tous cas, à des tournures moins évocatrices, telles que «déplacement» ou «non-retour». L'explication est directement en rapport avec la délimitation du domaine de la Convention. Sur ce point, comme nous l'avons souligné ci-dessus (voir Nos 12 à 16), une étude du sujet dont s'occupe la Convention met en relief qu'en ce qui concerne aussi bien les rapports normalement existants entre «enleveur» et «enfant» que les intentions du premier, nous sommes fort loin des délits visés sous les dénominations d'«enlèvement», «*kidnapping*» ou «*secuestro*». Comme on est fort éloignés des problèmes propres au droit pénal, on a donc évité d'utiliser dans le texte de la Convention des appellations pouvant avoir une signification équivoque. Par contre, on a cru souhaitable de retenir le terme d'«enlèvement» dans le titre de la Convention, étant donné son emploi habituel par les «mass-media» et son retentissement dans l'opinion publique. Néanmoins, pour éviter toute équivoque, ce même titre précise, comme le faisait déjà le titre de l'avant-projet, que la Convention n'a pour objet que de régler les «aspects civils» du phénomène visé. Si tout au long de ce Rapport nous employons de temps en temps des expressions telles qu'«enlèvement» ou «enleveur», comme on les trouve d'ailleurs dans la formule modèle, c'est parce qu'elles permettent parfois une rédaction plus aisée; mais il faudra en tout état de cause les entendre avec les nuances que comporte leur application au problème spécifique dont la Convention s'occupe.

Deuxième partie – Commentaire des articles de la Convention

CHAPITRE PREMIER – CHAMP D'APPLICATION DE LA CONVENTION

54 Le chapitre premier définit le domaine d'application de la Convention quant à la matière et aux personnes concernées (domaine d'application *ratione materiae* et *ratione*

Articles 22 to 26 and 30 (like the aforementioned articles 27 and 28) deal with certain technical matters regarding proceedings and the costs which can result from applications submitted pursuant to the provisions of the Convention. Articles 29 and 36 reflect the 'non-exclusive' view which prevailed during the preparation of the Convention in stating, on the one hand, that applications may be submitted directly by individuals to the judicial or administrative authorities of the Contracting States, outwith the framework of the provisions of the Convention, and on the other hand that Contracting States have the acknowledged right to derogate by agreement from the restrictions which the present Convention allows to be imposed upon the return of the child. Articles 31 to 34 refer to States with more than one system of law and to the Convention's relations with other conventions. Lastly, articles 37 to 45 contain the Final Clauses.

B *Terminology used in the Convention*

53 Following a long-established tradition of the Hague Conference, the Convention avoided defining its terms, with the exception of those in article 5 concerning custody and access rights, where it was absolutely necessary to establish the scope of the Convention's subject-matter. These will be examined in their context. At this point we wish merely to consider one aspect of the terminology used which in our opinion merits a brief comment. It has to do with lack of correspondence between the title of the Convention and the terms used in the text. Whilst the former uses the phrase 'international child abduction', the provisions of the Convention avail themselves of circumlocutions or at any event of less evocative turns of phrase, such as 'removal' or 'retention'. The reason for this is quite in keeping with the Convention's limited scope. As was stressed above (see Nos 12 to 16), studies of the topic with which the Convention deals show clearly that, with regard both to the relationship which normally exists between 'abductor' and 'child' and to the intentions of the former, we are far removed from the offences associated with the terms 'kidnapping', '*enlèvement*' or '*secuestro*'. Since one is far removed from problems peculiar to the criminal law, the use in the text of the Convention of possibly ambiguous terms was avoided.

On the other hand, it was felt desirable to keep the term 'abduction' in the title of the Convention, owing to its habitual use by the 'mass media' and its resonance in the public mind. Nonetheless, so as to avoid any ambiguity, the same title, as in the Preliminary Draft, states clearly that the Convention only aims to regulate the 'civil aspects' of this particular phenomenon. If, in the course of this Report, expressions such as 'abduction' or 'abductor' are used from time to time, and one will find them also in the model form, that is because they sometimes permit of easier drafting; but at all events, they will have to be understood to contain nuances which their application to the specific problem with which the Convention deals may call for.

Second Part – Commentary on the specific articles of the Convention

CHAPTER ONE – SCOPE OF THE CONVENTION

54 The first chapter defines the scope of the Convention as regards its subject-matter and the persons concerned (its scope *ratione materiae* and *ratione personae*). However, so as

personae). Cependant, pour avoir une perspective globale du domaine conventionnel, il faut considérer aussi l'article 34 sur les relations avec d'autres conventions, l'article 35 concernant son domaine d'application dans le temps et les articles 31 à 33 qui ont trait à l'application de la Convention dans les Etats plurilégislatifs.

Article premier – Les objectifs de la Convention

a Observations générales

55 Cet article expose en deux paragraphes les objectifs conventionnels que nous avons traités assez largement dans la première partie de ce Rapport. Il est donc évident que l'absence de parallélisme entre le titre et le contenu de la Convention va plus loin que la question purement terminologique.[22] De toute façon, il faut reconnaître que les termes employés dans le titre, malgré leur manque de rigueur juridique, ont un pouvoir évocateur et une force qui attirent l'attention, ce qui est l'essentiel.

56 En ce qui concerne la nature des espèces réglées, une remarque de portée générale s'impose. Quoique la Convention n'inclue aucune disposition proclamant le caractère international des situations envisagées, une telle conclusion découle aussi bien du titre que des divers articles. Or, dans le cas présent, le caractère international provient d'une situation de fait, à savoir de la dispersion des membres d'une famille entre différents pays. Une situation purement interne lors de sa naissance peut donc tomber dans le domaine d'application de la Convention par le fait, par exemple, qu'un des membres de la famille se soit déplacé à l'étranger avec l'enfant, ou du désir d'exercer un droit de visite dans un autre pays où réside la personne qui prétend avoir ce droit. Par contre, la différence de nationalité des personnes concernées n'implique pas nécessairement que nous soyons devant un cas d'espèce international auquel la Convention doive s'appliquer, bien qu'il s'agisse d'un indice clair d'une internationalisation possible, au sens où nous l'avons décrit.

b Lettre a

57 L'objectif d'assurer le retour immédiat des enfants déplacés ou retenus illicitement a été déjà longuement présenté. D'ailleurs, la Quatorzième session n'a changé en rien la teneur littérale de la formule élaborée par la Commission spéciale. Nous ne ferons donc ici que deux brèves considérations d'éclaircissement relatives à son libellé. La première concerne la caractérisation des comportements que l'on voudrait éviter par la réalisation de cet objectif. En résumé comme nous le savons déjà, il s'agit de toute conduite qui altère les rapports familiaux existant avant ou après toute décision judiciaire, en utilisant un enfant, transformé par ce fait en instrument et principale victime de la situation. Dans ce contexte, la référence aux enfants «retenus illicitement» entend couvrir les cas où l'enfant qui se trouvait dans un lieu autre que celui de sa résidence habituelle – avec le consentement de la personne qui exerçait normalement sa garde – n'est pas renvoyé par la personne avec laquelle il séjournait. C'est la situation type qui se produit quand le déplacement de l'enfant est la conséquence d'un exercice abusif du droit de visite.

[22] Voir sur ce point Rapport de la Commission spéciale, No 52.

to have an overall picture of the Convention's scope, one must consider also article 34 which deals with the Convention's relationship with other conventions, article 35 which concerns the Convention's temporal application, and articles 31 to 33 which relate to the application of the Convention in States with more than one legal system.

Article 1 – The aims of the Convention

a General observations

55 This article sets out in two paragraphs the objects of the Convention which were discussed in broad terms in the first part of this Report. It is therefore clear that the lack of correspondence between the title and the specific provisions of the Convention is more than merely a matter of terminology.[22] In any event, it must be realized that the terms used in the title, while lacking legal exactitude, possess an evocative power and force which attract attention, and this is essential.

56 As for the nature of the matters regulated by the Convention, one general comment is required. Although the Convention does not contain any provision which expressly states the international nature of the situations envisaged, such a conclusion derives as much from its title as from its various articles. Now, in the present case, the international nature of the Convention arises out of a factual situation, that is to say the dispersal of members of a family among different countries. A situation which was purely internal to start with can therefore come within the scope of the Convention through, for example, one of the members of the family going abroad with the child, or through a desire to exercise access rights in a country other than that in which the person who claims those rights lives. On the other hand, the fact that the persons concerned hold different nationality does not necessarily mean that the international type of case to which the Convention applies automatically will arise, although it would clearly indicate the possibility of its becoming 'international' in the sense described.

b Sub-paragraph a

57 The aim of ensuring the prompt return of children wrongfully removed or retained has already been dealt with at length. Besides, the Fourteenth Session in no way altered the literal meaning of the wording devised by the Special Commission. Thus only two brief points by way of explanation will be put forward here. The first concerns the characterization of the behaviour which the realization of this objective seeks to prevent. To sum up, as we know, the conduct concerned is that which changes the family relationships which existed before or after any judicial decision, by using a child and thus turning it into an instrument and principal victim of the situation. In this context, the reference to children 'wrongfully retained' is meant to cover those cases where the child, with the consent of the person who normally has custody, is in a place other than its place of habitual residence and is not returned by the person with whom it was staying. This is the typical situation which comes about when the removal of the child results from the wrongful exercise of access rights.

[22] See the Report of the Special Commission, No 52.

58 En second lieu, le texte commenté précise que les enfants dont on essaie d'assurer le retour sont ceux qui ont été déplacés ou retenus «dans tout Etat contractant». Une telle précision a une double signification. D'une part, en ce qui concerne la disposition contenue à l'article 4, elle délimite le domaine d'application *ratione personae* de la Convention aux enfants qui, ayant leur résidence habituelle dans un des Etats contractants, sont déplacés ou retenus sur le territoire d'un autre Etat contractant.

59 Mais ces quelques mots ont aussi une signification toute différente. En effet, par ce biais, l'objectif de la Convention examinée, considéré en soi ou par rapport à la disposition de l'article 2, devient général, c'est-à-dire applicable à tous les enfants qui, dans les conditions décrites, se trouvent dans un Etat contractant. Pourtant, il y aura toujours une différence dans la situation juridique entre les enfants qui avaient leur résidence habituelle, avant le déplacement, dans un autre Etat contractant et les autres enfants. Ainsi, la situation des premiers devra être résolue par application directe des dispositions conventionnelles. Par contre, l'obligation des Etats envers les autres sera plus nuancée, dans la mesure où elle découlerait (abstraction faite de la législation interne) du devoir consacré par l'article 2, qui pourrait être décrit comme celui de prendre les mesures appropriées pour éviter que leurs territoires ne se convertissent en lieux de refuge d'éventuels «enleveurs».

c Lettre b

60 L'objectif conventionnel visé à ce sous-alinéa a été clarifié dans la rédaction qu'il a reçue lors de la Quatorzième session.[23] En ce qui concerne son domaine, il est maintenant manifeste que les situations considérées sont les mêmes que celles auxquelles s'applique la Convention, c'est-à-dire les situations internationales qui mettent en relation deux ou plusieurs Etats contractants. La précision n'est pas superflue, surtout si l'on tient compte du fait que le texte de l'avant-projet permettait d'autres interprétations, notamment la référence à des situations internes.

61 Quant à savoir quelle est la portée qu'on a voulu donner à l'objectif qui y est consacré, il s'impose de faire une distinction entre droit de garde et droit de visite. En ce qui concerne le droit de garde, on peut dire que la Convention n'a pas essayé de le développer de manière autonome. C'est donc dans l'obligation générale exprimée dans l'article 2, ainsi que dans la régulation du retour de l'enfant – basée, comme nous le verrons dans le cadre du commentaire à l'article 3, sur le respect d'un droit de garde effectivement exercé et attribué par le droit de l'Etat de la résidence habituelle – qu'on doit trouver la suite de la disposition qui nous occupe à cet égard. Par contre, le droit de visite a eu un sort plus favorable et les bases sur lesquelles doit se construire son respect effectif apparaissent fixées, au moins dans leurs grandes lignes, dans le contexte de l'article 21.

Article 2 – Obligation générale des Etats contractants

62 En étroite relation avec les objectifs vastes et souples de l'article 1*b*, cet article consacre une obligation générale de comportement des Etats contractants; il s'agit donc d'une obligation qui, à l'encontre des obligations de résultat, normalement incluses dans une convention, n'exige pas de

[23] *Cf.* Doc. trav. No 2 (*Proposal of the United Kingdom delegation*) et P.-v. No 2.

58 Secondly, the text states clearly that the children whose return it is sought to secure are those who have been removed to, or retained in, 'any Contracting State'. This wording is doubly significant. On the one hand, the provision in article 4 limits the scope of the Convention *ratione personae* to those children who, while being habitually resident in one of the Contracting States, are removed to or retained in, the territory of another Contracting State.

59 But these same words also have a quite diferent meaning. In fact, through this formulation this particular object of the Convention, whether considered in its own right or in relation to article 2, becomes indirectly a general one, applicable to all children who, in the circumstances set forth, are in any Contracting State. However, there will always be a difference between the legal position of those children who, prior to their removal, were habitually resident in another Contracting State, and that of other children. The position of the former will have to be resolved by the direct application of the provisions of the Convention. On the other hand, the duty of States towards the other children is less clear (leaving aside provisions of internal law) in so far as it derives from the obligation stated in article 2, which could be described as a duty to take appropriate measures to prevent their territory being turned into a place of refuge for potential 'abductors'.

c Sub-paragraph b

60 The aim of the Convention contained in this sub-paragraph was clarified in the course of drafting at the Fourteenth Session.[23] So far as its scope is concerned, it is now clear that the situations under consideration are the same as those to which the Convention applies, that is to say international situations which involve two or more Contracting States. It should not be thought that precision in this matter is unnecessary, especially when one considers that the text of the Preliminary Draft allowed of other interpretations, and in particular a reference to internal situations.

61 As for knowing the desired meaning of the aim stated therein, it is necessary to draw a distinction between custody rights and access rights. With regard to custody rights, it can be said that the Convention has not attempted to deal with them separately. It is thus within the general obligation stated in article 2, and the regulation governing the return of the child – which is based, as we shall see in the commentary on article 3, upon respect for custody rights actually exercised and attributed under the law of the child's habitual residence – that one must look in order to find the consequences of the provision which concerns us here. On the other hand, access rights are treated more favourably, and the foundations upon which respect for their effective exercise seem fixed, at least in broad outline, within the context of article 21.

Article 2 – General obligation of Contracting States

62 Closely related to the objects stated in broad and flexible fashion in article 1*b* is the fact that this article sets forth a general duty incumbent upon Contracting States. It is thus a duty which, unlike obligations to achieve a result which are normally to be found in conventions, does not require

[23] *Cf.* Working Document No 2 (Proposal of the United Kingdom delegation) and *P.-v.* No 2.

réalisations concrètes, mais plus simplement l'adoption d'une attitude déterminée en vue d'aboutir à de telles réalisations. Dans le cas présent, l'attitude, le comportement demandé aux Etats se traduit par le fait de prendre «toutes les mesures appropriées pour assurer, dans les limites de leur territoire, la réalisation des objectifs de la Convention». La Convention essaie ainsi, tout en sauvegardant le caractère *self-executing* de ses autres articles, d'encourager les Etats contractants à s'inspirer de ces normes pour résoudre les situations similaires à celles dont elle s'occupe, mais ne rentrant pas dans son domaine d'application *ratione personae* ou *ratione temporis*. D'une part, cela doit conduire à une considération attentive des normes conventionnelles quand l'Etat envisagera une modification de sa législation interne en matière de droits de garde ou de visite; d'autre part, l'extension des objectifs de la Convention à des cas non couverts par ses dispositions devrait influencer l'action des tribunaux et se traduire par une diminution du jeu de l'exception d'ordre public au moment de se prononcer sur des relations internationales tombant hors du domaine d'application de la Convention.

63 De plus, dans sa dernière phrase, l'article précise une des mesures envisagées, en soulignant l'importance accordée par la Conférence à l'utilisation de procédures rapides dans les affaires concernant les droits de garde ou de visite. Pourtant, cette disposition n'impose pas aux Etats l'obligation d'adopter dans leur loi interne de nouvelles procédures; la concordance établie entre le texte français et le texte anglais cherche justement à éviter une telle interprétation, que le texte français original rendait possible. Elle se limite donc à demander aux Etats contractants d'utiliser, dans toute question concernant la matière objet de la Convention, les procédures les plus urgentes figurant dans leur propre droit.

Article 3 – Le caractère illicite d'un déplacement ou d'un non-retour

a Observations générales

64 L'ensemble de l'article 3 constitue une disposition clé de la Convention, puisque de son application dépend le déclenchement des mécanismes conventionnels en vue du retour de l'enfant; en effet, la Convention n'impose l'obligation de retourner l'enfant que lorsqu'il y a eu un déplacement ou un non-retour considérés par elle comme illicites. Or, en précisant les conditions que doit réunir une situation pour que son altération unilatérale puisse être qualifiée d'illicite, cet article met indirectement en relief les rapports que la Convention entend protéger; ces rapports sont basés sur un double élément: *primo*, l'existence d'un droit de garde attribué par l'Etat de la résidence habituelle de l'enfant; *secundo*, l'exercice effectif de cette garde, avant le déplacement. Examinons de plus près la teneur des conditions mentionnées.

b L'élément juridique

65 En ce qui concerne l'élément des situations visées qu'on pourrait appeler juridique, ce que la Convention se propose de défendre ce sont les relations qui se trouvent déjà protégées, au moins par l'apparence d'un titre valable sur le droit de garde, dans l'Etat de la résidence habituelle de l'enfant; c'est-à-dire par le droit de l'Etat où ces relations se déroulaient avant le déplacement. L'affirmation antérieure exige certaines précisions sur deux points. Le premier aspect que nous devons considérer a trait au droit dont la violation détermine l'existence d'un déplacement ou d'un non-retour illicites, au sens de la Convention. Il s'agit, comme nous venons de le dire, du droit de garde; en effet, bien qu'au

that actual results be achieved but merely the adoption of an attitude designed to lead to such results. In the present case, the attitude and behaviour required of States is expressed in the requirement to 'take all appropriate measures to secure within their territories the implementation of the objects of the Convention'. The Convention also seeks, while safeguarding the 'self-executing' character of its other articles, to encourage Contracting States to draw inspiration from these rules in resolving problems similar to those with which the Convention deals, but which do not fall within its scope *ratione personae* or *ratione temporis*. On the one hand, this should lead to careful examination of the Convention's rules whenever a State contemplates changing its own internal laws on rights of custody or access; on the other hand, extending the Convention's objects to cases which are not covered by its own provisions should influence courts and be shown in a decreasing use of the public policy exception when questions concerning international relations which are outwith the scope of the Convention fall to be decided.

63 Moreover, the last sentence of the article specified one of the particular means envisaged, while stressing also the importance placed by the Convention on the use of speedy procedures in matters of custody or access rights. However, this provision does not impose an obligation upon States to bring new procedures into their internal law, and the correspondence now existing between the French and English texts rightly seeks to avoid such an interpretation, which the original French text made possible. It is therefore limited to requesting Contracting States, in any question concerning the subject-matter of the Convention, to use the most expeditious procedures available in their own law.

Article 3 – The unlawful nature of a removal or retention

a General observations

64 Article 3 as a whole constitutes one of the key provisions of the Convention, since the setting in motion of the Convention's machinery for the return of the child depends upon its application. In fact, the duty to return a child arises only if its removal or retention is considered wrongful in terms of the Convention. Now, in laying down the conditions which have to be met for any unilateral change in the *status quo* to be regarded as wrongful, this article indirectly brings into clear focus those relationships which the Convention seeks to protect. Those relationships are based upon the existence of two facts, firstly, the existence of rights of custody attributed by the State of the child's habitual residence and, secondly, the actual exercise of such custody prior to the child's removal. Let us examine more closely the import of these conditions.

b The juridical element

65 As for what could be termed the juridical element present in these situations, the Convention is intended to defend those relationships which are already protected, at any rate by virtue of an apparent right to custody in the State of the child's habitual residence, *i.e.* by virtue of the law of the State where the child's relationships developed prior to its removal. The foregoing remark requires further explanation in two respects. The first point to be considered concerns the law, a breach of which determines whether a removal or retention is wrongful, in the Convention sense. As we have just said, this is a matter of custody rights. Although the problems which can arise from a breach of

cours de la Quatorzième session les problèmes pouvant dériver de la violation d'un droit de visite, surtout quand le titulaire de la garde déplace l'enfant à l'étranger, aient été soulevés, l'opinion majoritaire a été qu'on ne peut pas assimiler une telle situation aux déplacements illicites qu'on essaie de prévenir.[24]
Cet exemple, et d'autres similaires où la violation du droit de visite altère profondément l'équilibre de la situation établie par une décision, sont certes la preuve de ce que les décisions sur la garde des enfants devraient toujours être susceptibles de révision. Mais ce problème échappe à l'effort de coordination entrepris par la Conférence de La Haye; on aurait abouti à des résultats contestables si, à travers une égale protection accordée aux droits de garde et de visite, l'application de la Convention avait conduit, au fond, à la substitution des titulaires de l'un par ceux de l'autre.

66 La deuxième question à examiner se réfère au droit choisi pour évaluer la validité initiale du titre invoqué. Nous ne nous arrêterons pas ici sur le concept de la résidence habituelle; il s'agit en effet d'une notion familière à la Conférence de La Haye, où elle est comprise comme une notion de pur fait, qui diffère notamment de celle de domicile. D'ailleurs, le choix du droit de la résidence habituelle en tant que critère déterminant de la légalité de la situation violée par l'enlèvement est logique. En fait, aux arguments qui ont agi en faveur de lui accorder un rôle prééminent en matière de protection des mineurs, comme dans la Convention de La Haye de 1961, vient s'ajouter la propre nature même de la Convention, c'est-à-dire sa portée limitée. En ce sens, il faut faire deux considérations: d'une part, la Convention n'essaie pas de régler définitivement la garde des enfants, ce qui affaiblit considérablement les arguments favorables à la loi nationale; d'autre part, les normes conventionnelles reposent, dans une large mesure, sur l'idée sous-jacente qu'il existe une sorte de compétence naturelle des tribunaux de la résidence habituelle de l'enfant dans un litige relatif à sa garde.
Dans une perspective différente, nous devons aussi attirer l'attention sur le fait que la Convention parle du «droit» de l'Etat de la résidence habituelle, s'écartant ainsi de la tradition bien établie par les Conventions de La Haye sur la loi applicable, élaborées à partir de 1955, qui soumettent la réglementation du sujet dont elles s'occupent à une loi interne déterminée. Certes, dans ces cas, le terme de «loi» doit être compris dans son sens le plus large, celui qui recouvre aussi bien les règles écrites et coutumières – quel qu'en soit le rang – que les précisions apportées par leur interprétation jurisprudentielle. Cependant, l'adjectif «interne» implique l'exclusion de toute référence aux règles de conflit de la loi désignée. Donc, si la Convention a abandonné la formule traditionnelle pour parler du «droit de la résidence habituelle», la différence ne saurait être purement terminologique. En effet, comme le montrent les travaux préparatoires,[25] dès le début, l'intention a été d'élargir davantage l'éventail des dispositions qui doivent être prises en considération dans ce contexte. En fait, il y a même eu, au cours de la Quatorzième session, une proposition tendant à expliciter dans cet article que la référence au droit de la résidence habituelle s'étend à ces normes de droit international privé; si la proposition a été rejetée, c'est parce que la Conférence était convaincue qu'une telle inclusion était superflue et s'avérait implicite du moment que le texte

[24] *Cf.* Doc. trav. No 5 (Proposition de la délégation canadienne) et P.-v. No 3.

[25] *Cf.* le Rapport de la Commission spéciale, No 62, *supra*, p. 90.

access rights, especially where the child is taken abroad by its custodian, were raised during the Fourteenth Session, the majority view was that such situations could not be put in the same category as the wrongful removals which it is sought to prevent.[24]

This example, and others like it where breach of access rights profoundly upsets the equilibrium established by a judicial or administrative decision, certainly demonstrate that decisions concerning the custody of children should always be open to review. This problem however defied all efforts of the Hague Conference to co-ordinate views thereon. A questionable result would have been attained had the application of the Convention, by granting the same degree of protection to custody and access rights, led ultimately to the substitution of the holders of one type of right by those who held the other.

66 The second question which should be examined concerns the law which is chosen to govern the initial validity of the claim. We shall not dwell at this point upon the notion of habitual residence, a well-established concept in the Hague Conference, which regards it as a question of pure fact, differing in that respect from domicile. Moreover, the choice of the law of habitual residence as the factor which is to determine the lawfulness of the situation flouted by the abduction is logical. In actual fact, to the arguments in favour of its being accorded a pre-eminent role in the protection of minors, as in the Hague Convention of 1961, must be added the very nature of the Convention itself, *viz.* its limited scope. In this regard, two points must be made: on the one hand, the Convention does not seek to govern definitively questions concerning the custody of children, a fact which weakens considerably those arguments favouring the application of national law; on the other hand, the rules of the Convention rest largely upon the underlying idea that there exists a type of jurisdiction which by its nature belongs to the courts of a child's habitual residence in cases involving its custody.
From a different viewpoint, our attention should also be drawn to the fact that the Convention speaks of the 'law' of the State of habitual residence, thus breaking with a long-established tradition of Hague Conventions on applicable law since 1955, which refer to a particular internal law to govern the matters with which they deal. Of course, in such cases, the word 'law' has to be understood in its widest sense, as embracing both written and customary rules of law – whatever their relative importance might be – and the interpretations placed upon them by case-law. However, the adjective 'internal' implies the exclusion of all reference to the conflict of law rules of the particular legal system. Therefore, since the Convention has abandoned its traditional formulation by speaking of 'the law of the habitual residence', this difference cannot be regarded as just a matter of terminology. In fact, as the preliminary proceedings of the Commission demonstrate,[25] it was intended right from the start to expand considerably the range of provisions which have to be considered in this context. Actually, a proposal was made during the Fourteenth Session that this article should make it clear that the reference to the law of the habitual residence extends also to the rules of private international law. The fact that this proposal was rejected was due to the Conference's view that its inclusion was unnecessary and became implicit anyway

[24] *Cf.* Working Document No 5 (Proposal of the Canadian delegation) and *P.-v.* No 3.

[25] *Cf.* the Special Commission Report, No 62, *supra*, p. 90.

n'exclut ni directement ni indirectement les règles en question.[26]

67 Les considérations antérieures nous montrent que l'invocation du droit de la résidence habituelle de l'enfant est aussi large que possible. De même, les sources dont peut découler le droit de garde qu'on essaie de protéger sont toutes celles qui peuvent fonder une réclamation dans le cadre du système juridique en question. A cet égard, l'alinéa 2 de l'article 3 considère certaines – les plus importantes sans doute – de ces sources, mais en soulignant la nature non exhaustive de l'énumération; cet alinéa dispose en effet que «le droit de garde visé en *a* peut notamment résulter . . .», en soulignant de la sorte l'existence possible d'autres titres non considérés dans le texte. Or, comme nous le verrons dans les paragraphes suivants, les sources retenues couvrent un vaste éventail juridique; la précision de leur caractère partiel doit donc être surtout comprise comme favorisant une interprétation souple des concepts employés, qui permette d'appréhender le maximum d'hypothèses possibles.

68 La première des sources à laquelle l'article 3 fait allusion est la loi, quand il dit que la garde peut «résulter d'une attribution de plein droit». Cela nous amène à insister sur l'un des traits caractéristiques de cette Convention, nommément son applicabilité à la protection des droits de garde exercés avant toute décision en la matière. Le point est important, car on ne peut pas ignorer que, dans une perspective statistique, les cas où l'enfant est déplacé avant qu'une décision concernant sa garde n'ait été prononcée sont assez fréquents. D'ailleurs, dans de telles situations, les possibilités existantes, en marge de la Convention, pour le parent dépossédé de récupérer l'enfant sont presque nulles, sauf s'il recourt à son tour à des voies de fait toujours pernicieuses pour l'enfant. A cet égard, en introduisant ces cas dans son domaine d'application, la Convention a progressé de manière significative dans la solution des problèmes réels qui échappaient auparavant, dans une large mesure, aux mécanismes traditionnels du droit international privé.
Quant à savoir quel est, selon la Convention, le système juridique qui peut attribuer le droit de garde qu'on désire protéger, il nous faut en revenir aux considérations développées au paragraphe précédent. Ainsi donc, la garde *ex lege* pourra se baser soit sur la loi interne de l'Etat de la résidence habituelle de l'enfant, soit sur la loi désignée par les règles de conflit de cet Etat. Le jeu de la première option est parfaitement clair; en ce qui concerne la seconde, elle impliquerait, par exemple, que le déplacement par son père français d'un enfant naturel ayant sa résidence habituelle en Espagne où il habitait avec sa mère, tous les deux étant aussi de nationalité française, devrait être considéré comme illicite au sens de la Convention, par application de la loi française désignée comme compétente par la règle de conflit espagnole en matière de garde et indépendamment du fait que l'application de la loi interne espagnole aurait vraisemblablement conduit à une autre solution.

69 La deuxième source du droit de garde, retenue à l'article 3, est l'existence d'une décision judiciaire ou administrative. Etant donné que la Convention n'ajoute aucune précision sur ce point, il faut considérer, d'une part que le mot «décision» est utilisé dans son sens le plus large, de manière à embrasser toute décision ou élément de décision (judiciaire ou administrative) concernant la garde d'un

[26] *Cf.* Doc. trav. No 2 (*Proposal of the United Kingdom delegation*) et P.-v. No 2.

once the text neither directly nor indirectly excluded the rules in question.[26]

67 The foregoing considerations show that the law of the child's habitual residence is invoked in the widest possible sense. Likewise, the sources from which the custody rights which it is sought to protect derive, are all those upon which a claim can be based within the context of the legal system concerned. In this regard, paragraph 2 of article 3 takes into consideration some – no doubt the most important – of those sources, while emphasizing that the list is not exhaustive. This paragraph provides that 'the rights of custody mentioned in sub-paragraph *a* above may arise in particular', thus underlining the fact that other sorts of rights may exist which are not contained within the text itself. Now, as we shall see in the following paragraphs, these sources cover a vast juridical area, and the fact that they are not exhaustively set out must be understood as favouring a flexible interpretation of the terms used, which allows the greatest possible number of cases to be brought into consideration.

68 The first source referred to in article 3 is law, where it is stated that custody 'may arise . . . by operation of law'. That leads us to stress one of the characteristics of this Convention, namely its application to the protection of custody rights which were exercised prior to any decision thereon. This is important, since one cannot forget that, in terms of statistics, the number of cases in which a child is removed prior to a decision on its custody are quite frequent. Moreover, the possibility of the dispossessed parent being able to recover the child in such circumstances, except within the Convention's framework, is practically non-existent, unless he in his turn resorts to force, a course of action which is always harmful to the child. In this respect, by including such cases within its scope, the Convention has taken a significant step towards resolving the real problems which in the past largely escaped the control of the traditional mechanisms of private international law.

As for knowing the legal system which, according to the Convention, is to attribute the custody rights, which it is desired to protect, it is necessary to go back to the considerations developed in the previous paragraph. Thus, custody *ex lege* can be based either on the internal law of the State of the child's habitual residence, or on the law designated by the conflict rules of that State. The scope of the first option is quite clear; the second implies, for example, that the removal by its French father of a child born out of wedlock which had its habitual residence in Spain where it lived with its mother, both mother and child being of French nationality, should be considered wrongful in the Convention sense, by means of the application of French law designated as applicable by the Spanish conflict rule on questions of custody, quite independently of the fact that application of internal Spanish law would probably have led to a different result.

69 The second source of custody rights contained in article 3 is a judicial or administrative decision. Since the Convention does not expand upon this, it must be deemed, on the one hand, that the word 'decision' is used in its widest sense, and embraces any decision or part of a decision (judicial or administrative) on a child's custody and, on the other hand, that these decisions may have been issued by the courts of

[26] *Cf.* Working Document No 2 (Proposal of the United Kingdom delegation), and *P.-v.* No 2.

enfant; d'autre part que les décisions visées peuvent avoir été rendues aussi bien par les tribunaux de l'Etat de la résidence habituelle de l'enfant que par ceux d'un Etat tiers.[27] Or, dans cette dernière hypothèse, c'est-à-dire lorsque le droit de garde s'exerçait dans l'Etat de la résidence habituelle de l'enfant sur la base d'une décision étrangère, la Convention n'exige pas qu'elle ait été formellement reconnue. En conséquence, il doit suffire aux effets considérés que la décision soit telle au regard du droit de l'Etat de la résidence habituelle, c'est-à-dire, en principe, qu'elle présente les caractéristiques *minima* pour pouvoir déclencher une procédure en vue de son homologation ou de sa reconnaissance;[28] interprétation large qui se trouve d'ailleurs confirmée par la teneur de l'article 14 de la Convention.

70 Finalement, le droit de garde peut découler, d'après l'article 3, «d'un accord en vigueur selon le droit de cet Etat». En principe, les accords envisagés peuvent être de simples transactions privées entre les parties, au sujet de la garde des enfants. La condition d'être «en vigueur» selon le droit de l'Etat de la résidence habituelle, a été introduite au cours de la Quatorzième session en substitution de l'exigence d'avoir «force de loi», qui figurait dans l'avant-projet. La modification répond à un désir de clarification, mais aussi d'assouplissement, autant que possible, des conditions posées à l'acceptation d'un accord en tant que source de la garde protégée par la Convention. Sur le point précis de savoir ce qu'est un accord «en vigueur» selon un droit déterminé, il nous semble que l'on doive inclure sous cette appellation tout accord qui ne soit pas interdit par un tel droit et qui puisse servir de base à une prétention juridique devant les autorités compétentes. Or, pour en revenir au sens large que la notion «droit de l'Etat de la résidence habituelle de l'enfant» a reçu dans cet article 3, le droit en question peut être aussi bien la loi interne de cet Etat que la loi désignée par ses règles de conflit; le choix entre les deux branches de l'option appartient aux autorités de l'Etat concerné, quoique l'esprit de la Convention semble incliner pour celle qui, dans chaque cas d'espèce, légitime la garde effectivement exercée. D'autre part, la Convention ne précise point les conditions de fond ou de forme que ces accords doivent remplir; elles changeront donc selon la teneur du droit impliqué.

71 Tout en ajournant l'étude de la personne qui peut être titulaire d'un droit de garde au commentaire de l'article 4 sur le domaine d'application *ratione personae* de la Convention, il convient d'insister ici sur le fait qu'on s'est proposé de protéger toutes les modalités d'exercice de la garde d'enfants. En effet, aux termes de l'article 3, le droit de garde peut avoir été attribué, seul ou conjointement, à la personne qui demande qu'on en respecte l'exercice. Il ne pouvait en être autrement à une époque où les législations internes introduisent progressivement la modalité de la garde conjointe, considérée comme la mieux adaptée au principe général de la non-discrimination à raison du sexe. D'ailleurs, la garde conjointe n'est pas toujours une garde *ex lege*, dans la mesure où les tribunaux se montrent de plus en plus favorables, si les circonstances le permettent, à partager entre les deux parents les responsabilités inhérentes au droit de garde. Or, dans l'optique adoptée par la Convention, le déplacement d'un enfant par l'un des titulaires de la garde

[27] Cette interprétation s'appuie sur les travaux qui ont conduit à l'adoption d'un texte, similaire à l'actuel, au sein de la Commission spéciale. Voir Rapport de la Commission spéciale, No 64, *supra*, p. 191-192.

[28] Sur l'intérêt de ce que la Convention inclue un tel cas, voir le Doc. trav. No 58. «Document de clarification présenté par la délégation italienne».

the State of the child's habitual residence as well as by the courts of a third country.[27] Now, in the latter case, that is to say when custody rights were exercised in the State of the child's habitual residence on the basis of a foreign decree, the Convention does not require that the decree had been formally recognized. Consequently, in order to have the effect described, it is sufficient that the decision be regarded as such by the State of habitual residence, *i.e.* that it contain in principle certain minimum characteristics which are necessary for setting in motion the means by which it may be confirmed or recognized.[28] This wide interpretation is moreover confirmed by the whole tenor of article 14.

70 Lastly, custody rights may arise according to article 3, 'by reason of an agreement having legal effect under the law of that State'. In principle, the agreements in question may be simple private transactions between the parties concerning the custody of their children. The condition that they have 'legal effect' according to the law of the State of habitual residence was inserted during the Fourteenth Session in place of a requirement that it have the 'force of law', as stated in the Preliminary Draft. The change was made in response to a desire that the conditions imposed upon the acceptance of agreements governing matters of custody which the Convention seeks to protect should be made as clear and as flexible as possible. As regards the definition of an agreement which has 'legal effect' in terms of a particular law, it seems that there must be included within it any sort of agreement which is not prohibited by such a law and which may provide a basis for presenting a legal claim to the competent authorities. Now, to go back to the wide interpretation given by article 3 to the notion of 'the law of the State of the child's habitual residence', the law concerned can equally as well be the internal law of that State as the law which is indicated as applicable by its conflict rules. It is for the authorities of the State concerned to choose between the two alternatives, although the spirit of the Convention appears to point to the choice of the one which, in each particular case, would recognize that custody had actually been exercised. On the other hand, the Convention does not state, in substance or form, the conditions which these agreements must fulfil, since these will change according to the terms of the law concerned.

71 Leaving aside a consideration of those persons who can hold rights of custody, until the commentary on article 4 which concerns the scope of the Convention *ratione personae*, it should be stressed now that the intention is to protect *all* the ways in which custody of children can be exercised. Actually, in terms of article 3, custody rights may have been awarded to the person who demands that their exercise be respected, and to that person in his own right or jointly. It cannot be otherwise in an era when types of joint custody, regarded as best suited to the general principle of sexual non-discrimination, are gradually being introduced into internal law. Joint custody is, moreover, not always custody *ex lege*, in as much as courts are increasingly showing themselves to be in favour, where circumstances permit of dividing the responsibilities inherent in custody rights between both parents. Now, from the Convention's standpoint, the removal of a child by one of the joint holders without the consent of the other, is equally wrongful, and

[27] This interpretation is based upon the deliberations of the Special Commission which led to its adopting a similar text to the current one. See Report of the Special Commission, No 64, *supra*, pp. 191-192.

[28] See Working Document No 58, '*Document de clarification présenté par la délégation italienne*', for the desirability of including such a case in the Convention.

conjointe, sans le consentement de l'autre titulaire, est également illicite; ce caractère illicite proviendrait, dans ce cas précis, non pas d'une action contraire à la loi, mais du fait qu'une telle action aurait ignoré les droits de l'autre parent, également protégé par la loi, et interrompu leur exercice normal. La véritable nature de la Convention apparaît plus clairement dans ces situations: elle ne cherche pas à établir à qui appartiendra dans l'avenir la garde de l'enfant, ni s'il s'avérera nécessaire de modifier une décision de garde conjointe rendue sur la base de données qui ont été altérées par la suite; elle essaie plus simplement d'éviter qu'une décision ultérieure à cet égard puisse être influencée par un changement des circonstances introduit unilatéralement par l'une des parties.

c L'élément de fait

72 Le deuxième élément qui caractérise les rapports protégés par la Convention est que le droit de garde, qu'on prétend violé par le déplacement, ait été exercé de façon effective par son titulaire. En effet, du moment qu'on a choisi une approche du sujet conventionnel s'écartant de la pure et simple reconnaissance internationale des droits de garde attribués aux parents, la Convention a mis l'accent sur la protection du droit des enfants au respect de leur équilibre vital; c'est-à-dire du droit des enfants à ne pas voir altérées les conditions affectives, sociales, etc., qui entourent leur vie, à moins qu'il n'existe des arguments juridiques garantissant la stabilité d'une nouvelle situation. Cette approche est reflétée dans la limite du domaine d'application de la Convention aux droits de garde effectivement exercés. De plus, une telle conception se trouve justifiée dans le cadre des relations internationales par un argument complémentaire, touchant au fait que, dans ce contexte, il est relativement fréquent qu'il existe des décisions contradictoires peu à même de servir de base à la protection de la stabilité de la vie d'un enfant.

73 En réalité, cette conception a été à peine contestée. Pourtant, plusieurs propositions[29] ont été présentées en vue de supprimer de l'article 3 toute référence à l'exercice effectif de la garde; la raison en était que, par ce biais, on imposait au demandeur le fardeau d'une preuve sur un point qui serait parfois difficile à établir. La situation semblait encore plus compliquée si on tenait compte du fait que l'article 13 consacré aux exceptions possibles à l'obligation de faire retourner l'enfant exige, de «l'enleveur» cette fois, la preuve que la personne dépossédée n'exerçait pas effectivement la garde qu'elle réclame maintenant. Or, c'est justement en rapprochant les deux dispositions que l'on fait apparaître nettement la véritable nature de la condition prévue à l'article 3. En effet, cette condition, en délimitant le domaine d'application de la Convention, n'exige du demandeur qu'une première évidence du fait qu'il exerçait réellement les soins sur la personne de l'enfant; cette circonstance doit être, en général, assez facile à établir. D'ailleurs, le caractère non formel de cette exigence est mis en relief à l'article 8 lorsque, parmi les données que doit contenir la demande introduite auprès des Autorités centrales, il indique simplement sous *c* «les motifs sur lesquels se base le demandeur pour réclamer le retour de l'enfant».
Par contre, l'article 13 de la Convention (12 de l'avant-projet) nous place devant un véritable fardeau de la preuve à la charge de «l'enleveur»; c'est en effet lui qui doit établir,

[29] *Cf.* Doc. trav. No 1 (*Proposal of the United States delegation*) et No 10 (*Proposal of the Finnish delegation*), ainsi que le P.-v. No 3.

this wrongfulness derives in this particular case, not from some action in breach of a particular law, but from the fact that such action has disregarded the rights of the other parent which are also protected by law, and has interfered with their normal exercise. The Convention's true nature is revealed most clearly in these situations: it is not concerned with establishing the person to whom custody of the child will belong at some point in the future, nor with the situations in which it may prove necessary to modify a decision awarding joint custody on the basis of facts which have subsequently changed. It seeks, more simply, to prevent a later decision on the matter being influenced by a change of circumstances brought about through unilateral action by one of the parties.

c The factual element

72 The second element characterizing those relationships protected by the Convention is that the custody rights which it is claimed have been breached by the child's removal were actually exercised by the holder. In fact, as soon as an approach to the subject-matter of the Convention was adopted which deviated from the pure and simple international recognition of custody rights attributed to parents, the Convention put its emphasis on protecting the right of children to have the stability which is so vital to them respected. In other words, the Convention protects the right of children not to have the emotional, social etc. aspects of their lives altered, unless legal arguments exist which would guarantee their stability in a new situation. This approach is reflected in the scope of the Convention, which is limited to custody rights actually exercised. What is more, such a notion is justified within the framework of international relations by a complementary argument which concerns the fact that contradictory decisions arise quite frequently in this particular context, decisions which are basically of little use in protecting the stability of a child's life.

73 Actually, this idea was not opposed to any extent. However, several proposals[29] were put forward for the deletion from article 3 of any reference to the actual exercise of custody rights. The reason for this was that its retention could place on the applicant the burden of proving a point which would sometimes be difficult to establish. The situation became even more complicated when account was taken of the fact that article 13, which concerns the possible exceptions to the obligation to order the return of the child, requires the 'abductor' this time to prove that the dispossessed party had not actually exercised the custody rights he now claims. Now, it is indeed by considering both provisions together that the true nature of the condition set forth in article 3 can be seen clearly. This condition, by defining the scope of the Convention, requires that the applicant provide only some preliminary evidence that he actually took physical care of the child, a fact which normally will be relatively easy to demonstrate. Besides, the informal nature of this requirement is highlighted in article 8 which simply includes, in sub-paragraph *c*, 'the grounds on which the applicant's claim for return of the child is based', amongst the facts which it requires to be contained in applications to the Central Authorities.
On the other hand, article 13 of the Convention (12 in the Preliminary Draft) shows us the real extent of the burden of proof placed upon the 'abductor'; it is for him to show, if he

[29] *Cf.* Working Documents Nos 1 (Proposal of the United States delegation) and 1((Proposal of the Finnish delegation), and also *P.-v.* No 3.

pour éviter le retour de l'enfant, que le gardien n'exerçait pas effectivement le droit de garde. Donc, nous pouvons en arriver à la conclusion que l'ensemble de la Convention est construit sur la présomption non explicite que celui qui a le soin de la personne de l'enfant en exerce effectivement la garde; cette idée devra être détruite en vertu de l'inversion du fardeau de la preuve qui est le propre de toute présomption, (par «l'enleveur» s'il veut éviter que l'enfant ne soit renvoyé).

74 Cependant, la Convention inclut expressément dans le domaine qu'elle entend protéger la situation qui se pose quand la garde n'a pas pu devenir effective à cause précisément du déplacement de l'enfant; c'est en ce sens que se prononce le dernier membre de phrase de la lettre *b* de l'article 3. En théorie, l'idée sous-jacente s'accorde parfaitement avec l'esprit qui inspire la Convention; c'est donc d'un point de vue pratique qu'on peut se demander si un tel ajout était nécessaire.[30] Dans cette optique, les hypothèses que cette précision essaie de protéger visent deux situations type possibles, dont l'une rentrerait clairement dans le domaine d'application de la Convention, tandis que l'autre, à défaut de cette norme, exigerait vraisemblablement une interprétation trop forcée de ses dispositions. Il s'agit, d'une part, des cas soulevés lorsqu'une première décision sur la garde est mise en échec par le déplacement de l'enfant; or, dans la mesure où une telle décision suit, dans un délai raisonnable, la rupture de la vie familiale commune, on peut considérer que le titulaire de la garde l'avait exercée au préalable et qu'en conséquence la situation décrite remplit toutes les conditions que fixe le domaine d'application conventionnel. Pourtant, si nous nous plaçons devant une décision sur la garde, rendue par les tribunaux de la résidence habituelle de l'enfant, qui modifie une décision précédente et dont l'exécution est rendue impossible par l'action du ravisseur, il peut se trouver que le nouveau titulaire de la garde ne l'ait pas exercée dans un délai étendu; les difficultés qu'on rencontrerait dans de telles situations, et peut-être dans d'autres non visées dans ces lignes, pour invoquer la Convention sont évidentes. En conclusion, et quoiqu'il faille s'attendre à ce que le jeu de cette disposition ne soit pas fréquent, nous devons conclure que son inclusion dans la Convention peut s'avérer utile.

Article 4 – Domaine d'application ratione personae

75 Cet article ne concerne que le domaine d'application *ratione personae* de la Convention par rapport aux enfants protégés. Pourtant dans un souci de systématisation, nous traiterons aussi dans son contexte les autres aspects du problème, c'est-à-dire les titulaires possibles des droits de garde et de visite et les personnes qui pourraient être considérées comme «enleveurs», aux termes de la Convention.

a Les enfants protégés

76 La Convention s'applique aux enfants âgés de moins de seize ans qui avaient «leur résidence habituelle dans un Etat contractant immédiatement avant l'atteinte aux droits de garde ou de visite». En relation avec l'exigence concernant la résidence habituelle, il faut revenir aux considérations émises sur la nature de la Convention, qui aboutissent à la conclusion qu'une convention de coopération entre

[30] *Cf.* Doc. trav. No 2 (*Proposal of the United Kingdom delegation*) et les débats sur ce point aux P.-v. Nos 3 et 13.

wishes to prevent the return of the child, that the guardian had not actually exercised his rights of custody. Thus, we may conclude that the Convention, taken as a whole, is built upon the tacit presumption that the person who has care of the child actually exercises custody over it. This idea has to be overcome by discharging the burden of proof which has shifted, as is normal with any presumption (*i.e.* discharged by the 'abductor' if he wishes to prevent the return of the child).

74 However, there is expressly included amongst the matters which the Convention is intended to protect the situation which arises when actual custody cannot be exercised precisely because of the removal of the child; that is the situation envisaged in the last alternative set out in article 3*b*. Theoretically, the underlying idea is perfectly in keeping with the spirit of the Convention, and it is therefore from a practical point of view that it may be wondered whether such a provision needed to be added.[30] From this viewpoint, the hypothetical situations which this provision is designed to protect are of two types, one of which falls clearly within the scope of the Convention, while the other, failing this rule, would probably require too strained an interpretation of its provisions. On the one hand, there are cases where an initial decision on custody is rendered worthless by the removal of the child. In so far as such a description follows the disruption of normal family life after a reasonable lapse of time, the holder of the rights could be regarded as having exercised them from the outset, so that the situation described fulfils all the conditions laid down within the scope of the Convention. However, if a decision on custody by the courts of the child's habitual residence is considered, which modifies a prior decision and cannot be enforced because of the action of the abductor, it could be that the new holder of the right to custody has not exercised it within the extended time-limit. The difficulties which would be encountered in seeking to apply the Convention to such situations and perhaps to others not herein mentioned, are obvious. To conclude, although this provision must not be expected to come into play very often, it has to be said finally that its inclusion in the Convention might prove to be useful.

Article 4 – Convention's scope ratione personae

75 This article concerns only the Convention's scope *ratione personae* as regards the children who are to be protected. However, for the sake of completeness, we shall also deal with the other aspects of the problem in their proper context, that is to say those potential holders of custody and access rights and those who could be regarded as 'abductors', within the terms of the Convention.

a The children protected

76 The Convention applies to children of less than sixteen years of age, who were 'habitually resident in a Contracting State immediately before any breach of custody or access rights'. As regards the requirement that they be habitually resident, reference must again be made to those considerations previously expressed about the nature of the Convention, which lead to the conclusion that a convention

[30] *Cf.* Working Document No 2 (Proposal of the United Kingdom delegation) and the debate on this point in *P.-v.* Nos 3 and 13.

autorités ne peut atteindre toute son efficacité que si les rapports visés se produisent entre Etats contractants.

77 L'âge limite pour l'application de la Convention soulève deux questions importantes. La première, la question de l'âge *stricto sensu*, a été à peine débattue. La Convention retient l'âge de seize ans, consacrant ainsi une notion d'enfant plus restrictive que celle admise par d'autres Conventions de La Haye.[31] La raison découle des objectifs conventionnels eux-mêmes; en effet, une personne de plus de seize ans a en général une volonté propre qui pourra difficilement être ignorée, soit par l'un ou l'autre de ses parents, soit par une autorité judiciaire ou administrative.

Quant à la détermination du moment où cet âge interdit l'application de la Convention, celle-ci, parmi les diverses options possibles, retient la plus limitative; en conséquence, aucune action ou décision basée sur les dispositions conventionnelles ne peut être adoptée à l'égard d'un enfant après son seizième anniversaire.

78 Le deuxième problème a trait à la situation des enfants âgés de moins de seize ans qui ont le droit de fixer leur lieu de résidence. Compte tenu du fait que ce droit fait en général partie du droit de garde, une proposition a été faite dans le sens de la non-application de la Convention dans de tels cas.[32] Cependant, cette proposition a été rejetée sur la base de divers arguments, parmi lesquels on peut citer: 1) la difficulté de choisir le système juridique qui devrait consacrer l'existence d'une telle possibilité, étant donné qu'il existe au moins trois possibilités qui sont, respectivement, la loi nationale, la loi de la résidence habituelle avant le déplacement et la loi de l'Etat de refuge; 2) la limitation excessive que cette proposition apporterait au domaine d'application de la Convention, par rapport notamment au droit de visite; 3) le fait que la faculté de décider du lieu de résidence d'un enfant n'est qu'un élément possible du droit de garde qui n'en épuise pas le contenu.

D'autre part, la décision prise à cet égard ne peut pas être isolée de la disposition de l'article 13, alinéa 2, qui donne la possibilité aux autorités compétentes de tenir compte de l'opinion de l'enfant sur son retour, dès qu'il atteint un âge et une maturité suffisants; en effet, cette norme permettra aux autorités judiciaires ou administratives, quand il sera question du retour d'un mineur ayant capacité de décider sur son lieu de résidence, de considérer que l'opinion de l'enfant est toujours déterminante. On peut arriver ainsi à l'application automatique d'une disposition facultative de la Convention, mais une telle conséquence semble préférable à la réduction globale du domaine d'application de la Convention.

b Les titulaires des droits de garde et de visite

79 Les problèmes soulevés à cet égard par l'un et l'autre des droits visés sont nettement différents. D'abord, en ce qui concerne le droit de visite, il est évident que par la nature même des choses, ses titulaires seront toujours des personnes physiques, dont la détermination dépendra de la loi appliquée à l'organisation de ce droit. En principe, ces personnes appartiendront à la proche famille de l'enfant, et il s'agira normalement soit du père, soit de la mère.

[31] Par exemple: *Convention sur la loi applicable aux obligations alimentaires envers les enfants, du 24 octobre 1956* (article premier); *Convention concernant la reconnaissance et l'exécution des décisions en matière d'obligations alimentaires envers les enfants, du 15 avril 1958* (article premier); *Convention concernant la compétence des autorités et la loi applicable en matière de protection des mineurs, du 5 octobre 1961* (article 12); *Convention concernant la compétence des autorités, la loi applicable et la reconnaissance des décisions en matière d'adoption, du 15 novembre 1965* (article premier).

[32] *Cf.* Doc. trav. No 4 (Proposition de la délégation belge) et P.-v. No 4.

based on co-operation among authorities can only become fully operational after the relationships envisaged come into existence as among Contracting States.

77 The age limit for application of the Convention raises two important questions. Firstly, the matter of age in the strict sense gave rise to virtually no dispute. The Convention kept the age at sixteen, and therefore held to a concept of 'the child' which is more restrictive than that accepted by other Hague Conventions.[31] The reason for this derives from the objects of the Convention themselves; indeed, a person of more than sixteen years of age generally has a mind of his own which cannot easily be ignored either by one or both of his parents, or by a judicial or administrative authority.

As for deciding upon the point at which this age should exclude the Convention's application, the most restrictive of the various options available was retained by the Convention. Consequently, no action or decision based upon the Convention's provisions can be taken with regard to a child after its sixteenth birthday.

78 The second problem deals with the situation of children under sixteen years of age who have the right to choose their own place of residence. Considering that this right to choose one's residence generally forms part of the right to custody, a proposal was put forward to the effect that the Convention should not apply in such cases.[32] However, this proposal was rejected on various grounds, *inter alia* the following: (1) the difficulty of choosing the legal system which should determine whether such a possibility exists, since there are at least three different laws which could be applicable, namely, national law, the law of habitual residence prior to the child's removal, and the law of the State of refuge; (2) the excessive restriction which this proposal would place upon the scope of the Convention, particularly with regard to access rights; (3) the fact that the right to decide a child's place of residence is only one possible element of the right to custody which does not itself deprive it of all content.

On the other hand, the decision taken in this regard cannot be isolated from the provision in article 13, second paragraph, which allows the competent authorities to have regard to the opinion of the child as to its return, once it has reached an appropriate age and degree of maturity. Indeed this rule leaves it open to judicial or administrative authorities, whenever they are faced with the possibility of returning a minor legally entitled to decide on his place of residence, to take the view that the opinion of the child should always be the decisive factor. The point could therefore be reached where an optional provision of the Convention becomes automatically applicable, but such a result seems preferable to an overall reduction in the Convention's scope.

b The holders of custody and access rights

79 The problems raised by both of these rights in this regard are quite different. Firstly, as regards access rights, it is obvious, by the very nature of things, that they will always be held by individuals, whose identity will depend on the law which applies to the organizing of these rights. These persons will as a rule be close relatives of the child, and normally will be either its father or mother.

[31] For example: *Convention of 24 October 1956 on the Law Applicable to Maintenance Obligations in Respect of Children* (article 1); *Convention of 15 April 1958 on the Recognition and Enforcement of Decisions Relating to Maintenance Obligations in Respect of Children* (article 1); *Convention of 5 October 1961 Concerning the Powers of Authorities and the Law Applicable in Respect of the Protection of Minors* (article 12); *Convention of 15 November 1965 on Jurisdiction, Applicable Law and Recognition of Decisions Relating to Adoptions* (article 1).

[32] *Cf.* Working Document No 4 (*Proposition de la délégation belge*) and *P.-v.* No 4.

80 Par contre, des personnes morales peuvent aussi être titulaires d'un droit de garde, au sens de la Convention. A cet égard, l'article 3 considère la possibilité de l'attribution du droit de garde à «une institution ou tout autre organisme», en utilisant sciemment une expression vague et large. En effet, au cours de la Quatorzième session, l'inclusion dans le domaine conventionnel des hypothèses où la personne de l'enfant est confiée à une institution a été acceptée sans débats. Or, étant donné qu'il y a des organismes autres que les institutions qui ont à leur charge les soins de certains enfants, on a élargi l'expression utilisée pour y faire rentrer aussi bien les organismes ayant une personnalité juridique que ceux qui sont liés à l'organisation étatique et dépourvus d'une personnalité indépendante.

c Les éventuels «enleveurs»

81 La Convention ne contient aucune disposition expresse à ce propos. Néanmoins, de l'ensemble du texte, nous pouvons déduire deux remarques qui éclairent cet aspect relatif au domaine d'application *ratione personae* de la Convention. La première concerne les personnes physiques qui peuvent être responsables du déplacement ou du non-retour d'un enfant. Sur ce sujet, la Convention maintient le point de vue adopté par la Commission spéciale de ne pas attribuer de telles actions exclusivement à des parents.[33] L'idée de famille étant plus ou moins large selon les différentes conceptions culturelles, il est préférable de s'en tenir à une vue large qui permette, par exemple, de qualifier d'enlèvement d'enfant, au sens de la Convention, les déplacements faits par un grand-père ou un père adoptif.

82 La deuxième remarque a trait à la possibilité de ce qu'une «institution ou tout autre organisme» agisse comme «enleveur». A cet égard, il est difficilement imaginable qu'un organisme quelconque puisse déplacer, par la force ou par la ruse, un enfant d'un pays étranger vers son propre pays. D'autre part, si un enfant a été confié, par une décision judiciaire ou administrative (c'est-à-dire, au cas d'un placement forcé de l'enfant), à un tel organisme dans le pays de sa résidence habituelle, le parent qui prétend obtenir la jouissance effective d'un droit de garde sur celui-ci aura peu de chance de pouvoir invoquer la Convention. En effet, du fait que les organismes visés exercent en principe leurs compétences, abstraction faite de l'éventuelle reconnaissance de l'autorité parentale,[34] une telle prétention ne rentrerait pas dans le domaine conventionnel, puisque la garde au sens de la Convention appartiendrait à l'organisme en question.

Article 5 – De certaines expressions utilisées dans la Convention

83 Suivant une tradition bien établie de la Conférence de La Haye, la Convention ne définit pas les concepts juridiques dont elle se sert. Pourtant, dans cet article, elle précise le sens dans lequel sont utilisées les notions de droit de garde et de droit de visite, étant donné qu'une interprétation incorrecte de leur portée risquerait de compromettre les objectifs conventionnels.

84 En ce qui concerne le droit de garde, la Convention se limite à souligner qu'il comprend «le droit portant sur les soins de la personne de l'enfant», en marge des mécanismes

[33] Une approche plus restrictive se trouvait initialement dans le Rapport Dyer, cité *supra*, intitulé *Rapport sur l'enlèvement international d'un enfant par un de ses parents*.
[34] Voir sur ce point, Cour internationale de Justice, Arrêt du 28 novembre 1958, Affaire relative à l'application de la Convention de 1902 pour régler la tutelle des mineurs, *Recueil des arrêts* 1958, p. 55 et suiv.

80 On the other hand, legal persons can also, in terms of the Convention, hold rights of custody. Article 3 envisages the possibility of custody rights being attributed to 'an institution or any other body', and is expressed in deliberately vague and wide terms. In fact, during the Fourteenth Session, the inclusion within the scope of the Convention of situations in which the child is entrusted to an institution was not challenged. Now, since there are bodies other than institutions which have children in their care, the term used was extended so as to apply equally to those bodies with legal personality and to those which, as an arm of the State, lack separate personality.

c The potential 'abductors'

81 The Convention contains no express provision on this matter. Nevertheless, two comments may be drawn from the text as a whole, which shed light upon this question in relation to the Convention's scope *ratione personae*. The first concerns the physical persons who may be responsible for the removal or retention of a child. On this, the Convention upholds the point of view adopted by the Special Commission by not attributing such acts exclusively to one of the parents.[33] Since the idea of 'family' was more or less wide, depending on the different cultural conceptions which surround it, it was felt better to hold a wide view which would, for example, allow removals by a grandfather or adoptive father to be characterized as child abduction, in accordance with the Convention's use of that term.

82 The second comment relates to the possibility of an 'institution or any other body' acting as an 'abductor'. In this regard, it is difficult to imagine how any body whatever could remove, either by force or by deception, a child from a foreign country to its own land. On the other hand, if a child were entrusted, by virtue of a judicial or administrative decision (*i.e.* compulsory placement of the child) to such a body in the country of its habitual residence, the parent who sought to obtain the actual enjoyment of custody rights would stand little chance of being able to invoke the provisions of the Convention. In fact, by virtue of the fact that such bodies would as a rule exercise jurisdiction, except as regards the possible recognition of parental authority,[34] such a claim would not come within the scope of the Convention, since custody, in the sense understood by the Convention, would belong to the body in question.

Article 5 – Certain terms used in the Convention

83 The Convention, following a long-established tradition of the Hague Conference, does not define the legal concepts used by it. However, in this article, it does make clear the sense in which the notions of custody and access rights are used, since an incorrect interpretation of their meaning would risk compromising the Convention's objects.

84 As regards custody rights, the Convention merely emphasizes the fact that it includes in the term 'rights relating to the care of the person of the child', leaving aside the

[33] A more restrictive approach was to be found initially in the Dyer Report, referred to above, entitled *Report on international child abduction by one parent*.
[34] See the Judgment of the International Court of Justice, dated 28 November 1958, on the case concerning the application of the Convention of 1902 for regulating the guardianship of minors, *ICJ Reports* 1958, p. 55 *et seq.*

possibles de protection de ses biens. Il s'agit donc d'une notion plus restrictive que celle de «protection des mineurs»,[35] malgré les tentatives faites au cours de la Quatorzième session pour introduire l'idée de «protection», en vue surtout de couvrir les cas des enfants confiés à des institutions ou organismes. Mais, tous les efforts faits pour préciser la notion de droit de garde par rapport à ces situations ayant échoué, il faut s'en tenir au concept générique mentionné ci-dessus. La Convention essaie de le préciser en mettant en relief, comme indice des «soins» dont il s'agit, le droit de décider du lieu de résidence de l'enfant. Cependant, lorsque l'enfant, quoique mineur du point de vue juridique, a la faculté de fixer lui-même son lieu de résidence, le contenu du droit de garde sera déterminé en fonction des autres droits portant sur sa personne.

D'autre part, bien que dans cet article rien ne soit dit sur la possibilité que la garde soit exercée par son titulaire seul ou conjointement, il est évident que cette possibilité est envisagée. En effet, une règle classique du droit des traités exige que l'interprétation de ses termes soit effectuée dans son contexte et en tenant compte de l'objet et du but du traité;[36] or, la teneur de l'article 3 ne laisse pas de doute sur l'inclusion de la garde conjointe parmi les situations que la Convention entend protéger. Quant à savoir quand existe une garde conjointe, c'est une question qui doit être déterminée dans chaque cas d'espèce à la lumière du droit de la résidence habituelle de l'enfant.

85 Quant au droit de visite, la lettre *b* de cet article se limite à signaler qu'il comprend «le droit d'emmener l'enfant pour une période limitée dans un lieu autre que celui de sa résidence habituelle». L'intention de la Convention n'est évidemment pas d'exclure toutes les autres modalités du droit de visite; plus simplement, elle a voulu souligner que cette notion s'étend aussi au droit dit d'hébergement, manifestation du droit de visite que la personne qui a la garde de l'enfant redoute spécialement. De plus, étant donné que cette norme explicative ne qualifie point ce «lieu autre» où l'enfant peut être emmené, il faut conclure que le droit de visite, selon la Convention, inclut également le droit de visite transfrontière.

86 Une proposition a été faite en vue d'inclure dans cet article une définition des autorités judiciaires ou administratives visées tout au long des normes conventionnelles.[37] Les difficultés rencontrées tant pour la localisation d'un point de vue systématique que pour trouver une rédaction large qui englobe toutes les hypothèses possibles ont conseillé sa non-inclusion. Or il est clair qu'il s'agit, comme nous l'avons déjà souligné,[38] des autorités compétentes pour décider soit de la garde, soit de la protection des enfants, d'après la loi interne de chaque Etat contractant. D'ailleurs, c'est justement en raison des différences entre ces lois que l'on parle toujours des autorités «judiciaires ou administratives», en vue de recouvrir toutes les autorités ayant compétence en la matière, sans égard à la qualification juridique qu'elles reçoivent dans chaque Etat.

CHAPITRE II — AUTORITÉS CENTRALES

Article 6 — Création des Autorités centrales

87 Le rôle joué par les Autorités centrales, pièces clés dans

[35] Voir par exemple la *Convention concernant la compétence des autorités et la loi applicable en matière de protection des mineurs, du 5 octobre 1961*.
[36] En ce sens, l'article 31, alinéa premier, de la Convention de Vienne sur le droit des traités du 23 mai 1969.
[37] Voir Doc. trav. No 7 (*Proposal of the United States delegation*) et P.-v. Nos 4 et 14.
[38] Voir *supra* No 45.

possible ways of protecting the child's property. It is therefore a more limited concept than that of 'protection of minors',[35] despite attempts made during the Fourteenth Session to introduce the idea of 'protection' so as to include in particular those cases where children are entrusted to institutions or bodies. But since all efforts to define custody rights in regard to those particular situations failed, one has to rest content with the general description given above. The Convention seeks to be more precise by emphasizing, as an example of the 'care' referred to, the right to determine the child's place of residence. However, if the child, although still a minor at law, has the right itself to determine its own place of residence, the substance of the custody rights will have to be determined in the context of other rights concerning the person of the child.

On the other hand, although nothing is said in this article about the possibility of custody rights being exercised singly or jointly, such a possibility is clearly envisaged. In fact, a classic rule of treaty law requires that a treaty's terms be interpreted in their context and by taking into account the objective and end sought by the treaty,[36] and the whole tenor of article 3 leaves no room for doubt that the Convention seeks to protect joint custody as well. As for knowing when joint custody exists, that is a question which must be decided in each particular case, and in the light of the law of the child's habitual residence.

85 As regards access rights, sub-paragraph *b* of this article merely points out that they include 'the right to take a child for a limited period of time to a place other than the child's habitual residence'. Clearly, therefore, it is not intended that the Convention exclude all other ways of exercising access rights. Quite simply, it seeks to emphasize that access rights extend also to what is called 'residential access', that aspect of access rights about which the person who has custody of the child is particularly apprehensive. Moreover, since this explanatory provision in no way qualifies this 'other place' to which the child may be taken, one must conclude that access rights, in terms of the Convention, also include the right of access across national frontiers.

86 A proposal was made to include in this article a definition of the judicial or administrative authorities mentioned throughout the Convention's rules.[37] The difficulties encountered as much in reaching a systematic viewpoint on this as in devising a definition wide enough to encompass all possible contingencies made for its exclusion. Now, as was mentioned earlier,[38] it is clear that these are the authorities who have the power, according to the internal law of each Contracting State, to determine questions concerning a child's custody or protection. Besides, it is precisely because of differences amongst these laws that reference is always made to 'judicial or administrative' authorities, so as to embrace all authorities which have jurisdiction in the matter, without regard to their legal characterization in each State.

CHAPTER II — CENTRAL AUTHORITIES

Article 6 — Creation of Central Authorities

87 The role played by the Central Authorities, crucial

[35] See, for example, the *Convention of 5 October 1961 concerning the powers of authorities and the applicable law in respect of the protection of minors.*
[36] See article 31(1) of the Vienna Convention of 23 May 1969 on the law of treaties.
[37] See Working Document No 7 (Proposal of the United States delegation) and *P.-v.* Nos 4 and 14.
[38] See *supra*, No 45.

l'application de la Convention, a déjà été longuement présenté.[39]
En ce qui concerne les Etats susceptibles de désigner plus d'une Autorité centrale, c'est l'idée que le critère déterminant à cet effet devait être l'existence de plusieurs organisations territoriales en matière de protection des mineurs qui a prévalu. En conséquence, on a ajouté aux hypothèses des Etats fédéraux et plurilégislatifs le cas des Etats «ayant des organisations territoriales autonomes», expression qui doit être interprétée dans un sens large.

Article 7 – Obligations des Autorités centrales

88 Cet article résume le rôle des Autorités centrales dans la mise en oeuvre du système instauré par la Convention. L'article est structuré en deux alinéas, dont le premier, rédigé en termes généraux, établit une obligation globale de coopération, tandis que le second énumère, de la lettre *a* à la lettre *i*, quelques-unes des principales fonctions que les Autorités centrales doivent remplir. Tous deux sont le résultat du compromis entre, d'une part les délégations qui désiraient des Autorités centrales fortes avec des compétences d'action et d'initiative amples et d'autre part les délégations qui envisageaient lesdites Autorités comme de simples mécanismes administratifs pour faciliter l'action des parties. Or, puisque ces diverses attitudes reflétaient la plupart des profondes différences existant entre les systèmes représentés à la Conférence, la solution à retenir devait être souple, de manière à permettre à chaque Autorité centrale d'agir selon le droit dans lequel elle est appelée à s'insérer. Donc, bien que la Convention précise les principales obligations confiées à la charge des Autorités centrales, elle laisse à chaque Etat contractant la détermination des mesures appropriées pour les exécuter. D'ailleurs, c'est dans ce sens qu'il faut interpréter la phrase qui introduit le second alinéa, et qui spécifie que les Autorités centrales doivent remplir les fonctions énumérées «soit directement, soit avec le concours de tout intermédiaire»; c'est à chaque Autorité centrale de choisir entre l'une ou l'autre option en fonction de son propre droit interne et dans l'esprit du devoir général de coopération que lui impose le premier alinéa.

89 Comme nous venons de le dire, la norme insérée dans le *premier alinéa* énonce l'obligation générale de coopérer des Autorités centrales, en vue d'assurer l'accomplissement des objectifs de la Convention. Une telle coopération doit se développer à deux niveaux: les Autorités centrales doivent d'abord coopérer entre elles; mais, de surcroît, elles doivent promouvoir la collaboration entre les autorités compétentes pour les matières visées dans leurs Etats respectifs. La réalisation effective de cette promotion dépendra dans une large mesure de la capacité d'action que chaque droit interne accorde aux Autorités centrales.

90 Les fonctions détaillées au *deuxième alinéa* essaient de suivre, dans leurs grandes lignes, les différents stades de l'intervention des Autorités centrales dans un cas type de déplacements d'enfants. Néanmoins, il est évident que cette énumération n'est pas exhaustive; par exemple, puisque l'intervention des Autorités centrales exige qu'elles aient été saisies au préalable, soit directement par le demandeur, soit par l'Autorité centrale, d'un autre Etat contractant, dans la seconde hypothèse, l'Autorité centrale initialement saisie de

[39] Voir *supra* Nos 43 à 48.

factors as they are in the application of the Convention, has already been dealt with at length.[39]
As for those States which may appoint more than one Central Authority, the idea which prevailed was that the determining factor should be the existence of several territorial organizations for the protection of minors. Thus there was added to those cases of Federal States and States with more than one system of law that of States 'having autonomous territorial organizations', a term which is to be interpreted broadly.

Article 7 – Obligations of Central Authorities

88 This article summarizes the role played by Central Authorities in bringing into play the system established by the Convention. The article is structured in two paragraphs, the first of which, drafted in general terms, sets out an overall duty of co-operation, while the second lists, from sub-paragraphs *a* to *i*, some of the principal functions which the Central Authorities have to discharge. Both result from a compromise between, on the one hand, those delegations which wanted strong Central Authorities with wide-ranging powers of action and initiative, and on the other hand those which saw these Authorities as straightforward administrative mechanisms for promoting action by the parties. Now, since these diverse attitudes reflected most of the deep differences which existed amongst the systems represented at the Conference, the ultimate solution had to be flexible, and such as would allow each Central Authority to act according to the law within which it has to operate. Therefore, although the Convention clearly sets out the principal obligations laid upon the Central Authorities, it lets each Contracting State decide upon the appropriate means for discharging them. And it is in this sense that the sentence occurring at the beginning of the second paragraph must be understood, which states that the Central Authorities are to discharge their listed functions 'either directly, or through any intermediary'. It is for each Central Authority to choose one or the other options, while working within the context of its own internal law and within the spirit of the general duty of co-operation imposed upon it by the first paragraph.

89 As we have just said, the rule in the *first paragraph* sets out the general duty of Central Authorities to co-operate, so as to ensure the Convention's objects are achieved. Such co-operation has to develop on two levels: the Central Authorities must firstly co-operate with each other; however, in addition, they must promote co-operation among the authorities competent for the matters dealt with within their respective States. Whether this co-operation is promoted effectively will depend to a large extent on the freedom of action which each internal law confers upon the Central Authorities.

90 The functions listed in the *second paragraph* seek to trace, in broad outline, the different stages of intervention by Central Authorities in the typical case of child removal. Nonetheless, it is clear that this list is not exhaustive. For example, since the intervention of Central Authorities necessarily depends on their having been initially seized of the matter, either directly by the applicant or by the Central Authority of a Contracting State, then in the latter case the Central Authority initially seized will have to send the

[39] See *supra*, Nos 43 to 48.

l'affaire devra transmettre la demande à l'Autorité centrale de l'Etat où l'on suppose que l'enfant se trouve. Or, cette obligation n'est pas précisée à l'article 7, mais plus tard, dans le contexte de l'article 9. D'autre part, il est évident aussi que les Autorités centrales ne sont pas tenues de remplir, dans chaque cas d'espèce, toutes les obligations énumérées dans cet article; en effet, ce sont les circonstances du cas précis qui vont déterminer les démarches à faire par les Autorités centrales: par exemple, on ne peut pas soutenir qu'une Autorité centrale quelconque soit tenue de «localiser» l'enfant quand le demandeur sait avec exactitude où se trouve celui-ci.

91 En plus de la localisation de l'enfant, chaque fois que cela s'avère nécessaire (lettre *a*), l'Autorité centrale doit prendre ou faire prendre toute mesure provisoire qui semble utile pour prévenir de «nouveaux dangers pour l'enfant ou des préjudices pour les parties concernées» (lettre *b*). La rédaction de ce sous-alinéa met à nouveau en relief un fait souligné auparavant: la capacité d'agir des Autorités centrales peut varier d'un Etat à un autre. Quant au fond, les mesures provisoires qui ont été envisagées se centrent tout particulièrement sur l'idée d'éviter un nouveau déplacement de l'enfant.

92 La lettre *c* consacre le devoir des Autorités centrales d'essayer de trouver une solution extrajudiciaire à l'affaire. En effet, d'après l'expérience évoquée par certains délégués, le nombre de cas qu'il est possible de résoudre sans avoir besoin de recourir aux tribunaux est considérable. Mais, encore une fois, c'est l'Autorité centrale qui, dans ces étapes précédant une éventuelle procédure judiciaire ou administrative, dirige l'évolution du problème; donc c'est à elle de décider à quel moment les tentatives faites, soit pour assurer la «remise volontaire» de l'enfant, soit pour faciliter une «solution amiable», ont échouées.

93 La lettre *d* porte sur les échanges d'informations relatives à la situation sociale de l'enfant. L'obligation à cet effet est subordonnée au critère des Autorités centrales impliquées dans chaque cas d'espèce. En effet, l'introduction du membre de phrase «si cela s'avère utile» montre que l'on n'a pas voulu imposer une obligation rigide sur ce point: la possibilité qu'il n'existe pas d'informations à fournir, ainsi que la peur qu'elles puissent être employées dans le cadre d'une tactique dilatoire des parties, sont quelques-uns des arguments qui ont conseillé cette attitude. D'autre part, on a rejeté une proposition rendant possible que certaines informations soient transmises à condition qu'elles restent confidentielles.[40]

94 L'obligation faite aux Autorités centrales de fournir des informations sur le contenu du droit dans leur Etat pour l'application de la Convention apparaît à la lettre *e*. Ce devoir couvre notamment deux aspects: d'une part dans le cas où le déplacement s'est produit avant qu'il n'y ait eu une décision sur la garde de l'enfant, l'Autorité centrale de l'Etat de la résidence habituelle de l'enfant pourra produire une attestation sur le contenu du droit de cet Etat, en vue de l'application de la Convention; d'autre part, l'Autorité centrale devra renseigner les particuliers sur le fonctionnement de la Convention et des Autorités centrales, ainsi que sur les procédures possibles à suivre. Par contre, la possibilité d'aller plus loin, c'est-à-dire d'obliger les Autorités centrales à donner des conseils juridiques sur des cas concrets, n'est pas envisagée dans cette norme.

[40] Voir Doc. trav. No 9 (*Proposal of the United Kingdom delegation*) et P.-v. No 5.

application to the Central Authority of the State in which the child is thought to be. Now, this obligation is not spelled out in article 7, but later, in the context of article 9. On the other hand, it is also clear that the Central Authorities are not obliged to fulfil, in every specific case, all the duties listed in this article. In fact, the circumstances of each particular case will dictate the steps which are to be taken by the Central Authorities; for example, it cannot be maintained that every Central Authority must discover the whereabouts of a child when the applicant knows full well where it is.

91 In addition to finding the whereabouts of the child, where necessary (sub-paragraph *a*), the Central Authority must take or cause to be taken any provisional measures which could help prevent 'further harm to the child or prejudice to interested parties' (sub-paragraph *b*). The drafting of this sub-paragraph clearly brings out once again a fact which was emphasized above, namely, that the ability of Central Authorities to act will vary from one State to another. Basically, the provisional measures envisaged are designed in particular to avoid another removal of the child.

92 Sub-paragraph *c* sets out the duty of Central Authorities to try to find an extrajudicial solution. In actual fact, in the light of experience as spoken to by some delegates, a considerable number of cases can be settled without any need to have recourse to the courts. But, once again, it is the Central Authorities which, in those stages preceding the possible judicial or administrative proceedings, will direct the development of the problem; it is therefore for them to decide when the attempts to secure the 'voluntary return' of the child or to bring about an 'amicable resolution', have failed.

93 Sub-paragraph *d* relates to the exchange of information about the social background of the child. This duty is made subject to the criteria adopted by the Central Authorities involved in a particular case. Indeed, the insertion of the phrase 'where desirable' demonstrates that there is no wish to impose an inflexible obligation here: the possibility of there being no information to provide, as well as the fear that reference to this provision might be used by the parties as a delaying tactic, are some of the arguments which prompted this approach. On the other hand, a proposal which would have made the transmission of certain information conditional upon its remaining confidential, was rejected.[40]

94 The obligation laid upon Central Authorities to provide information on the content of the law in their own States for the application of the Convention appears in sub-paragraph *e*. This duty applies in particular to two situations. Firstly, where the removal occurs prior to any decision as to the custody of the child, the Central Authority of the State of the child's habitual residence is to produce, for the purposes of the Convention's application, a certificate on the relevant law of that State. Secondly, the Central Authority must inform the individuals about how the Convention works and about the Central Authorities, as well as about the procedures available. On the other hand, the possibility of going further, by obliging the Central Authorities to give legal advice in individual cases, is not envisaged by this rule.

[40] See Working Document No 9 (Proposal of the United Kingdom delegation) and *P.-v.* No 5.

95 Quand il est nécessaire, pour obtenir le retour de l'enfant, de faire intervenir les autorités judiciaires ou administratives de l'Etat où il se trouve, l'Autorité centrale doit introduire elle-même – si cela est possible selon son droit interne – ou favoriser l'ouverture d'une procédure; obligation qui s'étend aussi aux procédures qui s'avèrent nécessaires pour permettre l'organisation ou l'exercice effectif du droit de visite (lettre *f*).

96 Dans les cas où l'Autorité centrale ne peut pas saisir directement les autorités compétentes dans son propre Etat, elle doit accorder ou faciliter au demandeur l'obtention de l'assistance judiciaire, aux termes de l'article 25 (lettre *g*). Il convient de préciser très brièvement que l'expression «le cas échéant» dans ce sous-alinéa fait référence à la carence de ressources économiques du demandeur, sur la base des critères établis par la loi de l'Etat où cette assistance est sollicitée; elle ne fait donc pas allusion à des considérations abstraites sur la convenance ou non de l'octroyer.

97 Au terme du processus suivi par ce paragraphe, la lettre *h* inclut, parmi les obligations des Autorités centrales la mise en oeuvre des mesures administratives nécessaires et opportunes dans chaque cas d'espèce, pour assurer le retour sans danger de l'enfant.

98 En dernier lieu, la lettre *i* énonce une obligation des Autorités centrales qui ne concerne pas directement les particuliers mais la Convention elle-même: il s'agit du devoir de «se tenir mutuellement informées sur le fonctionnement de la Convention et, autant que possible, de lever les obstacles éventuellement rencontrés lors de son application». Cette obligation devra jouer à deux niveaux complémentaires: d'une part, sur le plan des relations bilatérales entre Etats parties à la Convention; d'autre part, au niveau multilatéral, en participant le cas échéant aux commissions réunies à cet effet par le Bureau Permanent de la Conférence de La Haye.

CHAPITRE III – RETOUR DE L'ENFANT

Article 8 – La saisine des Autorités centrales

99 D'après le *premier alinéa*, une demande en vue d'obtenir le retour d'un enfant peut être adressée à toute Autorité centrale qui, dès lors, sera tenue par toutes les obligations conventionnelles. Cela signifie que le demandeur est libre de saisir l'Autorité centrale qu'il estime la plus adéquate; néanmoins, pour des raisons d'efficacité, une mention expresse de l'Autorité centrale de la résidence habituelle de l'enfant est faite dans le texte – mention qui ne doit pourtant pas être interprétée comme signifiant que les demandes adressées aux autres Autorités centrales devraient être exceptionnelles.

100 Etant donné que l'utilisation de la formule modèle est simplement recommandée, il était indispensable d'inclure dans le texte de la Convention les éléments que doit contenir une demande introduite devant une Autorité centrale pour être recevable, ainsi que les documents facultatifs qui peuvent accompagner ou compléter une telle demande. Les éléments que doit contenir toute demande adressée à une Autorité centrale, dans ce contexte, sont énumérés au *deuxième alinéa* de l'article 8. Il s'agit notamment des données qui permettent l'identification de l'enfant et des parties concernées, ainsi que de celles qui peuvent aider à localiser l'enfant (lettres *a*, *b* et *d*). En ce qui concerne l'information sur la date de naissance de l'enfant, la Convention signale qu'elle sera apportée seulement «s'il est possible de se la procurer». Par cette précision, on a entendu favoriser l'action du demandeur qui ignore une telle circonstance; il

95 When it is necessary, in order to obtain the child's return, for the judicial or administrative authorities of the State in which it is located to intervene, the Central Authority must itself initiate proceedings (if that can be done under its internal law) or facilitate the institution of proceedings. This duty also extends to proceedings which prove to be necessary for organizing or securing the effective exercise of rights of access (sub-paragraph *f*).

96 Where the Central Authority is not able to apply directly to the competent authorities in its own State, it must provide or facilitate the provision of legal aid and advice for the applicant, in terms of article 25 (sub-paragraph *g*). It is appropriate to point out here very briefly that the phrase 'where the circumstances so require' in this sub-paragraph refers to the applicant's lack of economic resources, as determined by the criteria laid down by the law of the State in which such assistance is sought, and that it does not therefore refer to abstract considerations as to the convenience or otherwise of granting legal aid.

97 Following the method adopted by this paragraph, sub-paragraph *h* includes among the Central Authorities' obligations the bringing into play in each case of such administrative arrangements as may be necessary and appropriate to secure the safe return of the child.

98 Finally, sub-paragraph *i* sets forth an obligation on the part of Central Authorities which does not directly concern individuals but only the Convention itself. It is the duty 'to keep each other informed with respect to the operation of the Convention, and, as far as possible, to eliminate any obstacles to its application'. This obligation is to operate on two complementary levels, firstly at the level of bilateral relations between States which are Party to the Convention, and secondly on a multilateral level, through participating when required in commissions called for this purpose by the Permanent Bureau of the Hague Conference.

CHAPTER III – RETURN OF THE CHILD

Article 8 – Applications to Central Authorities

99 In terms of the *first paragraph*, an application for the return of a child can be addressed to any Central Authority which, from that point, will be bound by all the obligations laid down by the Convention. This demonstrates that the applicant is free to apply to the Central Authority which in his opinion is the most appropriate. However, for reasons of efficiency, the Central Authority of the child's habitual residence is expressly mentioned in the text, but this must not be understood as signifying that applications directed to other Central Authorities are to be regarded as exceptional.

100 Since use of the model form is merely recommended, it was necessary to include in the text of the Convention the elements which any application submitted to a Central Authority must contain in order to be admissible, as well as the optional documents which may accompany or supplement such an application. The elements which every application to a Central Authority must contain, in this context, are those listed in the *second paragraph* of article 8. In particular, they are facts which allow the child and interested parties to be identified, such as those which may be able to help in locating the child (sub-paragraphs *a*, *b*, and *d*). As regards information on the child's date of birth, the Convention makes it clear that this should be supplied only 'where available'. This provision is intended to favour action by an applicant who is ignorant of such a fact but who will, however, always have to supply precise information on the

devra pourtant toujours fournir des indices exacts sur l'âge de l'enfant, étant donné que le contenu de l'article 4 de la Convention peut déterminer le rejet de sa demande aux termes de l'article 27.

De plus, il faut que la demande contienne «les motifs sur lesquels se base le demandeur pour réclamer le retour de l'enfant» (lettre *c*). Ceci est une exigence logique, qui permettra d'ailleurs l'application de l'article 27 concernant la faculté qu'ont les Autorités centrales de rejeter les demandes manifestement non fondées. Les motifs invoqués doivent, en principe, se référer aux deux éléments, juridique et de fait, retenus à l'article 3. Or, puisque l'élément juridique peut notamment s'appuyer sur le contenu du droit de la résidence habituelle de l'enfant, sur une décision ou sur un accord, on aurait pu songer à exiger un soutien documentaire à ce stade initial. Pourtant, la Convention a choisi une voie différente et place cette preuve parmi les documents qui, d'une manière facultative, peuvent accompagner ou compléter la demande. La raison en est que l'obtention des documents en question sera parfois difficile; de plus, elle peut exiger un temps précieux pour une localisation rapide de l'enfant. D'ailleurs, chaque fois que l'Autorité centrale réussit à obtenir la remise volontaire de l'enfant ou une solution amiable de l'affaire, ils peuvent apparaître comme accessoires.

101 En ce sens, les deux premières lettres du *troisième alinéa* concernant la documentation facultative qui peut accompagner, ou compléter à un moment ultérieur, la demande, se réfèrent aux documents qui sont à la base de la réclamation en retour de l'enfant. A cet effet, il faut souligner d'abord que l'exigence que les copies de toute décision ou tout accord soient authentifiées ne s'oppose pas à la disposition de l'article 23, d'après laquelle «aucune légalisation ni formalité similaire ne sera requise dans le contexte de la Convention». Il s'agit simplement de vérifier des copies ou des documents privés à l'origine pour en garantir la concordance avec les originaux et en assurer, par ce biais, la libre circulation.

En second lieu, la preuve du contenu du droit de l'Etat de la résidence habituelle de l'enfant peut être établie soit par une attestation, soit par une déclaration avec affirmation, c'est-à-dire moyennant des documents incorporant des déclarations solennelles qui engagent la responsabilité de leurs auteurs. Quant à savoir qui peut produire lesdites déclarations, la Convention a choisi une formule large, qui doit faciliter la tâche du demandeur (lettre *f*). Ainsi, en plus des Autorités centrales et des autres autorités compétentes de l'Etat de la résidence habituelle de l'enfant, elles peuvent émaner de toute personne qualifiée – par exemple, d'un notaire, d'un avocat ou d'institutions scientifiques.

D'autre part, il convient de souligner que dans une phase ultérieure, c'est-à-dire quand les autorités judiciaires ou administratives de l'Etat de refuge sont appelées à intervenir, celles-ci peuvent demander, selon l'article 15, la production de certains des documents considérés comme facultatifs au moment de la saisine des Autorités centrales.

Finalement, la Convention admet la possibilité que la demande soit accompagnée ou complétée par «tout autre document utile» (lettre *g*). En principe, étant donné que la demande est introduite par le gardien dépossédé, c'est lui qui pourra apporter ces documents complémentaires. Ce qui n'empêche pas que, si la demande est transmise à une autre Autorité centrale, l'Autorité centrale initialement saisie puisse accompagner la demande notamment des informations relatives à la situation sociale de l'enfant – si elle en dispose et les considère utiles –, en vertu de la fonction que lui attribue l'article 7, alinéa 2*d*.

age of the child, since the provisions of article 4 may result in his application being rejected, in terms of article 27.

Moreover, the application must contain 'the grounds on which the applicant's claim for return of the child is based' (sub-paragraph *c*). This requirement is logical, in that it allows the application of article 27 concerning the right of Central Authorities to reject applications which are clearly not well-founded. The grounds must in principle refer to the two elements, legal and factual, contained in article 3. Now, since the legal element in particular may depend on the provisions of the law of the child's habitual residence, or upon a decision or agreement, it might have been expected that documentary support would be required at this initial stage. However, the Convention chose to follow a different route and placed this evidence amongst those documents which may, optionally, accompany or supplement the application. The reason for this is that obtaining the documents in question is sometimes difficult and, what is more, could take up precious time better spent in speedily discovering the whereabouts of the child. Moreover, whenever a Central Authority succeeds in bringing about the voluntary return of the child or an amicable resolution of the affair, such requirements may seem merely accessory.

101 Understood thus, the first two sub-paragraphs of the *third paragraph*, dealing with the optional provision of documents which may accompany or supplement applications, are seen to refer to documents which are fundamental to a claim for the return of the child. It must be emphasized firstly that the requirement that copies of any decision or agreement be authenticated in no way contradicts the provision in article 23 that 'no legalization or similar formality may be required in the context of this Convention'. It is simply a matter of verifying what were originally copies or private documents so as to guarantee that they correspond to the originals and thus to secure their free circulation.

Secondly, proof of the substantive law of the State of the child's habitual residence may be established by either certificates or affidavits, that is to say documents which include solemn statements for which those who make them assume responsibility. As regards those persons who may adduce such statements, the Convention chose to define them widely, a fact which must make the task of the applicant easier (sub-paragraph *f*). Thus, they may emanate from any qualified person – for example, an attorney, solicitor, or barrister or research institution – as well as from the Central Authorities and the other competent authorities of the State of the child's habitual residence.

On the other hand, it should be stressed that at a later stage, when the judicial or administrative authorities of the State of refuge have been called upon to intervene, they may, in terms of article 15, request the production of certain documents which were considered to be optional at the time of application to the Central Authorities.

Lastly, the Convention acknowledges that the application may be accompanied or supplemented by 'any other relevant document' (sub-paragraph *g*). In theory, since it is the dispossessed guardian of the child who brings the application, it is for him to provide these supplementary documents. This does not preclude the Central Authority to which the application was originally made, where the application is sent to another Central Authority, from accompanying the application by, *inter alia*, information concerning the social background of the child (if it has such information at its disposal and considers it to be useful), by virtue of the task laid upon it by article 7, paragraph 2*d*.

Article 9 – Transmission de la demande à l'Autorité centrale de l'Etat où se trouve l'enfant

102 Une conséquence directe de la liberté dont jouit le demandeur de s'adresser à l'Autorité centrale de son choix est l'obligation qui pèse sur celle-ci de transmettre la demande à l'Autorité centrale de l'Etat où elle a des raisons de penser que l'enfant se trouve; obligation qui va aussi se présenter quand l'Autorité centrale qui connaît d'une affaire par une autre Autorité centrale arrivera à la conclusion que l'enfant se trouve dans un pays différent. Il s'agit là d'une fonction qui vient compléter le cadre esquissé à l'article 7, puisqu'elle est en rapport direct avec l'obligation de coopérer entre Autorités centrales qu'établit le premier alinéa dudit article.

Or, si le sens de l'article 9 est clair, sa rédaction n'en est pas très heureuse. «L'Autorité centrale requérante» à laquelle cet article se réfère existe seulement lorsque la demande introduite conformément à l'article 8 a été transmise à une *autre* Autorité centrale aux termes de l'article 9 lui-même. En conséquence, l'obligation d'informer une «Autorité centrale requérante» n'existe que lorsque la demande a été transmise à une troisième Autorité centrale, l'enfant ne se trouvant pas dans l'Etat de la deuxième Autorité centrale saisie. Par contre, l'obligation de transmettre une demande en vertu de cet article incombe à *toute* Autorité centrale, indépendamment du fait qu'elle soit première saisie ou saisie par l'intermédiaire d'une autre Autorité centrale, en raison du fait que cette disposition doit être interprétée comme s'appliquant aux deux hypothèses qu'elle a l'intention de couvrir.

Article 10 – La remise volontaire de l'enfant

103 La fonction des Autorités centrales visée à l'article 7, alinéa 2*c* de «prendre toutes les mesures appropriées pour assurer la remise volontaire de l'enfant», trouve à cet article un traitement préférentiel qui met en relief l'intérêt accordé au recours à cette voie. Dans le texte de la Convention, on a supprimé le membre de phrase qui introduisait, dans l'avant-projet, cette disposition et qui situait dans le temps («avant l'ouverture de toute procédure judiciaire ou administrative») l'obligation qu'elle incorpore. La raison en était la difficulté éprouvée par certains systèmes juridiques pour accepter qu'une autorité publique, telle que l'Autorité centrale, puisse agir avant l'introduction d'une demande auprès des autorités compétentes; la teneur de la disposition conventionnelle n'empêche pas que les Autorités centrales des autres Etats agissent de la sorte. D'autre part, il ne sera jamais question d'une obligation rigide, dans un double sens: d'une part, les efforts pour la remise volontaire de l'enfant peuvent se poursuivre après la saisine des autorités judiciaires ou administratives s'ils ont commencé avant; d'autre part, dans la mesure où l'initiative en vue du retour de l'enfant ne se transfert pas à ces autorités, c'est l'Autorité centrale qui doit décider si les tentatives en vue de tel objectif ont échoué.

D'ailleurs, il est entendu que les démarches visées dans cet article ne doivent pas préjuger de l'action des Autorités centrales pour empêcher un nouveau déplacement de l'enfant, selon l'article 7, alinéa 2*b*.

Article 11 – L'utilisation des procédures d'urgence par les autorités judiciaires ou administratives

104 L'importance du facteur temps dans toute la matière apparaît de nouveau dans cet article. Si l'article 2 de la Convention impose aux Etats contractants l'obligation d'utiliser des procédures d'urgence le *premier alinéa* de cet article reproduit cette obligation à l'égard des autorités de

Article 9 – Transmission of the application to the Central Authority of the State where the child is located

102 A direct consequence of the applicant's right to apply to the Central Authority of his choice is the duty imposed on the latter to transmit the application to the Central Authority of the State in which it has reason to believe the child is located; this duty arises also when the Central Authority which is informed of a case by another Central Authority reaches the conclusion that the child is in fact located in a different country. This is a task which supplements the framework of duties outlined in article 7, since it relates directly to the duty of co-operation amongst Central Authorities established by the first paragraph of that article.

Now, although the meaning of article 9 may be clear, it has not been very artfully drafted. The 'requesting Central Authority' to which this article refers exists only where the application submitted in accordance with article 8 has been transmitted to *another* Central Authority in terms of article 9 itself. Consequently, the duty to inform a 'requesting Central Authority' exists only when the application has been transmitted to a third Central Authority, the child not being located in the State of the second Central Authority to which the application was sent. But on the other hand, the duty to transmit an application in terms of this article devolves upon *any* Central Authority, independently of the fact that it was seized of the matter either directly or through the intervention of another Central Authority, since this provision must be understood as applying to both of the cases it is meant to cover.

Article 10 – Voluntary return of the child

103 The duty of Central Authorities, stated in article 7(2)(*c*), to 'take all appropriate measures to secure the voluntary return of the child', is given preferential treatment in this article, which highlights the interest of the Convention in seeing parties have recourse to this way of proceeding. The phrase 'before the institution of any legal or administrative proceedings' which preceded this provision in the Preliminary Draft, and restricted the duty included within it to a particular point in time, was deleted from the text of the Convention. The reason for this deletion is the difficulty experienced by some legal systems in accepting that a public authority, such as a Central Authority, could act before an application had been brought before the competent authorities; however, the whole tenor of the provision shows that the Central Authorities of other States are not precluded from acting in that way. On the other hand, it is in no way an inflexible obligation, for two reasons: firstly, efforts to secure the voluntary return of the child which were begun prior to the referral of the matter to the judicial or administrative authorities may be pursued thereafter, and secondly, in so far as the initiative for the return of the child has not been transferred to those authorities, it is for the Central Authority to decide whether the attempts to achieve this objective have failed.

Moreover, the measures envisaged in this article are not intended to prejudice the efforts of Central Authorities to prevent further removals of the child, pursuant to article 7(2)(*b*).

Article 11 – The use of expeditious procedures by judicial or administrative authorities

104 The importance throughout the Convention of the time factor appears again in this article. Whereas article 2 of the Convention imposes upon Contracting States the duty to use expeditious procedures, the *first paragraph* of this article restates the obligation, this time with regard to the authori-

l'Etat où l'enfant a été emmené et qui doivent statuer sur la remise de celui-ci. L'obligation considérée a un double aspect: d'une part, l'utilisation des procédures les plus rapides connues par leur système juridique; d'autre part le traitement prioritaire, dans toute la mesure du possible, des demandes visées.

105 Dans son désir de pousser les autorités internes à accorder une priorité maximum aux problèmes soulevés par les déplacements internationaux d'enfants, le *deuxième alinéa* établit un délai non contraignant de six semaines, après lequel le demandeur ou l'Autorité centrale de l'Etat requis peuvent solliciter une déclaration sur les motifs du retard. De plus quand l'Autorité centrale de l'Etat requis aura reçu la réponse, elle aura à nouveau une obligation de renseignement, soit envers l'Autorité centrale de l'Etat requérant, soit envers le demandeur, si c'est lui qui l'a directement saisie. En somme, l'importance de cette disposition ne peut pas être mesurée par rapport à l'exigibilité des obligations qu'elle consacre, mais par le fait même qu'elle attire l'attention des autorités compétentes sur le caractère décisif du facteur temps dans les situations concernées et qu'elle fixe le délai maximum que devrait prendre l'adoption d'une décision à cet égard.

Articles 12 et 18 – Obligation de retourner l'enfant

106 Ces deux articles peuvent être examinés ensemble car, malgré leur nature différente, ils présentent un certain caractère complémentaire.
L'article 12 constitue une pièce essentielle de la Convention, étant donné que c'est lui qui précise les situations dans lesquelles les autorités judiciaires ou administratives de l'Etat où se trouve l'enfant sont tenues d'ordonner son retour. C'est pourquoi il convient de souligner, une fois encore, que la remise non volontaire d'un enfant s'appuie, d'après la Convention, sur une décision adoptée par les autorités compétentes à cet égard dans l'Etat requis; en conséquence, l'obligation de retour dont traite cet article s'impose auxdites autorités. A cet effet, l'article distingue deux hypothèses: la première concerne le devoir des autorités lorsqu'elles ont été saisies dans le délai d'un an après le déplacement ou le non-retour illicites d'un enfant; la seconde a trait aux conditions qui entourent ce devoir quand l'introduction de la demande est postérieure au délai susmentionné.

107 Dans le premier alinéa, l'article apporte une solution unique au problème soulevé par la détermination de la période pendant laquelle les autorités en question doivent ordonner le retour immédiat de l'enfant. Le problème est important car, dans la mesure où le retour de l'enfant est envisagé dans son intérêt, il est certain que lorsque l'enfant est intégré dans un nouveau milieu, son retour ne devrait se produire qu'après un examen du fond du droit de garde – ce qui nous situe en dehors de l'objectif conventionnel. Or, les difficultés que rencontre toute tentative de traduire le critère de l'intégration de l'enfant sous forme d'une norme objective ont conduit à la fixation d'un délai, qui est peut-être arbitraire, mais qui constitue la «moins mauvaise» réponse aux soucis exprimés sur ce point.

108 Dans l'approche adoptée, il a fallu affronter une pluralité de questions: *primo*, le moment à partir duquel commence le délai; *secundo*, l'extension du délai; *tertio*, le moment d'expiration du délai. En ce qui concerne le premier point, c'est-à-dire la détermination du moment où commence à courir le délai, l'article se réfère au déplacement ou non-retour illicites; la concrétisation de la date décisive en cas de non-retour devant être entendue comme celle à laquelle l'enfant aurait dû être remis au gardien, ou à laquelle le titulaire de la garde a refusé son consentement à

ties of the State to which the child has been taken and which are to decide upon its return. There is a double aspect to this duty: firstly, the use of the most speedy procedures known to their legal system; secondly, that applications are, so far as possible, to be granted priority treatment.

105 The *second paragraph*, so as to prompt internal authorities to accord maximum priority to dealing with the problems arising out of the international removal of children, lays down a non-obligatory time-limit of six weeks, after which the applicant or Central Authority of the requested State may request a statement of reasons for the delay. Moreover, after the Central Authority of the requested State receives the reply, it is once more under a duty to inform, a duty owed either to the Central Authority of the requesting State or to the applicant who has applied to it directly. In short, the provision's importance cannot be measured in terms of the requirements of the obligations imposed by it, but by the very fact that it draws the attention of the competent authorities to the decisive nature of the time factor in such situations and that it determines the maximum period of time within which a decision on this matter should be taken.

Articles 12 and 18 – Duty to return the child

106 These two articles can be examined together since they complement each other to a certain extent, despite their different character.
Article 12 forms an essential part of the Convention, specifying as it does those situations in which the judicial or administrative authorities of the State where the child is located are obliged to order its return. That is why it is appropriate to emphasize once again the fact that the compulsory return of the child depends, in terms of the Convention, on a decision having been taken by the competent authorities of the requested State. Consequently, the obligation to return a child with which this article deals is laid upon these authorities. To this end, the article highlights two cases; firstly, the duty of authorities where proceedings have begun within one year of the wrongful removal or retention of a child and, secondly, the conditions which attach to this duty where an application is submitted after the aforementioned time-limit.

107 In the first paragraph, the article brings a unique solution to bear upon the problem of determining the period during which the authorities concerned must order the return of the child forthwith. The problem is an important one since, in so far as the return of the child is regarded as being in its interests, it is clear that after a child has become settled in its new environment, its return should take place only after an examination of the merits of the custody rights exercised over it – something which is outside the scope of the Convention. Now, the difficulties encountered in any attempt to state this test of 'integration of the child' as an objective rule resulted in a time-limit being fixed which, although perhaps arbitrary, nevertheless proved to be the 'least bad' answer to the concerns which were voiced in this regard.

108 Several questions had to be faced as a result of this approach: firstly, the date from which the time-limit was to begin to run; secondly, extension of the time-limit; thirdly, the date of expiry of the time-limit. As regards the first point, *i.e.* how to determine the date on which the time-limit should begin to run, the article refers to the wrongful removal or retention. The fixing of the decisive date in cases of wrongful retention should be understood as that on which the child ought to have been returned to its custodians or on which the holder of the right of custody refused to agree to

un prolongement du séjour de l'enfant dans un autre lieu que celui de sa résidence habituelle. En second lieu, la consécration d'un délai unique d'un an, abstraction faite des difficultés rencontrées dans la localisation de l'enfant, constitue une amélioration substantielle du système prévu dans l'article 11 de l'avant-projet élaboré par la Commission spéciale. En effet, par ce biais on a clarifié l'application de la Convention, en éliminant les difficultés inhérentes à la preuve des éventuels problèmes suscités par la localisation de l'enfant. Troisièmement, en ce qui concerne le *terminus ad quem*, l'article retient le moment de l'introduction de la demande, au lieu de la date de la décision, le retard possible dans l'action des autorités compétentes ne devant pas nuire aux intérêts des parties protégées par la Convention.

En résumé, chaque fois que les circonstances que nous venons d'examiner se trouvent réunies dans un cas d'espèce, les autorités judiciaires ou administratives doivent ordonner le retour immédiat de l'enfant, sauf si elles constatent l'existence d'une des exceptions prévues par la Convention elle-même.

109 Le deuxième alinéa répond à la nécessité, ressentie tout au long des travaux préparatoires,[41] d'assouplir les conséquences de l'adoption d'un délai rigide passé lequel la Convention ne pourrait pas être invoquée. La solution finalement retenue[42] étend nettement le domaine d'application de la Convention en consacrant, pour une période indéfinie, une véritable obligation de retourner l'enfant. De toute façon, on ne peut pas ignorer qu'une telle obligation disparaît si on arrive à établir que «l'enfant s'est intégré dans son nouveau milieu». La disposition ne précise point qui doit prouver cette circonstance; pourtant, il semble logique de penser qu'une telle tâche incombe à l'enleveur ou à la personne qui s'oppose au retour de l'enfant, tout en sauvegardant l'éventuel pouvoir d'appréciation des autorités internes à cet égard. En tout cas, la preuve ou la constatation du nouvel enracinement de l'enfant ouvre la porte à la possibilité d'une procédure plus longue que celle visée au premier alinéa. En définitive, tant pour ces raisons que du fait que le retour se produira toujours, par la nature même des choses, beaucoup plus tard qu'un an après l'enlèvement, la Convention ne parle pas dans ce contexte de retour «immédiat», mais simplement de retour.

110 Un problème commun aux deux situations examinées est la détermination du *lieu* où il faut retourner l'enfant. A cet égard, la Convention n'a pas retenu une proposition tendant à préciser que le retour se ferait toujours vers l'Etat de la résidence habituelle de l'enfant avant son déplacement. Certes, une des raisons sous-jacentes à l'idée de retourner l'enfant est le souci d'éviter que la compétence «naturelle» des tribunaux de l'Etat de sa résidence ne soit bafouée par une voie de fait; néanmoins, l'inclusion d'une telle précision dans le texte de la Convention en aurait rendu l'application inutilement rigide. En effet, nous ne devons pas ignorer que ce qu'on entend protéger en luttant contre les enlèvements internationaux d'enfants, c'est le droit de ceux-ci à ne pas être écartés d'un certain milieu qui, parfois, sera fondamentalement familial. Or, si le demandeur n'habite plus l'Etat de la résidence habituelle antérieure au déplacement, le retour de l'enfant dans cet Etat poserait des problèmes pratiques difficiles à résoudre. Le silence de la Convention sur ce point doit donc être interprété comme permettant aux autorités de l'Etat de refuge de renvoyer

[41] Voir Rapport de la Commission spéciale No 92.
[42] Voir Doc. trav. No 25 (Proposition de la délégation de la République fédérale d'Allemagne), et P.-v. Nos 7 et 10.

an extension of the child's stay in a place other than that of its habitual residence. Secondly, the establishment of a single time-limit of one year (putting on one side the difficulties encountered in establishing the child's whereabouts) is a substantial improvement on the system envisaged in article 11 of the Preliminary Draft drawn up by the Special Commission. In fact, the application of the Convention was thus clarified, since the inherent difficulty in having to prove the existence of those problems which can surround the locating of the child was eliminated. Thirdly, as regards the *terminus ad quem*, the article has retained the date on which proceedings were commenced, instead of the date of decree, so that potential delays in acting on the part of the competent authorities will not harm the interests of parties protected by the Convention.

To sum up, whenever the circumstances just examined are found to be present in a specific case, the judicial or administrative authorities must order the return of the child forthwith, unless they aver the existence of one of the exceptions provided for in the Convention itself.

109 The second paragraph answered to the need, felt strongly throughout the preliminary proceedings,[41] to lessen the consequences which would flow from the adoption of an inflexible time-limit beyond which the provisions of the Convention could not be invoked. The solution finally adopted[42] plainly extends the Convention's scope by maintaining indefinitely a real obligation to return the child. In any event, it cannot be denied that such an obligation disappears whenever it can be shown that 'the child is now settled in its new environment'. The provision does not state how this fact is to be proved, but it would seem logical to regard such a task as falling upon the abductor or upon the person who opposes the return of the child, whilst at the same time preserving the contingent discretionary power of internal authorities in this regard. In any case, the proof or verification of a child's establishment in a new environment opens up the possibility of longer proceedings than those envisaged in the first paragraph. Finally, and as much for these reasons as for the fact that the return will, in the very nature of things, always occur much later than one year after the abduction, the Convention does not speak in this context of return 'forthwith' but merely of return.

110 One problem common to both of these situations was determining the *place* to which the child had to be returned. The Convention did not accept a proposal to the effect that the return of the child should always be to the State of its habitual residence before its removal. Admittedly, one of the underlying reasons for requiring the return of the child was the desire to prevent the 'natural' jurisdiction of the courts of the State of the child's residence being evaded with impunity, by force. However, including such a provision in the Convention would have made its application so inflexible as to be useless. In fact, we must not forget that it is the right of children not to be removed from a particular environment which sometimes is a basically family one, which the fight against international child abductions seeks to protect. Now, when the applicant no longer lives in what was the State of the child's habitual residence prior to its removal, the return of the child to that State might cause practical problems which would be difficult to resolve. The Convention's silence on this matter must therefore be understood as allowing the authorities of the State of refuge

[41] See Report of the Special Commission, No 92.
[42] See Working Document No 25 (Proposal of the delegation of the Federal Republic of Germany) and *P.-v.* Nos 7 and 10.

l'enfant directement au demandeur, sans égard au lieu de la résidence actuelle de celui-ci.

111 Le troisième alinéa de l'article 12 introduit une idée tout à fait logique, inspirée par des soucis d'économie procédurale, en vertu de laquelle les autorités qui connaissent d'une affaire peuvent suspendre la procédure ou rejeter la demande, lorsqu'elles ont des raisons de croire que l'enfant a été emmené dans un autre Etat. Les moyens par lesquels elles peuvent arriver à une telle conviction ne sont pas envisagés dans l'article; ils dépendront par conséquent du droit interne de l'Etat concerné.

112 Finalement, *l'article 18* signale que rien dans ce chapitre ne limite le pouvoir de l'autorité judiciaire ou administrative saisie d'ordonner le retour de l'enfant à tout moment. Rédigée sur la base de l'article 15 de l'avant-projet, cette disposition, qui n'impose aucune obligation, souligne la nature non exhaustive, complémentaire, de la Convention. En effet, elle autorise les autorités compétentes à ordonner le retour de l'enfant en invoquant d'autres dispositions plus favorables à ce but. Ceci peut surtout se produire dans les situations envisagées au deuxième alinéa de l'article 12, c'est-à-dire quand, du fait que l'autorité a été saisie après que se soit écoulé plus d'un an depuis le déplacement, le retour peut être refusé si l'enfant s'est intégré dans son nouveau milieu social et familial.

Articles 13 et 20 – Exceptions possibles au retour de l'enfant

113 Dans la première partie de ce Rapport nous avons commenté longuement la justification, l'origine et la portée des exceptions consacrées dans les articles examinés.[43] Nous nous limiterons ici à faire quelques considérations sur sa teneur littérale. En termes généraux, il convient d'insister sur le fait que les exceptions visées dans les deux articles en question ne sont pas d'application automatique, en ce sens qu'elles ne déterminent pas inévitablement le non-retour de l'enfant; par contre, la nature même de ces exceptions est de donner aux juges la possibilité – non pas de leur imposer l'obligation – de refuser le retour dans certaines circonstances.

114 En ce qui concerne *l'article 13*, le paragraphe introductif du premier alinéa met en relief que le fardeau de la preuve des circonstances énoncées aux sous-alinéas *a* et *b* est à la charge de celui qui s'oppose au retour de l'enfant, c'est-à-dire à une personne, institution ou organisme qui peut parfois ne pas coïncider avec l'enleveur. La solution retenue se limite certes à préciser une maxime générale de droit, selon laquelle celui qui invoque un fait (ou un droit) doit le prouver; mais en adoptant cette optique, la Convention a entendu équilibrer la position de la personne dépossédée par rapport à l'enleveur qui, en principe, a pu choisir le for de sa convenance.

115 Les exceptions retenues à la lettre *a* sont établies en raison du fait que la conduite du prétendu gardien permet de douter de l'existence d'un déplacement ou d'un non-retour illicites, au sens de la Convention. D'une part, il s'agit des situations où celui qui avait le soin de la personne de l'enfant n'exerçait pas effectivement le droit de garde à l'époque du déplacement ou du non-retour. La Convention

[43] Voir *supra* Nos 28 à 35.

to return the child directly to the applicant, regardless of the latter's present place of residence.

111 The third paragraph of article 12 introduces a perfectly logical provision, inspired by considerations of procedural economy, by virtue of which the authorities which are acquainted with a case can stay the proceedings or dismiss the application, where they have reason to believe that the child has been taken to another State. The reasons by which they may come to such a conclusion are not stated in the article, and will therefore depend on the internal law of the State in question.

112 Finally, *article 18* indicates that nothing in this chapter limits the power of a judicial or administrative authority to order the return of the child at any time. This provision, which was drafted on the basis of article 15 of the Preliminary Draft, and which imposes no duty, underlines the non-exhaustive and complementary nature of the Convention. In fact, it authorizes the competent authorities to order the return of the child by invoking other provisions more favourable to the attainment of this end. This may happen particularly in the situations envisaged in the second paragraph of article 12, *i.e.* where, as a result of an application being made to the authority after more than one year has elapsed since the removal, the return of the child may be refused if it has become settled in its new social and family environment.

Articles 13 and 20 – Possible exceptions to the return of the child

113 In the first part of this Report we commented at length upon the reasons for, the origins and scope of, the exceptions contained in the articles concerned.[43] We shall restrict ourselves at this point to making some observations on their literal meaning. In general, it is appropriate to emphasize that the exceptions in these two articles do not apply automatically, in that they do not invariably result in the child's retention; nevertheless, the very nature of these exceptions gives judges a discretion – and does not impose upon them a duty – to refuse to return a child in certain circumstances.

114 With regard to *article 13*, the introductory part of the first paragraph highlights the fact that the burden of proving the facts stated in sub-paragraphs *a* and *b* is imposed on the person who opposes the return of the child, be he a physical person, an institution or an organization, that person not necessarily being the abductor. The solution adopted is indeed limited to stating the general legal maxim that he who avers a fact (or a right) must prove it, but in making this choice, the Convention intended to put the dispossessed person in as good a position as the abductor who in theory has chosen what is for him the most convenient forum.

115 The exceptions contained in *a* arise out of the fact that the conduct of the person claiming to be the guardian of the child raises doubts as to whether a wrongful removal or retention, in terms of the Convention, has taken place. On the one hand, there are situations in which the person who had the care of the child did not actually exercise custody rights at the time of the removal or retention. The Conven-

[43] See *supra*, Nos 28 to 35.

n'inclut pas une définition de ce qu'il faut entendre par «exercice effectif» de la garde, mais cette disposition se réfère de façon expresse au soin de la personne de l'enfant; donc, si l'on en compare le texte avec celui de la définition du droit de garde contenue à l'article 5, on peut conclure qu'il y a garde effective quand le gardien s'occupe des soins de la personne de l'enfant, même si, pour des raisons plausibles (maladie, séjour d'études, etc.), dans chaque cas concret, enfant et gardien n'habitent pas ensemble. Il s'ensuit que la détermination du caractère effectif ou non d'une garde doit être établi par le juge d'après les circonstances qui entourent chaque cas d'espèce.
D'ailleurs en mettant en relation ce paragraphe avec la définition du déplacement ou du non-retour illicites de l'article 3, il faut conclure que la preuve que la garde n'était pas effective ne constitue pas une exception à l'obligation de retourner l'enfant lorsque le gardien dépossédé n'exerçait pas de façon effective son droit à cause précisément de l'action de l'enleveur. En effet, la délimitation des situations protégées, contenue à l'article 3, préside toute la Convention et on ne peut interpréter aucun de ses articles en contradiction avec cette délimitation.
D'autre part, la conduite du gardien peut aussi altérer la qualification de l'action du ravisseur, au cas où il aurait consenti ou acquiescé postérieurement au déplacement qu'il combat maintenant. Cette précision a donné la possibilité de supprimer toute référence à l'exercice de «bonne foi» du droit de garde, en évitant simultanément que la Convention puisse être utilisée comme instrument d'un «marchandage» possible entre les parties.

116 Les exceptions consacrées à la lettre *b* concernent des situations dans lesquelles l'enlèvement international d'un enfant s'est vraiment produit, mais où le retour de l'enfant serait contraire à son intérêt, tel qu'il est apprécié dans ce sous-alinéa. Chacun des termes employés dans cette disposition reflète un délicat compromis atteint au cours des travaux de la Commission spéciale et qui s'est maintenu inchangé; en conséquence, on ne peut pas déduire, *a contrario*, des interprétations extensives du rejet, au cours de la Quatorzième session, des propositions tendant à inclure une allusion expresse à l'impossibilité d'invoquer cette exception lorsque le retour de l'enfant pourrait nuire à ses perspectives économiques ou éducatives.[44]

117 Il n'y a rien à ajouter aux commentaires déjà faits sur le deuxième alinéa de cet article (notamment, *supra* No 31).

Quant au troisième alinéa, il contient une disposition de nature très différente; il s'agit, en effet, d'une disposition procédurale qui vise, d'une part, à équilibrer la charge de la preuve imposée à la personne qui s'oppose au retour de l'enfant et d'autre part, à renforcer l'utilité des informations fournies par les autorités de l'Etat de la résidence habituelle de l'enfant. De telles informations, qui peuvent émaner soit de l'Autorité centrale, soit de toute autre autorité compétente, peuvent en particulier être précieuses pour permettre aux autorités requises de constater l'existence des circonstances à la base des exceptions visées aux deux premiers alinéas de cet article.

118 La possibilité reconnue à *l'article 20* de ne pas retourner un enfant quand ce retour «ne serait pas permis par les principes fondamentaux de l'Etat requis sur la sauvegarde des droits de l'homme et des libertés fondamentales», a été placée significativement dans le dernier

[44] Voir Doc. trav. No 12 (*Proposal of the United States delegation*) et No 42 (Proposition de la délégation hellénique), ainsi que le P.-v. No 8.

tion includes no definition of 'actual exercise' of custody, but this provision expressly refers to the care of the child. Thus, if the text of this provision is compared with that of article 5 which contains a definition of custody rights, it can be seen that custody is exercised effectively when the custodian is concerned with the care of the child's person, even if, for perfectly valid reasons (illness, education, etc.) in a particular case, the child and its guardian do not live together. It follows from this that the question of whether custody is actually exercised or not must be determined by the individual judge, according to the circumstances of each particular case.
Moreover, by relating this paragraph to the definition of wrongful removal or retention in article 3, one must conclude that proof that custody was not actually exercised does not form an exception to the duty to return the child if the dispossessed guardian was unable actually to exercise his rights precisely because of the action of the abductor. In fact, the categorization of protected situations, contained in article 3, governs the whole Convention, and cannot be contradicted by a contrary interpretation of any of the other articles.
On the other hand, the guardian's conduct can also alter the characterization of the abductor's action, in cases where he has agreed to, or thereafter acquiesced in, the removal which he now seeks to challenge. This fact allowed the deletion of any reference to the exercise of custody rights 'in good faith', and at the same time prevented the Convention from being used as a vehicle for possible 'bargaining' between the parties.

116 The exceptions contained in *b* deal with situations where international child abduction has indeed occurred, but where the return of the child would be contrary to its interests, as that phrase is understood in this sub-paragraph. Each of the terms used in this provision is the result of a fragile compromise reached during the deliberations of the Special Commission and has been kept unaltered. Thus it cannot be inferred, *a contrario*, from the rejection during the Fourteenth Session of proposals favouring the inclusion of an express provision stating that this exception could not be invoked if the return of the child might harm its economic or educational prospects,[44] that the exceptions are to receive a wide interpretation.

117 Nothing requires to be added to the preceding commentary on the second paragraph of this article (notably in No 31, *supra*.
The third paragraph contains a very different provision which is in fact procedural in nature and seeks on the one hand to compensate for the burden of proof placed on the person who opposes the return of the child, and on the other hand to increase the usefulness of information supplied by the authorities of the State of the child's habitual residence. Such information, emanating from either the Central Authority or any other competent authority, may be particularly valuable in allowing the requested authorities to determine the existence of those circumstances which underlie the exceptions contained in the first two paragraphs of this article.

118 It is significant that the possibility, acknowledged in *article 20*, that the child may not be returned when its return 'would not be permitted by the fundamental principles of the requested State relating to the protection of human rights and fundamental freedoms' has been placed in the

[44] See Working Documents Nos 12 (Proposal of the United States delegation) and 42 (*Proposition de la délégation hellénique*), and also *P.-v.* No 8.

article du chapitre; on a voulu souligner de la sorte le caractère nettement exceptionnel que doit toujours revêtir son application. Quant à savoir quel est le contenu de cette disposition, nous nous limiterons à faire deux remarques: en premier lieu, même si sa teneur littérale rappelle fortement la terminologie des textes internationaux en matière de protection des droits de l'homme, cette norme ne vise pas les développements atteints sur le plan international; par contre, elle ne concerne que les principes admis dans le droit de l'Etat requis, soit par voie de droit international général ou conventionnel, soit par voie législative interne. En conséquence, pour pouvoir refuser un retour sur la base de cet article, il sera nécessaire que les principes fondamentaux en la matière acceptés par l'Etat requis ne le permettent pas; il ne suffit pas que le retour soit incompatible, ou même manifestement incompatible avec ces principes. En second lieu, l'invocation de tels principes ne devra en aucun cas être plus fréquente ni plus facilement admise qu'elle ne le serait pour régler des situations purement internes. Le contraire serait discriminatoire en soi, c'est-à-dire opposé à l'un des principes fondamentaux les plus généralement reconnus dans les droits internes. Or, l'étude de la jurisprudence des différents pays montre que l'application par le juge ordinaire de la législation concernant les droits de l'homme et les libertés fondamentales se fait avec une prudence qu'il faut s'attendre à voir maintenue à l'égard des situations internationales que vise la Convention.

Article 14 – Assouplissement de la preuve du droit étranger

119 Du moment que la Convention fait dépendre le caractère illicite d'un déplacement d'enfants du fait qu'il se soit produit en violation de l'exercice effectif d'un droit de garde attribué par le droit de la résidence habituelle de l'enfant, il est évident que les autorités de l'Etat requis devront prendre ce droit en considération pour décider du retour de l'enfant. En ce sens, la disposition incluse dans l'article 13 de l'avant-projet,[45] d'après laquelle ces autorités «tiendront compte» du droit de la résidence habituelle de l'enfant pouvait être considérée comme superflue. Cependant, une telle disposition, d'une part, soulignait bien qu'il ne s'agissait pas d'appliquer un droit, mais de l'utiliser comme instrument dans l'appréciation de la conduite des parties; d'autre part, dans la mesure où elle était applicable aux décisions qui pouvaient être à la base du droit de garde violé, elle faisait apparaître la Convention comme une sorte de *lex specialis*, d'après laquelle les décisions visées auraient eu dans l'Etat requis un effet indirect qui ne pouvait pas être conditionné par l'obtention d'un exequatur ou de toute autre modalité de reconnaissance des décisions étrangères.

Puisque le premier aspect découlait nécessairement d'autres dispositions conventionnelles, la teneur actuelle de l'article 14 s'occupe seulement du second. L'article se présente donc comme une disposition facultative concernant la preuve du droit de la résidence habituelle de l'enfant, en vertu de laquelle l'autorité saisie «peut tenir compte directement du droit et des décisions judiciaires ou administratives reconnues formellement ou non dans l'Etat de la résidence habituelle de l'enfant, sans avoir recours aux procédures

[45] Voir Rapport de la Commission spéciale, Nos 102-103.

last article of the chapter: it was thus intended to emphasize the always clearly exceptional nature of this provision's application. As for the substance of this provision, two comments only are required. Firstly, even if its literal meaning is strongly reminiscent of the terminology used in international texts concerning the protection of human rights, this particular rule is not directed at developments which have occurred on the international level, but is concerned only with the principles accepted by the law of the requested State, either through general international law and treaty law, or through internal legislation. Consequently, so as to be able to refuse to return a child on the basis of this article, it will be necessary to show that the fundamental principles of the requested State concerning the subject-matter of the Convention do not permit it; it will not be sufficient to show merely that its return would be incompatible, even manifestly incompatible, with these principles. Secondly, such principles must not be invoked any more frequently, nor must their invocation be more readily admissible than they would be in their application to purely internal matters. Otherwise, the provision would be discriminatory in itself, and opposed to one of the most widely recognized fundamental principles in internal laws. A study of the case law of different countries shows that the application by ordinary judges of the laws on human rights and fundamental freedoms is undertaken with a care which one must expect to see maintained in the international situations which the Convention has in view.

Article 14 – Relaxation of the requirements of proof of foreign law

119 Since the wrongful nature of a child's removal is made to depend, in terms of the Convention, on its having occurred as the result of a breach of the actual exercise of custody rights conferred by the law of the child's habitual residence, it is clear that the authorities of the requested State will have to take this law into consideration when deciding whether the child should be returned. In this sense, the provision in article 13 of the preliminary draft Convention,[45] that the authorities 'shall have regard to' the law of the child's habitual residence, could be regarded as superfluous. However, such a provision would on the one hand underline the fact that there is no question of applying that law, but merely of using it as a means of evaluating the conduct of the parties, while on the other hand, in so far as it applied to decisions which could underlie the custody rights that had been breached, it would make the Convention appear to be a sort of *lex specialis*, according to which those decisions would receive effect indirectly in the requested State, an effect which would not be made conditional on the obtaining of an *exequatur* or any other method of recognition of foreign judgments.

Since the first aspect of article 14 necessarily derives from other provisions of the Convention, the actual purport of article 14 is concerned only with the second. The article therefore appears as an optional provision for proving the law of the child's residence and according to which the authority concerned 'may take notice directly of the law of, and of judicial or administrative decisions, formally recognized or not in the State of habitual residence of the child, without recourse to the specific procedures for the

[45] See Report of the Special Commission, Nos 102-103.

spécifiques sur la preuve de ce droit ou pour la reconnaissance des décisions étrangères qui seraient autrement applicables». Il n'est pas nécessaire d'insister sur l'importance pratique que cette norme peut avoir pour aboutir aux décisions rapides qui sont à la base du mécanisme conventionnel.

proof of that law or for the recognition of foreign decisions which would otherwise be applicable'. There is no need to stress the practical importance this rule may have in leading to the speedy decisions which are fundamental to the working of the Convention.

Article 15 – Possibilité de demander une décision ou une attestation des autorités de la résidence habituelle de l'enfant

120 Cet article répond aux difficultés que les autorités compétentes de l'Etat requis peuvent éprouver à statuer sur la demande en retour de l'enfant sans être certaines de l'application au cas d'espèce du droit de la résidence habituelle de celui-ci. Si tel est le cas, les autorités en question peuvent demander «la production par le demandeur d'une décision ou d'une attestation émanant des autorités de l'Etat de la résidence habituelle de l'enfant». A ce propos, nous ferons seulement deux remarques. La première concerne la nature non contraignante de la pétition, en ce sens que le retour de l'enfant ne peut pas être conditionné par son accomplissement; une telle conclusion s'impose en effet au vu tant de la teneur littérale de l'article (qui parle de «demander» et non pas d'«exiger») que de la possibilité, reconnue par la même disposition, du fait que l'obtention des documents sollicités ne soit pas possible dans l'Etat de la résidence de l'enfant. Or, sur ce dernier point, l'obligation que l'article impose aux Autorités centrales d'assister le demandeur pour obtenir la décision ou attestation doit faciliter sa tâche, étant donné que l'Autorité centrale peut produire une attestation concernant son droit en matière de garde, selon l'article 8*f*. En second lieu, le contenu de la décision ou attestation doit porter sur le caractère illicite, au sens de la Convention, du déplacement ou du non-retour; cela signifie, à notre avis, que l'une ou l'autre devra se prononcer sur les deux éléments retenus à l'article 3, et donc constater que le déplacement a interrompu une garde effective et légitime *prima facie*, d'après le droit de la résidence habituelle de l'enfant.

Article 15 – The possibility of requesting a decision or other determination from the authorities of the child's habitual residence

120 This article answers to the difficulties which the competent authorities of the requested State might experience in reaching a decision on an application for the return of a child through being uncertain of how the law of the child's habitual residence will apply in a particular case. Where this is so, the authorities concerned can request 'that the applicant obtain from the authorities of the State of the habitual residence of the child a decision or other determination'. Only two comments will be made here. The first concerns the voluntary nature of the request, in the sense that the return of the child cannot be made conditional upon such decision or other determination being provided. This conclusion arises in fact as much from the actual terms of the article (which speaks of 'requesting' and not 'requiring') as from the fact acknowledged in the same provision, that it may be impossible to obtain the requested documents in the State of the child's residence. Now, with regard to this last point, the duty which the article places upon Central Authorities to help the applicant obtain the decision or determination must make his task easier, since the Central Authority can provide a certificate concerning its relevant law in terms of article 8(3)(*f*). Secondly, the contents of the decision or certificate must have a bearing upon the wrongful nature, in the Convention sense, of the removal or retention. This means, in our opinion, that one or the other will have to contain a decision on the two elements in article 3, and thus establish that the removal was in breach of custody rights which, *prima facie*, were being exercised legitimately and in actual fact, in terms of the law of the child's habitual residence.

Article 16 – Prohibition de statuer sur le fond du droit de garde

121 En vue de faciliter la réalisation de l'objectif conventionnel relatif au retour de l'enfant, cet article essaie d'éviter qu'une décision sur le fond du droit de garde ne soit prise dans l'Etat de refuge. Dans ce but, il interdit aux autorités compétentes de cet Etat de statuer sur ce point, si elles sont informées que l'enfant concerné a été déplacé ou retenu illicitement, selon la Convention. Cette prohibition disparaîtra: lorsqu'il sera établi qu'il n'y a pas lieu de renvoyer l'enfant, d'après la Convention; ou lorsqu'une période raisonnable ne se sera pas écoulée sans qu'une demande en application de la Convention ait été introduite. Les deux circonstances qui peuvent mettre fin au devoir consacré dans cet article sont très différentes, tant par leur justification que par leurs conséquences. En effet, il est absolument logique de prévoir que l'obligation cesse dès qu'on constate que les conditions pour un retour de l'enfant ne sont pas réunies, soit parce que les parties sont arrivées à une solution amiable, soit parce qu'il y a lieu d'apprécier une des exceptions prévues aux articles 13 et 20; de surcroît, dans de tels cas, la décision sur le fond du droit de garde réglera l'affaire de façon définitive.

Par contre, étant donné que «l'information» sur laquelle on peut justifier une prohibition de statuer doit procéder, soit de l'introduction d'une demande en retour de l'enfant,

Article 16 – Prohibition against deciding upon the merits of custody rights

121 This article, so as to promote the realization of the Convention's objects regarding the return of the child, seeks to prevent a decision on the merits of the right to custody being taken in the State of refuge. To this end, the competent authorities in this State are forbidden to adjudicate on the matter when they have been informed that the child in question has been, in terms of the Convention, wrongfully removed or retained. This prohibition will disappear when it is shown that, according to the Convention, it is not appropriate to return the child, or where a reasonable period of time has elapsed without an application under the Convention having been lodged. The two sets of circumstances which can put an end to the duty contained in the article are very different, both in the reasons behind them and in their consequences. In fact, it is perfectly logical to provide that this obligation will cease as soon as it is established that the conditions for a child's return have not been met, either because the parties have come to an amicable arrangement or because it is appropriate to consider on the exceptions provided for in articles 13 and 20. Moreover, in such cases, the decision on the merits of the custody rights will finally dispose of the case.

On the other hand, since the 'notice' which may justify the prohibition against deciding upon the merits of the case must derive either from an application for the return of the

directement par le demandeur, soit d'une communication officielle de l'Autorité centrale du même Etat, il est difficile d'imaginer que les cas où l'information n'est pas suivie d'une demande ne seraient pas compris dans la première hypothèse. D'ailleurs, si de telles situations existent, l'ambiguïté de l'expression «période raisonnable» peut conduire à l'adoption d'une décision avant l'expiration de la période d'un an, retenue à l'article 12, alinéa premier; or, dans un tel cas, la décision adoptée coexisterait avec l'obligation de retourner l'enfant, d'après la Convention, posant ainsi un problème dont traite l'article 17.

Article 17 – Existence d'une décision relative à la garde dans l'Etat requis

122 La genèse de cet article montre clairement l'objectif qu'il poursuit: la Première commission a initialement adopté une disposition qui donnait priorité absolue à l'application de la Convention, en faisant prévaloir l'obligation de retourner l'enfant sur toute autre décision relative à la garde, rendue ou susceptible d'être reconnue dans l'Etat requis. En même temps, elle a accepté la possibilité d'une réserve qui aurait permis de refuser ce retour, quand il se serait avéré incompatible avec une décision existant dans l'Etat de refuge, antérieure à «l'enlèvement».[46] Le texte actuel est donc le produit d'un compromis en vue d'éliminer une réserve dans la Convention, sans en diminuer le degré d'acceptabilité par les Etats.[47] En ce sens, on a remanié la disposition originale en soulignant que ne fera pas obstacle au retour de l'enfant la *seule* existence d'une décision, et en donnant la possibilité au juge de prendre en considération les motifs de cette décision pour décider sur la demande de retour.

123 La solution incorporée dans l'article s'accorde parfaitement au but conventionnel de décourager les éventuels enleveurs qui ne pourront protéger leur action ni par une décision «morte», antérieure au déplacement, mais jamais exécutée, ni par une décision obtenue postérieurement et qui sera, dans la plupart des cas, entâchée de fraude. Par conséquent, l'autorité compétente de l'Etat requis devra considérer la demande de retour comme la preuve de ce qu'un élément nouveau est intervenu, qui l'oblige à remettre en question une décision non effective, ou adoptée sur la base de critères abusifs de compétence, ou encore ne respectant pas les droits de défense de toutes les parties concernées. D'ailleurs, étant donné que la décision sur le retour de l'enfant ne concerne pas le fond du droit de garde, les motifs de la décision qui pourront être pris en considération se limitent à ce qui concerne «l'application de la Convention». Quant à la situation provoquée par une décision rendue par les autorités de l'Etat de la résidence habituelle de l'enfant avant son «enlèvement», accordant la garde à l'«enleveur», elle serait normalement résolue par l'application de l'article 3 de la Convention, puisque l'existence du droit de garde réclamé doit être apprécié selon le droit dudit Etat.

Article 19 – Portée des décisions sur le retour de l'enfant

124 Cette disposition exprime l'idée qui se trouve à la base même de toute la Convention; en fait, nous nous en sommes

[46] Doc. trav. No 53, paragraphe 2 (*Proposal of the United Kingdom delegation*), No 32, article XG (*Proposal of the Netherlands delegation*) et No 19 (*Proposal of the Japanese delegation*), ainsi que P.-v. No 12.
[47] Voir Doc. trav. No 77 (Proposition du Président, appuyée par le Rapporteur et les délégations de la République fédérale d'Allemagne, de l'Australie, du Canada, de l'Espagne, de la Finlande, de la France, de l'Irlande, du Royaume-Uni et de la Suisse) et le P.-v. No 17.

child which is submitted directly by the applicant, or from an official communication from the Central Authority of the same State, it is difficult to see how cases in which the notice is not followed by an application would not be contained within the first hypothesis. Moreover, if such situations do exist, the ambiguity in the phrase 'reasonable time' could lead to decisions being taken before the period of one year, contained in article 12, first paragraph, has expired; in such a case, this decision would coexist alongside the duty to return the child, in accordance with the Convention, thus giving rise to a problem which is dealt with in article 17.

Article 17 – The existence of a decision on custody in the requested State

122 The origins of this article clearly demonstrate the end pursued. The First Commission initially adopted a provision which gave absolute priority to the application of the Convention, by making the duty to return the child prevail over any other decision on custody, which had been issued or was likely to be issued in the requested State. At the same time, it accepted the possibility of a reservation allowing the return of the child to be refused, when its return was shown to be incompatible with a decision existing in the State of refuge, prior to the 'abduction'.[46] The current text is therefore the result of a compromise which was reached in order to eliminate a reservation in the Convention, without at the same time reducing the extent of its acceptability to the States.[47] In this way, the original provision was recast by emphasizing that the sole fact that a decision existed would not of itself prevent the return of the child, and by allowing judges to take into consideration the reasons for this decision in coming to a decision themselves on the application for the child's return.

123 The solution contained in this article accords perfectly with the object of the Convention, which is to discourage potential abductors, who will not be able to defend their action by means either of a 'dead' decision taken prior to the removal but never put into effect, or of a decision obtained subsequently, which will, in the majority of cases, be vitiated by fraud. Consequently, the competent authority of the requested State will have to regard the application for the child's return as proof of the fact that a new factor has been introduced which obliges it to reconsider a decision which has not been put into effect, or which was taken on the basis of exorbitant grounds of jurisdiction, or else failed to have regard to the right of all the parties concerned to state their case. Moreover, since the decision on the return of the child is not concerned with the merits of custody rights, the reasons for the decision which may be taken into consideration are limited to those which concern 'the application of the Convention'. A situation brought about by a decision issued by the authorities of the State of a child's habitual residence prior to its 'abduction' and which granted custody to the 'abductor', would normally be resolved by applying article 3 of the Convention, since the existence of a claimed right to custody must be understood in accordance with the law of that State.

Article 19 – Scope of the decisions on the return of the child

124 This provision expresses an idea which underlies the whole of the Convention; as a matter of fact, in this Report

[46] Working Documents Nos 53, paragraph 2 (Proposal of the United Kingdom delegation), 32, article XG (Proposal of the Netherlands delegation), and 19 (Proposal of the Japanese delegation), as well as *P.-v.* No 12.
[47] See Working Document No 77 (Proposal of the Chairman, supported by the Rapporteur and the delegations of Australia, Canada, Finland, France, the Federal Republic of Germany, Ireland, Spain, Switzerland and the United Kingdom) and *P.-v.* No 17.

déjà occupé à plusieurs reprises dans ce Rapport, en ce qui concerne tant sa justification que son commentaire. Cet article se limite à préciser la portée du retour de l'enfant que la Convention essaie de garantir; un retour qui, pour pouvoir être «immédiat» ou «rapide», ne doit pas préjuger du fond du droit de garde et qui cherche précisément à éviter qu'une décision ultérieure sur ce droit puisse être influencée par un changement des circonstances, introduit unilatéralement par une des parties.

CHAPITRE IV — DROIT DE VISITE

Article 21

125 Avant tout, il s'impose de reconnaître que la Convention n'essaie pas d'établir une réglementation exhaustive du droit de visite, ce qui aurait sans doute débordé les objectifs conventionnels. En effet, même si l'attention prêtée au droit de visite répond à la conviction qu'il doit être le corollaire normal du droit de garde, au niveau des buts de la Convention il suffisait d'assurer la coopération des Autorités centrales en ce qui concerne, soit son organisation, soit la protection de son exercice effectif. Par ailleurs le temps particulièrement court que lui a consacré la Première commission est peut-être le meilleur indicatif du haut degré de consensus atteint à son égard.

126 Comme nous venons de l'indiquer, l'article repose dans son ensemble sur la coopération entre Autorités centrales. Une proposition visant à introduire, dans un nouvel alinéa, la seule compétence en matière de droit de visite tant des autorités que de la loi de l'Etat de la résidence habituelle de l'enfant a été rejetée à une large majorité.[48] L'organisation et la protection de l'exercice effectif du droit de visite sont donc toujours envisagées par la Convention comme une fonction essentielle des Autorités centrales. En ce sens, le premier alinéa consacre deux points importants: d'un côté la liberté des particuliers pour saisir l'Autorité centrale de leur choix; de l'autre côté, l'objet de la demande adressée à l'Autorité centrale peut être, soit l'organisation d'un droit de visite, c'est-à-dire son établissement, soit la protection de l'exercice d'un droit de visite déjà déterminé. Or, surtout quand la demande vise l'organisation du droit prétendu, ou lorsque son exercice se heurte à l'opposition du titulaire de la garde, le recours à des procédures légales s'imposera très fréquemment; à cet effet, le troisième alinéa de l'article envisage la possibilité pour les Autorités centrales d'entamer ou de favoriser de telles procédures, soit directement, soit par des intermédiaires.

127 Les problèmes abordés au deuxième alinéa sont de nature très différente. Il s'agit d'assurer l'exercice paisible du droit de visite sans qu'il mette en danger le droit de garde. Dans ce sens, cette disposition contient des éléments importants pour atteindre ce but. Au centre même de la solution esquissée, il faut situer, une fois encore, la coopération entre Autorités centrales, une coopération qui vise tant à faciliter l'exercice du droit de visite qu'à garantir l'accomplissement de toute condition à laquelle un tel exercice serait soumis.

[48] Voir Doc. trav. No 31 (*Proposal of the Danish delegation*) et P.-v. No 13.

we have already been concerned on several occasions as much with the reasons for it as with commenting upon it. This article is restricted to stating the scope of decisions taken regarding the return of the child which the Convention seeks to guarantee, a return which, so as to be 'forthwith' or 'speedy', must not prejudge the merits of custody rights; this provision seeks to prevent a later decision on these rights being influenced by a change of circumstances brought about by the unilateral action of one of the parties.

CHAPTER IV — RIGHTS OF ACCESS

Article 21

125 Above all, it must be recognized that the Convention does not seek to regulate access rights in an exhaustive manner; this would undoubtedly go beyond the scope of the Convention's objectives. Indeed, even if the attention which has been paid to access rights results from the belief that they are the normal corollary of custody rights, it sufficed at the Convention level merely to secure co-operation among Central Authorities as regards either their organization or the protection of their actual exercise. In other respects, the best indication of the high level of agreement reached regarding access rights is the particularly short amount of time devoted to them by the First Commission.

126 As we have just pointed out, the article as a whole rests upon co-operation among Central Authorities. A proposal which sought to insert a provision in a new paragraph that both the authorities and the law of the State of the child's habitual residence should have exclusive jurisdiction in questions of access rights, was rejected by a large majority.[48] The organizing and securing of the actual exercise of access rights was thus always seen by the Convention as an essential function of the Central Authorities. Understood thus, the first paragraph contains two important points: in the first place, the freedom of individuals to apply to the Central Authority of their choice, and secondly the fact that the purpose of the application to the Central Authority can be either the organization of access rights, *i.e.* their establishment, or the protection of the exercise of previously determined access rights. Now, recourse to legal proceedings will arise very frequently, especially when the application seeks to organize rights which are merely claimed or when their exercise runs up against opposition from the holder of the rights of custody. With this in view, the article's third paragraph envisages the possibility of Central Authorities initiating or assisting in such proceedings, either directly, or through intermediaries.

127 The nature of the problems tackled in the second paragraph is very different. Here it is a question of securing the peaceful enjoyment of access rights without endangering custody rights. This provision therefore contains important elements for the attainment of this end. Once again, co-operation among Central Authorities is placed, of necessity, in the very centre of the picture, and it is a co-operation designed as much to promote the exercise of access rights as to guarantee the fulfilment of any conditions to which their exercise may be subject.

[48] See Working Document No 31 (Proposal of the Danish delegation) and *P.-v.* No 13.

Parmi les moyens concrets d'assurer l'exercice du droit de visite, l'article 21 en retient seulement un, lorsqu'il signale que l'Autorité centrale doit essayer que «soient levés, dans toute la mesure du possible, les obstacles de nature à s'y opposer»; obstacles qui, notamment, peuvent être légaux ou dérivés d'éventuelles responsabilités de type pénal. Le reste est laissé à la coopération entre Autorités centrales, considérée comme la meileure méthode pour obtenir que les conditions imposées à l'exercice du droit de visite soient respectées. En effet, ce respect constitue, pour le titulaire de la garde, la seule garantie qu'un tel exercice ne serait pas nuisible à ses propres droits.

128 Sur la question de savoir comment les Autorités centrales vont organiser cette coopération en vue d'assurer le caractère «innocent» de l'exercice d'un droit de visite, la Convention ne donne pas d'exemples, car ils auraient pu être interprétés restrictivement. On peut donc mentionner, à titre purement indicatif, comme le faisait le Rapport de l'avant-projet,[49] qu'il convient d'éviter que l'enfant figure sur le passeport du titulaire du droit de visite et, en cas de visite «transfrontière», qu'il serait judicieux que celui-ci prenne l'engagement, devant l'Autorité centrale de l'Etat de la résidence habituelle de l'enfant, de le renvoyer à une date précise en indiquant le ou les endroits où il a l'intention d'habiter avec l'enfant. Une copie d'un tel compromis serait, par la suite, transmise tant à l'Autorité centrale de la résidence habituelle du titulaire du droit de visite, qu'à celle de l'Etat où il a déclaré qu'il séjournerait avec l'enfant. Cela permettrait de connaître à tout moment la localisation de l'enfant et de déclencher la procédure pour assurer son retour, dès l'expiration du délai fixé. Evidemment, aucune des mesures avancées ne peut, à elle seule, assurer l'exercice correct du droit de visite; de toute façon nous ne croyons pas que ce Rapport puisse aller plus loin: les mesures concrètes que pourront prendre les Autorités centrales impliquées dépendront des circonstances de chaque cas d'espèce et de la capacité d'agir reconnue à chaque Autorité centrale.

CHAPITRE V — DISPOSITIONS GÉNÉRALES

129 Ce chapitre contient une série de dispositions hétérogènes en raison de la matière dont elles s'occupent, mais qu'il fallait traiter en dehors des chapitres précédents. Il s'agit, d'une part de certaines dispositions procédurales communes aux procès visant tant le retour de l'enfant que l'organisation du droit de visite; d'autre part de la réglementation des problèmes posés par l'application de la Convention dans les Etats plurilégislatifs, ainsi que de ses relations avec d'autres conventions et de son domaine d'application *ratione temporis*.

Article 22 – «Cautio judicatum solvi»

130 Suivant une tendance marquée en faveur de la suppression conventionnelle des mesures procédurales discriminatoires envers les étrangers, cet article déclare qu'aucune caution, qu'aucun dépôt, sous quelque dénomination que ce soit, ne peut être imposé dans le contexte de la

[49] Voir Rapport de la Commission spéciale, No 110.

Of all the specific ways of securing the execise of access rights, article 21 contains only one, where it points out that the Central Authority must try 'to remove, as far as possible, all obstacles to the exercise of such rights', obstacles which may be legal ones or may originate in possible criminal liability. The rest is left up to the co-operation among Central Authorities, which is regarded as the best means of ensuring respect for the conditions imposed upon the exercise of access rights. In fact, such respect is the only means of guaranteeing to the custodian that their exercise will not harm his own rights.

128 The Convention gives no examples of how Central Authorities are to organize this co-operation so as to secure the 'innocent' exercise of access rights, since such examples could have been interpreted restrictively. Mention could however be made purely indicatively as in the Report of the preliminary draft Convention,[49] of the fact that it would be advisable that the child's name not appear on the passport of the holder of the right of access, whilst in 'transfrontier' access cases it would be sensible for the holder of the access rights to give an undertaking to the Central Authority of the child's habitual residence to return the child on a particular date and to indicate also the places where he intends to stay with the child. A copy of such an undertaking would then be sent to the Central Authority of the habitual residence of the holder of the access rights, as well as to the Central Authority of the State in which he has stated his intention of staying with the child. This would enable the authorities to know the whereabouts of the child at any time and to set in motion proceedings for bringing about its return, as soon as the stated time-limit has expired. Of course, none of the measures could by itself ensure that access rights are exercised properly, but in any event we believe that this Report can go no further: the specific measures which the Central Authorities concerned are able to take will depend on the circumstances of each case and on the capacity to act enjoyed by each Central Authority.

CHAPTER V — GENERAL PROVISIONS

129 This chapter contains a series of provisions which differ according to the topics with which they deal, and which had to be dealt with outside the framework of the foregoing chapters. On the one hand, there are certain procedural provisions common both to the proceedings for the return of the child and to the organization of access rights, and on the other hand there are provisions for regulating the problems arising out of the Convention's application in States with more than one system of law, as well as those which concern its relationship with other conventions and its scope *ratione temporis*.

Article 22 – 'Cautio judicatum solvi'

130 Following a marked tendency to favour the deletion from the Convention of procedural measures which discriminated against foreigners, this article declares that no security, bond or deposit, however described, shall be required within the context of the Convention. Two short

[49] See Report of the Special Commission, No 110.

Convention. Le texte mérite deux brefs commentaires. Le premier concerne le domaine d'application *ratione personae* de la prohibition consacrée; sur ce point, la solution retenue est largement généreuse, comme l'exigeait une convention construite sur l'idée sous-jacente de la protection des enfant.[50] En second lieu, la caution ou dépôt dont sont exonérés les étrangers sont ceux qui, dans chaque système juridique et sous différentes dénominations, visent à garantir qu'ils respecteront le contenu des décisions en ce qui concerne le paiement des frais et dépens découlant d'un procès. Dans un souci de cohérence, l'article précise que la règle joue seulement par rapport aux «procédures judiciaires ou administratives visées par la Convention», en évitant une formule plus large qui aurait pu être interprétée comme s'appliquant, par exemple aux procès visant directement la détermination du fond du droit de garde. D'autre part, il se déduit clairement de ce qui précède qu'elle n'interdit pas d'autres cautions ou dépôts possibles exigés, notamment les cautions imposées en vue de garantir l'exercice correct d'un droit de visite.

Article 23 – Exemption de légalisation

131 Cet article reproduit à la lettre le texte de l'article parallèle de l'avant-projet, qui se limitait à exprimer dans une disposition séparée une idée contenue dans toutes les Conventions de La Haye, impliquant la transmission de documents entre Etats contractants. Il se déduit de sa rédaction ouverte qu'il n'interdit pas seulement les «légalisations diplomatiques», mais toute autre exigence de ce genre; cependant, reste en dehors de cette disposition l'exigence possible d'authentification des copies ou documents privés, selon la loi interne des autorités concernées.

Article 24 – Traduction des documents

132 En ce qui concerne les langues à utiliser dans les relations entre Autorités centrales, la Convention a maintenu la solution retenue dans l'avant-projet, en vertu de laquelle les documents seront envoyés dans leur langue d'origine et accompagnés d'une traduction dans une des langues officielles de l'Etat requis ou, lorsque cette traduction s'avère difficilement réalisable, d'une traduction en français ou en anglais.[51] Sur ce point, d'ailleurs, la Convention admet la possibilité de formuler une réserve aux termes de l'article 42, en vertu de laquelle un Etat contractant pourra s'opposer à l'utilisation d'une des langues de substitution; la réserve ne pourra évidemment pas exclure l'utilisation des deux langues. Finalement, il faut souligner, d'une part que le système établi prétend être un système de facilité *minimum*, qui peut être amélioré par d'autres conventions excluant entre les Etats parties toute exigence de traduction; d'autre part qu'il n'a trait qu'aux communications entre Autorités centrales. En conséquence de quoi, les demandes et autres documents adressés aux autorités judiciaires ou administratives internes devront respecter les règles imposées par la loi de chaque Etat en matière de traduction.

[50] Voir la construction plus restrictive incorporée à l'article 14 de la *Convention tendant à faciliter l'accès international à la justice*, Convention adoptée aussi au cours de la Quatorzième session de la Conférence.
[51] Une solution partiellement différente est consacrée à l'article 7 de la *Convention tendant à faciliter l'accès international à la justice*, citée *supra*.

comments are in order here. The first concerns the scope of the stated prohibition *ratione personae*; on this point, an extremely liberal solution was arrived at, such as was required by a convention built upon the basic idea of protecting children.[50] Secondly, the security, bond or deposit from which foreigners are exempt are those which, in any legal system and howsoever described, are meant to guarantee respect for decisions on the payment of costs and expenses arising out of legal proceedings. The article, in its concern for coherence, states that the rule will apply only to those 'judicial or administrative proceedings falling within the scope of the Convention', and avoids a wider formulation which could have been interpreted as applicable, for example, to proceedings raised directly for a decision on the merits of custody rights. On the other hand, it can clearly be inferred from the preceding observations that it does not prevent other types of security, bond or deposit being required, particularly those which are imposed so as to guarantee the proper exercise of access rights.

Article 23 – Exemption from legalization

131 This article repeats word for word the text of the equivalent article in the preliminary draft Convention, which merely set forth in a separate provision an idea which is to be found in all Hague Conventions, involving the transmission of documents among Contracting States. The fact that it has been drafted in wide terms means that not only 'diplomatic legalization', but also any other similar sort of requirement, is forbidden. However, any requirement of the internal law of the authorities in question that copies or private documents be authenticated remains outside the scope of this provision.

Article 24 – Translation of documents

132 As regards the languages which are to be used as among Central Authorities, the Convention upheld the approach in the Preliminary Draft, by which documents are to be sent in their original language, accompanied by a translation into one of the official languages of the requested State or, where that is not feasible, a translation into French or English.[51] In this matter, the Convention also allows a reservation to be made in terms of article 42, under which a Contracting State can object to the use of one or other of the substitute languages, but this reservation cannot of course exclude the use of both. Finally, it must be emphasized firstly that the scheme which has been chosen offers only a *minimal* facility and may be improved upon by other conventions which exclude any requirement of translation as among States which are Party to them, and secondly that it governs only communications among Central Authorities. Consequently, applications and other documents sent to internal judicial or administrative authorities will have to conform to the rules regarding translation laid down by the law of each State.

[50] See the more restrictive construction which was incorporated in article 14 of the *Convention on International Access to Justice*, also adopted during the Fourteenth Session of the Conference.
[51] A somewhat different approach is found in article 7 of the *Convention on International Access to Justice*, referred to *supra*.

Article 25 – Assistance judiciaire et juridique

133 La disposition sur ce point élargit le domaine de l'assistance judiciaire dans une double perspective: d'un côté, par l'inclusion parmi les éventuels bénéficiaires, en plus des nationaux des Etats parties, des personnes qui auraient dans ces Etats leur résidence habituelle; de l'autre, par l'extension de l'assistance visée à la consultation juridique, un aspect qui n'est pas toujours couvert par les divers systèmes étatiques d'assistance judiciaire.[52]

Article 26 – Frais découlant de l'application de la Convention

134 Le principe exprimé au premier alinéa, d'après lequel chaque Autorité centrale assumera ses propres frais en appliquant la Convention, n'a pas rencontré d'opposition. Il implique avant tout qu'une Autorité centrale ne peut pas réclamer ces frais à une autre Autorité centrale. Quant à savoir quels sont les frais visés, il faut convenir qu'ils dépendront des services réels offerts par chaque Autorité centrale, en accord avec les possibilités d'action que lui reconnaît la loi interne de l'Etat concerné.

135 Par contre, le second alinéa a trait à l'un des points les plus controversés au cours de la Quatorzième session et qui a finalement été résolu par l'acceptation de la réserve figurant au troisième alinéa de ce même article. En effet, on n'a pu mettre fin à la controverse entre les délégations qui voulaient assurer au demandeur la gratuité totale dans l'application de la Convention (en incluant l'exonération des frais et dépens non couverts par le système d'assistance judiciaire et juridique, qui pourraient découler d'un procès ou éventuellement, des frais entraînés par la participation d'un avocat), et les délégations favorables à la solution contraire retenue dans l'avant-projet,[53] que par l'inclusion d'une réserve en faveur des secondes. La raison en est que, étant donné que les différents critères prenaient leurs racines dans la structure des systèmes juridiques impliqués, toute tentative de faire prévaloir, en termes absolus, une position sur l'autre, aurait conduit à l'exclusion *a priori* de la Convention d'un certain nombre d'Etats; or, personne ne souhaitait un tel résultat.[54] Par contre, l'accord a été total en ce qui concerne la norme incluse dans la dernière phrase du deuxième alinéa, qui autorise les Autorités centrales à «demander le paiement des dépenses causées ou qui seraient causées par les opérations liées au retour de l'enfant«.

136 Le quatrième alinéa incorpore une disposition de nature tout à fait différente, en vertu de laquelle les autorités compétentes internes peuvent mettre à la charge de «l'enleveur» ou de celui qui empêche l'exercice du droit de visite, le paiement de certains frais engagés par le demandeur ou en son nom, notamment «des frais de voyage, des frais de représentation judiciaire du demandeur et de retour de l'enfant, ainsi que tous les coûts et dépenses faits pour localiser l'enfant». Mais étant donné qu'il s'agit d'une norme simplement facultative, qui respecte le pouvoir d'appréciation concrète des tribunaux dans chaque cas d'espèce, sa portée semble être surtout symbolique, celle d'un éventuel élément de dissuasion d'une conduite contraire aux objectifs conventionnels.

Article 25 – Legal aid and advice

133 The relevant provision here enlarges the scope of legal aid in two respects. Firstly, it includes among the possible beneficiaries persons habitually resident in a Contracting State as well as that State's own nationals. Secondly, the legal aid available is extended to cover legal advice as well, which is not invariably included in the various systems of legal aid operated by States.[52]

Article 26 – Costs arising out of the Convention's application

134 The principle enunciated in the first paragraph, under which each Central Authority bears its own costs in applying the Convention, met no opposition. Quite simply, it means that a Central Authority cannot claim costs from another Central Authority. It must however be admitted that the costs envisaged will depend on the actual services provided by each Central Authority, according to the freedom of action conferred upon it by the internal law of the State concerned.

135 On the other hand, the second paragraph refers to one of the most controversial matters dealt with by the Fourteenth Session, a matter which in the end had to be resolved by accepting the reservation in the third paragraph of the same article. In fact, the argument between those delegations which wanted the applicant to be exempt from all costs arising out of the application of the Convention (including exemption from all costs and expenses not covered by the legal aid and advice system such as those which arise out of legal proceedings or, where applicable, the participation of counsel or legal advisers), and those which favoured the opposite solution adopted by the preliminary draft Convention,[53] was resolved only by including a reservation favouring the latter's point of view. The reason for this was that, since different criteria for the granting of legal aid were rooted in the very structure of the legal systems concerned, any attempt to make one approach prevail absolutely over the others would have led to the automatic exclusion of certain States from the Convention, a result which no one wanted.[54] However, there was total agreement as regards the rule contained in the last sentence of the second paragraph, authorizing the Central Authorities to 'require the payment of the expenses incurred or to be incurred in implementing the return of the child'.

136 The fourth paragraph contains a quite different type of provision, by which the competent internal authorities may direct the 'abductor' or the person who prevented the exercise of access rights, to pay necessary expenses incurred by or on behalf of the applicant, including 'travel expenses, any costs incurred or payments made for locating the child, the costs of legal representation of the applicant, and those of returning the child'. But since this rule is only an optional provision, which recognizes the discretion which may be exercised by the courts in each case, its scope would seem to be particularly symbolic, a possible deterrent to behaviour which is contrary to the objects of the Convention.

[52] Voir, dans un sens similaire, les articles 1 et 2 de la *Convention tendant à faciliter l'accès international à la justice*, cité *supra*.
[53] Article 22, alinéa 2*a* de l'avant-projet élaboré par la Commission spéciale.
[54] Voir Doc. trav. Nos 51 et 61 (Propositions de la délégation belge) et Nos 57 et 67 (Propositions des délégations des Etats-Unis, du Canada et des Pays-Bas), ainsi que les P.-v. Nos 11 et 14.

[52] See, in similar vein, articles 1 and 2 of the *Convention on International Access to Justice*, referred to *supra*.
[53] Article 22(2)(*a*) of the Preliminary Draft prepared by the Special Commission.
[54] See Working Documents Nos 51 and 61 (*Propositions de la délégation belge*) and Nos 57 and 67 (Proposals of the Canadian, Netherlands and United States delegations) and also *P.-v.* Nos 11 and 14.

Article 27 – Possibilité de rejeter une demande

137 Le bon sens indique qu'on ne peut pas obliger les Autorités centrales à accepter les demandes qui se situent hors du domaine d'application de la Convention ou qui sont manifestement sans fondement. Dans ces cas-là, la seule obligation des Autorités centrales est d'informer «immédiatement de leurs motifs le demandeur ou, le cas échéant, l'Autorité centrale qui leur a transmis la demande». Cela signifie que le rejet d'une demande peut être fait tant de l'Autorité centrale directement saisie par le demandeur que d'une Autorité centrale saisie originairement par une autre Autorité centrale.

Article 28 – Procuration exigée par l'Autorité centrale

138 La disposition contenue dans cet article n'est qu'une autre manifestation du point de vue adopté par la Convention en ce qui concerne l'organisation et les compétences des Autorités centrales. Puisqu'on veut éviter que les Etats aient à changer leur droit pour pouvoir l'accepter, la Convention prend en considération le fait que, selon le droit des divers Etats membres de la Conférence, l'Autorité centrale pourra avoir besoin d'une autorisation du demandeur. De fait, la «formule modèle» introduit, comme exemple des pièces produites éventuellement (note au No IX), une référence à la «procuration conférée à l'Autorité centrale», procuration qui devra donc être jointe, chaque fois qu'une Autorité centrale l'exigera, aux éléments envisagés à l'article 8 et aux demandes introduites en application de l'article 21.

Article 29 – Saisine directe des autorités internes compétentes

139 La Convention n'essaie pas d'établir un système exclusif entre les Etats contractants pour obtenir le retour des enfants. Elle se présente au contraire comme un instrument complémentaire se proposant d'aider les personnes dont le droit de garde ou de visite a été violé. Par conséquent, ces personnes ont le choix entre recourir aux Autorités centrales – c'est-à-dire utiliser les mécanismes propres à la Convention – ou bien choisir la voie d'une action directe devant les autorités compétentes en matière de garde et de visite de l'Etat où se trouve l'enfant. Dans la seconde hypothèse, donc quand les personnes concernées optent pour saisir directement les autorités en question, elles peuvent encore faire un deuxième choix et introduire leur demande «par application ou non des dispositions de la Convention». Dans le dernier cas, évidemment, les autorités ne seront pas tenues d'appliquer les dispositions conventionnelles, à moins que l'Etat ne les ait converties en règles internes, suivant en cela l'article 2 de la Convention.

Article 30 – Recevabilité des documents

140 Par cette disposition, la Convention a entendu résoudre le problème existant dans certains Etats membres de la Conférence en ce qui concerne la recevabilité des documents. Il s'agit donc simplement de faciliter l'admission par les autorités judiciaires ou administratives des Etats contractants des demandes introduites directement ou par l'intermédiaire d'une Autorité centrale, ainsi que des documents pouvant être annexés ou fournis par les Autorités centrales. En effet, on ne doit pas interpréter cet article comme incorporant une règle sur la valeur de preuve qu'il faut accorder à ces documents; ce problème tombe absolument hors du domaine conventionnel.[55]

[55] Voir article 26 de l'avant-projet, Doc. trav. No 49 (*Proposal of the United States delegation*) et P.-v. No 11.

Article 27 – Possible rejection of an application

137 Common sense would indicate that Central Authorities cannot be obliged to accept applications which belong outside the scope of the Convention or are manifestly without foundation. In such cases, the only duty of Central Authorities is to 'inform forthwith the applicant or the Central Authority through which the application was submitted, as the case may be, of its reasons'. This means that an application may be rejected by the Central Authority to which the applicant applied directly as well as by a Central Authority which was initially brought into the case by another Central Authority.

Article 28 – Authorization required by the Central Authority

138 The provision in this article is merely another example of the Convention's attitude to the organization and powers of Central Authorities. Since the aim is to avoid requiring States to change their own law in order to be able to accept the Convention, the Convention takes into consideration the fact that, in terms of the law of various Member States of the Conference the Central Authority would have the power to require some authorization from the applicant. As a matter of fact, the 'model form', as an example of the documents which might be attached to an application (see note to No IX), brings in a reference to 'the authorization empowering the Central Authority to act on behalf of the applicant', an authorization which, every time it is required by a Central Authority, will have to accompany those matters listed in article 8 and the applications submitted under article 21.

Article 29 – Direct application to competent internal authorities

139 The Convention does not seek to establish a system for the return of children which is exclusively for the benefit of the Contracting States. It is put forward rather as an additional means for helping persons whose custody or access rights have been breached. Consequently, those persons can either have recourse to the Central Authorities – in other words, use the means provided in the Convention – or else pursue a direct action before the competent authorities in matters of custody and access in the State where the child is located. In the latter case, whenever the persons concerned opt to apply directly to the relevant authorities, a second choice is open to them in that they can submit their application 'whether or not under the provisions of this Convention'. In the latter case the authorities are not of course obliged to apply the provisions of the Convention, unless the State has incorporated them into its internal law, in terms of article 2 of the Convention.

Article 30 – Admissibility of documents

140 This provision was intended to resolve the problem which existed in some Member States regarding the admissibility of documents. It merely seeks to facilitate admission before the judicial or administrative authorities of Contracting States of applications submitted either directly or through the intervention of a Central Authority, as well as documents which may be attached or supplied by the Central Authorities. In fact, this article must not be understood to contain a rule on the evidential value which is to be placed on these documents, since that problem falls quite outwith the scope of the Convention.[55]

[55] See article 26 of the preliminary draft Convention, Working Document No 49 (Proposal of the United States delegation) and *P.-v.* No 11.

Articles 31 à 33 – Application de la Convention en ce qui concerne les Etats plurilégislatifs

141 Ces trois articles règlent l'application de la Convention en ce qui concerne les Etats à systèmes juridiques non unifiés. A l'instar des dernières conventions élaborées par la Conférence de La Haye, une distinction est faite entre les Etats ayant plusieurs systèmes de droit d'application territoriale, et les Etats ayant plusieurs systèmes de droit applicables à des catégories différentes de personnes. Plus précisément, les solutions retenues s'inspirent de celles adoptées dans les conventions élaborées au cours de la Treizième session de la Conférence.[56]

En ce qui concerne le premier groupe d'Etats, l'article 31 précise comment il faut comprendre, d'une part la référence à la résidence habituelle de l'enfant, et d'autre part la référence au droit de l'Etat d'une telle résidence.

En ce qui concerne le deuxième groupe d'Etats, l'article 32 confie la détermination du droit dont il faut tenir compte aux règles en vigueur dans chaque Etat.

Finalement, sur le contenu de ces deux articles, il faut souligner que leur intérêt ne se limite pas aux Etats directement envisagés; en effet, les normes en question devront être prises en considération par tout Etat contractant dans ses relations avec eux, par exemple chaque fois qu'un enfant sera déplacé d'un de ses Etats vers un autre Etat ayant un système de droit unifié ou non.

142 D'autre part, l'article 33 délimite les cas dans lesquels les Etats plurilégislatifs sont tenus d'appliquer la Convention, en excluant les situations où un Etat ayant un système de droit unifié ne serait pas tenu de le faire. En somme, cet article se limite à déclarer que la Convention n'est applicable qu'aux relations internationales, en même temps qu'il qualifie de relations internes toutes celles qui se passent à l'intérieur d'un Etat, plurilégislatif ou non.

Article 34 – Relations avec d'autres conventions

143 Cet article a été commenté dans la première partie de ce Rapport (Nos 39 et 40).

Article 35 – Domaine d'application ratione temporis *de la Convention*

144 La question de déterminer si la Convention devait s'appliquer aux enlèvements qui se seraient produits entre deux Etats contractants antérieurement à son entrée en vigueur, ou seulement à ceux qui auraient eu lieu après cette date, s'est vue proposer différentes solutions au cours de la Quatorzième session. La première était sans doute la plus généreuse, puisqu'elle prévoyait l'application de la Convention à tout «enlèvement», indépendamment du moment de sa réalisation.[57] Cependant, cette décision a été suivie plus tard par l'acceptation de la possibilité pour tout Etat contractant de faire une déclaration en vue de limiter l'application de la Convention aux «enlèvements» intervenus après son entrée en vigueur dans cet Etat.[58] La situation restait ainsi largement ouverte, tout en reconnaissant néanmoins à chaque Etat la possibilité de restreindre l'application de la Convention, s'il le jugeait nécessaire. Il est clair

[56] Voir notamment le Rapport de M. von Overbeck sur la Convention sur la loi applicable aux régimes matrimoniaux, *Actes et documents de la Treizième session*, tome II, p. 374 et s.
[57] Voir Doc. trav. No 53 (*Proposal of the United Kingdom delegation*) et P.-v. No 13.

[58] Voir Doc. trav. No 68 (Proposition de la délégation du Canada) et P.-v. No 15.

Articles 31 to 33 – Application of the Convention in relation to States with more than one system of law

141 These three articles govern the Convention's application to States with non-unitary legal systems. As in recent conventions of the Hague Conference, a distinction has been drawn between States which have several systems of law applicable in different territorial units, and those with several systems of law applicable to different categories of persons. To be more precise, the solution adopted received its inspiration from that reached by the conventions drawn up during the Thirteenth Session of the Conference.[56]

As regards the first group of States, article 31 explains how references to the child's habitual residence and to the law of the State of its habitual residence are to be understood.

As regards the second type, article 32 leaves the determination of the applicable law to the rules in force in each State.

Finally, it must be emphasized that the substantive provisions of these two articles are not restricted to the States directly concerned. In actual fact, the relevant rules are to be taken into consideration by all Contracting States in their relations with each other, for example whenever a child is removed from one of those States to another State with a unified or non-unified legal system.

142 On the other hand, article 33 limits the occasions where States with more than one system of law are obliged to apply the Convention, by excluding those in which a State with a unified system of law would not be bound to do so. Put shortly, this article merely states that the Convention applies only at the international level and at the same time characterizes as internal all those relationships which arise within a State, whether or not that State has more than one system of law.

Article 34 – Relationship to other conventions

143 This article was commented upon in the first part of the Report (Nos 39 and 40).

Article 35 – Scope of the Convention ratione temporis

144 The question as to whether the Convention should apply to abductions involving two States and which occurred prior to its entry into force or only to those occurring thereafter, was met with different proposed solutions during the Fourteenth Session. The first proposal was undoubtedly the most liberal, since it envisaged the Convention's applying to all 'abductions', irrespective of when it came into effect.[57] However, this decision was followed by acceptance of the idea that any Contracting State could declare that the Convention would apply only to 'abductions' which occurred after its entry into force in that State.[58] The situation therefore remained largely unresolved, with each State, where it deemed this necessary, being able to limit the Convention's application. It was clear that the operation of such declarations within a convention which is clearly bilateral in its application would create some technical problems, to

[56] See in particular Mr von Overbeck's Report on the Convention on the Law Applicable to Matrimonial Property Regimes, in *Acts and Documents of the Thirteenth Session*, Book II, p. 374 *et seq.*
[57] See Working Document No 53 (Proposal of the United Kingdom delegation) and *P.-v.* No 13.
[58] See Working Document No 68 (Proposal of the Canadian delegation) and *P.-v.* No 15.

que le jeu de telles déclarations dans le contexte d'une convention d'application nettement bilatérale posait quelques problèmes techniques. Pour y pallier, la Première commission s'est finalement prononcée en faveur de la solution contraire à la première, c'est-à-dire pour la plus restrictive. C'est donc celle qui apparaît à l'article 35, d'après lequel la Convention ne s'applique entre les Etats contractants, «qu'aux enlèvements ou aux non-retours illicites qui se sont produits après son entrée en vigueur dans ces Etats».[59] D'autre part, de l'ensemble des dispositions conventionnelles (et notamment de l'article 12, alinéa 2) on doit déduire qu'il n'existe pas de limite pour introduire l'action, dès lors que l'enfant n'a pas atteint l'âge de seize ans, selon l'article 4. En effet, l'introduction de l'action après l'expiration de la période d'un an, envisagée au premier alinéa de l'article 12, ne fait que nuancer l'obligation de faire retourner l'enfant, en admettant qu'elle ne s'impose pas lorsqu'il est établi que l'enfant s'est intégré dans son nouveau milieu.

alleviate which the First Commission finally pronounced itself in favour of the opposite solution to that first adopted, *i.e.* the more restrictive. It is seen therefore in article 35, by which the Convention is to apply as among Contracting States 'only to wrongful removals or retentions occurring after its entry into force in those States'.[59] On the other hand, the inference must be drawn from the Convention's provisions as a whole (and in particular article 12, second paragraph) that no time-limit is imposed on the submission of applications, provided the child has not reached sixteen years of age, in terms of article 4. In fact, the commencement of an action after the expiry of the one year period stated in the first paragraph of article 12, merely lessens the obligation to cause the child to be returned, whilst it is recognized that the obligation will not arise if the child is shown to have become settled in its new environment.

145 La disposition a sans doute le mérite d'être claire. On ne peut cependant pas ignorer que son application est destinée à frustrer les expectatives légitimes des particuliers concernés. Mais étant donné qu'il s'agit en définitive d'une restriction à l'obligation de retourner l'enfant, rien ne s'oppose à ce que deux ou plusieurs Etats conviennent entre eux d'y déroger conformément à l'article 36, c'est-à-dire qu'ils se mettent d'accord pour appliquer rétroactivement la Convention.

D'ailleurs, la disposition ne concerne que les dispositions conventionnelles visant le retour de l'enfant. En effet, la réglementation conventionnelle du droit de visite ne peut être invoquée, par la nature même des choses, qu'à propos du refus de son exercice s'étant produit ou continuant à se produire après l'entrée en vigueur de la Convention.

145 The provision certainly has the merit of being clear. However, it cannot be denied that its application is fated to frustrate the legitimate expectations of the individuals concerned. But since in the last resort it is a limitation on the duty to return the child, it in no way prevents two or more States agreeing amongst themselves to derogate from it in terms of article 36, by agreeing to apply the Convention retroactively.

Moreover, the provision concerns only those provisions in the Convention regarding the return of the child. In actual fact, the provision of the Convention governing access rights can, in the nature of things, only be invoked where their exercise is refused or continues to be refused after the Convention has come into force.

Article 36 – Possibilité de limiter conventionnellement les restrictions au retour de l'enfant

146 En concordance avec les principes généraux qui inspirent la Convention et sur la base de l'expérience d'autres Conventions de la Conférence de La Haye,[60] cet article admet la possibilité que deux ou plusieurs Etats contractants conviennent de déroger entre eux aux dispositions de la Convention pouvant impliquer des restrictions au retour des enfants, notamment celles visées aux articles 13 et 20. Cela montre d'une part le caractère de compromis de certaines dispositions conventionnelles et la possibilité d'adopter des critères plus favorables à l'objectif principal de la Convention dans les relations entre Etats de conceptions juridiques très homogènes, et d'autre part que, comme nous l'avons souligné à plusieurs reprises au cours de ce Rapport, la Convention n'est inspirée par aucune idée d'exclusivité dans son domaine d'application. Or, si de telles conventions complémentaires voient le jour, il faudrait éviter un effet négatif, redouté par certaines délégations: le fait qu'en dehors du domaine d'application géographiquement restreint de tels accords, les Etats parties soient tentés de donner une interprétation large aux restrictions incluses dans cette Convention, de manière à affaiblir sa portée.[61]

Article 36 – Possibility of limiting by agreement the restrictions on the return of the child

146 This article, conform to the general principles underlying the Convention, which are based on the experience derived from other Hague Conventions,[60] allows two or more Contracting States to agree to derogate as amongst themselves from any of the Convention's provisions which may involve restrictions on the return of the child, in particular those contained in articles 13 and 20. This demonstrates, on the one hand, the compromise character of some of the Convention's provisions and the possibility that criteria more favourable to the principal object of the Convention may be adopted to govern relationships among States which share very similar legal concepts, while on the other hand, as we have emphasized on several occasions throughout this Report, the Convention is not to be regarded as in any way exclusive in its scope. Now, if such supplementary conventions see the light of day, one negative consequence, feared by some delegations, will have to be avoided, namely that beyond the geographical limits of such agreements, the States concerned will be tempted to interpret the limitations contained in the Convention in a wide sense, thus weakening its scope.[61]

---

59 Voir Doc. trav. No 81 (Proposition du Président avec l'accord des délégations de l'Autriche, de la République fédérale d'Allemagne, de la Suisse et du Royaume-Uni) et P.-v. No 18. Une proposition orale du Rapporteur tendant à étendre la Convention aux situations créées au cours de l'année antérieure à son entrée en vigueur n'a pas été retenue.

60 Par exemple la *Convention relative à la procédure civile, du premier mars 1954*.

61 Voir sur cet article, les Doc. trav. No 70 (Proposition des délégations belge, française et luxembourgeoise) et No 80 (*Proposal of the United States delegation*), ainsi que les P.-v. Nos 15 et 18.

59 See Working Document No 81 (Proposal of the Chairman with the consent of the delegations of Austria, the Federal Republic of Germany, Switzerland and the United Kingdom) and *P.-v.* No 18. An oral proposal of the Reporter that the Convention be extended to cover situations which occurred during the year prior to its entry into force was not accepted.

60 See, for example, the *Convention of 1 March 1954 on civil procedure*.

61 See Working Documents Nos 70 (*Proposition des délégations belge, française et luxembourgeoise*) and 80 (Proposal of the United States delegation) as well as *P.-v.* Nos 16 and 18.

CHAPITRE VI — CLAUSES FINALES

147 Les clauses finales contenues aux articles 37 à 45 de la Convention sont rédigées conformément aux dispositions adoptées à cet effet par les dernières sessions de la Conférence de La Haye. Il n'est donc pas nécessaire d'en faire le commentaire détaillé et nous nous limiterons à quelques brèves remarques à leur propos.

La première concerne l'adaptation des clauses finales à la décision adoptée en ce qui concerne l'ouverture sous condition de la Convention à des Etats non-membres de la Conférence. Ce point ayant été déjà abordé auparavant,[62] il suffit de souligner ici que la nature semi-fermée de la Convention provient du mécanisme de la déclaration d'acceptation par les Etats parties et non pas de l'existence d'une restriction quelconque relative aux Etats pouvant y adhérer (article 38).

148 Quant au «degré» de l'acceptation de la Convention par les Etats qui comprennent deux ou plusieurs unités territoriales dans lesquelles des systèmes de droit différents s'appliquent aux matières régies par la Convention, l'article 40 prévoit qu'ils pourront déclarer – au moment de la signature, de la ratification, de l'acceptation, de l'approbation ou de l'adhésion – que la Convention s'applique à toutes ou seulement à certaines des unités territoriales en question. Cette déclaration pourra être modifiée à tout moment par une autre déclaration plus extensive. En effet, une modification de la déclaration tendant à restreindre l'application de la Convention devrait être considérée comme une dénonciation partielle selon l'article 44, alinéa 3.

D'après l'article 39, la même solution s'applique pour les territoires représentés sur le plan international par certains Etats; en effet, bien que de telles situations soient appelées à disparaître comme une conséquence logique de l'application progressive du principe qui proclame le droit des peuples à disposer d'eux-mêmes, la Conférence a considéré souhaitable de maintenir une clause qui peut encore s'avérer utile.

149 Il convient enfin de dire un mot sur l'article 41, la disposition étant tout à fait nouvelle dans une Convention de La Haye; elle fut introduite, de même d'ailleurs que dans l'autre Convention adoptée lors de la Quatorzième session, à savoir la *Convention tendant à faciliter l'accès international à la justice*, à la demande expresse de la délégation australienne.

Le but de cet article est de préciser que la ratification de la Convention par un Etat n'entraîne aucune conséquence quant à la répartition interne des autorités de cet Etat dans le partage des pouvoirs exécutif, judiciaire et législatif.

La chose semble aller de soi, et c'est bien dans ce sens qu'il faut comprendre l'intervention du chef de la délégation canadienne lors des débats de la Quatrième commission où fut décidée l'introduction de cette disposition dans les deux Conventions (voir P.-v. No 4 de la Séance plénière); la délégation canadienne, exprimant ouvertement l'opinion d'un grand nombre de délégations, estimait l'introduction de cet article dans les deux Conventions comme inutile. L'article 41 fut néanmoins adopté, en grande partie pour donner satisfaction à la délégation australienne, pour qui l'absence d'une telle disposition semblait poser une difficulté constitutionnelle insurmontable.

150 En ce qui concerne le problème des réserves, la Con-

[62] Voir *supra* No 42.

CHAPTER VI— FINAL CLAUSES

147 The final clauses in articles 37 to 45 of the Convention have been drafted in accordance with similar provisions adopted by the most recent sessions of the Hague Conference. No detailed commentary is therefore necessary and we shall make only a few brief comments on them.

Firstly, the adaptation of the final clauses to the decision which was taken on the conditional opening of the Convention to non-Member States. This point has been dealt with earlier,[62] and it is sufficient merely to emphasize here that the 'semi-closed' character of the Convention derives from the means by which States Parties may declare their acceptance and not from any restriction placed on the States which may accede to it (article 38).

148 With regard to the 'degree' of acceptance of the Convention by States which contain two or more territorial units in which different systems of law are applicable to matters dealt with in this Convention, article 40 provides that they may declare – at the time of signature, ratification, acceptance, approval or accession – that the Convention shall extend to all its territorial units or only to one or more of them. Such a declaration can be modified at any time by another more extensive declaration. Actually, any modification of a declaration which tends to limit the applicability of the Convention ought to be regarded as a partial denunciation in terms of article 44, third paragraph.

Under article 39, the same result will occur with regard to States which are responsible for the international relations of other territories. Although such situations are meant to disappear as a logical consequence of the progressive application of the principle which proclaims the right of peoples to self-determination, the Conference felt it advisable to keep a clause which might yet prove to be useful.

149 Finally, a word should be said on article 41, since it contains a wholly novel provision in Hague Conventions. It also appears in the other Convention adopted at the Fourteenth Session, *i.e.* the *Convention on International Access to Justice*, at the express request of the Australian delegation.

This article seeks to make it clear that ratification of the Convention by a State will carry no implication as to the internal distribution of executive, judicial and legislative powers in that State.

This may seem self-evident, and this is the point which the head of the Canadian delegation made during the debates of the Fourth Commission where it was decided to insert such a provision in both Conventions (see *P.-v.* No 4 of the Plenary Session). The Canadian delegation, openly expressing the opinion of a large number of delegations, regarded the insertion of this article in the two Conventions as unnecessary. Nevertheless, article 41 was adopted, largely to satisfy the Australian delegation, for which the absence of such a provision would apparently have created insuperable constitutional difficulties.

150 On the question of reservations, the Convention

[62] See *supra*, No 42.

vention ne permet que celles prévues aux articles 24 et 26. Aucune autre réserve ne sera admise. D'autre part, l'article 42 précise, comme il est habituel, qu'un Etat pourra «à tout moment, retirer une réserve qu'il aura faite».

151 Finalement, il convient de souligner l'importance accrue de l'obligation de notification assumée par le Ministère des Affaires Etrangères du Royaume des Pays-Bas (article 45), dans le contexte d'une convention comme celle-ci, en raison notamment du jeu des déclarations d'acceptation des adhésions éventuelles.

Madrid, avril 1981

ELISA PÉREZ-VERA

allows only those provided for in articles 24 and 26. No other reservation is permitted. Moreover, article 42 sets forth the customary provision whereby a State can 'at any time withdraw a reservation it has made'.

151 Finally, the importance placed on the duty which was assumed by the Ministry of Foreign Affairs of the Kingdom of the Netherlands (article 45) to notify Member States and Contracting States should be emphasized, particularly in view of the role played by declarations of acceptance of future accessions in a convention such as this.

Madrid, April 1981

ELISA PÉREZ-VERA

APPENDIX 3

International Child Abduction Remedies Act

TITLE 22. FOREIGN RELATIONS AND INTERCOURSE

CHAPTER 97. INTERNATIONAL CHILD ABDUCTION REMEDIES

22 USC § 9001 et. seq.
(International Child Abduction Remedies Act – ICARA)

§ 9001. Findings and declarations

(a) Findings. The Congress makes the following findings:

(1) The international abduction or wrongful retention of children is harmful to their well-being.

(2) Persons should not be permitted to obtain custody of children by virtue of their wrongful removal or retention.

(3) International abductions and retentions of children are increasing, and only concerted cooperation pursuant to an international agreement can effectively combat this problem.

(4) The Convention on the Civil Aspects of International Child Abduction, done at The Hague on October 25, 1980, establishes legal rights and procedures for the prompt return of children who have been wrongfully removed or retained, as well as for securing the exercise of visitation rights. Children who are wrongfully removed or retained within the meaning of the Convention are to be promptly returned unless one of the narrow exceptions set forth in the Convention applies. The Convention provides a sound treaty framework to help resolve the problem of international abduction and retention of children and will deter such wrongful removals and retentions.

(b) Declarations. The Congress makes the following declarations:

(1) It is the purpose of this Act to establish procedures for the implementation of the Convention in the United States.

(2) The provisions of this Act are in addition to and not in lieu of the provisions of the Convention.

(3) In enacting this Act the Congress recognizes--

(A) the international character of the Convention; and

(B) the need for uniform international interpretation of the Convention.

(4) The Convention and this Act empower courts in the United States to determine only rights under the Convention and not the merits of any underlying child custody claims.

§ 9002. Definitions

For the purposes of this Act--

(1) the term "applicant" means any person who, pursuant to the Convention, files an application with the United States Central Authority or a Central Authority of any other party to the Convention for the return of a child alleged to have been wrongfully removed or retained or for arrangements for organizing or securing the effective exercise of rights of access pursuant to the Convention;

(2) the term "Convention" means the Convention on the Civil Aspects of International Child Abduction, done at The Hague on October 25, 1980;

(3) the term "Parent Locator Service" means the service established by the Secretary of Health and Human Services under section 453 of the Social Security Act (42 U.S.C. 653);

(4) the term "petitioner" means any person who, in accordance with this Act, files a petition in court seeking relief under the Convention;

(5) the term "person" includes any individual, institution, or other legal entity or body;

(6) the term "respondent" means any person against whose interests a petition is filed in court, in accordance with this Act, which seeks relief under the Convention;

(7) the term "rights of access" means visitation rights;

(8) the term "State" means any of the several States, the District of Columbia, and any commonwealth, territory, or possession of the United States; and

(9) the term "United States Central Authority" means the agency of the Federal Government designated by the President under section 7(a) [22 USCS § 9006(a)].

§ 9003. Judicial remedies

(a) Jurisdiction of the courts. The courts of the States and the United States district courts shall have concurrent original jurisdiction of actions arising under the Convention.

(b) Petitions. Any person seeking to initiate judicial proceedings under the Convention for the return of a child or for arrangements for organizing or securing the effective exercise of rights of access to a child may do so by commencing a civil action by filing a petition for the relief sought in any court which has jurisdiction of such action and which is authorized to exercise its jurisdiction in the place where the child is located at the time the petition is filed.

(c) Notice. Notice of an action brought under subsection (b) shall be given in accordance with the applicable law governing notice in interstate child custody proceedings.

(d) Determination of case. The court in which an action is brought under subsection (b) shall decide the case in accordance with the Convention.

(e) Burdens of proof.

(1) A petitioner in an action brought under subsection (b) shall establish by a preponderance of the evidence--

(A) in the case of an action for the return of a child, that the child has been wrongfully removed or retained within the meaning of the Convention; and

(B) in the case of an action for arrangements for organizing or securing the effective exercise of rights of access, that the petitioner has such rights.

(2) In the case of an action for the return of a child, a respondent who opposes the return of the child has the burden of establishing--

(A) by clear and convincing evidence that one of the exceptions set forth in article 13b or 20 of the Convention applies; and

(B) by a preponderance of the evidence that any other exception set forth in article 12 or 13 of the Convention applies.

(f) Application of the Convention. For purposes of any action brought under this Act--

(1) the term "authorities", as used in article 15 of the Convention to refer to the authorities of the state of the habitual residence of a child, includes courts and appropriate government agencies;

(2) the terms "wrongful removal or retention" and "wrongfully removed or retained", as used in the Convention, include a removal or retention of a child before the entry of a custody order regarding that child; and

(3) the term "commencement of proceedings", as used in article 12 of the Convention, means, with respect to

the return of a child located in the United States, the filing of a petition in accordance with subsection (b) of this section.

(g) Full faith and credit. Full faith and credit shall be accorded by the courts of the States and the courts of the United States to the judgment of any other such court ordering or denying the return of a child, pursuant to the Convention, in an action brought under this Act.

(h) Remedies under the Convention not exclusive. The remedies established by the Convention and this Act shall be in addition to remedies available under other laws or international agreements.

§ 9004. Provisional remedies

(a) Authority of courts. In furtherance of the objectives of article 7(b) and other provisions of the Convention, and subject to the provisions of subsection (b) of this section, any court exercising jurisdiction of an action brought under section 4(b) of this Act [42 USCS § 11630(b)] may take or cause to be taken measures under Federal or State law, as appropriate, to protect the well-being of the child involved or to prevent the child's further removal or concealment before the final disposition of the petition.

(b) Limitation on authority. No court exercising jurisdiction of an action brought under section 4(b) [22 USCS § 9003(b)] may, under subsection (a) of this section, order a child removed from a person having physical control of the child unless the applicable requirements of State law are satisfied.

§ 9005. Admissibility of documents

With respect to any application to the United States Central Authority, or any petition to a court under section 4 [22 USCS § 9003], which seeks relief under the Convention, or any other documents or information included with such application or petition or provided after such submission which relates to the application or petition, as the case may be, no authentication of such application, petition, document, or information shall be required in order for the application, petition, document, or information to be admissible in court.

§ 9006. United States Central Authority

(a) Designation. The President shall designate a Federal agency to serve as the Central Authority for the United States under the Convention.

(b) Functions. The functions of the United States Central Authority are those ascribed to the Central Authority by the Convention and this Act.

(c) Regulatory authority. The United States Central Authority is authorized to issue such regulations as may be necessary to carry out its functions under the Convention and this Act.

(d) Obtaining information from Parent Locator Service. The United States Central Authority may, to the extent authorized by the Social Security Act [42 USCS §§ 301 et seq.], obtain information from the Parent Locator Service.

(e) Grant authority. The United States Central Authority is authorized to make grants to, or enter into contracts or agreements with, any individual, corporation, other Federal, State, or local agency, or private entity or organization in the United States for purposes of accomplishing its responsibilities under the Convention and this Act.

(f) Limited liability of private entities acting under the direction of the United States Central Authority.

(1) Limitation on liability. Except as provided in paragraphs (2) and (3), a private entity or organization that receives a grant from or enters into a contract or agreement with the United States Central Authority under subsection (e) of this section for purposes of assisting the United States Central Authority in carrying out its responsibilities and functions under the Convention and this Act, including any director, officer, employee, or agent of such entity or organization, shall not be liable in any civil action sounding in tort for damages directly related to the performance of such responsibilities and functions as defined by the regulations issued under subsection (c) of this section that are in effect on October 1, 2004.

(2) Exception for intentional, reckless, or other misconduct. The limitation on liability under paragraph (1) shall not apply in any action in which the plaintiff proves that the private entity, organization, officer, employee, or agent described in paragraph (1), as the case may be, engaged in intentional misconduct or acted, or failed to act, with actual malice, with reckless disregard to a substantial risk of causing injury without legal justification, or for a purpose unrelated to the performance of responsibilities or functions under this Act.

(3) Exception for ordinary business activities. The limitation on liability under paragraph (1) shall not apply to any alleged act or omission related to an ordinary business activity, such as an activity involving general administration or operations, the use of motor vehicles, or personnel management.

§ 9007. Costs and fees

(a) Administrative costs. No department, agency, or instrumentality of the Federal Government or of any State or local government may impose on an applicant any fee in relation to the administrative processing of applications submitted under the Convention.

(b) Costs incurred in civil actions.

(1) Petitioners may be required to bear the costs of legal counsel or advisors, court costs incurred in connection with their petitions, and travel costs for the return of the child involved and any accompanying persons, except as provided in paragraphs (2) and (3).

(2) Subject to paragraph (3), legal fees or court costs incurred in connection with an action brought under section 4 [22 USCS § 9003] shall be borne by the petitioner unless they are covered by payments from Federal, State, or local legal assistance or other programs.

(3) Any court ordering the return of a child pursuant to an action brought under section 4 [22 USCS § 9003] shall order the respondent to pay necessary expenses incurred by or on behalf of the petitioner, including court costs, legal fees, foster home or other care during the course of proceedings in the action, and transportation costs related to the return of the child, unless the respondent establishes that such order would be clearly inappropriate.

§ 9008. Collection, maintenance, and dissemination of information

(a) In general. In performing its functions under the Convention, the United States Central Authority may, under such conditions as the Central Authority prescribes by regulation, but subject to subsection (c), receive from or transmit to any department, agency, or instrumentality of the Federal Government or of any State or foreign government, and receive from or transmit to any applicant, petitioner, or respondent, information necessary to locate a child or for the purpose of otherwise implementing the Convention with respect to a child, except that the United States Central Authority--

(1) may receive such information from a Federal or State department, agency, or instrumentality only pursuant to applicable Federal and State statutes; and

(2) may transmit any information received under this subsection notwithstanding any provision of law other than this Act.

(b) Requests for information. Requests for information under this section shall be submitted in such manner and form as the United States Central Authority may prescribe by regulation and shall be accompanied or supported by such documents as the United States Central Authority may require.

(c) Responsibility of government entities. Whenever any department, agency, or instrumentality of the United States or of any State receives a request from the United States Central Authority for information authorized to be provided to such Central Authority under subsection (a), the head of such department, agency, or instrumentality shall promptly cause a search to be made of the files and records maintained by such department, agency, or instrumentality in order to determine whether the information requested is contained in any such files or records. If such search discloses the information requested, the head of such department, agency, or instrumentality shall immediately transmit such information to the United States Central Authority, except that any such information the disclosure of which--

(1) would adversely affect the national security interests of the United States or the law enforcement interests of the United States or of any State; or

(2) would be prohibited by section 9 of title 13, United States Code;

shall not be transmitted to the Central Authority. The head of such department, agency, or instrumentality shall, immediately upon completion of the requested search, notify the Central Authority of the results of the search, and whether an exception set forth in paragraph (1) or (2) applies. In the event that the United States Central Authority receives information and the appropriate Federal or State department, agency, or instrumentality thereafter notifies the Central Authority that an exception set forth in paragraph (1) or (2) applies to that information, the Central Authority may not disclose that information under subsection (a).

(d) Information available from Parent Locator Service. To the extent that information which the United States Central Authority is authorized to obtain under the provisions of subsection (c) can be obtained through the Parent Locator Service, the United States Central Authority shall first seek to obtain such information from the Parent Locator Service, before requesting such information directly under the provisions of subsection (c) of this section.

(e) Recordkeeping. The United States Central Authority shall maintain appropriate records concerning its activities and the disposition of cases brought to its attention.

§ 9009. Office of Children's Issues

(a) Director requirements. The Secretary of State shall fill the position of Director of the Office of Children's Issues of the Department of State (in this section referred to as the "Office") with an individual of senior rank who can ensure long-term continuity in the management and policy matters of the Office and has a strong background in consular affairs.

(b) Case officer staffing. Effective April 1, 2000, there shall be assigned to the Office of Children's Issues of the Department of State a sufficient number of case officers to ensure that the average caseload for each officer does not exceed 75.

(c) Embassy contact. The Secretary of State shall designate in each United States diplomatic mission an employee who shall serve as the point of contact for matters relating to international abductions of children by parents. The Director of the Office shall regularly inform the designated employee of children of United States citizens abducted by parents to that country.

(d) Reports to parents.

(1) In general. Except as provided in paragraph (2), beginning 6 months after the date of enactment of this Act [enacted Nov. 29, 1999], and at least once every 6 months thereafter, the Secretary of State shall report to each parent who has requested assistance regarding an abducted child overseas. Each such report shall include information on the current status of the abducted child's case and the efforts by the Department of State to resolve the case.

(2) Exception. The requirement in paragraph (1) shall not apply in a case of an abducted child if--

(A) the case has been closed and the Secretary of State has reported the reason the case was closed to the parent who requested assistance; or

(B) the parent seeking assistance requests that such reports not be provided.

§ 9010. Interagency coordinating group

The Secretary of State, the Secretary of Health and Human Services, and the Attorney General shall designate Federal employees and may, from time to time, designate private citizens to serve on an interagency coordinating group to monitor the operation of the Convention and to provide advice on its implementation to the United States Central Authority and other Federal agencies. This group shall meet from time to time at the request of the United States Central Authority. The agency in which the United States Central Authority is located is authorized to reimburse such private citizens for travel and other expenses incurred in participating at meetings of the interagency coordinating group at rates not to exceed those authorized under subchapter I of chapter 57 of title 5, United States Code [5 USCS §§ 5701 et seq.], for employees of agencies.

§ 9011. Authorization of appropriations

There are authorized to be appropriated for each fiscal year such sums as may be necessary to carry out the purposes of the Convention and this Act.

APPENDIX 4

State Department Legal Analysis

INTERNATIONAL PARENTAL ABDUCTION

The Hague Convention on the Civil Aspects of International Child Abduction

Legal Analysis

(51 Federal Register 10494)

Introduction

The Hague Convention on the Civil Aspects of International Child Abduction (Hague Abduction Convention) is the primary civil law mechanism for parents seeking the return of the children from other treaty partner countries. Countries that are party to the Convention have agreed that a child who was living in one Convention country, and who has been removed to or retained in another Convention country in violation of the left-behind parent's custodial rights, shall be promptly returned. Once the child has been returned, the custody dispute can then be resolved, if necessary, in the courts of that jurisdiction. The Convention does not address who should have custody of the child; it addresses where the custody case should be heard.

Each country party to the Convention designates a Central Authority, a specific government office, to carry out specialized Convention duties. Central Authorities communicate with each other and they assist parents in filing applications for return of or for access to their children under the Convention. The Department of State is the U.S. Central Authority for the Convention. The Department's Office of Children's Issues within the Bureau of Consular Affairs is responsible for administering the day-to-day functions of the U.S. Central Authority.

The Hague Abduction Convention consists of six chapters containing forty-five articles. This legal analysis was prepared to facilitate understanding of the Convention by the Senate and the use and interpretation of the Convention by parents, judges, lawyers and public and private agency personnel. The articles are analyzed and discussed in the categories outlined in the table of contents below.

For more information, please contact AskCI@state.gov.

For more information please see our website at travel.state.gov

A. International "child abduction" not criminal: Hague Convention distinguished from extradition treaties (Article 12)

B. "Wrongful removal or retention" (Articles 1, 3, 5(a))

1. Holders of rights protected by the Convention (*i.e.*, with respect to whom the removal or retention is wrongful)

(a) "Person, institution or other body" (Article 3(a), (b))

(b) "Jointly or alone" (Article 3(a), (b))

2. Defined

(a) Breach of "custody rights" (Articles 3(a), 5(a))

(b) "Custody rights" determined by law of child's habitual residence (Articles 3(a), 31, 32, 33)

(c) Sources of "Custody rights" (Article 3, last paragraph)

i. Operation of law (Articles 3, 15)

ii. Judicial or administrative decision (Article 3)

iii. Agreement having legal effect (Article 3)

(d) "Actually exercised" (Articles 3(b), 5, 8(c), 13)

III. Judicial Proceedings for Return of the Child

A. Right to seek return (Articles 29, 12, 34, 8)

B. Legal advice and costs (Articles 25, 26, 42)

C. Pleading requirements (Articles 8, 24)

D. Admissibility of evidence (Articles 30, 23)

E. Judicial promptitude/status report (Article 11)

F. Judicial notice (Article 14)

G. Court determination of "wrongfulness" (Articles 15, 3, 11, 12, 14)

H. Constraints upon courts in requested states in making substantive custody decisions (Article 16)

I. Duty to return not absolute

  1. Temporal qualifications

    (a) Article 4

    (b) Article 35

    (c) Article 12

  2. Article 13 limitations on return obligation

    (a) Legislative history (Articles 13, 20)

    (b) Non exercise of custody rights (Articles 13(a), 3(b))

    (c) Grave risk of harm/intolerable situation (Article 13(b))

    (d) Child's preference (Article 13)

    (e) Role of social studies

  3. Article 20

  4. Custody order no defense to return (Article 17)

J. Return of the child (Article 12)

  1. Return order not on custody merits (Article 19)

  2. Costs, fees and expenses shifted to abductor (Article 26)

IV. Central Authority

(Articles 1, 10, 21)

A. Establishment of Central Authority (Article 6)

B. Duties (Article 7)

C. Other Tasks (Articles 8, 9, 10, 11, 15, 21, 26, 27, 28)

  1. Processing applications (Articles 8, 9, 27, 28)

  2. Assistance in connection with judicial proceedings

    (a) Request for status report (Article 11)

    (b) Social studies/background reports (Article 13)

    (c) Determination of "wrongfulness" (Article 15)

(d) Costs (Article 26), reservation (Articles 42, 22)

V. Access Rights -- Article 21

A. Remedies for breach (Articles 21, 12)

B. Defined (Article 5(b))

C. Procedure for obtaining relief (Articles 21, 8, 7)

D. Alternative remedies (Articles 18, 29, 34)

VI. Miscellaneous and Final Clauses

A. Article 36

B. Articles 37 and 38

C. Articles 42, 43 and 44

D. Articles 39 and 40

E. Article 41

F. Article 45

Recommended Return Application Form

Bibliography

Guide to Terminology Used in the Legal Analysis

"*Abduction*" as used in the Convention title is not intended in a criminal sense. That term is shorthand for the phrase "wrongful removal or retention" which appears throughout the text, beginning with the preambular language and Article 1. Generally speaking, "*wrongful removal*" refers to the taking of a child from the person who was actually exercising custody of the child. "*Wrongful retention*" refers to the act of keeping the child without the consent of the person who was actually exercising custody. The archetype of this conduct is the refusal by the noncustodial parent to return a child at the end of an authorized visitation period. "Wrongful retention" is not intended by this Convention to cover refusal by the custodial parent to permit visitation by the other parent. Such obstruction of visitation may be redressed in accordance with Article 21.

The term "*abductor*" as used in this analysis refers to the person alleged to have wrongfully removed or retained a child. This person is also referred to as the "alleged wrongdoer" or the "respondent."

The term "*person*" as used in this analysis includes the person, institution or other body who (or which) actually exercised custody prior to the abduction and is seeking the child's return. The "person" seeking the child's return is also referred to as "applicant" and "petitioner."

The terms "*court*" and "*judicial authority*" are used throughout the analysis to mean both judicial and administrative bodies empowered to make decisions on petitions made pursuant to this Convention. "Judicial decree" and "court order" likewise include decisions made by courts or administrative bodies.

"*Country of origin*" and "*requesting country*" refer to the child's country ("State") of habitual residence prior to the wrongful removal or retention. "*Country addressed*" refers to the country ("State") where the child is located or the country to which the child is believed to have been taken. It is in that country that a judicial or administrative proceeding for return would be brought.

"*Access rights*" correspond to "*visitation rights.*"

References to the "reporter" are to Elisa Perez-Vera, the official Hague Conference reporter for the Convention. Her explanatory report is recognized by the Conference as the official history and commentary on the Convention and is a source of background on the meaning of the provisions of the Convention available to all States becoming parties to it. It is referred to herein as the "Perez-Vera Report." The Perez-Vera Report appears in *Actes et documents de la Quatorzieme Session (1980), Volume III, Child Abduction,* edited by the Permanent Bureau of the Hague Conference on Private International Law, The Hague, Netherlands. (The volume may be ordered from the Netherlands Government Printing and Publishing Office, 1 Christoffel Plantijnstraat, Postbox 20014, 2500 EA The Hague, Netherlands.)

I. Children Protected by the Convention

A fundamental purpose of the Hague Convention is to protect children from wrongful international removals or retentions by persons bent on obtaining their physical and/or legal custody. Children who are wrongfully moved from country to country are deprived of the stable relationships which the Convention is designed promptly to restore. Contracting States are obliged by Article 2 to take all appropriate measures to implement the objectives of the Convention as set forth in Article 1: (1) To secure the prompt return of children wrongfully removed to or retained in any Contracting State; and (2) to ensure that rights of custody and of access under the law of one Contracting State are effectively respected in other Contracting States. While these objectives are universal in their appeal, the Convention does not cover all children who might be victims of wrongful takings or retentions. A threshold inquiry, therefore, is whether the child who has been abducted or retained is subject to the Convention's provisions. Only if the child falls within the scope of the Convention will the administrative and judicial mechanisms of the Convention apply.

A. Age

The Convention applies only to children under the age of sixteen (16). Even if a child is under sixteen at the time of the wrongful removal or retention as well as when the Convention is invoked, the Convention ceases to apply when the child reaches sixteen. Article 4.

Absent action by governments to expand coverage of the Convention to children aged sixteen and above pursuant to Article 36, the Convention itself is unavailable as the legal vehicle for securing return of a child sixteen or older. However, it does not bar return of such child by other means.

Articles 18, 29 and 34 make clear that the Convention is a nonexclusive remedy in cases of international child abduction. Article 18 provides that the Convention does not limit the power of a judicial authority to order return of a child at any time, presumably under other laws, procedures or comity, irrespective of the child's age. Article 29 permits the person who claims a breach of custody or access rights, as defined by Articles 3 and 21, to bypass the Convention completely by invoking any applicable laws or procedures to secure the child's return. Likewise, Article 34 provides that the Convention shall not restrict the application of any law in the State addressed for purposes of obtaining the child's return or for organizing visitation rights. Assuming such laws are not restricted to children under sixteen, a child sixteen or over may be returned pursuant to their provisions.

Notwithstanding the general application of the Convention to children under sixteen, it should be noted that the wishes of mature children regarding their return are not ignored by the Convention. Article 13 permits, but does not require, the judicial authority to refuse to order the child returned if the child "objects to being returned and has attained an age and degree of maturity at which it is appropriate to take account of its views." The role of the child's preference in return proceedings is discussed further at III.I(2)(d), *infra*.

B. Residence

In order for the Convention to apply the child must have been "habitually resident in a Contracting State immediately before any breach of custody or access rights." Article 4. In practical terms, the Convention may be invoked only where the child was habitually resident in a Contracting State and taken to or retained in another Contracting State. Accordingly, child abduction and retention cases are actionable under the Convention if they are international in nature (as opposed to interstate), and provided the Convention has entered into force for both countries involved. *See* discussion of Article 38, VI.B, *infra*.

To illustrate, take the case of a child abducted to California from his home in New York. The Convention could not be invoked to secure the return of such child. This is true even if one of the child's parents is an American citizen and the other a foreign national. The Uniform Child Custody Jurisdiction Act (UCCJA) and/or the Parental Kidnapping Prevention Act (PKPA), domestic state and federal law, respectively, would govern the return of the child in question. If the same child were removed from New York to Canada, application under the Convention could be made to secure the child's return provided the Convention had entered into force both for the United States and the Canadian province to which the child was taken. An alternative remedy might also lie under other Canadian law. If the child had been removed from Canada and taken to the United States, the aggrieved custodial parent in Canada could seek to secure the child's return by petitioning for enforcement of a Canadian custody order pursuant to the UCCJA, or by invoking the Convention, or both.

C. Timing/Cases Covered

Article 35 states that the Convention shall apply as between Contracting States only to wrongful removals or retentions occurring after its entry into force in those States. Following a strict interpretation of that Article, the Convention will not apply to a child who is wrongfully shifted from one Contracting State to another if the wrongful removal or retention occurred before the Convention's entry into force in those States. However, under a liberal interpretation Article 35 could be construed to cover wrongful removal or retention cases which began before the Convention took effect but which continued and were ongoing after its entry into force.

D. Effect of Custody Order Concerning the Child

1. Existing Custody Orders

Children who otherwise fall within the scope of the Convention are not automatically removed from its protections by virtue of a judicial decision awarding custody to the alleged wrongdoer. This is true whether the decision as to custody was made, or is entitled to recognition, in the State to which the child has been taken. Under Article 17 that State cannot refuse to return a child solely on the basis of a court order awarding custody to the alleged wrongdoer made by one of its own courts or by the courts of another country. This provision is intended to ensure, *inter alia,* that the Convention takes precedence over decrees made in favor of abductors before the court had notice of the wrongful removal or retention.

Thus, under Article 17 the person who wrongfully removes or retains the child in a Contracting State cannot insulate the child from the Convention's return provisions merely by obtaining a custody order in the country of new residence, or by seeking there to enforce another country's order. Nor may the alleged wrongdoer rely upon a stale decree awarding him or her custody, the provisions of which have been derogated from subsequently by agreement or acquiescence of the parties, to prevent the child's return under the Convention. Article 3.

It should be noted that Article 17 does permit a court to take into account the reasons underlying an existing custody decree when it applies the Convention.

2. *Pre-Decree Removals or Retentions*

Children who are wrongfully removed or retained prior to the entry of a custody order are protected by the Convention. There need not be a custody order in effect in order to invoke the Convention's return provisions. Accordingly, under the Convention a child will be ordered returned to the person with whom he or she was habitually resident in pre-decree abduction cases as well as in cases involving violations of existing custody orders.

Application of the Convention to pre-decree cases comes to grips with the reality that many children are abducted or retained long before custody actions have been initiated. In this manner a child is not prejudiced by the legal inaction of his or her physical custodian, who may not have anticipated the abduction, and the abductor is denied any legal advantage since the child is subject to the return provisions of the Convention.

The Convention's treatment of pre-decree abduction cases is distinguishable from the Council of Europe's Convention on Recognition and Enorcement of Decisions Relating to the Custody of Children, adopted in Strasbourg, France in November 1979 ("Strasbourg Convention"), and from domestic law in the United States, specifically the UCCJA and the PKPA, all of which provide for enforcement of custody decrees. Although the UCCJA and PKPA permit enforcement of a decree obtained by a parent in the home state after the child has been removed from that state, in the absence of such decree the enforcement provisions of those laws are inoperative. In contrast to the restoration of the *legal* status quo ante brought about by application of the UCCJA, the PKPA, and the Strasbourg Convention, the Hague Convention seeks restoration of the *factual* status quo ante and is not contingent on the existence of a custody decree. The Convention is premised upon the notion that the child should be promptly restored to his or her country of habitual residence so that a court there can examine the merits of the custody dispute and award custody in the child's best interests.

Pre-decree abductions are discussed in greater detail in the section dealing with actionable conduct. *See* II.B(2)(c)(i).

II. Conduct Actionable Under the Convention

A. "International Child Abduction" Not Criminal: Hague Convention Distinguished From Extradition Treaties

Despite the use of the term "abduction" in its title, the Hague Convention is not an extradition treaty. The conduct made actionable by the Convention -- the wrongful removal or retention of children -- is wrongful not in a criminal sense but in a civil sense.

The Hague Convention establishes civil procedures to secure the return of so-called "abducted" children. Article 12. In this manner the Hague Convention seeks to satisfy the overriding concern of the aggrieved parent. The Convention is not concerned with the question of whether the person found to have wrongfully removed or retained the child returns to the child's country of habitual residence once the child has been returned pursuant to the Convention. This is in contrast to the criminal extradition process which is designed to secure the return of the fugitive wrong-doer. Indeed, when the fugitive-parent is extradited for trial or to serve a criminal sentence, there is no guarantee that the abducted child will also be returned.

While it is uncertain whether criminal extradition treaties will be routinely invoked in international custody cases between countries for which the Hague Convention is in force, nothing in the Convention bars their application or use.

B. Wrongful Removal or Retention

The Convention's first stated objective is to secure the prompt return of children who are wrongfully removed from or retained in any Contracting State. Article 1(a). (The second stated objective, i.e., to ensure that rights of custody and of access under the law of one Contracting State are effectively exercised in other Contracting States (Article 1(b)), is discussed under the heading "Access Rights," V., *infra.*) The removal or retention must be wrongful within the meaning of Article 3, as further clarified by Article 5(a), in order to trigger the return procedures established by the Convention. Article 3 provides that the removal or retention of a child is to be considered wrongful where:

(a) it is in breach of custody rights attributed to a person, an institution or another body, either jointly or alone, under the law of the State in which the child was habitually resident immediately before the removal or retention; and (b) at the time of the removal or retention those rights were actually exercised, either jointly or alone, or would have been so exercised but for the removal or retention.

This Article is a cornerstone of the Convention. It is analyzed by examining two questions:

1.) Who holds rights protected by the Convention (or, with respect to whom is the removal or retention deemed to be wrongful?); and

2.) What are the factual and legal elements of a wrongful removal or retention?

1. Holders of Rights Protected by the Convention

(a) *"Person, institution or other body".* While the child is the ultimate beneficiary of the Convention's judicial and administrative machinery, the child's role under the Convention is passive. In contrast, it is up to the "person, institution or other body" (hereinafter referred to simply as "the person") who "actually exercised" custody of the child prior to the abduction, or who would have exercised custody but for the abduction, to invoke the Convention to secure the child's return. Article 3 (a), (b). It is this person who holds the rights protected by the Convention and who has the right to seek relief pursuant to its terms.

Since the vast majority of abduction cases arises in the context of divorce or separation, the person envisioned by Article 3(a) most often will be the child's parent. The typical scenario would involve one parent taking a child from one Contracting State to another Contracting State over objections of the parent with whom the child had been living.

However, there may be situations in which a person other than a biological parent has actually been exercising custody of the child and is therefore eligible to seek the child's return pursuant to the Convention. An example would be a grandparent who has had physical custody of a child following the death of the parent with whom the child had been residing. If the child is subsequently removed from the custody of the grandparent by the surviving parent, the aggrieved grandparent could invoke the Convention to secure the child's return. In another situation, the child may be in the care of foster parents. If custody rights exercised by the foster parents are breached, for instance, by abduction of the child by its biological parent, the foster parents could invoke the Convention to secure the child's return.

In the two foregoing examples (not intended to be exhaustive) a family relationship existed between the victim-child and the person who had the right to seek the child's return. However, institutions such as public or private child care agencies also may have custody rights the breach of which would be remediable under the Convention. If a natural parent relinquishes parental rights to a child and the child is subsequently placed in the care of an adoption agency, that agency may invoke the Convention to recover the child if the child is abducted by its parent(s).

(b) *"Jointly or alone".* Article 3 (a) and (b) recognize that custody rights may be held either jointly or alone. Two persons, typically mother and father, can exercise joint custody, either by court order following a custody adjudication, or by operation of law prior to the entry of a decree. The Convention does not distinguish between these two situations, as the commentary of the Convention reporter indicates:

Now, from the Convention's standpoint, the removal of a child by one of the joint holders without the consent of the other, is wrongful, and this wrongfulness derives in this particular case, not from some action in breach of a particular law, but from the fact that such action has disregarded the rights of the other parent which are also protected by law, and has interfered with their normal exercise. The Convention's true nature is revealed most clearly in these situations: it is not concerned with establishing the person to whom custody of the child will belong at some point in the future, nor with the situations in which it may prove necessary to modify a decision awarding joint custody on the basis of facts which have subsequently changed. It seeks, more simply, to prevent a later decision on the matter being influenced by a change of circumstances brought about through unilateral action by one of the parties. Perez-Vera Report, paragraph 71 at 447-448.

Article 3(a) ensures the application of the Convention to pre-decree abductions, since it protects the rights of a parent who was exercising custody of the child jointly with the abductor at the time of the abduction, before the issuance of a custody decree.

2. *"Wrongful Removal or Retention" Defined*

The obligation to return an abducted child to the person entitled to custody arises only if the removal or the retention is wrongful within the meaning of the Convention. To be considered wrongful, certain factual and legal elements must be present.

(a) *Breach of "custody rights".* The removal or retention must be in breach of "custody rights," defined in Article 5(a) as "rights relating to the care of the person of the child and, in particular, the right to determine the child's place of residence."

Accordingly, a parent who sends his or her child to live with a caretaker has not relinquished custody rights but rather has exercised them within the meaning of the Convention. Likewise, a parent hospitalized for a protracted period who places the child with grandparents or other relatives for the duration of the illness has effectively exercised custody

(b) *"Custody rights" determined by law of child's habitual residence.* In addition to including the right to determine the child's residence (Article 5(a)), the term "custody rights" covers a collection of rights which take on more specific meaning by reference to the law of the country in which the child was habitually resident immediately before the removal or retention. Article 3(a). Nothing in the Convention limits this "law" to the internal law of the State of the child's habitual residence. Consequently, it could include the laws of another State if the choice of law rules in the State of habitual residence so indicate.

If a country has more than one territorial unit, the habitual residence refers to the particular territorial unit in which the child was resident, and the applicable laws are those in effect in that territorial unit. Article 31. In the United States, the law in force in the state in which a child was habitually resident (as possibly preempted by federal legislation enacted in connection with U.S. ratification of the Convention) would be applicable for the determination as to whether a removal or retention is wrongful.

Articles 32 and 33 also control, respectively, how and whether the Convention applies in States with more than one legal system. Perez-Vera Report, paragraphs 141 and 142 at 470.

(c) *Sources of "custody rights".* Although the Convention does not exhaustively list all possible sources from which custody rights may derive, it does identify three sources. According to the final paragraph of Article 3, custody rights may arise: (1) by operation of law; (2) by reason of a judicial or administrative decision; or (3) by reason of an agreement having legal effect under the law of that State.

i. *Custody rights arising by operation of law.* Custody rights which arise by operation of law in the State of habitual residence are protected; they need not be conferred by court order to fall within the scope of the Convention. Article 3. Thus, a person whose child is abducted prior to the entry of a custody order is not required to obtain a custody order in the State of the child's habitual residence as a prerequisite to invoking the Convention's return provisions.

In the United States, as a general proposition both parents have equal rights of custody of their children prior to the issuance of a court order allocating rights between them. If one parent interferes with the other's equal rights by unilaterally removing or retaining the child abroad without consent of the other parent, such interference could constitute wrongful conduct within the meaning of the Convention. (See excerpts from Perez-Vera Report quoted at II.B.1(b), *supra.*) Thus, a parent left in the United States after a pre-decree abduction could seek return of a child from a Contracting State abroad pursuant to the Convention. In cases involving children wrongfully brought to or retained in the United States from a Contracting State abroad prior to the entry of a decree, in the absence of an agreement between the parties the question of wrongfulness would be resolved by looking to the law of the child's country of habitual residence.

Although a custody decree is not needed to invoke the Convention, there are two situations in which the aggrieved parent may nevertheless benefit by securing a custody order, assuming the courts can hear swiftly a petition for custody. First, to the extent that an award of custody to the left-behind parent (or other person) is based in part upon an express finding by the court that the child's removal or retention was wrongful within the meaning of Article 3, the applicant anticipates a possible request by the judicial authority applying the Convention, pursuant to Article 15, for a court determination of wrongfulness. This may accelerate disposition of a return petition under the Convention. Second, a person outside the United States who obtains a custody decree from a foreign court subsequent to the child's abduction, after notice and opportunity to be heard have been accorded to the absconding parent, may be able to invoke either the Convention or the UCCJA. or both, to secure the child's return from the United States. The UCCJA may be preferable inasmuch as its enforcement provisions are not subject to the exceptions contained in the Convention.

ii. *Custody rights arising by reason of judicial or administrative decision.* Custody rights embodied in judicial or administrative decisions fall within the Convention's scope. While custody determinations in the United States are made by state courts, in some Contracting States, notably the Scandinavian countries, administrative bodies are empowered to decide matters relating to child custody including the allocation of custody and visitation rights. Hence the reference to "administrative decisions" in Article 3.

The language used in this part of the Convention can be misleading. Even when custody rights are conferred by court decree, technically speaking the Convention does not mandate recognition and enforcement of that decree. Instead, it seeks only to restore the factual custody arrangements that existed prior to the wrongful removal or retention (which incidentally in many cases will be the same as those specified by court order).

Finally, the court order need not have been made by a court in the State of the child's habitual residence. It could be one originating from a third country. As the reporter points out, when custody rights were exercised in the State of the child's habitual residence on the basis of a foreign decree, the Convention does not require that the decree have been formally recognized. Perez-Vera Report, paragraph 69 at 447.

iii. *Custody rights arising by reason of agreement having legal effect.* Parties who enter into a private agreement concerning a child's custody have recourse under the Convention if those custody rights are breached. Article 3. The only limitation is that the agreement have legal effect under the law of the child's habitual residence.

Comments of the United States with respect to language contained in an earlier draft of the Convention (*i.e.,* that the agreement "have the force of law") shed some light on the meaning of the expression "an agreement having legal effect". In the U.S. view, the provision should be interpreted expansively to cover more than only those agreements that have been incorporated in or referred to in a custody judgment. *Actes et documents de la Quatorzieme Session, (1980) Volume III. Child Abduction,* Comments of Governments at 240. The reporter's observations affirm a broad interpretation of this provision:

As regards the definition of an agreement which has "legal effect" in terms of a particular law, it seems that there must be included within it any sort of agreement which is not prohibited by such a law and which may provide a basis for presenting a legal claim to the competent authorities. Perez-Vera Report, paragraph 70 at 447.

(d) *"Actually exercised".* The most predictable fact pattern under the Convention will involve the abduction of a child directly from the parent who was actually exercising physical custody at the time of the abduction.

To invoke the Convention, the holder of custody rights must allege that he or she actually exercised those rights at the time of the breach or would have exercised them but for the breach. Article 3(b). Under Article 5, custody rights are defined to include the right to determine the child's place of residence. Thus, if a child is abducted from the physical custody of the person in whose care the child has been entrusted by the custodial parent who was "actually exercising" custody, it is the parent who placed the child who may make application under the Convention for the child's return.

Very little is required of the applicant in support of the allegation that custody rights have actually been or would have been exercised. The applicant need only provide some preliminary evidence that he or she actually exercised custody of the child, for instance, took physical care of the child. Perez-Vera Report, paragraph 73 at 448. The Report points out the informal nature of the pleading and proof requirements; Article 8(c) merely requires a statement in the application to the Central Authority as to "the grounds on which the applicant's claim for return of the child is based." *Id.*

In the scheme of the Convention it is presumed that the person who has custody actually exercised it. Article 13 places on the alleged abductor the burden of proving the nonexercise of custody rights by the applicant as an exception to the return obligation. Here, again, the reporter's comments are insightful:

Thus, we may conclude that the Convention, taken as a whole, is built upon the tacit presumption that the person who has care of the child actually exercises custody over it. This idea has to be overcome by discharging the burden of proof which has shifted, as is normal with any presumption (*i.e.* discharged by the "abductor" if he wishes to prevent the return of the child.) Perez-Vera Report paragraph 73 at 449.

III. Judicial Proceedings for Return of Child

A. Right to Seek Return

When a person's custody rights have been breached by the wrongful removal or retention of the child by another, he or she can seek return of the child pursuant to the Convention. This right of return is the core of the Convention. The Convention establishes two means by which the child may be returned. One is through direct application by the aggrieved person to a court in the Contracting State to which the child has been taken or in which the child is being kept. Articles 12, 29. The other is through application to the Central Authority to be established by every Contracting State. Article 8. These remedies are not mutually exclusive; the aggrieved person may invoke either or both of them. Moreover, the aggrieved person may also pursue remedies outside the Convention. Articles 18, 29 and 34. This part of the report describes the Convention's judicial remedy in detail. The administrative remedy is discussed in IV, *infra.*

Articles 12 and 29 authorize any person who claims a breach of custody rights within the meaning of Article 3 to apply for the child's return directly to the judicial authorities of the Contracting State where the child is located.

A petition for return pursuant to the Convention may be filed any time after the child has been removed or retained up until the child reaches sixteen. While the window of time for filing may be wide in a particular case without threat of technically losing rights under the Convention, there are numerous reasons to commence a return proceeding promptly if the likelihood of a voluntary return is remote. The two most crucial reasons are to preclude adjudication of custody on the merits in a country other than the child's habitual residence (see discussion of Article 16, *infra*) and to maximize the chances for the child's return by reducing the alleged abductor's opportunity to establish that the child is settled in a new environment (see discussion of Article 12, *infra*).

A petition for return would be made directly to the appropriate court in the Contracting State where the child is located. If the return proceedings are commenced less than one year from the date of the wrongful removal or retention, Article 12 requires the court to order the return of the child forthwith. If the return proceedings are commenced a year or more after the alleged wrongful removal or retention, the court remains obligated by Article 12 to order the child returned unless it is demonstrated that the child is settled in its new environment.

Under Article 29 a person is not precluded from seeking judicially-ordered return of a child pursuant to laws and procedures other than the Convention. Indeed, Articles 18 and 34 make clear that nothing in the Convention limits the power of a court to return a child at any time by applying other laws and procedures conducive to that end.

Accordingly, a parent seeking return of a child from the United States could petition for return pursuant to the Convention, or in the alternative or additionally, for enforcement of a foreign court order pursuant to the UCCJA. For instance, an English father could petition courts in New York either for return of his child under the Convention and/or for recognition and enforcement of his British custody decree pursuant to the UCCJA. If he prevailed in either situation, the respective court could order the child returned to him in England. The father in this illustration may find the UCCJA remedy swifter than invoking the Convention for the child's return because it is not subject to the exceptions set forth in the Convention, discussed at III.I., *infra.*

B. Legal Advice and Costs

Article 25 provides for the extension of legal aid and advice to foreign applicants on the same basis and subject only to the same eligibility requirements as for nationals of the country in which that aid is sought.

Article 26 prohibits Central Authorities from charging applicants for the cost and expenses of the proceedings or, where applicable, those arising from the participation of legal counsel or advisers. This provision will be of no help to an applicant, however, if the Contracting State in question has made a reservation in accordance with Articles 26 and 42 declaring that it shall not be bound to assume any costs resulting from the participation of legal counsel or advisers or from court proceedings, except insofar as those costs may be covered by its system of legal aid and advice.

It is expected that the United States will enter a reservation in accordance with Articles 26 and 42. This will place at least the initial burden of paying for counsel and legal proceedings on the applicant rather than on the federal government. Because the reservation is nonreciprocal, use of it will not automatically operate to deny applicants from the United States free legal services and judicial proceedings in other Contracting States. However, if the Contracting State in which the child is located has itself made use of the reservation in question, the U.S. applicant will not be eligible for cost-free legal representation and court proceedings. For more information on costs, including the possibility that the petitioner's costs may be levied on the abductor if the child is ordered returned, see III.J 2 and IV.C (d) of this analysis.

C. Pleading Requirements

The Convention does not expressly set forth pleading requirements that must be satisfied by an applicant who commences a judicial return proceeding. In contrast, Article 8 sets forth the basic requirements for an application placed before a Central Authority (discussed IV.C(1), *infra*) for the return of the child. Since the objective is identical -- the child's return -- whether relief is sought through the courts or through intercession of the Central Authority, it follows that a court should be provided with at least as much information as a Central Authority is to be provided in a return application filed in compliance with Article 8. To ensure that all necessary information is provided, the applicant may wish to append to the petition to the court a completed copy of the recommended model form for return of a child (see Annex A to this analysis).

In addition to providing the information set forth in Article 8, the petition for return should allege that the child was wrongfully removed or retained by the defendant in violation of custody rights that were actually being exercised by the petitioner. The petition should state the source of the custody rights, the date of the wrongful conduct, and the child's age at that time. In the prayer for relief, the petitioner should request the child's return and an order for payment by the abducting or retaining parent of all fees and expenses incurred to secure the child's return.

Any return petition filed in a court in the United States pursuant to the Convention must be in English. Any person in the United States who seeks return of a child from a foreign court must likewise follow the requirements of the foreign state regarding translation of legal documents. See Perez-Vera Report, paragraph 132 at page 467.

D. Admissibility of Evidence

Under Article 30, any application submitted to the Central Authority or petition submitted to the judicial authorities of a Contracting State, and any documents or information appended thereto, are admissible in the courts of the State. Moreover, under Article 23, no legalization or similar formalities may be required. However, authentication of private documents may be required. According to the official report, "any requirement of the internal law of the authorities in question that copies or private documents be authenticated remains outside the scope of this provision." Perez-Vera Report, paragraph 131 at page 467.

E. Judicial Promptitude/Status Report

Once an application for return has been filed, the court is required by Article 11 "to act expeditiously in proceedings for the return of children." To keep matters on the fast track, Article 11 gives the applicant or the Central Authority of the requested State the right to request a statement from the court of the reasons for delay if a decision on the application has not been made within six weeks from the commencement of the proceedings.

F. Judicial Notice

In ascertaining whether there has been a wrongful removal or retention of a child within the meaning of Article 3, Article 14 empowers the court of the requested State to take notice directly of the law and decisions in the State of the child's habitual residence. Standard procedures for the proof of foreign law and for recognition of foreign decisions would not need to be followed and compliance with such procedures is not to be required.

G. Court Determination of "Wrongfulness"

Prior to ordering a child returned pursuant to Article 12, Article 15 permits the court to request the applicant to obtain from the authorities of the child's State of habitual residence a decision or other determination that the alleged removal or retention was wrongful within the meaning of Article 3. Article 15 does not specify which "authorities" may render such a determination. It therefore could include agencies of government (*e.g.*, state attorneys general) and courts. Central Authorities shall assist applicants to obtain such a decision or determination. This request may only be made where such a decision or determination is obtainable in that State.

This latter point is particularly important because in some countries the absence of the defendant-abductor and child from the forum makes it legally impossible to proceed with an action for custody brought by the left-behind parent. If an adjudication in such an action were a prerequisite to obtaining a determination of wrongfulness, it would be impossible for the petitioner to comply with an Article 15 request. For this reason a request for a decision or determination on wrongfulness can not be made in such circumstances consistent with the limitation in Article 15. Even if local law permits an adjudication of custody in the absence of the child and defendant (*i.e.*, post-abduction) or would otherwise allow a petitioner to obtain a determination of wrongfulness, the provisions of Article 15 will probably not be resorted to routinely. That is so because doing so would convert the purpose of the Convention from seeking to restore the *factual* status quo prior to an abduction to emphasizing substantive legal relationships.

A further consideration in deciding whether to request an applicant to comply with Article 15 is the length of time it will take to obtain the required determination. In countries where such a determination can be made only by a court, if judicial dockets are seriously backlogged, compliance with an Article 15 order could significantly prolong disposition of the return petition, which in turn would extend the time that the child is kept in a state of legal and emotional limbo. If "wrongfulness" can be established some other way, for instance by taking judicial notice of the law of the child's habitual residence as permitted by Article 14, the objective of Article 15 can be satisfied without further prejudice to the child's welfare or undue delay of the return proceeding. This would also be consistent with the Convention's desire for expeditious judicial proceedings as evidenced by Article 11.

In the United States, a left-behind parent or other claimant can petition for custody after the child has been removed from the forum. The right of action is conferred by the UCCJA, which in many states also directs courts to hear such petitions expeditiously. The result of such proceeding is a temporary or permanent custody determination allocating custody and visitation rights, or joint custody rights, between the parties. However, a custody determination on the merits that makes no reference to the Convention may not by itself satisfy an Article 15 request by a foreign court for a determination as to the wrongfulness of the conduct within the meaning of Article 3. Therefore, to ensure compliance with a possible Article 15 request the parent in the United States would be well-advised to request an explicit finding as to the wrongfulness of the alleged removal or retention within the meaning of Article 3 retention within the meaning of Article 3 in addition to seeking custody.

H. Constraints Upon Courts in Requested States in Making Substantive Custody Decisions

Article 16 bars a court in the country to which the child has been taken or in which the child has been retained from considering the merits of custody claims once it has received notice of the removal or retention of the child. The constraints continue either until it is determined that the child is not to be returned under the Convention, or it becomes evident that an application under the Convention will not be forthcoming within a reasonable time following receipt of the notice.

A court may get notice of a wrongful removal or retention in some manner other than the filing of a petition for return, for instance by communication from a Central Authority, from the aggrieved party (either directly or through counsel), or from a court in a

Contracting State which has stayed or dismissed return proceedings upon removal of the child from that State.

No matter how notice may be given, once the tribunal has received notice, a formal application for the child's return pursuant to the Convention will normally be filed promptly to avoid a decision on the merits from being made. If circumstances warrant a delay in filing a return petition, for instance pending the outcome of private negotiations for the child's return or interventions toward that end by the Central Authority, or pending determination of the location of the child and alleged abductor, the aggrieved party may nevertheless wish to notify the court as to the reason(s) for the delay so that inaction is not viewed as a failure to proceed under the Convention.

I. Duty to Return not Absolute

The judicial duty to order return of a wrongfully removed or retained child is not absolute. Temporal qualifications on this duty are set forth in Articles 12, 4 and 35. Additionally, Articles 13 and 20 set forth grounds upon which return may be denied.

1. Temporal Qualifications

Articles 4, 35 and 12 place time limitations on the return obligation.

(a) *Article 4.* Pursuant to Article 4, the Convention ceases to apply once the child reaches age sixteen. This is true regardless of when return proceedings were commenced and irrespective of their status at the time of the child's sixteenth birthday. *See* I.A., *supra.*

(b) *Article 35.* Article 35 limits application of the Convention to wrongful removals or retentions oocurring after its entry into force between the two relevant Contracting States. *But see* I.C., *supra.*

(c) *Article 12.* Under Article 12, the court is not obligated to return a child when return proceedings pursuant to the Convention are commenced a year or more after the alleged removal or retention *and* it is demonstrated that the child is settled in its new environment. The reporter indicates that "[T]he provision does not state how this fact is to be proved, but it would seem logical to regard such a task as falling upon the abductor or upon the person who opposes the return of the child . . ." Perez-Vera Report, paragraph 109 at page 459.

If the Convention is to succeed in deterring abductions, the alleged abductor must not be accorded preferential treatment by courts in his or her country of origin, which, in the absence of the Convention, might be prone to favor "home forum" litigants. To this end, nothing less than substantial evidence of the child's significant connections to the new country is intended to suffice to meet the respondent's burden of proof. Moreover, any claims made by the person resisting the child's return will be considered in light of evidence presented by the applicant concerning the child's contacts with and ties to his or her State of habitual residence. The reason for the passage of time, which may have made it possible for the child to form ties to the new country, is also relevant to the ultimate disposition of the return petition. If the alleged wrongdoer concealed the child's whereabouts from the custodian necessitating a long search for the child and thereby delayed the commencement of a return proceeding by the applicant, it is highly questionable whether the respondent should be permitted to benefit from such conduct absent strong countervailing considerations.

2. Article 13 Limitations on the Return Obligation

(a) *Legislative history.* In drafting Articles 13 and 20, the representatives of countries participating in negotiations on the Convention were aware that any exceptions had to be drawn very narrowly lest their application undermine the express purposes of the Convention -- to effect the prompt return of abducted children. Further, it was generally believed that courts would understand and fulfill the objectives of the Convention by narrowly interpreting the exceptions and allowing their use only in clearly meritorious cases, and only when the person opposing return had met the burden of proof. Importantly, a finding that one or more of the exceptions provided by Articles 13 and 20 are applicable does not make refusal of a return order mandatory. The courts retain the discretion to order the child returned even if they consider that one or more of the exceptions applies. Finally, the wording of each exception represents a compromise to accommodate the different legal systems and tenets of family law in effect in the countries negotiating the Convention, the basic purpose in each case being to provide for an exception that is narrowly construed.

(b) *Non-exercise of custody rights.* Under Article 13(a), the judicial authority may deny an application for the return of a child if the person having the care of the child was not actually exercising the custody rights at the time of the removal or retention, or had consented to or acquiesced in the removal or retention. This exception derives from Article 3(b) which makes the Convention applicable to the breach of custody rights that were actually exercised at the time of the removal or retention, or which would have been exercised but for the removal or retention.

The person opposing return has the burden of proving that custody rights were not actually exercised at the time of the removal or retention, or that the applicant had consented to or acquiesced in the removal or retention. The reporter points out that proof that custody was not actually exercised does not form an exception to the duty to return if the dispossessed guardian was unable to exercise his rights precisely because of the action of the abductor. Perez-Vera Report, paragraph 115 at page 461.

The applicant seeking return need only allege that he or she was actually exercising custody rights conferred by the law of the country in which the child was habitually resident immediately before the removal or retention. The statement would normally include a recitation of the circumstances under which physical custody had been exercised, *i.e.*, whether by the holder of these rights, or by a third person on behalf of the actual holder of the custody rights. The applicant would append copies of any relevant legal documents or court orders to the return application. *See* III, C., *supra,* and Article 8.

(c) *Grave risk of harm/intolerable situation.* Under Article 13(b), a court in its discretion need not order a child returned if there is a grave risk that return would expose the child to physical harm or otherwise place the child in an intolerable situation.

This provision was not intended to be used by defendants as a vehicle to litigate (or relitigate) the child's best interests. Only evidence directly establishing the existence of a grave risk that would expose the child to physical or emotional harm or otherwise place the child in an intolerable situation is material to the court's determination. The person opposing the child's return must show that the risk to the child is grave, not merely serious.

A review of deliberations on the Convention reveals that "intolerable situation" was not intended to encompass return to a home where money is in short supply, or where educational or other opportunities are more limited than in the requested State. An example of an "intolerable situation" is one in which a custodial parent sexually abuses the child. If the other parent removes or retains the child to safeguard it against further victimization, and the abusive parent then petitions for the child's return under the Convention, the court may deny the petition. Such action would protect the child from being returned to an "intolerable situation" and subjected to a grave risk of psychological harm.

(d) *Child's preference.* The third, unlettered paragraph of Article 13 permits the court to decline to order the child returned if the child objects to being returned and has attained an age and degree of maturity at which it is appropriate to take account of the child's views. As with the other Article 13 exceptions to the return obligation, the application of this exception is not mandatory. This discretionery aspect of Article 13 is especially important because of the potential for brainwashing of the child by the alleged abductor. A child's objection to being returned may be accorded little if any weight if the court believes that the child's preference is the product of the abductor parent's undue influence over the child.

(e) *Role of social studies.* The final paragraph of Article 13 requires the court, in considering a respondent's assertion that the child should not be returned, to take into account information relating to the child's social background provided by the Central Authority or other competent authority in the child's State of habitual residence. This provision has the dual purpose of ensuring that the court has a balanced record upon which to determine whether the child is to be returned, and preventing the abductor from obtaining an unfair advantage through his or her own forum selection with resulting ready access to evidence of the child's living conditions in that forum.

3. Article 20

Article 20 limits the return obligation of Article 12. It states: "The return of the child under the provisions of Article 12 may be refused if this would not be permitted by the fundamental principles of the requested State relating to the protection of human rights and fundamental freedoms."

The best explanation for this unique formulation is that the Convention might never have been adopted without it. The negotiating countries were divided on the inclusion of a public policy exception in the Convention. Those favoring a public policy exception believed that under some extreme circumstances not covered by the exceptions of Article 13 a court should be excused from returning a child to the country of habitual residence. In contrast, opponents of a public policy exception felt that such an exception could be interpreted so broadly as to undermine the fabric of the entire Convention.

A public policy clause was nevertheless adopted at one point by a margin of one vote. That clause provided: "Contracting States may reserve the right not to return the child when such return would be manifestly incompatible with the fundamental principles of the law relating to the family and children in the State addressed." To prevent imminent collapse of the negotiating process engendered by the adoption of this clause, there was a swift and determined move to devise a different provision that could be invoked on the rare occasion that return of a child would utterly shock the conscience of the court or offend all notions of due process.

The resulting language of Article 20 has no known precedent in other international agreements to serve as a guide in its interpretation. However, it should be emphasized that this exception, like the others, was intended to be restrictively interpreted and applied, and is not to be used, for example, as a vehicle for litigating custody on the merits or for passing judgment on the political system of the country from which the child was removed. Two characterizations of the effect to be given Article 20 are recited below for illumination.

The following explanation of Article 20 is excerpted from paragraph 118 of the Perez-Vera Report at pages 461-2:

It is significant that the possibility, acknowledged in *article 20*, that the child may not be returned when its return 'would not be permitted by the fundamental principles of the requested State relating to the protection of human rights and fundamental freedoms' has been placed in the last article of the chapter; it was thus intended to emphasize the always clearly exceptional nature of this provision's application. As for the substance of this provision, two comments only are required. Firstly, even if its literal meaning is strongly reminiscent of the terminology used in international texts concerning the protection of human rights, this particular rule is not directed at developments which have occurred on the international level, but is concerned only with the principles accepted by the law of the requested State, either through general international law and treaty law, or through internal legislation. Consequently, so as to be able to refuse to return a child on the basis of this article, it will be necessary to show that the fundamental principles of the requested State concerning the subject-matter of the Convention do not permit it; it will not be sufficient to show merely that its return would be incompatible, even manifestly incompatible, with these principles. Secondly, such principles must not be invoked any more frequently, nor must their invocation be more readily admissible than they would be in their application to purely internal matters. Otherwise, the provision would be discriminatory in itself, and opposed to one of the most widely recognized fundamental principles in internal laws. A study of the case law of different countries shows that the application by ordinary judges of the laws on human rights and fundamental freedoms is undertaken with a care which one must expect to see maintained in the international situations which the Convention has in view.

A. E. Anton, Chairman of the Commission on the Hague Conference on Private International Law that drafted the Convention, explained Article 20 in his article, "The Hague Convention on International Child Abduction," 30 I.C.L.Q. 537, 551-2 (July, 1981), as follows:

Its acceptance may in part have been due to the fact that it states a rule which many States would have been bound to apply in any event, for example, by reason of the terms of their constitutions. The reference in this provision to "the fundamental principles of the requested State" make it clear that the reference is not one to international conventions or declarations concerned with the protection of human rights and fundamental freedoms which have been ratified or accepted by Contracting States. It is rather to the fundamental provisions of the law of the requested State in such matters . . . If the United Kingdom decides to ratify the Hague Covention, it will, of course, be for the implementing legislation or the courts to specify what provisions of United Kingdom law come within the scope of Article 20. The Article, however, is merely permissive and it is to be hoped that States will exercise restraint in availing themselves of it.

4. Custody Order no Defense to Return

See I.D.1, *supra, for discussion of Article 17.*

J. Return of the Child

Assuming the court has determined that the removal or retention of the child was wrongful within the meaning of the Convention and that no exceptions to the return obligation have been satisfactorily established by the respondent, Article 12 provides that "the authority concerned shall order the return of the child forthwith." The Convention does not technically require that the child be returned to his or her State of habitual residence, although in the classic abduction case this will occur. If the petitioner has moved from the child's State of habitual residence the child will be returned to the petitioner, not the State of habitual residence.

1. Return Order not on Custody merits

Under Article 19, a decision under the Convention concerning the return of the child shall not be taken to be a determination on the merits of any custody issue. It follows that once the factual status quo ante has been restored, litigation concerning custody or visitation issues could proceed. Typically this will occur in the child's State of habitual residence.

2. Costs, Fees and Expenses Shifted to Abductor

In connection with the return order, Article 26 permits the court to direct the person who removed or retained the child to pay necessary expenses incurred by or on behalf of the applicant to secure the child's return, including expenses, costs incurred or payments made for locating the child, costs of legal representation of the applicant, and those of returing the child. The purposes underlying Article 26 are to restore the applicant to the financial position he or she would have been in had there been no removal or retention, as well as to deter such conduct from happening in the first place. This fee shifting provision has counterparts in the UCCJA (sections 7(g), 8(c), 15(b)) and the PKPA *(28 U.S.C. 1738A* note).

IV. Central Authority

In addition to creating a judicial remedy for cases of wrongful removal and retention, the Convention requires each Contracting State to establish a Centeral Authority (hereinafter "CA") with the broad mandate of assisting applicants to secure the return of their children or the effective excercise of their visitation rights. Articles 1, 10, 21. The CA is expressly directed by Article 10 to take all appropriate measures to obtain the voluntary return of children. The role of the CA with respect to visitation rights is discussed in V., *infra.*

A. Establishment of Central Authority

Article 6 requires each Contracting State to designate a Central Authority to discharge the duties enumerated in Articles 7, 9, 10, 11, 15, 21, 26, 27, and 28.

In France, the Central Authority is located within the Ministry of Justice. Switzerland has designated its Federal Justice Office as CA, and Canada has designated its Department of Justice; However, each Canadian province and territory in which the Convention has come into force has directed its Attorney General to serve as local CA for cases involving that jurisdiction.

In the United States it is very unlikely that the volume of cases will warrant the establishment of a new agency or office to fulfill Convention responsibilities. Rather, the duties of the CA will be carried out by an existing agency of the federal government with experience in dealing with authorities of other countries.

The Department of State's Office of Citizens Consular Services (CCS) within its Bureau of Consular Affairs will most likely serve as CA under the Hague Convention. CCS presently assists parents here and abroad with child custody-related problems within the framework of existing laws and procedures. The Convention should systematize and expedite CCS handling of requests from abroad for assistance in securing the return of children wrongfully abducted to or retained in the United States, and will provide additional tools with which CCS can help parents in the United States who are seeking return of their children from abroad.

The establishment of an interagency coordinating body is envisioned to assist the State Department in executing its functions as CA. This body is to include representatives of the Departments of State, Justice, and Health and Human Services.

In addition to the mandatory establishment of a CA in the national government, Contracting States are free to appoint similar entities in political subdivisions throughout the country. Rather than mandating the establishment of a CA in every state, it is expected that state governments in the United States will be requested on a case-by-case basis to render specified assistance, consistent with the Convention, aimed at resolving international custody and visitation disputes with regard to children located within their jurisdiction.

B. Duties

Article 7 enumerates the majority of the tasks to be carried out either directly by the CA or through an intermediary. The CA is to take "all appropriate measures" to execute these responsibilities. Although they are free to do so, the Convention does not obligate Contracting States to amend their internal laws to discharge Convention tasks more efficaciously. *See* Perez-Vera Report, paragraph 63 at page 444.

The following paragraphs of subsections of Article 7 of the Convention are couched in terms of the tasks and functions of the United States CA. The corresponding tasks and functions of the CA's in other States party to the Convention will be carried out somewhat differently in the context of each country's legal system.

Article 7(a). When the CA in the United States is asked to locate a child abducted from a foreign contracting State to this country, it would utilize all existing tools for determining the whereabouts of missing persons. Federal resources available for locating missing persons include the FBI-operated National Crime Information Center (NCIC) computer (pursuant to Pub. L. No. 97-292, the Missing Children Act), the Federal Parent Locator Service (pursuant to section 9 of Pub. L. No. 96-611, the Parental Kidnapping Prevention Act) and the National Center for Missing and Exploited Children. If the abductor's location is known or suspected, the relevant state's Parent Locator Service or Motor Vehicle Bureau and the Internal Revenue Service, Attorney General and Secretary of Education may be requested to conduct field and/or record searches. Also at the state level, public or private welfare agencies can be called upon to verify discreetly any address information about the abductor that may be discovered.

Article 7(b). To prevent further harm to the child, the CA would normally call upon the state welfare agency to take whatever protective measures are appropriate and available consistent with that state's child abuse and neglect laws. The CA, either directly or with the help of state authorities, may seek a written agreement from the abductor (and possibly from the applicant as well) not to remove the child from the jurisdiction pending procedures aimed at return of the child. Bonds or other forms of security may be required.

Article 7(c). The CA, either directly or through local public or private mediators, attorneys, social workers, or other professionals, would attempt to develop an agreement for the child's voluntary return and/or resolution of other outstanding issues. The obligation of the CA to take or cause to be taken all appropriate measures to obtain the voluntary return of the child is so fundamental a purpose of this Convention that it is restated in Article 10. However, overtures to secure the voluntary return of a child may not be advisable if advance awareness by the abductor that the Convention has been invoked is likely to prompt further flight and concealment of the child. If the CA and state authorities are successful in facilitating a voluntary agreement between the parties, the applicant would have no need to invoke or pursue the Convention's judicial remedy.

Article 7(d). The CA in the United States would rely upon court personnel or social service agencies in the child's state of habitual residence to compile information on the child's social background for the use of courts considering exceptions to a return petition in another country in which an abducted or retained child is located. *See* Article 13.

Article 7(e). The CA in the United States would call upon U.S. state authorities to prepare (or have prepared) general statements about the law of the state of the child's habitual residence for purposes of application of the Convention in the country where the child is located, *i.e.*, to determine whether a removal or retention was wrongful.

Articles 7(f) and (g). In the United States the federal CA will not act as legal advocate for the applicant. Rather, in concert with state authorities and interested family law attorneys, the CA, through state or local bodies, will assist the applicant in identifying competent private legal counsel or, if eligible, in securing representation by a Legal Aid or Legal Services lawyer. In some states, however, the Attorney General or local District Attorney may be empowered under state law to intervene on behalf of the applicant-parent to secure the child's return.

In some foreign Contracting States, the CA may act as the legal representative of the applicant for all purposes under the Convention.

Article 28 permits the CA to require written authorization empowering it to act on behalf of the applicant, or to designate a representative to act in such capacity.

Article 7(h). Travel arrangements for the return of a child from the United States would be made by the CA or by state authorities closest to the case in cooperation with the petitioner and/or interested foreign authorities. If it is necessary to provide short-term care for the child pending his or her return, the CA presumably will arrange for the temporary placement of the child in the care of the person designated for that purpose by the applicant, or, failing that, request local authorities to appoint a guardian, foster parent, etc. The costs of transporting the child are borne by the applicant unless the court, pursuant to Article 26, orders the wrongdoer to pay.

Article 7(i). The CA will monitor all cases in which its assistance has been sought. It will maintain files on the procedures followed in each case and the ultimate disposition thereof. Complete records will aid in determining how frequently the Convention is invoked and how well it is working.

C. Other Tasks

1. Processing Applications

Article 8 sets forth the required contents of a return application submitted to a CA, all of which are incorporated into the model form recommended for use when seeking a child's return pursuant to the Convention (see Annex A of this analysis). Article 8 further provides that an application for assistance in securing the return of a child may be submitted to a CA in either the country of the child's habitual residence or in any other Contracting State. If a CA receives an application with respect to a child whom it believes to be located in another Contracting State, pursuant to Article 9 it is to transmit the application directly to the appropriate CA and inform the requesting CA or applicant of the transmittal.

It is likely that an applicant who knows the child's whereabouts can expedite the return process by electing to file a return application with the CA in the country in which the child is located. The applicant who pursues this course of action may also choose to file a duplicate copy of the application for information purposes with the CA in his or her own country. Of course, the applicant may prefer to apply directly to the CA in his or her own country even when the abductor's location is known, and rely upon the CA to transfer documents and communicate with the foreign CA on his or her behalf. An applicant who does not know the whereabouts of the child will most likely file the return application with the CA in the child's State of habitual residence.

Under Article 27, a CA may reject an application if "it is manifest that the requirements of the Convention are not fulfilled or that the application is otherwise not well founded." The CA must promptly inform the CA in the requesting State, or the applicant directly, of its reasons for such rejection. Consistent with the spirit of the Convention and in the absence of any prohibition on doing so, the applicant should be allowed to correct the defects and refile the application.

Under Article 28, a CA may require the applicant to furnish a written authorization empowering it to act on behalf of the applicant, or designating a representative so to act.

2. Assistance in Connection With Judicial Proceedings

(a) *Request for status report.* When an action has been commenced in court for the return of a child and no decision has been reached by the end of six weeks, Article 11 authorizes the applicant or the CA of the requested State to ask the judge for a statement of the reasons for the delay. The CA in the country where the child is located may make such a request on its own initiative, or upon request of the CA of another Contracting State. Replies received by the CA in the requested State are to be transmitted to the CA in the requesting State or directly to the applicant, depending upon who initiated the request.

(b) *Social studies/background reports.* Information relating to the child's social background collected by the CA in the child's State of habitual residence pursuant to Article 7(d) may be submitted for consideration by the court in connection with a judicial return proceeding. Under the last paragraph of Article 13, the court must consider home studies and other social background reports provided by the CA or other competent authorities in the child's State of habitual residence.

(c) *Determination of "wrongfulness".* If a court requests an applicant to obtain a determination from the authorities of the child's State of habitual residence that the removal or retention was wrongful, Central Authorities are to assist applicants, so far as practicable, to obtain such a determination. Article 15.

(d) *Costs.* Under Article 26, each CA bears its own costs in applying the Convention. The actual operating expenses under the Convention will vary from one Contracting State to the next depending upon the volume of incoming and outgoing requests and the number and nature of the procedures available under internal law to carry out specified Convention tasks.

Subject to limited exceptions noted in the next paragraph, the Central Authority and other public services are prohibited from imposing any charges in relation to applications submitted under the Convention. Neither the applicant nor the CA in the requesting State may be required to pay for the services rendered directly or indirectly by the CA of the requested State.

The exceptions relate to transportation and legal expenses to secure the child's return. With respect to transportation, the CA in the requested State is under no obligation to pay for the child's return. The applicant can therefore be required to pay the costs of transporting the child. With respect to legal expenses, if the requested State enters a reservation in accordance with Articles 26 and 42, the applicant can be required to pay all costs and expenses of the legal proceedings, and those arising from the participation of legal counsel or advisers. However, see III. J 2 of this analysis discussing the possibility that the court ordering the child's return will levy these and other costs upon the abductor. Even if the reservation under Articles 26 and 42 is entered, under Article 22 no security, bond or deposit can be required to guarantee the payment of costs and expenses of the judicial or administrative proceedings falling within the Convention.

Under the last paragraph of Article 26 the CA may be able to recover some of its expenses from the person who engaged in the wrongful conduct. For instance, a court that orders a child returned may also order the person who removed or retained the child to pay the expenses incurred by or on behalf of the petitioner, including costs of court proceedings and legal fees of the petitioner. Likewise, a court that issues an order concerning visitation may direct the person who prevented the exercise of visitation rights to pay necessary expenses incurred by or on behalf of the petitioner. In such cases, the petitioner could recover his or her expenses, and the CA could recover its outlays on behalf of the petitioner, including costs associated with, or payments made for, locating the child and the legal representation of the petitioner.

V. Access Rights - Article 21

A. Remedies for Breach

Up to this point this analysis has focussed on judicial and administrative remedies for the removal or retention of children in breach of custody rights. "Access rights," which are synonymous with "visitation rights", are also protected by the Convention, but to a lesser extent than custody rights. While the Convention preamble and Article 1(b) articulate the Convention objective of ensuring that rights of access under the law of one state are respected in other Contracting States, the remedies for breach of access rights are those enunciated in Article 21 and do not include the return remedy provided by Article 12.

B. Defined

Article 5(b) defines "access rights" as including "the right to take a child for a limited period of time to a place other than the child's habitual residence."

A parent who takes a child from the country of its habitual residence to another country party to the Convention for a summer visit pursuant to either a tacit agreement between the parents or a court order is thus exercising his or her access rights. Should that parent fail to return the child at the end of the agreed upon visitation period, the retention would be wrongful and could give rise to a petition for return under Article 12. If, on the other hand, a custodial parent resists permitting the child to travel abroad to visit the noncustodial parent, perhaps out of fear that the child will not be returned at the end of the visit, this interference with access rights does not constitute a wrongful retention within the meaning of Article 3 of the Convention. The parent whose access rights have been infringed is not entitled under the Convention to the child's "return," but may request the Central Authority to assist in securing the exercise of his or her access rights pursuant to Article 21.

Article 21 may also be invoked as a precautionary measure by a custodial parent who anticipates a problem in getting the child back at the end of a visit abroad. That parent may apply to the CA of the country where the child is to visit the noncustodial parent for steps to ensure the return of the child at the end of the visit -- for example, through appropriate imposition of a performance bond or other security.

C. Procedure for Obtaining Relief

Procedurally Article 21 authorizes a person complaining of, or seeking to prevent, a breach of access rights to apply to the CA of a Contracting State in the same way as a person seeking return of the child. The application would contain the information described in Article 8, except that information provided under paragraph (c) would be the grounds upon which the claim is made for assistance in organizing or securing the effective exercise of rights of access.

Once the CA receives such application, it is to take all appropriate measures pursuant to Article 7 to promote the peaceful enjoyment of access rights and the fulfillment of any conditions to which the exercise of those rights is subject. This includes initiating or facilitating the institution of proceedings, either directly or through intermediaries, to organize or protect access rights and to secure respect for conditions to which these rights are subject.

If legal proceedings are instituted in the Contracting State in which the noncustodial parent resides. Article 21 may not be used by the noncustodial parent to evade the jurisdiction of the courts of the child's habitual residence, which retain authority to define and/or condition the exercise of visitation rights. A parent who has a child abroad for a visit is not to be allowed to exploit the presence of the child as a means for securing from the CA (or court) in that country more liberal visitation rights than those set forth in a court order agreed upon in advance of the visit. Such result would be tantamount to sanctioning forum-shopping contrary to the intent of the Convention. Any such application should be denied and the parent directed back to the appropriate authorities in the State of the child's habitual residence for consideration of the desired modification. Pending any such modification, once the lawful visitation period has expired, the custodial parent would have the right to seek the child's return under Article 3.

The Perez-Vera Report gives some limited guidance as to how CA's are to cooperate to secure the exercise of access rights:

... it would be advisable that the child's name not appear on the passport of the holder of the right of access, whilst in 'transfrontier' access cases it would be sensible for the holder of the access rights to give an undertaking to the Central Authority of the child's habitual residence to return the child on a particular date and to indicate also the places where he intends to stay with the child. A copy of such an undertaking would then be sent to the Central Authority of the habitual residence of the holder of the access rights, as well as to the Central Authority of the State in which he has stated his intention of staying with the child. This would enable the authorities to know the whereabouts of the child at any time and to set in motion proceedings for bringing about its return, as soon as the stated time-limit has expired. Of course, none of the measures could by itself ensure that access rights are exercised properly, but in any event we believe that this Report can go no further: the specific measures which the Central Authorities concerned are able to take will depend on the circumstances of each case and on the capacity to act enjoyed by each Central Authority. Perez-Vera Report, paragraph 128 at page 466.

D. Alternative Remedies

In addition to or in lieu of invoking Article 21 to resolve visitation-related problems, under Articles 18, 29 and 34 an aggrieved parent whose access rights have been violated may bypass the CA and the Convention and apply directly to the judicial authorities of a Contracting State for relief under other applicable laws.

In at least one case it is foreseeable that a parent abroad will opt in favor of local U.S. law instead of the Convention. A noncustodial parent abroad whose visitation rights are being thwarted by the custodial parent resident in the United States could invoke the UCCJA to seek enforcement of an existing foreign court order conferring visitation rights. Pursuant to section 23 of the UCCJA, a state court in the United States could order the custodial parent to comply with the prescribed visitation period by sending the child to the parent outside the United States. This remedy is potentially broader and more meaningful than the Convention remedy, since the latter does not include the right of return when a custodial parent obstructs the noncustodial parent's visitation rights, *i.e.,* by refusing to allow the other parent to exercise those rights. It is possible that a parent in the United States seeking to exercise access rights with regard to a child habitually resident abroad may similarly find greater relief under foreign law than under the Convention.

VI. Miscellaneous and Final Clauses

A. Article 36

Article 36 permits Contracting States to limit the restrictions to which a child's return may be subject under the Convention, *i.e.,* expand the return obligation or cases to which the Convention will apply. For instance, two or more countries may agree to extend coverage of the Convention to children beyond their sixteenth birthdays, thus expanding upon Article 4. Or, countries may agree to apply the Convention retroactively to wrongful removal and retention cases arising prior to its entry into force for those countries. Such agreement would remove any ambiguity concerning the scope of Article 35. The Department of State is not proposing that the United States make use of this Article.

B. Articles 37 and 38

Chapter VI of the Hague Convention consists of nine final clauses concerned with procedural aspects of the treaty, most of which are self-explanatory. Article 37 provides that states which were members of the Hague Conference on Private International Law at the time of the Fourteenth Session (October 1980) may sign and become parties to the Convention by ratification, acceptance or approval. Significantly, under Article 38 the Convention is open to accession by non-member States, but enters into force only between those States and member Contracting States which specifically accept their accession to the Convention. Article 38.

C. Articles 43 and 44

In Article 43 the Convention provides that it enters into force on the first day of the third calendar month after the third country has deposited its instrument of ratification, acceptance, approval or accession. For countries that become parties to the Convention subsequently, the Convention enters into force on the first day of the third calendar month following the deposit of the instrument of ratification. Pursuant to Article 43, the Convention entered into force on December 1, 1983 among France, Portugal and five provinces of Canada, and on January 1, 1984 for Switzerland. As of January, 1986 it is in force for all provinces and territories of Canada with the exception of Alberta, the Northwest Territories, Prince Edward Island and Sasketchewan.

The Convention enters into force in ratifying countries subject to such declarations or reservations pursuant to Articles 39, 40, 24 and 26 (third paragraph) as may be made by each ratifying country in accordance with Article 42.

The Convention remains in force for five years from the date it first entered into force (*i.e.,* December 1, 1983), and is renewed tacitly every five years absent denunciations notified in accordance with Article 44.

D. Articles 39 and 40

Article 39 authorizes a Contracting State to declare that the Convention extends to some or all of the territories for the conduct of whose international relations it is responsible.

Under Article 40, countries with two or more territorial units having different systems of law relative to custody and visitation rights may declare that the Convention extends to all or some of them. This federal state clause was included at the request of Canada to take account of Canada's special constitutional situation. The Department of State is not proposing that the United States make use of this provision. Thus, if the United States ratifies the Convention, it would come into force throughout the United States as the supreme law of the land in every state and other jurisdiction.

E. Article 41

Article 41 is another provision inserted at the request of one country, and is best understood by reciting the reporter's explanatory comments:

Finally a word should be said on Article 41, since it contains a wholly novel provision in Hague Conventions. It also appears in the other Conventions adopted at the Fourteenth Session, *i.e.*, the *Convention on International Access to Justice,* at the express request of the Australian delegation.

This article seeks to make it clear that ratification of the Convention by a State will carry no implication as to the internal distribution of executive, judicial and legislative powers in that State.

This may seem self-evident, and this is the point which the head of the Canadian delegation made during the debates of the Fourth Commission where it was decided to insert such a provision in both Conventions (see P.-v. No. 4 of the Plenary Session). The Canadian delegation, openly expressing the opinion of a large number of delegations, regarded the insertion of this article in the two Conventions as unnecessary. Nevertheless, Article 41 was adopted, largely to satisfy the Australian delegation, for which the absence of such a provision would apparently have created insuperable constitutional difficulties. Perez-Vera Report, paragraph 149 at page 472.

F. Article 45

Article 45 vests the Ministry of Foreign Affairs of the Kingdom of the Netherlands, as depository for the Convention, with the responsibility to notify Hague Conference member States and other States party to the Convention of all actions material to the operation of the Convention.

Recommended Return Application Form

The following model form was recommended by the Fourteenth Session of the Hague Conference on Private International Law (1980) for use in making applications pursuant to the 1980 Hague Convention on the Civil Aspects of International Child Abduction for the return of wrongfully removed or retained children. The version of the form to be used for requesting the return of such children from the United States will probably seek additional information, in particular to help authorities in the United States in efforts to find a child whose whereabouts are not known to the applicant.

Request for Return

Hague Convention of 25 October 1980 on the Civil Aspects of International Child Abduction.

Requesting Central Authority or Applicant

Requested Authority

Concerns the following child: who will attain the age of 16 on , 19 .

Note. -- The following particulars should be completed insofar as possible.

I -- Identity of the Child and its Parents

1 Child

Name and first names

Date and place of birth

Passport or identity card No., if any

Description and photo, if possible (see annexes)

2 Parents

2.1 Mother:

Name and first names

Date and place of birth

Nationality

Occupation

Habitual residence

Passport or identity card No., if any

2.2 Father:

Name and first names

Date and place of birth

Nationality

Occupation

Habitual residence

Passport or identity card No., if any

2.3 Date and place of marriage

II -- Requesting Individual or Institution (who actually exercised custody before the removal or retention)

3 Name and first names

Nationality of individual applicant

Occupation of individual applicant

Address

Passport or identity card No., if any

Relation to the child

Name and address of legal adviser, if any

III -- Place Where the Child Is Thought To Be

4.1 Information concerning the person alleged to have removed or retained the child

Name and first names

Date and place of birth, if known

Nationality, if known

Occupation

Last known address

Passport or identity card No., if any

Description and photo, if possible (see annexes)

4.2 Address of the child

4.3 Other persons who might be able to supply additional information relating to the whereabouts of the child

IV -- Time, Place, Date and Circumstances of the Wrongful Removal or Retention

V -- Factual or Legal Grounds Justifying the Request

VI -- Civil Proceedings in Progress

VII -- Child Is To Be Returned To:

a. Name and first names

Date and place of birth

Address

Telephone number

b. Proposed arrangements for return of the child

VIII -- Other Remarks

IX -- List of Documents Attached *

* E.g. Certified copy of relevant decision or agreement concerning custody or access; certificate or affidavit as to the applicable law; information relating to the social background of the child; authorization empowering the Central Authority to act on behalf of applicant.

Date

Place

Signature and/or stamp of the requesting Central Authority or applicant

Bibliography

Explanatory Report by E. Perez-Vera, Hague Conference on Private International Law, Actes et documents de la Quatorzieme session, vol. III, 1980, p. 426.

Anton, A.E. -- The Hague Convention on International Child Abduction; *30 Int'l & Comp. L.Q. (1981), p. 537.*

Bodenheimer, B. -- The Hague Convention on International Child Abduction; XIV Fam. L.Q. (1980), p. 99.

Chatin, L. -- Les conflicts relatifs a la garde des enfants et au droit de visite en droit international prive; Travaux du Comite francais de droit international prive, Seance du 12 mai 1982, Publication du Ministere de la Justice.

Crouch, R.E. -- Effective Measures Against International Child Snatching; *131 New L.J. (1981), p. 592.*

Deschenaux, D. -- La Convention de La Haye sur les aspects civils de l'enlevement international d'enfants, du 25 octobre 1980; XXXVII Schweizerisches Jahrbuch fur internationales Recht (1981), p. 119.

Dyer, A. -- International child abduction by parents; 168 Recueil des Cours de l'Academie de droit international de La Haye (1980), p. 231.

Eekelaar, J.M. -- The Hague Convention on the Civil Aspects of International Child Abduction; Explanatory Documentation prepared for Commonwealth Jurisdictions, Commonwealth Secretariat, 1981.

Farquhar, K.B. -- The Hague Convention on International Child Abduction Comes to Canada; *4 Can. J. Fam. L. (1983), p. 5.*

Frank, R.J. -- American and International Responses to International Child Abductions, *16 N.Y.U.J. Int'l L. & Pol. (Winter 1984), p. 415.*

Hoff, P., Schulman, J. and Volenik, A. -- Interstate Child Custody Disputes and Parental Kidnapping: Policy, Practice and Law, Legal Services Corporation -- American Bar Association, 1982.

Huesstege, R. -- Internationale Kindesentfuehrungen und Landesverfassungsrecht; IPRax (1982), p. 95 -- Der Uniform Child Custody Jurisdiction Act -- Rechtsvergleichende Betrachtungen zu Internationalen Kindesentfuehrengen, Verlag fur Standesamtswesen, Frankfurt am Main, 1982.

Morgenstern, B.R. -- The Hague Convention on the Civil Aspects of International Child Abduction: The Need for Ratification; *10 N.C.J. Int'l L. & Com. Reg. (1985), p. 463.*

Reymond, P.H. -- Convention de La Haye et Convention de Strasbourg. Aspects comparatifs des conventions concernant l'enlevement d'un enfant par l'un de ses parents; Revue de droit suisse 1981, p. 329.

Schulman, J. -- cf. Hoff, P.

Vink, E.L.M. -- Enkele civielrechtelijke aspecten van de internationale ontvoeringen van kinderen door een van de ouders; Leiden, mai 1981.

Volenik, A. -- cf. Hoff, P.

Westbrook, G.R. -- Law and Treaty Responses to International Child Abductions; *20 Va. J. Int'l L. (1980), p. 669.*

APPENDIX 5

Application Under the Hague Convention on the Civil Aspects of International Child Abduction

U. S. Department of State

OMB NO. 1405-0076
EXPIRES 12/31/2012
Estimated Burden - 1 Hour

APPLICATION UNDER THE HAGUE CONVENTION ON THE CIVIL ASPECTS OF INTERNATIONAL CHILD ABDUCTION

FILL OUT ALL SECTIONS ON BOTH SIDES

**Provide Information Below to the extent that it is available*

This is an application for the ☐ **Return of** ☐ **Access to** the child/children listed below.

I. FIRST CHILD SUBJECT OF APPLICATION

Child's Name *(Last, First, MI)*		Date of Birth *(mm-dd-yyyy)*	Place of Birth
Address *(At Time of Removal)*		U.S. SSN*	Passport/Identity Card* Country Number
Address and Telephone Number of Child's Current Location *(If Known)*			Citizenship(s)
Height	Weight	Color of Hair	Color of Eyes
Name of Child's Father if not Listed in Section II or III.		Name of Child's Mother if not Listed in Section II or III.	

II. APPLICANT (PERSON SEEKING RETURN OF/ACCESS TO CHILD/CHILDREN)

Name *(Last, First, MI)*		Date of Birth *(mm-dd-yyyy)*	Place of Birth
Relationship to Child/ren	Citizenship(s)	U.S. SSN*	Passport/Identity Card* Country Number
Current Address, Telephone Number, and Email Address			Occupation
Name, Address, and Telephone Number of Legal Advisor*			

III. PERSON ALLEGED TO HAVE WRONGFULLY REMOVED OR RETAINED THE CHILD/CHILDREN

Name *(Last, First, MI)*		Date of Birth *(mm-dd-yyyy)*	Place of Birth
Relationship to Child/ren	Citizenship(s)	U.S. SSN*	Passport/Identity Card* Country Number
Occupation, Name, and Address of Employer *(If Known)*			Known Aliases
Address and Telephone Number of Current Location			
Height	Weight	Color of Hair	Color of Eyes

DS-3013
12-2009

Page 1 of 5

IV. ADDITIONAL CHILD/CHILDREN Subject of Application

Child's Name *(Last, First, MI)*		Date of Birth *(mm-dd-yyyy)*	Place of Birth
Address *(At Time of Removal)*		U.S. SSN*	Passport/Identity Card* Country Number
Address and Telephone Number of Child's Current Location *(If Known)*			Citizenship(s)
Height	Weight	Color of Hair	Color of Eyes
Name of Child's Father if not Listed in Section II or III.		Name of Child's Mother if not Listed in Section II or III.	
Child's Name *(Last, First, MI)*		Date of Birth *(mm-dd-yyyy)*	Place of Birth
Address *(At Time of Removal)*		U.S. SSN*	Passport/Identity Card* Country Number
Address and Telephone Number of Child's Current Location *(If Known)*			Citizenship(s)
Height	Weight	Color of Hair	Color of Eyes
Name of Child's Father if not Listed in Section II or III.		Name of Child's Mother if not Listed in Section II or III.	
Child's Name *(Last, First, MI)*		Date of Birth *(mm-dd-yyyy)*	Place of Birth
Address *(At Time of Removal)*		U.S. SSN*	Passport/Identity Card* Country Number
Address and Telephone Number of Child's Current Location *(If Known)*			Citizenship(s)
Height	Weight	Color of Hair	Color of Eyes
Name of Child's Father if not Listed in Section II or III.		Name of Child's Mother if not Listed in Section II or III.	
Child's Name *(Last, First, MI)*		Date of Birth *(mm-dd-yyyy)*	Place of Birth
Address *(At Time of Removal)*		U.S. SSN*	Passport/Identity Card* Country Number
Address and Telephone Number of Child's Current Location *(If Known)*			Citizenship(s)
Height	Weight	Color of Hair	Color of Eyes
Name of Child's Father if not Listed in Section II or III.		Name of Child's Mother if not Listed in Section II or III.	

DS-3013 Page 2 of 5

ADDITIONAL SHEETS MAY BE ATTACHED

V. TIME, PLACE, DATE AND CIRCUMSTANCES OF THE WRONGFUL REMOVAL OR RETENTION

Additional sheets may be attached.

VI. FACTUAL AND LEGAL JUSTIFICATION FOR THE REQUEST

Habitual Residence (Please provide details related to the child's place of habitual residence.)

Basis of Applicants' Custody Rights

Supporting Documentation: (Please check applicable boxes and attach.)

- [ ] Law/Statute of Child's Residence at Time of Alleged Removal or Retention
- [ ] Court Order in Effect at Time of Alleged Removal or Retention
- [ ] Legally Binding Agreement
- [ ] Marriage Certificate, If Applicable
- [ ] Child's Birth Certificate, Required
- [ ] Other

Are civil proceedings currently in progress? (If yes, please provide details.)

ADDITIONAL SHEETS MAY BE ATTACHED

VII. PROPOSED ARRANGEMENTS FOR RETURN TRAVEL OF CHILD/CHILDREN

VIII. OTHER PERSONS WITH ADDITIONAL INFORMATION RELATING TO THE WHEREABOUTS OF THE CHILD/CHILDREN

Preferably, in country of child's current location. Please include, name, address, telephone number, and /or email address.

IX. OTHER RELEVANT INFORMATION

Signature of Applicant *(Sign in Blue Ink)*	Date *(mm-dd-yyyy)*

PRIVACY ACT STATEMENT

AUTHORITY: The information solicited on this form is requested under the authority of the International Child Abduction Remedies Act, Public Law 100-300.

PURPOSE: The primary purpose for soliciting the information is to evaluate applicants' claims under the Hague Convention on the Civil Aspects of International Child Abduction, advise applicants about available legal remedies, and locate abducted children.

Furnishing your social security number, as well as the other information requested on this form, is voluntary. The social security number may be used, if necessary, to authenticate the identities of individuals that are listed in the applicant claim. Failure to submit this form or to provide all the requested information may result in delay in the processing of your application.

ROUTINE USES: The principal users of this information are offices within the U.S. Department of State's Bureau of Consular Affairs. The information will be used to assist in facilitating operations under the Convention and may be provided to governments of member countries, bar associations and legal aid services, local police, social service agencies, and parents. This information may also be released on a need-to-know basis to other government agencies, including foreign agencies, having statutory or other lawful authority to gain access to such information.

PAPERWORK REDUCTION ACT STATEMENT

*Public reporting burden for this collection of information is estimated to average 60 minutes per response, including time required for searching existing data sources, gathering the necessary data, providing the information required, and reviewing the final collection. You do not have to provide this information requested if the OMB approval has expired. Send comments on the accuracy of this estimate of the burden and recommendations for reducing it to: A/GIS/DIR, Room 2400, SA-22, U.S. Department of State, Washington, DC 20522-2202.

APPENDIX 6

Hague Convention—General Instructions

(FROM U.S. STATE DEPARTMENT)

General Instructions:

- To invoke the Hague Convention, submit TWO completed applications for EACH child. The application form may be photocopied.
- Type or print all information in black or blue ink.
- Furnish as much of the information called for as possible, using an additional sheet of paper if you need more space.
- If you have further questions about the form, you may wish to refer to the text of the Convention.
- You may also call the Office of Children's Issues (CA/OCS/CI) at 1-888-407-4747.
- Translation of the supporting documents into the official language of the receiving country may be necessary. Translations can speed up the overall process. Foreign attorneys and judges tend to respond more favorably with such documents. Ask CA/OCS/CI for more information about supporting documents.
- You may fax your Hague application to CA/OCS/CI fax number (202) 736-9132.
- Send originals and supporting documents by mail, express mail, or courier service to:

    Department of State, Office of Child/ren's Issues
    SA-29, 2201 C Street, NW
    U.S. Department of State
    Washington, DC 20520
    Note: Be sure to sign and date the application

Section Specific Checklist and Instructions for Completing the Hague Application

Section I: First Child Subject of Application

This section is for information concerning the child for whom you are invoking the Hague Convention.

- **Child's Name**—The child's full name: last name, first, middle
- **Date of Birth**—Month/Day/Year
- **Place of Birth**—City/State/Country
- **Address**—Child's address in the country of habitual residence at the time of the abduction or removal.
- **United States Social Security Number**—A nine-digit number: 000-00-0000 (if known)
- **Passport/Identity Card**—Issuing country and passport or I.D. number (if known)
- **Address and Telephone Number of Child's Current Location (if known)—**Please provide any address information or details that may help locate the child.
- **Citizenship**—Include all citizenships held by the child (e.g. U.S., Canadian).
- **Height**—Feet and inches
- ***Weight***—Pounds
- **Sex**—Male or Female
- **Color of Hair**—Child's hair color
- **Color of Eyes**—Child's eye color (Include color photo, if available.)
- **Name of Child's Father if not Listed in Section II or III**—The father's full name (if it is not listed later in section II or III)
- **Name of Child's Mother if not Listed in Section II or III**—The mother's full name (if it is not listed later in section II or III)

Section II: Applicant (Person Seeking Return of/Access to Child/ren)

This section is for information concerning the person or institution applying for access to or the return of the child to the United States.

- **Name**—Full name of applicant: last name, first, middle
- **Date of Birth**—Month/Day/Year
- **Place of Birth**—City/State/Country
- **Relationship to Child/ren-** Relationship of the applicant requesting access/return to the child (e.g. mother, father)
- **Citizenship(s)**—List all citizenships held by the requester (e.g. United States, Canadian)

- **United States Social Security Number**—A nine-digit number: 000-00-0000.
- **Passport/Identity Card**—Issuing country and passport or I.D. number.
- **Current Address, Telephone Number, and Email Address** – Include mailing address, home telephone, work telephone, fax number, and email address.
- **Occupation** – Occupation of the requester (if a person).
- **Name, Address and Telephone Number of Legal Adviser, if any**—Include zip code as well as telephone and fax numbers. Some of this information may be the same as that already given.

Section III: Person Alleged to Have Wrongfully Removed or Retained the Child/ren

This section is for information concerning the person alleged to have abducted or retained the child/ren. The information about the abducting parent is needed to assist in locating the child. Please provide all requested information and any additional facts that may help authorities locate the child.

- **Name**—Full name of parent alleged to have abducted or wrongfully retained the child.
- **Date of Birth**—Month/Day/Year
- **Place of Birth**—City/State/Country
- **Relationship to Child/ren**- Relationship of the alleged abductor/retainer to the child (e.g. mother, father)
- **Citizenship(s)**—List all citizenships held by the alleged abductor/retainer (e.g. United States, Canadian)
- **United States Social Security Number**—A nine-digit number: 000-00-0000 (if known).
- **Passport/Identity Card**—Issuing country and passport or I.D. number (if known).
- **Occupation, Name and Address of Employer**—Provide any employment information that may be helpful in locating the alleged abductor/retainer, such as usual type of work, potential employers or employment agencies.
- **Known Aliases**—Any other names the alleged abductor/retainer may use.
- **Address and Telephone Number of Current Location**—Of the alleged abductor/retainer in the country where the child was taken.

- **Height**—Feet and inches
- **Weight**—Pounds
- **Color of Hair** – Alleged abductor/retainer's hair color.
- **Color of Eyes**—Alleged abductor/retainer's eye color. (Include color photo, if available.)

Section IV: Additional Child/ren Subject of Application

This section is for information concerning any additional child/ren for whom you are invoking the Hague Convention. Provide the following information for EACH child.

- **Child's Name**—The child's full name: last name, first, middle
- **Date of Birth**—Month/Day/Year
- **Place of Birth**—City/State/Country
- **Address**—Child's address in the country of habitual residence at the time of the abduction or removal.
- **United States Social Security Number**—A nine-digit number: 000-00-0000 (if known)
- **Passport/Identity Card**—Issuing country and passport or I.D. number (if known)
- **Address and Telephone Number of Child's** Current Location (if known) – Please provide any address information or details that may help locate the child.
- **Citizenship**—Include all citizenships held by the child (e.g. U.S., Canadian).
- **Height**—Feet and inches
- **Weight**—Pounds
- **Sex**—Male or Female
- **Color of Hair**—Child's hair color
- **Color of Eyes**—Child's eye color (Include color photo, if available.)
- **Name of Child's Father if not Listed in Section II or III**—The father's full name (if it is not listed later in section II or III)
- **Name of Child's Mother if not Listed in Section II or III**—The mother's full name (if it is not listed later in section II or III)

Section V: Time, Place, Date, and Circumstances of the Wrongful Removal or Retention

This section is for the applicant to describe the circumstances under which the Child/ren were wrongfully removed or retained.

- Provide the date, to the best of your knowledge, that the child left the United States or when the wrongful retention began. Include the place from which the child was taken.
- Describe the legal relationship existing between you and the abducting parent when the child was removed.
- Describe the circumstances under which the child was removed/retained. What were the circumstances leading up to the removal or retention? How did you learn of the removal/retention? Did the other parent take the child during a scheduled visitation? Did the other parent take the child for what you believed would be a short visit and then inform you that they were staying? Did they purchase round-trip air tickets to show that they intended to return? Had you and your family moved to the other country, and then you decided to return to the United States?
- Take this opportunity to tell your story. Try to anticipate what claims the other parent may make and provide your explanation.
- Do not limit yourself to the space provided on the form. Additional pages may be attached to fully narrate the circumstances. However, please be concise.

Section VI: Factual and Legal Justification for the Request

This section is for the applicant to describe the legal basis for invoking the Hague Convention.

- Habitual Residence – Provide details that establish the child's place of habitual residence.
- Basis of Applicant's Custody Rights—Provide information and documentation establishing that you had, and were exercising, a right of custody at the time of the child's removal. Generally, a right of custody is created by a custody order when parents are divorced, or by operation of state law when parents are still married or were never married when the child was taken.—As stated, the Convention defines "rights of custody" as including "rights relating to the care of the child and, in particular, the right to determine the child's place of residence." Thus, you may have a "right of custody" as defined by the Convention even if you do not have court-ordered joint or sole custody of the child .

***IMPORTANT*:** If there is no applicable court order, please provide a copy of the state statute, case law, or an affidavit of law prepared by an attorney that establishes your right of custody at the time of the child's removal. This provision of the law may sometimes be found in the estate and wills section of the state code. Remember, you are not attempting to show that you would have an equal right to obtain custody in a subsequent custody proceeding, but that you had and were exercising a right of custody *when the child was taken.* **SEND IN YOUR HAGUE APPLICATION IMMEDIATELY. Do NOT wait to get an order of custody. Orders issued after removal/ retention are irrelevant in a Hague hearing.**

- **Are civil proceedings currently in progress?**—Indicate any civil action (in the United States or abroad) that may be pending (e.g.. custody, divorce). List court and hearing dates.

Section VII: Proposed Arrangements for Return Travel of Child

This section is for the applicant to describe how the return travel of the child/ren will be arranged.

Provide means by which you propose the child will return to the United States if this is ordered.

For example, would you travel to pick up the child, or would someone go in your place? Is the child old enough to travel by him or herself? Is there someone in the foreign country who could return with the child? Would the child travel by car, train, airplane? **Be specific. Include:**

- Name of person to whom child will be returned.
- Date of Birth of person to whom child will be returned.
- Place of Birth—of person to whom child will be returned.
- Address of person to whom child will be returned.
- Telephone Number of person to whom child will be returned.

Section VIII: Other Persons with Additional Information Relating to the Whereabouts of the Child/ren

This section is for the applicant to provide information concerning anyone else who may be able to provide information helpful in locating the child/ ren. These persons would preferably be in the country of the child/ren's current location.

- Provide names, addresses, telephone numbers, and email addresses of anyone who could potentially give the Central Authority in the country of the child/ren's current location information on the child's whereabouts.

Section IX: Other Relevant Information

This section is for the applicant to provide any other information that may be pertinent to the Hague application.

- State here whether you are applying for return or access under the Convention.
- You should include here any additional information that you believe may be pertinent to the Hague application.
- Sign and date the application in BLUE ink.

APPENDIX 7

Uniform Child Custody Jurisdiction and Enforcement Act

[ARTICLE] 1

GENERAL PROVISIONS

SECTION 101. SHORT TITLE. This [Act] may be cited as the Uniform Child-Custody Jurisdiction and Enforcement Act.

SECTION 102. DEFINITIONS. In this [Act]:

(1) "Abandoned" means left without provision for reasonable and necessary care or supervision.

(2) "Child" means an individual who has not attained 18 years of age.

(3) "Child-custody determination" means a judgment, decree, or other order of a court providing for the legal custody, physical custody, or visitation with respect to a child. The term includes a permanent, temporary, initial, and modification order. The term does not include an order relating to child support or other monetary obligation of an individual.

(4) "Child-custody proceeding" means a proceeding in which legal custody, physical custody, or visitation with respect to a child is an issue. The term includes a proceeding for divorce, separation, neglect, abuse, dependency, guardianship, paternity, termination of parental rights, and protection from domestic violence, in which the issue may appear. The term does not include a proceeding involving juvenile delinquency, contractual emancipation, or enforcement under [Article] 3.

(5) "Commencement" means the filing of the first pleading in a proceeding.

(6) "Court" means an entity authorized under the law of a State to establish, enforce, or modify a child-custody determination.

(7) "Home State" means the State in which a child lived with a parent or a person acting as a parent for at least six consecutive months immediately before the commencement of a child-custody proceeding. In the case of a child less than six months of age, the term means the State in which the child lived from birth with any of the persons mentioned. A period of temporary absence of any of the mentioned persons is part of the period.

(8) "Initial determination" means the first child-custody determination concerning a particular child.

(9) "Issuing court" means the court that makes a child-custody determination for which enforcement is sought under this [Act].

(10) "Issuing State" means the State in which a child-custody determination is made.

(11) "Modification" means a child-custody determination that changes, replaces, supersedes, or is otherwise made after a previous determination concerning the same child, whether or not it is made by the court that made the previous determination.

(12) Person" means an individual, corporation, business trust, estate, trust, partnership, limited liability company, association, joint venture, government; governmental subdivision, agency, or instrumentality; public corporation; or any other legal or commercial entity.

(13) "Person acting as a parent" means a person, other than a parent, who:

(A) has physical custody of the child or has had physical custody for a period of six consecutive months, including any temporary absence, within one year immediately before the commencement of a child-custody proceeding; and

(B) has been awarded legal custody by a court or claims a right to legal custody under the law of this State.

(14) "Physical custody" means the physical care and supervision of a child.

(15) "State" means a State of the United States, the District of Columbia, Puerto Rico, the United States Virgin Islands, or any territory or insular possession subject to the jurisdiction of the United States.

[(16) "Tribe" means an Indian tribe or band, or Alaskan Native village, which is recognized by federal law or formally acknowledged by a State.]

(17) "Warrant" means an order issued by a court authorizing law enforcement officers to take physical custody of a child.

SECTION 103. PROCEEDINGS GOVERNED BY OTHER LAW. This [Act] does not govern an adoption proceeding or a proceeding pertaining to the authorization of emergency medical care for a child.

SECTION 104. APPLICATION TO INDIAN TRIBES.

(a) A child-custody proceeding that pertains to an Indian child as defined in the Indian Child Welfare Act, 25 U.S.C. § 1901 et seq., is not subject to this [Act] to the extent that it is governed by the Indian Child Welfare Act.

[(b) A court of this State shall treat a tribe as if it were a State of the United States for the purpose of applying [Articles] 1 and 2.]

[(c) A child-custody determination made by a tribe under factual circumstances in substantial conformity with the jurisdictional standards of this [Act] must be recognized and enforced under [Article] 3.]

SECTION 105. INTERNATIONAL APPLICATION OF [ACT].

(a) A court of this State shall treat a foreign country as if it were a State of the United States for the purpose of applying [Articles] 1 and 2.

(b) Except as otherwise provided in subsection (c), a child-custody determination made in a foreign country under factual circumstances in substantial conformity with the jurisdictional standards of this [Act] must be recognized and enforced under [Article] 3.

(c) A court of this State need not apply this [Act] if the child custody law of a foreign country violates fundamental principles of human rights.

SECTION 106. EFFECT OF CHILD-CUSTODY DETERMINATION. A child-custody determination made by a court of this State that had jurisdiction under this [Act] binds all persons who have been served in accordance with the laws of this State or notified in accordance with Section 108 or who have submitted to the jurisdiction of the court, and who have been given an opportunity to be heard. As to those persons, the determination is conclusive as to all decided issues of law and fact except to the extent the determination is modified.

SECTION 107. PRIORITY. If a question of existence or exercise of jurisdiction under this [Act] is raised in a child-custody proceeding, the question, upon request of a party, must be given priority on the calendar and handled expeditiously.

SECTION 108. NOTICE TO PERSONS OUTSIDE STATE.

(a) Notice required for the exercise of jurisdiction when a person is outside this State may be given in a manner prescribed by the law of this State for service of process or by the law of the State in which the service is made. Notice must be given in a manner reasonably calculated to give actual notice but may be by publication if other means are not effective.

(b) Proof of service may be made in the manner prescribed by the law of this State or by the law of the State in which the service is made.

(c) Notice is not required for the exercise of jurisdiction with respect to a person who submits to the jurisdiction of the court.

SECTION 109. APPEARANCE AND LIMITED IMMUNITY.

(a) A party to a child-custody proceeding, including a modification proceeding, or a petitioner or respondent in a proceeding to enforce or register a child-custody determination, is not subject to personal jurisdiction in this State for another proceeding or purpose solely by reason of having participated, or of having been physically present for the purpose of participating, in the proceeding.

(b) A person who is subject to personal jurisdiction in this State on a basis other than physical presence is not immune from service of process in this State. A party present in this State who is subject to the jurisdiction of another State is not immune from service of process allowable under the laws of that State.

(c) The immunity granted by subsection (a) does not extend to civil litigation based on acts unrelated to the participation in a proceeding under this [Act] committed by an individual while present in this State.

SECTION 110. COMMUNICATION BETWEEN COURTS.

(a) A court of this State may communicate with a court in another State concerning a proceeding arising under this [Act].

(b) The court may allow the parties to participate in the communication. If the parties are not able to participate in the communication, they must be given the opportunity to present facts and legal arguments before a decision on jurisdiction is made.

(c) Communication between courts on schedules, calendars, court records, and similar matters may occur without informing the parties. A record need not be made of the communication.

(d) Except as otherwise provided in subsection (c), a record must be made of a communication under this section. The parties must be informed promptly of the communication and granted access to the record.

(e) For the purposes of this section, "record" means information that is inscribed on a tangible medium or that is stored in an electronic or other medium and is retrievable in perceivable form.

SECTION 111. TAKING TESTIMONY IN ANOTHER STATE.

(a) In addition to other procedures available to a party, a party to a child-custody proceeding may offer testimony of witnesses who are located in another State, including testimony of the parties and the child, by deposition or other means allowable in this State for testimony taken in another State. The court on its own motion may order that the testimony of a person be taken in another State and may prescribe the manner in which and the terms upon which the testimony is taken.

(b) A court of this State may permit an individual residing in another State to be deposed or to testify by telephone, audiovisual means, or other electronic means before a designated court or at another location in that State. A court of this State shall cooperate with courts of other States in designating an appropriate location for the deposition or testimony.

(c) Documentary evidence transmitted from another State to a court of this State by technological means that do not produce an original writing may not be excluded from evidence on an objection based on the means of transmission.

SECTION 112. COOPERATION BETWEEN COURTS; PRESERVATION OF RECORDS.

(a) A court of this State may request the appropriate court of another State to:
    (1) hold an evidentiary hearing;
    (2) order a person to produce or give evidence pursuant to procedures of that State;
    (3) order that an evaluation be made with respect to the custody of a child involved in a pending proceeding;

(4) forward to the court of this State a certified copy of the transcript of the record of the hearing, the evidence otherwise presented, and any evaluation prepared in compliance with the request; and

(5) order a party to a child-custody proceeding or any person having physical custody of the child to appear in the proceeding with or without the child.

(b) Upon request of a court of another State, a court of this State may hold a hearing or enter an order described in subsection (a).

(c) Travel and other necessary and reasonable expenses incurred under subsections (a) and (b) may be assessed against the parties according to the law of this State.

(d) A court of this State shall preserve the pleadings, orders, decrees, records of hearings, evaluations, and other pertinent records with respect to a child-custody proceeding until the child attains 18 years of age. Upon appropriate request by a court or law enforcement official of another State, the court shall forward a certified copy of those records.

[ARTICLE] 2

JURISDICTION

SECTION 201. INITIAL CHILD-CUSTODY JURISDICTION.

(a) Except as otherwise provided in Section 204, a court of this State has jurisdiction to make an initial child-custody determination only if:

(1) this State is the home State of the child on the date of the commencement of the proceeding, or was the home State of the child within six months before the commencement of the proceeding and the child is absent from this State but a parent or person acting as a parent continues to live in this State;

(2) a court of another State does not have jurisdiction under paragraph (1), or a court of the home State of the child has declined to exercise jurisdiction on the ground that this State is the more appropriate forum under Section 207 or 208, and:

(A) the child and the child's parents, or the child and at least one parent or a person acting as a parent, have a significant connection with this State other than mere physical presence; and

(B) substantial evidence is available in this State concerning the child's care, protection, training, and personal relationships;

(3) all courts having jurisdiction under paragraph (1) or (2) have declined to exercise jurisdiction on the ground that a court of this State is the more appropriate forum to determine the custody of the child under Section 207 or 208; or

(4) no court of any other State would have jurisdiction under the criteria specified in paragraph (1), (2), or (3).

(b) Subsection (a) is the exclusive jurisdictional basis for making a child-custody determination by a court of this State.

(c) Physical presence of, or personal jurisdiction over, a party or a child is not necessary or sufficient to make a child-custody determination.

1. Home State Jurisdiction. The jurisdiction of the home State has been prioritized over other jurisdictional bases. Section 3 of the UCCJA provided four independent and concurrent bases of jurisdiction. The PKPA provides that full faith and credit can only be given to an initial custody determination of a "significant connection" State when there is no home State. This Act prioritizes home state jurisdiction in the same manner as the PKPA thereby eliminating any potential conflict between the two acts.

The six-month extended home state provision of subsection (a)(1) has been modified slightly from the UCCJA. The UCCJA provided that home state jurisdiction continued for six months when the child had been removed by a person seeking the child's custody or for other reasons and a parent or a person acting as a parent continues to reside in the home State. Under this Act, it is no longer necessary to determine why the child has been removed. The only inquiry relates to the status of the person left behind. This change provides a slightly more refined home state standard than the UCCJA or the PKPA, which also requires a determination that the child has been removed "by a contestant or for other reasons." The scope of the PKPA's provision is theoretically narrower than this Act. However, the phrase "or for other reasons" covers most fact situations where the child is not in the home State and, therefore, the difference has no substantive effect.

In another sense, the six-month extended home state jurisdiction provision is this Act is narrower than the comparable provision in the PKPA. The PKPA's definition of extended home State is more expansive because it applies whenever a "contestant" remains in the home State. That class of individuals has been eliminated in this Act. This Act retains the original UCCJA classification of "parent or person acting as parent" to define who must remain for a State to exercise the six-month extended home state jurisdiction. This eliminates the undesirable jurisdictional determinations which would occur as a result of differing state substantive laws on visitation involving grandparents and others. For example, if State A's law provided that grandparents could obtain visitation with a child after the death of one of the parents, then the grandparents, who would be considered "contestants" under the PKPA, could file a proceeding within six months after the remaining parent moved and have the case heard in State A. However, if State A did not provide that grandparents could seek visitation under such circumstances, the grandparents would not be considered "contestants" and State B where the child acquired a new home State would provide the only forum. This Act bases jurisdiction on the parent and child or person acting as a parent and child relationship without regard to grandparents or other potential seekers of custody or visitation. There is no conflict with the broader provision of the PKPA. The PKPA in § (c)(1) authorizes States to narrow the scope of their jurisdiction.

2. Significant connection jurisdiction. This jurisdictional basis has been amended in four particulars from the UCCJA. First, the "best interest" language of the UCCJA has been eliminated. This phrase tended to create confusion between the jurisdictional issue and the substantive custody determination. Since the language was not necessary for the jurisdictional issue, it has been removed.

Second, the UCCJA based jurisdiction on the presence of a significant connection between the child and the child's parents or the child and at least one contestant. This Act requires that the significant connections be between the child, the child's parents or the child and a person acting as a parent.

Third, a significant connection State may assume jurisdiction only when there is no home State or when the home State decides that the significant connection State would be a more appropriate forum under Section 207 or 208. Fourth, the determination of significant connections has been changed to eliminate the language of "present or future care." The jurisdictional determination should be made by determining whether there is sufficient evidence in the State for the court to make an informed custody determination. That evidence might relate to the past as well as to the "present or future."

Emergency jurisdiction has been moved to a separate section. This is to make it clear that the power to protect a child in crisis does not include the power to enter a permanent order for that child except as provided by that section.

Paragraph (a)(3) provides for jurisdiction when all States with jurisdiction under paragraphs (a)(1) and (2) determine that this State is a more appropriate forum. The determination would have to be made by all States with jurisdiction under subsection (a)(1) and (2). Jurisdiction would not exist under this paragraph because the home State determined it is a more appropriate place to hear the case if there is another State that could exercise significant connection jurisdiction under subsection (a)(2).

Paragraph (a)(4) retains the concept of jurisdiction by necessity as found in the UCCJA and in the PKPA. This default jurisdiction only occurs if no other State would have jurisdiction under subsections (a)(1) through (a)(3).

Subsections (b) and (c) clearly State the relationship between jurisdiction under this Act and other forms of jurisdiction. Personal jurisdiction over, or the physical presence of, a parent or the child is neither necessary nor required under this Act. In other words neither minimum contacts nor service within the State is required for the court to have jurisdiction to make a custody determination. Further, the presence of minimum contacts or service within the State does not confer jurisdiction to make a custody determination. Subject to Section 204, satisfaction of the requirements of subsection (a) is mandatory.

The requirements of this section, plus the notice and hearing provisions of the Act, are all that is necessary to satisfy due process. This Act, like the UCCJA and the PKPA is based on Justice Frankfurter's concurrence in *May v. Anderson*, 345 U.S. 528 (1953). As pointed out by Professor Bodenheimer, the reporter for the UCCJA, no "workable interstate custody law could be built around [Justice] Burton's plurality opinion .... Bridgette Bodenheimer, The Uniform Child Custody Jurisdiction Act: A Legislative Remedy for Children Caught in the Conflict of Laws, 22 Vand.L.Rev. 1207,1233 (1969). It should also be noted that since jurisdiction to make a child custody determination is subject matter jurisdiction, an agreement of the parties to confer jurisdiction on a court that would not otherwise have jurisdiction under this Act is ineffective.

SECTION 202. EXCLUSIVE, CONTINUING JURISDICTION.

(a) Except as otherwise provided in Section 204, a court of this State which has made a child-custody determination consistent with Section 201 or 203 has exclusive, continuing jurisdiction over the determination until:

(1) a court of this State determines that neither the child, nor the child and one parent, nor the child and a person acting as a parent have a significant connection with this State and that substantial evidence is no longer available in this State concerning the child's care, protection, training, and personal relationships; or

(2) a court of this State or a court of another State determines that the child, the child's parents, and any person acting as a parent do not presently reside in this State.

(b) A court of this State which has made a child-custody determination and does not have exclusive, continuing jurisdiction under this section may modify that determination only if it has jurisdiction to make an initial determination under Section 201.

SECTION 203. JURISDICTION TO MODIFY DETERMINATION. Except as otherwise provided in Section 204, a court of this State may not modify a child-custody determination made by a court of another State unless a court of this State has jurisdiction to make an initial determination under Section 201(a)(1) or (2) and:

(1) the court of the other State determines it no longer has exclusive, continuing jurisdiction under Section 202 or that a court of this State would be a more convenient forum under Section 207; or

(2) a court of this State or a court of the other State determines that the child, the child's parents, and any person acting as a parent do not presently reside in the other State.

SECTION 204. TEMPORARY EMERGENCY JURISDICTION.

(a) A court of this State has temporary emergency jurisdiction if the child is present in this State and the child has been abandoned or it is necessary in an emergency to protect the child because the child, or a sibling or parent of the child, is subjected to or threatened with mistreatment or abuse.

(b) If there is no previous child-custody determination that is entitled to be enforced under this [Act] and a child-custody proceeding has not been commenced in a court of a State having jurisdiction under Sections 201 through 203, a child-custody determination made under this section remains in effect until an order is obtained from a court of a State having jurisdiction under Sections 201 through 203. If a child-custody proceeding has not been or is not commenced in a court of a State having jurisdiction under Sections 201 through 203, a child-custody determination made under this section becomes a final determination, if it so provides and this State becomes the home State of the child.

(c) If there is a previous child-custody determination that is entitled to be enforced under this [Act], or a child-custody proceeding has been commenced in a court of a State having jurisdiction under Sections 201 through 203, any order issued by a court of this State under this section must specify in the order a period that the court considers adequate to allow the person seeking an order to obtain an order from the State having jurisdiction under Sections 201 through 203. The order issued in this State remains in effect until an order is obtained from the other State within the period specified or the period expires.

(d) A court of this State which has been asked to make a child-custody determination under this section, upon being informed that a child-custody proceeding has been commenced in, or a child-custody determination has been made by, a court of a State having jurisdiction under Sections 201 through 203, shall immediately communicate with the other court. A court of this State which is exercising jurisdiction pursuant to Sections 201 through 203, upon being informed that a child-custody proceeding has been commenced in, or a child-custody determination has been made by, a court of another State under a statute similar to this section shall immediately communicate with the court of that State to resolve the emergency, protect the safety of the parties and the child, and determine a period for the duration of the temporary order.

SECTION 205. NOTICE; OPPORTUNITY TO BE HEARD; JOINDER.

(a) Before a child-custody determination is made under this [Act], notice and an opportunity to be heard in accordance with the standards of Section 108 must be given to all persons entitled to notice under the law of this State as in child-custody proceedings between residents of this State, any parent whose parental rights have not been previously terminated, and any person having physical custody of the child.

(b) This [Act] does not govern the enforceability of a child-custody determination made without notice or an opportunity to be heard.

(c) The obligation to join a party and the right to intervene as a party in a child-custody proceeding under this [Act] are governed by the law of this State as in child-custody proceedings between residents of this State.

SECTION 206. SIMULTANEOUS PROCEEDINGS.

(a) Except as otherwise provided in Section 204, a court of this State may not exercise its jurisdiction under this [article] if, at the time of the commencement of the proceeding, a proceeding concerning the custody of the child has been commenced in a court of another State having jurisdiction substantially in conformity with this [Act], unless the proceeding has been terminated or is stayed by the court of the other State because a court of this State is a more convenient forum under Section 207.

(b) Except as otherwise provided in Section 204, a court of this State, before hearing a child-custody proceeding, shall examine the court documents and other information supplied by the parties pursuant to Section 209. If the court determines that a child-custody proceeding has been commenced in a court in another State having jurisdiction substantially in accordance with this [Act], the court of this State shall stay its proceeding and communicate with the court of the other State. If the court of the State having jurisdiction substantially in accordance with this [Act] does not determine that the court of this State is a more appropriate forum, the court of this State shall dismiss the proceeding.

(c) In a proceeding to modify a child-custody determination, a court of this State shall determine whether a proceeding to enforce the determination has been commenced in another State. If a proceeding to enforce a child-custody determination has been commenced in another State, the court may:

(1) stay the proceeding for modification pending the entry of an order of a court of the other State enforcing, staying, denying, or dismissing the proceeding for enforcement;

(2) enjoin the parties from continuing with the proceeding for enforcement; or

(3) proceed with the modification under conditions it considers appropriate.

SECTION 207. INCONVENIENT FORUM.

(a) A court of this State which has jurisdiction under this [Act] to make a child-custody determination may decline to exercise its jurisdiction at any time if it determines that it is an inconvenient forum under the circumstances and that a court of another State is a more appropriate forum. The issue of inconvenient forum may be raised upon motion of a party, the court's own motion, or request of another court.

(b) Before determining whether it is an inconvenient forum, a court of this State shall consider whether it is appropriate for a court of another State to exercise jurisdiction. For this purpose, the court shall allow the parties to submit information and shall consider all relevant factors, including:

(1) whether domestic violence has occurred and is likely to continue in the future and which State could best protect the parties and the child;

(2) the length of time the child has resided outside this State;

(3) the distance between the court in this State and the court in the State that would assume jurisdiction;

(4) the relative financial circumstances of the parties;

(5) any agreement of the parties as to which State should assume jurisdiction;

(6) the nature and location of the evidence required to resolve the pending litigation, including testimony of the child;

(7) the ability of the court of each State to decide the issue expeditiously and the procedures necessary to present the evidence; and

(8) the familiarity of the court of each State with the facts and issues in the pending litigation.

(c) If a court of this State determines that it is an inconvenient forum and that a court of another State is a more appropriate forum, it shall stay the proceedings upon condition that a child-custody proceeding be promptly commenced in another designated State and may impose any other condition the court considers just and proper.

(d) A court of this State may decline to exercise its jurisdiction under this [Act] if a child-custody determination is incidental to an action for divorce or another proceeding while still retaining jurisdiction over the divorce or other proceeding.

SECTION 208. JURISDICTION DECLINED BY REASON OF CONDUCT.

(a) Except as otherwise provided in Section 204 [or by other law of this State], if a court of this State has jurisdiction under this [Act] because a person seeking to invoke its jurisdiction has engaged in unjustifiable conduct, the court shall decline to exercise its jurisdiction unless:
   (1) the parents and all persons acting as parents have acquiesced in the exercise of jurisdiction;
   (2) a court of the State otherwise having jurisdiction under Sections 201 through 203 determines that this State is a more appropriate forum under Section 207; or
   (3) no court of any other State would have jurisdiction under the criteria specified in Sections 201 through 203.

(b) If a court of this State declines to exercise its jurisdiction pursuant to subsection (a), it may fashion an appropriate remedy to ensure the safety of the child and prevent a repetition of the unjustifiable conduct, including staying the proceeding until a child-custody proceeding is commenced in a court having jurisdiction under Sections 201 through 203.

(c) If a court dismisses a petition or stays a proceeding because it declines to exercise its jurisdiction pursuant to subsection (a), it shall assess against the party seeking to invoke its jurisdiction necessary and reasonable expenses including costs, communication expenses, attorney's fees, investigative fees, expenses for witnesses, travel expenses, and child care during the course of the proceedings, unless the party from whom fees are sought establishes that the assessment would be clearly inappropriate. The court may not assess fees, costs, or expenses against this State unless authorized by law other than this [Act].

SECTION 209. INFORMATION TO BE SUBMITTED TO COURT.

(a) [Subject to [local law providing for the confidentiality of procedures, addresses, and other identifying information], in] [In] a child-custody proceeding, each party, in its first pleading or in an attached affidavit, shall give information, if reasonably ascertainable, under oath as to the child's present address or whereabouts, the places where the child has lived during the last five years, and the names and present addresses of the persons with whom the child has lived during that period. The pleading or affidavit must state whether the party:

(1) has participated, as a party or witness or in any other capacity, in any other proceeding concerning the custody of or visitation with the child and, if so, identify the court, the case number, and the date of the child-custody determination, if any;

(2) knows of any proceeding that could affect the current proceeding, including proceedings for enforcement and proceedings relating to domestic violence, protective orders, termination of parental rights, and adoptions and, if so, identify the court, the case number, and the nature of the proceeding; and

(3) knows the names and addresses of any person not a party to the proceeding who has physical custody of the child or claims rights of legal custody or physical custody of, or visitation with, the child and, if so, the names and addresses of those persons.

(b) If the information required by subsection (a) is not furnished, the court, upon motion of a party or its own motion, may stay the proceeding until the information is furnished.

(c) If the declaration as to any of the items described in subsection (a)(1) through (3) is in the affirmative, the declarant shall give additional information under oath as required by the court. The court may examine the parties under oath as to details of the information furnished and other matters pertinent to the court's jurisdiction and the disposition of the case.

(d) Each party has a continuing duty to inform the court of any proceeding in this or any other State that could affect the current proceeding.

[(e) If a party alleges in an affidavit or a pleading under oath that the health, safety, or liberty of a party or child would be jeopardized by disclosure of identifying information, the information must be sealed and may not be disclosed to the other party or the public unless the court orders the disclosure to be made after a hearing in which the court takes into consideration the health, safety, or liberty of the party or child and determines that the disclosure is in the interest of jus-

SECTION 210. APPEARANCE OF PARTIES AND CHILD.

(a) In a child-custody proceeding in this State, the court may order a party to the proceeding who is in this State to appear before the court in person with or without the child. The court may order any person who is in this State and who has physical custody or control of the child to appear in person with the child.

(b) If a party to a child-custody proceeding whose presence is desired by the court is outside this State, the court may order that a notice given pursuant to Section 108 include a statement directing the party to appear in person with or without the child and informing the party that failure to appear may result in a decision adverse to the party.

(c) The court may enter any orders necessary to ensure the safety of the child and of any person ordered to appear under this section.

(d) If a party to a child-custody proceeding who is outside this State is directed to appear under subsection (b) or desires to appear personally before the court with or without the child, the court may require another party to pay reasonable and necessary travel and other expenses of the party so appearing and of the child.

[ARTICLE] 3

ENFORCEMENT

SECTION 301. DEFINITIONS. In this [article]:

(1) "Petitioner" means a person who seeks enforcement of an order for return of a child under the Hague Convention on the Civil Aspects of International Child Abduction or enforcement of a child-custody determination.

(2) "Respondent" means a person against whom a proceeding has been commenced for enforcement of an order for return of a child under the Hague Convention on the Civil Aspects of International Child Abduction or enforcement of a child-custody determination.

SECTION 302. ENFORCEMENT UNDER HAGUE CONVENTION. Under this [article] a court of this State may enforce an order for the return of the child made under the Hague Convention on the Civil Aspects of International Child Abduction as if it were a child-custody determination.

SECTION 303. DUTY TO ENFORCE.

(a) A court of this State shall recognize and enforce a child-custody determination of a court of another State if the latter court exercised jurisdiction in substantial conformity with this [Act] or the determination was made under factual circumstances meeting the jurisdictional standards of this [Act] and the determination has not been modified in accordance with this [Act].

(b) A court of this State may utilize any remedy available under other law of this State to enforce a child-custody determination made by a court of another State. The remedies provided in this [article] are cumulative and do not affect the availability of other remedies to enforce a child-custody determination.

SECTION 304. TEMPORARY VISITATION.

(a) A court of this State which does not have jurisdiction to modify a child-custody determination, may issue a temporary order enforcing:

(1) a visitation schedule made by a court of another State; or

(2) the visitation provisions of a child-custody determination of another State that does not provide for a specific visitation schedule.

(b) If a court of this State makes an order under subsection (a)(2), it shall specify in the order a period that it considers adequate to allow the petitioner to obtain an order from a court having jurisdiction under the criteria specified in [Article] 2. The order remains in effect until an order is obtained from the other court or the period expires.

SECTION 305. REGISTRATION OF CHILD-CUSTODY DETERMINATION.

(a) A child-custody determination issued by a court of another State may be registered in this State, with or without a simultaneous request for enforcement, by sending to [the appropriate court] in this State:

(1) a letter or other document requesting registration;

(2) two copies, including one certified copy, of the determination

sought to be registered, and a statement under penalty of perjury that to the best of the knowledge and belief of the person seeking registration the order has not been modified; and

(3) except as otherwise provided in Section 209, the name and address of the person seeking registration and any parent or person acting as a parent who has been awarded custody or visitation in the child-custody determination sought to be registered.

(b) On receipt of the documents required by subsection (a), the registering court shall:

(1) cause the determination to be filed as a foreign judgment, together with one copy of any accompanying documents and information, regardless of their form; and

(2) serve notice upon the persons named pursuant to subsection (a)(3) and provide them with an opportunity to contest the registration in accordance with this section.

(c) The notice required by subsection (b)(2) must state that:

(1) a registered determination is enforceable as of the date of the registration in the same manner as a determination issued by a court of this State;

(2) a hearing to contest the validity of the registered determination must be requested within 20 days after service of notice; and

(3) failure to contest the registration will result in confirmation of the child-custody determination and preclude further contest of that determination with respect to any matter that could have been asserted.

(d) A person seeking to contest the validity of a registered order must request a hearing within 20 days after service of the notice. At that hearing, the court shall confirm the registered order unless the person contesting registration establishes that:

(1) the issuing court did not have jurisdiction under [Article] 2;

(2) the child-custody determination sought to be registered has been vacated, stayed, or modified by a court having jurisdiction to do so under [Article] 2; or

(3) the person contesting registration was entitled to notice, but notice was not given in accordance with the standards of Section 108, in the proceedings before the court that issued the order for which registration is sought.

(e) If a timely request for a hearing to contest the validity of the registration is not made, the registration is confirmed as a matter of law and the person requesting registration and all persons served must be notified of the confirmation.

(f) Confirmation of a registered order, whether by operation of law or after notice and hearing, precludes further contest of the order with respect to any matter that could have been asserted at the time of registration.

SECTION 306. ENFORCEMENT OF REGISTERED DETERMINATION.

(a) A court of this State may grant any relief normally available under the law of this State to enforce a registered child-custody determination made by a court of another State.

(b) A court of this State shall recognize and enforce, but may not modify, except in accordance with [Article] 2, a registered child-custody determination of a court of another State.

SECTION 307. SIMULTANEOUS PROCEEDINGS. If a proceeding for enforcement under this [article] is commenced in a court of this State and the court determines that a proceeding to modify the determination is pending in a court of another State having jurisdiction to modify the determination under [Article] 2, the enforcing court shall immediately communicate with the modifying court. The proceeding for enforcement continues unless the enforcing court, after consultation with the modifying court, stays or dismisses the proceeding.

SECTION 308. EXPEDITED ENFORCEMENT OF CHILD-CUSTODY DETERMINATION.

(a) A petition under this [article] must be verified. Certified copies of all orders sought to be enforced and of any order confirming registration must be attached to the petition. A copy of a certified copy of an order may be attached instead of the original.

(b) A petition for enforcement of a child-custody determination must state:

(1) whether the court that issued the determination identified the jurisdictional basis it relied upon in exercising jurisdiction and, if so, what the basis was;

(2) whether the determination for which enforcement is sought has

been vacated, stayed, or modified by a court whose decision must be enforced under this [Act] and, if so, identify the court, the case number, and the nature of the proceeding;

(3) whether any proceeding has been commenced that could affect the current proceeding, including proceedings relating to domestic violence, protective orders, termination of parental rights, and adoptions and, if so, identify the court, the case number, and the nature of the proceeding;

(4) the present physical address of the child and the respondent, if known;

(5) whether relief in addition to the immediate physical custody of the child and attorney's fees is sought, including a request for assistance from [law enforcement officials] and, if so, the relief sought; and

(6) if the child-custody determination has been registered and confirmed under Section 305, the date and place of registration.

(c) Upon the filing of a petition, the court shall issue an order directing the respondent to appear in person with or without the child at a hearing and may enter any order necessary to ensure the safety of the parties and the child. The hearing must be held on the next judicial day after service of the order unless that date is impossible. In that event, the court shall hold the hearing on the first judicial day possible. The court may extend the date of hearing at the request of the petitioner.

(d) An order issued under subsection (c) must state the time and place of the hearing and advise the respondent that at the hearing the court will order that the petitioner may take immediate physical custody of the child and the payment of fees, costs, and expenses under Section 312, and may schedule a hearing to determine whether further relief is appropriate, unless the respondent appears and establishes that:

(1) the child-custody determination has not been registered and confirmed under Section 305 and that:

(A) the issuing court did not have jurisdiction under [Article] 2;

(B) the child-custody determination for which enforcement is sought has been vacated, stayed, or modified by a court having jurisdiction to do so under [Article] 2; or

(C) the respondent was entitled to notice, but notice was not given in accordance with the standards of Section 108, in the proceedings before the court that issued the order for which enforcement is sought; or

(2) the child-custody determination for which enforcement is sought was registered and confirmed under Section 304, but has been vacated, stayed, or modified by a court of a State having jurisdiction to do so under [Article] 2.

SECTION 309. SERVICE OF PETITION AND ORDER. Except as otherwise provided in Section 311, the petition and order must be served, by any method authorized [by the law of this State], upon respondent and any person who has physical custody of the child.

SECTION 310. HEARING AND ORDER.

(a) Unless the court issues a temporary emergency order pursuant to Section 204, upon a finding that a petitioner is entitled to immediate physical custody of the child, the court shall order that the petitioner may take immediate physical custody of the child unless the respondent establishes that:

(1) the child-custody determination has not been registered and confirmed under Section 305 and that:

(A) the issuing court did not have jurisdiction under [Article] 2;

(B) the child-custody determination for which enforcement is sought has been vacated, stayed, or modified by a court of a State having jurisdiction to do so under [Article] 2; or

(C) the respondent was entitled to notice, but notice was not given in accordance with the standards of Section 108, in the proceedings before the court that issued the order for which enforcement is sought; or

(2) the child-custody determination for which enforcement is sought was registered and confirmed under Section 305 but has been vacated, stayed, or modified by a court of a State having jurisdiction to do so under [Article] 2.

(b) The court shall award the fees, costs, and expenses authorized under Section 312 and may grant additional relief, including a request for the assistance of [law enforcement officials], and set a further hearing to determine whether additional relief is appropriate.

(c) If a party called to testify refuses to answer on the ground that the testimony may be self-incriminating, the court may draw an adverse inference from the refusal.

(d) A privilege against disclosure of communications between spouses and a defense of immunity based on the relationship of husband and wife or parent and child may not be invoked in a proceeding under this [article].

SECTION 311. WARRANT TO TAKE PHYSICAL CUSTODY OF CHILD.

(a) Upon the filing of a petition seeking enforcement of a child-custody determination, the petitioner may file a verified application for the issuance of a warrant to take physical custody of the child if the child is immediately likely to suffer serious physical harm or be removed from this State.

(b) If the court, upon the testimony of the petitioner or other witness, finds that the child is imminently likely to suffer serious physical harm or be removed from this State, it may issue a warrant to take physical custody of the child. The petition must be heard on the next judicial day after the warrant is executed unless that date is impossible. In that event, the court shall hold the hearing on the first judicial day possible. The application for the warrant must include the statements required by Section 308(b).

(c) A warrant to take physical custody of a child must:

(1) recite the facts upon which a conclusion of imminent serious physical harm or removal from the jurisdiction is based;

(2) direct law enforcement officers to take physical custody of the child immediately; and

(3) provide for the placement of the child pending final relief.

(d) The respondent must be served with the petition, warrant, and order immediately after the child is taken into physical custody.

(e) A warrant to take physical custody of a child is enforceable throughout this State. If the court finds on the basis of the testimony of the petitioner or other witness that a less intrusive remedy is not effective, it may authorize law enforcement officers to enter private property to take physical custody of the child. If required by exigent circumstances of the case, the court may authorize law enforcement officers to make a forcible entry at any hour.

(f) The court may impose conditions upon placement of a child to ensure the appearance of the child and the child's custodian.

SECTION 312. COSTS, FEES, AND EXPENSES.

(a) The court shall award the prevailing party, including a State, necessary and reasonable expenses incurred by or on behalf of the party, including costs, communication expenses, attorney's fees, investigative fees, expenses for witnesses, travel expenses, and child care during the course of the proceedings, unless the party from whom fees or expenses are sought establishes that the award would be clearly inappropriate.

(b) The court may not assess fees, costs, or expenses against a State unless authorized by law other than this [Act].

SECTION 313. RECOGNITION AND ENFORCEMENT. A court of this State shall accord full faith and credit to an order issued by another State and consistent with this [Act] which enforces a child-custody determination by a court of another State unless the order has been vacated, stayed, or modified by a court having jurisdiction to do so under [Article] 2.

SECTION 314. APPEALS. An appeal may be taken from a final order in a proceeding under this [article] in accordance with [expedited appellate procedures in other civil cases]. Unless the court enters a temporary emergency order under Section 204, the enforcing court may not stay an order enforcing a child-custody determination pending appeal.

SECTION 315. ROLE OF [PROSECUTOR OR PUBLIC OFFICIAL].

(a) In a case arising under this [Act] or involving the Hague Convention on the Civil Aspects of International Child Abduction, the [prosecutor or other appropriate public official] may take any lawful action, including resort to a proceeding under this [article] or any other available civil proceeding to locate a child, obtain the return of a child, or enforce a child-custody determination if there is:

(1) an existing child-custody determination;

(2) a request to do so from a court in a pending child-custody proceeding;

(3) a reasonable belief that a criminal statute has been violated; or

(4) a reasonable belief that the child has been wrongfully removed or retained in violation of the Hague Convention on the Civil Aspects of International Child Abduction.

(b) A [prosecutor or appropriate public official] acting under this section acts on behalf of the court and may not represent any party.

SECTION 316. ROLE OF [LAW ENFORCEMENT]. At the request of a [prosecutor or other appropriate public official] acting under Section 315, a [law enforcement officer] may take any lawful action reasonably necessary to locate a child or a party and assist [a prosecutor or appropriate public official] with responsibilities under Section 315.

SECTION 317. COSTS AND EXPENSES. If the respondent is not the prevailing party, the court may assess against the respondent all direct expenses and costs incurred by the [prosecutor or other appropriate public official] and [law enforcement officers] under Section 315 or 316.

[ARTICLE] 4

MISCELLANEOUS PROVISIONS

SECTION 401. APPLICATION AND CONSTRUCTION. In applying and construing this Uniform Act, consideration must be given to the need to promote uniformity of the law with respect to its subject matter among States that enact it.

SECTION 402. SEVERABILITY CLAUSE. If any provision of this [Act] or its application to any person or circumstance is held invalid, the invalidity does not affect other provisions or applications of this [Act] which can be given effect without the invalid provision or application, and to this end the provisions of this [Act] are severable.

SECTION 403. EFFECTIVE DATE. This [Act] takes effect ....

SECTION 404. REPEALS. The following acts and parts of acts are hereby repealed:

(1) The Uniform Child Custody Jurisdiction Act;

(2) ....

(3) ....

SECTION 405. TRANSITIONAL PROVISION. A motion or other request for relief made in a child-custody proceeding or to enforce a child-custody determination which was commenced before the effective date of this [Act] is governed by the law in effect at the time the motion or other request was made.

APPENDIX 8

Sean and David Goldman International Child Abduction Prevention and Return Act of 2014

Public Law 113–150
113th Congress

An Act

To ensure compliance with the 1980 Hague Convention on the Civil Aspects of International Child Abduction by countries with which the United States enjoys reciprocal obligations, to establish procedures for the prompt return of children abducted to other countries, and for other purposes.

Aug. 8, 2014
[H.R. 3212]

Be it enacted by the Senate and House of Representatives of the United States of America in Congress assembled,

Sean and David Goldman International Child Abduction Prevention and Return Act of 2014. 22 USC 9101 note.

SECTION 1. SHORT TITLE AND TABLE OF CONTENTS.

(a) SHORT TITLE.—This Act may be cited as the "Sean and David Goldman International Child Abduction Prevention and Return Act of 2014".

(b) TABLE OF CONTENTS.—The table of contents for this Act is as follows:

SEC. 2. FINDINGS; SENSE OF CONGRESS; PURPOSES.

22 USC 9101 note.

(a) FINDINGS.—Congress finds the following:

(1) Sean Goldman, a United States citizen and resident of New Jersey, was abducted from the United States in 2004 and separated from his father, David Goldman, who spent nearly 6 years battling for the return of his son from Brazil before Sean was finally returned to Mr. Goldman's custody on December 24, 2009.

(2) The Department of State's Office of Children's Issues, which serves as the Central Authority of the United States for the purposes of the 1980 Hague Convention on the Civil

Aspects of International Child Abduction (referred to in this Act as the "Hague Abduction Convention"), has received thousands of requests since 2007 for assistance in the return to the United States of children who have been wrongfully abducted by a parent or other legal guardian to another country.

(3) For a variety of reasons reflecting the significant obstacles to the recovery of abducted children, as well as the legal and factual complexity involving such cases, not all cases are reported to the Central Authority of the United States.

(4) More than 1,000 outgoing international child abductions are reported every year to the Central Authority of the United States, which depends solely on proactive reporting of abduction cases.

(5) Only about one-half of the children abducted from the United States to countries with which the United States enjoys reciprocal obligations under the Hague Abduction Convention are returned to the United States.

(6) The United States and other Convention countries have expressed their desire, through the Hague Abduction Convention, "to protect children internationally from the harmful effects of their wrongful removal or retention and to establish procedures to ensure their prompt return to the State of their habitual residence, as well as to secure protection for rights of access."

(7) Compliance by the United States and other Convention countries depends on the actions of their designated central authorities, the performance of their judicial systems as reflected in the legal process and decisions rendered to enforce or effectuate the Hague Abduction Convention, and the ability and willingness of their law enforcement authorities to ensure the swift enforcement of orders rendered pursuant to the Hague Abduction Convention.

(8) According to data from the Department of State, approximately 40 percent of abduction cases involve children taken from the United States to countries with which the United States does not have reciprocal obligations under the Hague Abduction Convention or other arrangements relating to the resolution of abduction cases.

(9) According to the Department of State's April 2010 Report on Compliance with the Hague Convention on the Civil Aspects of International Child Abduction, "parental child abduction jeopardizes the child and has substantial long-term consequences for both the child and the left-behind parent."

(10) Few left-behind parents have the extraordinary financial resources necessary—

(A) to pursue individual civil or criminal remedies in both the United States and a foreign country, even if such remedies are available; or

(B) to engage in repeated foreign travel to attempt to obtain the return of their children through diplomatic or other channels.

(11) Military parents often face additional complications in resolving abduction cases because of the challenges presented by their military obligations.

(12) In addition to using the Hague Abduction Convention to achieve the return of abducted children, the United States has an array of Federal, State, and local law enforcement,

criminal justice, and judicial tools at its disposal to prevent international abductions.

(13) Federal agencies tasked with preventing international abductions have indicated that the most effective way to stop international child abductions is while they are in progress, rather than after the child has been removed to a foreign destination.

(14) Parental awareness of abductions in progress, rapid response by relevant law enforcement, and effective coordination among Federal, State, local, and international stakeholders are critical in preventing such abductions.

(15) A more robust application of domestic tools, in cooperation with international law enforcement entities and appropriate application of the Hague Abduction Convention could—

(A) discourage some parents from attempting abductions;

(B) block attempted abductions at ports of exit; and

(C) help achieve the return of more abducted children.

(b) SENSE OF CONGRESS.—It is the sense of Congress that the United States should set a strong example for other Convention countries in the timely location and prompt resolution of cases involving children abducted abroad and brought to the United States.

(c) PURPOSES.—The purposes of this Act are—

(1) to protect children whose habitual residence is the United States from wrongful abduction;

(2) to assist left-behind parents in quickly resolving cases and maintaining safe and predictable contact with their child while an abduction case is pending;

(3) to protect the custodial rights of parents, including military parents, by providing the parents, the judicial system, and law enforcement authorities with the information they need to prevent unlawful abduction before it occurs;

(4) to enhance the prompt resolution of abduction and access cases;

(5) to detail an appropriate set of actions to be undertaken by the Secretary of State to address persistent problems in the resolution of abduction cases;

(6) to establish a program to prevent wrongful abductions; and

(7) to increase interagency coordination in preventing international child abduction by convening a working group composed of presidentially appointed and Senate confirmed officials from the Department of State, the Department of Homeland Security, and the Department of Justice.

SEC. 3. DEFINITIONS. 22 USC 9101.

In this Act:

(1) ABDUCTED CHILD.—The term "abducted child" means a child who is the victim of international child abduction.

(2) ABDUCTION.—The term "abduction" means the alleged wrongful removal of a child from the child's country of habitual residence, or the wrongful retention of a child outside such country, in violation of a left-behind parent's custodial rights, including the rights of a military parent.

(3) ABDUCTION CASE.—The term "abduction case" means a case that—

(A) has been reported to the Central Authority of the United States by a left-behind parent for the resolution of an abduction; and

(B) meets the criteria for an international child abduction under the Hague Abduction Convention, regardless of whether the country at issue is a Convention country.

(4) ACCESS CASE.—The term "access case" means a case involving an application filed with the Central Authority of the United States by a parent seeking rights of access.

(5) ANNUAL REPORT.—The term "Annual Report" means the Annual Report on International Child Abduction required under section 101.

(6) APPLICATION.—The term "application" means—

(A) in the case of a Convention country, the application required pursuant to article 8 of the Hague Abduction Convention;

(B) in the case of a bilateral procedures country, the formal document required, pursuant to the provisions of the applicable arrangement, to request the return of an abducted child or to request rights of access, as applicable; and

(C) in the case of a non-Convention country, the formal request by the Central Authority of the United States to the Central Authority of such country requesting the return of an abducted child or for rights of contact with an abducted child.

(7) APPROPRIATE CONGRESSIONAL COMMITTEES.—The term "appropriate congressional committees" means the Committee on Foreign Relations of the Senate and the Committee on Foreign Affairs of the House of Representatives.

(8) BILATERAL PROCEDURES.—The term "bilateral procedures" means any procedures established by, or pursuant to, a bilateral arrangement, including a Memorandum of Understanding between the United States and another country, to resolve abduction and access cases, including procedures to address interim contact matters.

(9) BILATERAL PROCEDURES COUNTRY.—The term "bilateral procedures country" means a country with which the United States has entered into bilateral procedures, including Memoranda of Understanding, with respect to child abductions.

(10) CENTRAL AUTHORITY.—The term "Central Authority" means—

(A) in the case of a Convention country, the meaning given such term in article 6 of the Hague Abduction Convention;

(B) in the case of a bilateral procedures country, the official entity designated by the government of the bilateral procedures country within the applicable memorandum of understanding pursuant to section 103(b)(1) to discharge the duties imposed on the entity; and

(C) in the case of a non-Convention country, the foreign ministry or other appropriate authority of such country.

(11) CHILD.—The term "child" means an individual who has not attained 16 years of age.

(12) CONVENTION COUNTRY.—The term "Convention country" means a country for which the Hague Abduction

Convention has entered into force with respect to the United States.

(13) HAGUE ABDUCTION CONVENTION.—The term "Hague Abduction Convention" means the Convention on the Civil Aspects of International Child Abduction, done at The Hague October 25, 1980.

(14) INTERIM CONTACT.—The term "interim contact" means the ability of a left-behind parent to communicate with or visit an abducted child during the pendency of an abduction case.

(15) LEFT-BEHIND PARENT.—The term "left-behind parent" means an individual or legal custodian who alleges that an abduction has occurred that is in breach of rights of custody attributed to such individual.

(16) NON-CONVENTION COUNTRY.—The term "non-Convention country" means a country in which the Hague Abduction Convention has not entered into force with respect to the United States.

(17) OVERSEAS MILITARY DEPENDENT CHILD.—The term "overseas military dependent child" means a child whose habitual residence is the United States according to United States law even though the child is residing outside the United States with a military parent.

(18) OVERSEAS MILITARY PARENT.—The term "overseas military parent" means an individual who—

(A) has custodial rights with respect to a child; and

(B) is serving outside the United States as a member of the United States Armed Forces.

(19) PATTERN OF NONCOMPLIANCE.—

(A) IN GENERAL.—The term "pattern of noncompliance" means the persistent failure—

(i) of a Convention country to implement and abide by provisions of the Hague Abduction Convention;

(ii) of a non-Convention country to abide by bilateral procedures that have been established between the United States and such country; or

(iii) of a non-Convention country to work with the Central Authority of the United States to resolve abduction cases.

(B) PERSISTENT FAILURE.—Persistent failure under subparagraph (A) may be evidenced in a given country by the presence of 1 or more of the following criteria:

(i) Thirty percent or more of the total abduction cases in such country are unresolved abduction cases.

(ii) The Central Authority regularly fails to fulfill its responsibilities pursuant to—

(I) the Hague Abduction Convention; or

(II) any bilateral procedures between the United States and such country.

(iii) The judicial or administrative branch, as applicable, of the national government of a Convention country or a bilateral procedures country fails to regularly implement and comply with the provisions of the Hague Abduction Convention or bilateral procedures, as applicable.

(iv) Law enforcement authorities regularly fail to enforce return orders or determinations of rights of access rendered by the judicial or administrative authorities of the government of the country in abduction cases.

(20) RIGHTS OF ACCESS.—The term "rights of access" means the establishment of rights of contact between a child and a parent seeking access in Convention countries—

(A) by operation of law;

(B) through a judicial or administrative determination; or

(C) through a legally enforceable arrangement between the parties.

(21) RIGHTS OF CUSTODY.—The term "rights of custody" means rights of care and custody of a child, including the right to determine the place of residence of a child, under the laws of the country in which the child is a habitual resident—

(A) attributed to an individual or legal custodian; and

(B) arising—

(i) by operation of law; or

(ii) through a judicial or administrative decision; or

(iii) through a legally enforceable arrangement between the parties.

(22) RIGHTS OF INTERIM CONTACT.—The term "rights of interim contact" means the rights of contact between a child and a left-behind parent, which has been provided as a provisional measure while an abduction case is pending, under the laws of the country in which the child is located—

(A) by operation of law; or

(B) through a judicial or administrative determination; or

(C) through a legally enforceable arrangement between the parties.

(23) UNRESOLVED ABDUCTION CASE.—

Time period.

(A) IN GENERAL.—Subject to subparagraph (B), the term "unresolved abduction case" means an abduction case that remains unresolved for a period that exceeds 12 months after the date on which the completed application for return of the child is submitted for determination to the judicial or administrative authority, as applicable, in the country in which the child is located.

(B) RESOLUTION OF CASE.—An abduction case shall be considered to be resolved if—

(i) the child is returned to the country of habitual residence, pursuant to the Hague Abduction Convention or other appropriate bilateral procedures, if applicable;

(ii) the judicial or administrative branch, as applicable, of the government of the country in which the child is located has implemented, and is complying with, the provisions of the Hague Abduction Convention or other bilateral procedures, as applicable;

(iii) the left-behind parent reaches a voluntary arrangement with the other parent;

(iv) the left-behind parent submits a written withdrawal of the application or the request for assistance to the Department of State;

(v) the left-behind parent cannot be located for 1 year despite the documented efforts of the Department of State to locate the parent; or

(vi) the child or left-behind parent is deceased.

TITLE I—DEPARTMENT OF STATE ACTIONS

SEC. 101. ANNUAL REPORT.

22 USC 9111.

Public information. Web posting.

(a) IN GENERAL.—Not later than April 30 of each year, the Secretary of State shall submit to the appropriate congressional committees an Annual Report on International Child Abduction. The Secretary shall post the Annual Report to the publicly accessible website of the Department of State.

(b) CONTENTS.—Each Annual Report shall include—

(1) a list of all countries in which there were 1 or more abduction cases, during the preceding calendar year, relating to a child whose habitual residence is the United States, including a description of whether each such country—

(A) is a Convention country;

(B) is a bilateral procedures country;

(C) has other procedures for resolving such abductions; or

(D) adheres to no protocols with respect to child abduction;

(2) for each country with respect to which there were 5 or more pending abduction cases, during the preceding year, relating to a child whose habitual residence is the United States—

(A) the number of such new abduction and access cases reported during the preceding year;

(B) for Convention and bilateral procedures countries—

(i) the number of abduction and access cases that the Central Authority of the United States transmitted to the Central Authority of such country; and

(ii) the number of abduction and access cases that were not submitted by the Central Authority to the judicial or administrative authority, as applicable, of such country;

(C) the reason for the delay in submission of each case identified in subparagraph (B)(ii) by the Central Authority of such country to the judicial or administrative authority of that country;

(D) the number of unresolved abduction and access cases, and the length of time each case has been pending;

(E) the number and percentage of unresolved abduction cases in which law enforcement authorities have—

(i) not located the abducted child;

(ii) failed to undertake serious efforts to locate the abducted child; and

(iii) failed to enforce a return order rendered by the judicial or administrative authorities of such country;

(F) the total number and the percentage of the total number of abduction and access cases, respectively, resolved during the preceding year;

(G) recommendations to improve the resolution of abduction and access cases; and

(H) the average time it takes to locate a child;

(3) the number of abducted children whose habitual residence is in the United States and who were returned to the United States from—

(A) Convention countries;

(B) bilateral procedures countries;

(C) countries having other procedures for resolving such abductions; or

(D) countries adhering to no protocols with respect to child abduction;

(4) a list of Convention countries and bilateral procedures countries that have failed to comply with any of their obligations under the Hague Abduction Convention or bilateral procedures, as applicable, with respect to the resolution of abduction and access cases;

(5) a list of countries demonstrating a pattern of noncompliance and a description of the criteria on which the determination of a pattern of noncompliance for each country is based;

(6) information on efforts by the Secretary of State to encourage non-Convention countries—

(A) to ratify or accede to the Hague Abduction Convention;

(B) to enter into or implement other bilateral procedures, including memoranda of understanding, with the United States; and

(C) to address pending abduction and access cases;

(7) the number of cases resolved without abducted children being returned to the United States from Convention countries, bilateral procedures countries, or other non-Convention countries;

(8) a list of countries that became Convention countries with respect to the United States during the preceding year; and

(9) information about efforts to seek resolution of abduction cases of children whose habitual residence is in the United States and whose abduction occurred before the Hague Abduction Convention entered into force with respect to the United States.

(c) EXCEPTIONS.—Unless a left-behind parent provides written permission to the Central Authority of the United States to include personally identifiable information about the parent or the child in the Annual Report, the Annual Report may not include any personally identifiable information about any such parent, child, or party to an abduction or access case involving such parent or child.

(d) ADDITIONAL SECTIONS.—Each Annual Report shall also include—

(1) information on the number of unresolved abduction cases affecting military parents;

(2) a description of the assistance offered to such military parents;

(3) information on the use of airlines in abductions, voluntary airline practices to prevent abductions, and recommendations for best airline practices to prevent abductions;

(4) information on actions taken by the Central Authority of the United States to train domestic judges in the application of the Hague Abduction Convention; and

(5) information on actions taken by the Central Authority of the United States to train United States Armed Forces legal assistance personnel, military chaplains, and military family support center personnel about—

(A) abductions;

(B) the risk of loss of contact with children; and

(C) the legal means available to resolve such cases.

(e) REPEAL OF THE HAGUE ABDUCTION CONVENTION COMPLIANCE REPORT.—Section 2803 of the Foreign Affairs Reform and Restructuring Act of 1998 (42 U.S.C. 11611) is repealed.

(f) NOTIFICATION TO CONGRESS ON COUNTRIES IN NONCOMPLIANCE.—

(1) IN GENERAL.—The Secretary of State shall include, in a separate section of the Annual Report, the Secretary's determination, pursuant to the provisions under section 202(b), of whether each country listed in the report has engaged in a pattern of noncompliance in cases of child abduction during the preceding 12 months. Determination. Time period.

(2) CONTENTS.—The section described in paragraph (1)—

(A) shall identify any action or actions described in section 202(d) (or commensurate action as provided in section 202(e)) that have been taken by the Secretary with respect to each country;

(B) shall describe the basis for the Secretary's determination of the pattern of noncompliance by each country;

(C) shall indicate whether noneconomic policy options designed to resolve the pattern of noncompliance have reasonably been exhausted, including the consultations required under section 203.

SEC. 102. STANDARDS AND ASSISTANCE. 22 USC 9112.

The Secretary of State shall—

(1) ensure that United States diplomatic and consular missions abroad—

(A) maintain a consistent reporting standard with respect to abduction and access cases;

(B) designate at least 1 senior official in each such mission, at the discretion of the Chief of Mission, to assist left-behind parents from the United States who are visiting such country or otherwise seeking to resolve abduction or access cases; and

(C) monitor developments in abduction and access cases; and

(2) develop and implement written strategic plans for engagement with any Convention or non-Convention country in which there are 5 or more cases of international child abduction. Strategic plans.

SEC. 103. BILATERAL PROCEDURES, INCLUDING MEMORANDA OF UNDERSTANDING. 22 USC 9113.

(a) DEVELOPMENT.—

(1) IN GENERAL.—Not later than 180 days after the date of the enactment of this Act, the Secretary of State shall initiate a process to develop and enter into appropriate bilateral procedures, including memoranda of understanding, as appropriate, Deadline.

with non-Convention countries that are unlikely to become Convention countries in the foreseeable future, or with Convention countries that have unresolved abduction cases that occurred before the Hague Abduction Convention entered into force with respect to the United States or that country.

(2) PRIORITIZATION.—In carrying out paragraph (1), the Secretary of State shall give priority to countries with significant abduction cases and related issues.

(b) ELEMENTS.—The bilateral procedures described in subsection (a) should include provisions relating to—

(1) the identification of—

(A) the Central Authority;

(B) the judicial or administrative authority that will promptly adjudicate abduction and access cases;

(C) the law enforcement agencies; and

(D) the implementation of procedures to ensure the immediate enforcement of an order issued by the authority identified pursuant to subparagraph (B) to return an abducted child to a left-behind parent, including by—

(i) conducting an investigation to ascertain the location of the abducted child;

(ii) providing protection to the abducted child after such child is located; and

(iii) retrieving the abducted child and making the appropriate arrangements for such child to be returned to the child's country of habitual residence;

Deadline. (2) the implementation of a protocol to effectuate the return of an abducted child identified in an abduction case not later than 6 weeks after the application with respect to the abduction case has been submitted to the judicial or administrative authority, as applicable, of the country in which the abducted child is located;

(3) the implementation of a protocol for the establishment and protection of the rights of interim contact during pendency of abduction cases; and

(4) the implementation of a protocol to establish periodic visits between a United States embassy or consular official and an abducted child, in order to allow the official to ascertain the child's location and welfare.

22 USC 9114.

SEC. 104. REPORT TO CONGRESSIONAL REPRESENTATIVES.

(a) NOTIFICATION.—The Secretary of State shall submit written notification to the Member of Congress and Senators, or Resident Commissioner or Delegate, as appropriate, representing the legal residence of a left-behind parent if such parent—

(1) reports an abduction to the Central Authority of the United States; and

(2) consents to such notification.

(b) TIMING.—At the request of any person who is a left-behind parent, including a left-behind parent who previously reported an abduction to the Central Authority of the United States before the date of the enactment of this Act, the notification required under subsection (a) shall be provided as soon as is practicable.

TITLE II—ACTIONS BY THE SECRETARY OF STATE

SEC. 201. RESPONSE TO INTERNATIONAL CHILD ABDUCTIONS. 22 USC 9121.

(a) UNITED STATES POLICY.—It is the policy of the United States—

(1) to promote the best interest of children wrongfully abducted from the United States by—

(A) establishing legal rights and procedures for their prompt return; and

(B) ensuring the enforcement of reciprocal international obligations under the Hague Abduction Convention or arrangements under bilateral procedures;

(2) to promote the timely resolution of abduction cases through 1 or more of the actions described in section 202; and

(3) to ensure appropriate coordination within the Federal Government and between Federal, State, and local agencies involved in abduction prevention, investigation, and resolution.

(b) ACTIONS BY THE SECRETARY OF STATE IN RESPONSE TO UNRESOLVED CASES.—

(1) DETERMINATION OF ACTION BY THE SECRETARY OF STATE.—For each abduction or access case relating to a child whose habitual residence is in the United States that remains pending or is otherwise unresolved on the date that is 12 months after the date on which the Central Authority of the United States submits such case to a foreign country, the Secretary of State shall determine whether the government of such foreign country has failed to take appropriate steps to resolve the case. If the Secretary of State determines that such failure occurred, the Secretary should, as expeditiously as practicable— Time period.

(A) take 1 or more of the actions described in subsections (d) and (e) of section 202; and

(B) direct the Chief of Mission in that foreign country to directly address the resolution of the case with senior officials in the foreign government.

(2) AUTHORITY FOR DELAY OF ACTION BY THE SECRETARY OF STATE.—The Secretary of State may delay any action described in paragraph (1) if the Secretary determines that an additional period of time, not to exceed 1 year, will substantially assist in resolving the case. Time period.

(3) REPORT.—If the Secretary of State delays any action pursuant to paragraph (2) or decides not to take an action described in subsection (d) or (e) of section 202 after making the determination described in paragraph (1), the Secretary, not later than 15 days after such delay or decision, shall provide a report to the appropriate congressional committees that details the reasons for delaying action or not taking action, as appropriate.

(4) CONGRESSIONAL BRIEFINGS.—At the request of the appropriate congressional committees, the Secretary of State shall provide a detailed briefing, including a written report, if requested, on actions taken to resolve a case or the cause for delay.

(c) IMPLEMENTATION.—

(1) IN GENERAL.—In carrying out subsection (b), the Secretary of State should—

(A) take 1 or more actions that most appropriately respond to the nature and severity of the governmental failure to resolve the unresolved abduction case; and

(B) seek, to the fullest extent possible—

(i) to initially respond by communicating with the Central Authority of the country; and

(ii) if clause (i) is unsuccessful, to target subsequent actions—

(I) as narrowly as practicable, with respect to the agencies or instrumentalities of the foreign government that are responsible for such failures; and

(II) in ways that respect the separation of powers and independence of the judiciary of the country, as applicable.

(2) GUIDELINES FOR ACTIONS BY THE SECRETARY OF STATE.— In addition to the guidelines under paragraph (1), the Secretary of State, in determining whether to take 1 or more actions under paragraphs (5) through (7) of section 202(d) or section 202(e), shall seek to minimize any adverse impact on—

(A) the population of the country whose government is targeted by the action or actions;

(B) the humanitarian activities of United States and nongovernmental organizations in the country; and

(C) the national security interests of the United States.

22 USC 9122.

SEC. 202. ACTIONS BY THE SECRETARY OF STATE IN RESPONSE TO PATTERNS OF NONCOMPLIANCE IN CASES OF INTERNATIONAL CHILD ABDUCTIONS.

(a) RESPONSE TO A PATTERN OF NONCOMPLIANCE.—It is the policy of the United States—

(1) to oppose institutional or other systemic failures of foreign governments to fulfill their obligations pursuant to the Hague Abduction Convention or bilateral procedures, as applicable, to resolve abduction and access cases;

(2) to promote reciprocity pursuant to, and in compliance with, the Hague Abduction Convention or bilateral procedures, as appropriate; and

(3) to directly engage with senior foreign government officials to most effectively address patterns of noncompliance.

(b) DETERMINATION OF COUNTRIES WITH PATTERNS OF NONCOMPLIANCE IN CASES OF INTERNATIONAL CHILD ABDUCTION.—

Deadline.

(1) ANNUAL REVIEW.—Not later than April 30 of each year, the Secretary of State shall—

Time period.

(A) review the status of abduction and access cases in each foreign country in order to determine whether the government of such country has engaged in a pattern of noncompliance during the preceding 12 months; and

(B) report such determination pursuant to section 101(f).

(2) DETERMINATIONS OF RESPONSIBLE PARTIES.—The Secretary of State shall seek to determine the agencies or instrumentalities of the government of each country determined to have engaged in a pattern of noncompliance under paragraph (1)(A) that are responsible for such pattern of noncompliance—

(A) to appropriately target actions in response to such noncompliance; and

(B) to engage with senior foreign government officials to effectively address such noncompliance.

(c) ACTIONS BY THE SECRETARY OF STATE WITH RESPECT TO COUNTRY WITH A PATTERN OF NONCOMPLIANCE.—

(1) IN GENERAL.—Not later than 90 days (or 180 days in case of a delay under paragraph (2)) after a country is determined to have been engaged in a pattern of noncompliance under subsection (b)(1)(A), the Secretary of State shall— Deadlines.

(A) take 1 or more of the actions described in subsection (d);

(B) direct the Chief of Mission in that country to directly address the systemic problems that led to such determination; and

(C) inform senior officials in the foreign government of the potential repercussions related to such designation. Notification.

(2) AUTHORITY FOR DELAY OF ACTIONS BY THE SECRETARY OF STATE.—The Secretary shall not be required to take action under paragraph (1) until the expiration of a single, additional period of up to 90 days if, on or before the date on which the Secretary of State is required to take such action, the Secretary determines and certifies to the appropriate congressional committees that such additional period is necessary— Time period. Determination. Certification.

(A) for a continuation of negotiations that have been commenced with the government of a country described in paragraph (1) in order to bring about a cessation of the pattern of noncompliance by such country;

(B) for a review of corrective action taken by a country after the designation of such country as being engaged in a pattern of noncompliance under subsection (b)(1)(A); or

(C) in anticipation that corrective action will be taken by such country during such 90-day period.

(3) EXCEPTION FOR ADDITIONAL ACTION BY THE SECRETARY OF STATE.—The Secretary of State shall not be required to take additional action under paragraph (1) with respect to a country determined to have been engaged in a persistent pattern of noncompliance if the Secretary—

(A) has taken action pursuant to paragraph (5), (6), or (7) of subsection (d) with respect to such country in the preceding year and such action continues to be in effect;

(B) exercises the waiver under section 204 and briefs the appropriate congressional committees; or

(C) submits a report to the appropriate congressional committees that— Reports.

(i) indicates that such country is subject to multiple, broad-based sanctions; and

(ii) describes how such sanctions satisfy the requirements under this subsection.

(4) REPORT TO CONGRESS.—Not later than 90 days after the submission of the Annual Report, the Secretary shall submit a report to Congress on the specific actions taken against countries determined to have been engaged in a pattern of noncompliance under this section.

(d) DESCRIPTION OF ACTIONS BY THE SECRETARY OF STATE IN HAGUE ABDUCTION CONVENTION COUNTRIES.—Except as provided in subsection (f), the actions by the Secretary of State referred to in this subsection are—

(1) a demarche;

(2) an official public statement detailing unresolved cases;

(3) a public condemnation;

(4) a delay or cancellation of 1 or more bilateral working, official, or state visits;

(5) the withdrawal, limitation, or suspension of United States development assistance in accordance with section 116 of the Foreign Assistance Act of 1961 (22 U.S.C. 2151n);

(6) the withdrawal, limitation, or suspension of United States security assistance in accordance with section 502B of the Foreign Assistance Act of 1961 (22 U.S.C. 2304);

(7) the withdrawal, limitation, or suspension of assistance to the central government of a country pursuant to chapter 4 of part II of the Foreign Assistance Act of 1961 (22 U.S.C. 2346 et seq.; relating to the Economic Support Fund); and

(8) a formal request to the foreign country concerned to extradite an individual who is engaged in abduction and who has been formally accused of, charged with, or convicted of an extraditable offense.

(e) COMMENSURATE ACTION.—

Determination.

(1) IN GENERAL.—Except as provided in subsection (f), the Secretary of State may substitute any other action authorized by law for any action described in subsection (d) if the Secretary determines that such action—

(A) is commensurate in effect to the action substituted; and

(B) would substantially further the purposes of this Act.

Reports.

(2) NOTIFICATION.—If commensurate action is taken pursuant to this subsection, the Secretary shall submit a report to the appropriate congressional committees that—

(A) describes such action;

(B) explains the reasons for taking such action; and

(C) specifically describes the basis for the Secretary's determination under paragraph (1) that such action—

(i) is commensurate with the action substituted; and

(ii) substantially furthers the purposes of this Act.

(f) RESOLUTION.—The Secretary of State shall seek to take all appropriate actions authorized by law to resolve the unresolved case or to obtain the cessation of such pattern of noncompliance, as applicable.

(g) HUMANITARIAN EXCEPTION.—Any action taken pursuant to subsection (d) or (e) may not prohibit or restrict the provision of medicine, medical equipment or supplies, food, or other life-saving humanitarian assistance.

22 USC 9123.

SEC. 203. CONSULTATIONS WITH FOREIGN GOVERNMENTS.

As soon as practicable after the Secretary of State makes a determination under section 201 in response to a failure to resolve unresolved abduction cases or the Secretary takes an action under subsection (d) or (e) of section 202, based on a pattern of noncompliance, the Secretary shall request consultations with the government of such country regarding the situation giving rise to such determination.

SEC. 204. WAIVER BY THE SECRETARY OF STATE. 22 USC 9124.

(a) IN GENERAL.—Subject to subsection (b), the Secretary of State may waive the application of any of the actions described in subsections (d) and (e) of section 202 with respect to a country if the Secretary determines and notifies the appropriate congressional committees that— Determination. Notification.

(1) the government of such country—

(A) has satisfactorily resolved the abduction cases giving rise to the application of any of such actions; or

(B) has ended such country's pattern of noncompliance; or

(2) the national security interest of the United States requires the exercise of such waiver authority.

(b) CONGRESSIONAL NOTIFICATION.—Not later than the date on which the Secretary of State exercises the waiver authority under subsection (a), the Secretary shall— Deadline.

(1) notify the appropriate congressional committees of such waiver; and

(2) provide such committees with a detailed justification for such waiver, including an explanation of the steps the noncompliant government has taken—

(A) to resolve abductions cases; or

(B) to end its pattern of noncompliance.

(c) PUBLICATION IN FEDERAL REGISTER.—Subject to subsection (d), the Secretary of State shall ensure that each waiver determination under this section—

(1) is published in the Federal Register; or

(2) is posted on the Department of State website. Web posting.

(d) LIMITED DISCLOSURE OF INFORMATION.—The Secretary of State may limit the publication of information under subsection (c) in the same manner and to the same extent as the President may limit the publication of findings and determinations described in section 654(c) of the Foreign Assistance Act of 1961 (22 U.S.C. 2414(c)), if the Secretary determines that the publication of such information would be harmful to the national security of the United States and would not further the purposes of this Act. Determination.

SEC. 205. TERMINATION OF ACTIONS BY THE SECRETARY OF STATE. 22 USC 9125.

Any specific action taken under this Act or any amendment made by this Act with respect to a foreign country shall terminate on the date on which the Secretary of State submits a written certification to Congress that the government of such country— Certification.

(1) has resolved any unresolved abduction case that gave rise to such specific action; or

(2) has taken substantial and verifiable steps to correct such country's persistent pattern of noncompliance that gave rise to such specific action, as applicable.

TITLE III—PREVENTION OF INTERNATIONAL CHILD ABDUCTION

SEC. 301. PREVENTING CHILDREN FROM LEAVING THE UNITED STATES IN VIOLATION OF A COURT ORDER.

(a) IN GENERAL.—Subtitle C of title IV of the Homeland Security Act of 2002 (6 U.S.C. 231 et seq.) is amended by adding at the end the following:

6 USC 241.

"SEC. 433. PREVENTION OF INTERNATIONAL CHILD ABDUCTION.

"(a) PROGRAM ESTABLISHED.—The Secretary, through the Commissioner of U.S. Customs and Border Protection (referred to in this section as 'CBP'), in coordination with the Secretary of State, the Attorney General, and the Director of the Federal Bureau of Investigation, shall establish a program that—

"(1) seeks to prevent a child (as defined in section 1204(b)(1) of title 18, United States Code) from departing from the territory of the United States if a parent or legal guardian of such child presents a court order from a court of competent jurisdiction prohibiting the removal of such child from the United States to a CBP Officer in sufficient time to prevent such departure for the duration of such court order; and

"(2) leverages other existing authorities and processes to address the wrongful removal and return of a child.

"(b) INTERAGENCY COORDINATION.—

Establishment.

"(1) IN GENERAL.—The Secretary of State shall convene and chair an interagency working group to prevent international parental child abduction. The group shall be composed of presidentially appointed, Senate confirmed officials from—

"(A) the Department of State;

"(B) the Department of Homeland Security, including U.S. Customs and Border Protection and U.S. Immigration and Customs Enforcement; and

"(C) the Department of Justice, including the Federal Bureau of Investigation.

"(2) DEPARTMENT OF DEFENSE.—The Secretary of Defense shall designate an official within the Department of Defense—

"(A) to coordinate with the Department of State on international child abduction issues; and

"(B) to oversee activities designed to prevent or resolve international child abduction cases relating to active duty military service members.".

(b) CLERICAL AMENDMENT.—The table of contents of the Homeland Security Act of 2002 (6 U.S.C. 101 note) is amended by adding after the item relating to section 432 the following:

"Sec. 433. Prevention of international child abduction.".

22 USC 9141.

SEC. 302. AUTHORIZATION FOR JUDICIAL TRAINING ON INTERNATIONAL PARENTAL CHILD ABDUCTION.

(a) IN GENERAL.—The Secretary of State, subject to the availability of appropriations, shall seek to provide training, directly or through another government agency or nongovernmental organizations, on the effective handling of parental abduction cases to the judicial and administrative authorities in countries—

(1) in which a significant number of unresolved abduction cases are pending; or

(2) that have been designated as having a pattern of non-compliance under section 202(b).

(b) STRATEGY REQUIREMENT.—Not later than 180 days after the date of the enactment of this Act, the President shall submit a strategy to carry out the activities described in subsection (a) to— Deadline. President.

(1) the Committee on Foreign Relations of the Senate;

(2) the Committee on Foreign Affairs of the House of Representatives;

(3) the Committee on Appropriations of the Senate; and

(4) the Committee on Appropriations of the House of Representatives.

(c) AUTHORIZATION OF APPROPRIATIONS.—

(1) IN GENERAL.—There is authorized to be appropriated to the Secretary of State $1,000,000 for each of the fiscal years 2015 and 2016 to carry out subsection (a).

(2) USE OF FUNDS.—Amounts appropriated for the activities set forth in subsection (a) shall be used pursuant to the authorization and requirements under this section.

Approved August 8, 2014.

LEGISLATIVE HISTORY—H.R. 3212:

SENATE REPORTS: No. 113–204 (Comm. on Foreign Relations).
CONGRESSIONAL RECORD:
Vol. 159 (2013): Dec. 11, considered and passed House.
Vol. 160 (2014): July 16, considered and passed Senate, amended.
July 25, House concurred in Senate amendment.

○

APPENDIX 9

Uniform Child Abduction Prevention Act

drafted by the

NATIONAL CONFERENCE OF COMMISSIONERS
ON UNIFORM STATE LAWS

and by it

APPROVED AND RECOMMENDED FOR ENACTMENT
IN ALL THE STATES

at its

ANNUAL CONFERENCE
MEETING IN ITS ONE-HUNDRED-AND-FIFTEENTH YEAR
HILTON HEAD, SOUTH CAROLINA

July 7-14, 2006

WITH PREFATORY NOTE AND COMMENTS

ABOUT NCCUSL

The **National Conference of Commissioners on Uniform State Laws** (NCCUSL), now in its 115th year, provides states with non-partisan, well-conceived and well-drafted legislation that brings clarity and stability to critical areas of state statutory law.

Conference members must be lawyers, qualified to practice law. They are practicing lawyers, judges, legislators and legislative staff and law professors, who have been appointed by state governments as well as the District of Columbia, Puerto Rico and the U.S. Virgin Islands to research, draft and promote enactment of uniform state laws in areas of state law where uniformity is desirable and practical.

- NCCUSL strengthens the federal system by providing rules and procedures that are consistent from state to state but that also reflect the diverse experience of the states.

- NCCUSL statutes are representative of state experience, because the organization is made up of representatives from each state, appointed by state government.

- NCCUSL keeps state law up-to-date by addressing important and timely legal issues.

- NCCUSL's efforts reduce the need for individuals and businesses to deal with different laws as they move and do business in different states.

- NCCUSL's work facilitates economic development and provides a legal platform for foreign entities to deal with U.S. citizens and businesses.

- NCCUSL Commissioners donate thousands of hours of their time and legal and drafting expertise every year as a public service, and receive no salary or compensation for their work.

- NCCUSL's deliberative and uniquely open drafting process draws on the expertise of commissioners, but also utilizes input from legal experts, and advisors and observers representing the views of other legal organizations or interests that will be subject to the proposed laws.

- NCCUSL is a state-supported organization that represents true value for the states, providing services that most states could not otherwise afford or duplicate.

DRAFTING COMMITTEE ON UNIFORM CHILD ABDUCTION PREVENTION ACT

The Committee appointed by and representing the National Conference of Commissioners on Uniform State Laws in drafting this Act consists of the following individuals:

LYLE W. HILLYARD, 175 E. 1st N., Logan, Utah 84321, *Chair*
CYNTHIA BOSCO, California Department of Developmental Services, 1600 9th St., Room 240 MS 2-14, Sacramento, CA 95814
VINCENT C. DELIBERATO, JR., Legislative Reference Bureau, Room 641, Main Capitol Building, Harrisburg, PA 17120-0033
W. MICHAEL DUNN, P.O. Box 3701, 1000 Elm St., Manchester, NH 03105
GORMAN HOUSTON, JR., 400 20th St. North, Birmingham, AL 35203
PETER K. MUNSON, 123 South Travis St., Sherman, TX 75090
MARIAN P. OPALA, Supreme Court, State Capitol, Room 238, Oklahoma City, OK 73105
CAM WARD, P.O. Box 1749, Alabaster, AL 35007
LINDA D. ELROD, Washburn University School of Law, 1700 SW College, Topeka, KS 66621, *Reporter*

EX OFFICIO

HOWARD J. SWIBEL, 120 S. Riverside Plaza, Suite 1200, Chicago, IL 60606, *President*
TOM BOLT, Corporate Place, 5600 Royal Dane Mall, St. Thomas, VI 00802-6410, *Division Chair*

AMERICAN BAR ASSOCIATION ADVISOR

BRUCE A. BOYER, Loyola Child Law Clinic, 16 E. Pearson St., Chicago, IL 60611

EXECUTIVE DIRECTOR

WILLIAM H. HENNING, University of Alabama School of Law, Box 870382, Tuscaloosa, AL 35487-0382, *Executive Director*

Copies of this Act may be obtained from:
NATIONAL CONFERENCE OF COMMISSIONERS ON UNIFORM STATE LAWS
211 E. Ontario Street, Suite 1300
Chicago, Illinois 60611
312/915-0195
www.nccusl.org

UNIFORM CHILD ABDUCTION PREVENTION ACT

TABLE OF CONTENTS

UNIFORM CHILD ABDUCTION PREVENTION ACT

Prefatory Note

Child abduction is a serious problem both in scope and effect. A study commissioned by the Office of Juvenile Justice and Delinquency Prevention estimated that 262,100 children were abducted in 1999; 203,900 (78 per cent) of them were abducted by a parent or family member; approximately 1000 of the abductions were international.[1] The purpose of the Uniform Child Abduction Prevention Act is to deter both predecree and postdecree domestic and international child abductions by parents, persons acting on behalf of a parent or others. Family abductions may be preventable through the identification of risk factors and the imposition of appropriate preventive measures.

The Uniform Child Abduction Prevention Act is premised on the general principle that preventing an abduction is in a child's best interests. Abducted children may suffer long-lasting harm. Federal law recognizes that parental abduction is harmful to children.[2] Child abductions can occur before or after entry of a child-custody determination. This Act allows the court to impose abduction prevention measures at any time.

Many abductions occur before a court has had the opportunity to enter a child-custody determination. Children at the center of custody disputes are at the highest risk for potential abductions.[3] Jurisdictional laws help deter abductions by specifying the proper state to handle custody litigation. The Uniform Child Custody Jurisdiction Act[4] sets out four concurrent bases for jurisdiction. Congress passed the Parental Kidnapping Prevention Act of 1980 to deter abductions, discourage interstate conflicts, and promote cooperation between states about custody matters by resolving jurisdictional conflicts.[5] The Parental Kidnapping Prevention Act prioritizes the state in which the child has lived for six months preceding the filing of the petition (the home state) as the place for custody litigation[6] and prohibits a second state from assuming jurisdiction if there is an action pending in the state that has

---

[1] See DAVID FINKELHOR, HEATHER HAMMER & ANDREA J. SEDLAK, NATIONAL INCIDENCE STUDIES OF MISSING, ABDUCTED, RUNAWAY, AND THROWNAWAY CHILDREN, CHILDREN ABDUCTED BY FAMILY MEMBERS: NATIONAL ESTIMATE AND CHARACTERISTICS (Oct. 2002).

[2] International Child Abduction Remedies Act, 42 U.S.C. § 11601(a)(1)("The Congress makes the following findings: (1) The international abduction or wrongful retention of children is harmful to their well-being…"). *See also* Dorothy S. Huntington, Parental Kidnapping: A New Form of Child Abuse, available at http://www.hiltonhouse.com/articles/child_abuse=huntington.txt. (characterizing child abduction as abuse.)

[3] AMERICA'S HIDDEN CRIME: WHEN THE KIDNAPPER IS KIN 10-11 (Polly Klaas Foundation 2004). *See also* Janet R. Johnston et al., Early Identification of Risk Factors for Parental Abduction (OJJDP March 2001)(indicating that men are more likely to abduct before an order is entered while women are more likely to abduct after a child custody determination).

[4] 9 UNIF. L. ANN. Part I 115 (1988).

[5] Pub. L. No. 96-611, note 7 to 28 U.S.C. §1738A.

[6] 28 U.S.C. Section 1738A(c).

proper jurisdiction.[7] The Uniform Child Custody Jurisdiction and Enforcement Act,[8] now in 45 jurisdictions, also prioritizes home state jurisdiction notwithstanding the child's absence. Jurisdictional laws do not provide prevention measures for abduction.

Post-decree abductions often occur because the existing child-custody determinations lack sufficient protective provisions to prevent an abduction. An award of joint physical custody without a designation of specific times; a vague order granting "reasonable visitation"; or the lack any restrictions on custody and visitation make orders hard to enforce. The awareness of abduction risk factors and preventive measures available can reduce the threat of abduction by giving the court the tools to make the initial child-custody determination clearer, more specific, and more easily enforceable.

If an abduction occurs after a child-custody determination, all states have enforcement remedies. Forty-six jurisdictions use the procedures in Article 3 of the Uniform Child Custody Jurisdiction and Enforcement Act. In addition, courts can punish abductors for contempt and allow tort actions for custodial interference. Several federal laws help locate missing children[9] and criminalize international parental kidnapping.[10] While there is no federal law criminalizing interstate parental kidnapping, there is a mechanism for apprehending persons who violate state parental kidnapping laws and travel across state lines.[11] While every state criminally forbids custodial interference by parents or relatives of the child, the laws differ as to the elements of the offenses, the punishments given, and whether a child-custody determination must exist for a violation to occur.[12]

If the abduction is international, the Hague Convention on the Civil Aspects of International Child Abduction, currently in effect between the United States and fifty-five countries, facilitates the return of an abducted child to the child's habitual residence.[13] Many

---

[7] 28 U.S.C.A. Section 1738A(g).

[8] 9 UNIF. L. ANN. Part I 657 (1999).

[9] Missing Children Act, 28 U.S.C. § 534 (1982); Missing Children Search Assistance Act and the National Child Search Assistance Act, 42 U.S.C. § 5779 & § 5780 (1990); and the Prosecutorial Remedies and Other Tools to End the Exploitation of Children Today (PROTECT) Act of 2003, Pub. L. 108-21, 117 Stat. 650 (AMBER Alert Program).

[10] *See* International Parental Kidnapping Crime Act (IPKCA), 18 U.S.C. § 1204; The Fugitive Felon Act, 18 U.S.C. § 1073; and The Extradition Treaties Interpretation Act of 1998, 18 U.S.C. § 3181.

[11] Unlawful Flight to Avoid Prosecution, 18 U.S.C. § 1204; The Fugitive Felon Act, 18 U.S.C. § 1073. When enacting the Parental Kidnapping Prevention Act, Congress declared that the Unlawful Flight to Avoid Prosecution provision applies to cases involving parental kidnapping and interstate or international flight to avoid prosecution. Pub. L. No. 96-611, 10(a).

[12] Appendix A. Citation List of State Parental Kidnapping Statutes, National Clearinghouse for the Defense of Battered Women, The Impact of Parental Kidnapping Laws and Practice on Domestic Violence Survivors 32 (2005).

[13] *See* The Hague Convention on the Civil Aspects of International Child Abduction, 51 Fed. Reg. § 10494 et seq. (1986); the International Child Abduction Remedies Act (ICARA), 42 U.S.C. §§ 11601-11610. For a current

countries, however, have not ratified the Hague Convention on the Civil Aspects of International Child Abduction, the United States has not accepted all nations' accessions, and some countries that have ratified do not comply with the treaty obligations.

This Act is civil law and complements existing state law. This Act does not limit, contradict, or supercede the Uniform Child Custody Jurisdiction and Enforcement Act or the Uniform Child Custody Jurisdiction Act. This Act is not meant to prevent a legitimate relocation action filed in accordance with the law of the state having jurisdiction to make a child-custody determination nor to prevent a victim of domestic violence from escaping abuse.

The Uniform Child Abduction Prevention Act applies to predecree and intrastate cases, to emergency situations, and to cases in which risk factors exist and the current child-custody determination lacks abduction prevention measures. Only three states have enacted comprehensive child abduction prevention statutes;[14] two other states include provisions to reduce the risk of abduction.[15] This Act will fill a void in the majority of states by identifying circumstances indicating a risk of abduction and providing measures to prevent the abduction of children, predecree or postdecree.

---

list of United States treaty partners, visit www.travel.state.gov/family/abduction/hague_issues/hague_issues_1487.html.

[14] *See* ARK. STAT. ANN. § 9-13-401-407 (2005); CAL. FAM. CODE § 3048 (2004); TEX. FAM. CODE § 153.501- § 153.503 (2003).

[15] *See* FLA. STAT. § 61.45 (2005); OR. REV. STAT. § 109.035 (2005).

UNIFORM CHILD ABDUCTION PREVENTION ACT

SECTION 1. SHORT TITLE. This [act] may be cited as the Uniform Child Abduction Prevention Act.

SECTION 2. DEFINITIONS. In this [act]:

(1) "Abduction" means the wrongful removal or wrongful retention of a child.

(2) "Child" means an unemancipated individual who is less than 18 years of age.

(3) "Child-custody determination" means a judgment, decree, or other order of a court providing for the legal custody, physical custody, or visitation with respect to a child. The term includes a permanent, temporary, initial, and modification order.

(4) "Child-custody proceeding" means a proceeding in which legal custody, physical custody, or visitation with respect to a child is at issue. The term includes a proceeding for divorce, dissolution of marriage, separation, neglect, abuse, dependency, guardianship, paternity, termination of parental rights, or protection from domestic violence.

(5) "Court" means an entity authorized under the law of a state to establish, enforce, or modify a child-custody determination.

(6) "Petition" includes a motion or its equivalent.

(7) "Record" means information that is inscribed on a tangible medium or that is stored in an electronic or other medium and is retrievable in perceivable form.

(8) "State" means a state of the United States, the District of Columbia, Puerto Rico, the United States Virgin Islands, or any territory or insular possession subject to the jurisdiction of the United States. The term includes a federally recognized Indian tribe or nation.

(9) "Travel document" means records relating to a travel itinerary, including

travel tickets, passes, reservations for transportation, or accommodations. The term does not include a passport or visa.

(10) "Wrongful removal" means the taking of a child that breaches rights of custody or visitation given or recognized under the law of this state.

(11) "Wrongful retention" means the keeping or concealing of a child that breaches rights of custody or visitation given or recognized under the law of this state.

Comment

To the extent possible, the definitions track the Uniform Child Custody Jurisdiction and Enforcement Act. The definition of a child as a person under age 18 is the same as in Section 102(2) of the Uniform Child Custody Jurisdiction and Enforcement Act. State law determines when a child becomes emancipated before age 18. This Act is limited to the abduction of minors even though the risk of abduction may apply to a disabled adult who has an appointed adult guardian.

The definition of "child-custody determination" is the same as the definition in Section 102(3) of the Uniform Child Custody Jurisdiction and Enforcement Act. This Act uses the traditional terminology of "custody" and "visitation" because that is the language used in the Uniform Child Custody Jurisdiction and Enforcement Act although local terminology may differ. The definition of a child-custody proceeding differs insignificantly from Section 102(4) of the Uniform Child Custody Jurisdiction and Enforcement Act.

The definition of abduction covers wrongful removal or wrongful retention. The definition is broad enough to encompass not only an abduction committed by either parent or a person acting on behalf of the parent but also other abductions. Generally both parents have the right to companionship and access to their child unless a court states otherwise. Abductions can occur against an individual or other entity with custody rights, as well as against an individual with visitation or access rights. A parent with joint legal or physical custody rights, by operation of law, court order, or legally binding agreement, commits an abduction by wrongfully interfering with the other parent's rights. A removal or retention of a child can be "wrongful" predecree or postdecree. An abduction is wrongful where it is in breach of an existing "child-custody determination" or, if predecree, in violation of rights attributed to a person by operation of law. The term "breaches rights of custody" tracks Article 3 of the Hague Convention on the Civil Aspects of International Child Abduction.

SECTION 3. COOPERATION AND COMMUNICATION AMONG COURTS.

Sections [110], [111], and [112] of [insert citation to the provisions of the Uniform Child

Custody Jurisdiction and Enforcement Act or its equivalent in the state] apply to cooperation and communications among courts in proceedings under this [act].

Comment

It is possible, even likely, that abduction situations will involve more than one state. Thus, there is a need for mechanisms for communication among courts, for testimony to be obtained quickly by means other than physical presence, and for cooperation between courts in different states. Sections 110, 111, and 112 of the Uniform Child Custody Jurisdiction and Enforcement Act provide mechanisms to deal with these issues. States that do not have the Uniform Child Custody Jurisdiction and Enforcement Act may want to include these provisions or use some similar provision of existing state law.

SECTION 4. ACTIONS FOR ABDUCTION PREVENTION MEASURES.

(a) A court on its own motion may order abduction prevention measures in a child-custody proceeding if the court finds that the evidence establishes a credible risk of abduction of the child.

(b) A party to a child-custody determination or another individual or entity having a right under the law of this state or any other state to seek a child-custody determination for the child may file a petition seeking abduction prevention measures to protect the child under this [act].

(c) A prosecutor or public authority designated under [insert citation to Section 315 of the Uniform Child Custody Jurisdiction and Enforcement Act or applicable law of this state] may seek a warrant to take physical custody of a child under Section 9 or other appropriate prevention measures.

Comment

An abduction may occur before a child-custody proceeding has commenced, after the filing but before entry of a child-custody determination, or in violation of an existing child-custody determination. To obtain abduction prevention measures, either the court on its own may impose the measures or a party to a child custody proceeding or an individual or entity having the right to seek custody may file a petition seeking abduction prevention measures.

A court hearing a child custody case may determine that the evidence shows a credible risk of abduction. Therefore, even without a party filing a petition under this Act, the court on its own motion can impose appropriate abduction prevention measures. Usually, however, a parent who fears that the other parent or family members are preparing to abduct the child will file a petition in an existing custody dispute. An individual or other entity, such as the state child welfare agency, which has a right to lawful custody may file a petition alleging a risk of abduction and seeking prevention measures with respect to a child who is not yet the subject of a child-custody determination.

The Act allows a prosecutor or public authority designated in Section 315 of the Uniform Child Custody Jurisdiction and Enforcement Act to seek a warrant under Section 9 of this Act if there is an imminent risk of wrongful removal.

SECTION 5. JURISDICTION

(a) A petition under this [act] may be filed only in a court that has jurisdiction to make a child-custody determination with respect to the child at issue under [insert citation to Uniform Child Custody Jurisdiction and Enforcement Act or the Uniform Child Custody Jurisdiction Act].

(b) A court of this state has temporary emergency jurisdiction under [insert citation to Section 204 of the Uniform Child Custody Jurisdiction and Enforcement Act or Section 3(a)(3) of the Uniform Child Custody Jurisdiction Act] if the court finds a credible risk of abduction.

Comment

This Act complements, but does not limit, contradict, or supercede the Uniform Child Custody Jurisdiction and Enforcement Act, 9 U.L.A. Part I 657 (1999), or the Uniform Child Custody Jurisdiction Act, 9 U.L.A. Part I 115 (1988). A court must have jurisdiction sufficient to make an initial child-custody determination, a modification, or temporary emergency jurisdiction to issue prevention measures under this Act.

The Parental Kidnapping Prevention Act prioritizes the child's home state as the primary jurisdictional basis; prohibits a court in one state from exercising jurisdiction if a valid custody proceeding is already pending in another state; and requires that states give full faith and credit to sister state decrees made in accordance with its principles. The Uniform Child Custody Jurisdiction and Enforcement Act follows the Parental Kidnapping Prevention Act.

A court has temporary emergency jurisdiction under the Uniform Child Custody Jurisdiction and Enforcement Act only if the child has been abandoned or it is necessary in an emergency to protect the child because the child, or a sibling or parent of the child, is subjected to or threatened with mistreatment or abuse. This Act equates a credible risk of abduction with threatened mistreatment or abuse for emergency jurisdiction purposes.

If a state would be able to exercise emergency jurisdiction under Section 204 the Uniform Child Custody Jurisdiction and Enforcement Act, it can do so even if another court has issued a child-custody determination and has continuing exclusive jurisdiction. The reference to Section 204 brings in all of its provisions that include communication, length of time of temporary orders, and the like.

Under Section 208 of the Uniform Child Custody Jurisdiction and Enforcement Act, if a court has jurisdiction because a person seeking to invoke its jurisdiction has engaged in unjustifiable conduct, the court shall decline to exercise its jurisdiction. However, as the comment to Section 208 explains, domestic violence victims should not be charged with unjustifiable conduct for conduct that occurred in the process of fleeing domestic violence. Domestic violence also shall be considered in a court's inconvenient forum analysis under Section 207(b)(1) of the Uniform Child Custody Jurisdiction and Enforcement Act.

SECTION 6. CONTENTS OF PETITION. A petition under this [act] must be verified and include a copy of any existing child-custody determination, if available. The petition must specify the risk factors for abduction, including the relevant factors described in Section 7. Subject to [insert citation to Section 209(e) of the Uniform Child Custody Jurisdiction and Enforcement Act or cite the law of this state providing for the confidentiality of procedures, addresses, and other identifying information], if reasonably ascertainable, the petition must contain:

(1) the name, date of birth, and gender of the child;

(2) the customary address and current physical location of the child;

(3) the identity, customary address, and current physical location of the respondent;

(4) a statement of whether a prior action to prevent abduction or domestic

violence has been filed by a party or other individual or entity having custody of the child, and the date, location, and disposition of the action;

(5) a statement of whether a party to the proceeding has been arrested for a crime related to domestic violence, stalking, or child abuse or neglect, and the date, location, and disposition of the case; and

(6) any other information required to be submitted to the court for a child-custody determination under [insert citation to Section 209 of the Uniform Child Custody Jurisdiction and Enforcement Act or applicable law of this state].

Comment

The contents of the petition follow those for pleadings under Section 209 of the Uniform Child Custody Jurisdiction and Enforcement Act. The information is made subject to state law on the protection of names or identifying information in certain cases. A number of states have enacted laws relating to the protection of victims in domestic violence and child abuse cases by keeping confidential the victims' names, addresses, and other information. These procedures must be followed if the state law requires their applicability. If a state does not protect names and addresses, then a provision similar to Section 209(e) of the Uniform Child Custody Jurisdiction and Enforcement Act should be added. That provision reads:

> If a party alleges in an affidavit or a pleading under oath that the health, safety, or liberty of a party or child would be jeopardized by disclosure of identifying information, the information must be sealed and may not be disclosed to the other party or the public unless the court orders the disclosure to be made after a hearing in which the court takes into consideration the health, safety, or liberty of the party or child and determines that the disclosure is in the interest of justice.

The requirement for information on domestic violence or child abuse is to alert the court to the possibility that a batterer or abuser is attempting to use the Act. Domestic violence underlies large numbers of parental kidnapping. One study found that approximately one half of abductors had been violent toward the other parent during the marriage or relationship. Some batterers abduct their children during or after custody litigation; others abduct before initiating legal proceedings. The court should not allow a batterer to use this Act to gain temporary custody or additional visitation in an uncontested hearing. A person who has committed domestic violence or child abuse poses a risk of harm to the child. Such a person, however, may still seek relief in a contested hearing where the issues can be fully examined by the court. In order to screen for domestic violence or child abuse, the petition requires disclosure of all relevant information and the court can inquire about domestic violence at any hearing.

Notice and opportunity to be heard should be given according to the law of the state and may be by publication if other means are not effective. See Section 108(a) of the Uniform Child Custody Jurisdiction and Enforcement Act.

SECTION 7. FACTORS TO DETERMINE RISK OF ABDUCTION.

(a) In determining whether there is a credible risk of abduction of a child, the court shall consider any evidence that the petitioner or respondent:

(1) has previously abducted or attempted to abduct the child;

(2) has threatened to abduct the child;

(3) has recently engaged in activities that may indicate a planned abduction, including:

(A) abandoning employment;

(B) selling a primary residence;

(C) terminating a lease;

(D) closing bank or other financial management accounts, liquidating assets, hiding or destroying financial documents, or conducting any unusual financial activities;

(E) applying for a passport or visa or obtaining travel documents for the respondent, a family member, or the child; or

(F) seeking to obtain the child's birth certificate or school or medical records;

(4) has engaged in domestic violence, stalking, or child abuse or neglect;

(5) has refused to follow a child-custody determination;

(6) lacks strong familial, financial, emotional, or cultural ties to the state

or the United States;

(7) has strong familial, financial, emotional, or cultural ties to another state or country;

(8) is likely to take the child to a country that:

(A) is not a party to the Hague Convention on the Civil Aspects of International Child Abduction and does not provide for the extradition of an abducting parent or for the return of an abducted child;

(B) is a party to the Hague Convention on the Civil Aspects of International Child Abduction but:

(i) the Hague Convention on the Civil Aspects of International Child Abduction is not in force between the United States and that country;

(ii) is noncompliant according to the most recent compliance report issued by the United States Department of State; or

(iii) lacks legal mechanisms for immediately and effectively enforcing a return order under the Hague Convention on the Civil Aspects of International Child Abduction;

(C) poses a risk that the child's physical or emotional health or safety would be endangered in the country because of specific circumstances relating to the child or because of human rights violations committed against children;

(D) has laws or practices that would:

(i) enable the respondent, without due cause, to prevent the petitioner from contacting the child;

(ii) restrict the petitioner from freely traveling to or exiting from the country because of the petitioner's gender, nationality, marital status, or religion; or

(iii) restrict the child's ability legally to leave the country after the child reaches the age of majority because of a child's gender, nationality, or religion;

(E) is included by the United States Department of State on a current list of state sponsors of terrorism;

(F) does not have an official United States diplomatic presence in the country; or

(G) is engaged in active military action or war, including a civil war, to which the child may be exposed;

(9) is undergoing a change in immigration or citizenship status that would adversely affect the respondent's ability to remain in the United States legally;

(10) has had an application for United States citizenship denied;

(11) has forged or presented misleading or false evidence on government forms or supporting documents to obtain or attempt to obtain a passport, a visa, travel documents, a Social Security card, a driver's license, or other government-issued identification card or has made a misrepresentation to the United States government;

(12) has used multiple names to attempt to mislead or defraud; or

(13) has engaged in any other conduct the court considers relevant to the risk of abduction.

(b) In the hearing on a petition under this [act], the court shall consider any evidence that the respondent believed in good faith that the respondent's conduct was necessary to avoid imminent harm to the child or respondent and any other evidence that may be relevant to whether the respondent may be permitted to remove or retain the child.

Comment

The list of risk factors constitutes a summary of the wide variety of types of behaviors and characteristics that researchers have found to be present. The risk factors are based on research that has been done during the last twelve years. Research also shows that abducting parents dismiss the value of the other parent in the child's life; have young children or children vulnerable to influence; and often have the support of their family and others. Parents who have made credible threats to abduct a child or have a history are particularly high risk especially when accompanied by other factors, such as quitting a job, selling a home, and moving assets. *See* Janet Johnston & Linda Girdner, *Family Abductors: Descriptive Profiles and Preventative Interventions* (U.S. Dep't of Justice, OJJDP 2001 NCJ 182788); ABA, Early Identification of Risk Factors for Parental Abduction (NCJ185026). The more of these factors that are present, the more likely the chance of an abduction. However, the mere presence of one or more of these factors does not mean that an abduction will occur just as the absence of these factors does not guarantee that no abduction will occur. Some conduct described in the factors can be done in conjunction with a relocation petition, which would negate an inference that the parent is planning to abduct the child.

International abductions pose more obstacles to return of a child than do abductions within the United States. Courts should consider evidence that the respondent was raised in another country and has family support there, has a legal right to work in a foreign country and has the ability to speak that foreign language. There are difficulties associated with securing return of children from countries that are not treaty partners under the Hague Convention on the Civil Aspects of Child Abduction or are not compliant with the Convention. Compliance Reports are available at the United States Department of State website or may be obtained by contacting the Office of Children's Issues in Department of State.

Courts should be particularly sensitive to the importance of preventive measures where there is an identified risk of a child being removed to countries that are guilty of human rights violations, including arranged marriages of children, child labor, lack of child abuse laws, female genital mutilation, sexual exploitation, any form of child slavery, torture, and the deprivation of liberty. These countries pose potentially serious obstacles to return of a child and pose the possibility of harm.

Courts need to be sensitive to domestic violence issues. Batterers often abduct their children before as well as during and after custody litigation. However, courts also need to be aware of the dynamics of domestic violence. Rather than a vindictive reason for taking the child, a victim fleeing domestic violence may be attempting to protect the victim and the child. Almost half of the parents in one parental kidnapping study were victims of domestic violence and half of the parents who were contemplating abducting their children were motivated by the perceived need to protect their child from physical, sexual, and emotional abuse. Geoffrey L. Greif & Rebecca L. Hegar, When Parents Kidnap: The Families Behind the Headlines 8 (1993). Some of the risk factors involve the same activities that might be undertaken by a victim of domestic violence who is trying to relocate or flee to escape violence. If the evidence shows that the parent preparing to leave is fleeing domestic violence, the court must consider that any order restricting departure or transferring custody may pose safety issues for the respondent and the child, and therefore, should be imposed only when the risk of abduction, the likely harm from the abduction, and the chances of recovery outweigh the risk of harm to the respondent and the child.

The Uniform Child Custody Jurisdiction and Enforcement Act recognizes that domestic violence victims should be considered. The Comment to Section 208 of the Uniform Child Custody Jurisdiction and Enforcement Act (Jurisdiction Declined by Reason of Conduct) states that "Domestic violence victims should not be charged with unjustifiable conduct for conduct that occurred in the process of fleeing domestic violence, even if their conduct is technically illegal. An inquiry must be made whether the flight was justified under the circumstances of the case."

SECTION 8. PROVISIONS AND MEASURES TO PREVENT ABDUCTION.

(a) If a petition is filed under this [act], the court may enter an order that must include:

(1) the basis for the court's exercise of jurisdiction;

(2) the manner in which notice and opportunity to be heard were given to the persons entitled to notice of the proceeding;

(3) a detailed description of each party's custody and visitation rights and residential arrangements for the child;

(4) a provision stating that a violation of the order may subject the party in violation to civil and criminal penalties; and

(5) identification of the child's country of habitual residence at the time of the issuance of the order.

(b) If, at a hearing on a petition under this [act] or on the court's own motion, the court after reviewing the evidence finds a credible risk of abduction of the child, the court shall enter an abduction prevention order. The order must include the provisions required by subsection (a) and measures and conditions, including those in subsections (c), (d), and (e), that are reasonably calculated to prevent abduction of the child, giving due consideration to the custody and visitation rights of the parties. The court shall consider the age of the child, the potential harm to the child from an abduction, the legal and practical difficulties of returning the child to the jurisdiction if abducted, and the reasons for the potential abduction, including evidence of domestic violence, stalking, or child abuse or neglect.

(c) An abduction prevention order may include one or more of the following:

(1) an imposition of travel restrictions that require that a party traveling with the child outside a designated geographical area provide the other party with the following:

(A) the travel itinerary of the child;

(B) a list of physical addresses and telephone numbers at which the child can be reached at specified times; and

(C) copies of all travel documents;

(2) a prohibition of the respondent directly or indirectly:

(A) removing the child from this state, the United States, or another geographic area without permission of the court or the petitioner's written consent;

(B) removing or retaining the child in violation of a child-custody determination;

(C) removing the child from school or a child-care or similar facility; or

(D) approaching the child at any location other than a site designated for supervised visitation;

(3) a requirement that a party register the order in another state as a prerequisite to allowing the child to travel to that state;

(4) with regard to the child's passport:

(A) a direction that the petitioner place the child's name in the United States Department of State's Child Passport Issuance Alert Program;

(B) a requirement that the respondent surrender to the court or the petitioner's attorney any United States or foreign passport issued in the child's name, including a passport issued in the name of both the parent and the child; and

(C) a prohibition upon the respondent from applying on behalf of the child for a new or replacement passport or visa;

(5) as a prerequisite to exercising custody or visitation, a requirement that the respondent provide:

(A) to the United States Department of State Office of Children's Issues and the relevant foreign consulate or embassy, an authenticated copy of the order detailin passport and travel restrictions for the child;

(B) to the court:

(i) proof that the respondent has provided the information in subparagraph (A); and

(ii) an acknowledgment in a record from the relevant foreign consulate or embassy that no passport application has been made, or passport issued, on behalf of the child;

(C) to the petitioner, proof of registration with the United States Embassy or other United States diplomatic presence in the destination country and with the Central Authority for the Hague Convention on the Civil Aspects of International Child Abduction, if that Convention is in effect between the United States and the destination country, unless one of the parties objects; and

(D) a written waiver under the Privacy Act, 5 U.S.C. Section 552a [as amended], with respect to any document, application, or other information pertaining to the child authorizing its disclosure to the court and the petitioner; and

(6) upon the petitioner's request, a requirement that the respondent obtain an order from the relevant foreign country containing terms identical to the child-custody determination issued in the United States.

(d) In an abduction prevention order, the court may impose conditions on the exercise of custody or visitation that:

(1) limit visitation or require that visitation with the child by the respondent be supervised until the court finds that supervision is no longer necessary and order the respondent to pay the costs of supervision;

(2) require the respondent to post a bond or provide other security in an amount sufficient to serve as a financial deterrent to abduction, the proceeds of which may be used to pay for the reasonable expenses of recovery of the child, including reasonable attorneys fees and costs if there is an abduction; and

(3) require the respondent to obtain education on the potentially harmful effects to the child from abduction.

(e) To prevent imminent abduction of a child, a court may:

(1) issue a warrant to take physical custody of the child under Section 9 or the law of this state other than this [act];

(2) direct the use of law enforcement to take any action reasonably necessary to locate the child, obtain return of the child, or enforce a custody determination under this [act] or the law of this state other than this [act]; or

(3) grant any other relief allowed under the law of this state other than this [act].

(f) The remedies provided in this [act] are cumulative and do not affect the availability of other remedies to prevent abduction.

Comment

This act provides courts with a choice of remedies. Ideally the court will choose the least restrictive measures and conditions to maximize opportunities for continued parental contact while minimizing the opportunities for abduction. The most restrictive measures should be used when there have been prior custody violations and overt threats to take the child; when the child faces substantial potential harm from an abducting parent who may have serious mental or personality disorder, history of abuse or violence or no prior relationship with the child; or when the obstacles to recovering the child are formidable due to countries not cooperating and enforcing orders from the United States, not being signatories to the Hague Convention on the Civil Aspects of International Child Abduction or non-compliant. Section 8 lists the possible prevention measures categorized as travel restrictions, conditions on the exercise of custody and visitation, and urgent measures when abduction is imminent or in progress.

If a person files a petition under this Act, even if the court decides not to order restrictive measures or impose conditions, the court may clarify and make more specific the existing child-custody determination. To enter an abduction prevention order, the court must have jurisdiction to make a child-custody determination even if it is emergency jurisdiction. The court should set out the basis for the court's exercise of jurisdiction. The more apparent on the face of the document that the court issuing the order had proper jurisdiction, the more likely courts in other states and countries are to recognize it as valid. The court should also include a statement showing that the parties were properly served and given adequate notice. This makes it apparent on the face of the order that due process was met. *See* Sections 108 and 205 of the Uniform Child Custody Jurisdiction and Enforcement Act. States do not require personal jurisdiction to make a child-custody determination.

The court may make an existing child-custody order clearer and more specific. Vague orders are difficult to enforce without additional litigation. The term "reasonable visitation" can lead to conflicts between the parents and make it difficult for law enforcement officers to know if the order is being violated. The court may specify the dates and times for each party's custody and visitation, including holidays, birthdays, and telephone or Internet contact. Because joint custody arrangements create special enforcement problems, the court should ensure that the order specifies the child's residential placement at all times. Whenever possible, the residential arrangements should represent the parents' agreement. However, to prevent abductions, it is important for the court order to be specific as to the residential arrangements for the child. If there is a threat of abduction, awarding sole custody to one parent makes enforcement easier.

The court may also include language in the prevention order to highlight the importance of both parties complying with the court order by including in bold language: "VIOLATION OF THIS ORDER MAY SUBJECT THE PARTY IN VIOLATION TO CIVIL AND CRIMINAL PENALTIES."

Because every abduction case may be a potential international abduction case, the prevention order should identify the place of habitual residence of a child. Although the Hague Convention on the Civil Aspects of International Child Abduction does not define "habitual residence" and the determination is made by the court in the country hearing a petition for return of a child, a statement in the child-custody determination or prevention order may help. A typical statement reads:

> The State of ___________, United States of America, is the habitual residence of the minor children within the meaning of the Hague Convention on the Civil Aspects of International Child Abduction.

If the court finds a credible risk of abduction, this Act provides numerous measures to prevent an abduction. Courts can require a party traveling outside a specified geographical area to provide the other party with all relevant information about where the child will be and how to contact the child. The court can impose travel restrictions prohibiting the respondent from leaving the United States or a specific geographical area; from removing the child from school, day care or other facilities, and can restrict contact other than as specified in the order. The court may also impose passport restrictions and require the respondent to provide assurances and safeguards as a condition of traveling with the child.

The court may also choose to impose restrictions on custody or visitation. The most common, and one of the most effective, restrictions is supervised visitation. Visitation should remain supervised until the court decides the threat of abduction has passed. In addition, the court may require the posting of a bond sufficient to serve both as a deterrent and as a source of funds for the cost of the return of the child. If domestic violence is present, the court may want to order the abusive person to obtain education, counseling or attend a batterers' intervention and prevention program.

Because of international abduction cases are the most complex and difficult, reasonable restrictions to prevent such abductions are necessary. If a credible risk of international abduction of the child exists, passport controls and travel restrictions may be indispensable. It may be advantageous in some cases to obtain a "mirror"or reciprocal order. Before exercising rights, the respondent would need to get a custody order from the country to which the respondent will travel that recognizes both the United States order and the court's continuing jurisdiction. The foreign court would need to agree to order return of the child if the child was taken in violation of the court order. This potentially expensive and time consuming remedy should only be ordered when likely to be of assistance. Because the foreign court may subsequently modify its order, problems can arise.

The court may do whatever is necessary to prevent an abduction, including using the warrant procedure under this act or under the law of the state. Many law enforcement officers are unclear about their role in responding to parental kidnapping cases. One study showed that

70 percent of law enforcement agencies reported that they did not have written policies and procedures governing child abduction cases. A provision in the custody order directing law enforcement officer to "accompany and assist" a parent to recover an abducted child may be useful but is not included in this Act. The language tracks Section 316 of the Uniform Child Custody Jurisdiction and Enforcement Act that authorizes law enforcement to take any lawful action reasonably necessary to locate a child or a party and assist a prosecutor or appropriate public official in obtaining return of a child or enforcing a child-custody determination.

The remedies provided in this Act are intended to supplement and complement existing law.

SECTION 9. WARRANT TO TAKE PHYSICAL CUSTODY OF CHILD.

(a) If a petition under this [act] contains allegations, and the court finds that there is a credible risk that the child is imminently likely to be wrongfully removed, the court may issue an ex parte warrant to take physical custody of the child.

(b) The respondent on a petition under subsection (a) must be afforded an opportunity to be heard at the earliest possible time after the ex parte warrant is executed, but no later than the next judicial day unless a hearing on that date is impossible. In that event, the court shall hold the hearing on the first judicial day possible.

(c) An ex parte warrant under subsection (a) to take physical custody of a child must:

(1) recite the facts upon which a determination of a credible risk of imminent wrongful removal of the child is based;

(2) direct law enforcement officers to take physical custody of the child immediately;

(3) state the date and time for the hearing on the petition; and

(4) provide for the safe interim placement of the child pending further order of the court.

(d) If feasible, before issuing a warrant and before determining the placement of the child after the warrant is executed, the court may order a search of the relevant databases of the National Crime Information Center system and similar state databases to determine if either the petitioner or respondent has a history of domestic violence, stalking, or child abuse or neglect.

(e) The petition and warrant must be served on the respondent when or immediately after the child is taken into physical custody.

(f) A warrant to take physical custody of a child, issued by this state or another state, is enforceable throughout this state. If the court finds that a less intrusive remedy will not be effective, it may authorize law enforcement officers to enter private property to take physical custody of the child. If required by exigent circumstances, the court may authorize law enforcement officers to make a forcible entry at any hour.

(g) If the court finds, after a hearing, that a petitioner sought an ex parte warrant under subsection (a) for the purpose of harassment or in bad faith, the court may award the respondent reasonable attorney's fees, costs, and expenses.

(h) This [act] does not affect the availability of relief allowed under the law of this state other than this [act].

Comment

This section authorizes issuance of a warrant in an emergency situation, such as an allegation that the respondent is preparing to abduct the child to a foreign country and is on the way to the airport. The harm is the credible risk of imminent removal. If the court finds such a risk, the court should temporarily waive the notice requirements and issue a warrant to take physical custody of the child. Immediately after the warrant is executed, the respondent is to receive notice of the proceedings. This section mirrors Section 311 of the Uniform Child Custody Jurisdiction and Enforcement Act on warrants to pick up a child which are available when there is an existing child-custody determination. In many states, the term used in civil cases is "writ of attachment."

The court should hear the testimony of the petitioner or another witness before issuing the warrant. The testimony may be heard in person, by telephone, or by any other means acceptable under local law, which may include video conferencing or use of other technology.

Domestic violence includes "family" violence. Because some batterers may try to use the warrant procedure to prevent victims and the children from escaping domestic violence or child abuse, the court should check relevant state and national databases to see if either the petitioner or respondent's name is listed or if relevant information exists that has not been disclosed before issuing the warrant and ordering placement. Lundy Bancroft & Jay G. Silverman, The Batterer as Parent: Addressing the Impact of Domestic Violence on Family Dynamics 73, 75 (2002)(indicating that most parental abductions take place in the context of a history of domestic violence because threatening to take the child from the mother is a form of control).

Some courts have computer terminals on the bench and a database search takes seconds. Courts without computer access can seek the assistance of law enforcement. Unless impracticable, the court should conduct a search of all person databases of the National Crime Information Center system, including the protection order file, the historical protection order file, the warrants file, the sex offender registry, and the persons on supervised release file. In addition, it is recommended that courts run searches in the National Law Enforcement Telecommunication System in the petitioner's state of birth, current state of residence, and other recent states of residence. Civil courts are authorized by statute and National Crime Information Center policy to have access to information in several files for domestic violence and stalking cases. Because child abduction involves family members and can harm children, and violence between the parents is often a factor leading to child abduction, cases in which a parent alleges a risk of wrongful removal should permit access to the relevant databases.

The court should also view comparable state databases, such as the state department of social service registry of persons found to have abused or neglected children. If the petitioner or respondent are listed for a reason related to a crime of domestic or family violence, the court may refuse to issue a warrant or order any appropriate placement authorized under the laws of the state. The warrant must provide for the placement of a child pending the hearing. Temporary placement will most often be with the petitioner unless the database check reveals the petitioner is a likely or known abuser.

The court must state the reasons for issuance of the warrant. The warrant can be enforced by law enforcement officers wherever the child is found in the state. The warrant may authorize entry upon private property to pick up the child if no less intrusive means are possible. In extraordinary cases, the warrant may authorize law enforcement to make a forcible entry at any hour. This section also authorizes law enforcement officers to enforce out of state warrants.

Section 9 applies only to wrongful removals, not wrongful retentions. It does not hinder a court from issuing any other immediate ex parte relief to prevent a wrongful removal or retention as may be allowed under law other than this act.

SECTION 10. DURATION OF ABDUCTION PREVENTION ORDER. An

abduction prevention order remains in effect until the earliest of:

(1) the time stated in the order;

(2) the emancipation of the child;

(3) the child's attaining 18 years of age; or

(4) the time the order is modified, revoked, vacated, or superseded by a court with jurisdiction under [insert citation to Sections 201 through 203 of the Uniform Child Custody Jurisdiction and Enforcement Act or Section 3 of the Uniform Child Custody Jurisdiction Act and applicable law of this state].

SECTION 11. UNIFORMITY OF APPLICATION AND CONSTRUCTION. In applying and construing this uniform act, consideration must be given to the need to promote uniformity of the law with respect to its subject matter among states that enact it.

SECTION 12. RELATION TO ELECTRONIC SIGNATURES IN GLOBAL AND NATIONAL COMMERCE ACT. This [act] modifies, limits, and supersedes the federal Electronic Signatures in Global and National Commerce Act, 15 U.S.C. Section 7001, et seq., but does not modify, limit, or supersede Section 101(c) of the act, 15 U.S.C. Section 7001(c), or authorize electronic delivery of any of the notices described in Section 103(b) of that act, 15 U.S.C. Section 7003(b).

SECTION 13. EFFECTIVE DATE. This [act] takes effect on . . . .

Table of Cases

Index